SEVENTH EDITION

WORLD CRIMINAL JUSTICE SYSTEMS

A SURVEY

RICHARD J. TERRILL
PROFESSOR EMERITUS
GEORGIA STATE UNIVERSITY

World Criminal Justice Systems
Seventh Edition

Matthew Bender & Company, Inc., a member of the LexisNexis Group
New Providence, NJ

ISBN: 978-1-59345-612-2

Phone 877-374-2919
Web Site www.lexisnexis.com/anderson/criminaljustice

Library of Congress Cataloging-in-Publication Data

Terrill, Richard J.
World criminal justice systems : a survey / Richard J. Terrill.–7th ed.
p. cm.
Includes bibliographical references and index.
ISBN 978-1-59345-612-2 (softbound)
1. Criminal justice, Administration of. 2. Criminal justice, Administration of–Cross-cultural studies. I. Title.
HV7419.T47 2009
364–dc22
2009033503

Cover design by Tin Box Studio/ Cincinnati, OH
Chapter VII image by ©iStockphoto.com/
Amr abdelmonem abbas abdou

Editor Ellen S. Boyne
Acquisitions Editor Michael C. Braswell

To Justin

Table of Contents

Preface

Since the publication in 1984 of the first edition of this book, international developments throughout the world have illustrated in a special way the importance of comparative study at the macro level. Many of these events, in particular, point out the significance of comparative and international criminal justice studies. This book was originally conceived and written in the hope that it might be used as a tool to enhance American students' understanding of foreign justice systems. That remains the principal goal.

This edition has involved upgrading materials on the justice systems of the six countries presented in the text. The format for the coverage of each country essentially remains the same. Each chapter is devoted to a single country and attempts to describe the political, historical, organizational, procedural, and critical issues confronting that country's justice system. This format was originally selected because it is an effective method of introducing people to comparative studies. The acceptance of this book over the years appears to support that judgment.

This edition departs from this format with the addition of a chapter that is devoted to Islamic law. Obviously, there has been a heightened interest in Islam in recent years, and a central feature of that attention is with Islamic law in general and the role that it plays in criminal justice in particular. Unlike the other chapters, which focused on a single country and illustrated how a specific legal system contributed to the establishment of its criminal justice system, this chapter was designed to explain the various degrees in which Islamic law has influenced the justice system of a few countries that are associated with Islam. Please note that because there is not one standard method of transliteration of Arabic to English, names and terms often have several different spellings. I have attempted to use a simplified form that is free of many diacritical marks. Any quotations, however, are retained in the original form.

Over the years, I have been appreciative of the many kind words of encouragement from people who have commented on the text. Although this book was designed principally for use in college-level courses created to study foreign justice systems, it also has been utilized in other criminal justice courses and by other disciplines that have a tangential interest in the study of criminal justice. Moreover, it should also prove beneficial to the criminal justice practitioner or the general reader who appreciates the value of considering problems in our justice system from a different cultural and geographical perspective.

As is the case with any large project such as this, the author is indebted to a number of facilitators. Appreciation, therefore, is extended to a number of people, too numerous to mention individually, who work for either governmental or nongovernmental justice agencies in the countries that are presented in this book. They were most helpful in sending me information on their justice systems that was not readily available in this country. Much of the information contained in the introduction appeared previously in other formats. Therefore, a special note of thanks is extended to the Academy of Criminal Justice Sciences for permitting me to use my article, "Teaching Comparative Criminal Justice: Some Thoughts and Themes," which originally appeared in Harry R. Dammer and Philip L. Reichel, eds. (1997), *Teaching About Comparative/International Criminal Justice: A Resource Manual*, and to the publisher of the *Criminal Justice Review* for permission to use my 1982 article, "Approaches For Teaching Comparative Criminal Justice to Undergraduates."

I wish to thank Fred B. Rothman for permission to cite the translated laws of France and Sweden from the American Series of Foreign Penal Codes; to the Managing Director of Eibun-Horei-Sha, Inc., for permission to cite translated laws of Japan; and Mervyn Matthews, M.E. Sharpe Inc., who publishes Soviet Statutes and Decisions, and Martinus Nijhoff Publishers, who published F.J.M. Feldbrugge's translation of the 1977 Constitution of the USSR, for permission to cite various translated laws of the former Soviet Union.

Last, but certainly not least, I appreciate the support and work of my editor, Ellen S. Boyne. Authors of LexisNexis (Anderson Publishing) texts are fortunate to have her encouragement and expertise behind their projects.

Atlanta RJT

Introduction

Criminal justice has emerged as a field of study rather than an academic discipline. In many respects, this approach is analogous to the study of medicine. Medical students must be proficient in chemistry, biology, zoology, physics, and other academic disciplines before they are recognized as medical practitioners. Students of criminal justice also must have an understanding of a number of disciplines prior to considering themselves knowledgeable in their profession. Sociology, psychology, law, and public administration are a few of the more obvious disciplines in which students should possess some proficiency.

Many criminal justice programs are designed to train future practitioners in the techniques of problem solving and in the analysis of issues confronting the system. Among the paramount goals of this educational philosophy is the teaching of techniques for making more meaningful decisions for the system. The ability to understand and to utilize the decision-making process is central to this endeavor. Students are taught that the decision process involves a number of factors: (1) the availability of data on the status quo; (2) the decisionmaker's understanding, albeit a limited one, of the future state he or she wishes to achieve; (3) the comprehension of cost-benefit analyses that determine the direction and processes of moving from the present to the future; (4) the social-psychological makeup of the decisionmaker (that is, biases, prejudices, priorities, and assumptions); (5) the decisionmaker's understanding of his or her agency's place within the total system; and (6) the decisionmaker's skill at comprehending the environment existing beyond the justice process that enables the system to work. With the utilization of these techniques, significant strides have been made at improving the criminal justice system.

Even so, these processes and the academic field do suffer. They fail to recognize other approaches or points of focus that could improve the decision-making process in particular and benefit the academic field in general. For our purposes, the issue centers on our culturally provincial view of the administration of criminal justice. Criminal justice educators, practitioners, and students have had a tendency to think that the concerns within our system are in some way indigenous to it. Many have not considered the possibility that another country has confronted or may be facing a similar concern and that their means of resolving the issue may be of assistance to us. The technique designed to rectify this oversight is known as the comparative approach.

Comparative criminal justice could prove to be indispensable as a tool for the study of our own system, as it allows us to understand it better. It can play a role comparable to the study of history by giving us the perspective necessary to comprehend the dimensions of our system. It provides us with an associational view of our criminal justice institutions and rules that, without such a comparison, could lead us to a false belief in the necessity and permanency of the status quo. If criminal justice is studied only within the boundaries of our country, without taking into consideration foreign ideas and experiences, it will reduce significantly the knowledge and possible approaches to solving our problems. Therefore, the comparative approach does two things for current and future practitioners of criminal justice: it improves their personal freedom, as things are not absolute, and it permits a broader formulation of a philosophy toward the field of criminal justice.

COMPARATIVE METHOD

The comparative approach is one of the older methods of research and instruction. Since the time of the ancient Greeks, it has been utilized in some format by leading thinkers in the Western world. Aristotle, Machiavelli, Montesquieu, Karl Marx, and Max Weber employed it in some of their more significant works. Today, the comparative approach is used in anthropology, economics, law, history, political science, and sociology.

Comparative research involves the study of similarities and differences in cultures, societies, and institutions. The value of this kind of research may include one or more of the following purposes: to test generalizations based on data collected from a single unit of analysis, such as one society; to replicate the findings from one study, which centered on a single unit of analysis, with other studies that focused on similar units of analysis; and to determine under which conditions the conclusions of one study may be valid in the analysis of other studies that are similar.

As such, the comparative approach is not a true method of analysis. Rather, it is a particular approach that is dependent upon an established method of analysis. For example, if one decides to compare the sociological characteristics of two societies, we would expect the researcher to utilize a method compatible with the kinds of information necessary for comparison. Sociologists often employ the following methods: descriptive survey (questionnaire or interview), analytical survey (statistical) or experimental design (pretest/posttest or experimental/control group design) to achieve such ends. Thus, the methodological problems found in comparative studies are similar to any research endeavor utilizing some of these standard analytical tools. The problems are often compounded, however, because of the emphasis placed on studying more than one unit of analysis cross-culturally.

Comparative Criminal Justice

There are a number of approaches or models that are available when one embarks on the study of criminal justice from a comparative perspective. These models are borrowed from the more traditional academic disciplines that have been involved in comparative study for some time. There are at least five approaches to comparative criminal justice that are readily accessible at this time.

Anthropological-Historical Approach

Many criminal justice courses are guilty, by commission or omission, of portraying criminal justice as a static science. Students, however, should be prepared to expect change in the social ideas they are grappling with and with the institutions they will encounter professionally. If this is not achieved, students may be guided by dated or faulty theories of the past. Advocates of the anthropological-historical approach argue that the study of criminal justice emphasizes the present and future, with little regard for the past. They contend, therefore, that the future decisionmakers of the system lack a clear understanding of the system's past. An understanding of the evolutionary nature of society, its institutions and professions, and its philosophies is essential. The anthropological-historical approach prepares students to be part of a world of change. If this approach has value for the student studying his or her own criminal justice system, surely it is useful for understanding foreign justice systems.

Institutional-Structural Approach

Here the central goal is to acquaint the student with a panoramic view of a country's justice system. Proponents of this approach argue that students should be cognizant of the institutions, policies, and terms that give structure to a system. Just as students of one's own system need this kind of introduction, this is also true of the student of the comparative approach. Thus, this approach is directed at presenting organizational profiles of various foreign institutions in criminal justice.

Political-Legal Approach

Politics and the law are significant factors in our own justice system. Both go a long way toward explaining how and why we treat and process those individuals who have been characterized as deviant by our society. Proponents of this approach argue that the study of foreign criminal justice systems must also be placed in the realm of politics and the law. What is the role of government in relation to the justice system? What type of legal system exists in a country? These are two of the kinds of questions raised by this approach.

Social-Philosophical Approach

This approach places emphasis on the need to understand a society's consensus—or lack of consensus—regarding its criminological perspective. What are the prevailing views regarding the causes of crime and deviancy in a society? What are the philosophical approaches to resolving or coping with these views in the penal setting? The value of this approach rests on the idea that students should be introduced to the criminological perspectives of foreign countries. In the context of criminal justice, it provides an opportunity to examine the translation of these perspectives into policies adopted by the various components of the system. This approach also enables students to think through their own tentative views on criminal justice with this added dimension. If students are not exposed to different criminological views and policy implications, they will be limited in their attempts to offer solutions to problems in our society.

Analytical-Problems Approach

This final approach emphasizes the development of theory (be it organizational, legal, or criminological) and the testing of such theories with problems associated with the justice system. The analytical-problems approach defines problems, identifies goals, determines possible solutions, and considers the consequences of those solutions. This approach, more than any of the others mentioned, is future-oriented in terms of the state of the system.

Because this book is a survey of select criminal justice systems in the world, it would be inappropriate to focus solely on one of the aforementioned approaches. It would also be impossible to give equal weight to each. Thus, this text is designed to synthesize the significant benefits derived from each view.

FRAME OF REFERENCE

Before one begins the study of the criminal justice systems presented in this book, one caveat is in order. Although this text purports to be a comparative study of foreign justice systems, some purists might take issue with this liberal use of the term "comparative." This book is not an in-depth narrative comparison among these countries. Its purpose is to survey foreign justice systems. Thus, the format is similar to an introductory text on the criminal justice system of the United States. Also, many books of a comparative nature tend to include a chapter on the United States. The United States is not included here because there are a sufficient number of books published that introduce the reader to that system. It is assumed that the American reader who is interested in learning about the justice systems of other countries has already acquired at least a survey knowledge of the United States' system.

To assist the reader in making comparisons among the countries presented in this book or between a particular country and that of the United States, a strategy is needed to provide an appropriate frame of reference. At least five concepts come to mind that should provide the reader with that strategy. One or more of these concepts should facilitate a method of analysis that enables both a breadth of comparison and an opportunity to assess particular issues in greater depth. The five concepts suggested as points of reference are: the nation state, the legal system, democracy, rule of law, and systems theory.

Nation State

The concept of the nation state emerged in the eighteenth century and has been a significant political unit of analysis since that time. A number of characteristics are associated with the nation state. First, a nation state is an organization with its principal mission being to perform political activities. Second, a state occupies and has exclusive control over a specific territory. Third, a state is also sovereign, which means that its authority is not derived from nor shared with any other entity. Sovereign authority is illustrated by the power to make laws, the right to declare war and to make peace, and the power to grant pardons and appoint people to important governmental positions. Fourth, the population of a state often shares certain common societal features that facilitate a bonding of the people. These features may include: language, religion and a shared cultural or historical experience. The collective distinctiveness of the people helps establish a sense of belonging among the population. Fifth, the institutional development of a nation state has often placed a good deal of emphasis on law, because law has usually played a significant role in establishing various legitimate political processes. Finally, all states have developed bureaucracies that are designed to regulate and control and to provide various services.

As the twentieth century came to a close, the boundaries of the nation state were breaking down as a useful unit of analysis when studying issues like economics and business. That traditional perspective had been altered by the global economy. There remain instances, however, in which the nation state is an appropriate frame of reference. Criminal justice is one of them, in spite of the emergence of international crime cartels. As indicated earlier, the principal goal of this book is to introduce the American reader to justice systems of other countries in order to reduce our provincialism and expand our choice of action in resolving problems confronting our justice system. With the exception of the chapter on Islam, the countries selected for this book are considered powerful nation states, although the kind of power, level of industrialization, and degree of modernization varies among them. There are also differences in the nature of the crime problems confronting these countries. Nevertheless, an extensive and experienced bureaucracy has been established to address the issues of crime and justice that confront each country.

Legal System

Another point of reference is the legal system operable in each country. This factor is especially significant because criminal justice systems of modern industrialized countries are profoundly influenced by the legal system from which they have evolved and with which they are associated. According to René David and John E.C. Brierley, there are three prominent legal families that exist in the world, and they are referred to as: common law, Romano-Germanic, and socialist law [1985]. While these legal families originated in Europe, each has been transplanted to other parts of the world. There are a number of other legal families. The countries associated with these acknowledge the importance of law, but the purpose of law is distinct from that found in the West. This is because these countries embrace a philosophy that views the function of law in a different context from that which emerged in the West.

The common law family originated in England; therefore, it is appropriate to illustrate the characteristics of this law within the British context. Its development is linked to the establishment of royal power in medieval England. It was formulated primarily by judges, and its purpose was to resolve individual disputes on a case-by-case basis. Because of this tradition, the common law is not as philosophically abstract as the other legal families.

The Romano-Germanic family developed on the continent of Europe. The basic source of its creation was Roman law. Throughout the Middle

Ages and the early modern period of European history, this family was further developed by legal scholars. The significant characteristic of this family is its emphasis on the development of law in a codified form rather than on the resolution of individual disputes. French legal scholars were especially instrumental in the modern development of this legal family. Their legal tradition is traced directly to the Roman law. Thus, in this text, France represents one country's use of the Romano-Germanic law.

Another country that is part of the Romano-Germanic family is Sweden. It differs from France in that its development was not only influenced by Roman law but also by characteristics indigenous to many Germanic countries. Although Sweden's legal system is a part of the Romano-Germanic family, it illustrates that not all countries within this family have their origins solely in Roman law.

Some scholars have argued that the differences among legal families are not as pronounced as they once were. A number of countries that in the past were categorized under one family are now borrowing ideas from other legal systems. It is alleged by some that in time the differences among legal families will be negligible. To date, this has been especially noticeable in countries borrowing from common law and Romano-Germanic families. Japan represents a country that has been in the process of borrowing from these two legal families for more than a century. Since the Meiji Restoration, the Japanese have been assimilating a good deal of Western law into their legal system. During the nineteenth century, there was a significant French influence. This was followed by a strong German influence during the first half of the twentieth century. Thus, Japan was borrowing from the Romano-Germanic tradition. Throughout this period, the common law was virtually unknown to them, but with the Allied occupation following World War II, the Japanese were introduced to the common law family and have incorporated parts of it since the post-war years. Some scholars consider the period from the Meiji Restoration through the post-war years as a transitional period in the evolution of Japanese law. The desire now is to synthesize the benefits of both the Romano-Germanic and common law systems within the Japanese context.

Until 1991, socialist law was the third major legal family. Even before that time, however, it was at risk, as countries that formerly subscribed to socialist ideals began to abandon them. It should be pointed out that countries that had ascribed to the socialist legal tenets were often formerly associated with the Romano-Germanic tradition. Many of the legal rules and terminology utilized in the socialist family are traced to the Romano-Germanic system. What made the socialist family unique was the revolutionary nature that was often attributed to it. This family originated in the former Soviet Union and had been emerging as a significant family since the 1917 Revolution. In addition to its Romano-Germanic foundation, the country's legislature, which was influenced and directed by the Communist Party, was the source of socialist law.

The Russian Federation represents another example of a country borrowing legal ideas from other legal families. What makes the Russian case significantly different from the Japanese experience of blending ideas is that it offers a unique illustration of a country presently in the throes of making the most basic yet important decisions about how it wishes to govern itself. To date, the Russians have retained aspects of the old socialist legal system while blending them with ideas from the Romano-Germanic and common law families. In light of the fact that several countries in recent years have attempted to engage in the introduction of market economics and democratic principles, the Russian Federation serves as a useful case study of how this impacts the justice system.

The People's Republic of China offers a particularly interesting case study about the role of a legal system for two reasons. First, it is the last major country in the world that continues to embrace communism. As a result, it has retained many of the features of the socialist legal system that it acquired from the Soviet Union and introduced into the country during the 1950s. Second, China is an example of a country that historically never gave law the significant role that it achieved in the West. This cultural view continued even with the advent of communism and the introduction of socialist law. As such, law is not the only method of regulating human behavior and retaining social order. Harmony can be achieved and conflict reduced through mediation and reconciliation. Today, the importance of law has been acknowledged in China, but often for a specific purpose. Presently, law is recognized as a necessary vehicle in the efforts to modernize the country's economy.

Finally, it was mentioned that some countries view the purpose and function of law in a different context from that which emerged in the West. For our purposes, Islamic law will illustrate this fact. It is important to point out that Islam is primarily a religion, a belief system that espouses a specific moral code. Islam means submitting to God's will. The ultimate goal of Islam has been to establish a theocratic society. In such a context, the state is viewed as a vehicle to enhance and foster the revealed religion throughout the community of believers.

Islamic law is but one feature of this religion. Islamic law is based on divine revelation. For devout Muslims, it is the will of Allah (the preferred word for God) that was revealed to Muhammad, the Prophet of Islam. The Quran, Islamic scripture, is the primary source of these revelations. Obviously, this law is distinct from the other legal families mentioned in this book that are based on the will of legislators and judges. As mentioned in the Preface, Islamic law will not be examined in the context of a single country, but rather it will be viewed in the manner in which it has influenced the justice system of a few countries associated with Islam.

Democracy

The decline in the prominence of communism as a political ideology has enhanced the interest in democracy, especially by countries that have emerged from the political changes in eastern Europe and the former Soviet Union. Many are attempting to adopt and implement a democratic form of government. For our purposes, democracy serves as another point of reference. Four of the countries—England, France, Sweden, and Japan—have long associated themselves with democracy. Russia serves as an illustration of a country that has recently adopted and is attempting to implement a democratic form of government. Only China does not fit into this category. Nonetheless, the Chinese claim to follow the political principles of socialist democracy. Finally, there has been a significant debate among scholars, both within and outside the Muslim community, over whether a country can embrace democratic principles while adhering to the tenets of Islam.

Americans often have a limited understanding of the application of democratic principles. They specifically associate democracy with the political structures found in the United States. These include: the federated nature of the country, the principle of separation of powers, and the importance placed on local self-government. Like other political systems, democracy is capable of adopting several different forms. In fact, the aforementioned items associated with the democratic structure of government in the United States are not essential to the application of democracy as a political system. Because there are variations in the form and function of democracy, it stands to reason that diversification is also found in the application of the core ideals associated with a modern democracy. Those ideals include: a recognition of the importance of government by rule of law, a goal to achieve equality for all members of the community, an objective to establish a right for all members of the community to participate in the conduct of government, and a policy to control and limit government by representatives of the community.

Rule of Law

In recent years, a good deal of interest in both academic scholarship and political discourse has focused on the extent to which a country has embraced the rule of law. The rule of law has deep historical roots in some countries; while for other countries, it has not been part of the political lexicon. As such, rule of law can mean different things to different people, depending on when it became a part of a country's legal tradition. Some countries associate themselves with the concept of rule by law, as if it were synonymous with rule of law. It is not. A country that subscribes to the rule by law employs law as a tool that is often designed to enhance further the authority of the state at the expense of the citizenry. A central feature to rule of law is the idea that the exercise of state power must be regulated by law. For a country to establish or attempt to establish the rule of law, it must embrace several principles or legal values that go to the heart of governance. Among the important principles are: the supremacy of law, the existence of procedural rules for making law, legal transparency, legal certainty, the protection of human rights, equality before the law, and the ability of the state to enforce the law. Because these are legal values, it is more appropriate to view the rule of law as an ideal that a country is attempting to embrace. As a result, the political climate of opinion at any given moment in a country may illustrate both successes and failures at achieving the rule of law.

Systems Theory

A final point of reference that is worth considering when comparing the criminal justice systems of different countries is the extent to which each country is attempting to apply systems theory to the various justice organizations of a country. It is interesting to differentiate the extent to which the justice systems of these countries are open and closed systems and to compare the extent to which these countries have attempted to incorporate systems characteristics, such as goal-seeking, steady state, self-correcting, information feedback, cost-analysis, synergism, and action model building, into the policy and planning process of the justice system.

From an organizational perspective, justice systems in common law countries tend to be more decentralized, while those found in the Romano-Germanic law and socialist law countries clearly display greater tendencies toward centralization. The decentralized approach tends to distribute authority horizontally to several distinct organizations within the total justice system. With a centralized approach, authority is distributed in a hierarchical fashion to officials. The basic process of the organization is divided into distinct stages and is regulated internally by networks of rules. It would appear that the legal family a country is associated with is a contributing factor to the differences in organizations. There are undoubtedly a host of other cultural factors and accidents of history that have influenced this development as well. At issue is the extent and manner in which the organizations of the justice systems of these countries have embraced the current views about administration and management that are associated with systems theory.

CONCLUSION

Criminal justice is a relatively new field of academic study. If it is to mature and become a viable academic endeavor, as well as to assure excellence in what it purports to be doing, it would be well served to learn from some of the more traditional disciplines in the social sciences. The comparative method has been included in sociology, political science, law, history, and economics for a number of years, and each discipline has benefited from it. If there is no reason to doubt that the problems in criminal justice are numerous and the issues are significant, then we should consider employing the comparative method as a tool to help analyze and resolve these difficulties. This text is designed to serve as a foundation for utilizing the comparative approach.

Concepts to Know

Statute of Winchester (1285)
Human Rights Act (1998)
home secretary
police authorities
Serious Organized Crime Agency
Independent Police Complaints Commission
British Crime Survey
Henry II
Lord Chancellor
Constitutional Reform Act (2005)
barrister
solicitors
Crown courts
lay magistrates
proof by ordeal
Fourth Lateran Council
Police and Criminal Evidence Act (1984)
Prison Service
NACRO
Children and Young Persons Act (1969)
Crime and Disorder Act (1998)
Youth Court

Chapter I

ENGLAND

INTRODUCTION

England is a small island country situated off the northern coast of France. Throughout its history, the country has been referred to as England, Great Britain, and the United Kingdom. The official name changes occurred as a result of England's political union with its territorial neighbors. For example, in 1706, England and Wales united with Scotland. This geographic alliance became known as Great Britain. When the southern counties of Ireland formed the Irish Free State in 1922, the official name of Britain changed again—this time to the United Kingdom of Great Britain and Northern Ireland.

In this chapter, we are concerned only with the geographical area known as England and Wales. The reasons for this are quite simple. Scotland is not a common law country; its criminal justice system consists of a mixture of common and civil law. This was a result of its political association with France in the sixteenth and seventeenth centuries. Scotland retained some of the legal characteristics that are indigenous to civil law countries such as France. Northern Ireland is not included in this study as a result of the problems that exist between the Protestant and Catholic factions of that country. The serious nature of these problems, although they are beginning to be resolved, has caused the criminal justice system to be altered somewhat from the common law system that exists in England and Wales.

England and Wales encompass an area of 58,350 square miles, which is a little larger than the state of Michigan. Many of the more than 54 million inhabitants live in the highly industrialized cities of the country. Although England no longer retains the industrial supremacy it once possessed, the country continues to be a world leader in the manufacture of heavy machinery. Agriculture, fishing, and oil are some of England's other important industries. The legacy that the people of England have given the rest of the world is significant and indeed remarkable. The English have made major contributions in science, philosophy, literature, and the arts, but their most important and striking contribution to the historical evolution of civilization has been the creation of the common law and the development of parliamentary democracy.

GOVERNMENT

The foundation for England's political and legal institutions was established between the eleventh and fourteenth centuries. It was at this time that the monarchy negotiated several compromises with the nobility and, in the process, asserted its central authority. Following the English Civil War, which occurred during the first half of the seventeenth century, the modern basis for the country's political institutions was established. The power of the monarchy was curtailed, the authority of the House of Commons was secured, and the emergence of political parties was established. Efforts at further reform and modernization were completed during the nineteenth century.

As the country prepared to enter the twenty-first century, it embarked upon an intense period of government reform. What is particularly striking about these reform efforts is the fact that much of it is devoted to significant constitutional issues. The adoption of these initiatives is designed to improve the effectiveness and efficiency of democratic government. While it is far too early to assess the impact that these reforms will have on governance, one consequence is clear: the role and power of some units of the central government have shifted.

The Constitution

Many countries throughout the world have a written document called a constitution in which the political and legal beliefs of the country are expressed. England does not have this type of constitution; it has been characterized as having an unwritten or, more appropriately, an uncodified constitution. The British constitution is a blend of statutory law, precedent, and tradition that dates back to the time of King Henry I

(1100). A large part of English constitutional law is based on statutes passed in Parliament. Statutory law is an important factor in the creation of this kind of "organic" constitution. This is best illustrated by citing some of the significant statutes that were instrumental in developing British constitutional principles. These, in turn, have had a profound impact on the creation of written constitutions in other countries.

Magna Carta The first document that carried with it this kind of significance was Magna Carta. In 1215, King John was forced by English nobles to sign this charter, which was an expression of rights and privileges of the upper class in medieval England. The charter consisted of 62 chapters or issues identified by the nobles. Chapter 39 was the most important and famous of these and happens to be particularly pertinent to criminal justice. It stated:

> No free man shall be taken, imprisoned, disseised, outlawed, banished, or in any way destroyed, nor will we proceed against or prosecute him, except by the lawful judgment of his peers and by the law of the land.

For a number of years, some of the chapters in Magna Carta were misinterpreted. For example, Chapter 39 was described as originating trial by jury and the writ of habeas corpus, but both assumptions are false. To the twenty-first-century reader, the real value of Magna Carta is that it is the first attempt to explain in legal terms the germ of the idea of government by a constitutional process.

The Bill of Rights Another important historical document is the statute known as the Bill of Rights. Before Parliament offered the English crown to William III and Mary II in 1688, it required their acquiescence to principles that became known as the Bill of Rights. Among the principles that appeared in the statute were: Parliament should meet frequently to redress grievances and pass legislation; members of Parliament should be elected freely; freedom of speech should be assured during the proceedings of Parliament; the Crown cannot suspend or create law without the consent of Parliament; and excessive bail or fines should not be imposed nor cruel and unusual punishments permitted. The principal significance of this statute was that it established a clear foundation on which to build a modern constitution.

The Act of Settlement The Act of Settlement of 1700 was another statute that proved beneficial in establishing the modern constitution. One of the most important provisions of this act was the recognition that judges should hold office only during good behavior and could be removed only with the consent of Parliament. These statutes, along with others, clearly stated that the monarch must govern by and through Parliament. Since the seventeenth century, there have been other significant statutes passed in Parliament that have in some way altered the British constitution. Unfortunately, they are too numerous to list within the confines of this text. These examples provide the reader with a sense of how some basic constitutional principles were incrementally introduced, which usually coincided with Parliament enhancing its authority.

The Human Rights Act As mentioned earlier, the government embarked recently upon an intense period of reform that has some important constitutional implications. One of the most significant of these initiatives was the passage of the Human Rights Act (1998). Although this legislation received the royal assent in 1998, all of the sections to the act were not in force until October 2000. The significance of this legislation is that it incorporates the European Convention on Human Rights into an English statute and thus enables violations of the Convention's provisions to be adjudicated in English courts.

The European Convention on Human Rights was ratified by the United Kingdom in 1951, but it was not incorporated into domestic law. Nevertheless, the country has been bound by its terms and court judgments under international law. The Convention is similar to a written constitution, like the Constitution of the Untied States, in that it is a listing of fundamental principles associated with a democratic form of government. The Convention consists of a series of articles that address such rights and freedoms as: the right to life; prohibition of torture; prohibition of slavery and forced labor; right to liberty and security; right to a fair trial; no punishment without law; right to respect for private and family life; freedom of thought, conscience, and religion; freedom of expression; freedom of assembly and association; right to marry; prohibition of discrimination; restrictions on political activity of aliens; prohibition of abuse of rights; limitation on use of restrictions on rights; protection of property; right to education; right to free elections; abolition of the death penalty; and death penalty in time of war.

In 1966, citizens of the United Kingdom were empowered to petition the European Court on Human Rights, which is based in Strasbourg (France), if they believed one of their aforementioned rights had been violated by the government or an agent of the government. Unfortunately, such an appeal was costly to the petitioner, as legal aid was not available and the process took a good deal of time in light of various court delays. Five years has often been cited as not being an uncommon length of time for a case to work its way through the court. By incorporating the Convention into domestic law through the Human Rights Act (1998), citizens of the United Kingdom can now initially petition an English court.

Many scholars view the Human Rights Act (1998) as a new chapter in the evolution of English constitutional law, because all public authorities now have a duty to comply with the Convention on Human Rights

(Wadham and Mountfield, 2000). It is important, however, to note the distinction between a statutory and a constitutional duty. Most European countries adopted the Convention as part of their fundamental or basic law. This kind of incorporation enables the courts of a country to rule that a national law is incompatible with the Convention. This type of adoption did not occur in the United Kingdom because the English judiciary does not have the authority to overturn parliamentary decisions, that is, to declare a law unconstitutional. Granting the judiciary that kind of power would be a rejection of the idea of parliamentary sovereignty.

The Human Rights Act (1998) does address the issue of English law being incompatible with rights spelled out in the Convention. According to Sections 3 and 4 of the act, English courts can issue a declaration of incompatibility. This enables courts to indicate to the government that remedial action should be taken to correct that portion of a domestic law that is not in compliance with the fundamental democratic principles represented in the Convention. Thus, although English courts do not have the power to override the authority of Parliament, the role of the judiciary has been enhanced considerably by this legislation. The judiciary has been given the authority to encourage both the executive and legislature to take corrective action when domestic legislation is not in compliance with human rights provisions.

It should be noted that there are derogation statements in both the Human Rights Act, Section 1(2), "[t]hose Articles are to have effect for the purpose of this Act subject to any designated derogation or reservation," and The European Convention on Human Rights, Article 15, "[i]n time of war or other public emergency threatening the life of the nation." The issuance of a derogation order is of particular relevance in recent years as a result of the international concern over terrorism. For example, the British government derogated from Article 5 of the Convention, which deals with a person's right to liberty and security, specifically as it relates to being arrested or detained by the police. This was necessary because parliament passed the Anti-Terrorism, Crime and Security Act (2001), which permits the detention of suspected terrorists for extended periods of time that would not be permitted under a typical criminal investigation.

The reader should also be cognizant of some other characteristics of the British constitution. First, Britain is a unitary country and not a federated state. Therefore, Parliament is supreme over the entire United Kingdom. Although this principle remains in place, it should be pointed out that as part of the recent constitutional reform effort, devolution has been granted to Scotland and Wales. In 1999, representatives were elected to the newly established Scottish Parliament and Welsh Assembly. Second, Parliament exercises supreme legal power in Britain. As a result, no English court can declare an act of Parliament unconstitutional. The limitations imposed on the authority of the courts in the Human Rights Act

(1998) illustrate the importance of this principle to English jurisprudence. Finally, there is a fusion of powers in Britain, rather than a separation of powers as is the case in the United States. Both the executive and legislative branches of government are found in Parliament. Until recently, the highest court in the land, the Appellate Committee of the House of Lords, was also situated in Parliament. With the passage of the Constitutional Reform Act (2005), however, the Supreme Court of the United Kingdom was created to replace the Appellate Committee and is scheduled to begin operating in October 2009.

The recent passage of the Human Rights Act (1998), House of Lords Act (1999), and the Constitutional Reform Act (2005) are illustrations of the "organic" nature of the British constitution. Moreover, the British have been viewed for a long time as a rule of law–based country. These statutes, each in their own distinct way, enhance that position even further.

Parliament

The British government has operated under the constitutional principle that the country should be governed by a fused power rather than a separated one. Parliament provides that leadership. It consists of three parts: the monarch, the House of Lords, and the House of Commons.

The Monarch The role of the monarch in Parliament has been declining for almost 300 years. The reason for this reduction in power is constitutionally and politically related to Britain's establishment of a government based on democratic principles. Today, the monarch's importance is symbolic; it represents the unity of the country. For example, all statutes passed in Parliament are carried out in the monarch's name. Despite a loss of power, the monarch legally retains some authority. The monarch convenes Parliament after an election and dissolves Parliament when an election is required. The monarch calls for the leader of the political party who was victorious in the election campaign to form a government—or, more accurately, an administration for the government.

The House of Lords Like the monarchy, the power of the House of Lords has diminished considerably. The historical roots of this body are almost as ancient as the monarchy itself. Early English kings traditionally had a great council that consisted of a group of nobles who advised the king on domestic and foreign affairs. The House of Lords is the political descendant of the great council and is considered to be the upper house of Parliament. Its authority has declined, especially during the past 100 years, because the idea of popular democracy is theoretically at cross-purposes with such an unrepresentative element in government.

The House of Lords performs several duties. Until 2009, it was the highest court of appeal in the country, but when it sat as a court, only the lords of appeal in ordinary, also referred to as law lords, took part in the proceedings. The House does a considerable amount of committee work; that is, it examines and revises legislation proposed in the House of Commons. It has been suggested that the House of Commons benefits from this because it has restrictions placed on its time for scrutinizing legislation. The Lords' most controversial power is the constitutional power to delay the enactment of legislation passed in the House of Commons. With the exception of budget bills, which are the sole prerogative of the House of Commons, the House of Lords may delay the enactment into law of any public bill passed in the House of Commons. This delay cannot exceed one year; if it does, the bill becomes law without the House of Lords' assent.

While the upper House of Parliament continues to provide a valuable service to the country, the composition of its membership changed with the passage of the House of Lords Act (1999). This was another piece of reform legislation that was designed to reduce the number of hereditary peers sitting in the House. The objective was to eliminate a political anachronism from a governmental process that is based on democratic principles.

To understand the significance of the House of Lords Act (1999), it is useful to consider the composition of the House before the passage of this legislation. The House of Lords was composed of approximately 1,200 members who fell into one of three categories. First, there was a special group that consisted of the archbishops of York and Canterbury; the bishops of London, Durham, and Winchester; and 21 senior bishops of the Church of England. Also included in this special category were the law lords, who were responsible for performing judicial duties for the House, which was the court of highest appeal. Second, the group of hereditary peers made up the majority in the House of Lords, consisting of about 800 members. Although some of these people were very capable, they did not hold their seat in the House because of their ability to deal with legislative matters. Rather, they were members because they held the noble rank of duke, marquess, earl, viscount, or baron—a distinction conferred upon one of their ancestors by an English monarch at some point in the family's history. Thus, they had the hereditary right to sit in the House of Lords. The third category consists of life peers. The Life Peerage Act (1958) enables the government, through the monarch, to recognize people who have been outstanding public servants or who have made some significant achievement in industry or the professions by appointing them to the House of Lords. Unlike the hereditary peers, a life peer cannot pass the title onto his or her children.

The House of Lords Act (1999) is considered the first of a two-part phase in the reform of the House of Lords. This act eliminated the automatic right of a hereditary peer to sit in the House. It called for the election of 90 hereditary peers to continue to serve, along with the two peers that held the ancient titles of Lord Great Chamberlain and Earl Marshall, making the total 92. This is a considerable reduction from the roughly 800 people who were eligible to sit. The bishops of the Church of England were allowed to retain their seats, but members of the monarch's immediate family were excluded. The hereditary peers that were excluded from the House of Lords retain their title and are now eligible to stand for election to the House of Commons.

The House of Commons Today, the most important component of Parliament is the House of Commons. When people speak of Parliament, they are usually referring to the House of Commons. The origins of this House can be traced to the thirteenth century, but it was not until the seventeenth-century English Civil War that the Commons gained the political ascendancy in Parliament.

Presently, the House consists of 646 elected members. The typical member of the Commons (M.P. for Member of Parliament) is affiliated with either the Conservative or Labour parties. This House, more than the other two components of Parliament, represents the various social and political elements of the British population. The major responsibility of the House is to vote on legislative bills proposed by either the government or a member of the Commons. Another duty is to discuss issues and pending legislation. Members of the party in power are obviously attempting to support the government, while members of the opposition parties (the parties that are out of power) seek to criticize it.

The function of discussing issues and pending legislation also serves a political end for all parties, because England can be considered to be in a continuous election campaign. Statutory law requires that a general election be held every five years, but an election can be called before that time. For example, it is not uncommon for the party in power to call for an early election at a time when opinion polls indicate that it is riding a wave of popularity. In addition, if the government loses the support of a majority on an important vote in the Commons, it may request that the monarch dissolve Parliament and call for an election. Because election campaigns have usually lasted about three to four weeks, political parties must be continually capable of presenting their case to the people for either retaining power or gaining power in the Commons. Thus, the House of Commons continuously provides all parties with a forum for presenting their views to the British electorate.

Prime Minister

In the modern British constitution, the prime minister has become the fulcrum for the English form of parliamentary democracy. The way the political system works is largely dependent on the prime minister. The leader of the political party that has won a majority of seats in the House of Commons is selected to be the prime minister.

The qualities necessary for an effective prime minister are many; the person who occupies this position must be versatile. The reason for this is quite simple. The prime minister must combine into one job a set of responsibilities that in many countries are distributed among a number of people.

The prime minister is leader of the nation. National opinion polls are largely based on the personality and policies of the prime minister. Because the monarch has a right to be consulted on national issues, the prime minister is the personal advisor to the monarch. The prime minister is also leader of his or her political party. Although assisted in this leadership role by party whips, the prime minister nevertheless must function as a party manager and conciliator in keeping party members in line on important legislative issues before Parliament. Finally, the prime minister is chair of the cabinet, which is created by his or her appointments to it and which sets the goals and establishes the policies of the government.

The Cabinet

After the British electorate have voted for their candidates, it is the responsibility of the monarch to request that the leader of the victorious party—the one that has won a majority of seats in the House of Commons—form a government. The British executive branch is composed of members in Parliament whose political party commands a majority in the House of Commons. This group is referred to as the cabinet. Membership in the cabinet is dominated by the House of Commons, with a few members from the House of Lords.

Generally, the prime minister includes in the cabinet all of the outstanding leaders in the party. He or she is usually careful to include some younger members in order to groom them for future key leadership positions. The wise leader will also assure that the various points of view within the party are represented so that the cabinet serves as a microcosm of the entire party.

Each member of the cabinet is responsible to Parliament for the administration of his or her department. For example, the Chancellor of the Exchequer is responsible for the Treasury Department, while the foreign secretary is the chief executive of the Foreign Office. Collectively, the cabinet is accountable to Parliament for the administration of the entire government. Thus, the cabinet is responsible for three things: controlling the executive branch of government, coordinating the work of various departments, and determining government policy and submitting it to Parliament.

Political Parties

While England has had three parties vying for power for more than 100 years, the Conservative and Labour parties are considered the major political parties. The benefits of a two-party system are similar to those found in the United States. The party that wins the election usually has a clear majority in Parliament. The formation of a government by the majority party assures a stable and disciplined government. The British electorate have a clear choice at election time to retain the party in power based on its record or to select the opposition party based on its promises for the future.

Conservative Party The Conservative Party has a long heritage traceable to the seventeenth century. One of its remarkable achievements has been an ability to adapt to the changing political and social climate of opinion for more than 300 years. As is true of any conservative party, British conservatives support traditional institutions and political and social principles. Often they are devout defenders of the monarchy, the Church of England, and social class. Although they may accept change and innovation, they reject change for change's sake. They prefer to retain established institutions and principles that have stood the test of time. This attitude helps to explain why some members of the party are skeptical of the European Union, in particular, the issue of monetary union.

The Conservative Party supports the principles of free enterprise, private property, freedom of choice, self-interest, and reward for ability; yet, they have accepted in principle the concept of the welfare state. They differ, however, with the opposition regarding the degree and the means with which social services should be provided. So long as change occurs within the framework of the constitutional tradition of parliamentary government, the Conservative Party is willing to accept and endorse state activity in the private sector, as well as social reform in the public sector.

Labour Party The Labour Party was officially founded in 1900. The party's ideology can be traced back to the middle of the nineteenth century, when England was the most industrialized country in the world. Throughout the twentieth century, the party supported a socialist ideology. Their political platform emphasized a movement toward extending democratic principles of the political realm to the economic marketplace. Their goals included the nationalization of industries by the government, a more equal distribution of wealth through a progressive income tax and other forms of taxation, the institution of social welfare services for all citizens, and the elimination of a class-based society. Like their conservative counterparts, the Labour Party has been willing to achieve these ends gradually through the parliamentary process.

In the past few years, the Labour Party has attempted to become more mainstream or centrist. To illustrate, they have changed their long-standing commitment to the nationalization of industries. They support a dynamic capitalistic economy that is capable of balancing the objectives of the private sector with the public interest and can display social compassion for the less fortunate. They have espoused a policy that is tough on crime and its causes. Finally, they are leading the current efforts at constitutional reform.

Liberal Democratic Party In the late 1980s, the Liberal Democratic Party was created out of a merger of two small parties: the Liberal and the Social Democratic parties. The Liberal Party traced its ideological position back to the seventeenth century. For much of the twentieth century, however, they had a difficult time retaining a viable party membership because they had been out of political office since 1915. Early in 1981, some discontented moderates of the Labour Party resigned their positions and formed a new political party called the Social Democratic Party as an alternative to the extreme leftist positions that were being espoused by the Labour Party at that time.

Presently, the Liberal Democratic Party has tended to attract the interests of the suburban middle class. They are the party of the individual versus the collective. They are public sector–minded, with a strong power base in local government. They support the European Union, the reform of Parliament, and the reduction of tax breaks for the wealthy. While the Liberal Democrats claim to be the party of the center, they remain a fairly small party because the leadership of the Labour and Conservative parties have tempered their more extreme positions.

The Crown

The Crown is the constitutional office that symbolically unites the people of England. This institution, because of its ancient heritage and the associated pageantry, is revered by a large segment of the British population. The monarch is the person who occupies this office. The degree of affection drawn by a monarch is based on both personality and approach to the office. Throughout the long history of the monarchy, the English have had a number of popular and unpopular monarchs. Despite the unpopularity of a particular monarch, the people usually were capable of making a distinction between the person and the office. Thus, they have continued to show deference to the Crown. Like the House of Lords, the monarchy is the antithesis of democracy. The monarchy, however, remains a powerful and useful symbol for the country, and a majority of the public appears to acknowledge this fact.

Most of the powers and duties of the monarch have already been suggested. There is one final personal prerogative that a monarch can exercise: the right to be consulted. This means that all important government business must be available for the monarch's perusal. The significance of this right generally increases with the length of the monarch's reign. Political leaders come and go, but the monarch often reigns for a number of years. The monarch can gain considerable insight into the affairs of state and view current policies with a historical and associational perspective that a political leader may lack. This position can enable a diligent monarch to influence the leaders who ultimately must decide policy. Although there is no way of measuring the effects of this situation, it is a fact that must be reckoned with when considering the utility of the Crown in twenty-first-century politics.

Administration

Although England is a unitary state, there are areas of government that are not the sole responsibility of Parliament. England has had a long history of county and municipal government—working either in association with Parliament or separated from it—that dates back to medieval times. Occasionally, it was deemed appropriate to allow local governments to administer certain matters at the local level. Sewage, water, and parks and recreation are examples of local responsibilities.

After World War II, the national government stepped up its efforts to nationalize industries, substituting private ownership with public ownership. Obviously, this increased the scope of its power. One of the hallmarks of Prime Minister Margaret Thatcher's government was to reverse this trend of nationalizing industries by returning them to the private sector.

The areas of responsibility in which the national government has complete or almost complete control include matters pertaining to defense, foreign affairs, law, economics, social matters, and internal order. The national government has a significant role in judicial matters. Until 2006, the Lord Chancellor, who is appointed by the prime minister and is a member of the cabinet from the House of Lords, was ultimately responsible for appointing all judges. With the passage of the Constitutional Reform Act (2005), that responsibility passed to the Judicial Appointments Commission, whose members are selected by the Lord Chancellor. Internal order is a matter of shared responsibility between the national and local governments. For example, the police are accountable to the home secretary, who is also a member of the cabinet. This office establishes standards for all police forces and provides grants-in-aid equaling at least 51 percent of the costs for maintaining each of the forces. Local governments also have some control, for they are responsible for hiring officers and providing about 49 percent of the expenses needed to maintain their force.

Since the 1960s, the national government has made a concerted effort to control the planning and administration of the criminal justice system. The Lord Chancellor was concerned with the efficiency and effectiveness of the courts, while the home secretary had increased authority for law enforcement and the prison service. This development was a direct result of the government having to deal with crises within various components of criminal justice. This arrangement, however, was becoming increasingly untenable. Critics raised several concerns, of which some cited constitutional issues. For example, questions were raised about the independence of the judiciary, while others focused on the incompatible responsibilities of the home secretary: policing and maintain public order with prisons and protecting civil rights and reforming the criminal law. The ongoing furtherance of constitutional reform has attempted to rectify some of these problems. In 2007, a new Ministry of Justice was created and given responsibility for the courts, criminal law, prison and probation, and criminal justice reform. The Home Office had its focus narrowed to crime and policing, counter-terrorism, and immigration.

Over the course of the past three decades, almost every aspect of the criminal justice system has been the subject of interest to a government commission, an independent inquiry, or academic research. This has led to the passage of a significant amount of legislation directly impacting how the justice system is organized and administered. What happened in England during the 1980s and early 1990s is strikingly similar to what occurred in the United States during the 1960s and 1970s. The study of criminal justice has become a significant issue for the government and has emerged as an important field of study within England's system of higher education.

Police

The English have prided themselves on initiating a system of policing based at the local level but also mandated and in some fashion controlled by the central government. This shared responsibility for policing has existed throughout much of the country's history. Prior to the creation of the Metropolitan Police of London in 1829, this tradition of shared responsibility took four distinct forms.

The tithing was the earliest type of community-organized policing; references are made to it in Anglo-Saxon dooms. Historians refer to the period before the Norman invasion of 1066 as the Anglo-Saxon era. Dooms were the statutes or ordinances enacted during that period. The tithing was based on principles of self-help and collective responsibility. Each tithing consisted of 10 men who were accountable for policing each other. If one of their either accused of a crime, they were responsible for producing the defendant before a local court, and if they failed to surrender the individual, the court could impose a fine on the other members of the tithing. Supervision of the tithing was a responsibility of the sheriff, the local representative of the king. Therefore, during this early medieval period, the sheriff was the link between the local and the central government for criminal justice administration.

The creation of the office of constable was the next significant development in law enforcement. It occurred as a direct result of England emerging as a feudal society, following the Norman Conquest of 1066. With the advent of feudalism, the manor became the principal unit of local government. People worked on large tracts of land owned by the lord of a manor in return for economic and social security. The lord of a manor appointed officers to provide a number of services for the manor community. The ale-taster and bread-weigher were two of these officers, as was the position of constable. The constable replaced the tithing as the primary source for policing a manor. Long after feudalism ceased to exist, the constable continued in this role—recognized by the king as the principal officer responsible for maintaining the peace of the kingdom at the local level.

Throughout the twelfth and thirteenth centuries, English kings significantly increased the extent of their political authority. Whereas the tithing system and the office of constable evolved from custom and feudalism, respectively, future innovations were initiated because of the king's demand. These royal commands were given expression in statute law. The Statute of Winchester (1285) initiated a precedent that became the basis for the organization of English police to this day. It established the notion that policing was a responsibility shared between the central government of the king and the local communities.

The Statute of Winchester was the first public measure designed to systematize police efforts in towns. It retained some of the features of previous eras, especially the notion of local responsibility for policing. Specifically, it called for the introduction of town watchmen who would stand guard between sunset and sunrise. It revived the Anglo-Saxon "hue and cry" in which the whole community was expected to pursue a fleeing felon when a loud outcry was sounded. It also emphasized the maintenance of the "assize of arms," in which every male between the ages of 15 and 60 was required to own a weapon for defensive purposes.

Constables were responsible for seeing that each town adhered to the statute.

In 1361, the Justices of the Peace Act further clarified the approach to policing English society. Keepers of the peace for each shire or county had been established by the Justices of the Peace Act of 1327. The 1361 statute gave these keepers formal recognition as justices. The justices were usually owners of large tracts of land in their county. The king appointed and enabled them to maintain the peace and to administer justice at the local level. The Act reiterated the three points presented in the Statute of Winchester and supplemented them with two additional principles. One emphasized the duty of every citizen to keep the peace by permitting everyone to arrest offenders, while the other mandated that the constable present those accused of crimes before the local court. The Winchester and the Justices of the Peace statutes explained the official approach to policing that existed in England until the early nineteenth century.

By the late seventeenth and early eighteenth centuries, this system of policing had become ineffective. During the eighteenth century, a number of notable police practitioners—among them Henry Fielding, John Fielding, and Patrick Colquhoun—attempted to persuade Parliament to reform the police. Politicians, however, feared that improvements in police efficiency would enhance the authority of the monarchy. This was considered unacceptable at that time because a majority in Parliament were attempting to reduce monarchical power. Politicians often cited the efficient police system of France's *ancien regime* to illustrate their concern. Therefore, the suggestions of police reformers were not implemented, and the assessment of English politicians to curtail monarchical power was given further credence with the outbreak of the French Revolution.

During the 1820s, a few politicians realized that something had to be done about police inefficiency—especially in the greater metropolitan area of London. Robert Peel, a leading politician of the day, committed himself to a resolution of the problem. While serving as home secretary, Peel introduced a bill in Parliament calling for the creation of a metropolitan police force. The bill mandated that: (1) two justices of the peace would create and administer a force that would police the metropolitan areas of London, (2) police personnel would be sworn as constables, thereby having all the powers, duties, and privileges accorded a constable under common law, and (3) the two justices would exercise their authority and be responsible to the home secretary.

With scarcely any debate in Parliament, the bill became law on June 19, 1829. Peel appointed Colonel Charles Rowan, a retired army officer, and Richard Mayne, an Irish lawyer, to the posts of justices of the peace. They were soon referred to as commissioners of police. Upon Rowan's death, Mayne continued as the single commissioner of police for metropolitan London. The tradition of a single commissioner continues to this day. Rowan and Mayne planned, organized, and recruited the force, and on September 29, 1829, the "new police" began to patrol the streets of metropolitan London.

After a few difficult years, the force became recognized throughout many parts of the world as the first modern police force. During the 1830s, this model was accepted by the rest of the English citizenry. The Municipal Corporations Act of 1835 enabled towns to create police forces. In 1838, the City of London established a force modeled along these lines. Finally, the County Police Act of 1839 reformed the police in rural areas. At the turn of the twentieth century, there were 197 police forces scattered across the country.

One of the most important developments in twentieth-century British policing has been the extent to which these forces have been amalgamated. Today, there are 43 local forces serving the people of England and Wales. Consolidation has had a significant impact on the long-standing notion that policing is a responsibility shared by central and local governments.

Organization and Administration of the English Police

The English have long rejected the idea that they have a national police service. To prove the historical validity of their argument, they frequently cite a long list of statutes that date back to the Statute of Winchester (1285). In both theory and fact, however, the central government has enormous control and influence over the police, and it appears to be increasing. Despite this apparent contradiction, the management of police remains a shared responsibility between the central government and the local authorities. The following is a description of the organization of the English police (see Figure 1.1).

The Home Office At the top of the organizational hierarchy is the secretary of state for the Home Office, a civilian politician who is more commonly referred to as the home secretary. As previously mentioned, the home secretary is one of the senior officials in the prime minister's cabinet and is, therefore, a member of Parliament. The powers and duties of the home secretary, as they relate to police, are clearly explained in statutory law. The significance of this approach assures members of Parliament that one of their own, as well as a member of the government, is ultimately responsible for police throughout the country. This enables members to question the home secretary regarding the police service while Parliament is in session.

Figure 1.1

ORGANIZATION OF THE ENGLISH POLICE

Home Office

Office of Inspectors of Constabulary	Metropolitan Police Service
Serious Organized Crime Agency	City of London Police
Independent Police Complaints Commission	41 Provincial Police Forces

The home secretary's responsibilities are significant and comprehensive. They illustrate the centrality of this position's administrative authority. For example, the home secretary is consulted on the appointment of senior administrative positions to all forces and has the authority to remove these senior administrators from their positions. He or she can require the chief executive of a police force to submit a report on any aspect of policing for which the executive is responsible, and can appoint people to investigate any issue dealing with a police force. The home secretary also can make regulations regarding the organization and administration of police. This includes rank, qualifications of service, promotions, suspensions, authorized strength of a force, hours of duty, pay, and records. Also within the jurisdiction of the home secretary are regulations in reference to matters pertaining to training, the kinds of equipment used, and the number of buildings authorized for each force as well as appeals from members of a force who have been disciplined.

Three of the home secretary's most important powers are: the issuance of administrative circulars that impact considerably on the management of all forces throughout the country; the provision of 51 percent of monetary funds needed for the budget of each force; and the establishment of levels of performance throughout the police service. The home secretary prepares an annual National Policing Plan that discusses the objectives and performance targets. Finally, the home secretary has the ultimate administrative authority for the Inspectors of Constabulary, the Independent Police Complaints Commission, and the Serious Organized Crime Agency. The specific duties of these agencies are explained below.

Although the home secretary possesses administrative power and control over the police service in England, the use of such authority is limited. Thus, the chief constables and the local authorities of each force are afforded a good deal of discretion to operate their police service in a manner suitable to their needs. It should be emphasized at this point that the home secretary and the local authorities do not have the power to direct or to order police in their specific law enforcement duties. Rather, they are responsible as executive overseers for the management of the forces.

Chief Constables The chief administrative officer for each of the 41 provincial forces is called a chief constable. Appointed by the local police authority with the approval of the home secretary, the chief constable administers and manages the daily operations of the force. The chief constable is assisted in administrative duties by assistant chief constables and superintendents. The chief administrative officers for the Metropolitan Police Service and the City of London are called commissioners. The commissioner of police for the Metropolis is appointed by the monarch through the home secretary.

Police Authorities A unique administrative feature of the English police is the role played by police authorities, which have been utilized throughout the service for almost 100 years. There are 43 police authorities, which correspond to the 43 local police forces. The police authority serving the 41 provincial forces is a committee usually consisting of 17 members. Nine of the committee members are politicians from the local county council (or councils, in the event the police force serves more than one county). They are elected by their council colleagues to serve on the authority. Three of the members are magistrates (lower-court judges who adjudicate cases in the provincial region). The other five members are appointed by members of the police authority from a list of names prepared by the home secretary.

The police force for London has a separate and distinct police authority: the city council of London. Until 2001, the police authority for the Metropolitan Police Service had been the home secretary, who served alone in that capacity. In that year, however, the Metropolitan Police Authority was established. The new Authority consists of 23 members. The mayor selects 12 from those serving on the Greater London Assembly. Four magistrates and seven independent members are also selected to serve with one of the independents appointed by the home secretary.

Each police authority has five general functions. First, the police authority serves as an advisory body to the police force. In this capacity it is concerned with maintaining an efficient and effective force for its police area. This is accomplished in part by: (1) providing the area with an adequate police force (It accomplishes this task by providing 49 percent of the financial costs. With the approval of the home secretary, it maintains buildings for the police and provides vehicles, clothing, and other equipment necessary for the force.); and (2) consulting with the chief constable on local issues. The second function of the police authority is appointing the chief constable for the force, subject to the approval of the home secretary. After consulting with the chief constable, the authority appoints the assistant chief constables. These also are subject to the approval of the home secretary. In addition, the authority determines the size of the force and the number of people needed for each rank. This is accomplished in consultation with the aforementioned officials. Third, although the home secretary is empowered to remove a chief constable or an assistant chief constable, the police authority also has this right, with the approval of the home secretary. Fourth, disciplinary actions against an officer are the responsibility of the chief constable, but the police authority has a right and an obligation to be kept informed on such matters. Finally, the police authority provides funds to cover the liability for a tort committed by a member of the force while on duty.

In theory, the existence of a police authority enables each force to maintain a degree of local autonomy and assures public input into the organization and management of the force. In fact, the authority's actual role has declined over the years. Scholars have alleged that the authorities have abdicated their responsibilities and are now viewed as rubber stamps for chief constables (Brogden, 1982; Lustgarten, 1986; Oliver, 1987; Reiner, 1985). Several factors have been cited as possible reasons for this development. One is a result of the consolidation of the forces. The increased size of the new police bureaucracies may be reducing the police authorities' willingness to assert their power over the forces. Another is the home secretary's authority to issue administrative circulars, in addition to the new responsibility of establishing levels of performance throughout the police service. Both of these duties impact considerably on the management of the forces. The Research and Planning Unit and the Central Planning and Training Unit within the Home Office also may be hindering the police authorities' utility. No one is suggesting that these units are not needed, but bureaucratic technocrats have been known to intimidate local politicians on police authorities. These units also increase the power of the home secretary, if one accepts the notion that a key source of organizational power is the control and dissemination of information. Finally, the enhanced position and deference paid to chief constables has diminished the position of police authorities. Each of these factors gives further credence to the claim that England is moving toward a national police service.

Metropolitan Police Service The Metropolitan Police Service is responsible for providing police services to the greater metropolitan area of London. This area encompasses 620 square miles and contains a population of more than 7 million. The Metropolitan Police consists of more than 31,000 officers, 13,600 staff, and 2,100 police community support officers.

The head of the Metropolitan Police is the Commissioner, who has spent a professional career in law enforcement. The Metropolitan Police (often referred to as The Met) are organized in the following manner. Territorial Policing is concerned with regular daily policing issues found in the 33 operational command units that make up the metropolitan area. The Specialist Crime Directorate is composed of various specialized units, such as: intelligence; protection of politicians, embassies, and royalty; and certain categories of serious crime, which include violent crime, racial hatred, and terrorism. Central Operations also consists of specialized units. These include: Traffic, Air Support Unit, Marine Support Unit, Public Order, Mounted Branch, and the Dog Support Unit. The Met has a large administrative and support staff devoted to such functions as recruitment and training, information technology, and publicity and communications.

City of London Police It should be noted that the one-square-mile City of London has its own police agency. The City of London Police consists of approximately 800 officers and 400 civilians who are responsible for the policing needs of the roughly 6,000 residents of the city and the 350,000 commuters who work in the city, as well as a significant influx of tourists throughout the year.

Serious Organized Crime Agency Since 1965, England has had regional crime squads that were cooperative and collaborative ventures among regional constabularies. In 1997, these squads were merged into a National Crime Squad (NCS) with a mandate to prevent and detect serious crime. In 1992, the National Criminal Intelligence Service (NCIS) was created in an effort to establish proactive models of policing throughout the English police service. There were several operational units within NCIS that illustrated the range of its domestic responsibilities. They included the organized crime unit, the drugs unit, the economic crimes unit, and the football unit, which focuses on disruptive soccer fans. A specialist crime unit also dealt with kidnap and extortion, counterfeit currency, stolen vehicles, and pedophiles. The NCIS coordinated the collection, storage, and analysis of information about serious crime and criminals at the regional, national, and international levels. It provided criminal intelligence to police forces and other law enforcement agencies. Thus, it served as a national support unit for various law enforcement agencies.

In 2006, the Serious Organized Crime Agency (SOCA) assumed the functions of the NCS and NCIS. This agency is also responsible for drug trafficking, financial crimes, and organized immigration crime. The home secretary establishes the strategic priorities for the agency and appoints the chair and director general of SOCA. The chair is responsible for the overall performance of the agency, while the director general is charged with the administration and operations of the agency.

Other Police Organizations The British government has found it prudent over the years to establish several centralized law enforcement and investigative agencies that specialize in police matters. To illustrate, there is the Ministry of Defense Police, which is a civilian force with full police powers; it is responsible for the land, property, and personnel of the Ministry of Defense. The British Transport Police is responsible for the national railway network and the London Underground. Another national police force is the Atomic Energy Authority Constabulary, which protects nuclear materials and the sites of the Atomic Energy Authority.

Police Powers by Civilians Civilians have long been employed in police organizations and have usually been associated with the administrative and technical support staff. With the passage of the Police Reform Act (2002), civilians were given the opportunity to perform specific duties that had often been solely associated with the police. The objective of this change is to free up the regular police officers and thus enable them to use their law enforcement and order maintenance skills in a more effective and efficient manner. Within the first year of its existence, approximately 65 percent of the police forces were participating in this venture (Jason-Lloyd, 2003).

According to Section 38 of the Police Reform Act (2002), a civilian can exercise police powers if he or she is employed by the police authority of a force and is under the direction of the chief officer of that force. The chief officer of the force determines the extent to which these civilians will be permitted to exercise a wide range of special powers mentioned in the statute. Moreover, the civilians can perform one or more of the following duties: community support officer, investigating officer, detention officer, and escort officer. The community support officers wear a distinct uniform and are utilized in particular as an additional visible patrol presence in specific areas to address quality-of-life and safety issues in a community. The investigating officer enhances the status and authority of the civilian crime scene officers that have been utilized for many years. In light of the sophisticated financial and information technology crimes, this statute also enables the use of other civilian specialist detectives. Detention officers can be either employed by the police force or contracted out to a private firm. Their responsibility is to care for suspects summoned and detained at a police station. Finally, escort officers can also be either employed by the force or contracted out; their principal job is to transport people who are under arrest when the need arises.

A Non-Police Organization Although it is not a police organization, brief mention should be made of the Security Service for the United Kingdom, which is more commonly referred to as MI5. MI5 is responsible for protecting the country against threats to its national security. While it is accountable to the home secretary, it is not a part of the Home Office.

The origins of the Security Service are generally traced back to the sixteenth century, when Sir Francis Walsingham established a spy network to protect Queen Elizabeth I. In the early twentieth century, a number of British military intelligence units were designated by a section number. MI5 was responsible for counterintelligence and security. Its mandate was to protect the British political system and economic interests. Today, the Security Service collects and analyzes secret intelligence in order to protect the country from espionage, sabotage, and terrorism. It provides advice on security matters to both public and private organizations. It is a civilian investigative agency that does not have the power to detain or arrest but does share information with law enforcement agencies. MI6, a separate agency, is the Secret Intelligence Service that is responsible for the external security of the country. In that context, MI6 is similar to the Central Intelligence Agency of the United States.

Office of Inspectors of Constabulary This agency is mandated to assure efficiency and effectiveness in the British police service. The County and Borough Police Act created the office in 1856. The inspectorate has offices in London, along with three regional offices. The London office focuses on such issues as: crime and operational policing; community relations; personnel and training; and race and diversity. Until recently, inspectors of constabulary were all former chief constables who had been seconded to the inspectorate. Now, some inspectors do not have a background in policing; rather, they often have experience in the management of private or public-sector organizations.

The inspectorate provides two services to the home secretary and the various police forces. As originally mandated in 1856, it continues to assess the efficiency of forces and serves as a link between the research units of the various forces. The inspectorate encourages and facilitates the sharing of new ideas among forces. The most visible duty performed by the inspectorate is providing an annual report to the home secretary on a variety of aspects of the police service. The report discusses the recruitment and strength of forces, training and promotions, crime and traffic statistics, scientific and technical developments, community relations, complaints and discipline, and welfare.

Independent Police Complaints Commission For more than three decades, the British government has attempted to improve police community relations by permitting civilian participation in the determination of alleged police misconduct. Prior to this change, the police were solely responsible for policing themselves. Some citizens questioned the efficacy of this approach and were successful at convincing Parliament to amend the process. With the passage of the Police Act (1976), the Police Complaints Board was established. The board was essentially composed of part-time members, and its role was one of passive oversight in handling complaints. Critics of the board pointed out that it did not have adequate contact with the police or sufficient powers in the complaints process (Brown, 1987; Terrill, 1983).

Criticism of the Police Complaints Board's authority led to it being replaced with the Police Complaints Authority (PCA), through the passage of the Police and Criminal Evidence Act (1984). The PCA was composed of citizens who were appointed to full-time duty by the home secretary. Excluded from service were all current and former English police officers. Under this system, the authority was more actively involved in the complaints process. For example, it supervised investigations of all serious complaints. "Serious" was defined as allegedly causing death or serious bodily injury to a person. In such instances, the authority must be notified of the complaint. Less serious complaints that might be criminal as well as disciplinary in nature were also immediately called to the attention of the authority. In these cases, the authority simply supervised the investigation. All other complaints were either formally investigated or informally resolved.

In the 1990s, there was again a growing level of criticism directed at the PCA. Questions were raised over the extent to which the PCA was independent of the police. Some critics cited the European Convention on Human Rights and suggested that the PCA was an inadequate mechanism for enforcing Article 13 of the Convention, which states: "Everyone whose rights and freedoms as set forth in this Convention are violated shall have an effective remedy before a national authority notwithstanding that the violation has been committed by persons acting in an official capacity." It should be noted that while much of the European Convention on Human Rights was incorporated into the country's Human Rights Act (1998), Article 13 was excluded from the statute. Nevertheless, British courts have an obligation to note the developments in European Convention case law.

The Police Reform Act (2002) created the third and most recent iteration of civilian involvement with the process of investigating police misconduct by establishing the Independent Police Complaints Commission (IPCC). The IPCC became operational in April of 2004. Section 9 of the statute addresses the matter of the Commission's independence. It points out that the Commission is a corporate body rather than a "servant or agent of the Crown." Thus, it is a public organization that is independent from the government.

The IPCC consists of a chairperson and at least 10 other members who are appointed by the home secretary. No former or active police officer or member of the National Criminal Intelligence Service or National Crime Squad is eligible to serve on the Commission. While previous oversight mechanisms focused on complaints against regular police officers, the authority of the IPCC is broader. It includes all regular police, civilians with police authority (for example, the community support officers), and civilian employees.

Section 12 of the statute clarifies the scope or nature of complaints that can be filed with the IPCC. The complainant must be either a victim, a witness, or a person adversely affected by the conduct in question. Complaints can be filed with the IPCC, a police authority, or a chief officer of a force. It should be noted that a complaint can be informally resolved, but the complainant must agree to this method of handling the matter.

Depending on the nature of the alleged misconduct, an investigation into a complaint might take one of four forms. First, an investigation might be conducted in-house without the input of the IPCC. Second, an investigation might be supervised by the IPCC because the matter raises probable public concerns. Third, an investigation might be managed by the IPCC; that is, it would merit direct control by the IPCC because of the probable public concerns over the incident. Finally, an investigation might be conducted by the IPCC because of the nature of the incident and the heightened level of public concern.

Following the investigation, if the matter is noncriminal in nature, the chief officer has two avenues available. If the officer admits guilt, a sanction can be imposed. The IPCC and the complainant must be informed of the recommended sanction. If the officer does not admit guilt, a disciplinary hearing would be conducted. If found guilty, a sanction would be imposed. If there is a finding that a crime was committed, the case would be sent to the Director of Public Prosecutions. (This office will be explained in the section on the judiciary.)

Throughout the complaint process, the IPCC is either actively or passively monitoring how the case is being handled. What is particularly new to this complaints procedure is the degree to which the complainant can be actively involved in the process. For example, the complainant must consent to an informal resolution of a complaint. The IPCC must consider the complainant's preference for the type of investigation undertaken. The complainant is kept apprised of the case through progress reports and may appeal to the IPCC during the various stages of the process. Finally, the complainant may attend the disciplinary hearing. Obviously, all of these steps are designed to make the handling of alleged complaints against the police more transparent so that the public has a greater faith in the integrity of the system.

Representative Organizations Brief mention should be made of the various police representative institutions. Police unions in the United States have been a long-standing and controversial issue in police literature. A powerful union can frequently influence policy development and management directives. English police officers are not permitted to join a union or any other group whose purpose is to represent police on issues involving salary, pensions, or working conditions.

There are three police associations representing the various ranks in the English police service. The Police Federation, which was established in 1919, was formed because of a number of police strikes that occurred during and after World War I. The Federation represents all police below the rank of superintendent. The Association of Chief of Police Officers (ACPO) traces its origins to the 1890s and represents those of the rank of assistant chief constable and above. The Superintendents Association was founded in 1920 and was established primarily because officers with the rank of superintendent were not represented in the other two associations. Representatives from these three organizations serve on both the Police Council and the Police Advisory Board. Thus, although the English police are not allowed to join unions, they do have representatives on the committees that decide salaries, pensions, and working conditions.

The Police Council for Great Britain has been in existence since 1919. It is composed of members from various police authorities as well as representatives of the various police associations. The council handles such issues as salaries, hours of duty, pensions, and equipment. The Police Advisory Board for England and Wales was established in 1964; its membership consists of representatives from police authorities and police associations. It advises the home secretary on general issues affecting police, particularly promotions and disciplinary matters.

Police Functions The primary duties of police were explained in the 1962 Report of the Royal Commission on the Police. The Commission stated:

> First, the police have a duty to maintain law and order and to protect persons and property.
>
> Secondly, they have a duty to prevent crime.
>
> Thirdly, they are responsible for the detection of criminals and, in the course of interrogating suspected persons, they have a part to play in the early stages of the judicial process, acting under judicial restraint.
>
> Fourthly, the police in England and Wales have the responsibility of deciding whether or not to prosecute persons suspected of criminal offences.
>
> Fifthly, in England and Wales the police themselves conduct many prosecutions for the less serious offences.
>
> Sixthly, the police have the duty of controlling road traffic and advising local authorities on traffic questions.
>
> Seventhly, the police carry out certain duties on behalf of Government Departments—for example, they conduct enquiries into applications made by persons who wish to be granted British nationality.
>
> Eighthly, they have by long tradition a duty to befriend anyone who needs their help, and they may at any time be called upon to cope with minor or major emergencies.

The fourth and fifth responsibilities were altered somewhat with the introduction of the Crown Prosecutor Service through the Prosecution of Offenses Act (1985). This service will be discussed in the section on the judiciary.

Legal Status

The English police trace the origin of their office back to the constable, the local representative of the king who emerged as a prominent figure in the twelfth century. The police also claim that the powers of their office are derived from common law. In 1929, the Report of the Royal Commission of Police Powers and Procedures explained what is meant by the common law origins of the constable's powers.

> The police of this country have never been recognized, either in law or by tradition, as a force distinct from the general body of citizens. Despite the imposition of many extraneous duties on the police by legislation or administrative action, the principle remains that a policeman, in the view of the common law, is only "a person paid to perform, as a matter of duty, acts which if he were so minded he might have done voluntarily."

Thus, in theory, the English view their police as citizens who happen to be in uniform. In the execution of their duties, the police are limited to the powers that have been prescribed by law.

Over the years, there has emerged a body of statutes, case law, and administrative directives designed to grant special powers and controls to the English constable when questioning people, arresting suspects, searching people, and seizing evidence. The use of such authority has been the subject of much discussion in England, as it has in the United States. In January 1981, the Royal Commission on Criminal Procedure issued a report that was to become the basis for the Police and Criminal Evidence Act (1984). In light of some highly publicized miscarriages of justice, the Royal Commission on Criminal Justice was created in 1991. It issued a report that subsequently led to the passage of the Criminal Justice and Public Order Act (1994). The implications of these pieces of legislation on police powers will be examined in the law section of this chapter.

Like their American counterparts, the British police utilize a good deal of discretion in carrying out their responsibilities. Probably the most interesting characteristic of the English police, from an American point of view, is that they are not legally accountable to the municipality they serve for the performance of their duties. The English constable is acting as a servant of the Crown and not as an employee of the provincial police authority that hired him or her.

This independent status of the constable has been supported for some time by the courts. In the case of *Enever v. The King* (1906), the court ruled that: "The powers of a constable ..., whether conferred by common or statute law, are exercised by him by virtue of his office, and cannot be exercised on the responsibility of any person but himself. ... A constable, therefore, when acting as a peace officer, is not exercising a delegated authority, but an original authority." This judgment was affirmed in the often-cited case of *Fisher v. Oldham Corporation* (1930): "[A] police constable is not the servant of the borough [town]. He is a servant of the State, a ministerial officer of the central power, though subject, in some respects, to local supervision and local regulation."

These decisions obviously do not allow a police officer to act as a "free spirit" but as a member of a highly disciplined organization who is subject to the orders and directives of superiors. This fact was clearly enunciated in the case of *R. v. Commissioner of the Metropolis, ex parte Blackburn* (1968). The court ruled:

> Although chief officers of police are answerable to the law, there are many fields in which they have a discretion with which the law will not interfere. For example, it is for the Commissioner of Police or chief constable, as the case may be, to decide in any particular case whether enquiries should be pursued or whether an arrest should be made, or a prosecution brought. It must be for him to decide on the disposition of his Force and the concentration of his resources in any particular area.

Thus, a constable is responsible and accountable to the chief constable of the force in which he or she serves. Today, British police officials view these court decisions as an assurance that police have a degree of impartiality in carrying out their duties. This independence is assured by freeing them from the controls of the local government. Therefore, local politics are significantly removed from the police force.

The Police and the Public

When the Metropolitan Police of London was created in 1829, there was a recognized need to win public support and cooperation for the scheme because many people feared this kind of centralized police force. From its inception, the founders instilled in the rank and file the importance of public acceptance. For more than 175 years, police throughout England gained the trust and the support of a large segment of the British populace. For more than two decades, however, the English police have been the subject of a good deal of criticism. Much of it was initiated as a reaction to their handling of urban riots and public order demonstrations

(Brogden, 1982; Lustgarten, 1986; Oliver, 1987; Reiner, 1985; Scarman, 1981). This was followed by allegations of racism and most recently concerns over the mistreatment of ethnic minorities. Whereas respect for police was largely assumed in the past, there is now a recognition that it must be earned.

In addition to the aforementioned concerns, there is also the issue of crime and the public's perception of it in their community. For some time now, the British have been collecting two types of data on crime. One is the recorded crime figures reported to the police. The other is data collected from the British Crime Survey (BCS). The BCS seeks to get a more accurate reading on the degree and nature of crime by asking people about their personal experiences. This is done in recognition of the fact that not all people who are victims of crime report it to the police. As a note of caution, it is important to cite an acknowledgment by the BCS that it does not collect information on crimes against businesses or commercial property.

Crime peaked in England and Wales in 1995 when 5,252,980 offenses were reported to the police. The BCS estimated at the time that the actual number of crimes was possibly four times the number recorded by the police. Based on interviews taken in 2005–2006, it is estimated that roughly 10.9 million crimes have occurred against adults living in private households. This represents a 44 percent decrease or 8.4 million fewer crimes compared to 1995. Domestic burglary and vehicle crimes have declined by 59 percent and 60 percent, respectively, while violent crime has dropped by 43 percent. The risk of being a victim of a crime was reduced from 40 percent in 1995 to 23 percent in 2006. This is the lowest figure since the BCS was initiated in 1981.

Although the crime rate has fallen, a high proportion of people still believe that crime is increasing. According to the BCS, people are concerned about burglary, car crime, and violent crime. They are also concerned about the level of antisocial behavior in their neighborhoods. It is interesting to note that the BCS found people who read a national tabloid are twice as likely to think crime has increased than readers of a national newspaper (39% and 19%, respectively). When asked about their views on the criminal justice system, the public's confidence varied across the various components of the system. For example, 80 percent are of the opinion that the accused are treated fairly. Only 26 percent felt the system dealt with young people effectively. With regard to the police, 58 percent of the victims were satisfied with how the police handled their case, while 59 percent of witnesses that had contact with the police were satisfied.

Recruitment and Training The British have always prided themselves on maintaining a professional police service. This idea has taken on a new meaning and emphasis in recent years because of criticisms directed at the service. Central to professionalism are the recruitment, training, and educational opportunities extended to members of the police service. A good deal of effort has been directed at evaluating and amending training programs for police, and it appears that this kind of focus will continue.

The Criminal Justice and Police Act (2001) gave the home secretary a good deal of authority over police training. Centrex, the Central Police Training and Development Authority, was established as a result of this legislation. The headquarters of Centrex was Bramshill House, which was the home of the Police Staff College. Centrex provided a number of training services for the police, of which many are priorities for improving police activities that are highlighted in the home secretary's National Policing Plan. The Centrex staff included civilians with various expertise in training and education and police officers who had been seconded to assist with improving professional practices. In 2007, the National Policing Improvement Agency (NPIA) became operational and assumed the responsibilities of Centrex. Its mandate is to improve the way police organizations work across a variety of areas of policing. In addition to training, NPIA's responsibilities include: modernizing the workforce, improving professional practice, developing leadership and learning programs, assisting in the achievement of national standards, developing and maintaining a national police computer and database infrastructure, and delivering major change programs designed to improve the performance of the police service.

In terms of recruitment, there has been a national advertising campaign funded by the central government for some time now. Through a series of exercises designed by Centrex, a recruit is evaluated as to his or her competencies for police work. Until recently, the initial training was often teacher-centered and presented with a rigid, one-dimensional view of policing. Now the training philosophy emphasizes student-centered learning, with an eye to the development of the individual and a recognition of individual differences to some extent. There is also an emphasis on team activities. These new dimensions in training were introduced as a result of the Scarman Report following urban disorders. This report, along with published findings of several academic researchers, pointed out the problem of racial intolerance within the police service and the lack of understanding of the multiethnic society that England was quickly becoming. While the police had long been told that they had to secure the support and consent of the public, what had been lacking was a recognition that ethnic minorities constituted an important element of that public. As a result, training today not only consists of the acquisition of knowledge and skills but also includes an examination of attitudes (Southgate, 1988). The present recruit training program that embraces those values was designed by Centrex.

All recruits start their careers at the rank of constable. Thus, the British do not subscribe to the multiple-level entry scheme common in some countries in continental Europe. Each recruit is placed on probation during the initial two years of service. Their first indoctrination to police work is presented at one of the regional training centers. Basic training is a mixture of theory and practice, including courses in patrol procedures, law, report writing, traffic safety, first aid, and physical education. Following the initial training phase, recruits return to their force, where the force's training department offers a three-week course indoctrinating the officers in local procedural issues. This is followed by 10 weeks in the field under the guidance of a tutor constable. The rest of the probationary period is spent on a beat under regular supervision. During this period, there is some additional classroom training.

English police officers are offered a wide range of courses to assure technical competence and to aid people seeking promotion to middle-management positions. Centrex had been actively involved in the design of new courses and methods of testing the participants. There are refresher courses offered to people who are already in a technical field or position of management. Technical courses for the specialist include investigation, driving, photography, dog handling, communications, crowd control, crime prevention, first aid, and the use of firearms. It should be pointed out that since the inception of the police in 1829, the typical English police officer does not carry a gun. This is one of the unique and often-discussed features of English policing.

Officers are encouraged to continue their studies in institutions of higher education. Through the Bramshill scholarship, officers have attended Oxford University, Cambridge University, the London School of Economics, and many other British institutions of higher education. They have studied such diverse subjects as anthropology, economics, history, law, management, political science, psychology, and sociology. In addition to providing officers an opportunity to attend college, the police service also has attempted to recruit college graduates. Although all recruits must start at the rank of constable, the college graduate is placed in a graduate-entry scheme designed to promote him or her through the ranks faster than the nongraduate.

The British police service has attempted to improve its professional stature with the public by continuing to improve its recruitment campaign and basic training course and by emphasizing the need for people in the service to pursue studies in institutions of higher education. One problem area remains, however: minority recruitment. Although efforts have been made to recruit members from minority groups to various forces, the rate of success has been disappointing. Thus, the white majority continues to police racial minorities. Although minority recruitment will not totally eradicate racial tensions (this has already been proved in the United States), it should begin to help alleviate some of the discord and tension.

Crime Prevention The English police service has long been committed to crime prevention and for a number of years had offered specialist training in crime prevention at Staffordshire. The police have been experimenting with several strategies to enhance their crime prevention role. For example, crime prevention officers are found on every force. In addition to emphasizing the involvement of the community in crime prevention, the specialists also must convince their colleagues that crime prevention is the responsibility of all officers. One method of indoctrinating all officers to crime prevention is to orient the tutor constables to the work of crime prevention. Another strategy is to have a crime-prevention component included in all training (see Harvey, Grimshaw, and Pease, in Morgan and Smith, 1989).

Focused policing was another strategy that had been tried in some forces. In this design, beat officers focused their attention on particular crime problems in their patrol areas during periods when their time was uncommitted. Neighborhood watch programs also had been introduced. These programs included the four basic strategies of: having people watch their own neighborhoods and report concerns to police, marking personal property through the use of identification kits provided by police, providing home security surveys, and establishing community crime prevention and environmental awareness programs (Morgan and Smith, 1989). Presently, there are thousands of neighborhood watch programs established throughout the country (Home Office, 2001). A final strategy, tried in some forces, was the permanent or home-beat community constable. This involved the long-term assignment of an officer to a specific beat area, with an emphasis placed on crime fighting (particularly regarding property offenses) in the hope of establishing better contact with the community (see Fielding, Kemp, and Norris, in Morgan and Smith, 1989).

While the aforementioned strategies were each designed to contribute to the crime-prevention effort, there has been an interest in encouraging cost-effective initiatives in the management of police organizations. At a time when efficiency and effectiveness are the buzz words in policing, there arose suggestions that police must prioritize their work. This would undoubtedly have an impact on crime prevention strategies. In one study, police and public attitudes toward crime were considered along with the issue of prioritization. Prioritization implies that police can either respond to a call, ignore it, or pass it on to another service agency. It was discovered that the English police respond to almost all calls received. Thus, they continued to perceive themselves as the one all-purpose emergency agency. Moreover, surveys of the public suggest that they want more officers on foot patrol, that a priority be given to serious crimes, and that problems of youths, noise, and vandalism be left to the permanent beat officer and the community (see Shapland and Hobbs, in Morgan and Smith, 1989).

With the passage of the Police and Magistrates' Courts Act (1994), the police are required to prioritize their work. After consulting with the chief constable and the community, the police authorities are expected to establish local policing plans. The plan is to include specific objectives identified by either the home secretary or the local police authority, along with a budget for the resources necessary to implement the plan.

The Home Office has established a campaign of citizen-focused policing. The goal is to improve the public's confidence in the police through increasing the public's involvement with identifying the needs of the community and hence its expectations regarding law enforcement, order maintenance, and general service. Obviously, the local priorities will involve such issues as: reducing crime, investigating crime, promoting public safety, and providing assistance.

The community support officer scheme, which was mentioned earlier, has an important role to play in this effort. Community support officers are civilians who have been given limited police powers. Their principal job is to patrol areas either to assure the maintenance of quality-of-life issues or to identify safety issues in the community and seek methods to rectify specific problems. The use of community support officers is expanding throughout the country.

For some time now, the Metropolitan Police Service had established a Victim Support Scheme that was designed to encourage victims to seek support and assistance. They have specially trained officers to aid sexual assault victims. Recently, the Met has created community safety units. These units have received special training in community relations, specifically in local cultural issues. One of the tasks assigned to the community safety units is to assist with addressing the problem of hate crimes. The units are designed to provide advice or offer referrals to other organizations. The unit will investigate allegations of hate. If it is determined a crime was committed, the unit will offer support through the prosecutorial process.

Public Perceptions of Police Like their American counterparts, English police officers—especially those assigned to urban areas—consider themselves part of a minority that is grossly misunderstood. By and large, they have developed this attitude because of their contact with only a small segment of the population. That segment, rightly or wrongly, has been deemed criminal or deviant by society. Because of their infrequent contact with the nonoffender, police do not realize that a large segment of the population generally views their service in a favorable light.

Police and independent researchers have recognized that this feeling of support for the police and sense of cooperation with the white adult population does not exist to the same degree with young people and minority groups. Of particular note are personal criticisms about rudeness, bad tempers, and dishonesty. General criticisms of police are also cited, such as the abuse of powers of search and arrest, methods of obtaining information, and the concealment of complaints filed against police.

The Policy Studies Institute published a study of citizen attitudes toward police from data collected between 1980 and 1982 (Smith and Gray, 1985). The study found that public confidence in police with regard to their handling of crime matters remained fairly high, but that the public felt streets were not safe at night and that police were failing in this regard. Nevertheless, the public did not express alarm with the level of crime in general or with police performance in particular. In addition, police service to victims of crime was generally viewed as satisfactory.

The study also raised the question of police exceeding their powers: 46 percent expressed the view that police never exceed their powers, 29 percent were of the opinion that certain groups did not receive fair treatment (three-quarters of this group singled out minorities as recipients of unfair practices), and 25 percent had no opinion. Moreover, one in 10 lacked a general confidence in police standards of conduct, but even these people did not think that there was a pattern of frequent or usual misconduct.

The study clearly pointed out that it was the relations with specific minority groups that created divisive attitudes. One-third of young white people between 15 and 24 years of age thought police used threats and unreasonable pressure in questioning, and one-fifth felt that police employed excessive force in making an arrest. People of West Indian origin in this same age group were the most critical of police: 62 percent thought police used threats and unreasonable pressure in questioning, 53 percent felt police used excessive force in making an arrest, and 43 percent were of the opinion that police fabricated evidence. Despite these findings, a majority of these minority groups were willing to cooperate with police to a considerable extent.

When asked if an increased recruitment of minorities to the police would make a difference, a little more than one-half felt that it would make no difference. One-third thought that it would lead to improvements. All groups—whites, Asians, and West Indians—appeared supportive of hiring more minorities to the police.

Until the 1980s, the government and senior police officers had not publicly acknowledged the existence of these problems. Many were unwilling to admit that the police service and the public of the 1970s had changed considerably from those of previous generations. Moreover, to help bolster that sense of false security, confrontations between the police and the public had not been as violent, or as prevalent, as was the case in the United States. This situation changed in the 1980s, however. England experienced the rise of a vocal minority that was willing to be both verbally and physically hostile toward the police. For the most part, these minority groups were demanding the same kinds of changes that fostered the American civil rights movement of the 1960s—and for the same reasons.

To rectify these concerns, police have made an effort to improve relations with the general public, particularly with youth and minority groups. Training in police-community relations is an important part of the basic training and continuing education programs for officers. Government and independent researchers continue to recommend further improvements in police-community relations. These are similar to those mentioned in the literature on American policing. They include: the continuation and intensification of police instruction in community relations; the retraining of officers who are abusing police powers; the dissemination of information to the public about police with regard to their role, duties, and powers; the expansion of personal contact between the police and the public; and, in particular, an improvement in race relations.

For several years, specialists in police-community relations have been working to create liaison offices between the police and the public. This was given greater weight with the passage of the Police and Criminal Evidence Act (1984), which specifically called for the creation of methods by which people can express their views regarding police in their area. In light of this, the Home Office recommended the creation of police consultative committees (PCCs). The PCCs have four specific objectives: (1) to permit citizens to express their views about policing in their area, (2) to improve the citizens' understanding of the police role, (3) to resolve conflicts between police and a particular group, and (4) to encourage community participation in crime prevention efforts (Morgan and Smith, 1989).

In more recent years, the British Crime Survey has attempted to collect evidence regarding the public's perception of the police. Several points have been raised from this data, some of which are not surprising. Knowledge of and experience with the police vary greatly among the public. People who make contact with the police because of a crime problem are less satisfied with the outcome than those who contact the police for other reasons. The police are more apt to be viewed negatively by ethnic minority groups, specifically Asians and Afro-Caribbeans, than by whites (Morgan and Newburn, 1997). The 2004–05 British Crime Survey again examined citizen attitudes who had reported a crime to the police. Fifty-eight percent of white respondents were satisfied with the police response, whereas 48 percent of Asians, 53 percent of blacks, and 61 percent of Chinese and other minorities were satisfied.

In 1999, Sir William Macpherson published his report, *The Stephen Lawrence Inquiry*, looking into the racist murder of a young black man. The inquiry was originally designed to examine the police response to the Lawrence murder investigation. The report concluded that the investigation was handled incompetently. It further considered the issue of police community relations and questions of discriminatory behavior on the part of the police. While claims of racism and sexism within the police establishment had been made in the past, the Macpherson report concluded that there was "institutional racism" in the police service and singled out the London Metropolitan Police in particular.

A good deal of debate has been generated by Macpherson, and the police have promised to enhance their efforts at addressing both racism and relations with minority communities. In recent years, however, the tensions between the police and some minority communities have been heightened further because of terrorist attacks in England and the police response to terrorist threats. At issue are the threats directed at Muslims because of prejudice directed at Islam and those threats initiated by a small minority of Muslims involved in terrorist activity (Rowe, 2007).

JUDICIARY

Scholars of English legal and constitutional history are generally in agreement that King Henry II (1133–1189) was the principal facilitator in the development of English common law and the judicial machinery used to administer it. When Henry became king in 1154, he wanted to strengthen both his political and economic positions. To assist in achieving these ends, he synthesized both old and new ideas with regard to centralizing the administration of justice.

Prior to Henry's reign, the administration of justice was essentially carried out at the grassroots level. While there were a number of local courts with varying degrees of jurisdiction, the shire or county courts were the most significant before the Norman invasion of 1066. The principal officers of the shire courts were wealthy landowners, the bishop, and the reeve of the shire (who later would be referred to as the sheriff). Social rank, rather than knowledge of law, was the criterion used to determine who judged cases.

Feudalism was firmly established after the Norman invasion. As noted earlier, feudalism provided social and economic security for people who worked the land for a lord of the manor. One of the responsibilities of a lord was to administer justice; this was carried out in the manor court. Lords of the manor were a powerful political force for the king to consider. It was from this group that Henry II enhanced his political power by wrestling from them the authority to administer justice. He accomplished this by utilizing several different strategies.

First, some people had become dissatisfied with the administration of justice at the manorial level. They wanted the king, who in theory was the source of justice, to decide their cases. Kings of England had for years relied upon their Curia Regis, or Great Council, for advice. The Curia Regis counseled the king on domestic, foreign, and military affairs, and served as a court to settle disputes among powerful lords of the kingdom. It was from the Curia Regis that Henry created and permanently established three courts at the city of Westminster. The Court of Exchequer decided questions between the Crown and the taxpayer. The Court of Common Pleas had original jurisdiction in both civil and criminal cases between subjects of the king. The Court of King's Bench had original jurisdiction in cases between the lords of the realm, as well as appellate jurisdiction for certain cases from Common Pleas and other local courts.

Second, if subjects could not come to the courts that permanently sat at Westminster, royal justice would come to them in the form of a circuit judge. Henry II borrowed this idea from his grandfather, King Henry I (1068–1135), but expanded its use to a considerable degree. By the fourteenth century, royal justice was expanded further at the grassroots level with the introduction of the office of justice of the peace. The principal responsibilities of the justices of the peace included making arrests, receiving indictments, and hearing and determining minor cases.

From the fifteenth century through the nineteenth century, other specialized courts were added, and the court hierarchy was occasionally reorganized. While some of these specialized courts have been abolished, others remain as modern administrative courts. Thus, a highly centralized court hierarchy with specialized jurisdiction was established quite early in England, as compared to other European countries.

Third, while Henry II strengthened his political position among the lords through the centralization of his royal courts, he also enhanced his financial status. Royal justice was indeed becoming available to more people—but for a price. In order to gain entry into a royal court, a person had to purchase a writ. Although many of the early writs dealt with property rights, a series of important writs designed to address civil and criminal procedure were developed during the medieval period. Quo warranto considered how much legal and political power a lord could exercise. Certiorari enabled proceedings in an inferior court to be brought to King's Bench or some other superior court. Habeas corpus was designed to assure the presence of a person before the proper court. Prohibition forbade proceedings in inferior courts, and mandamus ordered inferior courts to perform their legal functions in a manner that would correct a previous error. Like the centralization of the courts, the writ system has remained an integral part of the legal system in countries tracing their origins to English common law.

Fourth, the jury is a legal institution that has been synonymous with the evolution of the common law. Although the jury was utilized before his reign, Henry II is credited with extending and formalizing its use. Originally, the jury was conceived as an administrative mechanism calling together a group of men who presumably knew certain facts and were sworn to reveal information requested by the king. Although Henry II continued this administrative practice, he expanded the jury's use in other ways. Through the Assize of Clarendon (1166), a grand jury in each county was established for criminal cases. Grand juries were originally composed of 12 people; later, the number increased to 24. Its responsibility was to identify people suspected of committing serious crimes. Until the fifteenth century, grand jury members were presumed to have personal knowledge of the case. By the end of the century, however, grand juries were no longer composed of people conversant with a case; rather, they were a group mandated to examine evidence presented to them. With the abolition of trials by ordeal in 1215, resulting from the pronouncement of the Fourth Lateran Council, the petty or trial jury was created. (Trials by ordeal will be explained in the next section on the law.) A trial jury was composed of 12 people who were to determine the guilt or innocence of a person.

The centralization of the royal courts, the establishment of circuit courts, the utilization of legal writs, and the creation of the grand and petty juries were largely the work of Henry II. Each became a significant feature in the administration of justice by the end of the thirteenth century.

It was also during the medieval period that a distinct legal profession emerged. For some time, English kings had appointed to the Curia Regis men who were learned in law, and this tradition increased after the Norman invasion. These men were essentially clergy who had studied either Roman law or the canon law of the Roman Catholic Church. As legal servants of the Crown, they were the precursors of the English legal profession. They served as judges who adjudicated cases brought to the king's courts. These judges were assisted in their work by clerks. Clerks were younger clerics who often possessed a formal education as well as the practical experience of aiding judges. As a result, they were frequently appointed to fill judicial vacancies. Thus, the notion that a practical apprenticeship in a courtroom was a criterion for judicial appointment was adopted quite early in England and remains an important factor to this day.

By the late thirteenth century, legal work had been taken over by laypersons, and two distinct professional classes were emerging. As early as Henry I's reign, litigants who were accused of a crime other than a felony were permitted the assistance of a friend in court to help plead their case. By the thirteenth century, a professional class of pleaders who performed this task had been developed. The demise of the use of clerics as legal advisors and judges led to the tradition of appointing pleaders (because of their extensive courtroom experience) to judicial vacancies.

Attorneys were the other emerging class of legal specialists. They were individuals appointed (or "attorned") to represent a person. English kings had frequently given power of attorney to men who represented them in their absence. The performance of this service was gradually popularized to the extent that people began to represent clients in court. Thus, a new occupation was created: a professional class of attorneys was firmly established by the late thirteenth century.

By the fourteenth century, then, two professional classes learned in the common law were established: pleaders and attorneys. It was also in that century that significant steps were taken to establish a specific form of legal education. Originally, legal training had been largely an informal matter. Members of the legal profession, however, were in the habit of frequenting certain inns or taverns when they were in the city of Westminster practicing before the royal courts. Young men who aspired to a career in the law would go to these inns and listen to lawyers discussing cases. They also would attend court and observe the proceedings.

It was during the fourteenth century that Gray's Inn, Lincoln's Inn, the Inner Temple, and the Middle Temple were taken over by the legal profession and transformed into a collegiate type of training center for young men who wanted to become pleaders. These legal societies established rules and regulations by which each student was required to abide. After a period of approximately seven years of study, a student was called to the bar. Thus, pleaders became known as barristers.

By the sixteenth century, those men who were not interested in a career at the Bar but who wanted to represent and advise clients as attorneys became known as solicitors. England's legal profession consisted of two separate branches quite early in its development, and the divisions have been retained to this day. Just as pleaders were selected to become judges during the middle ages, barristers—the direct descendants of pleaders—are the branch of the legal profession generally selected to serve as judges today.

Finally, the kind of legal education offered in England differed significantly from that of countries on the continent of Europe, where the course of study for law students was presented at a university and was essentially theoretical in content. England's common law students received what one might call a vocational-style training, for they were required to attend and to observe proceedings in royal courts. This was supplemented by a loosely structured academic component of lectures and readings at the inn with which they were associated. During the seventeenth and eighteenth centuries, the inns were closed, and law students were totally dependent on studying the law independently with a barrister. Although William Blackstone did lecture on English law at Oxford University during the late eighteenth century, it was not until the nineteenth century that English universities began to offer courses on English common law, which eventually led to a university degree.

Organization and Administration of the Courts

Before the English court hierarchy can be understood, it is important to explain the responsibilities of several officer holders.

Lord Chancellor The role of Lord Chancellor has changed significantly in recent years. Until 2006, the Lord Chancellor was the head of the judiciary of England and Wales and also charged with making all judicial appointments to the courts. This changed with the passage of the Constitutional Reform Act (2005). For a considerable period of time, criticism has been raised about the independence of the judiciary. In reference to the Lord Chancellor, how can a member of the prime minister's cabinet (executive branch) and a member of the House of Lords (legislative branch) be the head of the judiciary and make all judicial appointments? By making two significant changes, the statute is designed to correct the perception that the process is flawed and lacks transparency.

First, the Lord Chancellor is no longer the head of the judiciary of England and Wales. That title passed to the Lord Chief Justice, who is the presiding judge of the criminal division of the Court of Appeal. According to Section 7 of the statute, the Lord Chief Justice will hold the office of President of the Courts of England and Wales and is thus head of the judiciary. As president, he is responsible:

> (a) for representing the views of the judiciary of England and Wales to Parliament, to the Lord Chancellor and to Ministers of the Crown generally; (b) for the maintenance of appropriate arrangements for the welfare, training and guidance of the judiciary of England and Wales within the resources made available by the Lord Chancellor; (c) for the maintenance of appropriate arrangements for the deployment of the judiciary of England and Wales.

Second, the Lord Chancellor is no longer responsible for judicial appointments. The Constitutional Reform Act (2005) also created the Judicial Appointments Commission. This Commission is composed of 15 commissioners who are appointed by the monarch on the recommendation of the Lord Chancellor. The chair of the Commission must be a layperson. Among the other commissioners, five are members of the judiciary, two lawyers (one barrister and one solicitor), five laypersons, one lay magistrate, and one tribunal member (such as a member of the Immigration Appeal Tribunal).

The selection of people to the judiciary will continue to be based on merit. The goal, however, is to encourage a wider pool of well-qualified candidates to apply. To illustrate, in 1998, about 10 percent of the judges were women, and less than 2 percent were from minority backgrounds. By 2005, those figures had improved to some extent, with just under 17 percent of judges being women and more than 3 percent from minority backgrounds (Department of Constitutional Affairs, 2006). The goal is to diversify the judiciary further. Recently, it was reported that there are slightly more women than men serving as justices of the peace in the

Magistrates' Courts. In 1990, there were 16,090 men and 12,577 women serving; in 2008, there were 14,672 men and 14,747 women (Ministry of Justice, 2008). This is important because these part-time justices, along with 500 full-time district judges, handle 96 percent of the criminal cases.

In 2007, the Lord Chancellor was named to head a new cabinet-level department, the Ministry of Justice. The head of this ministry has two titles, Lord Chancellor and Secretary of State for Justice (or Minister of Justice). Moreover, in the past, the Lord Chancellor was a member of the House of Lords and presided over that House as its speaker. The new arrangement calls for the Lord Chancellor to no longer be the speaker of the House of Lords, and he or she can be a member of either house of Parliament. Finally, the Lord Chancellor is no longer required to be a lawyer.

The Ministry of Justice has an enormously broad and complex range of responsibilities. These are divided into four major categories. First are issues pertaining to democracy, the constitution, and law. Specifically, this encompasses constitutional reform, democracy and human rights, and law reform. Second are matters concerned with access to justice. They include: courts service, legal aid, legal services, civil justice, regulating the legal profession, and the parole board. Third is the National Offender Management Service, which involves both public and private prison services and probation boards. A fourth and final category involves criminal justice. This includes: criminal law, sentencing policy, criminal justice reform, and the Youth Justice Board.

Attorney General Although each cabinet minister has a legal branch within the department, the Attorney General, as legal advisor to the Crown and the Houses of Parliament, usually handles the government's controversial issues. The Attorney General and subordinate, the Solicitor General, are referred to as the law officers of the Crown. They are appointed by the prime minister. They possess distinguished legal careers and are notable politicians.

The Attorney General has four major responsibilities: (1) The Attorney General is the guardian of the public interest and accountable to the House of Commons for the criminal process in the courts. This area is somewhat limited, however, because administering the national prosecutorial system is the responsibility of the Director of Public Prosecutions, and initiating criminal law reform is the responsibility of the minister of justice. (2) As the guardian of the public interest, the Attorney General may bring civil actions and intervene in civil issues as amicus curiae when the government is not a party. (3) The Attorney General is also responsible for answering law reform questions in the House of Commons and is charged with rejecting or accepting bills dealing with such reform. (4) As titular head of the Bar of England and Wales, the Attorney General takes an active interest in the maintenance and enhancement of its professional status.

Director of Public Prosecutions The Director of Public Prosecutions is a professional barrister or solicitor, appointed by the home secretary but supervised by the attorney general. The director administers a large staff of lawyers specializing in criminal law and procedure. Prior to 1986, the principal task of this office was the prosecution of a few specific cases required by statute law, such as murders and cases against police officers. They also were mandated to advise police on their prosecutorial proceedings upon request. In this context, the office was to secure uniformity and consistency in prosecutions. Because police initiated most prosecutions, however, this goal was not achieved. Moreover, police often only consulted the office on borderline cases, so the office did not have a significant role in deciding to prosecute most cases.

Various interest groups and government commissions had expressed concern that police were both investigating and determining whether to prosecute in most cases. One of the specific criticisms directed at this arrangement was that too many cases presented by the police for prosecution were being dismissed by the courts. Critics felt that an independent assessment of the evidence in a case might then lead to greater consistency in the prosecution of cases. Although police hired local solicitors' offices to work for them at the actual prosecution stage, those solicitors were not accountable to any government office.

It was suggested that an independent prosecutor service be established, and this occurred with the passage of the Prosecution of Offenses Act (1985), creating the Crown Prosecution Service. Thus, the power to prosecute was removed from the police. Throughout its brief history, the Service has been confronted with various administrative problems. For example, criticism has been directed at the management of the organization, suggesting that it is too centralized and that this fact has contributed to inefficiencies in the Service. At the time, the administration of the Service was divided into 13 areas that covered England and Wales. In a 1998 study of the Crown Prosecution Service, it was recommended, among other things, to decentralize the Service. This reorganization has been accomplished with the establishment of 42 local areas. These areas correspond with the boundaries of the 43 police forces of the country, with one exception: the Metropolitan Police of London and the City of London Police represent a single area of the Crown Prosecution Service. Each area is headed by a Chief Crown Prosecutor who is appointed by the Director of Public Prosecutions.

The goals of the Crown Prosecutor Service are to assure independence and uniformity in the prosecution of cases, to enhance the quality of prosecutions with the public interest in mind, and to improve efficiency and effectiveness in prosecuting cases. It is the responsibility of the area Crown prosecutors to review police evidence and to determine if a case should be prosecuted. If the decision is in the affirmative, the Crown prosecutors must also decide whether the case should be presented in a Crown court or a magistrates' court.

The decision to prosecute is guided by two tests found in the Code for Crown Prosecutors. The evidential test is concerned with the prospect of convicting the accused based upon the quality and quantity of evidence collected. Within this context, the Crown prosecutor is obviously concerned with the reliability of the evidence and the likelihood of it being admitted or excluded at trial. Assuming a case meets the requirements of the first test, the second test is then considered. The second test is referred to as the public interest test. At issue here, as the name of the test suggests, is whether it is in the public interest to prosecute or possibly decline prosecution. Factors that favor a prosecution include: the seriousness of the offense, the use of a weapon or violence, evidence of premeditation, the vulnerability of the victim, and the defendant's previous convictions. Factors that might determine that a prosecution is not necessary include: the nature of the offense (a genuine misunderstanding or misjudgment), the likelihood of a small penalty, a long delay in reaching a trial date, the age or health of the defendant at the time of the offense, and the victim's physical and mental health. Although the decision in this test involves weighing the public interest, the victim's interests have a significant role to play in ultimately determining what the public interest is. According to the Code for Crown Prosecutors, the "Crown Prosecution Service will only start or continue a prosecution when the case has passed both tests."

The creation of the Crown Prosecution Service has reduced considerably the types of cases that are directly handled by the Office of the Director of Public Prosecutions, which now includes terrorist cases, Official Secrets Act violations, and local cases that are considered too sensitive for handling by the local Crown prosecutor because of a possible conflict of interest.

It should also be noted that the Crown Prosecution Service has long employed caseworkers who assist prosecutors in preparing cases for trial. In 1998, some caseworkers, who were not trained as lawyers, were selected to review and present a select group of cases in magistrates' courts that involved guilty pleas. These specially trained caseworkers are under the supervision of a Crown prosecutor. The caseworkers essentially review cases at police stations that involve such offenses as shoplifting, cannabis possession, and noncontentious traffic offenses; they then represent the Crown in the magistrates' court. This is another example of the justice system attempting to utilize its resources in a more cost-effective manner.

Following this brief explanation of the role of the government's principal court personnel is a description of the English court hierarchy, with emphasis placed on those courts that are involved in the criminal process (see Figure 1.2). Therefore, all the English courts and legal tribunals are not examined here.

Figure 1.2

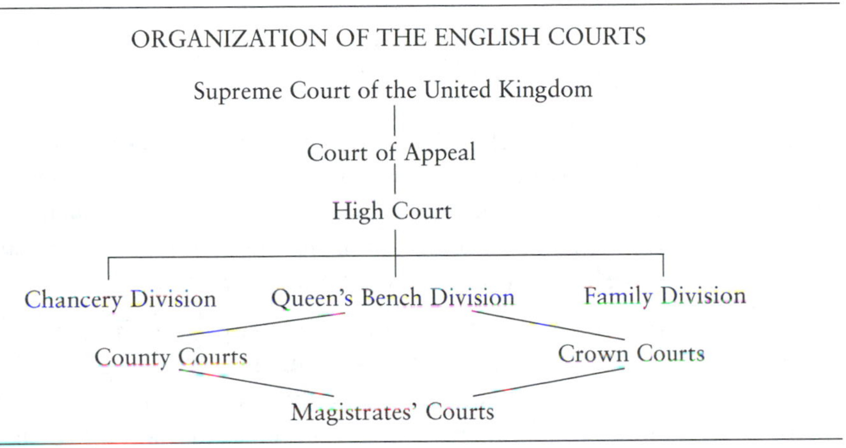

Supreme Court of the United Kingdom Until 2009, the oldest common law court was Parliament. The judicial functions of Parliament were exercised by the House of Lords. In theory, the judicial proceedings were the responsibility of the entire House. In fact, however, they were handled by a small group in the House who were specifically selected for this purpose and known as the Appellate Committee of the House of Lords. This group consisted of the Lord Chancellor, the lords of appeal in ordinary (usually referred to as law lords), and any member of the House who had held high judicial office in the past (such as former Lord Chancellors from previous governments).

In practice, the law lords heard most of the judicial business of the House. There were usually nine, but the number could not exceed 11. Most law lords were selected from members of the Court of Appeal. Thus, they easily met the criteria for appointment—either holding high judicial office for two years or being a practicing barrister for 15 years. Although law lords retired at age 75, they remained members of the House of Lords and could continue to participate in the nonjudicial work of the House.

The House of Lords' jurisdiction was almost entirely limited to civil and criminal appeals from the Court of Appeal and, in exceptional cases, from the High Court. The House heard only a limited number of appeals—approximately 50 a year. The amount was largely controlled by the House and the Court of Appeal. Generally, a dissatisfied litigant in the Court of

Appeal sought permission from that court to appeal to the House of Lords. If the court granted approval, the litigant could proceed. If the court denied the request, the litigant could still petition the House through a procedure that is similar to the certiorari proceedings utilized with the Supreme Court of the United States. Because the House entertained only those cases that were of significant public interest, the latter approach was rare.

These aforementioned duties will be assumed by a new court, the Supreme Court of the United Kingdom, which was created by the Constitutional Reform Act (2005). The first justices to serve on this 12-member court will be the law lords, and they will remain members of the House of Lords. Thereafter, all new appointments to the court will be called justices of the Supreme Court and will no longer be members of the House of Lords. When needed, a commission will be formed to fill vacancies on the court, and membership on the commission will include the President and Deputy President of the Supreme Court.

The Court of Appeal The Court of Appeal is the intermediate appellate court for the entire English system. It consists of a civil and a criminal division. The presiding judge of the civil division is the Master of the Rolls. (This unusual title is a remnant from England's medieval past.) The presiding judge of the criminal division is the Lord Chief Justice. There are approximately 20 lord justices of appeal who constitute the rest of the court. In order to qualify for a position on the court, the candidate must be a judge from the High Court or have had the right of audience in the High Court for 10 years. They are required to retire from the court at age 75. The Lord Chancellor can supplement this group by assigning judges from the High Court to sit and hear specific cases; this frequently is done when an appeal involves a criminal case.

The High Court The High Court is a single court with both original and appellate jurisdiction. It is divided into three divisions: (1) Chancery, (2) Queen's Bench, and (3) Family. The Chancery Division has original jurisdiction in matters dealing with property, trusts, wills, and estates. Although their jurisdiction is primarily original, they also hear appeals involving income tax and bankruptcy.

The Queen's Bench Division is the largest division of the three because its jurisdictional scope is broader. It is concerned with civil and criminal matters and has both original and appellate jurisdiction. Its original jurisdiction consists of actions in torts, contracts, commercial, and admiralty cases. Its appellate jurisdiction is solely concerned with criminal appeals from Crown courts and magistrates' courts.

The Family Division is the third component of the High Court, and it has both original and appellate jurisdiction. Its original jurisdiction includes matters involving matrimony, guardianship and wardship, and adoption. Guardianship and adoption are also the principal sources of its appellate jurisdiction.

High Court judges may sit in any division of the court, but the tendency is to assign judges to the division in which they have the greatest legal expertise. While all cases involving original jurisdiction are handled by a single judge, appeals are usually heard by two—but not more than three—judges. About half of the court's business is conducted at the Royal Courts of Justice in London. The other half is handled by judges, particularly from the Queen's Bench and Family divisions, while on circuit. For this purpose, the country is divided into six judicial circuits outside the metropolitan area of London.

The High Court consists of about 80 judges. In order to qualify for appointment to this court, a person must be a circuit judge for two years or have the right of audience in the High Court for 10 years. Members of the court are subject to mandatory retirement at age 75.

Crown Courts The Crown courts have exclusive jurisdiction over all major criminal cases; they also handle appeals from people convicted summarily in a magistrates' court. Crown courts exist in approximately 78 cities, but the Lord Chancellor has the power to order a court to sit anywhere.

Three kinds of judges preside over Crown court trials. Justices from the Queen's Bench Division of the High Court are assigned to handle the most serious cases. Approximately 400 circuit judges preside over the less serious cases, while about 500 recorders (part-time judges) assist the circuit judges with their caseloads. Circuit court judges are selected from barristers of 10 years standing; they may serve until they reach the age of 72. Circuit judges generally sit in a single Crown court. Recorders are part-time judges who are either barristers or solicitors of at least 10 years standing. Appointment is contingent upon an applicant's willingness to serve four weeks out of the year as a recorder over a three-year term. Serving as a recorder frequently results in financial loss to their private practice. The benefit to this scheme, however, is that a recorder can consider a career on the bench without making a total commitment to a career change. Trials in the Crown courts are heard by a judge and a jury.

County Courts Although they are not involved with the criminal justice system, brief mention should be made of the county courts. The jurisdiction of these courts is limited to civil matters. They are primarily concerned with small claims arising from cases in contract or tort. Their jurisdiction has been expanded to include estates and trusts when the value is small. The judges assigned to county courts are the circuit judges who also sit in Crown courts.

Magistrates' Courts The workhorse of the English court system is the magistrates' courts. There are more than 500 of these distributed among local government areas, and they handle about 96 percent of the criminal cases. Commonly referred to as the inferior criminal courts of the system, magistrates' courts also have some civil jurisdiction, including revocation and renewal of licenses, enforcement of marital separation decrees, orders involving child custody, and some adoption proceedings.

The criminal jurisdiction consists of two types. Minor crimes are tried summarily in these courts; that is, magistrates determine the outcome of these cases without a jury. Traffic offenses constitute a significant portion of the summary offenses. Moreover, all persons charged with a criminal offense are initially brought before a magistrate to determine if the case should be handled by the magistrates' court or transferred to a Crown court. The magistrates' court also serves as the juvenile court in the English system, handling both criminal prosecutions involving juveniles and child protection cases of a noncriminal nature.

There are two types of magistrates who sit in these courts. District judges, who were known as stipendiary magistrates until 2000, are people trained in the law and have been either a barrister or solicitor for at least seven years. There are approximately 130 district judges serving throughout England; more than half of these work in the greater London area. District judges sit alone when hearing cases. The age of retirement from the court is 70.

The other 30,000 magistrates are laypersons who are referred to as justices of the peace. Local advisory commissions recommend to the Lord Chancellor people who are willing to serve on these courts without financial remuneration. Justices of the peace are expected to serve at least one day biweekly, and the position is considered a status symbol in the community. Their term of service is six years, which can be renewed for an additional term that is supposed to be the maximum. Lay magistrates sit in panels of three to hear cases. Although lay magistrates go through a short period of training following their appointment, their knowledge of the law remains inadequate. As a result, each magistrates' court has a clerk who answers questions of substantive or procedural law for justices of the peace (Astor, 1986). The clerks do not rule on cases brought before the court, for that is the responsibility of the justices of the peace.

The Legal Profession

The most striking feature of the English legal profession is its bifurcated form. The division of the legal profession into two branches (barristers and solicitors) is a long-standing tradition dating back to medieval times. In examining differences between these two professions, the medical analogy of the general practitioner and the specialist surgeon is frequently utilized. The role of a solicitor is that of the legal generalist, while a barrister is the specialist.

Solicitors There are approximately 116,000 solicitors in England and Wales. They are the office lawyers—the legal advisors to the public. They draft wills and contracts, handle commercial and land transactions, and deal with probate and divorce issues. They are not completely isolated from the courtroom, however. They have the right of audience in magistrates' and county courts and a limited audience in Crown courts. With the passage of the Courts and Legal Services Act (1990), the right of audience for some solicitors has been expanded even further.

Although some solicitors practice alone, most form partnerships. This enables the legal generalist in larger firms to specialize in a particular branch of law, such as probate, real estate, or criminal law. When a member of the public needs legal advice, he or she turns to a solicitor for guidance; in most cases, that is the extent to which the public has contact with the legal profession.

The Law Society is the solicitor's professional organization, mandated by statutory law to assure professional conduct among solicitors and to safeguard the public interest. The Society administers a compensation fund used to indemnify a client against a solicitor's default in the handling of a client's money. The Society, however, does not discipline its members. An independent disciplinary committee has been empowered by statute to handle such matters. Statute law also regulates the fees that solicitors may charge clients.

For those seeking a career as a solicitor, the most common approach is to complete a university undergraduate law degree. If the person has a degree in another field of study, they must pass the Common Professional Examination. All candidates then participate in a one-year Legal Practice Course, which is designed to train the candidate in various skills, such as interviewing clients and advocacy techniques. Upon completion of this course, the candidate secures a two-year training contract. The training contract can be with a firm of solicitors in private practice or with a government department, such as the Crown Prosecution Service. Obviously, the contract provides the candidate with a good deal of practical experience. During this period, the candidate also completes a short Professional Skills Course. Once the person has completed all of these aforementioned requirements, they are admitted to the Law Society as a solicitor.

Barristers In most countries, judges decide issues at trial based on the written evidence submitted. Although this kind of evidence is important in English trials, the tradition of presenting oral arguments is central to British legal procedure. This practice calls for the specialized talents of a barrister. Although solicitors are consulted for legal advice, barristers present the cases in court. When a litigant is faced with a trial in the High Court (and in many Crown court cases) or is appealing a case to the Court of Appeal or the Supreme Court, the litigant's solicitor must seek the services of a barrister.

A purported expertise at oral advocacy is one reason for the selection of a barrister, but equally important is the fact that solicitors have not had the right of audience in the aforementioned courts. As was indicated earlier, however, the Courts and Legal Services Act (1990) has changed this rule to a limited degree. In all likelihood, some solicitors will have a right of audience extended to Crown courts as it relates to specific cases. The solicitor generally prepares the case by interviewing the client and the witnesses, but has the barrister argue the case before the court. Thus, the solicitor becomes a client of the barrister.

There are approximately 14,600 barristers in England and Wales, some of whom specialize in a particular branch of law. Barristers are subject to a strict code of professional conduct. For example, they cannot advertise their services, and they are dependent on solicitors coming to them with legal briefs. In addition, barristers cannot form a contract with a solicitor and be paid a salary. Their fees are negotiated with the solicitor based upon each case. Although barristers are forbidden by their code to form partnerships, the bar is organized into chambers or offices from which they practice. More than half of these are found in the greater London area.

In each chamber, barristers are divided into two groups: Queen's Counsel (QC) and juniors. Junior barristers are those who have been practicing law for less than 10 years. Once a junior barrister has accrued 10 years experience, he or she may apply to the Lord Chancellor for appointment as Queen's Counsel. This process is known as "taking silk" because, if accepted, the barrister wears a silk gown in court rather than a cotton one. Acceptance also means that the barrister is permitted to add the letters "QC" after his or her name and may sit in the front-row seats in the courtroom. (Junior barristers must sit behind Queen's Counsel.) More importantly, the practice of a QC is limited because most of his or her time is spent handling cases on appeal. About 10 percent of barristers are QCs, and it is from the ranks of the QCs that most judges are selected.

Anyone seeking a career as a barrister must obtain an undergraduate law degree from a university. If the person has a degree in another field of study, he or she must pass the Common Professional Examination. The candidate then takes the Bar Vocational Course, which is designed to prepare the person for a career as an advocate. All persons seeking a career as a barrister must join one of the four ancient Inns of Court: Gray's Inn, Lincoln's Inn, the Inner Temple, or the Middle Temple. The candidate is required to dine at the selected inn on certain occasions, and the inn provides additional courses of instruction focusing on some of the more practical aspects of the law not covered in university courses. These courses supplement a candidate's preparation for the bar examination required for entrance to the profession.

Once a candidate has successfully completed these requirements, he or she is called to the Bar, officially becoming a barrister. The training does not end, however, with a candidate being called to the Bar. A young barrister must arrange a pupilage; that is, the new barrister must find a junior barrister who is willing to take him or her on as a pupil for a period of one year. This period of apprenticeship introduces the young barrister to the practical work of the barrister in chambers and in the courtroom. When a junior barrister (referred to as the master) is satisfied with a candidate's pupilage, the candidate seeks admittance to a chamber. Ideally, the young barrister will attempt to join the chamber of the master, if a seat is available. In recent years, young barristers have found it increasingly difficult to secure a pupilage. This is largely the result of an overabundance of people entering the profession and a shortage of junior barristers having the time to serve as masters. The inns are attempting to resolve this problem by taking a more active role in the placement process.

Judges English judges do not constitute a separate tier in the legal profession as is the case in many countries. Judges are selected from either practicing barristers or (to a lesser extent) trained solicitors. Until recently, judicial appointments were made by the Lord Chancellor, but in 2006 the Judicial Appointments Commission assumed that responsibility. It should be further noted that the bar of England and Wales does not evaluate a candidate's suitability, which is a method frequently employed in the United States. Nor is a candidate subject to a confirmation hearing before Parliament, a device used in the United States when appointing people to the federal judiciary. Once the candidate is nominated, the monarch signs the person's commission. Thereafter, the person is a judge with permanent tenure in office (based on good behavior) until attainment of the age of retirement.

Over the course of the last few decades, criticism has been leveled at English judges for their lack of judicial activism. This criticism frequently cites the American judiciary and its activist role in civil rights and criminal procedure as a model that should be emulated. If one examines the backgrounds of English judges and their perception of their role, it becomes clear why they have not taken an activist stance. Various studies have confirmed that English judges, excluding to some extent the magistrates, are selected from a fairly narrow segment of the population. Most judges have come from the upper or upper-middle classes. Generally, they attended exclusive boarding schools and continued their education at either Oxford or Cambridge, the country's two ancient and prestigious universities.

Because Britain is a unitary country rather than a federated state, the future judge studies a unitary application of the law rather than a multi-jurisdictional approach. This political fact lends itself to a system of legal education that is based on learning a specific approach for resolving each legal problem confronted. This method has a tendency to foster among students a more certain and assured view of their legal system. Moreover, membership in the ancient inns perpetuates this rather narrow educational experience in the law.

Another factor that contributes to the lack of judicial activism is that most judges are selected when they are in their late forties or early fifties. Thus, their years of training and extensive experience as a practicing advocate have further enhanced their assurance in the virtues of the legal system, as well as their desire to maintain the status quo. The system of judicial promotion also assures that justices at the appellate level will be older than their counterparts in the United States. Moreover, there is a notable degree of judicial restraint among appellate justices with regard to developing new rules. It has been suggested that, as former trial judges, appellate justices appreciate the problems of the trial judge. Thus, they are unwilling to devise new rules to overturn lower-court judgments based on sound precedent, regardless of how dated the precedent might be.

English judges have had a narrower view of their role in the judicial system than their American counterparts. English judges have perceived their role to be that of applying existing law rather than creating new law. Historically, English judges helped formalize the common law, but this changed in time as most law is created in the form of a statute passed in Parliament, the supreme legal authority in England. The supremacy of Parliament assures the system that no English court will declare an act unconstitutional. English judges have interpreted and applied the law; they have not made it. That latter role has been the responsibility of legislators (Griffith, 1991).

With the passage of the Human Rights Act (1998), the criticism directed at the lack of judicial activism will inevitably change. The principal question is the degree to which the judiciary will assert itself. Admittedly, the Human Rights Act (1998) does not authorize courts to declare legislation unconstitutional. It does authorize courts to declare that an English law is not compatible with the fundamental principles represented in the European Convention on Human Rights. Issuing such a declaration of noncompliance enables judges to indicate to the government and Parliament that remedial action should be taken to correct the inconsistency. This kind of judicial activism enhances the role of the judiciary considerably.

Juries

Juries have long been synonymous with the evolution of the common law. They are often considered one of the cornerstones of the administration of justice. Today, only the petty or trial jury is used in England—and even this jury is employed rather sparingly. The grand jury became obsolete as the jury of presentment when justices of the peace gradually took over that responsibility. In 1948, the grand jury was officially abolished. At this point, the modern system of preliminary investigations became the sole responsibility of magistrates.

Although the right to trial by jury has not been eliminated, it has been severely restricted. The use of a jury in civil cases has declined considerably since 1933. Statutory law has limited its use to only a few actions, such as libel and slander. In all other civil suits, a jury is granted only through the court's direction. Generally cited as reasons for the decline are the proliferation of civil suits and the loss of faith in the jurors' ability to grapple with highly complex and technical civil trials. The belief that the interests of justice would be better served by a professional judge individually deciding civil cases has gained considerable support throughout this century.

The use of a jury in a criminal trial is determined by statute. People accused of an indictable offense have the right to a jury trial in Crown courts, while summary offenses are heard in magistrates' courts without a jury. Because the number of indictable offenses is rather small compared to the summary offenses, the use of the jury is reduced. Moreover, only one in every 20 eligible defendants elects a jury trial.

Eligibility to serve as a juror is based on three criteria: one must be between the ages of 18 and 70, be a registered voter, and have resided in the United Kingdom for five years since his or her thirteenth birthday. There are various ways to elude jury duty. People can be disqualified if they have been convicted of a crime and served a sentence of more than a specific period of time. Anyone sentenced to more than five years imprisonment is disqualified for life. People are declared ineligible if they are employed in the administration of justice. People can be excused from service if they are a member of Parliament, a healthcare professional, or military personnel. In addition, anyone between the ages of 65 and 70 has an automatic right to be excused from jury duty.

During the process of selecting people to serve on a jury, both the defense and prosecution can challenge for cause the seating of a specific juror. The English eliminated the use of peremptory challenges, which had been reserved exclusively for the defense and limited to three challenges. English juries are composed of 12 people, but a verdict does not have to be unanimous. Verdicts with a majority of at least 10 are permitted.

Critical Issues

Legal Profession Two concerns are paramount regarding the state of the legal profession: (1) its bifurcated organization, and (2) gender and racial issues. Concerning its bifurcated form, some criticism has questioned the need for two distinct classes of lawyers: barristers and solicitors. Although the issue has been debated intermittently for almost 100 years, there has been a renewed and intense discussion during the past decade. Until recently, the Law Society was reluctant to support the idea of merging these classes, and the Bar has been downright hostile toward it.

The belief that the bifurcated legal system fosters monopolistic and inefficient practices precipitated the notion of merging the two professions. Despite the fact that solicitors' fees are regulated by statute, it is alleged that the schedule and rules permit solicitors to charge exorbitant fees when handling certain types of legal transactions. The criticism of barristers centers on issues of effectiveness and efficiency. It is not unusual for a barrister to receive the brief that he or she will plead only a week before the hearing. As a result, not enough time and care may be given to a case because of a lack of preparation.

In addition, efficiency of cost in cases bound over to a Crown court is a considerable concern. A QC handling a case has a junior barrister assisting. When the role of the solicitor is added to this system, a client may end up with as many as three attorneys handling the case. Critics note that yet another concern is that more than half of all cases sent to Crown courts could be tried in a magistrates' court. They are heard in a Crown court because the defendant had a choice as to where the case would be heard. Even though many of the defendants plead guilty when the case reaches the Crown court, the attorneys must still be paid (at a considerable expense to the government).

The Courts and Legal Services Act (1990) may resolve some of these concerns, but it will probably be years before the total impact of this legislation takes effect. Because the legislation did not resolve all of the concerns of the critics, arguments for merging the two professions will probably continue. Proponents of the merger scheme have maintained that it would not lead to the demise of the general practitioner and the specialist, which is what the Bar fears. Proponents cite the fact that in countries with a single legal profession, there have emerged both specialists and generalists within the ranks. There is no reason to doubt that this would happen in England, especially considering that the practice is already in place (Hazell, 1978; Marre, 1988).

The other concern confronting the legal profession is the issue of gender and racial bias. From its inception, the study of law has been dominated by white males. In 1991, there was only one black judge in England. Part of this is explained by the limited number of blacks in the legal profession. On the other hand, in recent years, women have been making considerable strides within the profession. However, men continue to dominate positions on the judiciary. Part of the reason for this is that women have been underrepresented as QCs, which is the source for judicial selection. It has been suggested that charges of gender discrimination will really be tested in the coming years. By then, a significant number of women who entered the legal profession will be in a position to apply for the status of QC and will thus be eligible for appointment to the judiciary (Pearson and Sachs, 1980; Zander, 1989).

Unfortunately, there has been a limited number of women and minorities who have been appointed QCs, in light of the significant increase of both entering the legal profession in the 1990s. To address this problem, an Independent Selection Panel that includes both lay members and people from the legal profession was created in 2005. The Panel submits its recommendations to the Lord Chancellor, who has neither the power to reject nor to add candidates to the list. The entire application process is designed to establish a selection procedure that is merit-based. When this process was implemented for the first time in 2006, 49 percent of the women and 42 percent of the minority applicants were approved (Malleson, 2007).

Law

One of the basic distinctions made in law is the difference between civil justice and criminal justice. Civil litigation involves a resolution of private wrongs between two individuals. Criminal litigation is concerned with a public wrong, a crime in which someone has transgressed the public order of the state by inflicting some kind of harm, usually on a private individual. In criminal litigation, it is the state rather than the individual harmed that seeks a just treatment for the offender. This is to assure that public order is maintained and that the wronged individual's desire for revenge or retribution is satisfied.

The distinction between these two forms of justice has been present for so long that there is a tendency to assume that they have always existed. That assumption is false, however. In order for criminal law to exist in the aforementioned format, the state must be a strong and viable instrument of authority. The Norman Conquest in 1066 has often been identified as an important date in the history of England, and reference has already been made to it. The period after the conquest is often attributed with initiating the gradual merger of local legal customs into a law that was common throughout England. It was from this development that the term "common law" emerged.

Before the arrival of the Normans, the Anglo-Saxons had developed an extensive body of written law called dooms. Early dooms identified many of the more obvious forms of criminal conduct, such as murder, rape, robbery, and theft. Dooms also explained the procedures utilized to determine guilt or innocence and methods for sanctioning offenders.

Outlawry was one of the early methods for punishing those who repeatedly refused to observe the community's laws. Limited to the more serious offenders, under this system a person simply was placed outside the law. The individual was ordered to leave the community and was threatened with death upon return. Once the authority of the king increased, outlawry ceased as a method of punishment and instead became a form of assuring that a person would submit to a hearing in a judicial tribunal.

The blood feud was another primitive procedural approach that was explicitly based on a desire for revenge. A victim was often dependent on their kindred to seek retribution, and kindreds were based on blood relationships. Regulated by a system of rules, a blood feud sought an exact compensation that often followed literally the principle of "an eye for an eye and a tooth for a tooth."

Gradually, a monetary compensation plan was introduced to replace the blood feud. By the ninth century, a schedule of tariffs was established and recorded. With the creation of this scheme, the king was not only beginning to assert his authority in judicial matters but was also recognized in theory as a victim of crime. When a crime was committed, the victim was compensated by a monetary payment called a *wer*. The wer was the value placed on an individual, determined by the individual's rank in society. The king was considered a victim of the criminal act because the crime disrupted the general or public peace of the kingdom. He, therefore, was compensated by a monetary payment called a wite.

The monetary compensation scheme illustrates a method for sanctioning. The procedure devised by local Anglo-Saxon courts to determine liability was referred to as compurgation. Usually, a victim went to the local court and made an oath that the accusation was being made in good faith. The accusation was supported by offering material evidence and securing oaths of affirmation from oath-helpers. It was not uncommon to secure oath-helpers from one's tithing, that early form of Anglo-Saxon law enforcement. Both the quality of evidence and the number of oath-helpers necessary was dependent on the gravity of the accusation and the social rank of the plaintiff.

The defendant was then permitted to make an oath of denial. The defendant also had to secure oath-helpers. The number of oath-helpers was determined by the nature of the charge and the accused's social rank. Severe fines were levied against all parties concerned who falsely swore an oath.

Some defendants were not permitted to use compurgation. Instead, they had to submit to an ordeal, which was another form of proof. Defendants who were required to submit to an ordeal included: those who were unable to secure a sufficient number of oath-helpers to comply with the compurgation scheme, those who had an extensive record of accusations brought against them and were no longer considered oath-worthy, and those caught in the act of committing a crime or in possession of stolen property. Proof by ordeal was based on a belief that the gods or a god would intervene with a sign that would determine guilt or innocence. While ordeals had their origins in primitive societies, the practice was transformed into a Christian ritual by the Roman Catholic Church.

There were three types of ordeals that were frequently utilized. The plaintiff in a case usually determined which ordeal would be employed. The ordeal of cold water involved placing the defendant into a pool of blessed water. If the person sank, they were innocent; if they splashed about, they were considered guilty. The ordeal of hot iron and hot water were similar to one another. The ordeal of hot iron required the defendant to carry a hot iron bar nine feet, while the ordeal of hot water involved removing a stone from a cauldron of boiling water. All of the instruments in these ordeals were blessed by a priest. In these instances, the defendant's hand was bandaged and three days later the bandages were removed. If the skin was healing, the person was considered innocent; if the skin was infected, the person was obviously guilty. Thus, the Christian application of the ordeals was based on a belief that God would provide a sign as to the truth of the matter for the court. Although ordeals may appear to be a form of punishment, they were simply a method of determining guilt or innocence. People found guilty by an ordeal would then have to submit to a prescribed sanction, frequently involving monetary compensation.

By the time of the Norman Conquest, the Anglo-Saxons had developed an extensive body of written law. Their system was superior to that of their Norman invaders, who relied upon oral tradition rather than written custom. This may be the reason why the Normans did not tamper with Anglo-Saxon law following their conquest. If change was not in the offing as a result of the Conquest, why is the event considered such an important date in the development of English law? Norman kings were interested in centralizing their political control over their English kingdom. It was through the enhancement of their political position that the law was gradually transformed into a unified system, a common law for the whole kingdom.

The emergence during the medieval period of centralized royal courts, circuit courts, royal writs, and the jury has already been discussed in a previous section of this chapter. This period also experienced changes in the principles of criminal liability and in criminal procedure. For example, Anglo-Saxon law had not developed the notion that a crime requires a finding of *mens rea* or criminal intent. People were liable for all their actions. By the thirteenth century, however, a distinction was made between a crime and a tort. Although the term *mens rea* was not in use, there was a recognition of criminal intent. For example, people were granted pardons for death by misadventure. This would not have occurred during the Anglo-Saxon period. In addition to differentiating between a crime and a tort, a distinction was made between felonies and misdemeanors.

The term *felony* was used in statutes on a limited basis as early as the twelfth century; by the thirteenth century, serious crimes such as murder, robbery, rape, theft, and arson were classified as felonies.

Another significant procedural change occurred in 1215 as a result of the meeting of the Fourth Lateran Council. At this meeting, Pope Innocent III (1160/1161–1216) declared that clergy were to cease participating in trials involving bloodshed. With the clergy removed from the administration of ordeals, the procedure lost its significance. Before the Pope's declaration, the grand jury of indictment was utilized in England, and even the petty jury was employed in some cases to determine guilt or innocence. As a result of the Lateran Council's pronouncement, the use of juries gained in popularity and became a standard component of the English criminal trial.

The emergence of a unified legal system common throughout the kingdom was another significant factor in the development of English law following the Conquest. Despite the fact the Anglo-Saxon dooms had standardized some law and procedure, a good deal of regional custom remained prevalent in the local courts. The advent of royal courts—especially the use of circuit judges—changed that. Royal courts were superior to local courts, and thus, their decisions were binding on local courts. As royal court decisions became systematized, there gradually emerged a unified or common interpretation of the law. The roots of the common law are found in the decisions of the justices of the royal courts, in some of the Anglo-Saxon dooms, and in statutes passed after the Norman Conquest.

Criminal Law

The primary sources of English law are (1) common law, (2) legislation, and (3) equity, but only the first two are considered the basis of criminal law. The earliest common law offenses were felonies, and they were punishable by death or mutilation and by forfeiture of property. Murder, robbery, rape, arson, and larceny are examples of these early common law felonies. As other less serious offenses were identified by the judiciary, they were called misdemeanors. By the nineteenth century, the legislature became the principal source for identifying new forms of criminal behavior. Today, most common law crimes have been codified and are contained in statutes.

Until 1967, the English classified crimes by the traditional categories of treason, felonies, and misdemeanors. With the passage of the Criminal Law Act (1967), this old distinction was abolished, largely because it had become obsolete. As a result of this act, a dual system of categorization was created based upon substantive and procedural classification schemes.

Offenses are now referred to as arrestable or nonarrestable. Arrestable offenses are defined in the Act as: "offenses for which the sentence is fixed by law or for which a person (not previously convicted) may under or by virtue of any enactment be sentenced to imprisonment for a term of five years, and to attempts to commit any such offense." Thus, the most serious crimes are arrestable offenses; all others are deemed nonarrestable offenses.

The major significance of this legislation involved the power of arrest without a warrant. Under common law, this power was limited to treason, felonies, and breaches of the peace. Under the new substantive scheme, the power to arrest without a warrant was extended to all arrestable offenses.

It is the act's procedural classification scheme that determines how a case is handled. All offenses are tried either summarily in a magistrates' court or on indictment in a Crown court. Offenses are procedurally classified into one of the following categories: (1) Most serious offenses are triable on indictment before a judge and a jury in a Crown court. These include murder, manslaughter, rape, burglary, and assault with intent to rob. (2) Some indictable offenses may be tried summarily in a magistrates' court. Among the offenses that fall under this category are malicious wounding, assault, many thefts, some burglaries, and arson. The accused must give consent to the summary proceedings, however. (3) Statute law has created a small number of offenses that may be tried either summarily or on indictment. These offenses are commonly referred to as "hybrid" offenses. These cases are tried on indictment, unless the prosecutor applies to a magistrates' court for the case to be heard summarily. Examples of these offenses include driving under the influence, carrying a weapon, and cruelty to children. (4) Some summary offenses may be tried on indictment. These include those summary offenses in which the accused can claim a right to a jury trial, such as selling liquor without a license and illegal entry by immigrants. (5) Some summary offenses are tried in a magistrates' court without a jury. The vast majority of offenses in English law are summary in nature; they include drunk and disorderly conduct, loitering and soliciting, and most traffic offenses.

As previously mentioned, by the thirteenth century, the English recognized the principle of criminal intent. Today, there are two general principles establishing criminal liability. One is the *actus reus*, that is, the act of commission or omission forbidden by the criminal law. Each crime contains specific elements that define a particular crime and thus establish the *actus reus*. For example, the Theft Act (1968) defines robbery as: "[a] person is guilty of robbery if he steals, and immediately before or at the time of doing so, and in order to do so, he uses force on any person or puts or seeks to put any person in fear of being then and there subjected to force." The elements of stealing and using force or fear indicate the *actus reus*.

The other general principle is the *mens rea*, that is, the accused possessed the necessary intent to commit the crime. Like the *actus reus*, the *mens rea* of each crime is different. For example, theft requires the intent to permanently deprive the owner, while a forgery case requires the intend to defraud or deceive. Obviously, the *mens rea* is complex and at times difficult to prove because the accused's state of mind is being scrutinized. In order to prove that a crime was committed, it is the responsibility of the prosecutor to prove that both *actus reus* and *mens rea* existed in each particular case.

Criminal Procedure

The examination of English criminal procedure is divided into two categories: the pretrial process, which includes police powers and procedures, bail, and the preliminary hearing; and the trial process, which explains the procedures for trials on indictment, summary proceedings, and appellate reviews.

The English criminal justice system in general, and criminal procedural issues in particular, have received significant attention in recent years. The issue of police powers was the subject of a massive and extensive examination by the Royal Commission on Criminal Procedure (1981). The commission's report focused on (among other things) police powers of arrest, search, and questioning.

Because police powers were scattered throughout common law, case law, and statute law, critics were of the opinion that police authority should be reviewed and systematized in a coherent fashion. The Royal Commission on Criminal Procedure agreed with this position and offered a general recommendation that police powers be codified. The rationale was based on two objectives. First, the police argued that they preferred to have a clear understanding of the limits of their authority and that framing these powers in a statute would assist in eliminating existing ambiguities. Second, the citizenry had a right to be apprised of these powers, for this is a basic tenet of any country that claims to be founded on democratic principles. An even more pragmatic reason centered on the need for the citizen's willingness to cooperate with police when such powers were exercised. The assumption was that if the citizenry had a clear understanding of the extent of police powers, they would be more apt to cooperate.

The commission specifically suggested that the power to arrest without a warrant be more consistent. Arrests without a warrant were acceptable if the alleged violation was an arrestable offense or if another statute granted such a power. The commission recommended that there be one single power to arrest all accused of an imprisonable offense and that the power to stop and search a person should be based on a statute. The Commission would permit searches of stolen property or prohibited items in the event that an officer has a reasonable suspicion that a person possessed such property or items. Additionally, warrants to enter and search a premise should specifically detail the place to be searched and the items to be seized. General searches would be unacceptable.

In addition, the police power to question a suspect and take testimony was controlled by the Judges' Rules and the Administrative Directions on Interrogation and the Taking of Statements. Collectively, these rules called for voluntary confessions, enumerated a person's right to remain silent, enabled private consultations with a solicitor, and required that the person in custody be informed of these rights orally and that the rights be posted and displayed in a prominent place in police stations.

Although these rules served a similar purpose to that of the *Miranda* warning in the United States, they were not legally binding. Breaches, therefore, did not lead automatically to the exclusion of evidence at trial. It was the responsibility of the judge to make a determination on the admissibility of evidence. Moreover, it was suggested that people in custody had not been routinely informed of their qualified right to speak to a solicitor or to friends; and when they had been informed, many were denied this right. Compounding the problem was the fact that solicitors were not always willing to come to a police station at all hours of the night.

There emerged a concern among some critics of police procedures that citizens—especially the poor, illiterate, and uninformed—were victims of these and other unnecessary breaches of the rules. Critics contended that all citizens would become potential victims of these breaches if they were allowed to continue. Though in the past police had relied on public trust in their judgments and an almost unquestioned deference to agents of authority, the composition and attitudes of English society had changed considerably since World War II. Distinctions in the various segments of the population were more pronounced, and people were often unwilling to exhibit complete deference to the wishes and practices of police.

The Royal Commission recognized these concerns and offered two recommendations: the treatment of a suspect in custody should be regulated by statute, and the right of access to a solicitor should be improved by the establishment of a duty solicitor scheme. Although a few areas of the country had already developed such a scheme, the commission recommended that defendants throughout the country be given access to a solicitor on a 24-hour basis. The likelihood that such a scheme could work would be enhanced by guaranteeing solicitors a remuneration for their services.

As a result of the commission's work, Parliament passed the Police and Criminal Evidence Act (1984), often referred to as PACE. This act essentially encompasses in a single statutory instrument all of the aforementioned procedural issues relating to police. In addition to the act, the Home Secretary issued Codes of Practice designed to assist police with interpreting the statute. Like the act, the Codes of Practice were subject to the approval of Parliament.

In 1991, the Royal Commission on Criminal Justice was established after several high-profile convictions were overturned. Although the original convictions in some of these cases predated the passage of PACE, that was not the case with all of them, thus raising questions about PACE. The new Royal Commission was given a broad mandate to consider the effectiveness of the criminal justice system—specifically, how to assure the conviction of the guilty and the acquittal of the innocent. The work of this Commission, along with various other committees, led to the passage of the Criminal Justice and Public Order Act (1994) and the Police and Magistrates' Courts Act (1994). Unlike the Police and Criminal Evidence Act (1984), which essentially placed all procedural issues related to police under one statutory instrument, the new pieces of legislation deal with a host of issues that involve criminal law, criminal procedure, and the administration of the justice system (Bridges, 1994; Bridges and McConville, 1994; Zander, 1994). Since that time, more recent legislation impacts how the police perform their duties as it relates to criminal procedure. This legislation includes: the Terrorism Act (2000); Anti-Terrorism, Crime and Security Act (2001); the Anti-Social Behaviour Act (2003); and the Criminal Justice Act (2003).

Power to Stop and Search Under PACE, police have the power to stop anyone who is in a place to which the public has access and to speak with them briefly in order to decide if there are grounds to conduct a search. Before a stop occurs, police must have established reasonable suspicion for doing so, based on the probability that stolen goods or prohibited items will be found either on the person or in a vehicle. Prohibited articles consist of offensive weapons and items made or adapted for use in the commission of various offenses (which, for the most part, involve burglary or theft).

In order to carry out a search, an officer is expected to inform the person to be searched about the officer's name and police station, to identify the object of the proposed search, to explain the grounds for the search, and to inform the person of his or her right to receive a copy of the record of the search. The police also must keep a record of a search as long as it is practical to do so.

PACE also addressed the stopping and searching of vehicles and the issue of road checks. In the case of stopping and searching a vehicle, an officer must have reasonable suspicion that the vehicle contains stolen goods or prohibited articles. A search of an unattended vehicle is permitted as long as reasonable suspicion has been established. Road checks normally should be approved in advance by an officer of the rank of superintendent or above and an explanation given for the purpose of the check. The grounds for establishing a road block are: to apprehend a person who committed a serious offense, to secure a witness to a serious offense, to stop a person intending to commit a serious offense, or to apprehend an escaped prisoner.

Power to Enter, Search, and Seize A key issue in searching premises is whether an officer has secured a search warrant. Usually, a warrant is needed to search a residence, but the statute offers some exceptions to the general rule. For example, a person who occupies a residence may consent to a warrantless search. The Code of Practice, however, states that a person is not obligated to consent to a search. In the event a person does agree, the consent must be in writing and the person must be informed that anything seized may be used as evidence. Warrantless searches also can be used to prevent or stop a breach of the peace that is imminent or taking place, to rescue a person in danger, or to prevent serious property damage. Arresting a person in cases in which an arrest warrant has been issued or arresting a person for an arrestable offense are also acceptable reasons. Upon entering a premise to arrest a person, police must have reasonable grounds to believe that evidence of an offense or similar offenses will be found. Two final reasons for a warrantless search include situations in which the defendant was at a premises immediately before an arrest or in which the intent is to recapture an escaped prisoner.

The application for a search warrant is covered under PACE. Under the act, a magistrate must be satisfied that there are reasonable grounds to suspect that an arrestable offense was committed and that relevant admissible evidence will be found. There are two exceptions to this rule: legal privilege and excluded material. Legal privilege involves the communications between a professional legal advisor and his or her client. Excluded material includes personal records, a journalist's materials, and human tissue or tissue fluids. Although the last two are fairly self-explanatory, it should be noted that the Criminal Justice and Public Order Act (1994) amended this provision. As such, police powers have been extended to take intimate and nonintimate samples in select circumstances. Personal records include the records of healthcare professionals, clergy, counselors, and agencies dealing with personal welfare issues. Certain materials held on a confidential basis, such as bank records, may be seized following an application for a warrant to a circuit judge. Under normal conditions, this application is sought in the presence of the person on whom the order is being made.

PACE also established a uniform procedure for carrying out a search warrant. The request for a warrant must be made in writing, and an officer must be put under oath to answer questions of a magistrate concerning the request. The warrant can be used only once and must be executed within a period of one month. When executing a warrant, an officer must identify himself or herself and present a copy of the warrant to the occupant of the premises. The search should also occur at a reasonable hour. Police can seize any item covered by the warrant or reasonably believed to be evidence of an offense.

Finally, it is important to note that not all searches are governed only by PACE. Some specific police powers are found in other statutes. A sample of these include: the Theft Act (1968), the Misuse of Drugs Act (1971), the Aviation Security Act (1982), the Road Traffic Act (1988), the Offensive Weapons Act (1996), and the Terrorism Act (2000).

Power to Arrest The power to arrest involves two general sets of circumstances: cases of arrest with a warrant and cases of arrest without a warrant. Various statutes authorize arrest with a warrant. It is the issue of arresting without a warrant that is often complicated and controversial. PACE attempts to clarify the circumstances in which it is permissible. Police can arrest without a warrant if they have reasonable grounds to believe that a suspect has or is about to commit an arrestable offense. They also can arrest people without a warrant for common law offenses carrying a sentence of five or more years imprisonment or for specific offenses listed in Section 24 of the statute.

A person must be informed when he or she is under arrest and be provided reasons for the arrest. Once a person is arrested, he or she can be searched. The search must be based on reasonable grounds that the person poses a present danger to himself or herself or others, possesses evidence of a crime, or possesses items that could be used for escape.

Power to Detain The act and the accompanying code designate certain police stations to receive people for detention. Each of these stations has a custody officer at or above the rank of sergeant. Once a suspect arrives at a police station, the custody officer decides whether there is sufficient evidence to charge the person with a crime. Suspects who have not been charged can be detained if the custody officer believes that it is necessary in order to secure or preserve evidence. The custody officer also oversees the treatment of suspects who are being detained.

PACE calls for a periodic review of the detention of suspects who have been charged. A review officer is responsible for this task. The officer must be at least the rank of inspector and cannot be involved in the case under review. PACE mandates that the first review occur within the first six hours of detention, followed by further reviews at nine-hour intervals.

If police wish to continue to hold a suspect who has not been charged for longer than 24 hours, they must have the detention authorized by a person at the rank of superintendent or higher. If police wish to hold a suspect beyond 36 hours, they must seek the approval of a magistrate. Magistrates cannot authorize the holding of a suspect beyond 96 hours. The suspect or the suspect's representative must be informed of these continuances so that oral or written statements can be made with regard to the detention.

At least two magistrates and the court clerk must be present at a detention hearing. The suspect must be given a copy of the police application for further detention and be notified of the right to legal representation. Acceptable reasons for a continuance of detention are: the necessity to secure or preserve evidence, the fact that the allegation is a serious arrestable offense, and the assurance that the investigation is being conducted in an expeditious manner. These are the same criteria used by a superintendent in determining a continuance of the 24-hour period.

Once a person is charged with an offense, the reasons for detention change. The statute lists several reasons, including: to establish the suspect's name and address, to detain (upon reasonable grounds) a person for his or her own protection, to prevent a suspect from causing physical injury to another person or damage to property, to assure appearance in court, or to prevent any interference with the administration of justice. In the case of a juvenile, detention might be continued on the basis that it is in the best interests of the young person.

Under the old law, a person charged and held in custody would be brought to court as soon as it was practical. PACE retained this rule and strengthened it somewhat. If a magistrates' court is not sitting on the day of the charge or the next day (with the exception of Sundays and a few holidays), the custody office must request that the clerk of the court hold a special hearing for the suspect.

Power to Question Although a police officer has a right to ask a person anything, a person has an absolute right to remain silent. A person taken into custody also has a right to inform a friend, relative, or other person who will take an interest in their welfare. It is assumed that this will be done without delay, but there are circumstances in which delays are permissible—for example, if the suspect is being detained as a result of a serious arrestable offense. In addition, an officer of the rank of superintendent or above may delay the process if he or she believes it is possible that there will be interference with the investigation, that harm might come to other people, that other suspects might be alerted, or that the recovery of evidence might be hindered. The act further states that the maximum period of delay should not exceed 36 hours.

The Codes of Practice state that a detained person may receive visits at the custody officer's discretion. The detained person also has access to a telephone, unless any of the aforementioned reasons for holding a suspect incommunicado are in force. A police officer may listen to the contents of a telephone call unless the call is being made to a solicitor.

PACE also addresses the controversial issue of access to a lawyer. A suspect not involved in a serious arrestable offense has an absolute right to see a lawyer. Police are permitted to initiate questioning before the solicitor arrives, however. The code explains the circumstances in which this is permissible—including when a superintendent believes that a delay in questioning may cause harm to a person or risk the loss of (or damage to) property or believes that an unreasonable delay in the investigation would occur as a result of waiting for the solicitor. The suspect may agree in writing or on tape that the questioning may proceed without a solicitor.

Suspects detained because of alleged involvement in a serious arrestable offense also have an absolute right to see a lawyer, but access can be delayed up to 36 hours in most cases. In cases of terrorism, the delay can extend up to 48 hours. The reasons for delay are the same as those stated in the previous paragraph. The code clearly states that delays in access to a solicitor cannot be based on a concern that a solicitor might advise the suspect not to speak.

The suspect can name a particular solicitor, or the police will provide a list of solicitors available for such work. Many jurisdictions have developed a duty solicitor scheme, which consists of solicitors who are available on a 24-hour basis for suspects. Access to a solicitor is available free of charge.

A person who has asked for legal advice should not be interviewed until the solicitor arrives, unless the aforementioned exceptions are in effect. The solicitor may be present during the police interview. However, an officer of the rank of superintendent or above can ask that the solicitor withdraw because of misconduct and may report such behavior to the Law Society.

Probably the most controversial issue is the point at which a person must be informed of his or her rights. The answer is dependent on whether the person is under arrest. If a person is not under arrest, he or she must be told of his or her rights when cautioned. Circumstances in which a caution must be given are explained in the code under Section 10:

> 10.1 A person whom there are grounds to suspect of an offence must be cautioned before any questions about it (or further questions if it is his answers to previous questions that provide grounds for suspicion) are put to him for the purpose of obtaining evidence which may be given to a court in a prosecution. He therefore need not be cautioned if questions are put for other purposes, for example, to establish his identity, his ownership of, or responsibility for, any vehicle or the need to search him in the exercise of powers of stop and search.
>
> 10.2 When a person who is not under arrest is initially cautioned before or during an interview at a police station or other premises, he must at the same time be told that he is not under arrest, is not obliged to remain with the officer and may obtain legal advice if he wishes.
>
> 10.3 A person must be cautioned upon arrest for an offence unless (a) it is impracticable to do so by reason of his condition

> or behaviour at the time; or (b) he has already been cautioned immediately prior to arrest in accordance with paragraph 10.1 above.
>
> 10.4 The caution shall be in the following terms: "You do not have to say anything unless you wish to do so, but what you say may be given in evidence." Minor deviations do not constitute a breach of this requirement provided that the sense of the caution is preserved.
>
> 10.5 When there is a break in questioning under caution the interviewing officer must ensure that the person being questioned is aware that he remains under caution. If there is any doubt the caution should be given again in full when the interview resumes.
>
> 10.6 A record shall be made when a caution is given under this section, either in the officer's pocket book or in the interview record as appropriate.

A person under arrest must be told of his or her rights upon arrival at a police station.

A person must be informed of: the reasons for the detention, the right to inform someone of the detention, the right to see a copy of the codes, and the right to legal advice. The person must be told of these rights orally, and he or she has a right to a copy of the custody record. If a person has come to a police station voluntarily and has been cautioned, he or she must be advised of these rights as well as the right to leave the station, if desired.

Finally, the code offers several rules that relate to how police may question a person. Over any 24-hour period, eight continuous hours (which should occur at night) must be permitted for rest. Breaks should occur at two-hour intervals, but these can be delayed if there is a reasonable belief that harm could come to a person, that there is a risk of loss or damage to property, that there might be prejudice to the investigation, or that a delay would prevent a person's release from custody. Three meals must be provided over a 24-hour period. A person cannot be required to stand for questioning. If it is necessary to take a person's clothing for investigative purposes, replacements must be provided. The use of oppression in questioning a person also is forbidden.

While a person has a right to remain silent, the Criminal Justice and Public Order Act (1994) has altered the manner in which that principle has been interpreted. In the past, the right to silence assisted the accused in two ways: (1) a person could not be required to incriminate himself or herself while in police custody, and (2) as a result of exercising that right, one could not infer guilt at trial. The new legislation does away with this second benefit. Thus, the inference of guilt may be present. This, in turn, puts pressure on the accused to waive the right to silence when questioned by the police (Dennis, 1995; Pattenden, 1995).

It should also be noted that the issue of questioning a person has raised several problems. The code calls for police to keep an accurate record of each interview with a suspect. In light of this, officers had been required to write down each question and the suspect's answer before proceeding to a next question. The police had been critical of this requirement because it often breaks up the flow of an interrogation. This problem has been resolved as police use tape recorders for interrogations.

Bail Another significant procedural issue frequently addressed during the pretrial stage is the approval or denial of bail. The Bail Act (1976) explains the general rights and conditions under which bail may be granted. In general, the act presumes that any person accused of a crime is entitled to release on bail. Those who do not enjoy this presumed right are: fugitives, people who have been previously convicted of the offense with which they are now charged, people who have been released on bail and have been arrested for absconding or breach of bail, and those who are accused of crimes for which the punishment is imprisonment. The court may refuse bail under this last category for various reasons, including a belief that the person would not surrender to custody, that he or she may commit another offense while on bail, or that he or she may obstruct justice or interfere with witnesses. Before refusing bail, the court is obliged to consider the seriousness of the offense, the defendant's character, community ties, previous record, and the strength of the evidence.

Bail, when granted, can be either unconditional or conditional. Unconditional bail requires that the person surrender to the court on a specific date; failure to do so can lead to imprisonment, a fine, or both. Conditional bail is granted to assure that the defendant will surrender to custody, will not commit another offense while on bail, and will not obstruct justice or interfere with witnesses. The court may attach to the bail any condition that it deems appropriate. Among the most common stipulations are: to reside at a particular address, to inform police of any change of address, to report regularly to a police station, to avoid contact with the victim and potential witnesses, and to refrain from frequenting specific places.

Another condition for release on bail might be to provide sureties. Sureties are people who agree to assure the court that the defendant will appear when required. Should the defendant not appear, the surety must pay the Crown a sum of money. Sureties do not deposit money with the court until the defendant has actually failed to appear at the appointed time.

If a court refuses to grant bail or limits the conditions of bail, reasons must be given. Bail may be granted either before the trial or at any stage during the proceedings. If the defendant is not released on bail, he or she must be brought before a magistrates' court as soon as possible.

Bail is generally granted by the magistrates' court or the Crown court, but there is one exception to this rule. A police officer at or above the rank of inspector may grant bail to a defendant who is in custody after being arrested without a warrant. This bail is granted without conditions, with or without sureties, if the officer concludes that the offense is not serious.

The Criminal Justice and Public Order Act (1994) has added a new feature to bail decisions. Like the courts, the police have now been granted the authority to impose conditions (the common stipulations referred to earlier) when granting bail. The intent of this change was to improve the efficiency of the process, but questions have been raised about the potential for abuse. While the previous method of granting conditional bail was authorized by a magistrate or judge and occurred in a judicial setting with the prosecution and defense present, concerns have been expressed that this new responsibility will be added to the duties of the custody officer of the police cells (Raine and Willson, 1995).

Legal Aid The issue of legal aid frequently is addressed during the preliminary hearing. England has not developed a public defender system, but has established a legal aid scheme that is regulated by the Legal Aid Act (1974). Under the act, a magistrates' court may grant aid to a defendant appearing before it or to a person who has been convicted and wants to appeal to a Crown court. A Crown court may grant aid to an accused person appearing before it or to a person who has been convicted and plans to appeal to the Court of Appeal. The Court of Appeal or the Supreme Court of the United Kingdom may grant aid to a person appealing a case to the Supreme Court. If legal aid is granted, the accused is free to select any private solicitor willing to handle legal aid work. In cases in which the services of a barrister are needed, the solicitor seeks appropriate counsel for the client.

Legal aid is provided by state funds. In order to qualify for aid, the applicant faces means and merits tests. The means test determines whether the person is actually in financial need of either total or partial assistance. Therefore, the court can require that an applicant furnish proof of financial status. In Crown court cases, the merits test is usually satisfied by the fact that the case will be heard in a Crown court, which hears only the more serious cases. Guidelines have been established for determining the merits of granting legal aid for cases heard in a magistrates' court: the charge is a serious one in which the accused may lose his or her liberty, the charge raises a significant legal issue, or the nature of the case requires interviewing of witnesses and the ability to cross-examine witnesses effectively.

Trial on Indictment Procedures for a trial on indictment in a Crown court are similar to those for a jury trial in the United States. One judge and a jury would sit to hear the case. As was mentioned above, only one in 20 people accused of an indictable offense elects a jury trial. Trials on indictment involving adults must be conducted in public, and the press may fully report the proceedings.

The first stage of the trial is the arraignment. Although the accused does not have to be represented by counsel, the overwhelming majority employ counsel—especially in light of the availability of legal aid. If a person chooses to conduct his or her own case, the judge assists the accused on legal points that arise during the course of the trial. The accused, however, cannot appeal the case on the grounds that it was not properly conducted. When representing oneself, the accused is required to be present at the arraignment to hear the reading of the indictment and to answer the charge. Although there are several formal pleas, this text will limit the description to pleas of guilty and not guilty. If a person pleads guilty, the judge examines the accused to assure the court that the person understands the consequences of the plea. Once satisfied, the judge proceeds to impose a sentence. If the accused pleads not guilty, the trial continues.

The second stage of the trial involves the selection of a jury. A jury consists of 12 people between the ages of 18 and 70, who are registered voters, who have been a resident of the United Kingdom for five years since their thirteenth birthday, and who are eligible to serve. Various groups of people may be disqualified, deemed ineligible, or excused from jury duty. Specific rules for this were enumerated in the section on the judiciary. The defense and prosecution have an unlimited number of challenges for cause, but the use of peremptory challenges has been eliminated in England. Once a jury has been selected, the third stage of the trial begins. This stage is the oral presentation of the case by both sides in court. The standard procedure includes the following steps:

1. The prosecuting counsel gives an opening speech in which he or she outlines for the court the evidence that will be presented.
2. The prosecuting counsel then calls and examines witnesses. To assure that a witness will not hear the evidence of others, witnesses are normally not allowed to remain in the courtroom until after they have given their testimony.
3. Defense counsel is permitted to cross-examine witnesses as they appear.
4. The prosecutor then may reexamine the witness.
5. If the defense counsel plans to call witnesses other than the accused, counsel is permitted to make an opening statement that outlines defense evidence for the court.
6. An accused who chooses to give evidence is called first (although one cannot be compelled to do so). Once the

accused chooses to give evidence, he or she is then required to answer all questions, including those that are incriminating.

7. Other defense witnesses then are called.
8. The prosecution is permitted to cross-examine each witness.
9. This may be followed by a reexamination by the defense.
10. The prosecutor then offers a closing speech.
11. The defense counsel follows with a closing statement.
12. The judge then summarizes the case for the jury. Two duties are encompassed in the summarization: first, the judge discusses the specific law, its applicability to the case, and the burden of proof required to establish the accused's guilt; second, the judge sums up the evidence presented by both parties.
13. The jury then retires to consider a verdict. It can return a general, partial or special verdict. A general verdict covers all the charges in the indictment. A partial verdict indicates that the jury finds the accused guilty or not guilty on a limited basis. For instance, they may acquit the accused for the offense charged but find him or her guilty of another offense for which he or she was not charged. A special verdict frequently involves the jury's decision that the accused is not guilty by reason of insanity. The jury may reach a unanimous verdict or a majority verdict. The Juries Act (1974) provides for majority verdicts of 10 when the jury is composed of 11 or 12 people. Majority verdicts are accepted only if the jury deliberates for at least two hours or longer, if the court believes it is reasonable. If the jury is unable to reach a verdict, it is discharged and the accused may be tried again.

The division of labor between a judge and a jury in an English trial is similar to that found in the United States. The jury is limited to determining the facts in the case and returning a verdict. The judge determines the conduct of the trial, rules on all questions of law, guides the jury, and passes sentence.

The first two items may need further clarification. For example, the judge must rule on all motions raised by both sides during the trial. Following the prosecutor's presentation of the case, the judge must decide if the prosecution has presented sufficient evidence against the accused to warrant a continuance of the trial. The judge has the power to exclude evidence from the case if it was obtained illegally or is deemed inadmissible. In addition, if inadmissible evidence is presented, and the judge believes the defendant would not get a fair trial, the jury may be discharged.

A defendant who is found not guilty is released immediately. When the jury returns a verdict of guilty, the trial moves to the fourth and final stage: sentencing. Although all indictable offenses are punishable by imprisonment (the length of time controlled by statute), the judge usually receives two reports to assist in determining the appropriate sentence. One report is prepared by the prosecutor and contains such items as the age, education, employment, and past convictions record. The other report is prepared by a probation officer in conjunction with other nonlegal specialists. It pertains to the medical, psychological, and social condition of the defendant.

Section 142 of the Criminal Justice Act (2003) explains the purpose of sentencing.

> (1) Any court dealing with an offender in respect of his offence must have regard to the following purposes of sentencing-
>
> (a) the punishment of offenders,
>
> (b) the reduction of crime (including its reduction by deterrence),
>
> (c) the reform and rehabilitation of offenders,
>
> (d) the protection of the public, and
>
> (e) the making of reparation by offenders to persons affected by their offences.
>
> (2) Subsection (1) does not apply-
>
> (a) in relation to an offender who is aged under 18 at the time of conviction,
>
> (b) to an offence the sentence for which is fixed by law,
>
> (c) to an offence the sentence for which falls to be imposed under section 51A(2) of the Firearms Act 1968 (c. 27) (minimum sentence for certain firearms offences), under subsection (2) of section 110 or 111 of the Sentencing Act (required custodial sentences) or under any of sections 225 to 228 of this Act (dangerous offenders), or
>
> (d) in relation to the making under Part 3 of the Mental Health Act 1983 (c. 20) of a hospital order (with or without a restriction order), an interim hospital order, a hospital direction or a limitation direction.

Clearly, this legislation continues to make a distinction between an adult offender and a youthful offender.

Sentences are essentially divided into two general categories: custodial and noncustodial. The custodial sentences consist of imprisonment and youth custody for people under 18 years of age at the time of conviction.

Noncustodial sentences include: probation orders, various community service orders, and fines.

In addition to the custodial and noncustodial sentences, there are a few miscellaneous orders that the court may issue. For example, for certain traffic offense convictions, the court may suspend the offender's driving privileges. The Crown court also may order costs to be paid out of the central fund or by one of the parties. Costs paid out of the central fund may be ordered for the prosecution and witnesses. Defense counsel also may have costs paid if the defendant is acquitted. The Crown court, however, may order a convicted offender to pay all or part of the prosecution's costs or require that the prosecution pay all or part of the costs of an acquitted defendant.

People who are injured or have their property damaged or lost as a result of a crime may be awarded compensation by the court. The court may order the offender to pay compensation, but it must take into consideration the person's ability to pay. Injuries, losses, or damages that occur during a traffic accident are excluded from this scheme unless the injury or damage was the result of an offense under the Theft Act (1968). If the injuries result from a violent crime, the victim can apply to the Criminal Injuries Compensation Board, which may award compensation from public funds. A person convicted of a theft also may be ordered to make restitution to the victim. Finally, the court may order the forfeiture of an offender's property if the offender is sentenced to prison for more than two years and the property was used to commit or assist in the commission of any offense. If no other party has claimed a right to the property in question, the property is disposed of by police.

Following conviction and imposition of a sentence the defendant may appeal the case to the Criminal Division of the Court of Appeal, which handles such proceedings from trials on indictment. The defendant must file the appeal within 28 days of the conviction. The prosecution in a criminal case cannot appeal. Thus, the Criminal Division exists solely for the benefit of the convicted offender.

If the appeal involves a question of law, the person has a right to appeal. Only a small number of cases are appealed on such grounds. Most appeals involve questions of fact (or a mixture of fact and law), rejections of evidence at trial, or sentences imposed. In these cases, the court must grant leave to hear the case. Only one judge from the court examines the issue and determines the granting of leave for the whole court. Generally, if the judge rejects the case, the proceedings stop. If the judge grants leave, the matter comes before a panel of three judges of the court. Only oral arguments are heard; any written material is usually reviewed after the hearing. *Per curiam* decisions are handed down in criminal cases.

In comparison to appeals in the United States, English appeals are handled quickly because they do not require lengthy written opinions.

The Court of Appeal can dismiss an appeal, uphold the lower court's decision, quash the conviction, or reverse and remand the case back to the trial court with its instructions. In appeals involving the sentence, the court may reduce the sentence but cannot increase its severity.

Both the defense and the prosecution may appeal to the Supreme Court. The court hears only a limited number of appeals, and these are controlled by the court and the Court of Appeal. Generally, a dissatisfied defendant in the Court of Appeal must seek permission from that court to appeal to the Supreme Court. If the court grants approval, the defendant can proceed. If the court denies the request, the defendant can still petition the court through an application for leave. This is similar to the certiorari proceedings of the U.S. Supreme Court. This latter approach is rare, because the court entertains only those cases that are of significant public interest.

Once a case reaches the court, the President of the Supreme Court normally assigns the issue to five justices. Only oral arguments are presented by counsel; written briefs are not filed. A simple majority determines the outcome. Justices may deliver any of the judgments that are available to the Court of Appeal or may remit the case to the Court of Appeal.

Summary Proceeding Trial by jury remains one of the most significant contributions that the English have made to the evolution of legal procedure. Today, however, more than 90 percent of the criminal cases heard in England are handled at a summary proceeding, which is a trial in a magistrates' court without a jury. Either one district judge or three lay magistrates would sit to hear a case in a magistrates' court. The criminal jurisdiction of a magistrates' court consists of indictable offenses that also may be tried summarily, "hybrid" offenses that are triable either on indictment or summons, and offenses that can only be tried summarily.

A summary trial must be held in open court. The trial is based upon information that has been presented to the court by the prosecution, consisting of the offense, the facts of the case, and the offender's statement. Most summary offenses are initiated by a summons directing the accused to appear before a specific magistrates' court at a given date and time. Some summary offenses, like loitering or vagrancy, are initiated by an arrest without a warrant. Throughout proceedings that are based on a summons, the accused is not held in custody. The accused is deprived of liberty only after being convicted and sentenced to a period of incarceration.

It is significant to point out that the Magistrates' Courts Act (1957) permits the accused who has been sent a summons to plead guilty without attending court. In such a case, the offender would mail in a plea of guilty, the clerk of the court would inform the prosecutor, and the court would proceed to dispose of the case. The court does not have to accept the plea. If the court does accept it, the accused has to appear in court for sentence.

The first stage of a summary proceeding involves reading the information and hearing the accused's plea. The accused, as a general rule, does not have to be present at any stage in a summary trial. If the accused is absent, the court proceeds as though there were a plea of not guilty. If the accused is present, he or she is permitted to plead in open court. Pleas of guilty are followed by an examination by the magistrate to assure the court that the offender understands the consequences of the plea. Once satisfied, the magistrate imposes the sentence. If the accused pleads not guilty, the trial proceeds to the next stage.

The second stage of a summary proceeding is the oral presentation of the case by both sides in court. The procedure is similar to that of a trial on indictment but is not as formal. The procedure is as follows:

1. Although it is not necessary to state a case, the prosecution may make an opening statement.
2. The prosecution presents the evidence and then witnesses are examined, cross-examined, and (if necessary) reexamined.
3. The accused or the accused's counsel may make an opening statement.
4. The accused may make an unsworn statement.
5. Evidence for the accused is presented; if the accused is to give sworn testimony, he or she must do so before other witnesses are called. Witnesses are examined, cross-examined, and (if necessary) reexamined.
6. The prosecution addresses the court.
7. Finally, the defense counsel addresses the court.

Throughout the trial, the magistrate may refuse to accept inadmissible evidence, may ask questions of the witnesses, and may call witnesses to the stand. Usually, the clerk of the court will examine the witnesses for the magistrate. Guidelines have been established to determine when this is proper: to clarify ambiguous testimony, to question an incompetent person, or to assure that the interests of justice are served. It is not proper to question a witness if the accused is legally represented or is competent to conduct his or her own examination.

The third stage of the proceedings is the court's decision on the guilt or innocence of the accused. If the magistrates are not in agreement, they may retire to discuss the matter. Difficulties that arise because of questions of law (or law and fact) are referred to the clerk of the court, who is supposed to be a trained solicitor or barrister. The authority of the clerk in such matters is particularly acute in light of the fact that most magistrates are laypersons. Decisions in these cases are reached by a simple majority. If there is a tie vote that cannot be broken by a compromise, the magistrates must call for a rehearing before a court comprised of different magistrates.

The fourth and final stage of a summary hearing is the determination of a sentence. Sentences imposed in a magistrates' court are essentially the same as those imposed in a Crown court, but the degree of punishment is considerably less severe. For example, the length of a prison sentence is dependent on the nature of the offense, but the maximum sentence for a summary offense usually does not exceed six months. The noncustodial sanctions and miscellaneous orders that are available to Crown court judges and mentioned above are also applicable in the magistrates' courts.

Appellate review is also available for the parties of a case heard in a magistrates' court. The right to appeal a case to a Crown court is limited to the defendant. A defendant who pleaded guilty may appeal to the court against the sentence; a defendant who pleaded not guilty may appeal against the conviction or the sentence. If the appeal is against the sentence, the court hears only the evidence relevant to the sentence. If the appeal is against the conviction, the appeal takes the form of a rehearing of the case.

The appellate proceedings follow the pattern of a summary trial, though less formal. Witnesses may be recalled and new evidence introduced. When hearing an appeal, the Crown court sits without a jury. The appeal is heard by a circuit judge or a recorder and two magistrates. Judgments are reached by a simple majority. The court has the power to confirm, reverse, or vary the decision of the magistrates' court.

Both parties may appeal a case from a magistrates' court to the Queen's Bench Division of the High Court if the dispute involves a question of law. At least two Queen's Bench judges (usually three) hear the appeal. The Lord Chief Justice presides over the case, which consists of legal arguments presented by counsel on both sides. The court has the power to confirm, reverse, or vary the decision of the magistrates' court. Remissions are granted when the magistrates' court has made an error that requires a hearing or rehearing of authority.

Finally, both parties may appeal to the Supreme Court if the issue involves a point of law of general public importance. An application must first be registered with the Queen's Bench Division to certify the point of law. If approved, the procedure for appeal is the same as an appeal from a case tried on indictment. If the court refuses to approve the request, the appellant may petition the House directly. Again, the procedure would be the same as an appeal from a case tried on indictment.

Critical Issues

Plea Bargaining The procedure known as plea bargaining has received some notable attention. The significance of this interest lies in the fact that the British had assumed that plea bargaining did not take place in England, at least not on the scale it is utilized in the United States. Although critics admit that this is true, inducements to plead guilty are as formidable in England as they are in the United States. For example, in the United States, about 90 percent of the defendants plead guilty before a trial. In England, 58 percent of the defendants in Crown court cases plead guilty, while 88 percent of the defendants in magistrates' courts do the same.

Moreover, plea bargaining in the United States is considered an acceptable, even necessary, part of the system—centering on the prosecutor's willingness and promise to recommend a reduced sentence. Such prosecutorial conduct had been considered unethical in England. Thus, plea bargaining was viewed as being more within the discretionary province of the courts than of the prosecutor, and the Criminal Division of the Court of Appeal had placed restrictions on the practice.

The Court of Appeal established four principles to govern the plea bargaining process. These principles, expressed in the case *R. v. Turner* (1970), have been the focus of some criticism. They are:

> 1. Counsel must be completely free to do what is his duty, namely, to give the accused the best advice he can, and if needed, advise in strong terms. This will often include advice that a plea of guilty, showing an element of remorse, is a mitigating factor which may well enable the court to give a lesser sentence than would otherwise be the case. Counsel of course will emphasize that the accused must not plead guilty unless he has committed the acts constituting the offense charged.
>
> 2. The accused, having considered counsel's advice, must have a complete freedom of choice whether to plead guilty or not guilty.
>
> 3. There must be freedom of access between counsel and judge. Any discussion, however, which takes place must be between the judge and both counsel for the defense and counsel for the prosecution. If a solicitor representing the accused is in court he should be allowed to attend the discussion if he so desires.
>
> 4. The judge should … never indicate the sentence which he is minded to impose. A statement that, on a plea of guilty, he would impose one sentence but that, on a conviction following a plea of not guilty, he would impose a severer

> sentence is one which should never be made. This could be taken to be undue pressure on the accused, thus depriving him of that complete freedom of choice which is essential.

Criticism of the *Turner* decision centered on two procedural issues. First, will a plea of guilty serve as an independent element in determining the sentence? Rule 4 suggests that the judge should not imply to either counsel what he or she intends to do, but Rule 1 makes it explicit that counsel for the accused may advise in strong terms that a plea may lead to a lesser sentence. At issue is why counsel would encourage a client to plead guilty in the hope that a lesser sentence is forthcoming, unless the idea is transmitted in some fashion by the judge. Second, Rule 3 emphasizes the key role the judge must play in the bargaining process. It is alleged that, in the past, informal discussion went on between the police, counsel for both sides, and the accused. A bargain could be struck in these preliminary informal discussions before approaching the judge. Rule 3 implies that this should not occur because it might hamper the efficiency of the process and lead to unnecessary delays.

In studying the outcome of jury trials in the Birmingham Crown court, it was discovered that many of the cases that were earmarked for a jury trial were abruptly ending in pleas of guilty (Baldwin and McConville, 1978). The frequency of this occurrence piqued the authors' curiosity and led to interviews with 121 defendants who had pleaded guilty out of a total sample of 150. What Baldwin and McConville attempted to do with the data was to dismiss, once and for all, the myth that strong inducements to plea bargain are not a significant part of the pretrial process in England. They concluded that such inducements come from a number of sources. First, the British prosecutors' practice of charging the defendant with all possible counts in the indictment helps produce a climate that is very conducive to bargaining. Second, defense counsel's assumption that judges almost automatically reward pleas of guilty with reduced sentences is communicated to the defendant. Thus, the defendant perceives the judge in a different light even if the judge is not directly putting pressure on the accused to plead guilty. Third, because of the nature of the prosecution's case, defense counsel usually puts the greatest pressure on a defendant to plead guilty. Frequently, the most damaging evidence consists of the verbal statements attributed to the accused by police or the written statements signed by the defendant following a police interrogation. Although the defendant often claims that these statements are untrue or exaggerated by police, there is simply no way of determining the efficacy of the defendant's charge. The defense counsel could challenge these statements in court, but in most cases the judge believes the police rather than the defendant. This last concern is likely to change with the introduction of tape recordings of police interviews.

Baldwin and McConville did not offer a solution to the problem of plea bargaining, but they noted that it does enhance the bureaucratic efficiency of the administration of criminal justice. They contended, however—as some civil libertarians have in the United States—that the defendant's freedom of choice is compromised, that some innocent people may be induced to plead guilty, and that it leads to inequitable treatment. Thus, there is a serious question as to whether plea bargaining in its present form serves the interests of justice as well as it does the system's efficiency.

In the early 1990s, the Royal Commission on Criminal Justice found that a majority of barristers and judges favored plea discussions between the judge and counsel. In his *Review of Criminal Courts of England and Wales* (2001), Justice Auld called for a more transparent approach to plea bargaining. Some improvement has resulted from the Criminal Justice Act (2003), as section 144 states that a court must take into account:

> (a) The stage in the proceedings for the offence at which the offender indicated his intention to plead guilty, and
>
> (b) The circumstances in which this indication was given.

Victim Assistance Concern for assistance to victims of crime has become an important issue on the agendas of most criminal justice systems in the industrialized world. The first victim support scheme in England was established in Bristol in 1974. Today, there are more than 250 support groups established throughout the country. In addition, there is a national association that aims to coordinate the goals, resources, and standards of the various support schemes. Much of this victim support work is provided by volunteers. The various schemes are concerned not only with aiding the victims of crime and their family members but also with advising witnesses of crime. The schemes also have been active advocates for improving the system of compensation for criminal injuries.

Some recent accomplishments include providing information to victims of crime about the progress of their case, criminal injuries compensation, victim support, and crime prevention. Another information packet specifically designed for witnesses of crimes includes advice about the court and its personnel, giving evidence, claiming expenses, and how to ask for assistance. The victim support schemes also have been influential in getting legislation passed with regard to criminal injuries compensation, enhancing the authority of the courts with regard to compensation, protecting children who give evidence by allowing testimony through closed-circuit television, and allowing the acceptance of children's testimony without corroboration. Finally, they also have been instrumental in increasing the funding for victim support schemes.

While a good deal of work to assist victims has been carried out by volunteer groups, it is important to point out that various components of the criminal justice system are making significant efforts to aid victims. Some of the efforts by the police were outlined in the section of this chapter devoted to police. In addition, the government has established a number of magistrates' courts that specialize in domestic violence cases. These courts are designed to bring the various components of the justice system—police, Crown prosecutors, magistrates, probation service, and victim support services—together to facilitate moving these cases through the system in a more efficient manner. While the rate of convictions of domestic violence cases has increased in recent years irrespective of the type of court, the conviction rate in domestic violence courts has reached 71 percent, according to the Home Office. Presently, there are 98 courts that specialize in domestic violence cases.

Corrections

The importance of the juxtaposition of penal theory and the architectural design of correctional institutions is a notion that emerged in England during the late eighteenth century. At roughly the same time, police practitioners began in earnest to support improvements in law enforcement. People were questioning some of the basic assumptions behind the administration of justice, just as they were questioning many of the established political, religious, scientific, and social assumptions on which society was based.

Many of these basic tenets had been introduced originally during the middle ages, a period that some have referred to as the Age of Faith. The eighteenth century was a markedly different period, known by contemporaries as the Enlightenment, the Age of Reason—espousing a belief that the individual was a free, rational, and equal member of society. Such notions were obviously at cross-purposes with established custom and authority.

The eighteenth century serves as a useful benchmark for the emergence of the modern development of English corrections. It was during this time that people consciously and rationally attempted to study the purposes of and the conditions for incarcerating law violators. In order to appreciate the contributions of Enlightenment thinkers, it is useful to examine the state of corrections at earlier points in time. Anglo-Saxon dooms and medieval statutes enable us to piece together that history.

The stocks were probably the earliest form of imprisonment, though they were not suited for people who were sentenced to an extended period of custody. It is assumed that as early as the eighth century some type of prison existed, because owners of large tracts of land were frequently awarded the right of infangthief and outfangthief. *Infangthief* was the right to bring a thief caught on your land to the lord's court; *outfangthief* was the right to bring a thief caught beyond your land to the lord's court.

By the ninth and tenth centuries, it was common for courts to sentence thieves to 40 days in custody before releasing them on the condition that they pay the compensation that had already been awarded by the court. Such a sanction obviously required that a suitable place be available to hold suspects and individuals sentenced to a period of confinement. It is assumed that either a hut or cage on a manor, a room in a county town, or a designated area of a castle was used for this purpose.

Following the Norman Conquest in 1066, the use of imprisonment appears to have declined somewhat. Two possible explanations have been offered for this development. On the one hand, imprisoning people was a costly enterprise for the captor. On the other hand, alternatives to incarceration did exist. For example, death, mutilation, and outlawry had long been established methods for punishing serious offenders, while compensation was considered an appropriate sanction for less serious offenses.

The use of custody achieved a greater degree of certainty by the twelfth century as the king expanded royal authority in the administration of justice. Sheriffs were required to detain suspects of serious crimes until the trial was completed. People defaulting on the payment of their taxes to the king were imprisoned not only as a means of securing payment but also as a form of punishment for being delinquent. Originally, trespassing was considered a tort action but, by the thirteenth century, it was viewed as an indictable action. The reasoning was that the defendant had not only acted against the plaintiff but also had violated the peace of the kingdom. In addition, those convicted of larceny were imprisoned at a rate of one week for each penny stolen.

The Statute of Acton Burnell (1283) and the Statute of Merchants (1285) enabled private creditors to have debtors imprisoned until payment was made. Because the state did not provide funds for their upkeep, those who were incarcerated were almost totally dependent on their family and friends for their maintenance. As not all prisoners had family or friends, it is assumed that some probably starved to death. Members of the general public, however, did assist prisoners; it was not uncommon for people to give alms to inmates as they did to the poor. By the fourteenth century, prisoners frequently were permitted to beg while chained to posts outside prisons.

Throughout the medieval period, the spiritual well-being of prisoners appears to have been of greater concern than their physical health. Religious services were readily available, but impure drinking water and a general lack of sanitary conditions led to illnesses that occasionally reached epidemic proportions. Attempts also were made to separate felons from debtors and women from men, but not all facilities provided this type of segregation. Therefore, it is assumed that many prisoners associated freely with one another.

By the eighteenth century, prison conditions had reached an intolerable state. Criticism was directed at the use of institutions as a method of deterring and isolating offenders from society for a period of time. It is estimated that by the end of the century Parliament had also created about 200 statutes calling for the death penalty. A number of these statutes dealt with crimes that would be considered petty property offenses by today's standards. A small group of reformers began to question the propriety of incarcerating some offenders—especially in light of the poor facilities in which they were housed, as well as the rationale for dramatically increasing the death sentence.

Although rehabilitation, deterrence, and isolation are often presented as rationales for prisons today, they are considered to be at cross-purposes with one another. During the second half of the eighteenth century, the emerging view was that each of these rationales served as a component to a larger theory that justified the development of prisons. Reformers saw the need to deter and isolate offenders but were also concerned about efforts at rehabilitation.

It must be remembered that one of the principal tenets of Enlightenment philosophy was that humankind is malleable. The theorists were not so idealistic as to believe that all individuals had reached the state of being free, rational, and equal in society, but they did believe that everyone was capable of being led to that state of freedom. John Howard held this Enlightenment view. His contribution to prison reform illustrates its application to penal theory.

Howard serves as a representative of a larger movement. Cesare Beccaria, William Eden, Samuel Romilly, and Jeremy Bentham also were instrumental in encouraging change, but Howard was one of the first reformers in England to see a relationship between penal theory and the architectural design of facilities for housing the offender. This merger of theory and design was presented in his treatise, *State of the Prisons in England and Wales* (1777).

Howard argued that prisoners' accommodations should be clean and that nutritious food should be provided. Although his views were partly based on humanitarian grounds, he also thought that prisoners had more potential for being reformed if they were treated correctly. The key component of his rehabilitative philosophy involved prison design. Howard was either the discoverer of the cellular prison or one of its early and most ardent proponents. He was of the opinion that the reform of prisoners would be enhanced if they were lodged in separate cells. This view obviously had significant implications for the architectural design of prisons. Although rehabilitation has not always been at the forefront for justifying this design, the cellular prison has been a central issue in prison design since the late eighteenth century.

Throughout the nineteenth century, other reformers continued the movement to transform the purpose of corrections. Sir Walter Crofton's Irish system and Alexander Maconochie's attempt to change the regime on Norfolk Island are notable examples. While holding the position of home secretary, Robert Peel was instrumental in significantly reducing the number of death penalty statutes.

The key issue that was raised throughout much of the nineteenth century was: who should administer the prison system? The Prison Act (1877) resolved that question. Before the act's passage, the British had created two kinds of prisons. The first kind were convict prisons controlled by the central government. These prisons were designed to house offenders sentenced to penal servitude, wherein a prisoner spent the first nine months in solitary confinement and served the remainder working on public works projects. Local prisons, on the other hand, handled offenders sentenced to imprisonment, a sentence different from penal servitude in that it was considerably shorter—with a two-year maximum permitted by common law.

Because the central government was not involved in the administration of local prisons, there was a notable difference in the regimes established at each prison. Generally, local prisons adopted one of two popular systems: associated or separate. Under the associated scheme, prisoners worked together in workshops during the day but were segregated in their cells the rest of the time. The separate system kept prisoners segregated in their cells all of the time. Though the separate scheme obviously limited the kind of work assigned to prisoners, it tended to be the more popular of the two systems.

The Prison Act (1877) accomplished two things: it brought local prisons under the control of the central government, and it created a Board of Prison Commissioners. The Board's first chair, Sir Edmund Du Cane, was instrumental in developing a uniform policy by which prisons would operate. That policy consisted of establishing a prison regime based on the separate system. Although modifications in the scheme were introduced from time to time, it became an intricate part of the prison regime well into the twentieth century.

As the nineteenth century drew to a close, a series of articles was published that painted a bleak picture of the system of local prisons. Critics noted overcrowding, poor diet, inhumane treatment by guards, and the separate system. A committee formed to investigate the charges issued a report in 1895. Although the report addressed itself to the original criticisms and offered a series of reforms, it has been suggested that the report's most noteworthy achievement is found in the recommendations proposed for the future development of penal policy. The most significant examples that have come to fruition in the twentieth century are: the establishment of separate institutions for offenders between the ages of 16 and 23, the segregation of habitual criminals under special conditions, and the creation of a prerelease prison. Youth custody, preventive detention, and hostels have respectively transformed those suggestions into intricate parts of the British correctional system.

Sentencing Philosophy

Throughout the twentieth century, the British have been confronted with two major problems in sentencing that have also created controversy in the United States. One of these is the existence of multiple sentencing aims instead of a single unifying purpose. Sentencing with multiple aims may not be a bad idea, but it does compound the problems facing prison authorities and other social service agencies. The second problem involves judicial discretion. Depending upon the sentencing philosophy of the individual judge, any of a number of sentencing aims may determine the rationale for imposing a particular sanction.

Sentencing Aims There are essentially four categories of rationales in sentencing: retribution, isolation, deterrence, and rehabilitation. In the past, retribution was closely linked to vengeance, specifically the ancient Hebraic idea of "an eye for an eye." Because that rationale for sentencing has largely been discredited, a more modern perception has developed. Today, its justification rests on the belief that courts have an obligation to display society's collective disapproval of crime. Sanctions should serve as a means of condemning the guilty by punishing offenders in proportion to their culpability for criminal activity. Hence, the old term of retribution has been replaced with the label—"just deserts"—to capture this sentencing rationale.

Isolation is another aim based on the premise that society should be protected from dangerous and violent offenders. However, society is assured that this rationale works only when a person is sentenced to life imprisonment and actually serves the entire term. Like most modern justice systems, the British are usually unwilling to enforce this aim completely. Although a life sentence or a long prison term attempts to fulfill the goal of isolation, most prisoners do not serve the total period imposed. Thus, the objective is achieved for only a limited time, and citizens are often surprised or angered to discover the actual amount of time served.

Critics of isolation have raised another concern with regard to its purpose. Although dangerous and violent offenders are removed from society for a time, they are simply transferred to another society—the closed world of the prison—where they often inflict their violent tendencies on other inmates. Critics contend that this imposes an added punishment on other inmates and is therefore unjust.

Deterrence is frequently cited as one of the principal aims of sentencing. Although its effectiveness is usually difficult to prove, deterrence has a dual purpose. One is to deter a specific offender from violating the law. Research and the opinions of those working in the field suggest that this kind of individual deterrence is largely dependent on the type of offense committed. Fear of punishment may deter some property crimes, for example, but this aim is unlikely to reduce violent crimes, which frequently occur on impulse. Moreover, the character and personality of the offender also influences the utility of this aim.

The other purpose is to deter others who may intend to violate the law in the future. This is referred to as general deterrence, because it is directed at the general public as a type of crime prevention tactic. The success of this tactic is based on the premise that if the public is knowledgeable of the sanctions imposed for a particular offense, they will be discouraged from committing such an offense. For this to work, citizens must possess a respect for the law and display a degree of deference toward the agents administering the justice system. The case for general deterrence is probably stronger than that for individual deterrence, but in both instances the effectiveness is difficult to prove.

Finally, rehabilitation has become an important goal of sentencing for many professionals working in the justice system. Although the aim is highly desirable, it has not totally superseded the others in significance. The lack of consensus on rehabilitative objectives is usually attributed to limited knowledge with regard to which techniques work and the fact that some of the other sentencing aims are better suited to handling certain offenders. Nevertheless, significant attempts are made to divert offenders from traditional correctional settings to those that have a community-based correctional philosophy. These diversionary programs occur in the closed prison setting as well as in the community. Each program is designed to enhance efforts at rehabilitation.

The British have generally adopted a dual purpose for sentencing. Presently, under the guise of isolation, an offender is sentenced to a prison term that reflects his or her culpability. The rationale is designed to protect the public from a dangerous offender. The other purpose for sentencing is rehabilitative. The British are making a conscious effort to move toward noncustodial programs based on a treatment philosophy, because they acknowledge that rehabilitation is not as likely to work in a confined setting.

Judicial Discretion An issue of paramount importance to the sentencing process is the amount of discretion awarded judges. Judicial discretion is a modern phenomenon that was almost unknown in the nineteenth century. Under common law, discretion was not permitted in felony cases, with the exception that a capital sentence could be substituted with a transportation order to one of the British colonies. During the first half of the nineteenth century, some statutes were enacted that enabled judges to substitute transportation for a sentence to penal servitude.

At the beginning of the twentieth century, the general absence of judicial discretion was altered considerably. Appellate review of sentences was introduced in 1907 in an attempt to assure that the sentence imposed would fit the individual rather than the crime committed. The Probation of Offenders Act became law in the same year; it permitted the issuance of probation orders as a substitute for imprisonment. The following year saw the passage of the Prevention of Crime Act (1908), which introduced two new sentences: borstal detention for young adults and preventive detention for habitual offenders. Thus, individualized sentencing had arrived—and with it, judicial discretion. The Criminal Justice Act (1948) extended sentencing options further, and other alternatives were added over the past 40 years, most notably noncustodial sentences.

In recent years, a central topic of discussion has been the use of mandatory and minimum custodial sentences. Those issues, along with others, have guided judges in their sentencing decisions. A number of pieces of legislation have introduced sentencing guidelines for judges, and these include: the Criminal Justice Act (1991), the Criminal Justice Act (1993), the Crime (Sentences) Act (1997), and the Criminal Justice Act (2003).

Organization and Administration of the Prison Service

Throughout the 1970s, England's economic stability suffered considerably from a number of setbacks. Inflation, high unemployment, wildcat strikes (i.e., strikes not authorized by the union representing the workers) in key industries, and the burdens of an extensive social welfare program were well publicized. When a country finds itself faced with this dilemma, the government frequently attempts to cut spending in the public sector in the hope that it will stimulate economic growth in the private sector. Generally, social services are asked to bear an unusually large portion of the cuts. Even under favorable economic conditions, prisons are considered a low-priority item in most countries. This was also true in England. Though partly a reflection of the public's narrow understanding and knowledge of the purposes of such institutions, this sense of indifference was also displayed by elected representatives. During periods of extreme economic difficulty, prisons are subjected to an even lower status.

General State of Prisons The general state of prisons in England has been a long-standing critical issue confronting the justice system. Part of this dilemma can be attributed to the financial crises that have plagued the country. Despite efforts to utilize noninstitutional methods, England's prisons have been overcrowded. Following World War II, the inmate population was estimated at almost 16,000. By 1980, the figure had risen to approximately 45,000. The figure peaked at more than

50,000 in 1988, declined somewhat in the early 1990s, but rose again to more than 66,500 by 1998. In early January of 2006, the inmate population was at 74,679 in a system that has a useable operational capacity of 78,619. In a report issued by the Home Office, the prison population is projected to continue to increase over the next several years. It is important to point out that these figures include adults and young people sentenced to incarceration along with people held while awaiting trial.

Efforts to close old prisons and build new ones had not kept pace with the increase in the prison population. Successive governments established plans to undertake extensive building and remodeling programs, but schedules to implement the work were often set aside because of financial crises. Thus, many of the prisons were antiquated structures built during the previous century. These conditions created serious problems. Cells that were designed to hold one person now held two or three. The cells were without toilets, so slop buckets were used. The redesign of plumbing at the older correctional facilities has eliminated the need for slop buckets in most institutions. Poor ventilation created a hot and stuffy living environment, and there were inadequate bathing facilities. Each of these factors contributed to unsanitary conditions as well as to low morale among inmates, who already suffered from various states of depression (Stern, 1987). The state of the English prisons was the principal cause for several disturbances in the early 1980s at facilities housing long-term prisoners and at high-security institutions. By 1986, a series of riots occurred at a variety of prisons. The physical conditions of the facilities remained a central concern. Thus, the protest spread throughout the system (Cavadino and Dignan, 2004; Vagg, 1994).

Another perspective was offered on the financial state of prisons. One study concluded that the neglected condition of prisons was actually limited to the overworked and overcrowded local prisons (King and Morgan, 1979). Training prisons, especially those housing long-term dangerous offenders, were built after World War II. The study found that, though funding was available for prison construction and remodeling, the issue centered on how the money was actually spent. The greatest criticism centered on the Home Office's adoption of the dispersal policy. The dispersal policy was the Prison Service's method of handling dangerous offenders who had been processed through the system. More than three decades ago, the prison service was concerned with providing maximum-security conditions only for prisoners sentenced to a life term. Because many of these inmates were guilty of domestic murders, and thus not considered dangerous to society, they were dispersed throughout the system.

During the 1960s, it became apparent that the system was incarcerating a new class of offender, either for a long term or for life. This class included members of the underworld and professional criminals who were considered violent and dangerous. These people, too, were being dispersed throughout the system. Following a number of successful escapes, the Home Office decided to inquire into prison security. It appointed Lord Mountbatten to conduct an investigation. Mountbatten suggested that all prisoners considered dangerous to the public be placed in a high-security-risk prison. Opponents contended that the Mountbatten scheme would make the prison too difficult to manage.

Opposition to the idea led to the creation of a second committee appointed to investigate prison security. This committee, headed by Sir Leon Radzinowicz, opposed the single high-security prison. It recommended that such inmates should continue to be dispersed to reduce the likelihood of concentrating potential unrest in a single prison; the dispersals were to be limited to a few secure facilities. Periodically, inmates could be transferred to another secure facility in order to reduce any tensions that might be developing among some of the high-risk prisoners. The Radzinowicz proposal was adopted, and funds were used to assure that a number of the institutions were indeed secure.

During the 1970s, the dispersal scheme apparently backfired—at least in the eyes of some critics. Violent confrontations and riots occurred in these high-security prisons. On economic and humanitarian grounds, it has been suggested that the Prison Service consider adopting the original Mountbatten proposal of concentrating the high-risk prisoners in one or two maximum-security prisons, but this has not been implemented.

Despite the government's attempt to improve the conditions within prisons, riots continued to occur in the early 1990s. This resulted in a review of the entire prison system by a senior judge, Justice Woolf. The Woolf Report was published in 1991. It offered several conclusions as to why the disturbances occurred and several recommendations for alleviating the problems. In addition to management concerns, such as inadequate staffing and communications problems, the inmates raised several objections that have been identified as standard complaints, following prison riots in most countries. They included: overcrowding, type and quality of food, availability of work and educational opportunities, visitation rights and restrictions, ineffective grievance procedures, and the number of petty prison regulations.

A central feature of the Woolf Report was the strategy offered to assure that a more stable environment be established throughout the prison system. The report suggested that the goal of stability could be achieved only through security, control, and justice. Security focused on the need to prevent inmates from escaping. Control centered on the need to curb the disruptive behavior of inmates. Finally, justice suggested that inmates should be treated with a greater degree of humanity and fairness.

The Woolf Report maintained that the governance of prisons should be based on principles that address how inmates are to be treated. For example, it suggests that inmates take some responsibility for their lives while in prison, which in turn would make them accountable for their actions. Inmates should expect to be treated with justice, thus reducing arbitrary decisions and capricious actions by staff. Finally, the notion that privileges be awarded at the discretion of the prison governor should be eliminated. Many of the privileges mentioned, such as the use of a radio and the purchase of books or a newspaper, should be considered a norm by today's standards. These principles are obviously designed to improve the relations between inmates and staff.

Only time will tell if the adoption of Woolf's recommendations, coupled with the building of new prisons and the modernization of others, will reduce the concerns raised about the state of the English prisons. Early indications are that the problems raised by prisoners and confirmed by the Woolf Report persist. It has been suggested that part of the reason has to do with the fact that the government accepted only two of the three methods for achieving greater stability. Since Woolf, security and control have been emphasized throughout the prison service at the expense of even considering the third element—justice—in the stability equation (Cavadino and Dignan, 2004).

In his book, *Prison Crisis*, journalist Peter Evans pointed out that it would take a considerable amount of time to improve the prisons. He stated that "[the] system is now in such a state of decay and the backlog of replacing obsolete prisons so great that even if it were possible to replace one every two years, beginning in 1980, the last Victorian prison would not be phased out until 2060" (1980). Over the past 20 years, in part because of the improved economic conditions of the country, the government has committed itself to addressing the prison crisis by moving ahead with an aggressive building program. Twenty-one new prisons have been built since 1980, and another six are under construction. In addition, temporary facilities have been opened at army bases. Finally, attempts also have been made to modernize some of the existing facilities.

Ministry of Justice Since the nineteenth century, the British have been enacting legislation to assure a centralized administration of England's correctional system. Initially, the Home Secretary was the civilian politician responsible for prisons. As indicated earlier, the Lord Chancellor was named in 2007 to head a new cabinet-level department, the Ministry of Justice. As such, the Lord Chancellor is also referred to as the minister of justice. Placing the correctional system in the hands of a senior cabinet officer who is also a member of Parliament enables members of the legislative branch to question the executive branch on policies, procedures, and critical issues of the prison system (see Figure 1.3).

The Prison Act (1952) was the principal legislative instrument that explained the powers and duties of the home secretary (now minister of justice). According to the act, the key functions included: having general powers and jurisdiction over all prisons and prisoners, appointing people to various boards or committees that deal with correctional issues, establishing rules for prison personnel, ordering the transfer of a prisoner from one institution to another, granting a temporary discharge of a prisoner because of ill health, having the power to enlarge or build new prisons with the approval of the Treasury, ordering the closing of a prison, issuing a yearly report to Parliament on the state of the prisons, and having similar powers of control and jurisdiction over juvenile justice facilities.

Figure 1.3

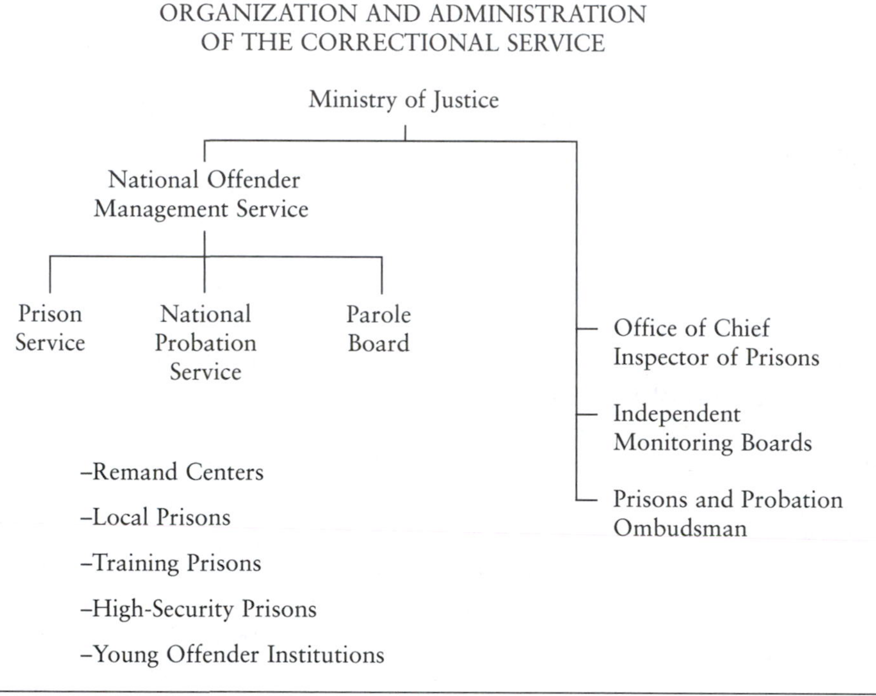

National Offender Management Service The National Offender Management Service (NOMS) was created in 2004. A review of the correctional system identified gaps in the work of the prison and probation services. NOMS was established to bridge the gaps and to improve the efficiency and effectiveness of the total correctional service. The chief executive and board of NOMS report to the minister of justice. NOMS is responsible for strategic planning, policy development, and financial leadership of the correctional service. It is also linked to other national and local government organizations, like the National Health Service, to enhance the quality of service provided and also to improve the public's confidence in these components of the criminal justice system. NOMS is organized into 10 regions (nine in England and one in Wales). Each region is responsible for planning the offender's supervision while in custody and the logical transition of the offender when released back into the community.

The Prison Service Until recently, the British correctional system had been administered centrally. The Prison Board, composed of a director general and five additional board members, was responsible for the formulation and implementation of prison policy and the overall management of the service. In an effort to reduce the size of government, an attempt is underway to decentralize the administration of the correctional system. This process began in 1993 when the Prison Service was granted agency status. Agency status essentially means that while the government will fund the correctional system and the employees will remain civil servants, the administration of the system will be more in line with that of a corporation in the private sector. Under this new arrangement, a chief executive officer administers the Prison Service, along with a board of management. This officer has authority over how the budget for the Service will be allocated. In addition, the number of administrative restrictions has been reduced to enhance efficiency and effectiveness. This includes giving prison governors more discretion in the daily management of their prisons (Ruggiero, Ryan, and Sim, 1995; Vagg, 1994).

With this agency status, the Prison Service is administered and managed in the following way. The director general of the Prison Service is the chief executive officer and is appointed by the minister of justice. The director general is responsible for the management of the Service, which includes the establishment of an organizational plan, performance targets, budget issues, and personnel matters. The director general is aided in long-term planning, policy, and fiscal development by NOMS.

As was mentioned earlier, one of the goals of the Ministry of Justice is to transform the administration of the correctional system so that it would operate along the lines of a corporate organization. One attempt at mirroring the private sector is illustrated by the adoption of a vision statement for the service titled: The Prison Service's Statement of Purpose.

> *Statement of Purpose*
> Her Majesty's Prison Service serves the public by keeping in custody those committed by the courts. Our duty is to look after them with humanity and help them lead law-abiding and useful lives in custody and after release.
>
> *Our Vision*
> To provide the very best prison services so that we are the provider of choice
>
> To work towards this vision by securing the following key objectives.
>
> *Objectives*
> To protect the public and provide what commissioners want to purchase by:
>
> Holding prisoners securely
>
> Reducing the risk of prisoners re-offending
>
> Providing safe and well-ordered establishments in which we treat prisoners humanely, decently and lawfully.

> *Our Principles*
> In carrying out our work we:
>
> Work in close partnership with out commissioners and others in the Criminal Justice System to achieve common objectives
>
> Obtain best value from the resources available using research to ensure effective correctional practice
>
> Promote diversity, equality of opportunity and combat unlawful discrimination, and
>
> Ensure our staff have the right leadership, organisation, support and preparation to carry out their work effectively.

The Prison Service is expected to continue to explore the notion of privatization of and within prisons, something that has received a good deal of attention in England. Privatization can include the design, construction, management, and funding of a facility or a combination of this kind of involvement. Presently, seven prisons are managed by private-sector organizations. Although the director of a private prison and the prison staff are employees of the contracting organization, they are subject to the same kind of oversight provided to public-sector prisons. Moreover, the director general of the Prison Service must approve the appointment of a director of a private-sector prison (Bryans and Jones, 2001).

Office of the Chief Inspector of Prisons The responsibility of this office is general oversight of the English prison system. It is also mandated to inspect young offender institutions and immigration removal centers. The office was created in 1981 to assure a degree of independence in the inspection of prisons. The chief inspector reports directly to the minister of justice rather than to the director general of the Prison Service. Because the inspectorate does not have any administrative authority over prisons and cannot impose any sanctions, its principal role is to identify problems in the Service and, on occasion, to offer strategies for resolving them. An actual inspection is carried out by a team composed of a prison governor and a senior prison officer who have been seconded from the Prison Service, as well as a civil servant. Other people may be added to the team because of their expertise. Doctors, lawyers, and building inspectors have been utilized in the past. Ultimately, it is the responsibility of the minister of justice to accept, reject, or delay addressing the issues identified by this office.

Independent Monitoring Boards For many years, the British have prided themselves on the use of lay volunteers to assist in the administration of justice. The local police authorities and the Independent Police Complaints Commission are examples of citizen participation in law enforcement, while lay magistrates illustrate this in the courts. Until 2003, these independent monitoring boards were referred to as boards of visitors. Under either name they reflect the use of lay participation in various penal establishments, and one exists for each correctional institution and immigration removal center. Board members are appointed by the minister of justice; they receive a training course designed to prepare them for their work; and they spend two to three days a month working as a board member. Presently, there are more than 1,800 members from a variety of walks of life who are serving in this capacity.

Board members have the responsibility of general oversight of prisons. Based on frequent visits by individual board members, each board produces a report on its institution for the minister of justice. The report examines the physical conditions of the establishment, the prison's administration and staff, and the various treatment programs that are available. Inmates also have access to board members, especially if they wish to raise a grievance about their treatment.

Irrespective of their good intentions, the boards have been the subject of various criticisms over the years. One is that the composition of the boards are too middle-class and disproportionately middle-aged. As many inmates are fairly young, it has been suggested that boards should have some representation from the prisoners' peer group. Unfortunately, board work generally requires that members have some control over their personal work schedule. Many young people have not gained that kind of freedom at their place of employment. Even the basic purpose of these boards has been a subject of criticism. Do boards contribute to an improvement of efficiency within the penal system, as their mandate implies, or are they merely window dressing for the Ministry of Justice? The same concern, you may recall, was raised regarding the role of local police authorities. Especially significant in this case, however, is the fact that some of these comments are being voiced by members of the boards.

Much of the criticism centers on their frustration with not being able to change the conditions that exist within correctional facilities. Board members have expressed concern about the types and conditions of work provided inmates and the low pay awarded. They also have pointed out that improvements should be made in educational and recreational programs. Little has been done to implement their suggestions, though, and the reasons most often cited for this inadequacy are financial. Some board members identify another more serious factor. They do not think the prison staff takes the work of the boards seriously. This is further compounded by the poor communication channels that exist between boards and the Ministry of Justice. Thus, board members feel thwarted by the prison establishment, both at the local level and at the top of the bureaucratic hierarchy. It will be interesting to see if the recent changes in the administration of the prison service resolve some of these concerns about the boards of visitors or possibly complicate the board's role further.

Prisons and Probation Ombudsman One of the concerns identified in the Woolf Report, which had looked at the causes for the proliferation of prison riots in the second half of the 1980s, was the lack of an independent oversight mechanism for the complaint process within the prison system. The Prisons and Probation Ombudsman is an attempt to address that concern. Created in 1994, the office is ultimately accountable to the minister of justice. The ombudsman's principal responsibility is to investigate complaints about how those in custody are treated throughout the prison and probation services. He or she also serves as the prisoners' final source of appeal from the internal disciplinary system of the prison authority. Finally, the ombudsman is responsible for investigating all deaths of prisoners, residents of probation hostels, and residents of immigration detention facilities.

In addition to the chief ombudsman, there are nine assistant ombudsmen and a staff of complaints investigators and fatal incidents investigators. Because the ombudsman is largely dependent on prison staff when conducting investigations, questions have already been raised about whether the ombudsman can reduce the inmates' concern that the disciplinary system is essentially unfair. It has been suggested that this system is too new to determine if it has brought a degree of fundamental fairness to the prison disciplinary system (Cavadino and Dignan, 2004).

Types of Prisons As was mentioned earlier, the British have adopted two sentencing rationales. For people found guilty of serious crimes, the sentencing aim is to incarcerate the person for an extended period of time, thereby protecting the public from a dangerous offender. Every effort should be made to impose a noncustodial sentence on other offenders in an effort to encourage these people to seek a treatment program. While the British acknowledge that custodial settings are often not suitable environments for serious attempts at treatment, they have recognized the need to provide opportunities within prisons that are specifically designed to encourage inmates not to reoffend upon release. As a result, programs have been designed to enable inmates: to improve basic educational skills, to provide meaningful work training, to address substance abuse, and to plan for outside accommodation and employment upon release from prison (Bryans and Jones, 2001).

An examination of the data provided by the Research and Statistics Department of the Ministry of Justice indicates how this sentencing philosophy has impacted the English prison system. By the end of 1996, the prison population for England and Wales was 55,300. Toward the end of 2008, it had risen to 83,714. Of that total, 13,598 were being held in remand prisons. Of the total prison population, 71,256 were adults (21 years of age and older), 9,641 were young adults (between 18 and 21 years of age), and 2,358 were under 18 years of age. The population consisted of 78,956 males and 4,758 females.

The British have established five types of prisons: (1) remand centers, (2) local prisons, (3) closed and open training prisons, (4) high-security prisons, and (5) closed and open young offender institutions. Each is designed to serve a specific purpose and is intended for a different kind of prisoner. Remand centers hold people who are awaiting trial or sentencing; they serve as distribution centers for the rest of the prison system and can be used to house inmates serving very short sentences of imprisonment. If an area does not have a remand center, the local prison will serve those functions. Thus, the purpose of local prisons in England is similar to that of jails in the United States.

One report, "Crisis in the Prisons: The Way Out," suggested that local prisons are also used to house people who will be incarcerated for an extended period of time (King and Morgan, 1979). It is not uncommon to find a person serving a four-year sentence in a local prison. The authors contend that this is a direct result of a policy of keeping the population low at some of the prisons that hold dangerous offenders. When Ministry of Justice officials talk about prison overcrowding, it is argued that the officials are really referring to the conditions in local prisons. For example, in 2006, the populations of remand centers represented 17 percent of the average population in custody (Cavadino and Dignan, 2007).

Since 1948, an attempt has been made to transform all prisons into corrective training centers. This has led to the establishment of the training prisons. The British pride themselves on the fact that about one-third of these correctional facilities are open institutions; that is, there are no walls or fences to prevent escape. All of the training facilities have as a primary goal the rehabilitation of inmates. Attempts are made to achieve this rehabilitative ideal by providing work and therapy for inmates.

Critics have taken issue with the supposed rehabilitative purpose of prisons and the lack of revenue to enhance rehabilitative programs. They contend that the rehabilitative goal of prisons is in a serious state of disillusionment in England and that it has been replaced by a new goal of the prison service: assuring secure and humane containment for inmates. While funds have been readily available to achieve the security objective, they have not been forthcoming in attaining a humane setting. Critics point out that this is illustrated by the fact that counseling, vocational, educational, and work programs are actually available to only a small number of inmates.

If the National Offender Management Service's strategy for protecting the public and reducing reoffending among inmates comes to practical fruition, some of the criticism may subside. One principal strategy is to manage offenders—both inmates and those in the community—more effectively. The plan calls for each offender to have an offender manager "who will be responsible for making sure that they are both punished and rehabilitated properly." The plan is designed to have the prison service and probation service interact more effectively. Related to this effort is an attempt to develop partnerships across government in areas like health, education, employment, housing, finance, and social and family ties. This is intended specifically to address issues related to recidivism.

Prison Staff The personnel working in a prison facility generally fall into one of three categories: the governor grade, the uniformed staff, and the professional and technical staffs. The governor grade consists of governors and assistant governors. A governor is the chief administrative officer of an institution and thus has the same responsibilities as a warden in a correctional facility in the United States. Assistant governors are assigned to a wing of a prison; their principal responsibilities focus on the rehabilitative care of inmates entrusted to them. Unlike the British police, the Prison Service is not unified. Therefore, the personnel do not all begin their careers at the lowliest ranks in the system and gradually work their way up through competitive promotions. The governor grade illustrates this fact, because governors traditionally have been recruited from outside the Service. Presently, there are three fast-track methods available to candidates for governor grade. An accelerated promotion scheme was implemented for both college graduate and veteran prison officials who aspire to administrative positions. The direct entry scheme permits managers of people-oriented organizations or prison staff entry to governor grade training. Finally, a cross-hierarchical scheme enables people who have an established career in another branch of the civil service to move into the Prison Service. Many of these people are appointed to the governor grade of the service. Once recruited, governors attend the Prison Staff College before being assigned to an institution. They also are encouraged to attend university courses dealing with counseling techniques and management skills.

Recruitment of uniformed staff is conducted both nationally and locally. Although there are no educational requirements beyond a high school diploma, selection standards are considered fairly rigorous. Candidates participate in a series of job simulation exercises that include testing their skills of: listening, calming, dealing with criticism, and offering constructive criticism. Candidates are also tested on their analytical skills and report-writing capabilities. The successful candidates would then participate in the prison officer initial training course. This is an 11-week course that begins with the candidate spending the first week essentially observing at the prison where they will eventually begin their career. This is followed by four weeks of training, one week at their prison, four more weeks of training, and one more week at their prison. Throughout this training period, candidates must pass a series of tests in order to gain certification. Approximately 9 percent of the candidates either fail the course or resign before its completion (Bryans and Jones, 2001). Although training traditionally has emphasized custody techniques and methods of supervising work and recreation, increased attention has focused on the officer's role as a treatment agent. In-service training is made available through refresher courses, and officers are encouraged to enroll in courses offered by other educational institutions.

The professional and technical staffs represent the third personnel category. They include: the medical staff, chaplains, psychologists, social workers, educational organizers, and prison industries instructors. The medical and psychological staff, as well as the chaplains, consist of both full-time and part-time personnel. Under the Education Acts, it used to be the sole responsibility of the local authority in which a prison was located to provide inmates with educational programs. Now private suppliers of educational services can compete for these contracts. Full-time and part-time educational organizers develop courses for inmates, and the costs for this service are reimbursed by the Ministry of Justice. Finally, civilian instructors (who are a part of the civil service but are not members of the uniformed staff) are hired to supervise and instruct inmates in prison industries. Some uniformed staff also assist the civilians in this capacity.

In recent years, there has been a growing degree of unrest among the staff of prisons. Much of this is directed at the government for essentially three reasons. First, an increase in the number of offenders placed in prisons has led to overcrowding, which in turn raises concerns about security and control among uniformed staff, who have already had to cope with prison riots. Second, budget cuts have inhibited or frustrated long-term planning, and this raises concerns about possible reductions in prison jobs. Finally, the introduction of privatization in the field of corrections on a limited scale has contributed to the sense of uncertainty among prison staff.

Parole The Criminal Justice Act (1967) introduced the parole system. Based upon the same premise as the United States' system, parole is designed to provide an inmate with an early release from a correctional institution. The Criminal Justice Act (1991) has revised the method of granting early release by establishing three strategies that are related to the inmate's length of sentence.

One strategy is the automatic unconditional release that is granted to all inmates serving less than 12 months. Eligibility occurs after one-half of the sentence is served, and there is no supervision unless the inmate is a young offender. If a person is convicted of a second offense while on early release, the court not only can impose a sentence for the new offense but also can reactivate all or part of the time remaining on the original sentence.

A second strategy is the automatic conditional release that is granted to all inmates sentenced from 12 months to less than four years. They are released after serving one-half of the sentence. Under this strategy, supervision is compulsory until at least three-quarters of the sentence is completed. If a person fails to adhere to the conditions of the early release, he or she can be fined or imprisoned for up to six months or have the time remaining on the original sentence reactivated if that is longer than six months.

The third strategy is the discretionary conditional release. This is available to inmates serving a term of more than four years. The inmate becomes eligible for consideration after serving one-half of the sentence, and it is the parole board that considers these cases. If an inmate is serving a sentence of less than seven years, the authority to release is given to the parole board. If the sentence is longer than seven years, the decision of the parole board is in the form of a recommendation to the minister of justice, who would make the final decision. Under this strategy, supervision is compulsory until at least three-quarters of the sentence is completed. In those cases in which the inmate is not considered for release under this strategy, the person would automatically be released after serving two-thirds of his or her sentence. Any breach of the conditions under this release strategy are handled by the parole board.

With the passage of the Crime and Disorder Act (1998), electronic tagging was introduced. This enabled the possibility of an earlier release by two months from the normal release date. This is known as the home detention curfew.

The Criminal Justice Act (2003) introduced some further changes to parole that went into effect in 2005. First, for sentences of less than 12 months that have an automatic release mechanism, there is a minimum period of incarceration of 13 weeks and a maximum period of 26 weeks. Second, once released, the remainder of the sentence is served in the community. Thus, supervision for all sentences, irrespective of the length of the initial sentence, is in force until the end of the sentence. Third, whereas home detention curfew was previously only available for short-term inmates, it is now available for all fixed-term prisoners.

Finally, the distinction between short- and long-term prisoners has been eliminated under the Criminal Justice Act (2003). Under normal circumstances, inmates will be released from prison after serving one-half of their sentence. For a typical fixed-term prisoner, the Parole Board will not be involved in the process, irrespective of the length of the original sentence. The Parole Board is expected to focus its attention on those inmates who are incarcerated for either violent or sexual offenses. These inmates are not eligible for the automatic release at the half point of their sentence. They will be released only when the Parole Board grants this order. Moreover, at the end of the custodial sentence, these types of offenders are subject to additional supervision: in the case of violent offenders, for five years, and in the case of sexual offenders, for eight years.

The Parole Board consists of about 20 members. It includes: judges, psychiatrists, a retired police officer, and others having expertise in social work and criminology. These individuals sit in panels to determine cases. When an inmate is released and supervision is called for, this responsibility would be handled by a probation officer.

Noninstitutional Sanctions

While the Prison Service is the unit within the Ministry of Justice that handles institutional treatment, the administration of noninstitutional programs is the responsibility of the National Probation Service. At the end of 2007, there were 150,179 people being supervised by the probation service. Of these probationers, 111,454 were issued community orders by a court, while 28,721 were people released from prisons on parole. This illustrates an attempt to impose noncustodial sentences on those who are guilty of offenses that are not considered violent or serious.

In the recent past, there were 55 local probation authorities responsible for probation services, with approximately 80 percent of the funds provided by the Ministry of Justice. The local probation authorities had a good deal of local control over these services. In 2001, it was reorganized into the National Probation Service. The reorganization also extended to the local probation authorities, with the 55 areas being reduced to 42. These new areas correspond with the boundaries of the 43 police forces of the country, with one exception. The Metropolitan Police of London and the City of London Police represent a single area of the National Probation Service. Each local area has a committee that is composed of magistrates and citizens from the area who assist in coordinating the programs and services provided to probationers of the area.

In the past, probation officers were not required to meet specific educational and training standards; in fact, many were volunteers. Today, the Central Council of Education and Training in Social Work controls the selection and training process. There has been a considerable influx of new probation officers holding university degrees in recent years. These people view themselves not as mere officers of the court but rather as a professional class of social workers allied more frequently with their clients than with the court. It appeared for a time that the probation service would be exclusively populated by these professionals, but increased caseloads and a recognition that lay volunteers would enhance the work of the service has led to a return to the utilization of volunteers.

Britain's justice system has become increasingly committed to the rehabilitative aims of sentencing. This conscious effort has led to an increased use of noninstitutional programs and the development of more nonpunitive methods within the community. What follows is a description of some of the more popular sentences that embody the community-based corrections philosophy.

Probation was the earliest form of noninstitutional sentencing. Its purpose is to allow the offender to remain in the community while under the supervision of a probation officer. A court will issue a probation order if the following criteria are met: the offense and the offender's record are such that incarceration is inappropriate; society is not being placed in danger by the release of the offender; the offender needs supervision; and the kind of supervision required is best provided while the offender is allowed to remain free in society.

Probation orders contain some standard conditions, such as maintaining good behavior, keeping in touch with the probation officer, and notifying the officer of any change in address. A court may impose additional requirements that include: specifying the place of residence, requiring medical or psychiatric treatment, and prohibiting association with certain people or the frequenting of specific places. If a court deems it necessary to place a restriction on the probationer's place of residence, or if the person does not have a fixed residence, the court orders the person to reside at a probation hostel. These facilities, run by either volunteer groups or the National Probation Service, are designed to provide the probationer with a residence while he or she works in the community during the day. Group treatment is frequently available at the hostel. Probation centers also have been established to assist probationers in acquiring basic skills that will enable them to secure employment. Probation orders are issued for a period of at least one year but not more than three. Failure to comply with a probation order generally leads to a fine or an order to perform community service.

Criticism has focused on the kinds of people utilizing hostels and probation centers. Hostels were originally designed to help improve employment skills of probationers. As the prison system attempts to reduce the number of people incarcerated, parolees are being sent to hostels. During periods of high unemployment, it was difficult to assist these people in finding work. Besides, many parolees at this stage of their release are in need of general coping skills for life. Another concern is that the number of offenders who suffer from alcohol or other drug abuse creates disruptive problems for hostels and day centers because it makes the offenders' behavior unpredictable (Smith, 1985). For some time, there had been a recognition that the number of hostels should be increased. The government had planned to expand the number but then abandoned the idea. In fact, they closed some of the existing hostels because of cost.

In the early 1970s, the British began experimenting with the community service order. The order requires an offender to perform 40 to 240 hours of unpaid community service. Such an order is generally served within a year's time, but it may be extended beyond that. Community service orders are frequently viewed as an alternative to a custodial sentence. Many offenders who have participated in this scheme are between the ages of 16 and 21; they have been sentenced in the past to custody or probation, so they are not first-time offenders. Noncompliance to a community service order may lead to a fine or to the revocation of the order and substitution of another sentence. The types of orders issued by a court under the program have included: hospital work, care of the elderly, the running of employment bureaus for ex-offenders, land reclamation projects, and work with youth organizations.

Although the number of offenders sentenced to community service continues to rise, probation officers have identified two areas of concern. The first involves the probation officers' perception of their role in the community service plan. Probation officers are accustomed to active participation with offenders. Under community service orders, an officer is initially involved with an offender as attempts are made to place the person with an organization. Once placed, however, it is advisable that an officer maintain a low profile. The burden of proving that the sentence was the correct one is almost totally in the hands of the offender. Some probation officers are finding it difficult to adapt to this new posture.

The second concern centers on the fact that the imposition of community service orders appears to have a multifaceted purpose. These orders can be viewed as punitive, rehabilitative, or as a form of compensation to the community. A number of critics have suggested that this clouds the purpose of the order and that it should actually have only a single objective. It has been suggested that this would enable the establishment of a clearer method for evaluating the entire program.

Community service orders are in part designed to fulfill a basic need of human nature: to feel wanted. Many offenders have been rejected by their families or society. Community service makes an attempt to reverse that sense of alienation. Moreover, the long-established view that correctional rehabilitation should be based on the premise that the offender needs help is altered considerably. With community service, offenders are not considered the recipients of help but rather as dispensers of it. Given the philosophical assumption behind the order, some have suggested that offenders should be paired with volunteer probation workers rather than professional probation officers. This notion is based on the belief that an offender should come in contact with the value system of a volunteer who is also displaying the need to feel wanted.

The Criminal Justice Act (1991) introduced a new sentence called the combination order. This order combines aspects of probation and community service. The period of probation must be at least 12 months but no longer than three years, while the community service hours range from 40 up to 100 hours. This sanction is available to any offender over the age of 16.

Another sentence introduced through the Criminal Justice Act (1991) is the curfew order. This order requires the offender to remain at a specific place for up to 12 hours a day. The act permits monitoring the curfew through an electronic device. Curfew orders can be imposed for up to six months.

Like many European countries, England utilizes the fine as a penal sanction for offenses other than traffic violations. Although it can be used in place of a custodial sentence, fines are imposed in addition to custodial sentences if the person is convicted on indictment. Unless a maximum amount is cited in a statute, a Crown court has unlimited power to fix a fine. Magistrates' courts, however, are limited in the amount that they can impose. Both courts consider the offender's income and general financial situation before imposing this sanction. Failure to pay can lead to a custodial sentence.

Other types of monetary sanctions include compensation and restitution orders. People who are injured or have property damaged (with the exception of traffic offenses) may be awarded compensation by a court. The order would be based on the offender's ability to pay. Offenders convicted of theft may be ordered to make restitution to the victim.

Another method of reducing the prison population was the development of the suspended sentence. The suspended sentence was first introduced under the Criminal Justice Act (1967). Courts that could impose a sentence of imprisonment for up to two years may suspend its enforcement if the time served is greater than six months. Offenders who are under a suspended sentence and who are subsequently convicted of another offense punishable by imprisonment would have the suspended sentence revoked. They would generally have to serve the remainder of the time in custody—in addition to serving the time for the new offense.

The Criminal Law Act (1977) introduced another method for employing the suspended sentence. Sentences ranging from six months to two years can be partially served and partially suspended. The suspended portion can range from one-fourth to three-fourths of a sentence. Offenders found guilty of a second offense while under this type of suspension are subject to the same rules spelled out in the Criminal Justice Act (1967). A court also can order the offender to seek treatment while on a suspended sentence.

A court may impose either an absolute or a conditional discharge in those cases in which a sentence is not fixed by law and the court believes that the character of the offender and the type of offense committed do not warrant imprisonment or a probation order. An absolute discharge is technically a conviction with exemption from any type of custody. A conditional discharge is the immediate release of an offender with the condition that the person not commit another offense over a specific period of time. This period cannot extend beyond three years. With a discharge order, a court can still require the person to pay compensation or restitution.

Finally, the Criminal Justice Act (1972) introduced deferred sentences. Under this type of sentence, a court defers the sanctioning of an offender for up to six months to determine if the person's conduct will change. If the person is convicted of another offense before the termination of the grace period, the court can impose a sanction for the original offense for which the offender received the deferment.

NACRO The impetus for developing a community-based corrections philosophy has not been fostered solely by courts and corrections personnel. Voluntary organizations have played a considerable role in introducing innovative rehabilitation programs. One of the leaders in this endeavor has been the National Association for the Care and Resettlement of Offenders (NACRO). NACRO was founded in 1966 by volunteer prisoners and societies in order to assist in the training of hostel staffs and the advising of those planning to develop hostels. Although it receives grants from the Ministry of Justice, it remains the major nongovernmental agency working to initiate new techniques and improve existing rehabilitation programs.

NACRO has been a particularly influential advocate in three areas of community-based corrections. First, it has been a vocal proponent of the use of volunteers. Specifically, it has urged the probation service to take a more active role (and greater care) in the placement of volunteers so as to assure the system that volunteers' time and energies are effectively utilized.

Second, it has been an innovator in the testing of diversionary programs. These programs are designed to help both those who have already been involved in the criminal justice system and those who are prime candidates for possible entry into the system. Among the projects developed by NACRO were: the Whitechapel Day Centre (which helps homeless offenders and ex-offenders by providing food, medical attention, counseling, job training, and placement); the NACRO Education Project (which offers placement in high schools, vocational schools, and colleges for offenders who started such a program while in prison); the Onward Workshop Project (which is designed to counsel drug users and their families); and the Lance Project (which assists the homeless who are perceived as potential delinquents by establishing hostels and offering referrals to other assistance agencies in the community).

Finally, NACRO has continued to play an important role in recommending to Parliament additional reforms regarding the handling of offenders. For example, it has called for a reduction in the maximum sentence for a number of offenses; it has urged abolishing sanctions of incarceration for drunkenness, marijuana use, vagrancy, begging, and soliciting; and it has proposed a broader use of alternatives to prisons. Thus, NACRO has played a major role in implementing and encouraging the use of noninstitutional treatment programs throughout England (Dodge, 1979).

In recent years, NACRO has been critical of the increase in the number of people sentenced to prison. Paul Cavadino, the Chief Executive of NACRO, has pointed out in their Corporate Plan for 2004–2007:

> NACRO aims to reduce crime by giving disadvantaged people, both offenders and those at risk of offending, a positive stake and place in our society. We work to reduce crime in three main ways: by promoting the social inclusion of marginalised people who might otherwise commit crimes; by working for a just,

> effective and non-discriminatory criminal justice system; and by reducing reoffending through the resettlement of offenders.

Among the specific concerns of NACRO are: the increase in the number of women, minorities, and mentally disturbed inmates; the length of the sentences; the difficulties of resettlement that confront the short-term prisoner; and the high level of unemployment among ex-offenders in general. Today, NACRO has established a comprehensive agenda for itself. It is involved in the management of more than 200 projects that include: housing for ex-offenders and other homeless people; employment training centers; informational and training services for prison inmates; structured activities for disadvantaged children; mediation and advice services for families; training for young people who have left school; and joint efforts with schools and outreach work to contact youths about education, training, and employment opportunities. These projects serve more than 60,000 people.

Critical Issue

Most modern correctional systems face a crisis of purpose and direction, and England's is no exception. This is in part due to the fact that the system frequently has established multiple goals for itself. When faced with this dilemma, conflict over which goal should take precedence is often inevitable. To compound the problem further, more than one component of the justice system has an impact on determining which direction the correctional system will take. As a result, goals and objectives are frequently imposed from outside and may be at cross-purposes with the goals established internally. Thus, corrections is not simply the official business of the Ministry of Justice. Parliament (with its lawmaking powers) and courts (with their sanctioning authority) play an important role in the development and execution of correctional policy.

Over the course of the past 30 years, various governments have initiated reform efforts to address the general state of prisons that were considered by many to be in a serious state of decay. Concerted attempts have been made to focus on improving the recruitment and training of employees of the Prison Service and with upgrading the quality of new and existing correctional facilities. Irrespective of the government in power, these efforts have been guided by two concepts—efficiency and effectiveness. When discussions focus on enhancing the efficiency and effectiveness of the Prison Service, it inevitably leads to a consideration of the role that prison privatization might play in the equation.

The privatization of prisons is not a new idea. From medieval times into the nineteenth century, prisons tended to be administered by private individuals. The idea of privatizing what had become an exclusive government function has been discussed in the context of reducing costs for the prison system. This is occurring at a time when there is a need to build more correctional facilities. While privatization can be implemented in a variety of ways, four approaches have dominated the discussion. One involves contracting out to the private sector the design and construction of prisons. Another focuses on having private firms finance the building of new prisons rather than using tax dollars. A third approach turns the ancillary services within a prison over to the private sector. These services usually include: catering, health care, education programs, and escorting prisoners. A final method involves transferring the management and administration of a prison facility over to a private firm. In this context, the government would continue to determine prison policy and monitor the administration of these facilities.

The British have elected to experiment with each of these approaches. Some of the future prisons are being financed, designed, and constructed by the private sector. Many of the ancillary services, such as catering, education, and prisoner escort, have been contracted out to a considerable degree. In early 1996, four prisons were being managed by a private firm. This number has risen to seven. Obviously, the ultimate goal for the government is to reduce the cost of the Prison Service.

Although privatization in any of its many formats is a relatively new endeavor, comments offered thus far provide a mixed review of these early efforts. Privately constructed prisons have been found to be similar in quality to those constructed by the public sector. Criticisms have been leveled that the various ancillary services, such as catering and educational programming, have been unsatisfactory. The private escort service has probably been the most noteworthy embarrassment. Shortly after assuming their duties, an escort service lost several prisoners and one died in their custody. An inquest found that the incidents could have been avoided. Finally, while costs are being reduced, staff levels in prisons run by the private sector are noticeably lower than those in the public sector. This has been made possible by the installation of high-technology security devices. It should also be pointed out that the staff hired by the private firms are paid less than those working in the public-sector prisons. Because privatization in the Prison Service is a new endeavor, only time will tell if its introduction was truly a cost-effective measure. Recently, it has been suggested that private prisoners might not be a solution to the problems confronting the Prison Service, but rather a factor that may aid in perpetuating them (Cavadino and Dignan, 2007)

Juvenile Justice

For centuries, the British seldom attempted to make a clear distinction between its poor and criminal classes. It was widely held that extreme poverty would inevitably lead to crime. Thus, legislation—in the form of a series of "poor laws"—was passed to cope with these problems. The laws were designed to serve two purposes: to aid the destitute in a humane fashion and to protect society from beggars and vagrants. A natural outgrowth of the poor laws was the development of a philosophy toward juvenile justice.

The emergence of a separate justice system for juveniles was based on the assumption that young people should be segregated from both the adjudication process and the penal system that had been established for adults. In part, this belief was based on humanitarian pity—especially for children of the poor—but there was also an element of self-interest underlying this philosophy. There was a fear that these children would inevitably become society's future criminals. The separate system was based on the premise that, because children were malleable, they could benefit from individual treatment, but that the rehabilitation process could only work if children were divorced from the adult justice system.

Another idea that emerged at approximately the same time suggested that the young should be treated as individuals possessing both needs and rights that the state should protect. This notion was directed at youths who had not violated the law but were orphans or victims of broken homes or child abuse. By the middle of the nineteenth century, the state commenced to expand its authority not only over the criminal behavior of the young but also over their noncriminal behavior.

Before these assumptions were introduced, young people were treated like adults. Juvenile delinquents were processed through the adult criminal justice system. They were tried in the same manner as adults and were sentenced to the same sanctions, including: death, transportation, and imprisonment. Actually, the implementation of the death sentence was rare, and although the law called for these harsh measures, they were modified in practice. For example, children were not always charged with the offenses they had been accused of committing, and when they were, juries often refused to convict them. Nevertheless, the system was harsh. Children were sentenced to transportation and imprisonment for what we would today consider minor offenses, and they served their term of imprisonment in adult prisons that were not conducive to the reformation of the child. Instead, these institutions tended to enhance the likelihood that the child would continue to violate the law.

Although attempts were made to introduce change during the first half of the nineteenth century, the reform movement failed to elicit the support of a majority in Parliament. With the passage of the Youthful Offenders Act (1854), efforts were realized to distinguish juveniles from adults in the justice system. This act created the reformatory school for juvenile offenders, which was later supplemented with the establishment of industrial schools for both offenders and nonoffenders. Although the reform and industrial schools were regulated by the Home Office and were eligible for government grants, they were usually run by volunteer organizations.

The development of these schools helped initiate a distinction between young and adult offenders, but children were still processed through the regular court system. Moreover, Parliament had not created alternative sanctions for juveniles. In 1887, however, the Probation of First Offenders Act introduced the suspended sentence. This was followed by the Probation of Offenders Act (1907), which established the probation scheme as we know it today.

Finally, the Children's Act (1908) created the juvenile court. This court is not a separate tribunal as was developed in the United States; rather, a juvenile court in England consists of a special sitting of a magistrates' court to handle juvenile matters. The Children's Act mandated that these courts adjudicate all offenses committed by children between the ages of seven and 16, with the exception of murder. It also authorized the court to decide issues involving the care of a child younger than 14. Among the circumstances identified as requiring attention were: children found begging, children in the company of dangerous persons, and children living with a drunken or criminal parent. Children considered beyond parental control were also subject to the court's jurisdiction. The act also expanded the court's choice of noninstitutional sanctions by developing various discharge and fining schemes.

Thus, the British introduced a juvenile court that remained a part of the regular court hierarchy. Other changes in juvenile justice occurred during the first half of the twentieth century, but for our purposes, the Children and Young Persons Act (1933) and its companion statute of the same name (introduced in 1969) are most significant. These pieces of legislation essentially explained the organization and administration of the juvenile justice system throughout much of the twentieth century. Of particular importance was the Children and Young Persons Act (1969), for it attempted to address the central issue confronting juvenile justice at that time: what was the most important goal of the juvenile justice system?

The original intention of the 1969 act was to bring about a major shift in policy through the introduction of a more liberal humanitarian view toward juvenile delinquency. The act called for de-emphasis of the punishment rationale and expansion of care services offered by social workers. These services would be determined at the local level by offering offenders assistance in their own community rather than sending them to an isolated institution. If the act had been fully implemented (something successive governments had not been willing to do), courts would have lost their power to determine specific kinds of residential and nonresidential treatment. Moreover, borstal training, detention centers, and attendance centers would have been phased out. Although borstal training was eliminated, it was replaced with youth custody, which is not without its critics.

Though the decade of the 1960s gave birth to this liberal philosophy, it was implemented during the 1970s, when the climate of opinion toward juvenile delinquency was changing considerably. This was illustrated by the fact that funds needed to implement the shift to community control were simply not forthcoming. This was partly the result of the national economic crisis. To implement the policy, more social workers would have to be hired, but neither the local authorities nor the national government were in a position to provide funds to hire the additional staff. More neighborhood care facilities would have to be established if the juvenile was to be treated in the community, but expenditures were not available for such projects. Thus, the system had to rely upon existing institutions whose design, location, and philosophy were in opposition to the intentions of the 1969 legislation.

During the 1970s, the number of juveniles involved in crime continued to rise, creating a public backlash favoring stricter measures in dealing with young offenders. Moreover, dropout rates among juveniles in treatment programs also rose significantly, something which did not enhance the cause of the treatment programs. These two factors helped to foster an ideological battle between magistrates and social workers. They also afforded the critics of community-based treatment an opportunity to attack one of its underlying assumptions: that of keeping the child in the community. At issue was the kind of community facility in which the delinquent would be housed. It was alleged that the material benefits found in community homes were creating an unrealistic environment for delinquents. Upon release, a considerable number of them would return to an environment that lacked these benefits. It was suggested that this could compound the delinquents' problems and lead to further violations of the law.

Finally, the act gave social workers more direct control over the juvenile when a care order or supervision order was issued. This created a jurisdictional and ideological battle between magistrates and social workers. Magistrates viewed the act as increasing the power of the executive and thus adversely affecting the impartiality of the judiciary. Because of the social workers' free rein in the implementation of care orders, magistrates believed their intentions for issuing such an order would be (and had been) altered by child care specialists. Because many magistrates had middle-class backgrounds and were sensitive to the public's demand for a more "law and order" philosophy, their conservative sentencing rationale was frequently at odds with that of caseworkers.

One study of the divergent views of magistrates and social workers toward psychiatric services lends credence to this point. It concluded that caseworkers displayed a greater degree of assurance in their expectations for psychiatric treatment than did magistrates. It suggested that this reflected the differences existing between the two groups with respect to their perception of role and status (Prins, 1975).

The implementation of some of the key provisions of the Children and Young Persons Act (1969) were halted. Reasons frequently mentioned for the failure to enact the entire piece of legislation included: the adverse change in the economy, the continued increase in juvenile crime, and the conflicting views among the decisionmakers and implementers of juvenile disposition orders. Some believed that this led to a serious crisis of purpose for those working in and treated by the juvenile justice system.

The Children and Young Persons Act (1969) was not able to resolve the question of what should be the ultimate goal of the juvenile justice system. Thus, the issue has remained a vexing problem, and the debate has continued over the kind of juvenile justice system that should be established and what that system's overriding goal should be. When considering the principal philosophical thrust of the juvenile justice system, a welfare model and a justice model are often pitted against each other. On the one hand, there is the liberal humanitarian notion that juvenile justice should have the welfare and protection of children as its goal. The most visible and vocal advocates of this approach are social workers. On the other hand, there remains a more conservative pragmatic philosophy that calls for a punitive approach—especially when dealing with those who are repeatedly at odds with the law. This has been reflected in the enhanced severity of institutional sanctions imposed by the courts (Pitts, 1988). In addition, the sentencing aim to isolate dangerous offenders or dangerous adult recidivists from the general population is finding support in the sanctioning of the serious juvenile offender.

Over the course of the past decade, the British have focused a good deal of attention on the desire to divert more young people away from the formal adjudicatory process, while also developing a strategy that deals with the most serious and persistent young offenders. Several pieces of legislation have been enacted that attempt to facilitate the administration and delivery of both objectives. They include: the Criminal Justice Act (1991), the Criminal Justice and Public Order Act (1994), the Crime and Disorder Act (1998), the Youth Justice and Criminal Evidence Act (1999), and the Criminal Justice Act (2003).

Prevention Many countries have recognized the need to direct some juvenile justice resources to the creation of diversion programs. Diversion (or prevention, as it is commonly referred to in England) attempts to direct juveniles away from the formal adjudication process. Its primary purpose is to prevent more juveniles from being labeled delinquent. Many of the programs are available for those who have had some contact with the system.

Ideally, all of the major components of the justice system should be involved in prevention. In England, each component contributes to this objective in varying degrees. In the area of corrections, probation officers and local caseworkers work with juveniles who have received a noncustodial sentence in the hope that they can divert these people from future criminal involvement that could lead to a custodial sentence. Some custodial sentences are even designed to prevent the continuance of delinquent acts at an early stage. The secure training order, created by the Criminal Justice and Public Order Act (1994), is a recent example of this policy. The underlying purpose of care orders and attendance centers also illustrates this position.

The youth courts' involvement in prevention is not as tangible, because they are not in the business of developing diversionary programs. Nevertheless, the courts contribute to the objectives when they issue noncustodial sentences such as absolute or conditional discharge, or a compensation, restitution, or hospital order. Issuing a care order to a nondelinquent is often a measure that the court will take in anticipation of future problems (possibly of a criminal nature) for the juvenile.

Police involvement in diversion generally takes two forms. One focuses on an officer's discretionary power to issue a reprimand or warning to a young person rather than formally charge them with an offense. The power to reprimand or warn was introduced by the Crime and Disorder Act (1998). This replaces the discretionary authority that police formerly had to caution a young person. This new authority may be exercised when: an officer has evidence that a young person has committed an offense, the officer is of the opinion that the person would be convicted based on the evidence, the offender admits guilt and has not been previously convicted of an offense, or the officer does not think that it is in the public interest to prosecute the case. A reprimand is given if the offender has not been previously reprimanded or warned; a warning is given if the offender has not been previously warned or the offense is serious. Moreover, when a warning is issued, the officer must refer the young person to a youth offending team, which is explained below.

The other avenue of police involvement with diversion is with the establishment of juvenile liaison schemes. These schemes are designed to show the public that police are not just involved with crime detection but that they are also committed to crime prevention. Within a constabulary, juvenile liaison officers are selected to work—with schools, neighborhood groups, and voluntary organizations—at diverting young people away from delinquent behavior. The officer, usually with the help of social workers, assists in organizing neighborhood groups. The goal is to establish a line of communication and foster a sense of cooperation between the group and the police. Juvenile liaison officers are also assigned to schools. Not sent to investigate crime or enforce school discipline, they are available to assist the school specifically in educating students about the administration of justice and more generally in the student's role as a socially aware and responsible citizen.

Through the Crime and Disorder Act (1998), the government introduced some additional measures that are examples of early intervention for children and young people at risk. For example, the act permits local government authorities to establish child curfews for children under the age of 10. Thus, children at or below that age cannot congregate during a specific time period (late night, early morning) unless they are supervised by a parent. Another measure is the child safety order, which authorizes a court to impose specific requirements on a child under the age of 10 who is at risk of becoming involved in crime. For example, such an order can impose a curfew and prohibit the child from associating with specific people or frequenting certain places. The order provides the child with supervision from a social worker for a period of roughly three months (and, in exceptional cases, 12 months). The objective is to assure that the child is receiving proper care, protection, support, and appropriate control so that the behavior that led to the safety order is eliminated or reduced considerably. Finally, while parents might not be blamed for specific actions of their children, they should be held responsible for their care and control. Unfortunately, it is believed that a significant number of juvenile offenders have not had an appropriate level of parental supervision. The act attempts to correct this deficiency through the establishment of the parenting order. A court can issue such an order to a parent of either a child (a person under the age of 14) or a young person (a person between the ages of 14 and 17). An order can exist for a period of up to 12 months and is generally designed to require that the parent receive counseling and guidance.

The Persistent Young Offender Toward the end of 1997, the government announced a new initiative regarding youth crime. While the government acknowledged that most young offenders infrequently commit offenses, they were concerned about a small group of persistent offenders. It was estimated that the persistent offenders consisted of approximately 100,000 active offenders and that they committed about one-half of all crimes. The profile of this group of 100,000 is: one-half were under 21 years of age, almost two-thirds abused hard drugs, three-quarters were out of work, more than one-third were in care as children, almost one-half were excluded from school, and one-half were without qualifications for employment. It also has been reported that this group fluctuates, in that approximately one-fifth will stop offending but will be replaced by another cohort (Home Office, 2001). The government's initiative to address the problem of the persistent offender is not limited to this issue; it is also intended to provide a broad-based effort at reform of the juvenile justice system.

The initiative is based on a systems approach to the problem. Several objectives have been identified, including: reducing delays in the adjudication of young people accused of crime; confronting the young offender with the consequences of his or her actions for himself or herself, his or her family, the victim, and the community; imposing a punishment that reflects the seriousness of the offense and the offender's history of criminal behavior; encouraging the offender to make reparations to the victim; reinforcing the parental responsibility for the young person; and assisting the young person in addressing issues surrounding his or her deviant behavior and developing a sense of personal responsibility for his or her actions.

A New National Strategy With the passage of the Crime and Disorder Act (1998) and the Youth Justice and Criminal Evidence Act (1999), the government introduced a new process and some additional administrative mechanisms that are designed to facilitate the establishment of a new national strategy to reform juvenile justice. Central to this effort is the desire to prevent young people from becoming involved in crime. If that effort initially fails, then the objective is to foster an approach for diverting young people away from the formal adjudication process when it is in the interests of the public and the young offender to do so. At the same time, the government acknowledges that greater effort must be devoted to focusing attention on the serious persistent young offender. As one might expect, the strategy is not without critics (Goldson, 2000).

The Youth Justice Board was created through the Crime and Disorder Act (1998). It is a group of approximately 12 people who have had extensive experience with juvenile justice issues. They are appointed by the minister of justice to a fixed term that cannot exceed five years. Their appointment can be renewed as long as the total years of service does not exceed 10 years. The Board has several responsibilities: to monitor the operation of the youth justice system, to advise the minister of justice on the effectiveness of the system and the establishment of national standards, to collect information from various groups working with young people in general and youth justice in particular, to publish information, to identify and acknowledge model programs, and to make grants available to local authorities and commissioned research. The results of much of this work will appear in an annual report. A key feature of the Board's responsibility will be the development of national standards that will be implemented at the local level.

The Crime and Disorder Act (1998) also calls for each local authority to develop and implement a youth justice plan. Part of this strategy involves bringing local politicians, social services, police, and educators together in an effort to address behavioral difficulties of young people in the community. A central feature of the plan is to prevent young people from reoffending. The act specifically calls upon each local authority to publish how they intend to provide and fund youth justice services. They must also explain how the youth offending teams will be utilized.

A key element in this new strategy is the establishment of youth offending teams. Each local authority is to establish at least one youth offending team. The team is composed of: a probation officer, police officer, social worker, educator, healthcare professional, and other people if the local authority deems them appropriate for the task at hand. The principal objective of the team is to address the behavior of the young offender. The probation officer and social worker are expected to play a central role in this strategy, with the ultimate goal of bringing about a change in the behavior of the person. Members of the team might be actively involved in a case. For example, one team member might supervise a child safety order while another team member supervises a parenting order. If the local authority has already established community-based intervention services, the team can also avail themselves of that support. Thus, the strategy calls for a focused response on the part of the team, while allowing them to utilize the social service infrastructure that is already in place.

The Crime and Disorder Act (1998) initiated the government's national strategy to reform juvenile justice and to address youth crime. With the passage of the Youth Justice and Criminal Evidence Act (1999), another component in this national strategy was introduced. Youth offender panels are that part of the administrative mechanism that focuses on requiring both young offenders and their parents to take responsibility for their behavior. More specifically, it is designed to allow the young offender active involvement in the justice process. This is an attempt to address an acknowledged fact that the traditional process of adjudication usually prevents the young offender from any meaningful participation.

The act creates a new sentence of referring the offender to a youth offender panel. The initial strategy is to limit this sentence to young people under the age of 18 who are being convicted for the first time. The terms of this referral order are expected to run from three to 12 months. It is the responsibility of the youth offending team to create a youth offender panel for each person sentenced in this manner. At least one member of a panel will be from the youth offending team. When such a referral order is issued to a young offender under the age of 16, at least one parent or guardian is expected to participate in the process, and the court can order that both parents be involved.

At the first meeting of the youth offending panel and the young offender, a contract will be agreed to that is designed to alter the young person's behavior and thus reduce the likelihood of reoffending. The conditions of the contract are likely to include such items as: reparation to the victim (not required), mediation session between offender and victim (if the victim agrees), community service, a home curfew, attendance at school or work, participation in certain activities like alcohol or other drug rehabilitation, avoiding certain people and places, and reporting to a local authority. Subsequent progress meetings would be held either at regular intervals or when deemed appropriate. If the young offender refuses to sign a contract or fails to appear for a scheduled meeting, he or she would be returned to court for resentencing.

Youth Court

Before the personnel and jurisdiction of the youth court are described, it is important to explain how the British classify juveniles according to their age and level of criminal responsibility.

Responsibility of Juveniles Anyone under the age of 17 is referred to as a juvenile, but a more intricate classification scheme has been established to differentiate people in this group. Anyone under the age of 14 is a child. Children are further divided into two groups: those who are under 10 years of age and those who are between 10 and 13. Children under the age of 10 cannot be prosecuted for any offense, while those between 10 and 13 can be prosecuted if the prosecution can prove that the child knew that his or her actions were wrong. A child in this latter group who is charged with murder or manslaughter may be tried on indictment.

Prosecuting a child above the age of 10 was a new feature introduced by the Crime and Disorder Act (1998). This was a change from the old common law principle of *doli incapax* (not capable of crime), which traces its origins to the reign of King Edward III (1312–1377). *Doli incapax* operated under the assumption that children under 14 years of age who had broken the law were too immature to know that what they were doing was wrong. Thus, they could not have criminal intent. With the 1998 statute, a case will go forward, if the prosecution can prove to the court through evidence that the child knew his or her actions were seriously wrong. As a result, young people are being held responsible and culpable for their actions at an earlier age. Some have suggested that this is one of many examples of the government's strategy to emphasize the deeds of young offenders rather than their needs (see Pitts in Matthews and Young, 2003).

A "young person" is defined as anyone between the ages of 14 and 17; these individuals are fully responsible for their actions under the criminal law. Young persons may be tried on indictment if they are charged with homicide or any offense that if committed by an adult would be punishable by imprisonment of more than 14 years, or if they are jointly charged with a person who is at least 18. This last category assures that the two would be tried together, which is necessary for the interests of justice. Finally, the term "juvenile adult" refers to anyone between the ages of 18 and 20. They are treated as adults for the purpose of trial, but special provisions have been devised for sentencing.

Court Personnel The Criminal Justice Act (1991) replaced the juvenile court with the youth court. The juvenile court was established at the beginning of the twentieth century. The youth court is a special sitting of a magistrates' court. Youth court magistrates are elected to a three-year term by and from the magistrates serving in a district. The selection is made from among the lay magistrates. Thus, district judges are rarely involved with youth court matters. Magistrates that are elected have displayed a specific interest in or experience with young people. In order to prepare them for this type of work, magistrates participate in a special training program. Although youth court magistrates cannot be over the age of 65, some criticism still remains regarding the apparent generation gap that exists between the justices and the young people brought before them. Magistrates sit in panels of three to hear cases; each panel must include at least one male and one female member.

The actual court proceedings are not open to the general public. The press, however, is allowed to attend and report on cases, as long as they do not disclose the identity of the child. Any details of a case that might lead to the child's identity are not disclosed. As the court is composed of lay magistrates, it is necessary to have a clerk present. The clerk of the court is a trained solicitor or barrister who is present to advise the justices on substantive and procedural points of law. Social workers are also in attendance. They include probation officers specializing in juvenile matters and members of the local authority's social service department.

Jurisdiction of the Court While the old juvenile courts had both civil and criminal jurisdiction for people under the age of 17, youth courts will only deal with criminal cases involving people under the age of 18. The court's original criminal jurisdiction over offenses excludes murder. There are some qualifiers on this. For example, a child under the age of 10 cannot be prosecuted for any offense, and a child between the ages of 10 and 13 can be prosecuted only if it is proved that he or she understood the consequences of their actions. The most controversial issues that have been raised about the court's jurisdiction have centered on its sanctioning authority. Some critics contend that the court should enhance its role as protector of the child's welfare, while others have called for a return to a more punitive sanctioning philosophy.

Procedures of the Youth Court

Pretrial Proceedures Generally, attempts are made to avoid referring a young person to a youth court for disposition. This position was adopted on the grounds that an appearance before a court has a tendency to stigmatize the juvenile. Thus, attempts are made to avoid labeling a young person delinquent, a position that also has been advocated throughout the United States. The police usually attempt to resolve the issue through consultations with the local authority, but if a decision is made to proceed through the court, the police either summon or arrest the juvenile (Maxim, 1986). When it is necessary to make such a referral, the law requires that the criminal charge be presented by a qualified person. In effect, this restricts the prosecution of juveniles to a Crown prosecutor.

Within 72 hours after being arrested, a juvenile must be brought before an examining magistrate. The court may permit the release of the juvenile into the parents' care or it can remand the young offender. The term "remand" means the person will be placed either in the care of the local authority or committed to a remand center. Remand is generally reserved for juveniles characterized as being dangerous or unruly. If a remand center is not available, the person is detained in a local prison. Remand centers are also used to hold juvenile adults who are awaiting trial or sentence. The normal period of remand before trial is usually a week. Criticism has been directed at placing young people in local prisons, but the shortage of remand centers and the increase in the number of juveniles being detained has left the courts with few alternatives.

Whereas the issue of juvenile rights has received a good deal of attention in the United States, it has not been the center of controversy in England because the youth courts' criminal jurisdiction has not been challenged. Moreover, statute law has assured juveniles the right to be notified of hearings, the right to bail, the right to legal aid, the right against self-incrimination, and the right of appeal. As in the United States, youth courts in England can transfer a case to an adult court. The transfer is made to the Crown court and is usually undertaken when one of two circumstances warrants such a move: (1) If a young person is charged with a serious crime and the court is of the opinion that he or she should be found guilty, the court may take the position that the offender should be sentenced to a long term of detention, which only a Crown court has the power to impose; or (2) If a young person is charged in conjunction with an adult for an indictable offense, the youth court may transfer the case to a Crown court in the interest of justice.

Trial Procedures For both trial on indictment and summary proceedings, the youth court employs the same basic procedures that are used in an adult court. The juvenile's right to appeal is also the same as that permitted an adult offender. At trial, a juvenile is given the same right to be legally represented as an adult. Parents of a young offender are allowed to assist in their child's defense if their child is not represented. Parents must attend all the court proceedings and can be issued a summons or warrant to assure their appearance. Moreover, the court is required to cross-examine witnesses if the juvenile is considered incompetent to do so.

Special provisions have been established for individuals who have been found guilty. For example, a juvenile and his or her parents are given the opportunity to address the court before the justices make their final disposition order. The court must also review the offender's presentence report. This includes information of the young person's medical history, performance at school, home surroundings, and general conduct. The parents and the juvenile—if old enough to comprehend the information—must be informed of the contents of the report by the court. If there is disagreement over the contents, the court will permit the juvenile or the parents to produce other information. Lastly, before the disposition order is announced, the court usually explains to the juvenile and parents its rationale for issuing the order.

Disposition

There are a number of options available to a court when it issues its disposition order. These are generally classified as being either noncustodial or custodial methods of treatment. Only noncustodial measures are discussed here. The custodial methods will be explained under the subsection dealing with treatment facilities.

Many of the noncustodial measures available to adults are deemed appropriate for young people. They include: absolute or conditional discharge, disqualification, fine, compensation, restitution, forfeiture of property, community service, and hospital orders. Each of these has been previously described in the sections on the law and corrections.

Since 1971, the court has had the power to issue supervision orders. These have largely replaced probation orders, which are no longer available to young people. With a supervision order, the person is placed under the supervision of either a caseworker from the local authority or a probation officer. Although the order is similar to that of probation, some of the conditions are different and the supervisor does not have to be a probation officer. The supervisor has the responsibility to advise and assist the person. Supervision orders are made for a period of up to three years or until the person reaches his or her eighteenth birthday. A supervisor can request that the court vary the conditions of the order during its term or replace it (usually with a care order). Once a person reaches 18 years of age, an adult magistrate's court can vary or cancel the order. If a person fails to abide by the conditions of the order, the court can impose a fine or order the person to an attendance center.

The court is permitted to impose specific conditions on the supervision order. For example, it can order a person to live with a specific individual or to reside at a particular place, such as a residential home. (Such an order cannot exceed 90 days, however.) It can order an offender to participate in certain activities that are designed to enhance the person's rehabilitation. Supervision orders also can restrict a person's night activity or require school attendance as part of the condition. If a court believes a person is suffering from a mental condition that has been diagnosed by a medical practitioner, it can order the person to seek psychiatric supervision.

In 2001, the intensive supervision and surveillance program was introduced as a rigorous strategy designed to target repeat offenders who commit the most serious crimes. With these offenders, the level of community-based surveillance is enhanced considerably. The program is designed to last six months. During the first three months of the program, the supervision averages about 25 hours per week. During the last three months of the program, the supervision is reduced to about five hours per week.

Treatment Facilities

The British started to eliminate sentences of imprisonment for juveniles in 1908. In that year, prison sentences for children between the ages of 14 and 16 were abolished. The minimum age for sentencing has since been raised to 17. Prior to sentencing anyone under 21 to a prison term, a court must first consider the alternative custodial institutions available. There are currently five types of custodial disposition orders that the court can issue for people under 21: (1) youth custody orders, (2) secure training orders, (3) detention center orders, (4) care orders, and (5) attendance center dispositions.

Youth custody has replaced borstal training. Borstal training was designed for offenders between the ages of 15 and 21 who had been convicted on indictment of an offense that was punishable by imprisonment. It was considered a reformative custodial sentence that varied in length from six months to two years. Magistrates' courts were prohibited from imposing this sentence because of its length, so a person was bound over to a Crown court to receive this disposition.

Borstals were introduced at the turn of the twentieth century and were designed to handle the juvenile adult. They attempted to combine vocational training, education, and counseling for those who had already established a pattern of criminality. Before its demise, however, trade school training and education had been abolished as features of this regimen. Although attempts were made to establish a relaxed atmosphere, the borstal regime came closest to that found in an adult prison, utilizing a collaborative treatment philosophy. Upon release from borstal training, the person was subject to a two-year period of supervision. Because of high recidivism rates, critics suggested that the system did not work.

Youth custody is designed for offenders between 15 and 20 years of age. For juveniles under 17, the maximum sentence is 24 months. Critics contend that its purpose is punishment, pure and simple. They point out that little in the way of counseling is achieved because generally only one probation officer is assigned to an institution. Moreover, many probation officers are of the opinion that they should concentrate their efforts on long-term offenders, which results in little help being directed at those who have received a short-term sentence. Some critics further contend that the overworked probation officers often find little time even to direct their efforts at the long-term offender (Pitts, 1988; Stewart and Smith, 1987).

Secure training orders were introduced with the Criminal Justice and Public Order Act (1994). They were designed to deal with young people who are considered persistent young offenders. A persistent young offender is defined as a person between 12 and 14 years of age who has committed three or more imprisonable offenses and fails to respond to noninstitutional sanctions. The maximum sentence for this order is two years—of which one-half is served at a secure training center and one-half is served under supervision within the community. The first secure training facility was operational in 1998.

With the passage of the Crime and Disorder Act (1998), the secure training order was replaced with the detention and training order. While this sentence is primarily designed for offenders between the ages of 12 and 17, it could be extended to offenders as young as 10. The detention and training order requires that the person is subject to a period of detention, which is then followed by a period of community supervision. This sanction is given only to young people who represent a high risk of reoffending, have a history of reoffending, and the nature of the offense is serious.

The following orders are designed for young people between the ages of 16 and 17. The community rehabilitation and punishment order can last between 12 months and 3 years. The young person is to perform unpaid community work for 40 to 100 hours. A community punishment order extends the time to perform unpaid community work to a period of between 40 and 240 hours. Finally, a community rehabilitation order is supervised by the youth offending team and may include activities in which the offender repairs the harm caused by his or her offense.

A supervision order is for a period of up to three years. It is generally used for more serious offenses. Specific activities can be attached to such orders—for example, participation in a drug treatment program or involvement in the intensive supervision and surveillance program mentioned above. Young people receiving such an order are also expected to participate in activities established by the youth offending team.

Care orders place a juvenile in the care of the local authority and remove all parental rights of control over the juvenile. The local authority may allow a person to live at home, in which case the supervision would be imposed through frequent visits by a caseworker. As an alternative, the local authority can require the person to reside in a community home, voluntary home, or foster home. Community homes are administered by the local authority and are regulated by the Ministry of Justice. Voluntary homes are run by volunteer organizations; they, along with foster homes, are subject to Ministry of Justice regulations.

Care orders cease to have the force of law when a juvenile reaches age 18, when the local authority informs the court that it would be more appropriate to impose a supervision order, or when the juvenile has reached the age of 15 and is considered a detriment to others in the home. In this last case, the person is sent to youth custody. A care order can be extended to a person's nineteenth birthday if the young person's mental condition warrants a continuance of the order. Interim care orders also can be issued to juveniles who have not been found guilty by a court; however, the term of the order is limited to 28 days.

Disposition to an attendance center is not strictly a custodial sentence. Instead, it is the imposition of a structured setting on an offender, which is administered by the local authority. Attendance centers are usually run by the local police or social service workers. They are only open on the weekend so they do not interfere with a young person's work or schooling. By and large, the centers are designed to teach juveniles how to utilize their free time constructively. Physical education and craft programs are offered to illustrate alternative methods of using idle time.

A court can order a young offender above the age of 10 to attend a center. Excluded from this type of order are those people who have already been sentenced to imprisonment, youth custody, or a detention center. The total number of hours imposed on the offender cannot exceed 36 hours. Because the offender attends a center for two or three hours at a time, an order can take several months to fulfill. Attendance center orders are imposed on young people who do not warrant a custodial sentence but require some restrictions placed on their time that are not available through the other types of dispositions. If the order is breached, a court can impose another kind of disposition.

Critical Issue One of the more important needs of the juvenile justice system is to provide the public with accurate information about youth crime and the youth justice system. The first national survey that explored public opinion on youth crime and justice in Britain was completed in 2003. In spite of the popular commentary about youth crime, the survey found that while the public acknowledges that youth crime is an important issue, it is not considered the most important issue or even the most important crime issue of the day. The survey found many misperceptions about youth crime. For example, people overestimated the amount of crime, particularly violent crime, in which young people were responsible. Most people were of the opinion that the sentences imposed on young offenders were too lenient, and they rated the youth courts as doing a poor job. This last finding is consistent with surveys conducted in other countries. The major conclusions from the study indicated that the public's pessimistic view is not justified by the official crime statistics. There is also a need to provide the public with quality information about youth crime and youth justice. Finally, the public favored alternatives to imprisonment for young offenders. When various restorative steps were explained to the participants, such as letters of apology and compensation to victims, the support for a custodial punishment declined even further (Hough and Roberts, 2004).

Summary

This chapter has offered an introduction to the English criminal justice system. The major components of the system—the police, judiciary, law, corrections, and juvenile justice—were surveyed, along with an overview of the political system. The history of each component was presented; the organization and administration were described; the role of practitioners was examined; the legal procedures were explained; and some of the critical issues facing each component of the system were assessed.

The English have long been recognized for their remarkable contribution to civilization through the creation of the common law and the development of parliamentary democracy. Of particular interest to the American observer is the fact that England is a unitary country rather than a federated state, and that political powers are fused in Parliament rather than separated. This political fact has important implications for the criminal justice system. The home secretary is responsible for crime and policing, counter-terrorism, and immigration. The Lord Chancellor (minister of justice) has extensive powers over the justice system. He or she is responsible for the reform of the criminal law and is the ultimate authority for the courts, legal profession, prison and probation service and criminal justice reform. Although the judiciary is independent of the influences of the political process, the national government has a degree of control over it as well. Moreover, in light of the fact that Parliament is supreme in matters of law, the judiciary does not rule on the constitutionality of legislation passed in Parliament.

There are also a number of substantive issues that are unique to the English justice system. Of particular interest are the legal status of the constable, the way judges are selected from a small group of lawyers, and the fact that the legal profession consists of two types of lawyers: solicitors and barristers.

Possibly the most interesting feature of English criminal justice is the extent to which laypersons are used in the day-to-day work of the system. Law enforcement uses the local police authorities and the Independent Police Complaints Commission. The courts rely upon magistrates (of which many are laypersons) to conduct summary trials. For a number of years, the prison department has been assisted by boards of lay visitors and has utilized lay volunteers in community-based corrections programs. Finally, lay volunteers have been active with juveniles found guilty of violating the law or in need of assistance in curbing their potential involvement in delinquent acts.

Concepts to Know

- Office of the President of France
- Ministry of the Interior
- National Gendarmerie
- Republican Security Company
- Constitutional Council
- court of assize
- National School for the Judiciary
- Ordinance of Villers-Cotterets (1539)
- Justinian's Code
- Code of Criminal Procedure
- *garde a vue*
- flagrant offense
- investigating judge
- liberty and custody judge
- chamber of instruction
- post-sentencing judge
- juvenile judge

Chapter II

FRANCE

Introduction

France is the largest country in continental Europe, consisting of 220,668 square miles. (Although Russia is larger, it occupies territory from eastern Europe across northern Asia.) The country's land borders are shared with Spain, Italy, Switzerland, Germany, Luxembourg, and Belgium, while the coastal boundaries include the English Channel, Atlantic Ocean, and Mediterranean Sea. When compared to the United States, France's almost 61 million inhabitants live in an area that is smaller than the state of Texas. A majority of the French people lived for centuries in the provincial areas of the country. This changed after World War II as people moved to urban areas in search of employment. Paris is the premier city in the country. Its significance is based on the fact that it is not only the political, financial, and cultural center of the country but also home to the largest number of industrial complexes.

The most notable change in the country's economy has been the emergence of more large-scale and sophisticated industries. Compared to England and Germany, France was slow to develop its industrial complex. Among the reasons frequently cited for this were the country's lack of natural resources, such as coal, and a preference for a rural environment. Today, France has established itself as a major industrial power. Its principal industries include automobiles, airplanes, chemicals, electronics, and energy.

The country appears fairly homogeneous on the surface. French is the official language, and the people are fiercely loyal to maintaining its linguistic purity. Moreover, the country is often referred to as the eldest daughter of the Catholic Church. Some of the most significant examples of French culture are its religious paintings and the architectural designs of its cathedrals. Its principal public holidays, with the exception of two, are Catholic holidays.

These are largely superficial displays of homogeneity, however. France may be a Catholic country, but only one-quarter of its citizens practice the religion with any degree of regularity. There are also significant and quite pronounced regional differences that include not only local customs that have existed for centuries but also more recent political and economic distinctions. For example, much of the industry is located in the north and northeast, whereas the west and southwest remain rural. Since the end of World War II, France has divested itself of what was once the second largest colonial empire. As a result, some of the people from these African, Middle Eastern, and Far Eastern holdings have emigrated to the mother country for political and economic reasons, thus diversifying the population further. Finally, French participation in the European Union has led to a large influx of guest workers from other European countries. Each of these factors has fostered the creation of a fairly heterogeneous society.

GOVERNMENT

The French have perceived themselves for centuries as either the leader (or at least at the center) of the development of European civilization. Indeed, the cultural contributions of the French people are beyond dispute. They have consistently made significant accomplishments in art, music, literature, science, and philosophy, and the country has never been isolated from the political events of Europe. Since the early medieval period, France has been at the center of European power struggles. In the early modern era, it attempted to rival Great Britain for colonial supremacy in the New World.

France's modern contributions to political and social theory are of particular interest for our purposes. They not only assist us in comprehending French perceptions of government and social order, but they also indicate the state's role in assuring that political and social mandates are carried out. If one were to ask a student of French politics to characterize the political climate of the country over the past 200 years, the response would most likely suggest a state of ambivalence, fragmentation, instability, and vacillation. No doubt, the student would also maintain that the principal reason for this state of uncertainty is the variation among individual perceptions regarding the historical significance of France's famous Revolution of 1789. Since the Revolution, the French have shown an affinity for two ideas that are often at cross-purposes with one another. They have had a long and deep attachment to personal liberty, yet they also have an abiding faith in authority—especially when the power is wielded by a hero who serves both as a symbol and as a catalyst for national unity.

In the realm of national politics, comparisons between England and France have proved especially instructive at illustrating the diverse methods for establishing democratic principles and institutions. The most striking difference between these two countries has been the issue of constitutional continuity. The British largely resolved their political differences in 1688 with their Glorious Revolution. Since that time, political revolution and violent change in government have been noticeably absent in Britain. The British view political change as essentially evolutionary, and they have tended to view their political past with an affection that allows them to retain many traditional institutions.

The French have largely rebelled against their past, at least as it pertains to their political system. After all, the purpose of the French Revolution was to overthrow the ancien regime, which had enabled the Bourbon monarchy to rule the country by retaining many of the remnants of France's feudal past while initiating a highly centralized and modern bureaucracy to govern the country. Unlike Britain's Glorious Revolution, which resolved the main political controversies once and for all, France's Revolution left the political debate unresolved. As such, the history of modern France has been one of recurrent revolution or threats of revolution. This is illustrated by the fact that since 1789 France has been governed by three constitutional monarchies, two empires, one semi-dictatorship, and five republics.

Another reason for the diversity between the modern political histories of Great Britain and France relates to a central feature of French political thought, that is, the ideological purity with which the French have often approached politics. Ideological purity enhances the likelihood that the political climate will be dominated by a sense of uncertainty, because the unbending commitment to political ideals leaves little room for pragmatic compromise. The French also have been fond of hero worship, especially in the political context. Heroes, of which the French have had many, have played an instrumental role in enhancing national unity.

Modern French political ideas have their basis in the eighteenth-century Enlightenment. Like other modern democracies, most notably England and the United States, the intellectual milieu of the Enlightenment *philosophes* had a profound impact on political theory. During the late eighteenth century, there emerged at least two major views as to how governmental reform should proceed in France.

On the one hand, there was a group of *philosophes* whose approach and attitude toward change was similar to that of the leaders of the American Revolution. In fact, some joined the American colonists in their cause and thus gained both intellectual and emotional sustenance for their own cause in France. This group believed in the inalienable rights of humankind and in the perfectibility of "man" through human progress. Thus, they were committed to overthrowing the political and religious tyranny that dominated eighteenth-century France and to the establishment of reason, humanitarianism, and individualism.

On the other hand, a second group—equally committed to the overthrow of tyranny—had a different perspective of the future. This group adopted the views expressed by Jean Jacques Rousseau. Rousseau exalted human instinct over reason and emphasized the community's interests over those of individual rights. For Rousseau, there were no inalienable rights, only the rule of the majority. Thus, political equality was more significant than political liberty. The right of all to participate in the governmental process was more important than the right to be protected against the will of the government.

Through its famous Revolution, France adopted many of the basic political principles that have become synonymous with democracy. Among these are a commitment to the principles of equal rights for all, equality of representation, derivation of government powers from the people, separation of church and state, and government under law. These principles were embodied in the French Declaration of the Rights of Man and of the Citizen (1789). To this day, they remain the central doctrines of French republicanism.

Constitution

The French government is organized and administered according to the Constitution of the Fifth Republic. This constitution is often referred to as Gaullist, because the document was essentially the creation of General Charles de Gaulle. On June 1, 1958, de Gaulle became prime minister of France while the Constitution of the Fourth Republic was still in effect. The general's mandate was to revise the constitution, and by September of that year, he submitted to the French people in a national referendum his constitution for the Fifth Republic.

Unlike many written constitutions, including the Constitution of the Fourth Republic, the new document did not contain a bill of rights that specifically clarified civil liberty issues. Article 2 simply states, "France is a Republic, indivisible, secular, democratic and social. It shall ensure the equality of all citizens before the law, without distinction of origin, race or religion. It shall respect all beliefs." Moreover, the preamble solemnly proclaims its attachment to "the Declaration of the Rights of

Man and reaffirms its commitment to the civil rights established in the Constitution of the Fourth Republic." However, the preamble does not have the force of law.

The entire document is divided into 24 titles, including a total of 92 articles. Each title is addressed to a particular aspect of constitutional authority. For example, Title I is concerned with sovereignty, while Titles II through IV are devoted respectively to the president, the government, and the parliament. The order in which each appears in the constitution is illustrative of the significant position that has been afforded the president and the secondary status of parliament. When compared to the Fourth Republic, these are important changes.

The Constitution of the Fifth Republic was unmistakably influenced by the political views of de Gaulle. Under the Fifth Republic, the president is vested with broad powers. The ultimate holder of state power, the president delegates authority and mediates between governmental authorities to assure that constitutional principles are safeguarded. De Gaulle tailored the office of presidency to fit the image that he perceived himself to exemplify.

President

As was previously indicated, the Office of the President of France is vested with extremely broad and independent powers. It is said that the presidency is a politically irresponsible position, because the other branches of government have an impotent check on the office. The president is elected to a five-year term by direct universal suffrage. Until 2008, there were no limits on the number of terms a president could serve. It is now limited to two. The president is the head of state, but this is not a mere figurehead position, for he or she is responsible for assuring the country's national independence and adherence to the constitution. According to Article 5, the president accomplishes these tasks through a position as mediator or arbitrator.

The constitution also gives the president a number of personally significant powers. The president appoints the premier, who is the head of the government. The president has the prerogative to dissolve the National Assembly on any issue at any time. There is one proviso, however; this can be done only once within a year's time. The president may also submit to the people, by way of referendum, certain issues that deal with governmental powers. Additionally, according to Article 16, if the country is in grave danger, or if the governmental authority created by the constitution is in some way disrupted, the president has the discretionary power to take appropriate measures to resolve the crisis. The Constitutional Council must first be consulted under such circumstances.

Finally, the president signs all decrees and ordinances prepared by the Council of Ministers and may question the constitutionality of any bill before parliament or law passed by it.

Premier

The premier (also referred to as the prime minister) is appointed by the president. According to the constitution, the premier is the head of the government (or administration), while the president is the head of state. The premier is not merely a ceremonial figure, but his or her status is less significant under the Fifth Republic than under the Fourth. Although the premier directs government operations, which define and conduct the policy of the nation, it is the president who actually decides government policy. The premier serves as a link between the president and parliament. He or she appears before parliament to defend or explain government policy, determines the composition of the Council of Ministers, presides over its meetings, and is responsible for the administration of the various governmental departments.

Council of Ministers

The Council of Ministers is the French equivalent to cabinet government. Members of the council are selected by the premier with the approval of the president. The size of the council varies with each government and is dependent on the particular needs of the times. The composition of the council has changed significantly under the Fifth Republic. The Council of Ministers is no longer composed of members of parliament, who in the past had to resign their legislative seat to serve in the council. Instead, presidents of the Fifth Republic have relied upon people who often have had no legislative experience. Increasingly, the council has been composed of three kinds of people: career civil servants, university professors, and technical experts. Like councils of ministers under previous regimes, the principle of cabinet responsibility is retained and is more effectively enforced because the premier and the ministers are dependent upon presidential power.

Parliament

The Fifth Republic retained the bicameral parliament. The parliament consists of the Senate (known as the upper chamber) and the National Assembly (referred to as the lower chamber). The Senate is composed of 330 senators who are elected to six-year terms, with one-third of the membership being elected every three years. Senators are not elected directly by the people; rather, an electoral college (which is composed of about 145,000 people) votes for the candidates. The college consists of members of department and municipal councils in addition to members of the National Assembly. The Senate shares the legislative powers with the National Assembly, but the lower chamber is considered more powerful than the upper chamber because the latter's authority does not allow them to dismiss a government.

The National Assembly is composed of 576 deputies, who are elected directly by the people to five-year terms. Although the National Assembly shares its legislative duties with the Senate, there are two exceptions to this principle. The National Assembly always examines the government's budget first, and the Council of Ministers is responsible only to the lower chamber. These exceptions tilt the balance of power between the two chambers toward the National Assembly.

The power of both chambers has been limited by the Fifth Republic. For example, each chamber holds two sessions during the course of a legislative term. One begins in October and is concluded in December, while the other session commences in April and ends in July. Extra sessions can be requested by the premier or by a majority in the National Assembly. Article 34 of the constitution is quite specific on the extent of parliament's law-making authority. All legislation that is not mentioned in the article is enacted by the government through decrees. Moreover, parliament no longer controls the order of its business, for this authority is now determined by the government. In addition, the government can reject any amendments attached to its bills by demanding a vote either on the bill it submitted or on only those amendments that it approves.

Political Parties

As was previously indicated, French politics tend to be unstable. This is caused in part by the manner in which French politicians and voters approach political issues. How individuals perceive the place of the French Revolution in history impacts upon their views of the politics of the present and the direction they advocate for the future. The French also have had a tendency to emphasize ideological purity and a commitment to political principles; as a result, they often have rejected compromises proposed for the pragmatic considerations at hand. This political posturing helped lead France to a multiparty system.

It has been suggested that the establishment of the Fifth Republic has had a significant impact on the party system, with regard to both the internal characteristics of parties and their willingness to work as coalition partners (Ehrmann, 1976). Unlike England and the United States, which tend to have fairly stable parties, France's system is unpredictable; political parties tend to emerge and decline. There has been a marked decline in membership in virtually all of the major political parties. This disenchantment has been attributed, in part, to domestic economic concerns and the uncertain future position of France with regard to the European Union.

With regard to presidential elections, it is interesting to note the relationship between political parties and presidential candidates. At times, the French approach can be somewhat different from that of the political processes in England and the United States in which a candidate from a party is selected to run for president. While some French candidates receive the endorsement of their party, there are cases in which a person announces candidacy and then seeks the endorsement of a political party or parties. Therefore, it is not necessary for a presidential candidate to have a close association with a political party, nor is it unusual for a political party not to have a presidential candidate. Finally, because of the multiparty system and the changing nature of the parties, political commentators have often grouped parties into one of three ideological categories: right, center, and left.

National Front The extreme right is represented by the National Front. It has received a good deal of attention for the past two decades, in part because of the tactics of its founder, Jean-Marie Le Pen. The principal item on the agenda of the National Front is its opposition to minority groups, particularly the influx of immigrants. The party alleges that immigrants take jobs away from French citizens and are responsible for a significant amount of crime. There are other small political parties or action groups of the far right that tend to support the National Front during presidential elections. These groups include: royalists, fascists, and Roman Catholics who have rejected the modernization within their church.

Movement for France The Movement for France is a relatively new political party that is also associated with the far right. It is similar to the National Front in that it opposes European Union and free trade and supports family, church, and law and order. It differs from the National Front in the manner in which it delivers its message of returning to traditional values. For example, on the issue of immigration, the position of the National Front is to deport all non-European immigrants and to expel any immigrant who is unemployed or convicted of a crime. The position of the Movement for France on this issue is to implement humane measures to stop the influx of more immigrants.

Union for a Popular Movement (UMP) The UMP (*Union pour un Mouvement Populaire*) is the most recent version of the party that supports the Gaullist movement. It is a fairly large party that manages to attract a good cross-section of the population. The party differs considerably from that of the RPF (*Rassemblement du Peuple Francais*), which served as the first standard-bearer of Gaullism. People who supported the RPF were primarily attracted to it because of de Gaulle's personality. Supporters of the UMP are more concerned with solving France's problems through a conservative platform than with holding on to an ideological past. The party favors a market economy, but it also supports a significant degree of state regulation by the central government.

Union for French Democracy (UDF) The UDF (*Union pour la Democratie Francaise*) is a center-right party that tends to attract the moderate and independent voter. It has been suggested that approximately 40 percent of the French people consider themselves part of the political center (Macridis, 1978). The UDF supports a market economy and tends to be more pro-European than the RPR. This party has had a problem within its ranks of agreeing upon a leader around which members can rally. As such, they have been unable to place a viable candidate on the presidential ballot. Valery Giscard d'Estaing has been identified as one of the party's leaders in recent years. However, he was an independent candidate when he won the presidential election in 1974.

Socialist Party The Socialist Party is the successor of the old SFIO (*Section Francaise de l'Internationale Ouvriere*), which at one time represented the cause of French socialism. Until the 1970s, most political commentators alleged that the principal problem facing the socialists was the fact that there was another viable political party in France that was even further to the left (that is, the Communist Party). As a result, the socialists failed to attract the necessary following to win the presidential election. In the early 1970s, however, the socialists reorganized under the leadership of Francois Mitterrand, and in 1981, Mitterrand won the presidential election. Two factors contributed to his success: a decline in support of the Communist Party and a public rejection of the continued governance by the political right, which had maintained power for more than 20 years. In 1988, he was reelected to a second term as president, with the goal of forming a center-left coalition. Today, the Socialists support a strong state and a mixed economy.

Communist Party (PCF) For a time, the French Communist Party attracted the support of the trade union movement. The PCF (*Parti Communiste Francais*) was allied with Moscow but often took a moderate stand in order to compete with socialists for votes. Throughout the 1960s and 1970s, it made respectable showings in various elections, but with the success of the Socialist Party in the 1980s, its influence declined. The party supports enhancing the social welfare system, increasing the minimum wage, reducing the income tax, and increasing the wealth tax.

Green Parties In countries that have a multiparty system, it has become increasingly common to find one that is identified as the principal advocate for ecological issues. They are often simply referred to as the Green Party. Presently, there are two groups associated with this movement in France; they are the Greens and the Ecologists. In addition to the environment, people associated with these parties also tend to support greater opportunities for women in politics.

Administration

Despite the inherent uncertainties of French politics and the various changes regarding the basic method of governance, there had been one factor that remained stable for more than 200 years, the bureaucracy or civil service. Unlike England and the United States, where there is a tradition of local participation and decisionmaking in government, the French have prized a highly centralized administrative system. This system has its origins in the seventeenth century when Cardinals Richelieu and Mazarin and Jean Baptiste Colbert created a bureaucracy that wrestled power from the nobility in the provinces and placed it firmly in the hands of the Bourbon monarchy. When Napoleon came to power, he simply streamlined the system further.

Although the national bureaucracy is highly centralized in Paris, one should not be left with the impression that all administrators are situated in that city. Most are located in the provinces, where they can implement policy directly. Since 1790, the departments (of which there are 96 on the mainland and four in the overseas territories) have been the basic units of French government. These units of administration are similar to counties. However, they do not establish local policies independently; rather they are viewed as subunits of the national government. Each department is administered by a prefect appointed by the government to enforce the laws and orders of the nation and, until recently, to supervise local units of government.

Communes are also a significant unit of government. They vary in size and are located in both urban and rural areas. Each commune has a municipal council elected by the people. The council, in turn, selects one of its own to serve as mayor. The mayor is expected to serve as both a national administrator and a municipal supervisor. The relationship of the mayor to both the national government and his or her local commune is illustrative of the manner in which the French have perceived local government.

With the election of Francois Mitterrand as president in 1981, significant changes were introduced regarding the nature of public administration. One of the principal pledges of the Socialist Party was to bring government closer to the people through a process of decentralization or self-management at the local level. One should not be left with the view that the goal of decentralization was unique to the Socialist Party, however. Previous governments of the Fifth Republic addressed this issue. In fact, a central feature of General de Gaulle's plans to modernize France involved regional administrative reforms, especially in the area of economics. Nevertheless, most experts are of the opinion that the reforms introduced by Mitterrand in 1982 were the most far-reaching since Napoleon introduced his structure of governance for the country in 1801.

Mitterrand's legislation was designed to enhance the role of local systems of government. While the prefects retained state powers over law and order, local systems of government could opt to hire their own executive to administer new local governmental functions. The local executive would be accountable to the mayor and locally elected officials. The new functions specifically earmarked for local governments include: urban planning, housing, transportation, job training, social services, some educational and cultural programs, environmental controls, and (most controversial of all) some local police services. The legislation permits communes to waive these new responsibilities, and some of the smaller ones that cannot afford to hire an executive have asked their prefect to help manage these new responsibilities. This is essentially what the prefects of the departments used to do before the introduction of efforts to decentralize the government.

Although Mitterrand's government was committed to decentralization and initiated the enabling legislation, these complex changes will take some time to implement. Some degree of consensus is needed with regard to identifying the responsibilities that are best left at the national level and those that are appropriate for local units of government. In addition, local governments have to be willing and capable of undertaking these new duties, while national units of government have to be willing to surrender some long-standing responsibilities.

A number of points described within the French political context have important implications for France's criminal justice system. Most significant is the fact that the country has had an unstable political past that has been accompanied by violent rhetoric and revolution. Central to French political thought are two conflicting views in perceiving the role of the individual citizen. One favors individual liberty, while the other embraces the belief that the community's interests should take precedence over individual rights. Moreover, the reliance of the French upon a centralized government bureaucracy is also important when assessing the organization and administration of the criminal justice system. The recent implementation of reforms designed to decentralize that authority could alter that assessment over time.

Police

Many countries throughout the world have established a national centralized police system as the principal vehicle for law enforcement responsibilities. From a Western perspective, this model traces its origins to the Roman style of policing, in which the central government created a police force for the community. Today, this approach is found in both democratic and nondemocratic countries. Unlike the fragmented police model, which is found in the United States and is attributed to the federated nature of the political system, the centralized police system is imposed on the people by the national government. Law enforcement is administered, supervised, and coordinated by that government. Moreover, the police are considered by both themselves and others as representatives of the state. For our purposes, France serves as an example of a democratic country that has established a national police system.

Throughout the history of France, Paris has had a unique place in the chronicles of the country. It is generally agreed that the French king, Hugh Capet (987–996), established the first police force when he created the position of Provost of Paris. This office combined three significant enforcement responsibilities: President of the Court of Justice, Military Governor, and Governor of the Police. The merger of these responsibilities was a result of Roman influence from when the ancient country of Gaul was part of the Roman Empire; it remained a characteristic of the French police establishment for centuries.

The provost was assisted in law enforcement duties by a number of forces. For example, at the disposal of the provost was an artillery company, a horse patrol, a foot patrol, and "watchmen." This array of units was reinforced further by constables and night watch sentries who were responsible for policing specific quarters (territorial divisions) of the city. Because French kings were politically weak, they were not in a position to impose their police system on the rest of the country. As a result, the nobles who controlled the provinces tended to rely upon their military troops to maintain order in the countryside. This dual system of Parisian and provincial law enforcement was to exist relatively unchanged until the seventeenth century.

French kings solidified their royal authority by the seventeenth century. Under the forceful administrations of Cardinals Richelieu and Mazarin, the reigns of Louis XIII and Louis XIV marked France's preeminence in the world. It was during this time that Jean Baptiste Colbert, Louis XIV's finance minister, created a truly national police force. The organization established in Paris is described here, but similar forces were created in the provinces on a modified scale.

The leader of the police in the city was called the lieutenant-general of police. Appointed by the king, the lieutenant-general was both magistrate and chief public safety officer. Thus, the Roman tradition of combining these duties (which was carried on by Hugh Capet in the medieval period) continued into the early modern era. Public safety at that time was not limited to controlling the criminal elements; it had a much broader connotation that encompassed political, social, and economic concerns. To illustrate, it was the lieutenant-general who developed fire brigades and ordered the streets cleaned.

Of particular interest is the elaborate police system that the lieutenants-general had at their disposal. It included commissioners of police who were distributed throughout the quarters of the city and served as both magistrates and police executives. Assigned to each quarter were police inspectors who served as the king's detectives. The maintenance of order in public places was the responsibility of police adjutants. They were assisted in their work by a special group of sentries who were seconded from the royal foot guards and garrisoned in the city. There were also 10 brigades of archers who patrolled the streets during the day. The watchguard, composed of both a foot and a horse patrol, patrolled the city at night. These forces were further supplemented by a military garrison quartered in Paris in the event that the civil forces were unable to handle a public disturbance. Finally, the lieutenants-general established an extensive spy system. The purpose of this group of spies, which was composed of people from all segments of society (including doctors, lawyers, waiters, domestic servants, and prostitutes), was to assist the police in compiling dossiers on a large segment of the population. This spy network, coupled with the fact that the police possessed both judicial and police powers, led to many abuses. This situation proved instrumental in rallying people to the cause of the revolutionaries in 1789.

Despite the Revolution, the police system of the ancien regime was not totally abandoned. The abuses of authority and the use of a spy network continued. The Marquis de Lafayette united former archers and constables in 1791 to establish the National Guard, which would eventually become the National Gendarmerie. In 1800, Napoleon resurrected the lieutenant-general system, made some alterations, and expanded it throughout the country. Although the old position of lieutenant-general was abandoned, in its place prefects were assigned to each of the original 95 departments—the new territorial divisions of the country. The prefects no longer served as magistrates, though. Compared to the English, French police powers remained quite broad. During the reign of Napoleon III, the police system was expanded further with the creation of the Sûreté in 1854. Originally a criminal investigation force, the Sûreté would eventually serve as both uniformed police and a detective force throughout France. The Sûreté was merged with the Police of Paris in 1966 to form the National Police.

In the previous section of this chapter, a comparison was made between France and England regarding the political history of the two countries. Because of their long historical association with one another, comparisons are often made between the two countries, and those comparisons related to the police are worth summarizing here. It is instructive for the reader to consider that these two countries, which claim a long association with the cause of democracy and liberty, established what some perceive as strikingly different roles for their police.

Among the characteristics worth comparing is the fact that the French police have been a part of the central government for centuries. The military tradition of the police is much more pronounced than that of the British, which, like the United States, has established a quasi-military character. Moreover, despite the frequent changes in the political regimes of France, each new government has enhanced the authority of the police. Thus, the mission of the police has remained fairly consistent, irrespective of the regime in power.

Another characteristic is the extent to which French police are allowed to intervene in the lives of citizens. While the British police have occasionally been accused of overstepping their bounds, they nevertheless see their role as largely the prevention and detection of crime. French police, however, claim a much more extensive right of intervention. This may in part be attributed to the acceptance of the philosophical position espoused by Jean Jacques Rousseau, which placed the collective needs of the majority over the individual's rights. This position is further supported by a more pragmatic rationale recognizing that the country's large land border has been frequently crossed by opposing armies—an unsettling source of concern realized in the twentieth century during the two World Wars. As a result, the need for internal security is a dominant concern.

The French police also have had a long and close relationship with judicial authorities. As was indicated, the lieutenants-general and the commissioners of police were magistrates. Although the police no longer have such powers, they do work in close conjunction with the judiciary because of the nature of the criminal procedural process. This will be clarified to some extent in this section and at greater length in the section on the law. In any event, French citizens usually do not make as clear a distinction between the role of the police and that of the judiciary as do British and United States citizens. Both police and judiciary are viewed as agents of the state with a common mission.

Finally, the involvement of local communities in providing police services offers an interesting comparison. In England, there has been a long-standing tradition of local community input. Although the success of this endeavor has become highly suspect in recent years, as more centralized administrative features appear in the English police service, at least the mechanism is in place. Moreover, the English are fond of proclaiming that the police are merely citizens in uniform. In France, throughout most of this century, the emphasis has been on establishing police forces that are essentially administered, supervised, and coordinated by the national government. Police are representatives of the state and perceive themselves as such. Recently, however, there has been an interest in establishing municipal police forces that are accountable to the local authorities.

Organization and Administration of the National Police

The National Police is the largest of the two principal police systems in France; it employs more than 145,000 people. The personnel include: more than 120,000 officers in the field, about 15,000 in administration, and almost 10,000 auxiliary police. The latter group consists of young people meeting their national service requirement. Accountable to the Ministry of the Interior, the National Police is responsible for policing any town with a population exceeding 10,000 (see Figure 2.1).

Figure 2.1

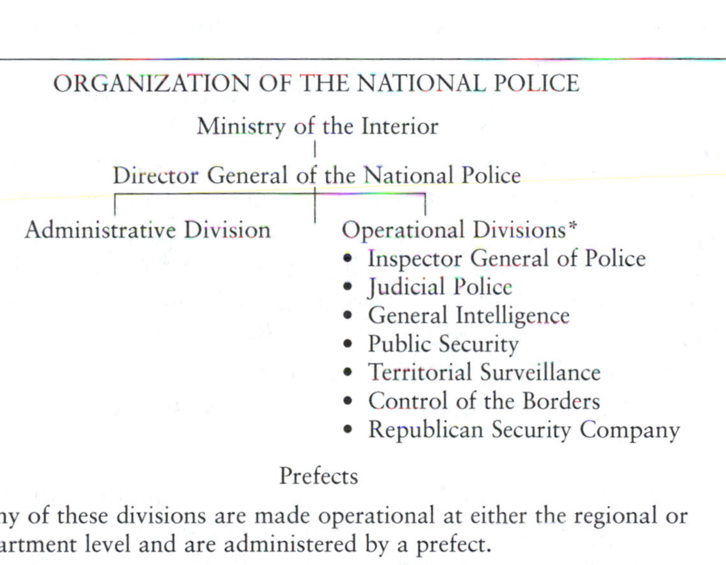

Ministry of the Interior The Ministry of the Interior is one of the most important ministries within the Council of Ministers. The minister of the interior is a civilian who has usually had a distinguished career in the civil service. The office is responsible for the administration, implementation, and supervision of many services provided by the national government. Among the most significant of these is law enforcement. The minister has the ultimate responsibility for the National Police force.

Director General of the National Police The director general is a civilian appointed to the position by the government. A career civil servant who has spent some time in the civilian branch of French law enforcement, the director general is concerned with the central administration of the National Police. Thus, as the organizational chart indicates, there are administrative and operational divisions that keep him or her abreast of all aspects of the police service. It is from the director general's office that the National Police are coordinated throughout the country.

Prefect In the previous section, it was noted that a characteristic of governments under the Fifth Republic has been to decentralize some governmental tasks to regional and local levels, while retaining ultimate control at the center. Traditionally, this has been accomplished by utilizing the 96 departments (counties) in which France is geographically divided for administrative purposes. The national executive officer of a department is called a prefect. One of the responsibilities of a prefect is to coordinate the work of the National Police within the department.

Prefects have a direct link to the Director General of the National Police. Unless there is an emergency, all directives from headquarters of the National Police and National Gendarmerie are first sent to the prefects. Prefects also meet frequently with the local directors of the National Police and National Gendarmerie. They are actively involved in and ultimately responsible for decisions made with respect to policing.

The National Police has established an organizational structure for purposes of efficiency and effectiveness that is made operational at different geographical levels, depending on the function. As such, some police work is organized at the regional level, some are accountable at the department level, and others are coordinated at the regional and departmental levels. When a task is organized at the regional level, a prefect from a department within the region is designated the chief administrator for the specific function.

Police Functions In 1995, the government adopted legislation that explained the role of law enforcement and the approach that it would take to assure greater public security for the country. Five goals were identified as special initiatives for the National Police. The goals include: (1) to assure a sense of public security, (2) to control the flow of illegal immigration, (3) to combat organized crime, especially major drug dealers, (4) to protect the country from terrorism, and (5) to maintain public order. By examining the operational divisions of the National Police in the organization chart (Figure 3.1), the reader is offered some understanding as to the breadth of this police agency's law enforcement responsibilities and its capacity to address the aforementioned goals.

The Office of the Inspector General of Police was mandated by a decree in 1974 to perform three tasks. It conducts a general inspection of all units of the National Police throughout the country. The purpose of this is to determine the effectiveness of the various forces. Another task is to investigate all alleged wrongdoing on the part of the police, including both internal and external complaints that have been brought to the attention of the inspector general. The office also takes an active role in determining the authenticity of such complaints. Finally, the Inspector General's office carries out studies that are designed to improve the efficiency of the police.

The Judicial Police are responsible for criminal investigations. The central administration of this directorate is divided into four subdirectorates: criminal affairs, economic and financial affairs, forensic science, and external liaison. The criminal affairs subdirectorate focuses on organized crime with the exception of economic and financial matters. Of particular concern are violent crimes; illegal drugs; trafficking in human beings; trafficking in cultural property; and trafficking in arms, explosives, and nuclear, biological, and chemical materials. The economic and financial subdirectorate is concerned with tax evasion, public corruption, counterfeiting, national fraud, serious financial crimes, and computer-related crime. The subdirectorate for forensic science includes a documentation branch, forensic laboratories, and the national research, documentation, and training center. The external liaison subdirectorate was added in 1995. It is involved with collecting crime statistics from the National Police and the National Gendarmerie and in maintaining cooperation with other countries participating in international police operations.

From an operations perspective, the judicial police are divided into 19 regions throughout France and are responsible for the investigation of serious crimes. In this context, they utilize several specialist squads, including theft, drugs, economic/financial, and counterfeit units. The judicial police are also found in each department to handle routine investigative matters. In terms of their accountability, the judicial police are unique. When criminal investigations are conducted by these detectives, they must notify either a procurator (if the offense is serious) or an investigating judge (if the offense is very serious) of their suspicions. In turn, a procurator or magistrate directs the actual investigation of these serious or very serious cases. Thus, in stark contrast to the common law system of criminal investigation, the French civil law system has a police investigator and a magistrate jointly conducting the examination of very serious cases. Moreover, the suspect is informed quite early that the police and an investigating judge are proceeding with such an investigation.

The General Intelligence Directorate illustrates the important role that the police force plays in collecting information for the national government. The members of this directorate are often referred to as the political police; the directorate has existed in some form since the eighteenth century. Today, the General Intelligence Directorate is responsible for the collection, examination, and centralization of political, social, and economic intelligence that the government considers necessary for the country's security. The directorate is specifically interested in preventing terrorism and monitoring groups that are viewed as a threat to national security. In recent years, there has been a specific concern for urban violence and ethnic organizations that have either been associated with such violence or are victims of such unrest.

The Public Security Directorate consists of the urban police or uniformed branch, which is responsible for patrolling the urban areas of the country. Members of this directorate are organized and administered from the departments. They are the most visible of all the directorates associated with the National Police because they handle most day-to-day police matters. Thus, they represent the initial efforts at both proactive and reactive policing.

The Territorial Surveillance Directorate is a specialized unit devoted to state security and counter-espionage activities. It is involved with the safety of people who are at risk from international terrorist attacks. It is also concerned with the protection of industrial, scientific, and technical information, and the prevention of the misuse of nuclear, biological, and chemical materials. As such, officers from this directorate are spread throughout the country in units with the objective of protecting French technology.

The Directorate for the Control of the Borders is concerned in particular with immigration issues. This directorate includes the Air and Border Police, which handle security matters at airports and along France's borders.

The Republican Security Company (CRS, for *les Compagnies Républicaines de Sécurité*) is another directorate that has been mandated specific law enforcement duties. The CRS is a highly disciplined militaristic unit. It is divided into 10 regions that correspond with France's 10 military regions and is organized into 61 companies, with 250 officers assigned to each company. The CRS is often referred to as the riot police. Indeed, they have the general responsibility to quell public disorders, but their mandate is not limited to controlling the periodic outbursts of student protests, industrial strikes, and other forms of social unrest. For example, the CRS is responsible for handling natural disasters (such as floods, avalanches, and forest fires), and they conduct rescue missions for stranded skiers and mountain climbers. They patrol camp sites and beaches during the summer months and serve as lifeguards. Because the CRS has a special duty to assist in the reduction of juvenile delinquency, they have established special clubs at beaches where they offer instruction in swimming, sailing, skin diving, and water skiing. Their interest in juveniles is carried over during the rest of the year through their participation in clubs that provide constructive leisure-time activities.

One of the primary responsibilities of the CRS is to assist the local police in the suburbs with their patrol functions. The CRS is also empowered to patrol the highways on the outskirts of large cities. Because they are noted as traffic specialists, they investigate accidents and conduct road safety campaigns. In addition to providing the president of France with a motorcycle escort, they are responsible for policing major sporting events.

Finally, it should be mentioned that there is a separate unit that is responsible for the security of the president of France, members of the government, and others who merit this kind of protection. This unit is also responsible for the protection of visiting dignitaries.

Representative Organizations Trade unions play a significant role in French society. Members of the National Police are represented by a number of unions. Presently, the number stands at about 30. Membership is based not only on the rank of the officer but is also influenced by the union's affiliation to a particular political party. Unions are capable of influencing policy on policing; they have the right to be consulted about policy changes. Union representatives sit on various committees that deal with general policy formation. They also participate in committees designed to address specific police issues (e.g., disciplinary committees). Finally, it has been suggested that unions have supported and been significant advocates for modernizing the police service (Horton, 1995).

Organization and Administration of the National Gendarmerie

The National Gendarmerie constitutes the other principal police force of France. It has been assigned three distinct tasks. It serves as the military police for the French army, air force, and navy. It also provides law enforcement services for French overseas territories. For our purposes, however, the gendarmerie is responsible for policing towns and rural areas in France where the population is under 10,000. The National Gendarmerie has approximately 104,000 employees, of which 15,000 are young people completing their national service as gendarmes.

The National Gendarmerie is administratively accountable to the Ministry of Defense, because its members belong to a military police force (see Figure 2.2). Since 2002, however, the Gendarmerie has been under the operational control of the Ministry of the Interior when it is carrying out its duties in France. The purpose of this change was designed to improve the cost-effectiveness of both the Gendarmerie and the National Police and to enhance the delivery of service.

Figure 2.2

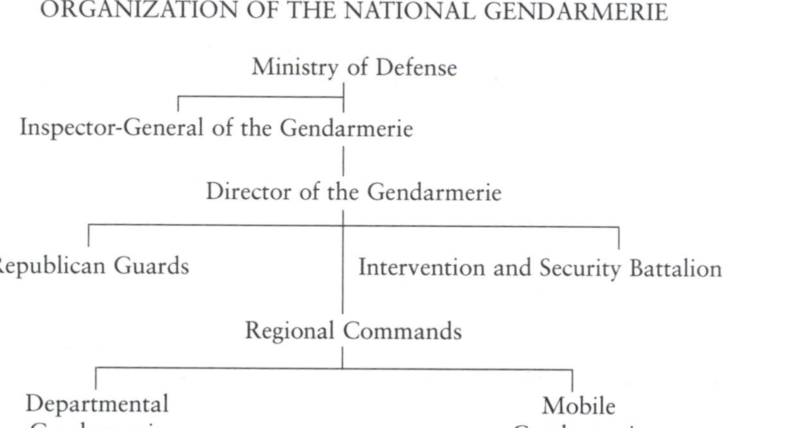

Ministry of Defense The Ministry of Defense is one of the more important ministries of the Council of Ministers. The minister of defense is responsible for the administration and coordination of the various branches of France's armed forces. This minister is also the cabinet officer who is ultimately responsible for the Gendarmerie. Assisting in the minister's duties are the director of the gendarmerie and the inspector general of the Gendarmerie. The director is trained in the law and is concerned with the central administration of the force. The Inspector General's Office is headed by an army general. Like the inspector general of the National Police, the Inspector General is responsible for conducting general inspections and examining ways to improve the effectiveness of the gendarmerie.

Gendarmerie Functions The Gendarmerie is considered a more highly disciplined force than the National Police because of its members' military backgrounds. Members have a tendency to view themselves as part of an elite law enforcement corps. The Gendarmerie is divided into 10 regional commands that correspond with the 10 military regions of France. It is divided essentially into three principal kinds of operational units.

The Departmental Gendarmerie is responsible for providing law enforcement services to small towns. Members are dispersed throughout the countryside in small brigades. Each Departmental Gendarmerie would have a judicial police unit as well as a uniformed unit for basic patrol. Depending on its location, the department could also have some specialized units, such as a motorcycle unit, a river unit, or a mountain unit.

The Mobile Gendarmerie is a regional unit that is mandated to provide the same kinds of services for areas that are offered by the Republican Security Company of the National Police. The Mobile Gendarmerie works with the departmental gendarmerie in assuring public security. It has a special responsibility to assist with rescue operations during natural disasters and in the control of large groups of people. Because it is a reserve force, the government can use it at home, in overseas territories, or abroad.

The Republican Guard, situated in Paris, is composed of three regiments: two infantry and one cavalry. They serve as honor guards, participate in colorful state parades, and assist in guarding government officials. Thus, they aid the National Police in protecting the capital.

In addition to these principal operational units, the Gendarmerie has established the Intervention and Security Battalion, which is an elite group of gendarmes drawn from three specialized units. The intervention unit assists with such incidents as terrorist attacks, prison riots, and hostage situations. The airborne intervention squadron is trained to deal with terrorism and other select crimes. Finally, the security unit of the President of the Republic is charged with maintaining the personal safety of the president.

Municipal Police

In a previous section of this chapter, it was pointed out that former President Mitterrand wanted to bring government closer to the people by way of decentralization and self-management at the local level. One of the more controversial aspects of this policy was permitting cities to establish municipal police forces that would be under the control of the mayor. Such forces existed to a limited degree before World War II, but their number and influence was reduced considerably by the two nationally centralized forces. To date, not all cities have established such a force, relying instead on either the National Police or the National Gendarmerie. Nevertheless, there are approximately 18,000 municipal police that are primarily operating in cities of more than 100,000 people.

Although municipal police are subject to national laws, the mayor is responsible for defining their specific mission. Presently, the principal responsibilities of municipal police include uniformed patrol and parking and traffic control. They do not have the authority to conduct a criminal investigation. As such, if they arrest a suspect, the person must be turned over to the National Police or the National Gendarmerie. Municipal police could assume other responsibilities. For example, with the increased fear of crime in general and property offenses in particular, another important responsibility could be crime prevention (Horton, 1995;

Journes, 1993, Kania, 1989; Levy and Ocqueteau, 1987). In a poll of mayors conducted in 2000, 64 percent considered security a matter for the state, while 31 percent thought it a municipal responsibility (de Maillard and Roche, 2004). In light of the current political climate on security matters, it does not appear that the central government will be surrendering any police powers to municipalities in the near future. Because the role of the municipal police has not been clearly defined at the national level, it has been recognized that steps are needed to control the use of municipal police. Efforts are under way to define their mission more clearly.

Legal Status

Because the police of France are considered civil servants, they are subject to the same civil service regulations as their counterparts in other units of government. Given the nature of their responsibilities, however, they are placed in situations that other civil servants would not generally confront. The kind of authority that the police exercise has led the public to refer to the police as "magistrates on their feet." This term acknowledges the close working relationship that exists between detectives and the examining magistrates who coordinate criminal investigations. In such investigative situations, the police are accorded special powers in the performance of their duties. As a result, many people find it difficult to make a distinction between an investigating officer and an examining magistrate. Both are viewed as agents of the state who are empowered with the same basic function.

Both the French Code of Criminal Procedure and the French Penal Code discuss the legal status of the police, along with other government agents. One should also keep in mind that the French parliament can pass legislation to amend the codified law. For example, the Security and Liberty Law of 1981 amended both the procedural and penal codes. More recently, the report of the Criminal Justice and Human Rights Commission (1993), chaired by professor Mireille Delmas-Marty, and the report by the Justice Commission (1997), chaired by Pierre Truche, president of the Court of Cassation, led to some significant reforms. In addition, the constitution allows the Council of Ministers to issue decrees and ordinances that have the force of law. Thus, the state is in a position to enhance the police authority with the powers that the government perceives to be vital to the performance of their duties. The police, in turn, view themselves as the principal defenders of the constitutional liberties of the state. Their devotion to this single purpose has provoked a number of comments regarding the relationship the police have with the public.

The Police and the Public

Since the 1960s, the French police have been confronted with a rising crime rate. As is the case in other industrialized countries, the most notable concern involves serious levels of juvenile delinquency. Like other European countries, this problem has focused in part on second- and third-generation immigrants and guest workers. Since the 1970s, particular attention has been directed at the *banlieues*, or deprived areas, which consist of large housing projects, often located on the outskirts of a city and home to many immigrant groups. These areas suffer from a lack of economic opportunity and a weak educational system. Recently, rioting erupted in these areas throughout a number of cities in the country. Over the course of the past decade, the police also have had to deal with an enhanced fear of crime among the citizenry, especially as it relates to property offenses.

Increased levels of crime, as well as fear of it, often result in the placement of law and order on the political agenda. France is no exception. While the political right was in power under the leadership of Valery Giscard d'Estaing, the strategy was to increase the number of police and to pass stricter law enforcement legislation, such as the Security and Liberty Law of 1981.

When the political left came to power in 1981 under Francois Mitterrand, the initial strategy called for a reform of the National Police. Essentially two objectives were being proposed. First, the police should focus their attention more on economic crimes and deemphasize their concern for public order maintenance and the collection of political intelligence in the name of national security. Second, greater controls should be placed on the police. Specific suggestions included establishing a code of professional ethics, reforming the inspector general's office, regulating certain police practices, and reinforcing the judicial authorities' responsibility to control police tactics (Levy and Ocqueteau, 1987).

The government, however, abandoned this scheme by 1985. Crime and the public's fear of it had remained. There was also renewed terrorist activity in the country that precluded the police from reducing their collection of political intelligence. A strategy was adopted to make the police more efficient through modernization. This included increasing the initial training of officers, establishing in-service training, providing police with state-of-the-art equipment, shifting officers from clerical tasks to actual police work, and increasing the police budget by 50 percent over the following five years ("Le Plan de Modernisation," 1985).

During the 2002 presidential election, the public's concern over crime and delinquency of immigrant youths in particular was a significant issue. To illustrate, the total number of people under investigation by the police rose from 717,116 in 1974 to 906,969 in 2002. This was an increase of

26 percent. When one considers the number of young people (under 18 years of age) who were under investigation during the same time period, the figures increased from 75,846 to 180,382. This was a 137 percent increase that was especially noticeable since the 1990s (de Maillard and Roche, 2004).

The police have had two additional problems that have, in light of the country's history, aggravated and frustrated their attempts at maintaining order. In May 1968, there were general strikes that were sparked in part by student unrest in the universities. With France's delicate political structure in a perpetual state of doubt, there was a real concern in some circles that the country might be faced with yet another change in its system of government. Strikes remain a common occurrence in France and are often brought about by organized labor groups and student protests.

The other problem, already alluded to, is the substantial number of terrorist acts in the country. Though in some cases these acts are not specifically directed at the French or their diplomatic position, terrorism nevertheless has been a problem with which the police are expected to contend. Islamic terrorism is a particular concern of the French government. France is now home to 5 million Muslims (out of a total population of almost 61 million), of which about half hold French citizenship. A good deal of the recent rioting in the aforementioned banlieues have involved Muslim youths. As a result, there has been a heightened effort by the police to improve its intelligence-gathering techniques and to focus more surveillance efforts on Muslim communities in general. It is interesting to note that while civil libertarian groups have voiced concerns over these tactics, the Muslim communities have not been among the vocal critics. It has been suggested that they are more focused on issues of cultural integration and economic opportunity (Laurence and Vaisse, 2006).

The level of crime, social unrest, and terrorist acts are bound to influence how law enforcement perceives the public and how the public develops its attitudes toward the police. Various indicators have been employed to gauge the opinions of both the police and the public. Three have been utilized here in the hope that this highly significant issue can be placed in perspective. What follows is an examination of police recruitment and training, efforts to establish crime-prevention programs, and the opinions of both police and the public regarding the police role in French society.

Recruitment and Training The French acknowledge that a central feature of police professionalism is the quality of recruitment, training, and educational opportunities extended to members of the police service. The recruitment and training of the National Police and National Gendarmerie are handled separately by each force. The National Police has had little difficulty finding people who are interested in a police career, and they have received a large number of applications from people who have attained a high level of education. In any event, it has been suggested that most recruits—even those who have achieved a high level of education—would not command the salaries they receive if they selected a career outside the police service. Thus, the National Police have not had to conduct vigorous recruitment campaigns.

The National Police have a four-tiered entry scheme: two tiers are designed for uniformed personnel, while the other two are for plainclothes officers. A recruit can enter the force as a uniformed patrol officer. Each recruit must be a French citizen, possess a driver's license, and meet the minimum height requirements (approximately 5'7"). The person must be of good character and in excellent physical condition. The French have a tendency to place a good deal of emphasis on the physical fitness of the candidate. Moreover, the age requirement is between 21 and 28 years of age. An exception is made for people recruited from the armed services who have not reached the age of 31. The minimum educational requirement is a certificate from elementary school. (Most people receive this at age 14.)

The entrance examination for the uniformed patrol officer includes a physical agility test and a scholastic aptitude test involving basic writing and mathematics skills. Those who are selected attend one of the eight regional training schools of the National Police. Basic training includes eight months at a school with a curriculum emphasizing both professional and physical education components. This is followed by four months of training in the field. If the candidate passes basic training, he or she is assigned to either a town or city police department, or to the Republican Security Company.

The other uniformed entry is that of lieutenant. The nationality, character, and physical fitness requirements are the same for this position as for that of the uniformed patrol officer, but the age limit is lowered to 19. The upper age level remains the same, and an exception again is made regarding those who have served in the armed forces. Vacancies in this rank are filled equally by two kinds of candidates. One-half are selected from the ranks of uniformed patrol. These candidates must have served a minimum of four years in that position to be eligible, and they must be under 35 years of age. The other half are selected from applicants who have obtained a French baccalaureate. (This is roughly equivalent to an associate's degree in the United States.) All candidates must pass a competitive entrance examination.

The candidate's period of training lasts 18 months. Nine months are spent in a formal education program at the National Police School for lieutenants at Nice. The subject matter includes professional courses (such as law and police organization) as well as traditional academic disciplines (such as sociology and psychology). If the candidate passes the examinations, the next phase of study includes a one-month stay with each of the uniformed branches of the National Police, the Republican Security Company, and the Police of Paris. Finally, six months of additional training is mandated.

The requirements to join the ranks of the plainclothes inspectors are essentially the same as those for lieutenant. The physical requirements are not as stringent, however. The manner of selecting the candidates is also the same as that for the lieutenants: one-half have spent at least four years in police service, while the remainder hold a degree. The inspectors' training program is conducted at special schools that are located at Toulouse, St. Malo, and Cannes-Ecluse. The program lasts about a year. The courses of instruction include: criminology, social psychology, criminalistics, and a number of law classes. Candidates for inspector also spend three months devoted to practical training in the field. Once they have completed their course of study, they will become members of the judicial police.

The final entry level is that of commissioners or chiefs of police. The general requirements are the same as those for detectives. In the case of commissioners, 60 percent are selected from among the candidates who hold a university degree. (This is equivalent to a master's degree or a law degree in the United States.) The other 40 percent are selected from candidates who have served in the National Police for at least four years. The entrance examination is highly competitive for candidacy and is composed of a written part that includes essays on: the political ideas and the social and economic problems of twentieth-century Europe, criminal law and procedure, and administrative law. The oral examination includes: a general interview, specific questions on law, and a test of the candidate's proficiency in a foreign language.

The successful candidates spend one year in training at the National Police College at Saint-Cyr. Courses taken there focus on five areas: (1) social sciences, (2) general police studies, (3) administrative law, (4) physical training, and (5) technical training. The second year of training is spent with each of the major branches of the police service. Candidates who complete the program are then appointed to a branch of the service that they have selected. Undoubtedly, they will eventually administer their own police force.

Although the French admit that their scheme reduces the promotional opportunities for those in the lower grades, they believe that such career disappointments are outweighed by the benefits that accrue to the organization. From their perspective, the multilevel entrance scheme enables the police to tap the creative resources of the university graduate. In turn, this leads to innovative problem-solving for the organization. The police are not unique in this regard, for the French have a tendency to emphasize the importance of obtaining university credentials—especially from their elite universities—for all the upper echelons of the government bureaucracy. Moreover, the university degree has traditionally been viewed as a mark of class distinction.

As was indicated earlier, the National Gendarmerie has a training program of its own. A candidate must be a French citizen, be between the ages of 18 and 35, and pass the psychological aptitude tests. The gendarmerie recruits many of its officers from the armed forces, army reserves, and its own noncommissioned ranks. The noncommissioned officers are usually selected from the ranks of noncommissioned personnel within the military. The gendarmerie has a number of training centers located throughout France at which emphasis is placed on police techniques, military tactics, and physical agility. It has been suggested that the gendarmerie generally attracts a better-educated group of candidates. They also tend to be much more disciplined as a result of their military training. These qualities have led members of the gendarmerie to view themselves as an elite law enforcement corps.

It also should be pointed out that France has a compulsory national service for young men. Since 1971, men have been able to meet this requirement by serving between 12 and 16 months as auxiliary members of the gendarmerie. They are assigned regular duties, except they do not handle public order incidents. These auxiliary gendarmes represent approximately 13 percent of the total force. In 1986, this method of meeting national service was extended to the National Police. While attempts are under way to have these auxiliary officers represent 10 percent of that force, presently they equal about 3 percent (Horton, 1995; Levy and Ocqueteau, 1987).

Until 1979, women were restricted to the plainclothes officers' unit of the National Police. Today, they are also members of the uniformed force. They represent approximately 6 percent of the total number of police serving in the National Police. Prior to 1983, women could only serve in clerical positions in the National Gendarmerie, but they are now recruited as police officers. They presently represent about 2 percent of the gendarmes. They have one restriction in their duties: they may not participate in handling public order incidents (Horton, 1995).

Finally, because of the heightened concern over crime among youths and the issue of Islamic terrorism, a greater effort has recently been initiated to promote community policing. One effort, which has not had much success at this time, is the recruitment of ethnic minorities to the police service. Another strategy has been the introduction of training in communication, conflict resolution, and cultural awareness for both new recruits and mid-level managers who are responsible for implementing any community policing program, especially those targeted to ethnic neighborhoods.

Crime Prevention The French police traditionally have approached their responsibility for crime control through two methods. One was a reaction to events after the crime had occurred, and the other was a proactive or crime prevention posture designed to control incidents before they happened. From the French perspective, both methods required the utilization of repressive measures to assure success. Although this observation has been expressed by people outside the police service, people within the police ranks also have admitted to the use of such measures.

In the past few decades, the French police have recognized that repressive measures are not always the most effective method for containing and preventing crime. Throughout the 1970s, they embarked upon several new crime prevention programs that correspond with tactics found in such countries as the United States, England, and Sweden. Among the crime prevention measures introduced were operations that significantly increased the number of police and gendarmes assigned to high-crime areas. The plan involved saturating an area that included a number of public buildings, with the goal of reducing the number of burglaries and muggings in the area. Thefts of automobiles (and of property from them) had also increased significantly. Officers affix to parked cars printed notices explaining how the owner can safeguard the car and its contents. Similar notices are posted in areas frequented by tourists, such as hotel lobbies.

Two additional crime prevention programs were introduced in 1975. One was called "Tranquillity-Vacations." Throughout the summer, but especially in August, a large number of people take vacations. Their deserted apartments have been prime targets for burglaries. "Tranquillity-Vacations" intensified the surveillance of these buildings with a good deal of success, not only in preventing crime but also in apprehending criminals. In that same year, the police launched a campaign to protect the elderly. This involved crime prevention seminars designed to educate the elderly to the unique dangers with which they are confronted.

A brochure was produced the following year that provided information about and techniques for protecting one's residence. The police have been assisted in this kind of endeavor by insurance companies and security firms. Moreover, the police also have been active in providing the business community with programs designed to protect their merchandise. Finally, like many police departments throughout the industrialized world, the French have returned to the establishment of the beat patrol system. Today, more officers are patrolling a specific beat either on foot, bicycle, or motorcycle with the goal of reestablishing closer contacts in the community.

Despite these efforts, thefts of (and from) automobiles, ordinary theft, and burglaries remain the principal crime concerns of the police, while violent crimes remain fairly infrequent. Only recently has the general public become aware of the difficulty police face in solving many property crimes—especially without sufficient information. This in part explains the heightened fear of crime among the French. It also explains the increased interest in personal security measures, as evidenced by the purchase of burglar alarms and reinforced doors and windows. In addition, insurance companies are now requiring that businesses utilize the services and devices of security firms.

By the 1980s, it was acknowledged that crime prevention was not and could not be solely the responsibility of the police. In fact, there tends to be agreement among the French that crime is the result of failed social policies coupled with an inability among many families to provide a moral foundation for their children. Crime prevention requires the cooperation of social service agencies that are generally found at the local level, the support of the private sector, and a degree of involvement by the citizenry. As a result, crime prevention committees have been formed in virtually every department, with more than 700 committees established throughout the country (Journes, 1993).

The Interministerial Committee on Cities Policy works with the local committees on funding various crime prevention projects. The prefect for the department serves as the link between the central and local government. The crime prevention programs that have received funding include: victim support, mediation and reparation of victims, work with offenders in the form of community service, initiatives on drugs, and developments with community policing. Community policing has tended to emphasize patrolling high-crime urban areas in pairs, either on foot or motorcycle. The police have established road safety and motorcycle training programs, distributed crime prevention information about theft (in particular, car theft), and given presentations on crime prevention for the elderly. Specific crime prevention measures also have been directed at the juvenile population. These will be discussed in the section devoted to juvenile justice.

It should also be pointed out that the issue of domestic abuse has received attention only in recent years. It was not until 1989 that the first major campaign raised a public awareness about domestic violence. The leadership for this came through various women's groups and the government's secretary of state for women. This led to the country's first domestic violence legislation in 1994. This has also led to a greater awareness of the problem of child abuse. With particular reference to domestic violence, the police introduced several initiatives. They include: making the police more aware of the problem through police training that includes the involvement of other agencies; increasing the number of female police officers; developing crime prevention policies that focus on the concerns of victims in general and women in particular; and establishing new cooperative efforts to work with other public and voluntary services (Horton, 1995).

Public and Police Perceptions of Law Enforcement The most common view expressed about the relationship between the police and the people of France is that it is one of strained tolerance. It has been suggested that the reason for citizen dislike of the police is partly political in nature. The French police perceive themselves as the guardians of French liberty and the protectors of the Fifth Republic. At times, there have been large groups of citizens who have wished to retain their freedom, but in a communist or socialist form, and they have been quite vocal in their opposition to the Fifth Republic and the kind of political, social, and economic principles it represents. Such convictions are bound to lead to antagonistic incidents between those segments of the public and the police. Some officers who were interviewed admitted sensing a dislike and distrust on the part of the public; nevertheless, they have a responsibility to protect the nation. Public image building is considered a secondary concern, and as was indicated earlier, this public attitude has not affected attempts to recruit candidates to the police service.

Indeed, the French police possess many of the powers that often are associated with a totalitarian regime. Although the powers may be available, the issue is whether they are utilized in a totalitarian manner to suppress individual freedoms. In his book, *The Police of Paris*, Philip John Stead concluded with the following statement:

> [The bitterest enemies of the Paris police] must concede that the city's frank, free enjoyment of the pleasures of the mind is still whole. Neither Lieutenants-General nor Prefects of Police, with whatever arbitrary powers they may have been invested, have stifled the spirit of liberty. The "police state" is still the land of Montaigne and Voltaire, of Moliere and Montesquieu, of Rabelais and Hugo. It is still the land of 1789, of 1830, of 1848, and 1870. It is the land of 1944. Those who have lived in real police states will hardly be disposed to regard France as one. (1957)

Although this comment was written 50 years ago, it appears to be applicable today. The present police system of France mirrors the country's political culture. There is, on the one hand, a deep attachment to personal liberty. On the other hand, there is an abiding faith in authority. If it were possible to curtail the powers of the French police, one would think it would have happened with the victory of the socialist president, Mitterrand. Although he initially introduced plans to reform the police (including some of their tactics), such plans were quickly set aside in favor of making the police more efficient in their law enforcement and order maintenance tasks.

JUDICIARY

It was pointed out in the chapter on England that King Henry II was largely responsible for developing the common law tradition by creating the necessary judicial machinery to administer it. Henry was able to accomplish this feat because he, along with the help of some of his predecessors, had undertaken the delicate process of consolidating royal political authority throughout the kingdom. As English monarchs claimed royal hegemony over the country, the common law and the royal administration of justice was firmly established during the medieval period.

Throughout the medieval period, France was politically decentralized. The French king's political power was limited to the area around Paris known as the Ile de France, while the rest of the country was controlled by the *grand seigneurs* (nobility). The absence of a centralized political authority in France had important implications for the legal system and the administration of justice.

There were basically four kinds of authorities that administered justice in medieval France. The ecclesiastical courts had jurisdiction over matters pertaining to the church, crimes committed by the clergy, and crimes that fell within its jurisdiction, irrespective of who might commit them (for example, adultery and heresy). Because the Fourth Lateran Council (1215) forbade the clergy from participating in trials that shed blood, some defendants who were found guilty in ecclesiastical courts had to be bound over to a secular court in order to have their sentences imposed and executed.

Another judicial authority was the communal court. Communal courts were found in the free cities. Although they were primarily concerned with commercial matters, they also handled civil and criminal matters within their territorial jurisdiction.

It was assumed throughout the medieval period that large landowners had a right to administer justice in their territory. This right was a characteristic of feudalism, which was the dominant economic and social system of the time. Thus, the principal source of justice was found in the seignorial courts of the great landowners. The law that was administered in these courts was essentially the local custom of the region. Because there were notable differences between regions, there was a lack of uniformity in the law.

The king of France also had the right to exercise judicial authority, for like the *grand seigneurs*, he was a feudal lord. Royal justice, however, was essentially limited to the king's land holdings around Paris. By the twelfth century, the legal position of the king began to change. There appeared at that time a popular theory arguing that the king was the source of all justice. This idea had its roots in Roman law, but the study of this law was abandoned following the collapse of the Roman Empire. It was not until the twelfth century that Roman law was rediscovered and introduced as one of the principal sources in the study of law on the continent of Europe.

As the French kings began to assume greater political control over their kingdom, their legal position was gradually enhanced to such an extent that they were sought out to administer justice in their Parlement (which consisted of a group of royal advisors who sat as the king's judicial tribunal). Appeals to the Parlement improved the king's political position further and gradually reduced the judicial position of the seigneurial courts. Toward the end of the thirteenth century, Parlement was divided into four courts in order to handle the increased caseload. The Court of Requests was responsible for petitions to the Parlement and determined which was the appropriate court to hear a case. The Chamber of Pleas heard most crown cases. The Court of Inquests entertained cases that were largely determined by written documents. Finally, the Tournelle was responsible for most criminal cases.

It was initially viewed as an honor to have one's case heard in a royal court. By the sixteenth century, however, all important cases were entertained in royal courts. This was deemed appropriate because of the king's enhanced position throughout the kingdom. With the increase in cases, provincial parlements were established to assist in the administration of royal justice. These parlements were equal to but independent from the Paris Parlement. Because of the variations in local legal custom, the provincial parlements were in a better position to consider the unique legal characteristics of a region when administering royal justice. Unfortunately, the provincial parlements were to prove divisive in the monarchy's attempt to unify the country. Ordinances that were applicable in one province might not have the same weight in another. As a result, chaos resulted that was not resolved until after the French Revolution. Thus, a royal court system was established throughout France by the eighteenth century. The central problem facing these courts was that they were not administering the same law.

As was the case in England, the clergy served as the first legal advisers to the kings and grand seigneurs of France. At a time when most of the population, including the nobility, was largely illiterate, many of the clergy could read and write. Some of them were either trained in (or at least familiar with) canon law. Canon law represented the legislation and legal opinions of the Roman Catholic Church. It was a complete legal system that was utilized at times by the various medieval kingdoms of Europe when they lacked a coherent unified legal system.

Dependence on the clergy for legal advice began to wane on the continent of Europe with the rediscovery of Roman law. What was actually being rediscovered and revived were the law books of Justinian (483–565), the Byzantine emperor from 527–565. Compiled during the sixth century, these books or codes had been lost for 500 years. They were brought to the University of Bologna, the premier center for the study of law on the continent, in the early twelfth century.

Justinian's Code, or the *Corpus Juris Civilis,* offered students a systematic view of law that was devoid of church doctrine; it was a secular codified system. Students from across Europe were attracted to Bologna to study this secular law. Once they had completed their studies, they either served as legal counsel to their family or gained employment with the king or a grand seigneur. The introduction of laypersons who were knowledgeable in law ended the dominant position of the clergy as judges and legal counsel.

By the thirteenth century, an occupational distinction was being made among French lawyers. The *avoue* served as a client's legal agent, while an *avocat* specialized in presenting oral arguments before a court. In comparison to the English, the avoue offered the kinds of services that were performed by a solicitor, whereas the avocat offered the skills associated with a barrister.

Another point of comparison between England and France was the tradition each brought to the study of law. It was explained in Chapter I that early English law students spent most of their time learning the law in the courtroom. Because the common law had no definitive text that could be studied, the English law student studied the law in action by observing courtroom procedure. This was supplemented by reading the decisions of previous cases. It was not until the nineteenth century that the common law was studied in a university setting, and this method was not popularized until the twentieth century.

In France, as well as other continental countries, the study of law was undertaken in a university. This tradition had its origins in twelfth-century Bologna and differed significantly from the study of law in England. The law that was studied on the continent was considered a science, and the principles of that legal science were found in authoritative texts, the first of these being Justinian's Code. Moreover, like the study of philosophy and theology, the study of law emphasized the analysis of the text. The purpose of this exercise was to discover general truths that had universal and transnational application. Thus, the law studied on the continent of Europe was more philosophical in content. The student learned to understand how law might become the model for social organization and intercourse and to grasp the essence of justice. The student was not trained in legal techniques or the practical aspects of law. The law professors considered their responsibility to be one of imparting an understanding of the law as a *Sollen* (what ought to be) rather than a *Sein* (what is done in fact). Therefore, an understanding of legal principles prevailed over the training of courtroom techniques. This approach to legal studies continues to this day and illustrates one of the marked differences in legal education between the common law system in England and the civil law system in France.

Organization and Administration of the Courts

There are two main branches or kinds of courts within the French legal system. The administrative courts are responsible for supervising the government. They entertain citizen complaints and attempt to balance the delicate relationship that exists when the state's general interests and the citizen's individual rights come into conflict. The other branch, known as the ordinary courts, handles the civil and criminal litigation. Both branches of the system have a separate court hierarchy. For our purposes, the five-tiered hierarchy of the ordinary courts are of particular interest. Before this court system is described, however, it may prove beneficial to explain the role of two additional judicial offices, which are not a part of the ordinary court hierarchy but have a significant responsibility to the administration of justice.

Ministry of Justice The Ministry of Justice is headed by the minister of justice, a member of the Council of Ministers. The minister's interest in the criminal justice system focuses on three areas: the correctional system, the selection and appointment of magistrates, and the general administration of the law. The last two responsibilities are of interest here.

The term "magistrate" is used to describe judges, procurators, and officials of the central administration of justice. According to the constitution, French judges are guaranteed independence in the performance of their judicial functions and are assured permanence in office. The minister of justice plays a role in the selection and appointment of judges. The minister, however, does not control or dominate the process, for judges are part of the French civil service. According to Article 65 of the constitution, the High Council of the Judiciary is mandated to make specific judicial appointments, including that of judges to the Court of Cassation, first presidents to the courts of appeal, and presidents of the courts of major jurisdiction. The High Council of the Judiciary includes: the president of France, the minister of justice, five judges from the civil courts, five judges from the criminal courts, one judge from the administrative courts, one member of the Public Ministry, and three people who are not judges or members of Parliament. The selection of the candidates to the other courts are made by the minister of justice on the advice of the High Council of the Judiciary.

Like judges, procurators are part of the civil service. Although procurators do not represent the interests of the state at a trial, they are responsible to the Ministry of Justice. The minister of justice appoints people to the Public Ministry and has the ultimate authority to discipline procurators. It should be pointed out that the High Council of the Judiciary plays a consultative role to the ministry in the appointment of procurators. When the High Council of the Judiciary meets for this purpose, its composition is different from when it offers advice on the appointment of judges. For the selection of procurators, the High Council consists of the president of France, the minister of justice, five members of the Public Ministry, one judge of the civil and criminal courts, and three independent people.

The members of the central administration of justice, the Chancellery (a part of the Ministry of Justice), are responsible for the general administration of the law. This is the other administrative issue with which the Ministry of Justice is concerned, and it is of particular interest to us at this time. Chancellery members draft statutes, publish reports on judicial decisions, develop statistical studies on the administration of justice, maintain personnel files on all magistrates, and prepare the budget for the administration of justice. They also are responsible for the administration and supervision of the prisons.

Finally, it should be pointed out that the Ministry has an Inspector General. This Office is responsible for inspecting the various departments or units within the Ministry of Justice and all of the courts, with the exception of the Court of Cassation. The minister of justice can also assign specific tasks that involve an assessment of any aspect of the judiciary. In 1988, the Modernization Commission was established under the direction of the Inspector General. The Commission is responsible for encouraging the introduction of modern administrative techniques throughout the judicial system.

The Constitutional Council In the United States, the Supreme Court has the principal responsibility of ruling on the constitutionality of all laws. This kind of judicial review is not practiced in France. The ordinary courts, in addition to the administrative courts, have refused to entertain this kind of legislative review. This decision was established in 1789, and with the exception of two incidents in 1851, French judges have not deviated from that position. Two kinds of arguments have been offered to explain this situation. One points out that courts are essentially administrative organs of the state and not considered a separate branch of government as that concept is used when discussing the idea of governmental separation of powers. In light of this, it has been suggested that the absence of judicial review is based on the belief that "no judicial body be 'this keeper of the nation's conscience' " (Tallon, 1979). Another rationale is based on history. Prior to the French Revolution, French judges wielded a good deal of power and independent discretion. The judges were essentially on the losing side of the Revolution. Since that time, the legislative branch has avoided granting the judiciary a role in the development of policy, which is clearly a feature of judicial review (Jacob et al., 1996).

The French have a Constitutional Council composed of nine members. Council members serve a nine-year term that is not renewable; one-third of the membership is appointed every three years. The president of France appoints three people, and the presidents of the Senate and the National Assembly are each responsible for selecting three members. In addition, all former presidents of the Republic serve as ex officio members.

The council has two responsibilities. One is handling election complaints in cases of irregularities or disagreements in the outcome. Another (more important for our purposes) is determining the constitutionality of legislation passed in parliament. Access to the council is quite limited; neither citizens nor members of the legal profession can request that a piece of legislation be reviewed on the grounds that they consider it unconstitutional. Constitutional issues are brought before the council from one of five sources: (1) from the council's inception, (2) from the president of the Republic, (3) from the premier, (4) from the president of the Senate, and (5) from the president of the National Assembly. Since 1974, an action can also be introduced by 60 members of parliament. The council's role is limited to acts passed in parliament, and the issue must be brought to their attention before it is signed into law by the president. Having explained the role of the Ministry of Justice and the Constitutional Council, a description of the hierarchy of France's ordinary courts follows (see Figure 2.3).

Figure 2.3

ORGANIZATION OF THE ORDINARY FRENCH COURTS

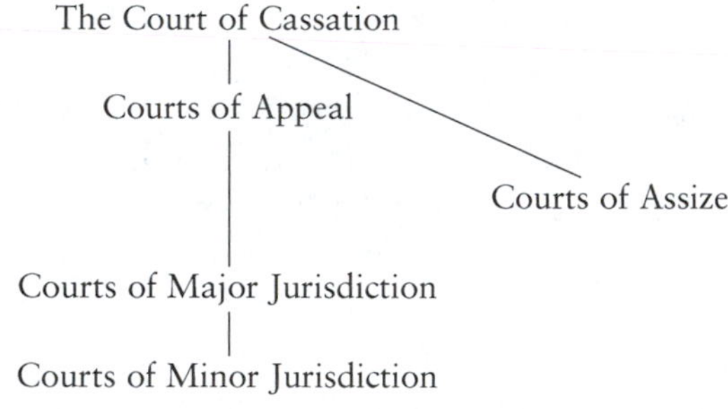

Court of Cassation The Court of Cassation is the highest court for civil and criminal appeals in France. The word "cassation" comes from the French *casser*, meaning "to shatter." In the context of judicial proceedings, this is figuratively what the court does, for it is responsible for ruling on appeals that involve a point of law. The Court of Cassation either can agree with the lower courts' original interpretation of the law, or it can quash (or shatter) the opinion of the lower court and have the case retried. Because, as a rule, the court entertains only issues involving a point of law, the entire case is not heard by the court. Usually, the court is interested only in determining if the lower court interpreted the law correctly. Thus, the principal role of the court is to assure that the law is interpreted uniformly throughout France.

The court is composed of six chambers. Three handle civil cases, while the others entertain social, commercial, and criminal matters, respectively. Each chamber has a judge who is called the president, and there is a first president who serves as the chief justice for the entire court. There are slightly more than 120 judges serving this court, and they are divided into two categories. The number of senior permanent appeals judges (or *conseillers*) is about 85. There are also approximately 40 career judges who are appointed to the court for a period of up to 10 years. They assist the senior judges of the court and are referred to as advisers. Following their term, they return to positions on a court of appeal. Each case heard in the court is handled by a minimum of seven judges and two advisers.

Courts of Appeal There are 33 courts of appeal that handle civil and criminal appeals from the lower courts. Each court is responsible for an area that usually encompasses between two and four departments. The issues brought before an appeals court can involve a point of law or some factual discrepancy in a case. Generally, for those cases in which the appeal is based solely on fact, this court will serve as the final arbiter. Issues involving law, however, can be appealed further to the Court of Cassation. Courts of appeal consist of four chambers that specialize in civil, social, correctional, and juvenile cases on appeal. Each case is handled by a three-judge panel (a presiding judge or president and two judges of appeal or *conseillers*).

Courts of Assize In each of the 96 departments of France, a court of assize sits with appellate and original jurisdiction in criminal matters. When the court hears appeals from a lower court, three judges handle the matter. It is also the court of first instance for all major felonies, which are referred to as crimes. As a tribunal of first instance, the court includes a panel of three judges (a presiding judge or president and two associate judges or *assesseurs*) and nine lay jurors. There are a few exceptions to the aforementioned composition of a court of assize. Some cases involving terrorism or drug dealing are handled by a three-judge panel without lay jurors. Assize courts are staffed by judges from the courts of appeal. Judges from local courts also can serve on a court of assize, but the presiding judge is always a member of a court of appeal. Courts of assize are divided into two chambers. One handles adult cases, while the other is responsible for juvenile offenders, usually between the ages of 16 and 17, accused of committing a serious crime.

Courts of Major Jurisdiction The next tier in the court hierarchy consists of the 181 courts of major jurisdiction. Each court is divided into three chambers. When judges sit to hear a civil matter, the court is called a civil court. Courts of major jurisdiction have unlimited jurisdiction in civil matters throughout the department in which they are located. When judges sit to hear a criminal matter, the court is called a correctional court. Courts of major jurisdiction handle serious misdemeanors, which are called *delits*. The court also sits as a juvenile court. Three-judge panels handle both the civil and criminal cases that come before the court. In 1995, the law was amended to permit a single judge to hear certain types of delits. These included some traffic offenses, the use of soft drugs, and the misuse of credit cards or checking accounts.

Courts of Minor Jurisdiction Last in the hierarchy are the 473 courts of minor jurisdiction. Each court is divided into two tribunals. Civil matters are heard in the civil tribunal. Minor misdemeanors and violations, which are called contraventions, are handled in the police tribunal. Contraventions include minor assaults, breaches of the peace, and traffic violations. This is the only court in the hierarchy that has a single judge sitting to decide a case.

The Legal Profession

For many years, a definite hierarchy has been established among members of the French legal profession. Law professors, magistrates, and avocats are distinguished not only by their professional titles but also by training, professional relationship, and responsibilities to the law. The more visible members of the legal profession are further divided into three groups: judges, procurators, and avocats. Members of each group have been professionally trained in the law. The law professors are considered at the pinnacle of the profession; their responsibilities will be discussed in the section concerning the French method of legal education.

Judges French judges are members of the tripartite judiciary. The other two groups are procurators and members of the central administration of justice, who work for the Ministry of Justice. As is the case in other civil law countries, the method of selecting and training judges in France is significantly different from that found in common law countries such as England, Canada, and the United States.

To become a judge, one must first obtain a law degree (a license in law) from a university law school. Typically, one must gain admission to the National School for the Judiciary at Bordeaux. This is the legal profession's *grande ecole*. France has a number of *grandes ecoles*, which are highly selective institutions that train the future professional elite of the country. The National School for the Judiciary is the special school designed to train people for careers as magistrates. This method of training is relatively new because the school has been in existence only since 1959. It complements the tradition long established in France of creating specialized professional schools; the school is modeled along the lines of the others. This method of instruction is a logical extension of the belief that French judges, as a part of the national civil service, need a specific kind of theoretical orientation and practical training before they are allowed to serve the state in this fashion. The school provides both scholarly and apprenticeship training components that take about three years to complete. Upon completing the program, the successful candidate joins the ranks of the judiciary as either a judge or a procurator.

This system enables French judges to begin their professional careers at a fairly young age. They are usually in their late twenties, which is noticeably younger than their colleagues in common law countries, who are often in their forties or fifties before they begin a career on the bench. Moreover, unlike their colleagues of the common law, French judges, for the most part, begin and end their legal careers as magistrates. It also should be noted that the National School for the Judiciary has a branch office in Paris that is responsible for all of its continuing education courses.

In recent years, because of the need to increase the number of judges serving in the criminal courts, some people have been recruited to the judiciary. People who have a legal background and at least 10 years of professional experience compete to secure a position. To gain entry, they must pass a written and oral examination.

In addition to the selection and training process, the nature of the job and the responsibilities of a judge also attract a certain type of personality to the profession. It has been suggested that people attracted to a career on the bench in France have a tendency to be unambitious (David, 1972). What is being alluded to is the fact that the position of a judge offers a fairly tranquil life, especially early in a career, when a judge is most likely to be assigned to a provincial city. Because judges are part of the civil service, their salary and tenure in office is secure. With the exception of the courts of minor jurisdiction, a French judge never has to rule alone on a decision. Thus, there is a collegiality in rendering a judicial opinion. Because the decisions are made secretly and issued without identification, each judge retains anonymity regarding his or her thoughts on a particular decision. The avoidance of undue pressure and public notoriety is enhanced further by the fact that judges in the ordinary courts do not rule on constitutional or administrative issues (which are more apt to attract public attention).

As more women enrolled in higher education in recent decades, they have gained a considerable presence in the legal profession. They represent a majority in the number of entrants to the National School for the Judiciary and those recruited who have already had a professional career in the law. To illustrate, women made up 28.5 percent of the trial judges in 1982, but by 2003, they represented 52.2 percent (Bell, 2006). While some women pursue careers as procurators, it has been suggested that the vast majority prefer a career on the bench, because the work schedule is more beneficial for those raising a family.

The manner in which judges render a decision is also of interest. A central characteristic of the judicial method is a judge's interest in and commitment to maintaining the theoretical purity and harmony of the legal system. Related to this kind of judicial posturing is the fact that a judge's professional career commences after the completion of theoretical training at the university and the National School for the Judiciary. This process has a profound impact on the way a judge perceives the law. It has been suggested that, within the legal profession, a judge has a much closer affinity to a law professor (the disinterested scholar of the law) than with a practicing attorney whose approach to the law is more pragmatic (David, 1972).

The commitment to theoretical purity and harmony of the legal system is best exemplified by the form of judicial decisions. Unlike English and American decisions, the French render rather abstract and brief rulings. According to legal scholars, these characteristics are largely attributable to philosophical and historical differences between the civil law and common law systems (Goutal, 1976). Regarding the abstract nature of a French decision, the French employ deductive logic rather than the induction or analogy usually utilized in common law countries. Because the codes are the principal source of French law, a French opinion begins with a general principle found in a code or a statute. The decision is designed to show clearly how it is in complete accord with the law. This method reduces significantly the likelihood that a judge will rely upon unwritten principles and be accused of arbitrariness.

Although French judges rely upon precedent, they are not obliged to do so. The principle of *stare decisis* does not exist. Actually, *stare decisis* is unnecessary because of the approach taken in rendering decisions. For example, when the Court of Cassation adds a new interpretation to the law, it simply states the new ruling. Given their authoritative position, judges do not feel compelled to justify their ruling by searching for precedents. Their attitude implies that although the court had never handed down such a ruling before, the ruling, nevertheless, should have been obvious all along. Thus, the fact that the court had not addressed itself to the issue before does not really make the opinion new or unique.

Unlike judges in the United States and England, French judges are required by law to offer a written opinion in a case. However, the decisions are noticeably brief. Whereas judges in the United States and England are apt to write lengthy decisions explaining the legislative history of an issue and a rationale for their opinion, French judges often render an opinion in less than one page. In fact, there is a rule that the decision of the court with respect to a specific legal issue be phrased in a single sentence. If more than one issue is a central feature of the case, then each issue is accorded a separate sentence in the decision. This tradition dates back to 1790, when the new legal system was established. Before the Revolution, judges were abusive and arbitrary in the exercise of their authority. As civil servants, however, judges of the post-Revolutionary era thought it advisable to be cautious in the exercise of their judicial powers. This attitude is illustrated by the judges' penchant for brief, impersonal opinions. Moreover, the fact that the decision is an anonymous ruling, which does not include dissenting opinions, further enhances the desire to maintain both judicial anonymity and collegiality. The absence of dissenting opinions also is designed to strengthen the authority of the decision (Wells, 1994).

According to Article 64 of the Constitution, "The President of the Republic shall be the guarantor of the independence of the judicial authority. ... Judges shall be irremovable." Thus, the basic principle of an independent judiciary is assured in the Constitution. A practical illustration of the manner in which judicial independence is carried out is with the selection of judges. As mentioned above, when the High Council of the Judiciary is selecting or promoting judges, it is composed of a number of judges. While there remains a significant number of political people on the Council, that number has decreased, and the number of judges has increased in recent years (Elliott and Vernon, 2000).

It should also be noted that while the Constitution suggests that a judge cannot be removed from office, this is not the case. If a judge is accused of serious malfeasance, the matter would be brought before the High Council of the Judiciary. In this context, the Council would sit as a court with the president of the Court of Cassation serving as the presiding judge. Neither the president of France nor the prime minister, both regular members of the High Council, serve when the Council is sitting as a court. This is another example of attempting to remove the appearance of politics in matters pertaining to the judiciary. While various sanctions exist, such as reprimand and demotion, the ultimate one is dismissal from office.

Procurators The procurators are another important branch of the French judiciary. Whereas judges are the *magistrats du siege* (the sitting magistrates), the procurators are commonly referred to as *magistrats debout* or *le parquet* (standing magistrates or "of the floor" rather than the bench). They undergo the same kind of training as judges (that is, a university legal education and further study at the National School for the Judiciary), and they are civil servants who work for the Public Ministry. Although it is unusual for a judge to request a transfer to the Public Ministry, it is not uncommon for a procurator to become a judge. Because both have been trained as members of the judiciary, this is not considered unusual.

The purpose and functions of the procurator are sometimes misinterpreted, especially by students of the common law tradition. Members of the Public Ministry appear to be a part of the executive branch of government and, thus, the defenders of that branch. Through the Ministry of

Justice, the executive appoints, promotes, disciplines, and discharges members of the Public Ministry. Procurators are organized in a hierarchy that corresponds to the court system. Procurators serving in lower courts are expected to comply with the orders that they receive from superiors who are assigned to appellate courts. The principal responsibility of procurators is to prosecute actions on behalf of the state.

These characteristics suggest that procurators are agents of the executive. This, however, is not the case, because procurators do not defend the interests of the state. Their responsibility is not to secure a conviction; it is to assure that justice is done and that society's interests are served. Thus, a distinction is made between the interests of the state or executive and those of society. Procurators are the guardians of the latter. When participating in the administration of justice, procurators enjoy an autonomy that befits their status as members of the judiciary. This is illustrated by the fact that when the state is involved in litigation before a civil or an administrative court, it must retain a lawyer to represent its side in the suit. The state does not turn the matter over to the Public Ministry to defend the state's specific interests.

There are two kinds of prosecutors in the French system. The state procurator acts on behalf of the public. If in the course of committing an offense, the accused has caused a person to suffer personal harm, which may be of either a physical or psychological nature, that person may bring a civil action against the accused. Counsel for the victim of this personal harm can appear in the criminal court and be considered a prosecutor for the civil party. Counsel for a victim is present primarily to argue for his or her client's right to collect compensation for damages.

Thus, although it is a civil claim, it can be heard concurrently with the criminal case. The victim, therefore, is considered a separate prosecuting party in the proceedings. In light of the fact that the victim has become a party to the proceedings, that person is prohibited from serving as a witness. This can obviously be a drawback to a procurator, whose case may be dependent on the victim's testimony. In the event the victim died, that person's heirs can also bring civil action. It should also be pointed out that the civil action can not only be brought against the accused but also against his heirs and any person who might be responsible for the offender, such as the accused's parents. Although it is less expensive and more efficient to attach a civil action to the criminal proceedings, because the victim benefits from the procurator's investigation into the case, it is important to note that a victim has the option of bringing a separate action in a civil court. Once this decision is made, however, it cannot be withdrawn in favor of having the matter heard concurrently with the criminal case.

In most cases, a public procurator decides whether a suit should be initiated. The manner and extent to which procurators utilize discretion has become a significant issue in recent years with the increase in crime and legislation creating additional offenses. Some critics have argued that this discretion should be eliminated by introducing the principle of mandatory prosecution that is found in other civil law countries. Mandatory prosecution requires the initiation of proceedings against the accused if guilt has been sufficiently established. If a procurator declines to prosecute, the victim can bring the matter before a trial court as a civil party complaint. Such an action thus forces the state procurator to initiate a public action. Victims are discouraged from bringing unjust claims or suits that lack sufficient grounds by a law permitting the accused individual, who is discharged following a trial, to initiate his or her own action against the civil party.

Another relatively new manner in which procurators can exercise discretion is in the mediation process of some criminal cases. Since 1993, this approach has been made available to victims and offenders who agree to this kind of procedure. In the event mediation fails, the procurator can still initiate a prosecution. Additional legislation was approved recently to expand the use of the mediation process. For example, all participants in the process have the right to a lawyer and a legal aid scheme is provided for those who are indigent. The procurator has an important role to play in the mediation process, for he or she has the power to impose various kinds of sanctions that include: compensation, fines, suspension of a driver's license, and community service. It should be pointed out that any order issued by a procurator must be approved by the court that would have entertained the case if the victim and offender had not agreed to mediation (Elliott and Vernon, 2000). Granting this kind of discretion is not considered unusual in the French context, in part because procurators are members of the judiciary.

Defense Counsel Until 1971, lawyers were divided into two groups: *avocats* and *avoues*. They were similar to English barristers and solicitors in terms of their specific legal duties. Following lengthy discussions and a good deal of pressure from the Ministry of Justice, however, the two professions merged in 1971. Today, the person who can represent a client in court and plead a case is called an avocat. Like other members of the legal profession, avocats must possess a license in law from a university law school. The law school graduate must also take a competency examination and then register with the local bar association, of which there are 180 throughout the country. Once a qualified individual is admitted to a local bar association, he or she can practice law throughout the country. There is one exception to this rule: there is a highly specialized group of senior avocats that are qualified to practice before the Court of Cassation. Finally, all certified law graduates serve as an apprentice avocat for a probationary period of at least three years. During the apprenticeship, an avocat must attend the special training center established by the court of appeal in his or her region.

Until recently, there was no national bar association in France. Each local association was independent and autonomous and had the authority to discipline its members. Legislation that went into effect in 1992 created a National Bar Council. It has been accorded three responsibilities: (1) to represent the profession before government authorities, (2) to establish a degree of uniformity in the rules and regulations developed by the local bar associations, and (3) to supervise the regional training centers (West, 1991).

Many avocats practice alone, but a change in legislation in the early 1970s permitted the formation of partnerships. Such partnerships have become more popular, but the associations are small when compared with those established in the United States. To some extent, avocats specialize in a particular branch of law, and the partnerships facilitate the arrangement. Avocats have been criticized by both judges and clients. The criticisms are similar to those that have been leveled against their counterparts in the United States. Clients question the competence and the cost of legal service, whereas judges complain about the lack of preparation for trials and the level of professional competence.

It was suggested that the profession of avocat was not as financially lucrative as it was during the early part of this century (Olivier, 1979). Part of the reason for this was the fact that another group within the hierarchy of the legal profession, *conseils juridiques*, handled most of the commercial and corporate legal work. That situation changed, because the 1992 legislation that created the National Bar Council also merged the professions of avocat and *conseil juridique*. Prior to this change, avocats had exclusive rights of audience in courts and could provide legal advice, while *conseils juridiques* were limited to providing legal advice and preparing legal documents. The 1992 legislation created a single profession, in which members are known as avocats, and all have rights of audience in courts, to provide legal advice, and to prepare legal documents.

The Jury

Although the jury was utilized in certain regions of medieval France, it was totally abandoned by the fifteenth century. Following the French Revolution, the jury was reintroduced, but its use was limited to the courts of assize, which handle the serious criminal cases. Critics of the French jury allege that it is a contradiction in that it has little impact on the administration of justice. Scholars point out that the jury is not rooted in French legal tradition; rather, it was borrowed from the British during the nineteenth century when judicial and political reforms were quite prevalent. It has been argued that the introduction of the jury was more of a political achievement than a judicial reform (Dunbar, 1968).

Moreover, it has been pointed out that the jury illustrates the acceptance of universal suffrage because jurors are selected from voting lists (David, 1972). In addition, it was originally viewed as a method of assuring that the public would share the burden of issuing capital punishment sanctions with the judges. Capital punishment, however, was abolished in France in 1981.

To serve on a jury, a person must be a French citizen, at least 23 years of age, able to read and write in French, and not be considered incapacitated or incompatible. People who have a criminal record or have been condemned to confinement or arrest are considered incapacitated. Among those considered incompatible are members of parliament, the Council of Ministers, magistrates, police, and military personnel.

Selection occurs through an annual list that is established from the voting rolls for each court of assize. Before the opening of the court session, the names of 35 jurors and 10 alternates are selected from the list through a lottery presided over by the president of the court. On the day of a trial, the jurors' names are drawn from an urn. The defense counsel can challenge five jurors, while the procurator can reject four. The reasons for the challenges need not be given. When nine names are selected, the jurors take their seats on either side of the three judges and are sworn in by the president of the court. A few alternate jurors are also selected in the event that they are needed.

Although jurors are mandated, along with the judges, to decide the ultimate fate of the defendant, they are considered an appendage of the judges. They are placed in this inferior position because they do not have access to the written record of the trial (which contains most of the evidence in a French trial), and they are not provided with a summing up of the law before deliberations commence. Thus, they are dependent on the judges for explanations of the law and many of the facts of the case on which they sit in judgment.

Legal Education

The French approach to legal education is strikingly different from that found in either England or the United States. This is largely attributed to the traditional approach that the French have taken toward higher education in general. The manner in which the current system of legal education is organized has been evolving since the post-Revolutionary period and is typical of the continental approach to higher education. France's universities are public institutions that are ultimately administered by the national government through the Ministry of National Education.

Students enter a university when they are approximately 18 years of age, after they have completed their high school education with an award of the baccalaureate diploma. Legal studies have been a traditional part of the general curriculum in French universities, and a significant number of students select it as a course of instruction. Students who select the legal studies curriculum are not necessarily planning on a career in law. Many plan to enter the civil service and view the law as an excellent preparation for that career.

Because the students are fairly young and inexperienced, the law curriculum is tailored along the lines of a general liberal arts education with a concentration in law. In 1997, the curriculum was revised to enhance student retention. A central feature of the reforms was the introduction of a series of foundation courses that are taken during the first semester. The foundation courses pay particular attention to study skills, which include a familiarity with learning resources, an ability to take lecture notes, and working in a group on a class project.

The pursuit of a legal education takes approximately four years and is divided into two phases. During the initial two-year phase, in addition to the aforementioned foundation courses, a student will study history, economics, political science, sociology, and finance, along with specific areas of law. These include constitutional law, administrative law, criminal law, contracts, property, and torts. The system was so developed because many of the social sciences are organized within the law faculties. Moreover, the French believe that it is essential to present the law in a general context in order for these young students to broaden their educational background. During the second two-year phase, a student begins to concentrate almost exclusively on legal studies. The more advanced courses include business law, civil liberties, employment law, and tax law. At the end of the third year, a student is awarded the degree of license in law, which is equivalent to a bachelor of law degree. Upon the completion of the fourth year, a student is granted a master of law degree.

The method of instruction is largely interdisciplinary during the first two years and is always theoretical in nature. This has been the source of some criticism directed at French legal studies programs. On the one hand, some students contend that the program does not prepare them immediately for a specific career. The law professors, on the other hand, argue that the study of law in the context of the university should be limited to the realm of ideas. Their responsibility is to train people to think like jurists, not to produce legal practitioners. Thus, a formal introduction to legal principles is imperative at this stage in the students' intellectual development. The professors expect that, following graduation, a student will learn the technical aspects of their craft through either apprenticeship programs or additional courses of study at a professional school.

The law professors appear to have won the argument to date. This is attributed in no small part to the fact that law professors traditionally have been considered to be at the apex of the entire legal profession. Law professors enjoy the status of the pure jurist. They are allowed to live in the realm of ideas and principles and are not relegated to the task of actually attempting to apply these principles to the practical problems confronting the rest of the legal profession.

Once a student is awarded a law degree, he or she must obtain professional qualifications to practice law. Students must first pass an entrance exam that will permit them to participate in a professional course of study that lasts one year. These professional programs are associated with the courts of appeal. It is in this program that the candidate learns about the rules of professional conduct and how to draft various documents. Students also participate in two internships of which one involves working with an avocat. At the end of the year, the candidate takes a test that consists of several practical exercises designed to certify the professional aptitude of the person. If the candidate successfully passes the examination, he or she begins a two-year apprenticeship with an avocat and must register with the local bar association.

Those who wish to pursue a career with the judiciary attend the National School for the Judiciary in Bordeaux. As alluded to earlier, this is the grande ecole of the legal profession, the professional school that prepares people to serve as judges, procurators, or members of the central administration of justice. Admission to the school is highly competitive and is based on a written and oral examination that focuses on a candidate's general educational background as well as knowledge of the law. The school admits approximately 200 people a year.

A successful candidate will spend 31 months in preparation to join the ranks of the judiciary. The first 11 months are spent in class at the school and participating in various public- and private-sector internships. These placements could include working with various correctional facilities, the National Police, the National Gendarmerie, or a psychiatric hospital. At the school, lectures and seminars are devoted to a wide range of legal topics and contemporary problems that are designed to prepare the candidates to function as members of the judiciary. The next 14 months are devoted to working with judges in various courts, in addition to time spent in the office of an avocat.

Candidates are graded on course work in the training classes and on the practical work out in the field. They must also pass a final series of oral and written examinations before a jury. The examining jury is composed of judges from various courts, a member of the Ministry of Justice, law professors, and a high-ranking government official. The jury can decide to pass, fail, or impose an additional year of study on the candidate. Those who fail usually enter the nonjudicial career of administration or research for the courts. Once the candidates successfully pass the examination, they spend the final six months of their training in their designated career field, either assisting a judge in a court of minor jurisdiction or working in an office of a procurator. Upon the completion of this six-month period of training, the person would begin his or her career as either a judge or a procurator. Promotions would occur through the Ministry of Justice with the advice of the High Council of the Judiciary.

Law

A distinction was made between civil law and criminal law when discussing the origins of English criminal law and procedure. The use of the term "civil law" in the common law context relates to litigation between private parties, such as issues involving torts, property, and contracts. Criminal law is concerned with a public wrong, a crime in which the defendant has transgressed the public order of society.

In this chapter, the term "civil law" is used to describe a legal system that is distinguishable from the common law system. The civil law system evolved on the continent of Europe and was influenced in its development initially by Roman law and the canon law of the Roman Catholic Church. It was influenced further by local custom. This civil law system is also referred to as the Romano-Germanic legal family.

France represents one of many European countries that adopted the civil law system. In fact, France was instrumental in establishing the Romano-Germanic family as a distinct legal system. Just as countries associated with the common law family have unique legal characteristics that distinguish them from other members of the family, so do nations within the Romano-Germanic family. Like the common law, Romano-Germanic law is found throughout the world in countries that were explored or colonized by Europeans. Until the advent of socialist law, the common law and the civil law were the most influential legal systems in the world, for they dominated the method of legal analysis.

Within its legal system, France has divided law into two general categories: public law and private law. The criminal law is part of public law, along with administrative law and constitutional law. The law governing issues involving two private parties is found under the general category of private law.

It was already pointed out earlier in the chapter that France lacked a powerful monarchy during the medieval period. This fact was instrumental in the development of law in the country. Without a dominant centralized administration, the various regions of the country were left to their own indigenous customs for the resolution of legal disputes. In the south of France, customs borrowed extensively from Roman law, a written law. In the northern provinces, the tendency was for local oral tradition or custom to dominate the formation of law. Legal principles from canon law were another distinct and important legal source. Finally, another source for resolving judicial disputes emerged upon the creation of provincial parlements. Because each parlement was independent, the resolution of the same type of dispute often differed from province to province. Thus, throughout the medieval period, legal decisions did not reflect a uniform standard.

Prior to the twelfth century, the French employed accusatory procedures similar to those used in England. The injured party had to make an oral complaint in court and the accused had to respond. Oath-helpers were used to support the positions of the victim and the accused. At first, monetary compensation was the dominant method of resolving disputes. Forms of corporal punishment or fines, however, were gradually introduced in the seigneurial courts.

The ordeals (explained in Chapter I on England) were also employed in France until they were banned by the Fourth Lateran Council in 1215. With the demise of the ordeals, the English adopted a new procedure that included the jury system. The French adopted a different approach. This new method had a profound impact on the future evolution of criminal procedure in France and led to the most notable distinction between the accusatory procedures established in the common law and the inquisitorial procedures of the Romano-Germanic law.

A primary source of France's new procedural system was the canon law of the Roman Catholic Church. Originally, canon law employed an accusatory procedure similar to that found in Roman law and Germanic custom. As early as the ninth century, however, the church initiated a change in procedure. If public opinion accused a person of committing a crime and the accusation was substantiated by a judge, the accused was compelled to prove his or her innocence. An accused person who refused or failed to prove his or her innocence was condemned. This early method of inquisition had not been a part of church custom; rather it was established through church legislation that often cited scripture as its justification. The inquisitorial procedures of the church were to achieve their most famous notoriety when the inquisition of heretics was undertaken in the thirteenth century. This procedure was to remain quite popular within the ecclesiastical community until the end of the fifteenth century.

Modifications in French accusatory procedure first appeared in the royal courts in the thirteenth century. What evolved was the establishment of two kinds of procedures. One was considered ordinary and accusatory in nature. The other was extraordinary, largely inquisitorial in style, and designed for use in more important and serious cases. The new inquisitorial style called for witnesses to appear before a court in a closed session. Judges acted as inquirers and collected witness testimony through an interrogation process that excluded the parties to the suit. The testimony was taken down in writing, and this marked the beginning of reliance upon written evidence in the form of a deposition. Once the inquisition was completed, the parties to the suit were brought together in open court to explain their positions. At that time, the accused had access to the written depositions and was allowed to introduce witnesses on his or her behalf.

By this time, the use of torture also was accepted as a mode of proof in the inquisitorial procedure. It has been suggested that the use of torture had its roots in Roman law. The Romans were apparently of the opinion that slaves only told the truth when subjected to pain. In ancient times, therefore, torture had become an important and universally acceptable method in cases involving people who were not free (Esmein, 1968). By the medieval period, it had become an acceptable mode of proof, irrespective of the accused's social standing.

From the thirteenth through the early sixteenth centuries, the French employed both accusatory and inquisitorial procedures. In 1539, however, King Francis I (1494–1547) issued the Ordinance of Villers-Cotterets, which called for the standardization and utilization of inquisitorial methods in all French courts. What follows are the major characteristics of that procedure. In every criminal case, the king's prosecutor became a party to the suit. Thus, the notion that trials were duels between private parties, which was developed under the accusatory scheme, ceased to exist. The state's interest, through the prosecutor, was recognized and aired in a criminal trial.

Two types of magistrates were used during the course of a criminal investigation and trial. One magistrate, called "the criminal judge," was responsible for collecting evidence and examining all parties in a case. The accused, when interrogated by the judge in private, was sworn to tell the truth but was not told of the accusation. Moreover, all interrogations of the accused, victim, and witnesses were reduced to a written transcript that became the principal source of evidence at the trial. The other kind of magistrate sat as part of a group to adjudicate the case. It was at this stage that the trial became public, and judges determined the accused's guilt or innocence. It was also at this time that the accused was confronted with the accusation and witnesses against him or her. Although a number of changes have been made since the sixteenth century, the Ordinance of Villers-Cotterets explains the basic characteristics of the inquisitorial procedure.

Today, much of the inquisitorial process remains closed to the public. In the more serious cases, judges retain an important role in the investigative process and the collection of evidence, of which written documentation is highly prized and considered central to a case. Once the case is bound over for trial, aspects of the adversarial process become apparent. The trial, for the most part, is open to the public, and the prosecution and defense are permitted to offer oral arguments. Nevertheless, the most important element of the trial is the written record of the pretrial investigation.

Finally, brief mention should be made of the codification movement. As was indicated in the previous section, the discovery of the law books of the Byzantine Emperor Justinian prompted a renaissance in legal studies during the twelfth century. These books were originally compiled around the year 534 and consisted of four parts. The Code was a collection of ordinances approved by Roman emperors before Justinian's time. The Novels contained the laws passed during Justinian's reign. The Digest was a collection of legal opinions by Roman jurists on a host of legal issues. The Institutes was a handbook designed to introduce students to the study of law. Collectively, these books are referred to as Justinian's Code or the *Corpus Juris Civilis*. Though these books do not constitute a code in the sense that the term has been used since the sixteenth century, the codification movement does trace its early origins to the discovery of Justinian's Code.

Throughout the sixteenth, seventeenth, and eighteenth centuries, attempts were made to establish a single legal code in France. The goal was to create some general statutes that would be enforceable throughout the country. This met with a moderate degree of success, but regional codes remained in force. It has been suggested that the evolution of the codification movement succeeded in establishing a number of characteristics that helped prepare the country for Napoleon's successful attempt at codification in the late eighteenth century (Maillet, 1969–70).

The codification movement attempted to establish a unified law and in the process solve the problem of social inequality. Under the ancien regime, different classes of people were subject to special rules that were based on social class. This feature of the ancien regime was one of the causes of the French Revolution. Codification eliminated that feature by establishing a single codified system of laws.

The codification movement also explained how the law would be administered. For example, because French jurists were trained in Roman law, they borrowed some of the substantive features of that system during their attempts at codification. In addition, judges, as officers of the king, were expected to interpret the law rather than to create new law or modify existing law in some fashion. Thus, judge-made law or case law had no place in the emerging French legal system.

As one might expect, the Revolution of 1789 totally disrupted French society. With the country in a state of disarray, it was imperative that the institutions of the ancien regime be transformed to meet the needs of the new social order—needs built on the social and political principles of the Enlightenment. The establishment of a new system for the administration of justice was central to this process. During the reign of Napoleon, a commission was created to codify the law. The Civil Code was completed in 1804, followed by the Code of Civil Procedure in 1807, the Code of Commerce in 1808, the Code of Criminal Procedure in 1808, and the Code Penal in 1810. These codes either have been completely revised since that time or have had parts superseded by statutes passed in parliament.

Criminal Law

The French criminal justice system is regulated by two principal legislative enactments: the Code of Criminal Procedure, which was completely revised in 1959, and the new Penal Code, which became law in 1994 and replaced the 1810 version that had been modified over the years. The Code of Criminal Procedure explains the methods of investigating and adjudicating a person charged with violating the criminal law. The Penal Code identifies the various types of offenses and the appropriate sanctions.

The most important source of criminal law is the Penal Code. The new code is divided into five books or parts. Book I explains the general provisions in the penal law, which include: criminal liability and responsibility, lengths of sentences, and kinds of punishments. Book II focuses on crimes (felonies) and delits (serious misdemeanors) against the person. These consist of offenses committed against an individual but also includes crimes against human rights. Book III deals with crimes and delits against property. Book IV is devoted to crimes and delits against the nation, the government, and the public order. Book V addresses other crimes and delits that are not associated with the categories already mentioned, such as crimes against the environment.

The French have divided criminal offenses into three categories: crimes, delits, and contraventions. This classification scheme not only makes distinctions between the gravity of the offense and the subsequent sanctions, but it also signifies which court in the hierarchy would hear the case. The French also include in the preliminary provisions of the code the principle that the law has no retroactive application; that is, an offender cannot be punished if the action was not illegal at the time it was committed. As was the case with the previous code, sections of it could be superseded in the future by statutes passed in parliament.

Criminal Procedure

It should be pointed out that for several years now there have been questions raised and a growing criticism of some basic criminal procedural issues. Specific concern has been directed at whether France was in compliance with the European Convention on Human Rights. Much of this criticism focused on matters of police custody and specifically whether France was in compliance with Article 5(2) of the Convention, which states: "Everyone who is arrested shall be informed promptly, in a language which he understands, of the reasons for his arrest and the charge against him." In addition, Article 6 of the Convention, which deals with rights to defend oneself of a criminal charge, has also received a good deal of attention from the critics of the status quo.

As was mentioned earlier, the 1993 report of the Criminal Justice and Human Rights Commission that was chaired by Professor Mireille Delmas-Marty proposed several significant reforms. One involved abolishing the position of investigating judge, because less than 10 percent of the criminal cases are supervised by such a judge. It was recommended that procurators assume the responsibility for all investigations. These recommendations have not happened. Another reform suggested that a defendant be permitted to have access to a lawyer during the *garde a vue*. The rationale for this recommendation was to assure that a defendant was aware of his or her rights, in particular the right to silence. While this right of access was approved in 1994, questions have been raised as to whether indigent defendants will actually see a lawyer. Finally, the commission recommended that the trial judge refrain from questioning the accused and witnesses during a trial. Instead, the judge should assume the role of arbitrator. Such a recommendation would transform the existing criminal procedure from an inquisitorial to an accusatorial method. This recommendation was rejected. Some have suggested the change in the political climate contributed to the limited success of the Commission's report (Trouille, 1994).

The issues of how a defendant was treated during the garde a vue and the number of people held on remand awaiting trial were raised in the 1997 report of the Justice Commission chaired by Pierre Truche, the president of the Court of Cassation. At issue was the need to protect the presumption of innocence. With regard to the garde a vue, the Truche Report recommended that a suspect have the right to see a lawyer at the beginning of the police custody. It was also suggested that police questioning should be recorded. In reference to the large number of people held on remand, the Truche Report recommended that custody decisions should be made by a panel of three judges rather than the investigating judge. While the government has implemented some reforms, it has been reluctant to adopt all the recommendations, especially in light of the public's concern over crime and order issues (Elliott and Vernon, 2000).

This examination of France's criminal procedure is divided into two categories. The first includes the preliminary investigation, which involves an examination of police powers and other pertinent pretrial procedural issues. The second category is concerned with the trial process, which consists of the main hearing and appellate review procedures. France's Code of Criminal Procedure is the legal document that essentially explains the manner in which these procedures are executed.

It should be noted that even before the Delmas-Marty and Truche reports were issued, there were proponents who had been recommending changes to the Code of Criminal Procedure. One such recommendation was to offer some basic guiding principles at the beginning of the Code. In 2000, a preliminary article was added to the Code that provided these principles.

I. Criminal procedure should be fair and adversarial and preserve a balance between the rights of the parties. It should guarantee a separation between those authorities responsible for prosecuting and those responsible for judging. Persons who find themselves in a similar situation and prosecuted for the same offences should be judged according to the same rules.

II. The judicial authority ensures that victims are informed and that their rights are respected throughout any criminal process.

III. Every person suspected or prosecuted is presumed innocent as long as his guilt has not been established. Attacks on his presumption of innocence are proscribed, compensated and punished in the circumstances laid down by statute. He has the right to be informed of charges brought against him and to be legally defended. The coercive measures to which such a person may be subjected are taken by or under the effective control of judicial authority. They should be strictly limited to the needs of the process, proportionate to the gravity of the offence charged and not such as to infringe human dignity. The accusation to which such a person is subjected should be brought to final judgment within a reasonable time. Every convicted person has the right to have his conviction examined by a second tribunal.

It is very important to clarify one word that is found in the first principle. The word is "adversarial." Adversarial is frequently associated with the procedures of the common law legal family, and it is often contrasted with the inquisitorial procedure that is associated with the Roman-Germanic legal family, of which France is a member. In the French context, adversarial means something different from the common law usage. It is meant to convey that all parties in a case are accorded the same rights in the procedural process. In particular, it is designed to assure that the defense will have an opportunity to review all of the evidence and be made aware of the case against the accused. This is designed to afford the accused an opportunity to answer the charges against him or her in a timely and thorough manner (Hodgson, 2005; Spencer, in Delmas-Marty and Spencer, 2002).

Preliminary Investigations Following the commission of an offense, a preliminary investigation is undertaken to determine who committed the act or who is reasonably suspected of involvement in the offense. According to Article 11, "[p]roceedings in the course of inquiry and investigation shall be secret, unless otherwise provided by law and without prejudice to the rights of the defense." The goal is to acquire an independent investigation of the facts in a case by an officer who impartially examines all aspects of the case.

During the early stages of an investigation, there is a concern regarding bias toward the person being questioned. The person held by the police for initial questioning (a process known as garde a vue) need only be told that they are assisting with a police investigation. Police do not have to provide a probable cause explanation. The person can be held for 24 hours without being formally charged, and this period of custody can be extended to 48 hours with the permission of a procurator. Although a person has a right to remain silent, there is no requirement that they be informed of this right. Moreover, a person does not have access to an avocat for the initial 20 hours of a garde a vue, and when they do, the meeting is limited to 30 minutes.

There are exceptions to these rules, however. Consultation with an avocat can be delayed even longer in certain circumstances. For example, in cases alleging conspiracy, aggravated extortion, or organized crime, a person can be prohibited from seeing an avocat for 48 hours. In those cases involving serious drug trafficking or terrorism, the garde a vue can last 96 hours and the consultation with an avocat delayed for 72 hours. When a detention involves drug offenses or terrorism, a judge from a court of major jurisdiction must approve the extension. In all the other instances, a judicial hearing is not provided to determine the validity of a detention. Finally, the French do not have a legal equivalent of a writ of habeas corpus.

Once a person is charged with an offense, the procurator and avocat for the defendant are given access to the findings of the investigator. Moreover, both parties can suggest specific kinds of leads for further inquiry. The principal participants involved in a preliminary investigation are the judicial police (who are members of the criminal investigation branch of the French police), a procurator, and—if the offense is serious—an investigating judge selected from the ranks of judges rather than from procurators of the judiciary.

If the offense is classified as flagrant, all of the above mentioned parties could be involved in the investigation. Article 52 explains what constitutes a flagrant offense.

> The felony or misdemeanor that is in the process of being committed or which has just been committed is a flagrant felony or flagrant misdemeanor. There is also a flagrant felony or misdemeanor when, in the period immediately following the act, the suspected person is pursued by clamor, or is found in possession of objects, or presents traces or indications, leading to the belief that he has participated in the felony or misdemeanor. Every crime or misdemeanor which, though not committed in the circumstances provided in the preceding paragraph, has been

> committed in a house the head of which asks the prosecuting attorney or an officer of the judicial police to establish it shall be assimilated to a flagrant felony or misdemeanor.

In cases of flagrant crimes or delits, the judicial police are expected to take immediate action. They are granted wide powers under the circumstances.

The first duty of the judicial police is to inform the procurator of the Republic. Within each of the 35 districts of the courts of appeal, there is a procurator of the Republic responsible for the prosecution of all cases in the district. The judicial police then are expected to go immediately to the scene of the offense. If the judicial police arrive before a procurator, they are empowered to do a number of things. For example, they preserve the crime scene, they search and seize all evidence and weapons pertinent to the case, and they interview and detain people at the crime scene who are knowledgeable about the case. These investigative responsibilities pass to the procurator upon arrival. Actually, the judicial police continue to perform these tasks, but under the procurator's direction.

In cases that are considered serious (that is, all crimes and many flagrant delits), the procurator of the Republic could request that an independent investigation be undertaken by an investigating judge, a judge responsible for conducting a complete and impartial examination of the facts. An investigating judge is mandated to conduct an instruction (or information). The mission of an investigating judge is to establish the truth in the matter. Assisted by the judicial police, the judge interviews witnesses and follows leads believed to be beneficial to the resolution of the case. The judge will issue the necessary warrants to have places searched and suspects and evidence seized. Once certain who has committed the offense, an investigating judge will issue a mandate that, depending on the type of case, authorizes the police either to bring the suspect before the investigating judge or to have the suspect arrested and held.

The obvious advantage to this system is that there is only one investigation. This eliminates the need for the police, procurator, and avocat for the defense to make separate inquiries into the matter, because the findings of the official investigation are made available to all parties in the case. Moreover, the procurator and the avocat can request an investigating judge to follow leads that they believe are pertinent to the case. The investigating judge, whose role is to discover the truth in the matter, is usually amenable to these suggestions.

It should be noted that the role of the investigating judge has been the subject of a good deal of controversy for some time. It has received the most media publicity of all the actors in the French criminal justice system. Some critics of the position allege that it provides too much power to a single individual. Given the complex nature of some criminal enterprises, questions have also been raised regarding the ability of some judges. This specific concern appears to have been addressed in 2008, when teams of investigating judges were assigned to complex cases. In early 2009, however, the president of France, Nicholas Sarkozy, proposed to eliminate the role of investigating judge and turn the investigative process over to the procurator. There were objections to this proposal from several groups. Only time will tell if this proposal is implemented.

In the more serious cases, a second review of the charges is entertained by a chamber of instruction before the case is brought to trial. Chambers of instruction are a permanent feature of courts of appeal. A chamber of instruction is composed of three judges from the local court of appeal. During this phase of the investigation, a hearing is conducted by the chamber, and briefs are filed by the parties to the case. The chamber also reviews petitions (for example, regarding the accused's detention) or appeals such as those involving the impropriety of the initial investigation. The chamber can order the appearance of the parties or evidence and can request a supplemental investigation if it deems it appropriate. An investigation can be directed by either a member of the chamber or an investigating judge. Following this hearing, the chamber can dismiss the case, issue an indictment that binds the accused over for trial, or reduce the charges to a misdemeanor violation and have the case heard in the appropriate court.

In cases that are not considered flagrant offenses, the judicial police have limited powers to conduct an investigation on their own or under the supervision of the procurator of the Republic. Thus, all other delits and contraventions are handled in this manner. The judicial police have the authority to question suspects and witnesses, to visit the scene if the owner agrees, and to decide if a person should be detained. In these less serious cases, a procurator directs the investigation.

Power to Detain and Arrest There are three instances under French procedural rules in which persons can be deprived of their liberty prior to the determination of guilt. One is the garde a vue, a temporary detention measure. This power may be utilized by the judicial police when they are conducting their preliminary investigation. According to the rules, the police have the authority to call on or summon any person who is capable of aiding in an investigation. This could include a suspect or a witness. If a person in unwilling to cooperate, the procurator has the authority to order the person to appear before the police. The police have the power to detain a suspect for up to 24 hours. If the police desire to extend the detention for a longer period, they must request an extension from either a procurator or an investigating judge. These requests are usually handled by a procurator, and an extension can be awarded for an additional 24-hour period. A liberty and detention judge or a chamber of instruction has the authority to cancel a detention measure if it is deemed unlawful. The role of the liberty and detention judge will be explained shortly. People who are detained under this procedure can be given a medical examination either during or after the termination of the 24-hour period.

Another method of depriving persons of their liberty before guilt has been determined is through the execution of a warrant. In cases involving flagrant crimes or delits, a procurator can issue a warrant for a suspect's arrest if an investigating judge has not as yet received the case. An investigating judge can issue four kinds of warrants: appearance, attachment, confinement, or arrest. Article 122 states:

> A warrant for appearance has as its object placing the accused under a duty to present himself before the judge on the date and at the hour indicated by the warrant. A warrant of attachment is the order given by the judge to the police immediately to produce the accused before him. A warrant for confinement is the order given by the judge to the supervisor of the jail to receive and to detain the accused. This warrant also permits searching for or transfer of the accused if he has been notified previously. A warrant of arrest is the order given to the police to seek out the accused and to produce him at the jail indicated in the warrant, where he shall be received and detained.

In cases involving a warrant for appearance, the investigating judge is expected to interrogate the person immediately. If this is not possible, the person can be held for 24 hours at most. A person held on a warrant for attachment also must appear before an investigating judge within 24 hours. Warrants for confinement are issued only after an investigating judge has already interrogated the suspect and the case begins to focus on a person who could be imprisoned for the offense if found guilty. Warrants for arrest require that the suspect be brought before an investigating judge for questioning within 48 hours of the time of the arrest.

The third method of depriving people of their liberty before trial is a result of the Security and Liberty Law of 1981. A procurator can request a judge of a court of major jurisdiction to restrict a defendant's liberty if the person is charged with a delit that is punishable by up to five years imprisonment.

It should also be pointed out that the Security and Liberty Law gives the police the legal authority to require any person to identify themselves during the course of a criminal investigation or during a public order disturbance. A person without adequate identification may be brought to a police station and permitted to contact people who can assist in their identification. In such instances, the person can be held for up to six hours. A person refusing to offer identification has the right to have a procurator notified. Refusal to cooperate in the identification process is an offense punishable by a jail sentence of 10 days to three months and a fine (Pugh and Pugh, 1982).

Interrogations The Code of Criminal Procedure makes a distinction between two kinds of interrogations: (1) the hearing of witnesses, and (2) interrogation and confrontations. In the hearing of witnesses, witnesses are placed under oath and examined separately by an investigating judge. The accused is not present at this proceeding. Witnesses who do not appear for questioning can be picked up by the police and fined. Witnesses who have declared knowledge of a crime or delit but refuse to answer questions posed by an investigating judge can be jailed for a period of at least 11 days but not more than one year. In addition, a fine also can be imposed in conjunction with a jail sentence.

Interrogations and confrontations involve the questioning of the accused and the civil party (or victim). The investigating judge must acquaint the parties with a number of rights. For example, an investigating judge must inform the accused of the offenses with which he or she is being charged and advise the accused of the right to remain silent and the right to an avocat for his or her defense. If the accused is willing to make a statement without counsel, the investigating judge is free to accept the information. The accused also must inform the investigating judge of his or her place of residence, whether he or she is being detained, and any change in residence. The civil party also has a right to be represented by counsel.

An accused individual who is being detained has a right to communicate with counsel. With the exception of counsel for the accused, an investigating judge can issue a prohibition that prevents the accused from communicating with other people. This right of prohibition lasts for 10 days and can be renewed only once for an additional 10-day period. The accused and victim cannot confront one another unless counsel is present or the right to have counsel present is waived. A procurator can assist an investigating judge in interrogating the accused or in hearing the victim. The procurator, counsel for the accused, and counsel for the victim can present only those questions that have been approved by the investigating judge. Even if the investigating judge rejects the question, it still appears in the official report.

Power to Search and Seize The powers of search and seizure are also governed by the Code of Criminal Procedure. A search and seizure can occur either with or without a warrant. Searches and seizures that are considered legal without a warrant involve offenses labeled flagrant crimes. Following the commission of a flagrant crime, the judicial police are expected to notify a procurator before proceeding to the scene of the offense. Upon their arrival, the police are expected to secure the crime scene and to collect evidence. According to Article 56 of the Code, if the judicial police believe additional evidence is likely to be uncovered at the residence of a suspect, they are expected to conduct a search of the premises immediately. Moreover, procedures require that either the suspect or a representative be present during the search. If this is not possible, the judicial police may select two witnesses to observe the search. Finally, Article 59 states that "the absence of a demand made from the interior of a house or the exceptions provided by law searches and domicility visits may not be begun before six o'clock in the morning or after nine o'clock at night."

These procedures are also followed in cases in which a flagrant delit has been committed and a suspect could be imprisoned if found guilty. Warrantless searches and seizures at any other location must have the written consent of the owners of the property. The police, however, are authorized to enter and search without a warrant under certain circumstances that have been established by specific statutes. These statutes deal with illegal gambling, immoral acts, and drug offenses.

According to Article 92, an investigating judge has the authority to "go anywhere in order there to effectuate all useful determinations or to conduct searches. He shall advise the prosecuting attorney, who may accompany him." In searching the residence of an accused or another person, an investigating judge is expected to follow the rules that apply to the judicial police.

Searches and seizures also are undertaken with a warrant issued by an investigating judge. The judicial police conduct the search. Before the search starts, the police are expected to identify themselves and present the warrant to the occupant. Either the occupant, a designated representative, or two witnesses must be present during a search. The police may search an occupant and the premises and are permitted to seize any item believed to be related to the offense. While searches of a person are conducted to secure evidence, a frisk of a person is also permissible to ensure the safety of a police officer.

It is the responsibility of the chamber of instruction to review the manner in which evidence is collected. The chamber has the authority either to void the proceedings because of illegal actions taken by the authorities or to exclude from the trial evidence that was obtained in an illegal manner. The judicial police who conducted the illegal activities also can be subject to a number of sanctions including: disciplinary procedures, temporary or permanent suspension from the ranks of the judicial police, penal sanctions, and civil proceedings.

Pretrial Detention and Supervision In law, detaining a person before trial is considered an exceptional measure. When it is instituted, it must comply with the rules that are explained in Articles 144 and 145 of the Code of Criminal Procedure. Article 144 states:

Pretrial detention may only be ordered or extended if it is the only way:

1. to preserve material evidence or clues or to prevent either witnesses or victims being pressured, or fraudulent conspiracy between persons under judicial examination and their accomplices;

2. to protect the person under judicial examination, to guarantee that he remains at the disposal of the law, to put an end to the offence or to prevent its renewal;

3. to put an end to an exceptional and persistent disruption of public order caused by the seriousness of the offence, the circumstances in which it was committed, or the gravity of the harm that it has caused.

Prior to 2000, it was primarily the responsibility of the investigating judge to determine if a defendant involved in a serious offense should be released or held in custody pending trial. In certain cases, pretrial detention could also be determined by a judge of the court of major jurisdiction or by the chamber of instruction. In 2000, however, as part of the effort to reform various procedures, the French introduced a new person in the criminal proceedings: the liberty and detention judge. Like the investigating judge, the liberty and detention judge is a member of the magistrates who elected a career as a judge. Like the investigating judge, the liberty and detention judge is assigned a specialized responsibility in French criminal procedure. As the name implies, the judge is the person primarily responsible for determining if a person will be released or detained prior to the trial. In certain cases, a judge of the court of major jurisdiction or the chamber of instruction retain the authority to detain a defendant.

The liberty and detention judge makes this determination to release or detain by holding an adversarial hearing. At this hearing the procurator, defendant, and the avocat for the defendant are given an opportunity to provide reasons and evidence as to why the defendant should be held or released. The judge must provide in writing the reasons for the decision, and the reasons must be based on the points mentioned above in Article 144 of the code—that is, preserve evidence, protect the person, or prevent public disorder.

Article 144-1 states: "Pre-trial detention may not exceed a reasonable length of time in respect of the seriousness of the charges brought against the person under judicial examination and of the complexity of the investigations necessary for the discovery of the truth." The length of a detention is determined by the nature of the offense. If the defendant is accused of a delit, the detention cannot exceed four months unless the person has already been sentenced for committing a crime or sentenced to a term of more than a year.

If the defendant is accused of a crime, he or she cannot be held for more than a year, unless the liberty and detention judge elects to extend the period of detention an additional six months following an adversarial hearing. Periods of pretrial detention are further elaborated in Article 145-3 of the code,

> The person under judicial examination may not be kept in custody for more than two years, where the applicable sentence is less than twenty years' imprisonment, and for more than three years in all other cases. The time limits are extended to three and four years respectively where one of the elements of the offence has been committed outside the national territory. The time limit is also four years where the person is being prosecuted for one or more felonies mentioned in Books II and IV of the Criminal Code, or for drug trafficking, terrorism, living off immoral earnings, extortion of money or for a felony committed by an organized gang.

Obviously, if a defendant is released, conditions are frequently imposed that restrict the accused's freedom of movement and spell out the obligations of the accused while at liberty.

It has been suggested that bail is not used much in France (Ingraham, 1987). Application for bail can be made by the accused or the accused's counsel at any time during a case. When bail is requested initially during an investigation into a serious offense, an investigating judge decides the matter. As the case proceeds during the pretrial phase, bail requests would transfer to the liberty and detention judge. Once bail is granted, the accused must inform the authorities of an established residence within the area of investigation.

Article 142 of the code explains how bail is secured and the methods by which it is either returned or forfeited, depending on the outcome of the trial. Before bail is granted, the judge can order the accused to furnish a security. A security is always in the form of money and is deposited with the clerk of the court. Moreover, the security is allotted for two purposes, and thus consists of two parts. Part of the security is designed to assure that the accused will appear at all stages of the trial. The other part is held in the event that costs are awarded to the civil or public party, a fine is imposed, or restitution and damages are awarded. The first part of the security is returned if the accused appears throughout the trial or is acquitted, or if the case is dismissed. The second part also is returned if the accused is acquitted or the case dismissed. In cases of conviction, only the balance of the security is returned after costs, fines, restitution, and damages are awarded. Those people who either were not detained or were released on bail during the preliminary investigation must surrender to the court no later than the evening before commencement of the trial.

Legal Aid Since the early 1970s, legal aid has become more readily available in France. Legal aid is granted either in total or in part, but the applicant must live in France and must be without sufficient means to pay for counsel. A person can apply for legal aid at any time during the course of a proceeding. A judge does not grant legal aid; instead, commissions have been established in courts of major jurisdiction, courts of appeal, and the Court of Cassation to dispense aid.

The commissions are composed of members of the judiciary, members of the legal profession, and local government authorities. Once legal aid is approved, the application is sent to the president of the local bar association, who then appoints counsel. Legal aid can be withdrawn during the course of the proceedings if the beneficiary acquires funds to employ his or her own counsel or if the commission discovers that a person did not accurately disclose his or her financial status.

Many lawyers appear to be either hostile or indifferent to the legal aid scheme. The opposition usually stems from two considerations. Legal aid means that an avocat is being financially supported by the state. Avocats oppose this on the grounds that they are indirectly becoming a part of the civil service. Moreover, legal aid only covers an avocat's expenses but does not provide a fee for services. At a time when the income of the profession has declined, this has resulted in avocats' lack of enthusiasm for the scheme.

The Trial There are three kinds of courts in France that are responsible for adjudicating specific types of criminal offenses. The courts of assize handle cases involving crimes. The courts of major jurisdiction entertain cases involving delits. The courts of minor jurisdiction hear cases involving contraventions. Each is examined here separately.

It should be pointed out that guilty pleas are not accepted unless the offense is a minor one that could lead only to the sanction of a fine. This essentially eliminates the possibility of plea bargaining as it is usually applied in the United States. Confessions before trial and guilty pleas at trial are simply treated as part of the evidence in the dossier. Obviously, an uncontested trial is considerably shorter, for all it requires is a confirmation of accuracy of the defendant's admission by the president of the court.

A court of assize exists in each of the 96 departments of France. It handles cases involving crimes that have been remanded on indictment. The court holds a regular assize every three months, but supplementary sessions can be called for by either the president of the court or the procurator of the Republic. The court is presided over by the president, who is a judge from the regional court of appeals. In addition to the president, the bench is composed of two assesseurs, who are judges from either a court of appeals or a court of major jurisdiction. Before a trial begins in a court of assize, a number of preliminary procedural issues must be completed. The accused, who has been remanded to the jail where the assize is held, is brought before the president or one of the assesseurs at the start of the assize. The judge confirms the identity of the accused, and if counsel has not been secured, permits the accused to select counsel from a list of avocats provided by the local bar association. If the accused does not select counsel, the judge will appoint an avocat.

At least 24 hours before the start of a trial, the parties in the case exchange lists of witnesses they wish to have called. The names of experts who assisted in the investigation and who will be called are supplied, and a list of potential jurors for the session is provided. In exceptional cases in which the president is not satisfied with the original inquiry, the president can call for the suspension of the trial and order the reopening of the preliminary investigation. Either the president, an assesseur, or an investigating judge can undertake this investigation. This is considered an exceptional matter because the case was originally investigated by an investigating judge (if it was a serious crime) and then it was sent to the chamber of instruction of the regional court of appeal for a second review.

Finally, at the opening of a session of the court, potential jurors are selected through a lottery method from an annual list of jurors. This lottery selects 35 potential jurors and 10 potential alternate jurors. The next step is the actual selection of the jurors for a trial. Although this was explained in the previous section on the judiciary, it is worth summarizing briefly how a French jury is formed. It is significant to note that this is the only French court that utilizes a jury.

In a public session before the accused, the names of the potential jurors are placed in an urn. The names of nine jurors must be drawn unchallenged before the jury is considered formed. If it is anticipated that a trial will be quite lengthy, one or more alternate jurors are selected at this time. As the name of each juror is drawn, the procurator and counsel for the accused have the opportunity to challenge the juror. Under the French system, this is simply a verbal challenge; counsel does not state a reason. The procurator is allowed no more than four challenges, while counsel for the accused has five challenges. Once nine jurors are selected, they take their seats beside the judges and are sworn in by the president of the court.

While most trials are open to the public, Article 306 of the code states that the "trial shall be public unless the publicity would be dangerous for public order or morals." It also states that "the president may prohibit access to the courtroom to all or some minors." The civil party in a case can request that the trial be closed to the public. For the most part, these requests are made when the case involves rape, sexual attacks that included torture, or some other barbaric activity.

The president is a principal participant in the trial, with significant discretionary powers. Criminal investigations in France traditionally have emphasized a thorough written record of the preliminary investigation. Thus, as was the case in centuries past, a dossier remains an important feature of a trial. In a case involving a crime, a dossier is prepared under the direction of an investigating judge. Despite extensive pretrial preparation, the president still can order the appearance of extra witnesses that may be of assistance and can request the collection of new or additional evidence. The president's mission during a trial is to see that all avenues are explored with the aim of discovering the truth.

The assesseurs and jurors also have an important role, but they must obtain the permission of the president to ask questions of witnesses or the accused during a trial. The procurator, who is representing the interests of society while prosecuting the case, may pose questions directly. The accused or the accused's counsel asks questions through the president. In cases in which a victim sues for damages and the suit is entertained jointly with the criminal trial, the civil party (or victim) or counsel also can raise questions through the president.

The standard trial procedure in a court of assize includes the following steps:

1. With all the principal participants of the trial in attendance, the president will ask the clerk to read the names of witnesses who will be heard for each party in the case. The witnesses will then be taken to a separate room where they will remain until it is their turn to testify. If a witness does not appear at the trial, the court can issue an order to the police to bring the person to the trial. Unless there is a legitimate excuse for nonappearance, the witness is charged the costs of being brought to the court. The court may not require the police to find witnesses and bring them to court because the witnesses' earlier testimony is already a part of the dossier.

2. The clerk of the court reads the decree of remand of the accused to the court. This is essentially a summary of the dossier and includes: the allegations, evidence of witnesses, and the defendant's response to the witnesses' evidence, the personal history of the defendant, the results of any psychological or psychiatric examinations, and the criminal history of the defendant.

3. The accused is afforded the opportunity to make a statement. This is followed by questioning from the president and procurator directly. Assesseur and jurors must seek the president's permission to ask questions. Finally, counsel for the civil party and defense must submit their questions to the president.

4. Each witness is called to testify separately. Usually, the police case officer is called first to give an account of the investigation. This is often followed by an expert witness, such as a psychiatrist. Witnesses first take an oath and are then free to make their statement. Witnesses are not interrupted when making their statement, as long as the testimony is relevant to the facts in the case. This is followed by questioning from the principal participants in the case. After completing his or her testimony, each witness remains in the courtroom unless the president grants them a leave of absence.

5. At any time during the testimony, the president can order evidence for the case presented to the court or the person on the witness stand.
6. The civil party or his or her counsel is then heard.
7. The procurator presents arguments.
8. The accused or his or her counsel offers the defense.
9. The civil party and the procurator are allowed to reply to the defense.
10. The accused or his or her counsel is offered a final opportunity to respond.
11. The president declares the termination of the trial. There is no summing up of the charges or of the defense. The president then suspends the hearing, and the judges and jurors retire to the court's conference room for deliberations.
12. After the judges and jurors have deliberated, they vote on secret written ballots regarding the charges against the accused. Unmarked ballots are considered favorable to the accused. To affirm a person's guilt, a majority of eight votes must favor conviction.
13. Once convicted, the judges and jurors vote to determine an appropriate sanction. Again, ballots are used and a majority must agree to the punishment.
14. The court then reconvenes with the accused present and the pronouncement is read. If the accused is acquitted, he or she is immediately set free. If convicted, the accused is informed of the sanction and told of the privilege to petition for a review of the case to the Court of Cassation. Petitions for review will be explained later in the chapter.
15. If a civil claim has been introduced, the judges retire alone to decide that issue. If the civil party is awarded damages, the accused must pay the costs. According to Article 372, "[t]he civil party, in case of acquittal as in the case of absolution, may request reparation of damages resulting from the fault of the accused to the extent that it results from the facts that were the object of the accusation." Article 375 states:

    > The civil party who has obtained damages shall never be held for [court] costs. One who has lost shall be condemned to costs only if he himself initiated the prosecution. However, even in that case he may, with regard to the circumstances of the case, be relieved of all or part of the costs by special decision of the court, stating reasons.

When a person is accused of committing a delit, the case is tried in a local court of major jurisdiction. Courts of major jurisdiction are divided into three divisions: civil, juvenile, and correctional courts. It is the correctional court that handles the adjudication of delits committed by adults. With one exception, the procedures and the participants are the same as those found in a court of assize. The exception is that the court is composed of three magistrates: the president of the court and two judges. Lay jurors are not used to deliberate a case involving a delit. As was indicated earlier, it is now permissible for a single judge of this court to hear cases involving certain kinds of delits, such as traffic offenses, some forms of drug abuse, and the misuse of a credit card.

With the passage of the Security and Liberty Law of 1981, summary procedures are now permitted in the correctional court. This procedure usually is invoked when the evidence clearly points to the guilt of a defendant. For example, when a person is caught committing a delit, the procurator brings the defendant to trial while still in police custody. Thus, the defendant's first appearance in court also serves as his or her trial. Defendants do have a right to postpone the trial for up to five days in order to secure an avocat and to prepare a defense. On the one hand, this law is designed to assure swift and certain punishment. On the other hand, critics are concerned about the consequences this process has for the defendant's rights; because trials are quickly handled, there is often an absence of counsel for the accused (Tomlinson, 1983).

Once a judgment is rendered in a correctional court of a court of major jurisdiction, all the principal parties involved in the case have the right to appeal to the court of appeal in that district. Appeals are based on either factual errors or on a point of law. A three-judge panel, consisting of the president of the court and two conseillers, hears the appeal. An appeal consists of an oral hearing, at which time witnesses can be called, the accused questioned, and arguments presented by the principal parties in the case. If the appeal is based solely on a factual discrepancy, the court of appeal serves as the final arbiter in the case. If the issue on appeal involves a point of law, the person can request that the Court of Cassation review the matter.

Depending on who initiated the appeal and what issue is involved, the court has a number of options available in deciding the case. For example, Article 515 indicates that when an issue is:

1. On appeal by prosecuting counsel, the Court of Appeal may either confirm the judgment or reverse it all or in part in a sense favorable or unfavorable to the accused.

2. The Court of Appeal may not, on the appeal only of the accused, of the person civilly responsible, of the civil party, or of the insurer of one of these persons, aggravate the position of the appellant.

3. The civil party may not form any new claim in a case on appeal; however, he may ask for an increase of the damages for prejudice suffered since the decision at trial.

Moreover, the court also can conclude that no offense was committed in cases in which there is insufficient evidence. Thus, the prosecution would be dismissed. According to Article 518, "[i]f the judgment is annulled because the Court of Appeal decides that the act constitutes only a contravention, it shall pronounce the penalty and decide on the civil action, if that is appropriate." Finally, Article 519 states that "[i]f the judgment is annulled because the Court of Appeal decides that the act is of such a nature as to be followed by a felony penalty the court shall declare itself incompetent. It shall remand to official counsel [procurator] that he may proceed as he sees fit." This could lead to the accused being brought to trial in a court of assize.

Finally, people accused of committing a contravention have the case heard in one of the 473 local courts of minor jurisdiction. Courts of minor jurisdiction are divided into two divisions: a civil tribunal for civil claims and a police court for criminal matters. The procedures are similar to those found in courts of major jurisdiction, but because of the nature of the offenses, they are generally handled in a summary fashion. The police court differs from the other tribunals in that a single judge hears the case.

A majority of cases in this court never go to trial. The procurator simply attaches to the dossier a request for a particular disposition. If the judge and defendant agree to the disposition, which is usually a fine, the case is terminated. Of course, if a judge or defendant oppose the disposition, the case is bound over for trial.

Cases heard in this court also can be appealed. Appeals involving facts or law are sent to the court of appeal in the district. If the matter involves a point of law that is not resolved in the court of appeal, the person can petition the Court of Cassation to review the matter further.

Among the ordinary courts in the French judicial hierarchy, the Court of Cassation is the tribunal of last resort. The role of the court is to assure that judicial decisions are consistent throughout France and are in conformity with the law. Although the court can intervene at any time on any issue to assure conformity, intervention is usually limited to points of law. It does not, as a rule, consider disagreements that involve facts. Those issues are brought to a court of appeal, which serves as the final arbiter.

In order to have a case brought to the Court of Cassation, a person must petition for a review with the court that handed down the decision that is being disputed. Criminal cases would go to the criminal chamber of the court. The chamber would be composed of about seven judges, who entertain only the disputed part of the case. The court can either reject the petition and let the original decision stand, or quash the original decision and send the matter back to a new court at the same level at which the case was originally heard. This new court is known as the court of rehearing. When it hears the case, it can adopt the position of the Court of Cassation in the matter. In such instances the decision is final. However, the court of rehearing is not obliged to follow the Court of Cassation's directions. If a second petition to the Court of Cassation results from the court of rehearing's unwillingness to follow the high court's direction, then the matter comes before the full court. If the full court quashes the decision and sends the matter back to a second court of rehearing, that court must comply with the wishes of the Court of Cassation.

It should be pointed out that a petition filed by a person convicted of a crime can be supported by the procurator. This may appear odd because the procurator was attempting to convict the accused during the course of trial. Nevertheless, if a person is convicted and sentenced to a sanction that does not apply to the crime committed, the convicted person could petition for a review of the sentence (for it is an issue that involves a point of law). The procurator may join in the petition in the interests of society.

Critical Issues

Procurator The heightened concern for swift and certain punishment and the enactment of the Security and Liberty Law have enhanced considerably the discretionary authority of the procurator. This has raised concerns among critics of the system. Procurators have long dominated the investigative stage, because they initiate investigations by filing the charge. This procedure is followed even if the offense is serious enough to require that an investigating judge oversee the actual investigation.

Because the number of investigating judges is small, they tend to be overworked. Procurators increasingly have been circumventing the investigating judge in the name of efficiency by reducing charges from a crime to a delit. Although defendants can protest this action, it is often not in their best interests to do so. As a result of the reduction in charges, investigating judges handle less than 10 percent of the cases under investigation (Levy, 1993; Hodgson, 2005; Tomlinson, 1983).

Critics are concerned that the exercise of this kind of discretion puts the legal rights of the defendant at risk. As indicated earlier, defendants are afforded more procedural rights when an investigation is supervised by an investigating judge than when it is handled initially and solely by the police. Circumventing the investigating judge has been resolved to some extent with the passage of the Security and Liberty Law, for this legislation changed the status of some offenses from a crime to a delit.

Another principal concern about procuratorial discretion involves the introduction of summary procedures in courts of major jurisdiction. Again, the defendant's legal rights are placed at risk. Summary procedures were introduced in these courts through the Security and Liberty Law, which was designed to assure swift and certain punishment, particularly when the guilt of a defendant was overwhelming. Critics argue that the swiftness of this process may inhibit a fair trial, especially if the defendant is pressured in some way against securing legal counsel.

With the issuance of the Truche Report in 1997 (mentioned earlier), procurators have once again been the subject of scrutiny. Of particular concern was the extent to which politicians may influence decisions of procurators. While procurators are trained as judges and considered part of the judiciary, they nevertheless are members of the Public Ministry and thus accountable to the Ministry of Justice. In recent years, a number of political corruption cases have been brought to the attention of procurators, in which they ruled that no further action was necessary. These cases are seen as illustrations of politicians interfering with the judicial process. These cases should not be judged in isolation, but rather considered in the larger context of procurators recommending no further action in cases. In 1995, for example, 5.2 million offenses were brought to the attention of procurators assigned to the courts of major jurisdiction. In one-half of these cases, a suspect was named in the case, yet 80 percent of the total number of cases (4.2 million) were classified as warranting no further action (Elliott and Vernon, 2000).

The policy of no further action has led to calls that the discretionary authority of procurators should be curbed. As mentioned earlier, some critics have argued that the introduction of the principle of mandatory prosecution, which is found in a number of civil law countries, would eliminate the concerns of procurators exercising too much discretion. The Truche Report did not support this idea. It favored retaining procuratorial discretion, for it is illustrative of the independent role that the judiciary plays in the judicial process. It did recommend the establishment of a right to appeal a decision of no further action. A number of recommendations of the Truche Report that would retain the independence of the procurators but also place a check on their discretion were submitted in the form of new legislation. Because of the ongoing concerns of a number of political factions, it has not been enacted into law.

Victim Assistance Another critical issue involves victim assistance. It has already been pointed out that a victim can sue for damages and that the suit can be entertained during a criminal trial. Although this is a progressive procedure, it has flaws. For example, the court is responsible only for enforcing the penal sanction, not the damages awarded a victim. Most damages, therefore, are not paid by the offender because the offender is indigent, refuses to pay, or possibly has not been identified.

Although very little research has been conducted on victimization in France, successive governments have taken steps to address the problem. The first state compensation law was adopted in 1977. It was initially designed for victims of bodily injury but has since been extended to include victims of burglary. Originally, the state was viewed as a secondary source for compensation. The victim was supposed to exhaust efforts at securing damages from the offender. Given the difficulty victims have had with collecting damages, another improvement in the law enables victims of serious bodily injury to collect compensation directly from the government. Legislation was passed in 1986 to create a special system for granting compensation to victims of terrorism.

In addition, the National Council for the Prevention of Delinquency was created in 1983. It has corresponding local councils at the department and municipal levels. There are presently more than 413 local associations. A National Institute has been established to train volunteers in victim assistance. The hope is that this training will be extended to include professionals in the field, such as police, judges, medical personnel, and social workers. The work of victim assistance illustrates the efforts to decentralize governmental administration in France. In addition to the formation of local associations, funding for these programs comes from the national ministries of Justice, Women's Rights, and Welfare, as well as from local grants (Piffaut, 1989).

CORRECTIONS

At the end of World War II, the Ministry of Justice turned its attention to reforming the correctional system through the introduction of a progressive regimen. The plan called for the use of a minimum amount of force when handling inmates and the establishment of treatment programs that would be both effective and humane. The scheme was directed at the entire prison population, including long-term prisoners. This progressive regimen was an indication of France's commitment to a rehabilitation scheme that was to serve as the principal function of the correctional system.

The regimen was composed of five phases. The first phase lasted nine months, during which time the inmate was kept in maximum-security isolation. The inmate was interviewed and evaluated by correctional counselors during this phase. At the end of this period, the inmate was either advanced to the second phase, transferred out of the progressive regimen, or retained in the first phase for further observation. Those who advanced to the second phase would continue to eat and sleep in isolation, but they would be given a work assignment to be performed with other inmates. At that time, the inmates were expected to work at some task, however menial, within the institution. This phase would continue for six to 12 months. The third phase, which lasted for approximately one year, kept the inmate in a separate cell during sleeping hours but allowed all other activities to be carried out in a group environment. Phase four was designed to allow the inmate to work in the private sector while continuing to reside at the prison. This phase could be in effect for up to six years. Finally, the fifth phase was the conditional release of the inmate without supervision, in which the person would be placed on parole for a period of one to three years and then be discharged (Conrad, 1965).

Attempts were also made to build new facilities or redesign old ones to meet the needs of the progressive regimen. Another concern centered on improving recruiting and training of the staff working in these facilities. Because of the lack of funding and—according to some critics—inadequate commitment, they were largely carried out in a piecemeal and sometimes insufficient fashion.

The next significant innovation to the correctional system was the passage of the Code of Criminal Procedure in 1958. That code legally created a new position that has had an important impact on the decision-making process of the release of inmates from French penal institutions. (Actually, the position was not new, because a 1945 regulation originally introduced the concept.) The position was that of the judge for the application of punishment, more commonly referred to as the post-sentencing judge. Like the investigating judge, this official is selected from the ranks of judges of the magistracy and serves a three-year term in this capacity.

With this change in the code, the judiciary formally accepted a responsibility that initially was the correctional administrator's, that is, determining the length of conditions and the appropriate conditions for a person's incarceration. Prison administrators opposed the concept of the post-sentencing judge from the beginning, on the grounds that judges were not adequately informed about the prison environment and that the scheme would reduce the role of correctional personnel. The role of the post-sentencing judge has received a good deal of attention over the years; its present status will be discussed shortly.

As was the case with many countries committed to a rehabilitation regimen, the French began to question its utility. By the early 1960s, greater attention was directed at making correctional institutions more secure. Although treatment programs were not totally abandoned, they were placed in a new perspective because of the unimpressive results of the existing rehabilitation programs. Moreover, a number of prison disturbances during the first half of the 1970s drew attention to the plight of the correctional community. The result was a series of reforms that were largely responsible for making the prison system what it is today.

According to the Ministry of Justice, the mission of the French penal system is "monitoring individuals placed under judicial authority and preparing them for their future social rehabilitation." This position is similar to that of many countries. Although this sentencing philosophy expounds multiple purposes for punishment, in the years since 1975, and particularly after 1980, much emphasis has been placed on protecting society and deterring known offenders. Thus, the French have introduced a "get tough" policy on criminals.

Although France has a much lower rate of violent crime than the United States, such crime has been increasing nevertheless. This has caused alarm among the public as well as among officials of the French criminal justice system. The Security and Liberty Law of 1981 had important implications for the correctional system in light of the rise in crime. Its principal goal was to assure swift and certain punishment for those found guilty of criminal offenses. For example, it called for increasing the certainty of sanctioning recidivists. In the past, a person was labeled a recidivist if he or she committed the same offense within five years. Under the Security and Liberty Law, the recidivist label would apply to offenders who committed a similar type of offense, in particular, crimes against the person and property. The law also called for minimum mandatory terms of imprisonment for certain offenses. In cases in which the maximum sentence was 10 years or more, a minimum sentence of two years was imposed. For offenses in which the maximum was less than 10 years, a minimum sentence of one year was called for. Finally, the use of suspended sentences and probation was reduced.

As a result of the changes in both attitude and legislation, the population in French correctional facilities, especially the jails, has dramatically increased. Between January 1975 and January 1995, the number of offenders incarcerated rose from 26,032 to 51,623, and in May of 1995, it reached a high of 55,479. In 1997, on average, there were more than 58,000 people incarcerated. During the early years of the period 1975 to 1981, the prison population increased because more offenders were being sentenced to a period of incarceration. From 1981 to 1988, the explanation for the size of the population was attributed to longer sentences of incarceration. Since 1988, longer sentences of incarceration continue to play a significant role in the size of the prison population. Two kinds of offenses—drug trafficking and breaches in the immigration laws—have had a significant role to play in the size of the prison population (Kensey and Tournier, 1997).

On January 1, 2005, the population of French prisons was 59,197. Approximately 66 percent had been sentenced to a term of incarceration, while 34 percent were awaiting trial and had not been convicted of anything. This clearly illustrates the French commitment to protecting society, irrespective of whether a person has yet been found guilty. Of the 39,041 convicted prisoners, 30 percent were serving a term of less than one year; 22.5 percent a term of between one and three years; 12.4 percent a period between three and five years; and 35.7 percent a term of more than five years. Of those receiving a long-term period of incarceration, 1.4 percent received a life sentence (Ministry of Justice,

2006). Although there has been a dramatic increase in incarcerating offenders, it must be placed in a French context, for they are still committed to utilizing noninstitutional sanctions.

The profile of the typical inmate is not surprising. In the prison population, of those sentenced and awaiting trial on January 1, 2005, male inmates represented more than 96 percent of the total population. Approximately 45 percent were under the age of 30, and more than 27 percent were between the ages of 30 and 39. French citizens made up more than 78 percent of the prison population, while more than 21 percent were represented by other nationalities (Ministry of Justice, 2006). The number of foreign prisoners has increased significantly in recent years. Part of the reason has to do with the fact that these offenders are less likely to receive a suspended sentence. The nature of their offenses, such as illegally entering the country, trafficking in drugs, and handling stolen goods, influence the decision to impose a period of incarceration (Kensey and Tournier, 1997).

As was mentioned in the last section, a new Penal Code was introduced in the 1990s. After three decades of work on the project, the code was implemented in 1994, thus replacing the much revised but archaic Napoleonic code of 1810. Unlike the old code, the new code does not stipulate a maximum or a fixed minimum sentence for all offenses. Although the new code often has increased the severity of the sanctions that can be imposed on an offender, it is important to note that imprisonment is no longer considered the principal method of punishment. Thus, judicial discretion has been enhanced.

The new code also recognizes degrees of culpability in several contexts. For example, it acknowledges more modern views regarding psychiatric disorders. While a person's diminished mental capacity may reduce his or her legal responsibility, it does not automatically eliminate it, as was the case with the old code. In addition, the old code did not draw a distinction between premeditated murder and second-degree murder; the sentence for both was life imprisonment. With the new code, premeditated murder is punishable with life imprisonment, while a person found guilty of second-degree murder could receive a 30-year sentence. Finally, members of organized crime are subject to harsher sanctions than non–gang members who commit the same offense.

The new code acknowledges the emergence of either totally new crimes or variations on old forms of deviance that have received a good deal of attention in the latter half of the twentieth century. Crimes against humanity and breaches of human rights are prominently featured. A significant innovation is the establishment of principles of liability for corporations, which was totally absent in the old code. Offenses associated with organized crime (such as racketeering) and terrorist activities are also acknowledged. Finally, environmental crimes are included, and sexual harassment is recognized as an offense.

The French have divided their criminal offenses into three categories. Crimes are the most serious offenses and can be punished by life imprisonment or a considerable number of years of imprisonment. The French abolished capital punishment in 1981. The principal purpose for sanctioning people who commit crimes in France is their removal from society. Delits are less serious offenses that are punishable by six months to 10 years of incarceration. The purpose of this type of sentence is to educate or coerce the offender. The new code raised the maximum penalty from five to 10 years; it also increased the minimum term of incarceration from two to six months. The justification offered for increasing the minimum term was that short periods of incarceration have failed to either intimidate or rehabilitate. Finally, because the new code abolished imprisonment for petty offenses, the sanctions prescribed for contraventions are either a fine or a noncustodial sentence. The goals of these punishments are to coerce people into obeying the law and to demonstrate to the public that justice is being done.

Organization of the Penitentiary Administration

It should come as no surprise that the correctional system is administered by a highly centralized national bureaucracy (see Figure 2.4). The most perplexing characteristic of the system is that although the French are often at the forefront of creating new ideas for corrections, they leave the actual development of the idea to practitioners in other countries. Parole is the most notable example of this phenomenon. Although its origins are traced to nineteenth-century France, the French did little in the way of experimenting and expanding its use until quite recently. The

Figure 2.4

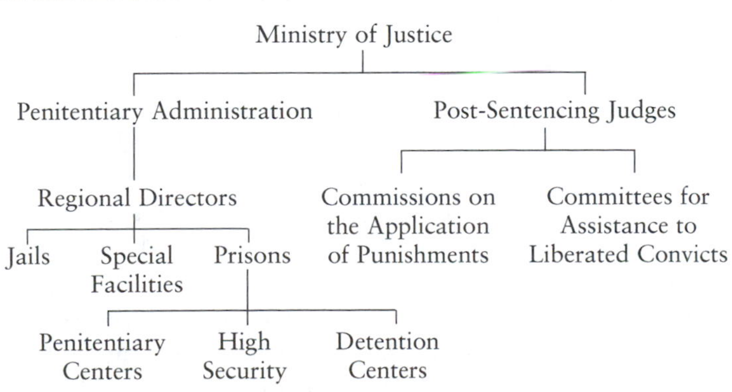

one possible exception to this trend is the extent to which they have created the role of the post-sentencing judge.

One possible reason for the apparent inability to follow through on their own creative ideas is that the French have lagged behind other countries in the study of criminology, despite the fact that they have established several institutes for that purpose. This can be attributed to both insufficient funding for research and a lack of interest in the study of criminal law. Another reason may be the traditionally low level of crime. In recent years, however, property crimes and certain types of offenses against the person have increased significantly, especially among the juvenile population. As a result, the French have attempted to improve or reform their correctional institutions, with a tendency to borrow quite heavily from the experiences of other countries.

Ministry of Justice The Ministry of Justice is responsible for the administration of the correctional system. It is responsible for the legal establishment that sentences people to imprisonment, and it coordinates the system for care and treatment of the offender.

Penitentiary Administration The Penitentiary Administration is the central bureaucracy (accountable to the minister of justice) that manages the administration of the entire correctional system, which includes the probation service. The central administration is responsible for the recruitment, training, and welfare of the personnel who work within the system. Correctional personnel are recruited civil servants and must sit for a competitive examination to qualify for the various levels within the organizational hierarchy. Personnel are trained at the National School for Penitentiary Administration. People initially pursuing a career as a guard must first pass an entrance examination that is designed to assess general knowledge and physical and psychological compatibility. If successful, the recruit would participate in an eight-month training program. The training would include theoretical courses at the school and an internship component at various correctional facilities. Traditionally, people were promoted from within the ranks of the French prison service. In recent years, however, university graduates have been recruited to enter the service at administrative levels within the bureaucracy.

To facilitate the work of the central administration, the prison service is divided into nine regions. Regional directors and prison wardens help to determine and coordinate the policies and procedures of their correctional facilities in accordance with the wishes of the central administration. Within any region, one is apt to find several different types of correctional units.

In addition, two centralized authorities have responsibility for inspecting the French correctional system. The Inspectorate for the Prison Services is part of the central bureaucracy. It performs five tasks: (1) investigating major disturbances, incidents, or escapes, (2) conducting routine inspections, (3) reviewing the security plans of the facilities, (4) examining system-wide correctional functions, and (5) overseeing the handling of probationers. The Inspectorate for Social Concerns has oversight responsibilities for the health of the inmates and the overall cleanliness of the correctional facilities. This Inspectorate reports to the minister of health (Vagg, 1994).

Types of Institutions The French have developed three general kinds of correctional facilities: jails, special institutions, and prisons. Each is designed for a particular type of offender. Jails are found throughout the country in close proximity to the courts of major jurisdiction. They are used to detain both the accused before trial as well as convicted offenders whose term of incarceration does not exceed one year. In comparison to most jails in the United States, French jails are small. They were originally built to accommodate 20 to 40 inmates, and the cells were originally designed for single occupancy. Because of the number of inmates being detained in these facilities, there is often serious overcrowding, with two or three people placed in a cell.

French jails have been criticized for many of the same weaknesses identified in the American and British systems. For example, the development of intensive rehabilitation programs has been hampered by the transient nature of the jail population. The French are making an effort to resolve another perennial problem by separating younger offenders from older recidivists. In addition, attempts at work release programs have proved somewhat unsuccessful because of the scarcity of jobs.

Special institutions are established for offenders who are also suffering from a physical handicap or a behavioral disorder that falls short of the legal definition of insanity. These facilities include health centers existing within correctional institutions or separate facilities such as sanatoriums or psychiatric hospitals. The French also have created special units for the chronic recidivist. This measure is referred to as penal guardianship.

Prisons are further subdivided into three categories: detention centers, penitentiary centers, and high-security facilities. A nationally centralized classification unit at Fresnes carries out diagnostic testing to determine where the convicted offender should serve time. Each institution, whether a detention center, penitentiary center or high-security facility, offers variations on the prison regimen designed to meet the diverse needs of the inmate population. For example, most high-security prisons follow a traditional model regarding inmate rules. Some have special security centers for the more dangerous offenders.

Detention centers have adopted a collaborative model intended to enhance the relationship between inmates and staff. Detention centers afford the offender greater degrees of freedom and individual responsibility, with both closed and open types of facilities. It should be noted that not all offenders are processed through the central classification unit at Fresnes. Inmates who serve a fairly short term of incarceration are classified at the local jail where they were held during the course of the trial.

Irrespective of which type of prison a person is sent to, one of the missions of the penal system is to prepare inmates for life outside the correctional facility. This is achieved through various activities. For example, prisoners have a right to work. Although work is voluntary, it enables the inmate to earn money. This kind of employment can occur within or outside the prison. Another activity is education or vocational training. It comes as no surprise that the illiteracy rate is higher in prisons than within the general population. The Ministry of Justice and the Ministry of Education have established agreements that enable inmates to pursue a wide variety of educational programs from literacy courses to preparation for admission to universities. The Ministry of Social Affairs, Employment, and Solidarity are active in providing inmates with vocational training programs. The Ministry of Culture assists with providing workshops in various fields of the arts. Public libraries assist with the operation of prison libraries. Finally, there are sports facilities located at almost 200 correctional institutions.

It was mentioned above that there has been a serious problem with overcrowding in French jails. The issue of overcrowding has also impacted the prison system. In 2002, the Ministry of Justice began a significant building project to address overcrowding in the prisons. A total of 27 facilities have either been built or are under construction. Of these, seven are specifically designed for young offenders.

Judge for the Application of Punishment With the passage of the Code of Criminal Procedure in 1958, the judge for the application of punishment (more commonly referred to as the post-sentencing judge) was given the responsibility of controlling the post-sentencing phase of the criminal process. The rationale for this innovation was based on the argument that both a judicial decision arrived at during the course of a trial and the implementation of that decision in a penitentiary were part of the same process. The thinking went that it was illogical and possibly harmful to disrupt the continuity of the decision by placing it in the hands of two distinct authorities. The post-sentencing judge was the French prescription for assuring that there would be continuity in the execution and application of the judicial decision.

The post-sentencing judge is a regular member of the branch of the magistracy that adjudicates cases in court. He or she is selected for a three-year term by the chief judge in a district of a court of major jurisdiction (although the nominee can refuse the appointment). The number of judges per district assigned to this special responsibility varies according to the type of correctional institutions found in each particular district. Thus, French judges serve the courts in one of four capacities: investigating judge, liberty and detention judge, trial judge, or post-sentencing judge. When not carrying out special sentencing responsibilities, the post-sentencing judge sits in a court and adjudicates cases with other judges.

Most who comment on the role of the post-sentencing judge have described it as having a dual purpose. One is administrative in nature, for the judge is part of the correctional institution's oversight committee. In this capacity, the judge receives copies of all instructions sent by the central prison authorities to the prisons and jails in his or her jurisdiction. He or she is informed of all changes in disciplinary and security matters and is kept apprised of all disciplinary actions. He or she is also expected to keep abreast of the conditions of the physical plant, inmate safety and security, and various rehabilitation programs. Additionally, the judge must visit the institution once a month and meet with individual inmates on request. Decisions that pertain to the management of the prison are not made by the judge, for he or she has no authority over the daily operations of the institution. Such responsibilities are left to the regional directors and wardens of the various correctional facilities.

The other responsibility of a post-sentencing judge is distinctly judicial in nature. It is in this context that the significant role of the magistracy's relationship to the correctional community becomes apparent. The judge has the authority to alter the inmate's sentence and to influence the individual's regimen. This is a central feature of the rehabilitation process for most inmates.

The role of the post-sentencing judge has been the subject of much criticism. Correctional administrators have long opposed the position on the grounds that although judges are not truly knowledgeable of the work in the correctional community, they are empowered to make decisions that influence the inmate population. Inmates, as well as some former post-sentencing judges, complained that judges are restricted in altering an inmate's sentence by the fact that they are largely dependent on information provided by the prison authorities. Some trial judges have opposed the independent nature of the office. Their complaint was that the post-sentencing judge's decision to change an offender's sentence (originally imposed by the trial judge) was not subject to appeal or review as was the case with the original sentence.

Because of adverse criticism from so many quarters, interest in serving as a post-sentencing judge declined. Trial judges who did accept the position were often viewed by their colleagues as "second-class" members of the magistracy. It was suggested that the system could be improved if the role and standing of the post-sentencing judge was altered somewhat. In particular, it was suggested that a method of reviewing the judge's decisions should be established (Chemithe and Strasburg, 1978).

As a result of these criticisms, the role of the post-sentencing judge has been clarified through a revision in the code. Article 722 of the Code of Criminal Procedure explains the principal duties.

> At each penitentiary establishment, the judge for the application of punishments shall determine for each convict the principal modalities of penitentiary treatment. In accordance with the limits and conditions provided by law, the judge shall accord placements on the outside, semiliberty, reductions, fractionings and suspensions of penalties, authorizations for leaves under escort, permissions for leave, [and] parole, or the judge shall bring the matter before the court competent to arrange the execution of the punishment. Except in emergency, the judge shall rule after advice from the commission on the application of punishments.

The commission on the application of punishments will be explained shortly. The code also states that "[e]xcept in emergencies the judge for the application of punishments shall also give his or her opinion, on the transfer of convicts from one establishment to another." Finally, in a decree issued in 1986, the status of the post-sentencing judge was raised to that of a specialist. It is hoped that this enhanced status will encourage more judges to serve in this capacity.

There are five principal methods by which a post-sentencing judge can act to alter an inmate's sanction of incarceration. Parole (traditionally called "conditional liberty") at one time could be granted only by the minister of justice. In 1972, the post-sentencing judge was delegated complete authority to issue a parole for inmates serving a term of three years or less. As approximately two-thirds of all sentences fall within this range, this first method was considered a significant change. For people serving a longer term, the judge may recommend parole but must have it approved by the minister of justice. Parole is usually granted to first-time offenders after one-half of the term is served, to recidivists after two-thirds of the term is served, to chronic recidivists after three-fourths of the term is served, and to people receiving a life sentence after 15 years (Chemithe and Strasburg, 1978). It is alleged that this change has enabled the system to work more effectively. This method of early release thus has been utilized more frequently.

The 1972 legislation that introduced changes in parole created a second method for reducing time served: sentence reduction. Each year, an inmate's disciplinary record is reviewed by the post-sentencing judge. In most cases, the judge reduces the person's sentence for good behavior. Reductions average about seven days per month for a sentence that is under one year, while inmates serving longer sentences have had as much as three months per year eliminated from their original sentence. Two groups of people, however, are excluded from this scheme: people sentenced to less than three months and chronic recidivists. A sentence is not necessarily a permanent reward for good conduct. A judge can retract all or part of the reduction if the inmate displays recalcitrant conduct in the future (Chemithe and Strasburg, 1978).

The third method, work release, is a system that allows the inmate to work outside the confines of the correctional institution. The nonworking hours are spent at a halfway house or a local jail. The costs of maintaining the inmate in the institution are deducted from his or her wages. Work release is usually granted to people during the last six to 12 months of their sentence. People who are about to be released on parole are also eligible for work release. This is usually done to test their ability to cooperate with the authorities under this regimen.

The fourth method, the granting of leaves from prison, originally was used for emergency purposes, such as an illness or death in the family. Since 1975, the scheme has been expanded to test the inmate's ability to function outside the confines of the prison for short periods of time. Inmates who are housed in detention centers and who have served one-third of their sentence are eligible for leaves of up to 10 days each year. Inmates who are being held in more secure facilities and who have approximately three years remaining on their sentence are granted three days' leave per year.

The fifth and final method, temporary suspension, has been available since 1975 but is used infrequently. It permits the judge to suspend the sentence of a person convicted of a misdemeanor for up to three months in cases of serious personal emergencies. An alternative to this scheme is to have the inmate continue to serve part of the sentence on weekends. In extraordinary situations, in which the request is for a period longer than three months, the judge's order must be approved by a court of major jurisdiction. The time suspended does not count toward the completion of the sentence.

Commission on the Application of Punishments The post-sentencing judge, though afforded a good deal of discretion in altering an inmate's sentence, is not totally independent. This point was reinforced in the aforementioned reference to Article 722 of the Code of Criminal Procedure. Judges are assisted in their work by a commission on the application of punishments, of which the judge serves as the president. Thus, it is a commission that annually reviews each case. A commission is created for each prison. Members include the warden, a procurator, the personnel director of the prison, the chief of supervision of the prison, a prison educator, a psychiatrist, a social worker, and a doctor. The post-sentencing judge also can appoint other people to serve on a temporary basis at his or her discretion.

Noninstitutional Sanctions

The French have been slow in developing noninstitutional sanctions. In recent years, they have explored alternatives to incarceration, partly because of the high cost of imprisonment. Currently, there are four methods for imposing a noninstitutional sentence.

A simple suspension is designed for the offender who has not been sentenced to imprisonment during the preceding five years. Article 735 of the Code of Criminal Procedure states that "[i]f the convict benefiting from the simple suspension of imprisonment does not commit, during a period of five years after the sentence, a common law felony or delit followed by a new sentence of either a felony penalty or a correctional prison penalty without suspension, the suspended conviction shall be considered void." The offender is still obliged to pay any damages or court costs rendered by the court.

The use of the suspended sentence received a good deal of adverse publicity in France, especially when a violent offender was freed through a suspended sentence and subsequently committed a second violent offense. The Security and Liberty Law of 1981 reduced the use of the suspended sentence. Now, anyone who is convicted of a violent crime must serve a minimum term in prison. Recidivists are no longer eligible for a suspended sentence. Civil libertarians opposed this measure for obvious reasons, and a large segment of the French trial judges opposed its passage on the grounds that it would curtail the independence of the judiciary.

A suspension of the sentence with probation is another alternative. What is required in such instances is that the offense is minor and the probability exists that the offender will not commit another offense. This is based on both the offender's previous record, if any, and his or her conduct during the course of the proceedings. The offender is placed on probation for a period of three to five years. If the person is not convicted of another offense, the sentence is nullified.

Each court of major jurisdiction has a committee devoted to assistance for liberated convicts. The committee is composed of probation officers, educators, and volunteers. Before 1986, the post-sentencing judge was the president of this committee. Today, that is no longer the case. Nevertheless, the work of the probation department is under the control of a post-sentencing judge. While a probation director is assigned the responsibility of organizing and managing the service, it is the post-sentencing judge who assigns to probation officers specific offenders who have been placed on probation, parole, or some other form of noninstitutional supervision. Probation officers attempt to assist the offender in resocialization efforts and are required to keep the judge apprised of the individual's progress. Whereas a post-sentencing judge has the authority to revoke a parole because of violations of the agreement, only a trial judge can revoke a probation order. A post-sentencing judge who thinks that the probation should be revoked must submit such a request for approval to the trial judge that originally ordered the probation.

The newest noninstitutional sanction is the community service order. Introduced in 1983, it involves performing 40 to 240 hours of unpaid work over a period of time that is not to exceed 18 months. It is designed for offenders who have a very limited criminal history and who have not been convicted of a serious offense in the previous five years. The order can be applied to adults and juveniles above the age of 16.

A community service order can be imposed along with other sanctions or used as a substitute for another form of punishment. Unlike other forms of sanctioning, the offender must agree to community service. This is required in order to comply with the European Convention on Human Rights, which states that a person cannot be "required to perform forced or compulsory labor." The work is performed for either a public organization, a public institution, or an approved association that has a social function. Much of the actual work involves the maintenance of the environment, buildings, or equipment of the organization. Although a trial judge imposes this sanction, it is the responsibility of a post-sentencing judge to oversee its execution.

Initially, the community service order was not utilized to any significant degree. In 1985, only 2 percent of those sentenced received such a sanction. Among the reasons cited for the paucity of its use were the difficulty in finding work, the absence of a work aptitude among the offenders, and the belief among judges that it be applied in a restrictive fashion. It appears that the community service order was used more often as a substitute sanction for driving offenses than for any other type of offense (Ezratty-Bader, 1989; Pradel, 1987). This view has changed significantly in recent years, as community service orders represent more than 16 percent of the noninstitutional sanctions.

Fines are another type of noninstitutional sanction. A fine can be imposed upon people who commit either a delit or a contravention. Fines can be imposed alone or along with another institutional or noninstitutional sanction.

JUVENILE JUSTICE

The French usually cite 1945 as the year in which they embarked upon a plan to develop a new juvenile justice system. Most authorities attribute the advent of this movement to the fact that the Ministry of Justice took over the administration of the correctional system from the Ministry of the Interior. Prior to that date, the treatment of juveniles was undertaken in the penitentiary setting.

Once the Ministry of Justice was charged with this new responsibility, change was in the offing. At first, the advances were largely in the areas of establishing new institutions and procedures in the processing of delinquents. The implementation of changes in the manner of treating juveniles was considerably slower. It has been suggested that this was attributed to the fact that France was still a rural society after the war (Poullain and Cirba, 1976). People were content to believe that social stability would return to both the home and personal lives of people during the postwar period. Moreover, they believed that there would be a resurgence in the adherence to and applicability of the Catholic ethics that had been the cornerstone of the rural social setting. This was not forthcoming.

As France became more urbanized and industrialized, the old rural values were swept aside. Changes in the social structure occurred more rapidly than ever before. Although the economic and social fortunes of a large segment of the population improved, this was accompanied by new forms of social maladjustment. It was not until the early 1950s that attempts were made to develop new methods of treatment and intervention for the delinquent youth.

Since the 1960s, the French have experienced an increase in juvenile crime. It was especially acute during the 1980s. Property crimes continue to lead the list of offenses, but there has been a marked rise in the number of violent offenses. The Ministry of the Interior has estimated that the number of juvenile delinquents has risen from 75,846 in 1974 to 180,382 in 2000. Moreover, 21 percent of all crime is attributed to them (Gendrot, in Muncie and Goldson, 2006). The juvenile justice system that was established after the war is the principal mechanism mandated to cope with this issue.

The juvenile justice system is based on two central premises. The juvenile judge is expected to be actively involved in the entire process, from the initial contact with the system through termination of the treatment program. The other premise emphasizes the importance of treatment, rather than punishment, for the delinquent offender. Therefore, the French juvenile justice system promotes a paternalistic social welfare-oriented approach to intervention. While principles of due process often are ignored in the application of this process, one must keep in mind that the juvenile is usually an active participant in decisions that relate to the treatment process (Hackler et al., 1986).

The French are committed, at least in theory, to a treatment model for juvenile delinquents. The model is based on four principles: (1) treatment must be individualized if the person is going to be stimulated to change in personality; (2) treatment should occur in an environment with which the juvenile is familiar (there is a recognition that a person may have to be temporarily removed from his or her environment, but attempts should not be made to sever established relationships);

(3) treatment must be available on a continuous basis if there is going to be a sincere commitment to transforming the delinquent's personality; and (4) treatment must be flexible. The judge as well as the staff of the rehabilitation program should be in frequent contact with one another to assure that the needs of the individual, rather than the goals of a particular institution, are being met. Thus, the institutional status quo should not be defended or justified at the expense of curtailing innovative programs or treatment methods (Poullain and Cirba, 1976).

Juvenile Courts

Before describing the jurisdiction of the juvenile courts and the personnel involved with the juvenile justice system, it is important to explain how juveniles are classified according to their age and level of criminal responsibility.

Responsibility of Juveniles In determining the age of criminal responsibility, the French take into consideration the age of the offender and the type of offense committed. The age of full adult responsibility in France is 18. If a person is between the ages of 16 and 17, a full penal sanction can be imposed if the judge deems it appropriate under the circumstances of the case, which usually focus solely on the type of offense committed.

Juveniles between the ages of 13 and 15 can also receive a penal sanction if the offense is serious, but the Penal Code requires that the sentence be shortened in these cases. Usually, the length of incarceration is one-half of that which could normally be imposed on an adult. In most cases, however, the judge attempts to impose a short noninstitutional sentence whenever possible.

Until recently, children under 13 years of age were protected from any type of criminal proceedings; they were dealt with informally by social welfare agencies or the juvenile court. This does not preclude the possibility that civil proceedings could be initiated with the purpose of protecting the child. In 2002, however, the law was changed that permitted, under exceptional circumstances, the imposition of a penal sanction on a child as young as 10.

Personnel Two kinds of courts in France's judicial hierarchy specialize in juvenile matters. Young people between the ages of 16 and 17 who have been charged with committing a crime have the case adjudicated in the court of assize for juveniles. This court of assize is composed of a judge from the district court of appeals, two juvenile judges, and nine jurors. It was pointed out earlier how a magistrate of the bench could specialize in certain judicial activities by becoming an investigating judge, a liberty and detention judge, or a post-sentencing judge. A fourth method of specialization is to become a juvenile judge. It is from the ranks of these juvenile judges that the rest of the bench is formed to hear cases in a court of assize for juveniles.

The juvenile judges not only work in this area full time, but they are also given special training to prepare them to carry out this responsibility. One of the criticisms of the French system, however, is the concern that the National School for the Judiciary does not offer enough training for these judges. Attempts are apparently under way to reform the curriculum and to offer a continuing education program for juvenile judges.

The other court that handles juvenile matters is the juvenile court, which is part of the court of major jurisdiction. This court is composed of one juvenile judge and two lay assessors. The assessors are citizens who have indicated a special interest in juvenile problems. Young people under the age of 18 who have either committed a delit or a contravention, or are considered in need of help, have the matter resolved in a juvenile court. The latter group are often victims of a noncriminal social condition beyond their control—an obvious example being child neglect. Thus, the juvenile court has both criminal and civil jurisdiction in matters involving young people.

The procurator is another person involved with juvenile matters. Responsible for initiating a public prosecution when a criminal offense has been committed, the procurator bases his or her decision upon either a police report or his or her own preliminary investigation into the matter. It already has been illustrated that procurators have an organizational hierarchy that in many respects roughly mirrors that of the courts. Unlike judges, who may specialize in juvenile matters, procurators do not complement that system with specialists of their own. This has been identified by some as an organizational problem facing the administration of the juvenile justice system. At this time, however, there does not appear to be any attempt to change the status quo. The reason for the lack of reform in this area may be attributed to the dominant role that the juvenile judge plays in the entire process. In addition to judges and procurators, probation officers and specialists who work for the various welfare agencies that provide treatment services for delinquents also have a significant role to play in the process of handling delinquent youths.

The procedures used in the courts of assize for juveniles are the same as those for adults who are tried in the regular courts of assize. The procedures in the juvenile courts are not as formal because the charges against the delinquent are not deemed as serious. Moreover, the philosophy of the juvenile court is similar to that found in some other countries; the court perceives its main task as determining an appropriate form of treatment for the child rather than establishing the offender's guilt.

Therefore, in civil and criminal cases in which the offense is not considered serious, the proceedings take on a protective appearance. What is deemed to be in the best interests of the child, at least from the court's point of view, is considered of paramount importance. In most cases, the juvenile is an active participant in determining the court's ultimate decision. The inquisitorial style of formal and informal proceedings allows the judge to play an active role in both questioning and negotiating with the juvenile as to what is in his or her best interests (Hackler et al., 1986; Hackler and Garapon, 1986).

The child and his or her parents or guardians must attend the juvenile hearing. In addition to the regular members of the court (judges, jurors or lay assessors, a procurator, defense counsel, and a probation officer), other experts that have knowledge of or expertise in the case (such as psychologists, teachers, and social workers) can be called to assist the court in the determination of the best course of action for the juvenile's welfare.

Disposition

How a case is disposed of is dependent on the nature of the offense and which agents of the justice system are involved in the case. If the police are initially involved, they can simply record the offense and then release the juvenile. If the offense is significant, the police turn the matter over to a procurator, because only the procurator can file formal charges. The police can detain a juvenile for up to 24 hours in a police cell. The period of detention for drug cases is extended to 48 hours.

Once the procurator receives a case, he or she can drop it, send it on to a juvenile judge, or—if the case involves a serious crime—request that an investigating judge conduct an investigation. A procurator may suggest that a juvenile be detained but does not have the authority to issue such an order. Only a juvenile judge or a liberty and detention judge has this authority. A juvenile who is detained would be placed in a juvenile wing of an adult prison.

Most delinquency cases are handled by a juvenile court judge. The manner in which the case is handled is largely dependent on whether the juvenile might be subjected to a period of incarceration. If incarceration is the recommended sanction, the case must be heard in a trial court. Most cases, however, do not lead to a period of incarceration. Instead, they are handled informally in the judge's office. Irrespective of the decision about whether to incarcerate, the ultimate goal of the sanction is, ideally, to reform the young offender. As noted earlier, as of January 1, 2005, the number of people either sentenced to prison or incarcerated while awaiting trial was 59,197. Of these, only 1.2 percent were under the age of 18 (Ministry of Justice, 2006).

The French emphasize cooperation of the juvenile, elicited through paternalistic persuasion by the juvenile judge. This approach is based on the premise that because the juvenile is involved in a conflict, the issue will not be resolved unless he or she actively participates in a meaningful way in its resolution (Hackler et al., 1986; Hackler and Garapon, 1986).

Juvenile Facilities

With the exception of the adult prisons that have a juvenile wing attached to them (which is often very small), there are no closed facilities for juvenile delinquents. Emphasis is placed on keeping the juvenile in close contact with the community at large. Recently, the French have established special institutions for young repeat offenders. They are closed secure facilities designed to handle about 12 young people, with a staff made up of social workers and educators. The French traditionally classify juvenile treatment centers as either long-term or temporary-care facilities.

Both types of facilities are referred to as *foyers*—which roughly means "places of welcoming"—and have the characteristics of group homes. Foyers can be a small homes or larger facilities. They can be run by public agencies, private agencies, or religious orders. They vary to some degree in their treatment philosophy: some have a strict regimen while others are more permissive.

No attempt is made to separate delinquent from nondelinquent youths in these facilities. The basic assumption is that both are in need of care. Thus, the reasons bringing them to the attention of the authorities are not significant at this stage of the process.

Irrespective of who operates the foyer, the juvenile judge has the authority of oversight. He or she ultimately determines where a juvenile will be sent for either long-term or temporary care. It has been suggested that delinquents in France view juvenile judges as a source of help because of their active involvement in the placement of a youth in a foyer and continued monitoring of the juvenile's progress with the probation or social worker assigned to the case (Hackler et al., 1986).

While many foyers offer residential facilities, some are designed as educational guidance and open treatment centers that provide training and counseling only during the day. Other methods of disposing of juvenile cases include fines, probation, suspended sentences, and community service orders. A juvenile court judge is expected to monitor the juvenile's progress in all cases. The judge has the authority to revise the sanction as he or she sees fit. Thus, the judge can modify the sentence, revoke the probation, order an early release, or impose an institutional sanction.

Earlier in this chapter the banlieues, or deprived areas, were mentioned. They are noted for a good deal of crime and on occasion civil unrest. In recent years, the Ministry of Justice has established "houses of justice' in these areas. They are designed to provide the youths of the deprived community with a variety of social services including: treatment, mediation, victim support, and information about rights. In 2002, there were 84 centers providing these kinds of services (de Maillard and Roche, 2004).

Critical Issues

The French have focused their attention on at least two critical issues that have confronted their juvenile justice system: treatment and diversion. Although there are other issues, such as the need to improve communications between professionals working in the system and to upgrade the training of these professionals, most of the attention appears to center on treatment and diversion.

The central issue confronting treatment programs is how to provide the most effective, yet open, style of regimen. Over the years, the French have made significant strides in moving away from a closed treatment model. Thus, like other countries, the French are grappling with the problem of developing programs that are open, humane, and individualized, yet also effective at lowering the rates of recidivism.

The French have recognized the value of developing diversion programs for both delinquent and nondelinquent youths. Juvenile court judges are attempting to divert more delinquents away from the formal adjudication process in order to avoid labeling the youths as delinquent. The educational guidance and open treatment centers assist in this process. The services at these centers also are utilized by nondelinquent youths. Young people in need of assistance can seek counseling at these centers without a referral from a juvenile court or a youth agency.

The police too have become more active in diverting juveniles away from the formal system. In addition to their involvement in youth clubs, which was explained in the section on the police, the police also have established juvenile squads. These squads have three principal responsibilities. They maintain a liaison with other professionals and agencies involved in the juvenile justice process in order to alert them to potential problems and to refer specific juveniles—who are in trouble and in need of assistance—to them. Additionally, they have established programs, conferences, and exhibits that are directed at informing juveniles about the dangers and consequences of involvement in criminal activity.

Another form of diversion is the community service order, introduced in France in 1983 and available to both adults and juveniles. Community service involves performing unpaid work for a specific number of hours over a predetermined period of time. It was suggested in the previous section that this type of sanction has not been utilized extensively. With reference to juveniles, part of the problem lies in the fact that work is difficult to find and many offenders lack an aptitude for it.

The government has also suggested an alternative scheme—based on the community service model but with a significant difference. What is being suggested is to offer a choice to young offenders between the ages of 16 and 25 who have received a prison sentence. They can either serve their time or participate in an occupational training program provided by private agencies. The offender is not to be paid, and the term of training mirrors the length of time served in a prison setting. The goal is to teach offenders basic work habits and possibly enable them to secure employment upon release (Pradel, 1987).

With the creation of the National Council for the Prevention of Delinquency in 1983, and the subsequent establishment of local councils for crime prevention, other strategies have been developed to address problems confronting young people. Job training programs have been established, and mentoring has been offered on how to find a job. National and local grants have been provided for both educational and recreational projects. In addition, programs have been created for youths involved with illicit drugs. The opportunity for disadvantaged youths to attend summer camps continues, and other organized activities have been developed for youths to participate in throughout the summer.

It has been suggested that one of the most important features of this endeavor is the permanent establishment of about 100 youth centers in many of the larger cities and towns. These centers provide a place for young people to associate with one another in a constructive setting and enable local individuals and organizations to work with young people.

SUMMARY

This chapter has presented the reader with an in-depth introduction to the French criminal justice system. Following a general appraisal of the government, the major components of the system—the police, judiciary, law, corrections, and juvenile justice—were surveyed. In addition to highlighting some of the historical antecedents, the organization and administration of the system was explained, the various roles of the practitioners were described, the legal process was examined, and some of the critical issues facing the system were assessed.

Although France has become an industrially prosperous country, its political history over the past 200 years has been characterized as unstable. This is partially attributed to the French penchant for approaching politics with an almost uncompromising ideological stance, as they have tended to commit themselves in an unbending fashion to the purity and rationality of their political ideas. This, in turn, has reduced their ability to resolve disputes through negotiation.

A central feature of French political thought since the Enlightenment has been the desire to establish a political system that assures liberty for all. However, the government often appears to stress the need for imposing an excessive amount of authority to assure that freedom. The political history of the country, with its curious juxtaposition of liberty and authority, has significant implications for the justice system.

For the student of the Anglo-American justice system, the French model clearly illustrates how the inquisitorial style of the Romano-Germanic law differs from that of the common law. Of particular interest is the role that the office of the judge plays in the criminal process. From the investigating judge at the preliminary investigation and the liberty and detention judge at the pretrial phase, to the trial judge in the courtroom, and on to the post-sentencing judge in the correctional community, these people have been trained and entrusted to assure that justice is served in the administration of that process. There is a rationality to this system that is alien to the common law tradition.

Finally, of equal interest is the extent to which a large, centralized bureaucracy can dominate and regulate the lives of the citizenry, yet maintain a commitment to democratic principles. In the realm of criminal justice, the law enforcement system is an example of that phenomenon in action. The form of the system's institutions and established procedures explain only part of the reason for the system's effectiveness, however. Another significant factor is related to the selection of the personnel who work within the system. The way the various branches of the legal profession are trained as well as the multiple-level entry scheme of the police are particularly noteworthy. Thus, the Romano-Germanic legal system serves as a striking contrast to the methods employed in the common law tradition: it offers a new perspective from which to reflect upon the numerous procedural, policy, and personnel issues that confront the student of criminal justice.

Concepts to Know

Riksdag

Office of the Parliamentary Ombudsman

National Police Board

Law Council

Temporary Custody Act (1973)

National Council for Crime Prevention

lay judges

principle of mandatory prosecution

public victims' counsel

furloughs

Act on Correctional Treatment in Institutions (1974)

day-fine

KRUM

social boards

social police

Chapter III

SWEDEN

Introduction

Sweden is a large, elongated country located on the eastern half of the Scandinavian peninsula. The Baltic Sea separates the country from its southern neighbors, Germany and Poland. Sweden encompasses an area of 173,731 square miles, which makes it the fourth largest country in Europe in terms of area and, by way of comparison, roughly the size of the state of California. Its population of more than 9 million is small compared to other European countries. About 90 percent of its inhabitants live in the southern half of the country, with one-third of the population living in the three major cities of Stockholm, Götenburg, and Malmö. The rest of the populace live in fairly small cities. This is largely the result of the highly decentralized nature of Sweden's industry.

Sweden was largely an agrarian country until the middle of the nineteenth century. Since that time, it has emerged as one of the most industrialized nations in the world. Included among the significant industries are: iron and steel, chemicals, pharmaceuticals, communications, electronics, paper, pulp and wood, and transportation equipment. The country has become so highly industrialized that only 2 percent of the labor force is now employed in agriculture. The majority of the farms in Sweden are small, family-owned units. With the possible exception of the United States, Sweden is the only industrialized country in the world that has the capacity to be relatively self-sufficient.

Since World War II, the greatest attention and interest in Sweden has been directed at two objectives: (1) its ability to achieve a high standard of living for its people through economic prosperity; and (2) an adherence to and expansion of its application of social welfare principles. There are a number of factors that were instrumental in securing the achievement of this successful merger of capitalism with socialism. The level of industrialization obviously enhanced the process, but there were other equally significant variables. For example, Sweden's foreign policy was one of neutrality in times of both peace and war. Thus, they were free to direct their attentions and resources to domestic affairs.

While most advanced societies are characterized as having some regional, linguistic, religious, racial, or ethnic heterogeneous qualities, only the Scandinavian countries, along with Japan, can claim to be homogeneous. The official language spoken is Swedish, and about 80 percent of the population are at least nominally members of the Lutheran State Church. Moreover, there have been only two native minority groups of any significance. The Sami or Lapps number about 17,000 and have lived in northern Sweden for centuries. In recent years, the Sami have begun to integrate into the general society as they abandon reindeer herding. The other minority group are the Finns, who number about 30,000 and have lived primarily near the Finnish border. The homogenous nature of the society has enabled the country to operate with an unusual degree of political and social stability.

A final factor, which was allegedly instrumental in securing a successful economic and social policy, was that government bureaucracy was decentralized. While the national government is located in Stockholm, it is largely administered at the provincial and local levels. This led to a further integration of society rather than a segregation of it.

The successful merger of capitalism with socialism began to experience some difficulty by the 1980s. Among the factors that contributed to these concerns was a reduction in the growth of the economy. There were also added pressures placed on the government's welfare budget. The welfare state had matured both in the sophisticated delivery of its services and in the number of people who were eligible for its benefits.

This last point is in part attributed to the previous decades of rapid industrialization, which led to demands for a larger labor force. As a result, there was an influx of immigrants from other Nordic countries and from the continent of Europe. In more recent years, the country has experienced an influx of immigrants who were also seeking political asylum. These included people from several eastern European countries, as well as refugees from Chile, Ethiopia, Iran, and Vietnam. In the late 1980s and early 1990s, Sweden began to experience racist incidents that were unheard of a decade earlier. This led to a good deal of discussion about restricting the country's immigration policy. The government initiated a campaign ahead of the 2006 parliamentary elections that was designed to increase participation in Swedish society, especially for those who had been excluded in the past. While all citizens were targeted, immigrants, along with people with disabilities, were singled out for particular attention.

Finally, it should be noted that Sweden became a member of the European Union (EU) on January 1, 1995. Sweden's neutral—and at times isolationist—foreign policy will undoubtedly be altered by this decision. Upon entering the EU, the country did reserve the right to abstain from participating in any defense alliances that the EU might establish.

GOVERNMENT

Sweden's political and legal institutions were largely indigenous creations that resulted from centuries of isolation from events on the continent of Europe. Sweden was an active participant in the European power struggles of the seventeenth and eighteenth centuries, but in the early nineteenth century, the country returned to a state of isolationism. Although its nonallied status in world politics enhanced its insular position, it is evident that this is not as pronounced as it once was. Ideas from France, Germany, England, and the United States have had a significant impact on Swedish society. Nevertheless, Sweden retains a degree of insularity that is unmatched by other industrialized countries. This will likely change to some extent as a result of joining the EU.

Although there have been concerns in the past decade with regard to racist incidents directed at immigrants, the country retains an enviable record of social cohesiveness. The political and legal history of Sweden is characterized by an unusual amount of stability. In the realm of politics, change has always been gradual. Thus, conflict among groups or alienation from the body politic has been negligible. An illustration of this is found in the number of female candidates who continue to make significant gains in local, county, and national elections. As a result of the 2006 general election, women occupy 47 percent of the seats in parliament. It should be noted that gender equality was not confined to this particular election. Women have held key positions in the government, as ministers of culture, foreign affairs, justice, and public administration, in addition to the position of speaker of the parliament. Following the 2006 election, the prime minister formed a cabinet of 21 ministers, of which 10 are headed by women.

Swedish historians attribute the unusual degree of social stability to a long-standing respect for the law that dates back to the Viking era. Swedes generally view law as an instrument that explains the limits of power and authority granted to those who govern. This attitude is reflected in their constitutional law.

The Constitution

Although Sweden's political system is characterized as stable, it is not stagnant. The constitutional arrangement has always been flexible in order to accommodate change. The country's constitutional law, which in Sweden is referred to as fundamental law, is composed of four parts or acts.

The Instrument of Government is considered the most important of the four acts. Its purpose is to explain how government is organized. Although the earliest version appeared in 1634, there were significant revisions in 1720, 1772, 1809, and 1975. The 1975 Instrument of Government, which has been amended, is similar to the original document in that it elaborates how government is organized and operated; thus, it is like the constitutions of other countries. While many constitutions contain a preamble or an introduction that declares some basic political principles, such a statement is found in Article 1 of Chapter 1 of the Act: "All public power in Sweden proceeds from the people. Swedish democracy is founded on freedom of opinion and on universal and equal suffrage. It shall be realized through a representative and parliamentary polity and through local self-government. Public power shall be exercised under the law."

The foreign observer is often surprised to discover that the Swedish constitution does not contain a bill of rights. Due process and civil rights concerns are expressed, however, in a number of provisions found in Chapter 2 of the 1975 Instrument of Government. The rights and freedoms elaborated in this chapter are divided into two kinds: (1) absolute rights and freedoms, and (2) rights and freedoms that may be restricted by law. Among the absolute rights are: freedom of worship; protection from compulsion to make known one's political, religious, cultural, or similar views; protection from compulsion to belong to a political association, a religious community, or other similar associations; prohibition against the registration of any person solely because of his or her political views; and protection of Swedish citizenship.

Some absolute rights and freedoms are of particular significance to understanding the country's justice system. They include: the right to have deprivation of liberty tried by a court of law or an authority of equal rank without undue delay; prohibition against corporal punishment, torture, and medical treatment to force people to make statements or keep silent; prohibition against retroactive penal legislation; and prohibition against capital punishment. Absolute rights and freedoms cannot be altered unless the fundamental law is amended.

Rights and freedoms that may be restricted by law include: freedom of speech, information, assembly, demonstration, and association; protection from personal search and from house search or similar intrusion; protection from examination of mail, wiretapping, and similar interference with confidential communication; protection from deprivation of liberty and other restraints on freedom of movement; and the right to public court proceedings.

It should be pointed out that when Sweden joined the European Union in 1995 it incorporated into its legal system the European Convention for the Protection of Human Rights and Fundamental Freedoms. Furthermore, a new provision of the Instrument of Government indicates that no law or regulation adopted in Sweden will contravene its commitment to the European Convention.

The second document that encompasses the fundamental law is the Act of Succession. It was first drawn up in 1810 and gave the right of succession to the Swedish throne to the male heirs of the Bernadotte family. This is referred to as an agnatic order of succession. In 1980, a new Act of Succession was adopted that was designed to assure gender equality. The new law simply states that the eldest child (male or female) of the monarch is considered heir to the throne. Thus, the change permits a full cognatic succession. Because Sweden is a constitutional monarchy with a parliamentary form of government, the monarch's duties are largely ceremonial. These include serving as Head of State, opening the Riksdag each year, and presiding over the cabinet when there is a change of government.

The third fundamental law document is the Freedom of the Press Act. This law was first enacted in 1766 and has been the subject of a number of revisions. The Act essentially enables people to publish materials without prior censorship from the government. The materials can be one's own thoughts and opinions, but may also include official documents. Chapter 2 of the Act explains what constitutes an official document. Basically, it includes materials held by a public authority and documents that were drawn up by a public authority and are registered in a final form.

While this Act provides people the right to express themselves in print, there are some restrictions. These are spelled out in Chapter 7 of the Act and include such offenses as: treason, espionage, insurrection, negligence injurious to the interests of the country, incitement to criminal acts, persecution of a population group, and defamation. Moreover, not all government documents are available to the public. The Secrecy Act provides guidance on such matters that pertain to national security interests and the protection of an individual's personal and financial information.

The issue of establishing rules for media other than print had been debated in Sweden since the 1970s. Initially, the attention was directed at radio and television but progressed to include film and other electronic recordings. The Fundamental Law on Freedom of Expression, which came into force on January 1, 1992, addresses those concerns and is the last of the four fundamental law documents. This Act utilizes the same principles that are spelled out in the Freedom of the Press Act, namely a prohibition on censorship and permitting free expression in the modern media. The principal exception to this policy is the provision for the review and licensing of films and videos designed for public viewing.

Finally, another characteristic of the Swedish constitutional scheme should be noted: that the government and administration are considered to have separate functions. Government ministries are primarily concerned with the preparation of new legislation that is submitted to the Riksdag. Once the legislation has received the assent of the government and the Riksdag, it is the responsibility of various central and county administrative agencies to implement the law.

The Riksdag

The Riksdag Act explains the operation of the Swedish parliament. While not a part of the fundamental law, this legislation is considered more significant than regular statute law. The Swedes have long considered the Riksdag a protector of their rights rather than a threat to their freedom. This faith was reinforced in 1809 when the Riksdag established the Office of Parliamentary Ombudsman, which has the responsibility of protecting the rights of citizens. Unlike most countries that have established a legislative branch of government, Sweden has maintained a unicameral parliament since 1971. A constitutional amendment abolished the bicameral system that had existed from 1866. The Riksdag is formed by direct election, and suffrage extends to all Swedes who have reached the voting age of 18. Swedish citizenship and attaining the voting age are also the basic eligibility requirements to run for a seat in the legislature.

The Riksdag is composed of 349 members, generally from county districts, who are elected to four-year terms. All the trades and professions are well represented and no individual group dominates the parliament. This comes as a surprise to those who expect legislatures to be dominated by lawyers. It is also worth repeating that 47 percent of the seats are currently held by women. Moreover, all elections are by proportional representation. This is achieved by having 310 seats assigned to specific electoral districts, while the remaining 39 seats are distributed at large. This assures that 39 seats are evenly distributed among the political parties in proportion to the votes that they receive nationally.

It was pointed out earlier that Sweden is noted for the unusual degree to which it has been able to maintain a highly stable political and social system. This is often attributed to a willingness to seek compromise and to reach consensus opinions. One could not find a better place to illustrate these qualities in action than in the work of the Riksdag.

It is also important to comment on two political characteristics that are common to Sweden as well as to other Scandinavian countries. These factors contribute significantly to our understanding of the parliamentary process in Sweden. First, it is generally assumed that when a political party receives a majority in an election, it will attempt to implement the policy presented to the electorate during the election campaign. This approach is common in countries such as the United States and England. In Sweden, however, the primary political criteria of the majority party does not hinge solely on the implementation of its policy. Rather, it is interested in reaching compromises with all power groups that will enable the enactment of consensus legislation.

Second, multiparty systems are generally associated with political instability. Countries such as France and Italy have suffered the consequences of having multiple parties throughout the twentieth century. This is often cited as a reason for abandoning such a scheme and adopting a two-party system. However, Sweden and the other Scandinavian countries prove to be an exception to the rule. Sweden has maintained a multiparty system and has achieved a high degree of political stability. The extent to which the Social Democratic Party has dominated Swedish politics since 1932, however, is a stabilizing influence.

The Cabinet

Most of the political power in Sweden rests with the cabinet and the political party or parties represented in it. The term "cabinet" is used interchangeably with "government," which is common in many European countries. Following an election, it is determined which of the major political parties is capable of governing the country and commanding support within the Riksdag. Once this is ascertained, the leader of the victorious party assumes the position of prime minister and selects people to join his or her cabinet. The cabinet includes the heads of the permanent ministries: agriculture, culture, defence, education and research, employment, enterprise, environment, finance, foreign affairs, health and social affairs, integration and gender equality, justice and public administration. In addition, several ministers-without-portfolio are appointed to the cabinet.

Although ministers-without-portfolio are generally members of the Riksdag, there is no regulation that limits selection from that body. Moreover, the prime minister may appoint people from another party in recognition of the political forces that are found in the Riksdag. Cabinet members represent the judicious choice of the prime minister; they are not subject to the approval of the Riksdag.

While members of the cabinet retain their seats in the Riksdag, they give up their right to vote in the parliament. Thus, another person assumes their parliamentary duties as long as they remain in the cabinet. Ministers, however, are permitted to address the Riksdag.

Swedish ministries are rather small, employing about 100 people, because they are not responsible for running the daily business of the government for which they have been assigned. Rather, their work is limited to initiating legislation that pertains to their area of government responsibility. The Swedish cabinet is similar to the British cabinet in that it practices collective responsibility. This means that each cabinet member is accountable to the Riksdag for the administration of the entire government. Although the cabinet does not have to be approved by the Riksdag, it can be voted out of office by the legislature.

Prime Minister

The political position of the Swedish prime minister is similar to that of his or her counterpart in England: political versatility is a must. The prime minister is the leader of the government and, therefore, is responsible both for initiating and defending policy in the Riksdag. As chair of the cabinet and leader of a political party, he or she assumes an important role at election time. Unlike other party leaders, the prime minister has greater access to information and is in a strategic position to influence the Riksdag, interest groups, and voters.

Political Parties

As was mentioned earlier, unlike most countries that have adopted a multiparty political system, Sweden retains an unusual degree of stability. Part of this success is attributed to the fact that from the 1920s until fairly recently, the same five parties have dominated the political scene. These parties include: (1) the Social Democrats, (2) the Left (formerly known as Communists), (3) the Liberals, (4) the Moderates (formerly known as Conservatives), and (5) the Center (formerly known as Agrarians).

For the most part, these parties have as their goal the furtherance of liberal democratic ideals. The differences among them have been found largely in the social and economic base of the party membership and in the speed with which they are willing to achieve their political objectives. Just as the French tend to divide their political parties into ideological categories, the Swedes often consider the Social Democrats and the Left as the socialist bloc and label the other parties as the nonsocialist bloc. When viewed as two political blocs, rather than distinct parties, the public has tended to support both blocs on an equal footing. Recently, two new parties—the Greens and the Christian Democrats—have emerged to compete with the traditional parties.

Social Democratic Party The Social Democratic Party is the largest of the five political parties. It usually receives approximately 40 percent of the votes during an election. Its success has been attributed to its ability to move from a party of ideology to one that is based on more pragmatic considerations. During the 1920s, the party abandoned its Marxist ideological stance and set out to achieve reform through another approach: by increasing its support at the ballot box. The party directed its attention to all employees and not just to the workers. While the Social Democratic Party has attracted the support of both blue-collar and white-collar workers, it has retained strong ties in particular to the National Swedish Confederation of Trade Unions. The party's goal of increasing welfare provisions for all citizens was aided by the extensive rate and success of industrialization that occurred in Sweden after the end of World War II. Current budget difficulties have led to a rethinking of the speed with which the party attempts to achieve its goal.

Liberal Party The Liberals are more apt to adhere to their ideological position than the others. Influenced by British and American forms of liberalism, they advocate popular democracy, individual freedom, free trade, and social reform. On social issues, they are similar to the Social Democrats in their belief that social welfare legislation should be expanded. In fact, this is their major source of criticism of the Social Democrats. The Liberals believe that the welfare system is inadequate and that the Social Democrats are guilty of poor planning of the welfare state when they are in power. The Liberals also tend to side with the Moderates in opposing the Social Democrats' attempts at economic leveling through a highly progressive tax system.

Moderate Party Like the Social Democrats, the Moderates (Conservatives) have made a pronounced shift from their original political stance. Before World War I, it was a party in opposition to the emergence of an industrialized society and the popular notion of parliamentary democracy. Although they have continued to support a strong national defense and the monarchy, the Moderates have become more liberal on issues of economic freedom and on social welfare issues impacting health care, education, childcare, and assistance for the elderly. The party is similar to the Conservative party of England.

Center Party Until 1958, the Center Party was referred to as the Farmers or Agrarian Party. Agrarian parties were a common feature of Scandinavian politics, and although the party was clearly an interest group, it did not attract the support of all their intended constituents. Owners of large farms tended to vote for the Moderates, while many agricultural workers supported the Social Democrats. The party usually appealed to the independent farmer. Since 1958, they have forged a new identity, along with a new name, and are identified with opposing high taxes and large state bureaucracy. In addition, they have gained the support of environmentalists because of their opposition to nuclear power.

Left Party Sweden's Left Party was originally the Communist Party of Sweden. The party took an independent approach to Marxism and did not align itself with either the Soviet Union or China. Since the fall of communism in eastern Europe, the party has not only changed its name, but also has attempted to expand its party base to include communists, disillusioned social democrats, and environmentalists. The Left Party's central policy still adheres to the need to eliminate class differences and to provide for the basic needs of all.

Green Party The Green Party was the first new party to emerge in Sweden since the early part of the twentieth century. Although the Center Party was largely viewed as Sweden's "green" party until the 1970s, it supported at that time the use of nuclear reactors and of toxic substances in agricultural production. With the nuclear accident at Chernobyl in the former Soviet Union in 1986, which affected Sweden directly with radioactive fallout, environmentalists established an organizational structure for a new political party and developed a comprehensive energy policy that is sensitive to environmental issues. The difficulty plaguing the Green Party is that it is perceived as a one-issue party. To help rectify this image, they have expanded their agenda to include grassroots democracy, social justice, and nonviolence issues.

Christian Democratic Party Many European countries have had political parties that place Christian philosophy at the core of their policies. The Christian Democratic Party was established in 1964 but was not viewed as a significant party until 1991, when it garnered enough votes (statute requires a 4 percent minimum) to gain representation in parliament. The party supports traditional moral and ethical values, placing an absolute value on human beings, defending human dignity, and supporting the right to life.

Administration

The administration of Sweden's government is carried out at three levels: national, county, and municipal. The national administration is conducted by government ministries, but as was pointed out earlier, these ministries are rather small and their principal duty is to initiate legislation in the Riksdag. Ministries, therefore, are not responsible for the daily administration of government business; that responsibility is handled by a number of central administrative agencies. For example, the Ministry of Justice is responsible for the police and the prison service, but the National Police Board and the National Prison and Probation Administration are authorized to manage these respective services.

Sweden is divided into 21 counties. Each county has a governor and a county administrative board. The governor is appointed by the government to a six-year term; thus, this person serves as the representative of the national government in the administration of the county. The governor and the county administrative board are primarily concerned with regional planning, social welfare issues, and police. Also found at the county level are county councils, whose members are elected by the popular vote of their constituents. These councils are responsible for the healthcare facilities and public transit of the county, and they impose an income tax on residents to provide these services.

The country is also divided into 290 municipalities. Municipal governments are responsible for housing, water and sewage, basic education, and public assistance. This work is funded by revenues from an income tax and a property tax.

Ombudsman

Although the government and the Riksdag play a significant role in checking the power and authority of Sweden's administrative bureaucracy, the position of ombudsman has long been synonymous with the country's attempt to curb government abuse. The word "ombudsman" means representative or attorney. There are hundreds of people throughout Sweden who are called ombudsmen. Labor unions, banks, and insurance companies have them, and the government has utilized the position to oversee antitrust, consumer, and equal rights issues.

Although there are several government-appointed ombudsmen—for example, the consumer ombudsman, the equal opportunities ombudsman, the ombudsman against ethnic discrimination, and the children's ombudsman—it is the Office of the Parliamentary Ombudsman that is of particular interest. This office was created in 1809 when the Swedish constitution made the holder of the position an officer of the Riksdag. Its purpose was to guarantee the citizenry that the judicial system and the government administration would not use oppressive measures in carrying out its duties.

Today, the office consists of four ombudsmen. The chief ombudsman handles issues involving taxation, in addition to the general duties of administering the internal workings of the office. One ombudsman supervises the military, the local governments, and the administrative courts, while another is responsible for social welfare and education programs. The fourth ombudsman supervises the courts of law, prosecutors, police, and the prison service. Each ombudsman is elected by the Riksdag to a four-year term that is renewable. It has been a tradition in Sweden that the ombudsman receives the support of all parties in the Riksdag. Prior to 1974, the law required that an ombudsman possess a legal education; as a result, most people who occupied the office were former members of the judiciary. There are no longer special qualifications for serving, but ombudsmen continue to be selected from the ranks of the judiciary.

Parliamentary ombudsmen perform three tasks. They periodically inspect the government agencies for which they are responsible; they conduct long-term investigations that are prompted by either individual complaints (or possibly an investigative article that has appeared in a magazine or a newspaper); and they deal with complaints from the public. Complaints often result from citizens being caught up in an agency's bureaucratic paperwork.

In its annual report covering the period from July 1, 2005, to June 30, 2006, there were 6,008 cases registered with the office. Of these, 5,804 were classified as complaints; 89 were cases initiated by an ombudsman; and 115 cases involved an ombudsman commenting on new legislation. Of the cases initiated by an ombudsman, the organization that received the most attention were: courts (7), police (8), prison administration (9) and social welfare (7). The organizations that attracted the most citizen complaints were: police (539), prison administration (912), social insurance (1,491), and social welfare (756).

The Office of the Parliamentary Ombudsman was originally viewed as that of a special prosecutor. A number of prosecutions were instituted during the nineteenth century. This is the exception today, however. The ombudsmen's principal weapon is to admonish or criticize officials who are at fault. In the process, they frequently suggest ways to rectify problems. On occasion, they may even recommend that a statute be amended. Ombudsmen, however, do not have the power to change an administrative decision or to order an official to take a specific course of action. Nevertheless, it is alleged that the office has enhanced the public's confidence in the courts and government agencies.

National Council for Crime Prevention

The National Council for Crime Prevention (NCCP) was established in 1974. Since 1994, it has been a government agency within the Ministry of Justice. The NCCP has a director-general and a board that is appointed by the government. The board includes representatives from various political parties in the Riksdag, undersecretaries from some ministries (such as Justice, Health and Social Affairs, and Education), representatives from county and local councils, and people from the private sector of labor and management. The purpose of the board is to establish the council's policies and priorities.

The NCCP has two advisory groups that assist in determining the priorities of the council. Members of the Scientific Council offer advice regarding research and development activities; specifically, this includes appropriate research methodologies, ethical questions about projects, and evaluation methods. The other body is called the Advisory Group; it recommends how research activities should be prioritized and encourages cooperative ventures between practitioners and scholars of the justice system.

The NCCP is essentially a research and information center on crime and criminal justice. It provides the government, the Riksdag, other justice agencies, and the public with information about crime, criminals, crime prevention, and the impact of reform in criminal policy. The specific work of the council is organized around eight divisions. The crime studies division examines trends in crime and social change. This includes special studies on recidivism, drugs and crime, and economic and organized crime, or it may focus on a specific group of offenders, such as juvenile delinquents. The individual change program division assesses the effects of various programs on offenders. This has included correctional treatment programs in general and an evaluation of electronic surveillance in particular. The statistical division produces the official justice statistics for the country. The methods and development division focuses on the research strategies of the council and also provides in-service training for people working in the justice system. The local crime prevention division provides the resources for various local crime prevention projects and particular attention has been directed at schools. The division is also responsible for evaluating these projects. The information and publication division disseminates the various materials that have been produced by the council. These include research reports, surveys, and evaluations. This division also organizes conferences. The international secretariat is designed to facilitate cooperative efforts between the NCCP and other international organizations. Finally, the administrative division handles the budgetary and personnel issues of the council.

In the past, the NCCP was credited with establishing working groups that attempted to improve efforts at coordinating activities between government agencies that are either directly or indirectly related to criminal justice. For example, they were active in improving cooperation among social welfare agencies, schools, and the police. They also considered ways in which the schools might instruct students about the law and the legal system. Of course, they disseminated information about crime and crime prevention through publications, exhibits, and conferences. Members of the NCCP have seen their principal duty as educating the citizenry regarding the fact that crime control is not just the responsibility of the criminal justice system, but also a duty involving all citizens.

This approach to issues of crime control was given a renewed impetus in 1996, when the government published *Our Collective Responsibility: A National Programme for Crime Prevention*. The government focused on three key initiatives to address the crime problem. The first was a recognition that general societal development, other social problems, and government decisions outside the realm of crime policy have all had a profound impact on crime. As such, the problem of crime needs to be addressed on a broad political front. This should include political leaders at the national, regional, and local level, but it would also include the private sector. The business community was singled out to become active in various initiatives in general and to assist in the reduction of certain types of crime in particular. For example, efforts to improve the manufacture of theft-proof cars were singled out for attention. The second initiative involves improving legislation and developing crime control policies that are more efficient. One objective is to write clear and comprehensible legislation that reduces the possibility of fraud or other abuse. Another objective is to reexamine the range of sentencing options in light of the view that imprisonment has not been an effective deterrent. The final initiative argues that the crime problem must be addressed at its source—the local level. Thus, cooperative efforts between government and citizens is imperative, and crime prevention strategies that have been initiated by citizens were singled out for particular attention (Ministry of Justice, 1997b). The NCCP is responsible for supporting and monitoring the crime prevention strategies that have emerged from these initiatives.

Among some of the NCCP's planned or recent projects are: an analysis and assessment of local crime prevention boards; an investigation of how courts take the needs of a child into account when sentencing a foreigner to deportation as a result of criminal activity; a trial study of providing long-term prisoners with the opportunity to serve the final four months of a sentence at home with electronic supervision; the development of a knowledge base on adults seeking contact with children via the Internet; and a national crime victim and security study that assesses levels of insecurity among victims and people exposed to crime.

POLICE

Until the middle of the nineteenth century, Swedish police forces were characterized as decentralized, unprofessional, and disorganized. Police forces in most European countries were suffering a similar stigma at that time. This is usually attributed to the fact that towns and cities were self-governing political units. As a result, policing the citizenry was considered a municipal concern. The responsibility for protecting a local community was considered a duty that was shared among police constables, town watchguards, fireguards, and, at times, a military garrison. Because many constables were employed at other occupations during the day, they were often limited to part-time duty at night.

Attempts were under way to reform the police service in Stockholm by the middle of the nineteenth century. The changes that were instituted over the next 100 years served as the model for law enforcement throughout the country. In 1850, for example, police districts were established within the city to improve patrolling techniques, whereas garrisons were primarily limited to policing the outskirts of the city. By 1864, the head of the detective department was also a public prosecutor who was given the authority to prosecute cases in the police court that handled minor criminal matters. Initially, the governor of Stockholm served as the judge in this court, but this responsibility was transferred to the police commissioner. Thus, minor offenses were detected, prosecuted, and adjudicated by the police.

Despite these improvements, the police service continued to suffer from a lack of training and discipline. In 1876, a special department was established to train officers. Other specialized units were created during the 1880s; among these were a mounted division, a riot squad, and an orderly department that was designed to aid people in need of assistance. Finally, there was a concerted effort to improve the selection of police personnel. Traditionally, police had been recruited from among the working class. Throughout the 1880s and 1890s, however, attempts were made to attract recruits from other classes by improving the wages of police. Moreover, as a condition of service, police were required to have military training. This was designed to improve discipline within the forces.

The idea that the police service should be nationalized was first raised in the 1920s. The Riksdag occasionally studied the issue during the 1930s and 1940s, but nothing resulted from these inquiries. In 1962, a study recommended that the service be nationalized, and changes were put into effect in 1965. Thus, in the course of about 100 years, the Swedish police service was transformed from a decentralized, unprofessional, and disorganized service into one characterized as centralized, professional, and systematized.

Organization and Administration of the Police

Although Sweden opted for a centralized national system in 1965, one of the paramount concerns over the course of the past three decades has been with the management of the service. At issue is the extent to which police should be administered by the national government or responsible and accountable to a local authority. As a result of the 1965 decision, a number of significant changes had an immediate impact on the law enforcement establishment. For example, the number of police districts was reduced from 554 to 118. This amalgamation was designed to make the system more efficient, because 70 percent of the 554 forces had less than 10 officers. Under the new scheme, law enforcement would be financed at the national level; thus, the police were no longer dependent on funding from the local district government in which they were serving. In turn, the responsibilities of police management were altered. Prior to centralization, the chief of police in most cities was also the public prosecutor and the distrainer. Distrainers are responsible for seizing the property of people who have failed to pay a debt or taxes. Under the new scheme, the chief of police was directly involved only with police work, and prosecutors and distrainers were found in separate departments.

The nationalization of the police service and the centralization of its management resulted in a good deal of criticism. Opponents of the new scheme initiated a campaign for reform that would both decentralize and democratize the police service (Akermo, 1986). Their concerns centered on the fact that the relationship between a local community and its police force had diminished and that decisions involving law enforcement were no longer being made at the local level. Rather, the National Police Board had established a virtual monopoly over policy, personnel, and process decisions. Moreover, the central police bureaucracy continued to expand. This was an important concern for those distrustful of the proliferation of government bureaucracy—especially when the agency was mandated to perform such sensitive duties as law enforcement and order maintenance.

Some critics also believed that contact between the police and the public had been further reduced during the 1970s with the advent of advanced technology in police work. They were of the opinion that this situation might lead to more coercive conflicts between police and citizens. The concept of democratization was directed in general at improving police-community relations and in particular at enhancing the authority of locally elected police boards.

In 1975, the government established a commission on the police to examine a host of issues, not the least of which were the criticisms generated by the 1965 move to nationalize the police. The commission was instructed to determine whether the police were adequately meeting the present needs of society. In its prefatory remarks, the commission pointed out that all government services had expanded considerably since the mid-1960s. This had created a need for closer coordination between the national and local governments, as they became more dependent on one another. As a result of this trend in government expansion, the police were no longer limited to law enforcement and order maintenance concerns, for they had increased their involvement in social service functions. Because of these added responsibilities, the commission believed that there must be a greater degree of cooperation between the National Police Board and local police agencies. Admittedly, the government and the Riksdag did not wish to relinquish their control over the police through the National Police Board, but the commission was of the opinion that the powers and authority of the Board should be eased somewhat.

The commission published its report recommending several approaches in which the management of the police could be decentralized (Government Commission on the Police, 1979). One of the commission's specific recommendations was that the regulations governing police be combined under one piece of legislation. The Police Act and a governmental Police Ordinance were enacted in 1984. Most of the commission's recommendations were contained in either the act or the ordinance, and they were implemented during the latter half of the 1980s. Subsequent changes were introduced so that now the police are governed by the 1999 edition of the Police Act. A description of the organization of the Swedish police service is found in Figure 3.1.

Figure 3.1

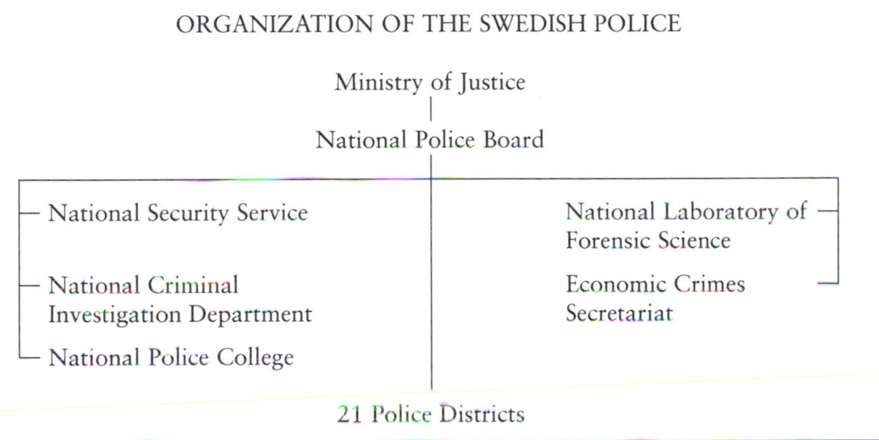

The Ministry of Justice The Ministry of Justice is a cabinet-level department in the Swedish government. The minister of justice is appointed by the prime minister and is usually a member of the Riksdag who is trained in law. The ministry consists of 18 divisions. Six of them are specifically responsible for matters that pertain to criminal justice: Division for Police and Prosecution Issues, Division for Procedural Law and Court Issues, Division for Penal Law, Division for Criminal Cases and International Judicial Cooperation, Division for Crime Policy, and Division for Constitutional Law. Thus, the minister of justice is the civilian politician who has the greatest responsibility for the Swedish criminal justice system.

The National Police Board It was pointed out earlier that cabinet ministries are primarily concerned with the initiation of legislation in the Riksdag. The actual day-to-day coordination of government is the responsibility of central administration. The central administration of police is entrusted to the National Police Board. The board includes the national police commissioner, the commissioner's deputy, and eight additional members. Both the commissioner and deputy are appointed by the government to six-year terms. Among the other eight members, two are representatives from the administrative staff of the board, and the other six are members of the Riksdag. All are appointed by the government. Thus, the minister of justice and the six board members from the Riksdag constitute a significant civilian element in the administration of the police.

The authority of the board is directed at coordinating improvements in the efficiency of police service throughout the country. The board's general responsibilities include: administration, budget, research and planning, computer services, equipment, and general inspection. The board also regulates the basic training scheme for all police districts and is responsible for the National Police College. Finally, the board administers the National Forensic Laboratory, the National Security Service, the National Criminal Investigation Department, and the Economic Crimes Secretariat.

The National Laboratory of Forensic Science provides forensic analysis primarily for the police service, but also offers professional assistance to other government agencies and organizations. The laboratory presents forensic training courses and conducts research into the development of new forensic techniques. It also has a cooperative relationship with a number of other forensic laboratories throughout the world.

The National Security Service is also under the direct control of the National Police Board. The board acknowledges that citizens have the right to know about the existence of the unit but are not willing, for obvious reasons, to explain in any detail the nature of the work. The basic purpose of the service is to collect information that affects the external and internal security of the country. As such, espionage and terrorist activities are the primary concerns of the service. Some of this work is also coordinated with the Swedish military and the Industrial Security Group. It also should be noted that the Security Service provides protection to government officials and foreign embassies and coordinates the security for state visits. Members of the service are recruited from the regular police service. They participate in an extensive training program that includes a basic training course followed by advanced training in firearms and driving.

The National Criminal Investigation Department (CID) is involved in the investigation and surveillance of all criminal activities that do not fall under the jurisdiction of the National Security Service or the Economic Crimes Secretariat. The National CID has essentially two responsibilities: (1) to investigate serious criminal activities that are either national or international in scope, such as organized crime, and (2) to provide support to local police districts in the investigation of serious crime, such as murder, drug offenses, and car-theft rings. Finally, the Economic Crimes Secretariat was established in 1998 to investigate, as its name suggests, the ever-increasing range of economic crimes.

Police Districts It was pointed out earlier that in the early 1960s Sweden was divided into 554 police districts. In 1965, efforts were initiated to centralize the police. One of the strategies employed to enhance the efficiency of law enforcement was to consolidate some of the police districts. In 1965, 554 districts were reduced to 118. Since that time, further efforts at consolidation have continued apace. Today, the police are divided along county lines. Thus, there are 21 police districts. The police authority for each district is a local police board, and the executive of the board is the county chief of police. The chief of police and other members of the local board are appointed by the government. Although they are provided with guidelines and priorities from the National Police Board, the local board is responsible for the organization and planning of their police district. The board is also responsible for a number of personnel issues including the establishment of an appropriate size for the force.

Each county also has an administrative board that is responsible for a host of regional and local government issues. Until recently, the county administrative board was responsible for its county police service. That is no longer the case, but the police authority is expected to keep the administrative board apprised of county-wide law enforcement issues. Ultimately, the supervision of each of the police districts rests with the National Police Board.

Each police district has the authority to establish its organizational structure. In addition to administration, which would handle personnel, finance, public relations, and other office matters, major divisions of responsibility also include public order and criminal investigation. Public order is the largest division and consists of uniformed patrol officers working a specific beat area and a traffic unit. Criminal investigation is usually divided into four squads: criminal investigation, drugs, economic crimes, and forensics.

Specialized Security Agencies Throughout the industrialized world, countries have established specialized security agencies to combat specific forms of criminal behavior. The very nature of certain crimes lends itself to this enforcement strategy. Sweden has established several agencies that fall into this category. Customs is involved with detecting the smuggling of drugs and illegal immigrants. The Financial Inspection Agency oversees banks and insurance companies and investigates insider trading in stocks and currencies. The Competition Agency is responsible for investigating monopolistic practices or other violations of the Competition Act. The Environmental Agency, along with various county and local boards, is concerned with crimes against the environment. For the most part, these agencies are empowered to investigate the aforementioned allegations. Unlike officers serving in the regular police service, these officers are not authorized to use force in the exercise of their duties.

Duties of the Police

In Sweden, most public-sector ventures, whether designed to address a problem or to create a new opportunity, are undertaken in cooperation with two or more groups. These groups might represent governmental departments exclusively or could include public interest groups or private organizations. Irrespective of the makeup of the groups, the underlying principle is one of inclusiveness. This notion of cooperation illustrates a specific approach of government and instills a particular attitude for government. This cooperative view is expressed in Section 1 of the Police Act, where it is acknowledged that police work is but "one aspect of community involvement in the promotion of justice and security."

Section 2 of the Act lists the responsibilities that have been deferred to the police. These include the prevention of crime and public order disturbances; the preservation of public order and safety by proactive and reactive strategies; the detection and investigation of crimes falling within the domain of public prosecution; the granting of protection, information, and assistance to the public; and the performance of functions that are incumbent on the police by special regulations.

Section 3 illustrates that police not only have to coordinate many of their efforts with other agencies that are clearly a part of the criminal justice system, but they also must cooperate with organizations whose principal mission may be outside the justice system. This section was specifically designed to stress the need of police to cooperate with social welfare agencies in their work. It further assumed that other organizations would reciprocate by assisting police in achieving their objectives.

The Swedish police are similar to other law enforcement personnel on the continent of Europe in that they carry firearms while performing many of their duties. The uniformed branch is always armed while on duty. Detectives, however, carry firearms only when they are sent to arrest someone or when they are conducting an investigation. Although the Swedish police retain their powers when they are off duty, they do not carry weapons. Firearms must be stored at the police station rather than at the officer's home. An officer who witnesses a crime while off duty is expected to inform his or her colleagues who are on duty. Although an off-duty officer may assist, he or she is expected to refrain from taking unnecessary risks.

The Police and the Public

Like their counterparts in other industrialized countries, the Swedish police have been faced with increases in serious crime since roughly the middle of the 1960s. Violent crime, narcotics offenses, property crime, and juvenile delinquency head the list of problems confronting the police. In reference to crime statistics, it is important to note that the method of counting criminal offenses varies among countries. In Sweden an attempted offense is counted along with completed offenses. Moreover, when multiple offenses are perpetrated on a victim during a single event, each offense is counted separately.

During 2007, 1,306,000 crimes were reported to police. This was a 7 percent increase from 2006. Crimes against the person represented 16 percent of this total. Among these crimes, assaults represented the largest proportion, at 82,000. Of these assaults, 4,750 involved rape and 8,700 were robberies. Crimes against property represented 45 percent of the total. Of these offenses, more than 576,000 involved theft, and slightly more than 16,900 were residential burglaries. Crimes inflicting damage to property increased by 35 percent and involved a total of 179,000 offenses, which includes graffiti crimes. Crimes against the Road Traffic Offences Act and the Narcotics Drugs Act were at 6 percent and 5 percent, respectively (National Council for Crime Prevention, 2008).

Although on a national scale morale remains generally high among police, this is not always the case in some major cities. This is reflected in part by the number of vacancies that exist in larger police districts, a problem that has lingered for at least the past three decades. Many veteran officers prefer to work in rural areas, where the chances of feeling alienated from the public are reduced significantly. Young officers recruited from the countryside are then assigned to police the urban areas. Many request a transfer back to a more rural setting once they have accrued a sufficient amount of time in the service.

Despite officer concerns over the public's attitude toward them, various independent surveys conducted during the 1970s suggested that the police were favorably perceived by a majority of the public. For example, in one survey, people were asked to rate various professions in terms of trustworthiness. Although judges and physicians were ranked higher than police, law enforcement personnel were rated above teachers, attorneys, cabinet ministers, union leaders, legislators, and print and video journalists (Becker and Hjellemo, 1976). Another survey revealed that 90 percent of the respondents were of the opinion that police were helpful and dependable. Eighty percent did not think police used excessive force or abused their authority in the performance of their duties (Snortum, 1979).

In a more recent study comparing the public's satisfaction with political and social institutions, police ranked at the top, with an 80 percent approval rating in 1981 and a 74 percent rating in 1990. In both surveys, the police led the educational system, legal system, and armed forces, which were the institutions that received the next highest rankings in public satisfaction (Petersson et al., 1999).

Finally, the Swedish Crime Survey for 2007 examined the public confidence in the criminal justice system. Across the system there were more higher levels of confidence than lower levels. The police received the highest levels of support, at 60 percent, and were followed by courts, at 56 percent. Only 14 percent of the participants ranked police as very low or fairly low, which was the same percentage of negative ranking achieved by courts. It was further discovered that the respondents to the survey who had been threatened or exposed to violent crime had more negative experiences with police than those who were victims of other kinds of crime. Not surprisingly, men had more negative experiences than women, and older people had more positive experiences in general (Toyra and Wigerhoit, 2008). The ability of the police to retain the support of the public is attributed to a number of factors. Among them are training programs established for recruits and veterans and the crime prevention programs that have been developed throughout the country.

Recruitment and Training The National Police Board has long been noted for its attempts to improve the quality of recruitment and training for law enforcement personnel. With regard to recruitment, the board has divided the country into six regions and has assigned seven recruitment consultants who work in each of the regions. Until recently, the central government determined the number of people recruited, but this responsibility has shifted to the local police authorities, who have a better sense of their personnel needs.

Sweden has established a dual entry scheme for those aspiring to a career in law enforcement. A candidate for the position of police commissioner must be a Swedish citizen, have a driver's license, be in good health, and possess a bachelor of law degree. Although there are usually a significant number of applicants (some being veteran police officers), only a small number are selected, after reference checks and employment interviews. Veteran police officers are usually well represented among the finalists for these positions.

Recruits for the position of police commissioner are sent to the National Police College at Sorentorp. For six months, they study general police duties as well as organization and management issues such as leadership, supervision, planning, and personnel administration. Following the completion of theoretical training, the recruit will spend the next two years acquiring practical experience within the criminal justice system. Six months are spent in a police district, followed by three months at the county level. The recruit is then assigned to a public prosecutor's office for three months, which is followed by 12 months of service at a district court. The candidate returns to the Police College for a two-month extension course. The training phase is concluded with a four-month assignment to the National Police Board. The candidate is then prepared to command a police district but is assigned to a district as a deputy police commissioner until a vacancy occurs.

Most candidates recruited to the police service begin their careers as line officers. To enter the service at this level, one must be a Swedish citizen at least 20 years of age, have passed the National University Admission Test or completed 20 or more academic credits, possess a driver's license, and meet the physical requirements. Additional qualifications that are sought include: university education, knowledge of languages and cultures, and work experience. It is the candidate's personality, however, that is the central factor in the recruitment process.

The successful recruit participates in a two-and-one-half year basic training program. The first two years are spent at the National Police College, where training consists of both theoretical and practical studies, with a greater emphasis placed on theory. Among the subjects presented are: general police theory, criminal law and procedure, criminology, road safety, criminal investigation, drug crimes, public disturbances, domestic violence, and young offenders. The full-time faculty consists of police instructors and various specialists in their respective disciplines. Much of the training focuses on problem-solving techniques. Thus, it is designed to improve the recruit's independence and critical assessment skills. Recently, the course offerings for this program were enhanced by developing partnerships with universities and research institutes. Once this phase of basic training is completed, the candidate begins six months of in-service training in a police district.

The National Police College also offers advanced police courses and courses for those officers aspiring to middle-management positions. Other specialized courses are offered throughout the country at select training centers. For example, various kinds of motor vehicle training, ranging from motorcycles to helicopters, are conducted at the Swedish Army Driving School. Some continuing training is also conducted at the district level and includes physical training and the use of service weapons.

It should be interjected at this point that women are eligible to serve in police forces. Unfortunately, they have suffered from many of the same skeptical attitudes that have confronted their counterparts in other parts of the world. Although their initial training and probationary period was the same as the male recruits, they were often assigned to be plainclothes detectives working as social and juvenile officers. These barriers are being removed as greater assurances are offered for equitable treatment and opportunities. Attempts are also under way to diversify the police service by recruiting more ethnic minorities.

Crime Prevention Programs The National Police Board has been active in establishing crime prevention programs, often in conjunction with the National Council for Crime Prevention. These strategies serve a dual purpose. They are principally designed either to curb a specific type of deviant behavior or to reduce crime in general. They also provide the police with an excellent opportunity to improve their public image with the citizenry. What follows are some of the crime prevention strategies employed in Sweden.

Crime prevention has been a long-standing feature of Swedish policing. Before it became fashionable in other parts of the world, each police district had at least one crime prevention officer. Although their primary responsibility was directed at residential burglaries, they were also involved with other types of crime, such as consumer fraud. In addition to advising homeowners about security measures, crime prevention officers consulted businesses about crime prevention techniques. The crime prevention officer was also involved with conducting classes on crime prevention for other officers in the district.

The block or neighborhood police officer scheme was established in 1959. Neighborhood police officers work out of informal storefront offices or apartment complexes. They interact with people in the neighborhood by walking a beat and distributing crime prevention literature from their offices. Because they are familiar with the neighborhood and its people, these officers are in an excellent position to establish close bonds with the immediate community. In addition to assuring that the law is enforced and that order is maintained throughout the neighborhood, the block officer also serves as a useful communications channel to police headquarters, city hall, or social service agencies when citizens have complaints or problems.

This position requires a long-term commitment by officers who are interested in specializing in this type of generalist work. This endeavor appears to work in many communities, but in larger cities, such as Stockholm and Malmö, it apparently is not as successful. One explanation is that larger cities tend to be policed by young recruits from the countryside. As such, their goal is to accumulate enough time to warrant a transfer back to a rural county force. Thus, a serious commitment to community policing in an urban setting is lacking to some extent in these young officers (Skolnick and Bayley, 1988).

Another type of crime prevention program was initiated in the early 1970s. It was specifically designed to improve the maintenance of public order in Sweden. Its implementation was a direct result of the urban disorders that plagued a number of European cities in the 1970s. The major difference between this program and other crime prevention measures is that it has the force of law. The Riksdag voted 288 to 16 to enact the Temporary Custody Act in 1973. The intent of this legislation is cited in Section 3. It states:

> He who, through his activities, disturbs the public order or constitutes an immediate danger for such shall be detained by a police officer, if it is necessary for the maintenance of order. Such detention shall also occur when it is needed to ward off a prosecutable offense.

With this legislation, the police have the authority to detain for up to six hours any person who is disrupting the public order and who is considered an immediate danger to the community. The person, however, is not subject to any legal consequences, nor is their name placed in official registers. This is clearly an example of a proactive crime prevention strategy that has the force of law.

Advocates of a continued reform of Sweden's justice system voiced some criticism of this law, focusing their concerns on three questions: (1) To what extent does this law serve a crime prevention role? (2) Is it a serious attack on one's human rights? (3) And is there adequate concern, either explicit or implicit, for the welfare of the person detained?

Eckart Kuhlhorn conducted an evaluation of the Temporary Custody Act (Knutsson, Kuhlhorn, and Reiss, 1979; Kuhlhorn, 1978). The study revealed that of all the people detained each year by police, only a small percentage are held as a result of this legislation. When detention was used, detainees were accused of active disturbances of the peace, such as violence, assaults, threats of violence, or loud noise in 67 percent of the cases. Gang behavior was responsible for 30 percent of the detentions, while conflicts with police were responsible for the remaining 3 percent. Kuhlhorn discovered that detainees were under the influence of alcohol or other drugs in approximately 66 percent of the cases, that the public had summoned police in 33 percent of the incidents, and that police attempted to resolve the problem without invoking the act in 60 percent of the cases.

Some critics were also concerned that police might use the legislation to curb political demonstrations, but Kuhlhorn's study found no evidence to support such a charge. Approximately 66 percent of those detained had been convicted of a serious crime in the past five years. These crimes often involved the use of violence in which alcohol or other drugs played a role.

The purpose of the Temporary Custody Act is to prevent through detention the commission of a criminal act. Kuhlhorn contends that every fifth detention prevented the continuance of a violent activity in a high-crime area. The act appears to help restrict criminal activity in high-crime areas. Finally, although only 6 percent of those detained were contacted by a social service agency, it is believed that this can be attributed to the fact that 60 percent of the people were already under some kind of social care. The use of the Temporary Custody Act will continue as long as the public remains concerned about the growth of violence and gang activity, especially in urban centers. Proponents of this legislation were given further assurances of its credibility when key provisions of the act were incorporated (at Sections 11 through 18) into the Police Act 1992.

In the late 1970s, Operation Identification was introduced with the hope of reducing residential burglaries. Two features differentiate the Swedish scheme from those introduced in the United States. In Sweden, all people use their identification number, received at birth by each citizen, for purposes of identifying their property. Each item is then recorded on the national police computer, along with the owner's identification number and the item's registration number.

Shortly after this scheme was made operational, one report suggested that police had improved their ability to return stolen property to the rightful owner (Snortum, 1983). Another study, however, attempted to evaluate the success of Operation Identification. It concluded that no crime prevention effect could be found with the scheme. It also pointed out that some items that are particularly attractive to burglars, such as jewelry and silver, are often too small to mark (Knutsson, 1984).

Since 1975, Sweden has had a policy of establishing random roadside police checks for drunk driving. One study conducted to test the merits of such checks found that of the 1,182,482 breath analysis samples collected, less than 1 percent showed violations of Sweden's drunk driving laws (Snortum, 1983). Other researchers have argued that this study, along with other data, suggests Sweden's drunk driving laws are effective (Shapiro and Votey, 1986).

The laws in question obviously relate to the possible sanctions involved. For first-time offenders with a blood alcohol level of 1.5 or more per thousand grams of blood, a one-month prison sentence is authorized. A second offense within three years calls for a two-month prison sentence. Later in this chapter it will be noted that Sweden's overall correctional policy tends either to limit or to avoid incarceration for most offenders. Those found with blood alcohol levels between .05 and .15 receive significant fines. The fine is the common method of sanctioning in Sweden. In addition, an offender with a blood alcohol level in excess of .08 may have his or her license suspended for one year.

In 1999, legislation was introduced to cover driving under the influence of drugs that can impair a person's ability to drive. This legislation also established two categories of "drink-driving"; in this context, drink-driving means under the influence of either alcohol or other drugs. The first category is called the offense of drink-driving, which can lead to either a fine or imprisonment of up to six months. The second category is gross drink-driving and is reserved for those offenders who are deemed seriously intoxicated. This category can lead to a term of imprisonment for up to two years. It is interesting to note that sanctions of either imprisonment or fine are decided by a district court, which is part of the regular court system of Sweden. However, a suspension of a driver's license is handled in a regional administrative court. The distinctions between regular courts and administrative courts are explained in the next section on the judiciary. In addition, the crime prevention strategy of random roadside checks may serve to disprove a common perception that Sweden is a fairly permissive society. This perception is based in part on the country's liberal social welfare policies. Admittedly, this liberal philosophy often comes into play within the justice system at the treatment phase, but that does not mean the country is without fairly strict laws and methods of enforcement.

In each of the aforementioned crime prevention strategies, the police have a central role to play in the development, implementation, and maintenance of the strategies. Recently, there has been a conscious effort to revise this approach by removing part of this exclusive burden from the police. Part of the reason for this change was the recognition that crime has continued to increase, despite the efforts of the police. For example, there has been a 500 percent increase in crime from 1950 to 1995 (Ministry of Justice, 1997b). What is particularly troubling is that the increases have included the serious categories of assault, robbery, theft, and drug abuse.

As was mentioned earlier, the country embarked on a national crime prevention program in 1996 that is based on the following premises. First, the government is ultimately responsible for crime policy. Second, crime policy should not be exclusively limited to crime issues but rather be inclusive of the social problems that are often associated with crime. Third, the causes of crime must be addressed where the problems exist, which is at the local level. Finally, a successful crime prevention strategy requires not only a commitment from the general public but also active citizen involvement in the effort.

A central feature of the crime prevention strategy is the adoption of a collaborative model to address the problem. The collaborative model is multifaceted and a truly system-wide endeavor. It seeks greater cooperation among agencies of the criminal justice system, in particular police, prosecutors, and juvenile justice. It attempts to establish an ongoing interaction among criminal justice agencies and other public- and private-sector groups. These groups include: welfare authorities, housing authorities, nursery schools, elementary and high schools, leisure centers for children, the business community, and residential neighborhoods.

The program has three goals: (1) to reduce opportunities for crime, (2) to reduce recruitment to criminal lifestyles, and (3) to reduce the criminal activity of persistent offenders. It is the responsibility of local crime prevention councils to develop plans to address these goals. It should be pointed out that the local crime prevention councils include a cross section of the community from the private- and public-sector groups. The specific crime prevention plans that a council identifies are expected to address one of four basic objectives: (1) make it more difficult to commit crime, (2) increase the risk of detection, (3) reduce the rewards of crime, or (4) make the justification of crime more difficult. From the perspective of the police, what has emerged from this government initiative is a renewed commitment to community policing with a specific focus on problem-oriented policing.

The National Council for Crime Prevention (NCCP) is available to support these local efforts throughout the country. The NCCP has been given four specific tasks. First, it is expected to stimulate local crime prevention efforts by assisting with basic issues of organization. Second, the NCCP will provide information on crime prevention. Third, it will facilitate or secure any training needs. Finally, it will monitor and evaluate a selection of these local crime prevention projects (Ministry of Justice, 1997b).

The emphasis placed on the importance of local crime prevention efforts has the support of local communities. As of 2000, 175 of Sweden's 289 municipalities had established a local crime prevention council. The NCCP facilitated these efforts by developing a "best practices" approach to organizing and integrating a crime prevention council in local communities. The Council has provided additional literature that is designed to target specific crime prevention issues. These include: assessing local problems, describing more than 30 different crime prevention projects, evaluating projects, mapping and crime prevention, neighborhood watch, the role of schools in reducing antisocial behavior, prevention of violence against women, and parental activities at the local level.

It also should be noted that Sweden has approximately 10,000 licensed security guards. The training of these guards is arranged through the local police. Some police authorities have the guards assemble at the local police station before their shift in order to update them on significant events. Other authorities have the guards prepare brief written reports on the state of security in their particular area.

The police also have devised some crime prevention programs specifically designed to meet the needs of young people. That subject is discussed in the section on juvenile justice.

Judiciary

Early in its history, Sweden's administration of justice was independent of royal authority. It was noted for being carried out at the grassroots level. Local custom remained the principal law in Sweden for resolving disputes until the sixteenth century. Throughout this period, Sweden was divided into districts called *lands*. Each land retained legislative and judicial powers over its territory. Within each land there was a local assembly called a *ting*, which was responsible for passing legislation and enforcing the customs of the district.

The principal administrative officer of a land was the lawman, who was learned in the customary law of the district. Throughout much of Europe, the people who were usually knowledgeable in law were members of the clergy (because they could read and write) or the wealthiest landowners in a territory (because of the economic power they wielded). This was not the case in Sweden, however. The lawman could be anyone in a community who understood the customary law and who had gained the trust of the electorate.

During the medieval period, some Swedish kings attempted to unify the law and the administration of justice. The method of codification was employed to establish a law that could be enforced throughout the country. Attempts at codification will be discussed later in the section on the law.

Efforts to unify the administration of justice were illustrated by attempts to centralize the courts. This was initiated by King Erik of Pomerania when he attempted to replace the tings with a royal court. According to his decree, which was handed down in 1413, judges would be appointed by the king and would sit with lawmen to hear cases. The court would also have appellate jurisdiction over the land-tings. Later, lower courts and an intermediate appellate court would be introduced. The king, however, was unable to gain the support of the people for this scheme.

It was not until the seventeenth century that King Gustavus II Adolphus (1611–1632) succeeded in centralizing the courts. He established a final court of appeals, the *Svea Hoffratt*; an intermediate appellate court, the *Hoffratt*; and general trial courts, *Radstuguratt*. As a result of these changes, the judge and *namnd* (a body of 12 citizens responsible for investigating pertinent facts in a case) would settle judicial disputes independently. Their decisions were no longer subject to the ratification of the ting. Gustavus Adolphus also had legislative authority transferred to the National Assembly, which was composed of nobles, clergy, property owners, and townspeople. Thus, the power and authority of the land-tings ceased to exist by the seventeenth century.

Although Sweden was the first Scandinavian country to establish a distinct legal profession, its development lagged behind that of many other European countries. Like other countries on the continent, the emergence of a legal profession was associated with a university education. The University of Uppsala was the first university established in Sweden. Before Uppsala was founded in 1477, Swedish students had to journey to continental universities. Because Uppsala did not have a law school, the universities at Paris, Leipzig, and Prague tended to attract Sweden's law students. While studying abroad, these students were introduced to the Romano-Germanic tradition.

Gustavus Adolphus's efforts to promote legal studies were realized in 1620 when a law school was established at Uppsala. For a number of years, Uppsala employed only one law professor, but the school eventually established a chair in Roman law in 1657. From its inception, the law school produced graduates who sought careers in government service, and this tradition has continued to this day. Another Swedish tradition also has been maintained: a person does not have to have the qualifications of a lawyer to represent people in court.

Organization and Administration of the Courts

Sweden has a three-tiered court hierarchy that is responsible for handling civil and criminal litigation. The Code of Judicial Procedure explains the organization and functions of these courts. Figure 3.2 illustrates the organization of Sweden's general courts. Before the general court system is described, it is important to mention briefly the role of a few government units that have a role to play in either the management or work of the courts and also to explain the purpose of the administrative courts.

National Courts Administration It was pointed out earlier that the Ministry of Justice is the cabinet-level department in the government that is responsible for the judiciary. In addition, it was mentioned that cabinet ministries are primarily concerned with the initiation of legislation in the Riksdag. The actual day-to-day coordination of government is the responsibility of central administration. With regard to courts, that responsibility falls to the National Courts Administration. Specifically, the administrative responsibilities include general courts, administrative courts, various tribunals, and the National Legal Aid Authority. It also coordinates training programs and is the source for information about the judiciary.

Figure 3.2

ORGANIZATION OF THE GENERAL COURTS

The Supreme Court

|

Courts of Appeal

|

District Courts

The Chancellor of Justice The Chancellor of Justice is the chief legal advisor to the cabinet and represents the state in civil litigation. The Chancellor also has an oversight responsibility. Attention was directed earlier at the role of the Office of the Parliamentary Ombudsman and its role in providing oversight of government bureaucracy in order to curb or prevent abuse. As mentioned, that office is accountable to the Riksdag, which created the position. The Chancellor of Justice provides a similar role to that of the ombudsman; in fact, the office utilizes many of the procedures followed by the ombudsman. One of the principal differences between the two is that the Chancellor of Justice is accountable to the government rather than to the Riksdag. The Chancellor provides an oversight function that is designed to ensure that officials of the government are in compliance with government regulations. Two of the more noteworthy pieces of legislation that it has a particular responsibility for are the Freedom of the Press Act and the Fundamental Laws on Freedom of Expression. These are two of the four pieces of legislation that make up the fundamental law, or constitutional law, of the country.

The Law Council The power of judicial review is one of the principal responsibilities of the U.S. Supreme Court. In Sweden, this type of review is not practiced because it is believed that the independent status of courts could be compromised. Swedish constitutional law has established the Law Council, which is composed of judges from the Supreme Court and the Supreme Administrative Court. The Law Council has the responsibility of reviewing bills presented to the Riksdag to assure that they do not violate constitutional law. Thus, before a bill becomes law, its constitutionality has already been carefully scrutinized. A panel of three justices usually provides an opinion, but it is important to note that the government is not required to adhere to the Council's opinion. Any grievance that questions the constitutionality of a law after it has been enacted is directed to an administrative tribunal or to an ombudsman.

Administrative Courts Administrative law involves matters of constitutional and political importance to the Swedish system of government Because issues of this kind have been deemed nonappealable through the general court hierarchy, a separate court system was established to handle such matters. This method of having judicial arbitrators, who are divorced from the general courts but responsible for controlling the government bureaucracy, is common in many European countries. In Sweden, administrative tribunals at the county level are responsible for adjudicating decisions of the local and county authorities. Some of these decisions can be appealed to one of the four fiscal courts of appeal, which are located in the country's principal cities. The highest administrative court is the Supreme Administrative Court; it hears only those cases that involve possible precedent-setting issues.

General Courts The judicial bodies that are a key component of Sweden's criminal justice system are collectively referred to as general courts. As is true in other countries, the judges of these courts occupy an important position and make a significant contribution to the political system of their country. It has been suggested, however, that their political role is not as pronounced as it is in other countries, such as the United States. The extent to which these judges are able to maintain their judicial independence from the political system is based on three factors: (1) judges are not appointed to the bench based on past political associations or favors; (2) they do not rule on administrative matters, for that is the province of administrative tribunals; and (3) there is no tradition of judicial review, as those types of issues already have been anticipated and generally resolved by the Law Council. Thus, these judges are left with the responsibility of handling civil and criminal litigation.

The Supreme Court Established in 1789, the Supreme Court is composed of at least 16 permanent justices. The cabinet appoints one of the justices to serve as president of the court. The court's jurisdiction is primarily limited to hearing appeals against decisions handed down in one of the courts of appeal. The court carefully scrutinizes the kinds of cases that it will hear, and generally accepts for review only those cases that may establish a precedent. There is an exception to this rule in that cases brought by the Director of Public Prosecutions will automatically be reviewed. In other instances, the decision to accept or reject a request for appeal is made by a panel of three justices. If the request is approved, usually five justices (but no more than seven) sit to hear the appeal. If during the course of a hearing a majority of the justices are inclined to overturn a legal principle previously established by the court, the justices may decide that the case should be heard by either the entire court or at least nine members. One might get the impression that the Swedish legal system adheres to the principle of *stare decisis*. That is not the case, however. Judges in Sweden apply the law as they interpret it; they are not obliged to follow precedent. While judges do appreciate the value of consistency and show deference to the Supreme Court's previous judgments, they are not bound by them.

Courts of Appeal There are six courts of appeal, and each is given a territorial jurisdiction as determined by the cabinet. These courts hear appeals from district courts. They also have limited powers to serve as courts of first instance in special cases. The courts are divided into two or more divisions. Civil matters are determined by five judges, whereas criminal appeals are heard by three judges and two lay judges (or lay assessors). The role of lay judges will be explained later in this section. Although each court handles most of the appeals from the city in which it is located, it may hold sessions in other locations within its circuit if the circumstances warrant it. The cabinet also can require a court of appeal to hold a session in another place within its circuit at specific times throughout the year.

District Courts The district courts are the principal courts of first instance in the Swedish court hierarchy. They handle about 95 percent of all litigation in the country. The cabinet determines how many district courts are needed to serve the country; currently there are 53. Each court is presided over by a chief judge and several assistant judges. The court may also be divided into divisions. The number of judges hearing a civil case may range between one and three. The number is dependent on the nature of the case, the degree of difficulty, and, in some cases, the agreement of the parties to the dispute. Criminal cases are handled by one judge and a panel of three lay judges. Cases of minor importance are heard by a single judge. If the legal issue involves a technical matter, the bench is composed of judges and technical experts. This is common in cases involving real estate.

Special Courts Although courts are essentially organized into the two categories of general or administrative courts, there are some additional courts that are detached from these categories and specialize in a very narrow branch of law. For example, the Labor Court handles all labor issues and has both original and appellate jurisdiction. A labor court includes at least seven people. The chairman and deputy chairman must be trained in law, while a third member does not have to be trained in law but must have expertise in labor market conditions. The other members of the court do not have to be trained in law; they include two people recommended by the employers' organization and two people recommended by the employees' organization.

Other special courts include the Market Court, which handles disputes about restraints on trade and marketing practices. The chair of this court is a legally trained judge, while the other members represent business, employee, and consumer interests. There is also a Housing Court as well as Rent and Leasehold Tribunals that are composed of some judges trained in law, while others represent landlord and tenant interests. In 1999, the enactment of an Environmental Code called for the establishment of Environmental Courts. Usually, this court is composed of a legally trained judge, an environmental advisor, and two environmental experts. One expert has experience in environmental protection, while the other has been involved with industrial or municipal organizations. The existence of these special courts is another illustration of how and why Sweden is noted for its highly stable social system. The composition of the bench for these courts is obviously an attempt to assure that compromises are sought and a consensus is achieved.

The Legal Profession

Once law students complete their legal studies at a law school, they choose a career path of either judge, prosecutor, or private counsel. Thus, the legal profession is divided into three distinct groups: judges, public prosecutors, and attorneys. Members of each group have been professionally trained in law. Although lay judges serve an important purpose in the judicial process, they are distinct from the legal profession.

Judges Judges represent a separate tier in the legal profession. They follow a tradition, long established in European countries, that has been influenced by the Romano-Germanic legal tradition. Graduates of a law school who have received a master of law degree and aspire to careers on the bench apply to the Ministry of Justice. If accepted, about 30 percent are successful, they begin their career in the judicial civil service with an assignment to one of the courts. Their principal duties are to assist judges in preparing to hear cases and to serve as court clerks. This period of training usually lasts two years. Once the training is completed and the candidates pass the appropriate test qualifying them for service on the bench, candidates are assigned to one of the district courts. At this point, the person is not considered a permanent judge. He or she is given a broad range of judicial assignments that can last up to eight years. Once a person secures one of the permanent judicial positions, the cabinet determines judicial appointments and promotions based on merit.

Judges who wish to serve at the appellate level usually must wait until they have accrued approximately 20 years of service. Supreme Court justices are generally selected from the ranks of the appellate judges. Occasionally, a law professor or a distinguished attorney is selected to serve on the high court.

Although the Swedish legal system has retained a number of characteristics that are indigenous to Sweden and its ancient legal tradition, it is nevertheless part of the Romano-Germanic family. That tradition started in the middle ages when students journeyed to France and Germany to acquire their legal education. This subsided somewhat during the seventeenth and eighteenth centuries but was renewed during the nineteenth century, when Swedish legal scholars were influenced by French and German legal thought.

Today, the method of judicial interpretation has been characterized as a mixture of that which was practiced in France and Germany and then in England and the United States. A good deal of importance is placed on statutory law, but the Swedes have not tried to establish an all-encompassing legal code, which is a characteristic of France and Germany. They do appreciate the significance of precedent, but Swedish judges are not bound by precedent. Thus, they do not rely upon judge-made law to the same extent as England or the United States. The Swedish judge applies the law based on his or her interpretation.

Public Prosecutors The organization of public prosecutors is under the administration of the Ministry of Justice. At the top of the administrative hierarchy is the Prosecutor-General, the individual directly responsible for the prosecutorial system. Appointed by the cabinet, the Prosecutor-General has the specific duty of prosecuting cases before the Supreme Court and is also responsible for initiating actions in lower courts when the accused is a civil servant, judge, or military commander who allegedly has violated the public trust. The most obvious grounds for such action would be charges of bribery.

The country is further divided into 43 local offices, which are administered by a chief district prosecutor. Among these offices, 35 are general public prosecution offices, while six deal with international cases. The remaining two are national prosecution offices: one deals with anti-corruption, and the other focuses on allegations of crime among police officers. It should be further noted that there is a special prosecutorial department, the Swedish National Economic Crimes Bureau, which deals with all matters associated with white-collar crime.

State prosecutors are responsible for public prosecutions within their district. They are actively involved in the preliminary investigation of cases, especially cases that are considered serious. Prosecutors decide whether to charge the accused and conduct any subsequent prosecution before the court. Thus, the prosecutor is afforded a good deal of power in the administration of justice. It should be noted that in cases involving young offenders the prosecutor may waive the proceedings and permit a local board to address the issue with the objective of developing a program of rehabilitation. Although most prosecutions are instituted by a prosecutor's office, the Code of Judicial Procedure permits injured parties to initiate prosecutions by applying to a court for a summons against the accused.

Graduates of law school who have received a master of law degree and aspire to prosecutorial careers apply to the Ministry of Justice. Once a candidate is accepted, the person begins a two-and-one-half-year training period. Part of the time is spent working in district offices of prosecutors. The rest of the training is spent with the police—especially the detective division—because one of the responsibilities of the Swedish prosecutor is to direct police in the preliminary investigation of alleged crimes. After this practical training is completed, the candidate attends a special prosecutors' course. The candidate is then prepared to begin a career as a prosecutor with civil service status.

Attorneys In Sweden, the accused is not required to employ an attorney for his or her defense. The accused may choose to defend himself or herself or select someone who is not trained in the law to represent his or her interests. This tradition is being phased out, however, as more people are either hiring an attorney or requesting that the court appoint one. When a court is asked to appoint a public defender, that person must be a member of the Swedish Bar Association. Compared with other countries, the number of attorneys in private practice is small. Approximately one-half of the attorneys in practice are members of a law firm. The size of the firms are also small, ranging between two and five members. The work of attorneys in Sweden is similar to that of lawyers in the United States in that they provide a variety of services. They have the responsibility of drawing up legal documents, advising clients, and representing them in court. Attorneys are not restricted with regard to where they plead cases; they can practice before any court in the country.

Attorneys gain admittance to the Swedish Bar Association after they have received a master of law degree and have practiced law with merit for at least five years. A board exists within this association that supervises members and has the authority to disqualify an attorney from practicing law. The Code of Judicial Procedure also has mandated to the attorney general the authority to request that the board take action against any attorney who has been negligent in his or her duties. Attorneys' fees are not monitored by an official schedule, but there are general rules regulating fees to assure that compensation is not unreasonable.

Lay Judges

The terms "lay judges," "lay assessors," "namnd," and "jurors" have been used synonymously to describe a component of Sweden's judicial system dating back to the medieval period. In order to reduce the likelihood of confusing the issue, this component will be referred to as lay judges. As was mentioned earlier in this section, lay judges had emerged by the thirteenth century as an important feature in Sweden's administration of justice. At that time, both parties to a suit selected six people to serve as lay judges. The lay judges would then collect the facts that were pertinent to the case. In conjunction with the lawman, the lay judges would decide the case based on their investigation of the facts and the oral testimony of the parties involved.

Although lawmen were replaced by professional judges in the seventeenth century, the role of lay judges was retained. Originally, lay judges were viewed as a check on royal authority in the context of the administration of justice, because the king had the power to appoint judges. Today, lay judges are viewed as an important feature of the democratic political system. This rationale is often given for the jury system in countries that ascribe to democratic principles.

While lay judges have one thing in common with Anglo-American and continental juries (that is, assuring civilian participation in the administration of justice), it is important to stress the fact that the Swedish scheme has a number of distinct characteristics setting it apart from both the common law and civil law jury systems. For example, lay judges are elected to serve in either a district court or one of the courts of appeal. Members of a municipal council select people to serve at the district level, while county council representatives elect people to serve in the appellate courts. Lay judges serve a four-year term, but they usually sit in court for only 10 days out of a year. Because the position of lay judge is renewable, some have served a number of years and have become quite knowledgeable in the law. Lay judges are not paid a salary, but they do receive a per diem allowance.

To be eligible to serve as a lay judge, one must be a Swedish citizen and under the age of 70. A person cannot refuse the appointment unless they have reached the age of 60 or have a valid excuse. Although the usual term of service is four years, a person can resign following the completion of his or her second year. The Code of Judicial Procedure also has identified certain categories of people who are excluded from participation. They are: judges, court officers and employees, public prosecutors, police, attorneys, and any others professionally engaged in judicial proceedings.

In district courts, lay judges are used in serious criminal cases and cases involving family matters. The bench is composed of one professional judge and three lay judges. In criminal matters, the entire bench decides issues of law and fact and imposes an appropriate sanction. Although it is rare, a majority of lay judges can prevail over the opinion of the professional judge. The courts of appeal use lay judges when hearing criminal cases. In the appellate courts, the bench is composed of three professional judges and two lay judges.

Lay judges can be disqualified from hearing a case. This usually occurs under one of five circumstances: (1) a lay judge or a relative has a special interest in the case by which they stand to gain from the outcome of the trial; (2) a lay judge is related to one of the parties in the case; (3) there is an adversarial relationship between one of the parties and a lay judge; (4) a lay judge already has been involved in the case but in a different context; or (5) the circumstances are such that a lay judge is unlikely to be impartial if permitted to hear the case. If a lay judge is disqualified from a case or fails to attend the session and no other lay judge is available, the professional judge can substitute anyone in the municipality or county who is eligible for election.

The effectiveness of this system of lay participation is dependent on the professional judge's ability to be patient and tolerant of the questions that are put by lay judges. Such questions frequently involve points of law. Lay judges generally respect the opinions of the professional judges with whom they work. Thus, the professional judge tends to influence the outcome of the trial.

Legal Education

Sweden's system of legal education resembles more closely the approach established on the continent of Europe than that which has evolved in England or the United States. Sweden has five law schools, which are located at the Universities of Uppsala, Lund, Stockholm, Göteborg, and Umeå. All were founded by the government, and the government remains the principal employer of many of the graduates.

Depending upon the pace with which the student wishes to proceed, a law student will spend four to five years pursuing the degree. The two principal areas of study are civil law and public law. Civil law consists of such subjects as contracts, torts, property, estates, criminal law and procedure, commercial law, and civil procedure. Public law includes constitutional law, administrative law, and finance and taxation. The mode of instruction is theoretical in nature and is not designed to enhance the student's ability to master the mechanical aspects of practicing law. Moreover, emphasis is placed primarily on studying the codes and statutes rather than case law because the doctrine of *stare decisis* is not applicable. Examinations for the courses may be taken any time a student feels ready to be tested on the material. Law schools do not administer a comprehensive examination to degree candidates; nor do graduates take a bar examination in order to practice law.

The number of law professors in Sweden is extremely small: approximately 100 people who teach law at the five schools. They are selected on the basis of their scholarly accomplishments and must hold a doctorate in law. In addition to teaching and individual scholarly pursuits, law professors often assist in drafting legislation and serve as advisors to various committees of the Riksdag.

LAW

Throughout the twentieth century, Scandinavian legal scholars have debated the issue of whether their law should be distinguished as a distinct legal family like the Romano-Germanic law and the common law. Central to this discussion is the extent to which Scandinavian law was influenced by Roman law in its development. At the turn of the twentieth century, many Scandinavian scholars rejected the contention that Roman law played a significant role in the evolution of their legal system. They were almost as vehement in their arguments as were the late nineteenth-century English scholars who advanced the unique and indigenous qualities of England's common law. Advocates of a separate Scandinavian family thesis suggested that Scandinavian law was markedly different in content from that which emerged on the continent of Europe.

Today, these arguments have been amended considerably. A number of Scandinavian legal scholars contend that their legal system is indeed part of the Romano-Germanic family. The basis for this contention is that the unity of the Romano-Germanic family is found in the formal techniques of the law rather than in its specific content. In support of this view, Jacob Sundberg (1969) cited two basic factors that have characterized the evolution of Romano-Germanic law. One is the conscious attempt to establish a simple and consistent approach to law through what Sundberg refers to as a conceptual apparatus. This apparatus includes the importance placed on codifying the law. Scandinavian countries had a long tradition of codification, dating back to the early Middle Ages when the development of provincial codes was largely based on customary law. Although the customary law may have been indigenously created, one can assume that law students who went to the continent to study Roman law must have brought back ideas to augment their existing system—especially if the customary law did not provide a resolution for all disputes.

During the early modern period, Scandinavian monarchs established national codes. Sweden developed its first national code in 1734 and has been revising it ever since. Admittedly, Sweden's codes are not as systematic as what one finds among other continental codes. Nevertheless, revisions of the codes were influenced by French and German legal thought during the nineteenth and early twentieth centuries, respectively. Moreover, convincing arguments have been offered for the reception of Roman law during the seventeenth century. For example, it has been suggested that Roman law was being used by the Svea Court of Appeals to settle commercial disputes (Jagerskiold, 1967). Thus, there is a strong case for the existence of Roman law influences since the early modern era, with the possibility that they extend even further back in time.

The other factor that Sundberg cited as characteristic of the evolution of Romano-Germanic law is the fact that medieval universities were founded largely by monarchs who viewed these institutions as training academies for civil servants. It follows that the legal process and, in particular, the legal education taught at these institutions were viewed as instruments by which the monarch could enhance the ability to govern. The close relationship of the legal profession to the executive branch of government has long been ingrained in Scandinavian countries. For example, Swedish judges are reluctant to interfere with the work of the legislature or the executive. They view themselves as civil servants whose responsibility is to carry out the politics of the ruling majority rather than developing their own particular point of view. Thus, although the content of the law may vary from country to country, it is the technique that unites those countries claiming membership in the Romano-Germanic family.

Criminal Law

Sweden's criminal justice system is regulated by legislation established by the Riksdag. The principal legislative enactments are found in the Code of Judicial Procedure, which explains the procedures for enforcing the criminal law, and the Penal Code, which identifies the various types of crimes and appropriate sanctions. Offenses are not categorized as felonies or misdemeanors, and all crimes are not listed in the Penal Code. There are a number of offenses that are described in separate statutes, including traffic offenses and narcotics violations.

Because Sweden has refrained from the large-scale codification that is common among other European countries, there is room for judicial interpretation. This has traditionally been viewed as a feature of the common law family. Thus, despite the fact that Sweden is considered a member of the Romano-Germanic family, the judiciary has a limited, although important, role in interpreting legislation. This has resulted in some scholars suggesting that Sweden's legal system occupies a halfway point between continental and Anglo-American legal systems.

The most important source of criminal law is the Penal Code. The current code came into force in 1965 and has been subjected to a number of revisions. The code is divided into three parts. The first part contains general provisions that are designed to explain the extent to which the criminal law may be applied. For example, a criminal act does not exist unless intent was established at the time of the act. Issues of intent and negligence are considered to be elements of a crime, but they are not defined in the Penal Code. It is the responsibility of the court to offer a conceptual definition as it applies to a particular case. While Sweden's criminal law does not distinguish offenses as felonies and misdemeanors, the law does make distinctions between punishments (imprisonment and fine), penal measures (conditional sentence, probation, and surrender for special care), and other legal consequences (forfeiture of property or liability for damages).

The second part of the Penal Code consists of a listing of many of the major crimes and the specific elements that constitute each offense. The type of sanction that may be imposed is also cited. The offenses listed in the code are divided into several categories, including: crimes against life and health; crimes against liberty and peace; theft, robbery, and other crimes of stealing; crimes against public order; and crimes against the security of the realm. It should be noted that Sweden does not have a separate military criminal code. Thus, the Penal Code includes a chapter devoted to crimes by members of the armed services. Finally, the third part of the code is concerned with principles for assessing sanctions. This includes the choice, limitations, and remission of sanctions.

Criminal Procedure

For our purposes, the examination of Sweden's criminal procedure is divided into two categories. The first involves the pretrial process, which includes an examination of police powers and other issues pertinent to the preliminary investigation. The second category is concerned with the trial process, which consists of the main hearing as well as appellate reviews. Sweden's Code of Judicial Procedure is the legal document that explains all of the aforementioned procedures. This code is not limited to criminal procedures, however. Procedural issues involving civil cases are also presented.

Preliminary Investigation Once it has been determined that a crime has been committed, a preliminary investigation is undertaken to determine who committed the act or who can be reasonably suspected of being involved in the crime. The principle of mandatory prosecution prevails throughout an investigation. This means that the authorities have a legal duty to prosecute anyone whose guilt has been substantially established. Preliminary investigations are conducted by either the police or the prosecutor. Police usually handle investigations that are fairly straightforward, but the prosecutor may issue instructions pertaining to the conduct of an investigation. Prosecutors conduct investigations with the aid of police when the matter is complex or when a person has been reasonably suspected of committing the crime.

The code is clear on the need to have a preliminary investigation conducted in as objective a manner as possible. Chapter 23, Section 4, states:

> At the preliminary investigation not only circumstances that are not in favour of the suspect but also circumstances in his favour shall be considered, and any evidence favourable to the suspect shall be preserved. The investigation should be conducted so that no person is unnecessarily exposed to suspicion, or put to unnecessary expense or inconvenience.

If reasonable suspicion focuses on an individual, the individual must be promptly informed of this so that a lawyer can be chosen and retained at public expense. Defense counsel will not usually conduct their own investigation because they have access to a copy of the prosecutor's investigative report. Moreover, the suspect or lawyer may request the prosecutor to question people or collect evidence that will assist in the defense. Such requests are complied with as long as they aid in the completion of an objective investigation. If the prosecution refuses a request, they must state their reasons. The defense then has the right to report the refusal to the court. The entire preliminary investigation significantly reduces the likelihood that surprise witnesses or evidence will be introduced at trial.

Any person who possesses information pertinent to a case may be questioned during a preliminary investigation. The interrogation of a person who is not under arrest or being detained cannot exceed six hours. The person is free to leave once an examination is completed and cannot be called back for further questioning until 12 hours have elapsed. The accused and his or her defense counsel may be present at an interrogation and may question the person who is being examined.

Whenever possible, the code also calls for the presence at examinations of "a reliable witness commissioned by the investigating authority." Since 1957, the municipal council of Götenburg has appointed local citizens and paid them a salary to attend interrogations in order to assure that a person's rights are protected during the preliminary examination. It has been suggested that this scheme should be implemented throughout the country. Once the prosecution has decided to prosecute, a summons application must be submitted to the court. The court then issues a summons to the defendant and requests a copy of the evidence that will be used at the main hearing for the defense.

Powers to Arrest and Detain A police officer's power to arrest involves two sets of circumstances: (1) cases of arrest with a detention order, and (2) cases of arrest without such an order. Following the commencement of a preliminary investigation, detention orders are issued by the court for an accused who could be imprisoned for at least two years; for suspects who could be imprisoned for at least one year and can be reasonably expected to flee, evade, or impede the legal proceedings; and for suspects in less serious cases who have no permanent residence and may flee. Thus, the standard fears of fleeing, collusion, or recidivism determine who will be arrested. When circumstances justify it, a person can be arrested while awaiting the court's formal order, but a person may not be detained if it is assumed that they will only be sentenced to a fine. There is one exception to this last rule, however.

> Any person suspected on probable cause of an offence may be detained regardless of the nature of the offence if: 1. his identity is unknown, and he either refuses to provide his name and address or he provides a name and address that can be assumed is false; or 2. he does not reside in the Realm and there is a reasonable risk that he will avoid legal proceedings or a penalty by fleeing the country.

Arrests without a detention order are permitted when the apprehended person "has committed an offence punishable by imprisonment, if he is caught in the very act of running away from the place. Anyone may also apprehend a person wanted for an offence. The apprehended person shall promptly be turned over to the first policeman encountered." Such people must be examined by the arresting authority as soon as possible.

Once an arrest has been made, the person must "be informed of the offense for which he is suspected. The household servants, or the immediate relatives, of the arrested person shall also be notified of the arrest as soon as this can be done without detriment to the investigation." The decision to detain a person is made by a professional judge at a court hearing. Suspects arrested by the police must be brought before a judge within 24 hours, but if a detention order is made, the initial appearance must occur within four days of the arrest. At this initial hearing, the court also determines when the main hearing will commence.

If the period of detention before the main hearing exceeds two weeks, the court must review its decision every two weeks and keep abreast of the prosecutor's preliminary investigation to assure that there are no unnecessary delays. If the case involves a fairly simple matter and the main hearing will occur within a week from the time of arrest, then a decision to detain can be made at the time of the main hearing. As a rule, the court must begin the main hearing within the week following the formal approval to prosecute.

Power to Search and Seize The powers to search and seize are also governed by the Code of Judicial Procedure. A search of a premise may be issued by either the police, the prosecutor, or the court. The rules under Chapter 28, Sections 1 and 2, explain when such searches may be conducted:

> Sec. 1. If there is reason to believe that an offence punishable by imprisonment has been committed, houses, rooms, or closed storage places may be searched to look for objects subject to seizure or to detect other information of potential importance to the inquiry of the offence.
>
> The premises of a person, other than one reasonably suspected of having committed the offense may not be searched unless the offence was committed there, or extraordinary reason indicates that the search will reveal an object subject to seizure or other information concerning the offence.
>
> A suspect's consent is not adequate to justify a search of his premises unless the suspect personally initiated the request for the search.
>
> Sec. 2. In order to find a person who is to be apprehended, arrested, detained, taken in custody for questioning or appearance in court or subjected to a body search or a body search conducted at his premises, or at another person's premises if there is extraordinary reason to assume that the person wanted is present there. The same applies to a defendant wanted for service of a summons application or summons to appear at the hearing if efforts to serve have failed or are considered pointless.

The code also calls for the authorities who conduct a search to secure a witness to the search. This could include the person whose premises are searched. If this is not possible, Chapter 28, Section 7, of the code states: "the person whose premises were searched must be notified of the search as soon as this is possible without detriment to the investigation." During the course of the search, any object that is considered important to the investigation can be seized. However, "[i]f a seizure is executed by anyone other than the investigating authority or the prosecutor, and neither of them has ordered the seizure, a report shall promptly be made to him, and he must then immediately consider and determine whether the seizure shall remain in effect."

An officer may conduct a search of a premise without a search order if the purpose is to apprehend, arrest, or detain a suspect. Moreover, body searches are considered reasonable "[i]f there is reason to believe that an offence punishable by imprisonment has been committed a person reasonably suspected of the offence may be subjected to a body search ..." Moreover, a person, who is not the suspect, "may be subjected to a body search if there is extraordinary reason to assume that an object subject to seizure thereby be discovered or it is otherwise of importance for investigating the offence."

Both the power to arrest and detain and to search and seize are viewed as awesome powers. Officials who fail to abide by the rules and instructions governing these powers may find themselves subject to punishment. The power to sanction irregular activities by any civil servant is found in the Penal Code. Chapter 20, Section 1, states, in part:

> A person who in the exercise of public authority by act or by omission, intentionally or through carelessness, disregards the duties of his office, shall be sentenced for misuse of office to pay a fine or imprisonment for at most two years. If, having regard to the perpetrator's official powers or the nature of his office considered in relation to his exercise of public power in other respects or having regard to other circumstances, the act may be regarded as petty, punishment shall not be imposed.
>
> If a crime mentioned in the first paragraph has been committed intentionally and is regarded as gross, a sentence for gross misuse of office to imprisonment for at least six months and at most six years shall be imposed. In assessing whether the crime is gross, special attention shall be given to whether the offender seriously abused his position or whether the crime occasioned serious harm to an individual or the public sector or a substantial improper benefit.

Travel Prohibitions Swedish constitutional law does not provide for a right to release on bail. When there is some risk that a defendant might attempt to flee the area, the Code of Judicial Procedure allows for the issuance of travel prohibitions as a substitute for detention. Travel prohibitions can be issued by the prosecutor or the court. If the order is issued by the prosecutor, the defendant can request the court to reconsider the order. A travel prohibition requires the person to obtain permission before leaving the area. Other restrictions are usually placed on the defendant with the issuance of such an order. For example, a defendant might be required to report daily (or several times a week) to local police or might be required to be present at his or her residence or place of employment at specific hours of the day. Failure to adhere to a travel prohibition or any other restriction can lead to the arrest and detention of the suspect.

Prosecutor and Defense Counsel Although the prosecutor and defense counsel have been alluded to earlier, a few additional comments are in order regarding procedural issues. As was pointed out, the principle of mandatory prosecution requires that a prosecutor commence proceedings against the accused if guilt has been sufficiently established. If a prosecutor initiates a prosecution that is not based on the probable guilt of the accused, the prosecutor may become the subject of a prosecution. Rules have been established to assist the prosecutor in deciding whether to prosecute. The exceptions for nonprosecution in cases in which guilt has been sufficiently established include: if the sanction is not more severe than a fine, if the public interest does not require prosecution, if the accused suffers from a mental abnormality in which he or she will be confined to an institution for treatment, or if the director of public prosecutions is of the opinion that a sanction is not required to prevent the suspect from further criminal activity. These rules illustrate the considerable discretionary authority of the prosecutor.

The breadth of prosecutorial discretion includes other issues as well. For instance, prosecutors may waive cases that are beyond the scope of the aforementioned rationales if it becomes obvious that a sanction is not needed to prevent future criminal activity or if special circumstances warrant refraining from initiating a prosecution. The enhancement of prosecutorial discretion was initiated more for economic reasons than for change in criminal policy. It was found that it would reduce the number of cases brought to court. Thus, although the rationale in law for prosecuting cases remains based on the mandatory prosecution principle, an economic principle founded on expediency has had a significant influence on the establishment of rules that supersede the mandatory prosecution principle. Finally, if the prosecutor decides not to prosecute, the injured party (or in the case of the victim's death, his or her descendants) may initiate the proceedings. However, private prosecutions are very rare.

Persons accused of a crime in Sweden have three options with regard to the manner in which they will be defended in court: (1) they may defend themselves, (2) they may hire their own attorney, or (3) they can ask the court to appoint a public defense counsel. The court will appoint a public defender if it finds the person is not capable of adequately defending himself or herself or protecting his or her own rights. Public defense counsel is not usually provided in minor criminal cases unless the accused is ill, is too old, or is a minor unable to safeguard his or her own rights. The right to select one's lawyer is considered an important principle in the judicial process. The actual selection of a public defender is made by the accused. However, the court may reject the choice if the defense counsel charges unusually high fees.

Public defenders are reimbursed for their services out of public funds that are based on a fee schedule. The fees can exceed the schedule if counsel can show that extensive work beyond the norm was required in the preparation of the case. If a defendant employs the services of a public defense counsel and is convicted, the defendant is liable to pay for part of the costs, based on economic status. The poor financial circumstances of many suspects usually eliminates that liability. A person who elects to pay for private counsel will have the costs reimbursed out of public funds if he or she is acquitted.

An outside observer may get the impression that defense lawyers in Sweden are passive parties to a trial. This is based on the fact that they rely upon the prosecutor's preliminary investigation and seldom make inquiries of their own, preferring instead to ask the prosecutor to supply the needed information. The issue is not one of indifference, but rather one of a difference in judicial tradition. Scandinavian lawyers do not view the trial as a battle. In fact, some view the American tradition of separate investigations and the occasional tactic of introducing surprise witnesses or evidence as bordering on being unethical. Scandinavian defense counsel perceive investigations undertaken by police and prosecutors to be objectively fair, thorough, and trustworthy. Thus, they usually consider a second investigation to be a superfluous exercise.

The Trial Swedish trials generally are governed by rules that are characteristic of many Romano-Germanic law countries. They differ in one noted respect, because over the past 50 years they have adopted the Anglo-American technique of allowing the prosecution and defense counsel to question both the accused and witnesses. In Romano-Germanic law countries, it traditionally has been the responsibility of the judge to examine the accused and witnesses.

Compared to a trial conducted in England or the United States, the Swedish trial might seem rather dull. Because the evidence pertaining to the case has already been revealed during the course of the preliminary investigation, there are few surprises uncovered during the trial. In addition, rules of evidence do not prohibit the introduction of hearsay evidence. Any information that is of significance to a case is admissible. This is based on the notion that the two parties should be permitted to submit their evidence and allow the court to decide the degree of its relevance.

The main hearing of a Swedish trial is generally open to the public. It is an oral hearing, which means that the parties involved may not read written statements or positions in the case. The principal participants in a trial are the district court, prosecutor, and defense counsel. The district court consists of one professional judge and three lay judges. In cases in which the maximum penalty is a fine, only one professional judge hears the case.

A victim may take an active part in a trial if he or she is seeking compensation for damages. In more serious cases, the court can appoint an aggrieved victim counsel to assist with the case. Serious crimes generally include those for which the sanction of imprisonment may be imposed.

Thus, the appointment of counsel cannot occur until after the preliminary investigation has been initiated. The cost of the aggrieved victim counsel is provided by public funds. If the accused is found guilty, the judgment of the court may include paying the costs of the aggrieved victim counsel.

The standard trial procedures for the main hearing include the following steps:

1. The prosecutor reads the summons application, which describes the crime and the circumstances in which it was committed and includes a statement of the reasons for charging the defendant with the crime. The prosecutor can claim compensation for damages for the injured party, or the victim may make this claim.

2. The professional judge then asks the defendant how he or she pleads and if he or she is willing to pay the compensation demanded.

3. If the defendant pleads not guilty, the prosecutor proceeds with the case by reporting on the evidence uncovered during the preliminary investigation.

4. If the injured party is to testify, he or she would go first. The injured person, as a party to the suit, does not take an oath. As is the case with all people who are placed on the witness stand, the victim is permitted to give a personal account of his or her story without interruption. This is then followed by questions posed by the prosecutor, defendant, and defense counsel.

5. The defendant takes the stand. As a party to the suit, he or she does not take an oath. The defendant tells his or her story uninterrupted and is then questioned by the prosecutor, injured party, and defense counsel.

6. One by one, the witnesses, who are under oath, are brought into the courtroom to tell what happened. They are subject to an interrogation.

7. Any other evidence to be introduced is presented at this time and examined by the court.

8. Next, the defendant's personal circumstances are taken into consideration. This may include an examination of the results of a psychiatric examination or an investigation into the personal finances of the defendant. This phase of the trial sometimes is conducted behind closed doors. Any doubts about the mental or emotional state of the defendant will be raised by the police or the prosecutor. In that event, the court would appoint psychiatric

experts to examine the defendant. Defense counsel rarely raises this issue. A defendant who is influenced by mental disease, feeblemindedness, or some other mental abnormality is subject to an order to surrender to an appropriate psychiatric facility. Self-induced intoxication is not considered a defense, however.

9. Following the investigation into the defendant's personal circumstances, final arguments are heard. The prosecutor and defense counsel summarize the case and then state which sentence they think is appropriate in the case the defendant is found guilty. Claims for reimbursement are also made at this time. The injured party and witnesses are eligible for travel expenses, daily allowance, and loss of earnings. The public defense counsel is reimbursed by the state for handling the case. The defendant who is acquitted is also eligible for reimbursement. A defendant who is found guilty may be partially or totally liable for repaying the state for its expenses in reimbursing the public defense counsel, the injured party and the witnesses. The amount is based on the defendant's income and the extent of obligations to dependents. People who are convicted and have a low annual income are often excused from paying any court costs.

10. Once the final arguments are made and the claims submitted, the judge declares the session closed. It is at this time that the court begins its deliberations. The professional judge and the lay judges are the only people who take part in these proceedings. They determine the guilt or innocence of the defendant and select an appropriate sanction. The Penal Code guides the judges in the determination of the sentence.

11. Finally, the judgment of the court is announced. The judge briefly explains the judgment and indicates how it may be appealed. If the judgment is not going to be announced immediately, the court will indicate this decision to the parties involved. Once the judgment is ready, the parties can come to the court and read the decision, or they can call the court and have it read over the telephone.

The Penal Code groups the types of sentences available into three categories. The most common punishment consists of fine and imprisonment. Disciplinary punishments are sanctions that can be imposed on public servants and members of the military forces. The third category includes conditional sentences, probation, and surrender for special care. The various types of sanctions that can be imposed on the civilian population will be explained in greater detail in the section on corrections.

One should not be left with the impression that people accused of a crime are necessarily going to be subjected to a trial. The Code of Judicial Procedure authorizes prosecutors and police to impose fines for minor offenses. This procedure has reduced considerably the number of cases that must be heard by the courts. It has been suggested that more than 80 percent of the crimes committed are handled in a summary fashion by prosecutors or police (Svensson, 1995).

The prosecutor may issue an order for this kind of summary punishment if the offense is punishable by a fixed fine, a day-fine, or imprisonment in which the term would not exceed six months. Orders for a summary punishment must be in writing and signed by a prosecutor, and the accused must be given a specific amount of time to consent to the order. To consent to the summary order, the accused must either do so in writing or pay the appropriate fine. Once accepted, the order has the same effect as a court judgment.

The offenses that are limited to the sanction of a fixed fine are referred to as breaches of regulations. The power to impose a breach-of-regulation fine is given to police, customs officers, and prosecutors. The Prosecutor-General and the National Police Board determine which types of offenses are included in the list of breaches of regulations. Breach-of-regulation orders must be in writing and signed by a police officer. The order either can be issued in the suspect's presence (in which case he or she can immediately agree to the order) or the officer can issue the order while permitting the accused to consent to it at a later date (if the order is issued in the suspect's absence or if the suspect wants time to think about the consequences of admitting guilt). If the suspect consents to the order, the order has the same effect as a court judgment.

It has been pointed out that once a trial is concluded, the parties have an opportunity to appeal the court's judgment to a court of appeal. As long as their petition is received by the district court within three weeks from when the court pronounced its judgment, both the defendant and the prosecutor have the right to appeal. In the petition for appeal, the appellant must state the factual or legal grounds for the appeal. If the appeal is granted, the prosecutor may be required to reopen the investigation into the case if the need arises.

At the main hearing, three professional judges and two lay judges from a court of appeal would hear the case. To the extent that it is relevant for the appeal, the parties are permitted to make an opening statement. This is followed by the presentation of evidence that is of importance to the appeal and may include a reexamination of witnesses. The parties are then given an opportunity to offer final arguments. All appeals are not resolved through a main hearing, however. If the prosecutor appeals for the defendant's benefit or if a defendant's appeal is supported by the other party, the court can dispose of the appeal without a main hearing.

After the court of appeal has heard the arguments presented, it must reach its decision in the case. It can let the judgment of the lower court stand, reduce the sentence imposed by the lower court, or change the sanction; it cannot impose a harsher sentence. Additionally, the court can vacate the lower court's judgment because of a grave procedural error, though this is a rare occurrence. The court may also vacate the lower court's judgment if the procedural error is not grave, but it is demonstrated that it affected the outcome of the trial.

The courts of appeal also entertain appeals based on orders issued by the lower court during the course of the proceedings. Chapter 49, Section 5, of the Code of Judicial Procedure lists a number of these; they include:

> 1. dismiss an attorney, counsel, or defence counsel or rejecting a request thereon;
> 2. reject an application by a third party to participate in proceedings as an intervenor or aggrieved person ... ;
> 3. direct a party or another person to produce a written evidence or to make an object accessible for view or inspection, or orders in which pursuant to the Freedom of Press Act ... or Fundamental Law on the Freedom of Expression ..., a court has found it to be of extraordinary importance that an information referred to there is provided on examination of a witness or party under truth affirmation;
> 4. determine an issue concerning final imposition of a default fine or detention, responsibility for a procedural offence, or liability of a person to pay litigation costs;
> 5. determine an issue concerning compensation or advance out of public funds to an aggrieved party, or concerning compensation or advance to counsel, defence counsel, witness, expert, or another;
> 6. determine an issue in civil cases concerning provisional attachment or measure pursuant to Chapter 15 or orders in criminal cases concerning detention ...;
> 7. reject a request for counsel or defence counsel, or appointing as such a person other than the one proposed by the party;
> 8. determine an issue concerning legal aid in accordance with the Legal Aid Act (1996:1619) in situations other than stated in items 5 or 7 above;
> 9. reject a request that compensation to a witness invoked by a private party shall be paid out of public funds...

These kinds of appeals are referred to as limited appeals.

Finally, appeals against judgments and orders handed down in a court of appeal are heard in the Supreme Court. In this event, the party must submit a review petition to the appellate court within four weeks of the appellate judgment. The petition must state the factual or legal grounds for the review petition.

Three justices of the Supreme Court determine whether a review of a case should be granted. Reviews are granted if the Supreme Court believes the issue requires legal guidance or if there is an extraordinary reason such as a procedural error or a gross oversight. Once the review is granted, the case is heard by five justices of the court. Most cases reach the Supreme Court because they raise an important issue in reference to the application of the law. These types of cases are usually significant because they entertain possible precedent-setting issues. The Supreme Court's formula for determining if a case will be heard with or without a main hearing is the same as the one applied to courts of appeal.

One must keep in mind that the Swedish Supreme Court does not rule on the constitutionality of a law. Justices from the Supreme Court and the Supreme Administrative Court, together as members of the Law Council, advise the Riksdag on the constitutionality of bills introduced in the legislature. Moreover, the Supreme Court does not rule on administrative law matters. That is the province of a separate tier of tribunals and courts, the highest of which is referred to as the Supreme Administrative Court.

Critical Issues

Throughout the twentieth century, Sweden was acknowledged as a leader in the extension of innovative social welfare policies for all of its citizens. Such creativity had been lacking somewhat in policies involving crime victims. Like other justice systems, Sweden tended to focus most of its effort on the social welfare of offenders rather than on victims of crime. This attitude has changed as the government has implemented several initiatives.

One should not be left with the impression that Sweden had no policy as it relates to crime victims. It simply had not been a leader in establishing creative programs and policies. Swedish law has long enabled the victim's claim for damages to be consolidated with the prosecution and heard in the criminal court. Under legal aid, the victim could also secure the services of a lawyer to assist in the claim at trial.

The State Compensation Act of 1971 enabled the awarding of compensation for personal injuries or property damage committed by offenders who had escaped from a state institution. Under this legislation, compensation was awarded if the offender could not pay or if payment was not awarded through insurance. In 1978, the Criminal Injuries Compensation Act created the Criminal Injuries Compensation Board, which is composed of people knowledgeable in either law, claims adjustments, or criminal policy. In addition to personal injury, property damage and financial loss are also covered when caused by escaped criminals, although there are some restrictions in these latter cases (Edqvist and Wennberg, 1983).

In the 1980s, various components of the justice system reexamined the plight of crime victims. Several changes were either implemented or recommended. As was the case in other countries, the principal catalyst for this reform was a growing recognition of and concern for women as victims in both sexual assault and domestic violence cases. This concern prompted government inquiries, changes in agency policies, and new legislation (Falkner, 1989).

For example, at the beginning of the 1980s, the prosecution was somewhat restricted in handling domestic violence cases. Prosecution was not forthcoming unless the victim reported the crime and supported the prosecution or unless the offense was clearly a grave crime for which it was in the public interest to prosecute. As such, many cases were not prosecuted. The new policy, based on the belief that it is in the public interest to try to prevent serious cases of domestic violence, enables the prosecution to initiate a case without the victim's support. Also in the past, the prosecution was apparently somewhat passive in pressing for damages in criminal proceedings. At the beginning of 1988, however, the Code of Judicial Procedure was changed to encourage the prosecution to take greater care in presenting damage claims of victims.

These changes have led to reforms in other branches of the justice system. For instance, courts now are expected to increase their attentiveness to prosecutorial claims for victim damages. Police are supposed to offer more help and support to crime victims and are expected to consider the issue of damages throughout their investigation of a crime. Both the police and prosecutors are expected to provide legal aid to victims and to inform them about filing a claim for financial compensation. They, along with courts, will assist in securing the appointment of an aggrieved victim counsel, if the offense was a crime against the person. The Ministry of Justice has produced a booklet for crime victims that explains the judicial process, the possibility of collecting damages, and the state compensation scheme. There are approximately 150 women's shelters that offer both practical and psychological support. In addition, 20 men's refuges have been established to support not only men who have been assaulted but also to provide help for men who have been violent toward women. Finally, the National Association of Victims' Assistance Agencies was created in 1988. This has led to the establishment of more than 100 victim assistance agencies at the local level.

In the 1990s, the Riksdag initiated two pieces of legislation designed to assist crime victims, specifically those associated with sexual assault and domestic violence. One involves expanding the legal aid scheme. In addition to providing legal services in pursuit of damages during the criminal proceedings, legal aid now offers a public victims' counsel. This person is appointed by the court (unless the victim does not need counsel) during the pretrial investigation. Public counsel not only offers help and support to the victim but also serves as an advocate for the victim's interests during the investigation. The other piece of legislation introduced protection orders that are designed to prevent female victims from being harassed by their assailants. A protection order can be initiated by a prosecutor or a court; its purpose is to prevent the accused from contacting the victim. Violation of the order can lead to a fine or up to six months' imprisonment.

A Victim Support Fund was introduced in July of 1994. This fund is used to benefit efforts at victim support, research, and education about the issue as well as the production of public information about victimization. Defendants found guilty of a crime that includes a sanction of imprisonment or those who accept a summary fine from a prosecutor are required as part of their sentence to pay a fee to the Victim Support Fund.

Two developments involving crime victims offer rather creative strategies for some long-standing problems. The first deals with the issue of domestic violence. In recent years, much interest has been expressed about viewing domestic abuse as a women's health issue. As a result, the Penal Code was amended in 1998 to include a new crime of gross violation of integrity. The Code states that "a person who commits criminal acts ..., if the acts form a part of an element in a repeated violation of that person's integrity and suited to severely damage that person's self-confidence, be sentenced for gross violation of integrity" (Penal Code, Chapter 4, Section 4a). The sanction for this offense is imprisonment for a minimum of six months to a maximum of six years. What this means is that under certain circumstances courts can sanction a domestic abuse offender for the original traditional offense (for example, assault) and also for a gross violation of the victim's integrity. In order for the justice system to utilize this new offense, courts will need to have knowledge of the woman's abusive circumstances. This will require abused women to seek medical treatment, which in the past they have often refused to do. The strategy is designed to have police, social workers, and healthcare professionals work together to address this problem. This will be achieved by encouraging the abused person to reveal the extent and length of abuse, collecting physical evidence, and addressing the victim's perceptions of self-worth. If these objectives are realized, this should empower the victim to seek assistance from the justice system, which will then be in a position to charge the offender with the offense of gross violation of integrity (Nylen and Heimer, 2000).

The other innovation deals with a new law on prostitution that went into effect in 1999. The law criminalizes the person who purchases sex rather than the prostitute. The rationale is based on the long-held view by people who have studied the problem that prostitution is another form of exploitation, usually with men taking advantage of women, and thus the prostitute should be viewed as a victim. The new law calls for a sanction of either a fine or imprisonment for a maximum term of six months (Boëthius, 1999).

Finally, the National Council for Crime Prevention has continued to consider the issue of victimization and has recommended further reforms. The council has suggested that victims be apprised of more information during the preliminary investigation, including decisions made by the police and prosecutor in the case. It has recommended that police be given more training in order to provide meaningful assistance to victims. The council also has argued that the state should take a greater role in assuring that the offender pays damages and that damage claims have a higher priority than they currently do when offenders file for bankruptcy. It also has recommended that government funding for the various components of victim assistance be increased.

Corrections

When a country's population is relatively homogeneous, the citizenry are more apt to agree on basic values and morals. We have already alluded to the importance placed on reaching consensus opinions in Sweden. This characteristic is equally evident in the criminal justice system. Although the pretrial process appears to reflect this quality, in the field of corrections—especially sanctioning rationales—an unusual degree of agreement has been reached. This section describes the building of consensus by examining the underlying philosophy behind sentencing and by explaining the organization and administration of both institutional and noninstitutional approaches to corrections.

Sentencing Philosophy

The Swedish prison system emerged in the nineteenth century. It adopted a model based on the principle of solitary confinement. It has been suggested that these early penitentiaries were very effective institutions at maintaining order and control of the inmates. Of course, by the beginning of the twentieth century, solitary confinement was beginning to be viewed as an extreme form of punishment (Nilsson, 2003). Since the 1940s, Sweden has embarked on an effort to make the field of corrections a more humane and morally just component of the justice system. Other countries have frequently looked to Sweden's correctional system and sentencing rationale as a model that should be emulated. To date, the planners and policymakers of the system have not been satisfied with the results, despite the fact that significant innovations have been introduced. From their perspective, more changes are in the offing. At issue are two policy questions with which they have been grappling for more than 40 years: What type of behavior should be criminalized in a country that prides itself on being democratic, prosperous, and highly industrialized? And what kinds of sanctions are effective for such a society (Sveri, 1981)?

An examination of the history of Sweden's attempts to answer these questions identifies two fairly distinct phases. The first phase started in the 1940s and became somewhat obsolete when the new Penal Code came into force in 1965. During this phase, attention focused more on the second question posed by Knut Sveri: What kinds of sanctions are effective for criminal behavior? The 1965 Penal Code was quite clear in enunciating an answer for civilians found guilty of violating the criminal law. Two types of sanctions were available. The common punishments consisted of fines and imprisonment; alternative sanctions included conditional sentence, probation, youth imprisonment, internment, and surrender for special care.

The first phase was marked by a firm belief in, and commitment to, a treatment philosophy. Criminologists and legislators joined in advocating and implementing a medical treatment model that relied on experts from the medical, psychological, and psychiatric professions.

The introduction of alternative sanctions was a central feature of this treatment philosophy. The conditional sentence was designed for people who could be punished by imprisonment but whose prognosis was such that incarceration was considered unnecessary. Probation was viewed as an alternative to imprisonment for those who had committed offenses punishable by imprisonment. It enabled the offender to remain free in the community while under supervision. Youth imprisonment was intended for people between 18 and 20 years of age who had committed an offense that was punishable by imprisonment. It was an indeterminate sentence involving both institutional care and a continuance of treatment and supervision upon release from an institution. Internment was an indeterminate sentence designed for dangerous offenders and recidivists. It was limited to offenders who had been convicted of crimes punishable by a minimum of two years of confinement. It involved both institutional and noninstitutional treatment, with an emphasis placed on institutional care. The internment board determined when a person was ready for release; once released, the offender was subject to both supervision and continued treatment outside the institution. Finally, surrender to special care enabled offenders to seek help beyond the correctional community.

This type of sanction was given to adults who were in need of psychiatric or alcohol treatment, as well as young people whose welfare could benefit from social or medical care.

In a slightly different context, imprisonment and fines played a significant role in the treatment model and the move to establish a more humane and just system of sanctioning. Sweden's policymakers realized that they could not totally abolish the sentence of imprisonment because those offenders committing serious crimes required a severe sanction. Because society would demand the retention of imprisonment for certain crimes, and because an alternative to incarceration had not been developed, imprisonment was retained. Every effort was made, however, to shorten the length of the sentence, to develop facilities that were designed to treat the inmate in a humane fashion, and to offer a number of rehabilitation programs. Monetary fines, especially the day-fine, were also developed further.

By the mid-1960s, however, critics had identified a number of flaws in the treatment model, not the least of which was the overly optimistic view of what it could realistically achieve. Sweden was obviously not alone in discovering the shortcomings of the treatment model; other correctional systems throughout the world were grappling with similar concerns. They also discovered defects in both the underlying assumptions of the treatment philosophy and in its practical application, especially in closed institutional settings.

Norman Bishop (1980) summarized a number of criticisms that dominated discussions in Sweden. Attempts were made from the start to standardize the treatment model. In turn, this led to a simplistic diagnosis of the offender's problems and the avoidance of an in-depth analysis of all possible causal factors. Some critics also argued that institutional treatment was not voluntary but coercive in nature. Thus, the inmate's rights and legal safeguards were often skirted in the name of humane treatment. The use of the indeterminate sentence for youth imprisonment and internment was especially susceptible to charges that the model was not as humane as some proponents alleged, based on the contention that it left inmates in a state of uncertainty regarding the actual length of time served. Others were concerned that institutionalization would merely reinforce the offender's negative self-image and sense of alienation. Moreover, the presence of high recidivism rates suggested that the approach to treatment was a failure. Finally, critics alleged that the correctional system had become too preoccupied with treatment at the expense of other valid reasons for sanctioning.

Critics of the treatment model were not suggesting that it be abandoned totally or that inmates be subjected to less-than-humane treatment. They were arguing that a more realistic sentencing philosophy be acknowledged, reflecting a belief that the sanctioning process could have multiple purposes other than rehabilitation and that these alternative purposes should be given equal weight at sentencing. In particular, sanctions should be viewed as having a general deterrent effect and used as a method of protecting society from serious law violators.

Since the mid-1960s, Sweden's policymakers embarked upon the second phase of their attempt to determine what types of behavior should be criminalized in a democratically prosperous country and what kinds of sanctions are effective. Erland Aspelin (1975) suggested that the greatest efforts at policy development focused on four areas of concern. First, attempts were made to decriminalize minor offenses and to develop nonpunitive reactions to such behavior. For example, full decriminalization has been addressed to issues involving offenses against the family and morality. Unlawful marriages, abortions, and certain sexual offenses are areas that have already been reformed. Attempts also have been made to depenalize certain offenses. This has been entertained because police and prosecutors already have tremendous caseloads, and depenalization would enable them to concentrate their efforts on more serious crimes. Some tax offenses, minor frauds, and minor property offenses could be handled by a fine, for example, rather than a custody sentence.

Second, because Sweden experienced an increase in serious crime, greater attention was directed at utilizing the justice system's limited resources to combat serious criminality. For example, because armed robbery and other similarly violent crimes escalated, efforts were made to impose harsher sanctions for illegal possession of weapons. Similarly, because narcotics offenses became a serious problem, the severity of sanctions was increased in an attempt to curb the problem. There also has been an attempt to expand the realm of criminality for certain serious offenses that are not violent in nature. Tax fraud, traffic offenses, and offenses against the environment are some of the crimes that have been targeted as warranting increased attention.

Third, efforts have been under way to limit the use of imprisonment. This argument is based on a belief that imprisonment is counterproductive for many offenders and that society does not actually benefit from its imposition. The long-standing criticism of the use of the indeterminate sentence was resolved with the abolition of youth imprisonment in 1979 and internment in 1981. Instead, the imposition of fines and noninstitutional sentences was increased.

Finally, greater attention has focused on the need to improve crime prevention strategies. These endeavors have included making citizens more aware of their role in preventing property crimes. The police have been attentive to this need by establishing the block police officer scheme and by creating the position of a crime prevention officer in each district. The National Council for Crime Prevention has been an important instrument in conducting research and evaluating prevention strategies since 1974, and it has a key role to play in the recent national crime prevention strategy that was explained in the section on police.

During this second phase in policy development, the government also addressed the concerns raised by critics of the treatment model. A shift in emphasis regarding the rationale for sanctions is illustrated by the 1988 annulment of Chapter 1, Section 7, of the Penal Code. The section stated "that the sanction shall serve to foster the sentenced offender's rehabilitation in society." According to the National Council for Crime Prevention, the abandonment of this policy reflects the view that a sanction should be based primarily on the nature of the crime in question, along with a proper consideration for both mitigating and aggravating circumstances—and not on the offender's rehabilitation. The council is of the opinion that this change in sentencing policy is directed at recidivists in particular. They also point out, however, that the "correctional system should continue to be based upon a humane orientation and should facilitate the sentenced person's re-adjustment to society with rehabilitative and supportive measures" (National Council for Crime Prevention, 1990).

Sweden, along with the other Scandinavian countries, has made a number of significant advances over the past 40 years toward establishing a more humane and morally just sentencing philosophy. They have reduced the number of offenses that warrant a prison sentence, in addition to reducing the actual amount of time served. With modifications in the sentencing rationale, Sweden has reduced the number of sanctions available. Presently, there are five types of sentences: (1) fines, (2) imprisonment, (3) conditional sentence, (4) probation, and (5) commitment for special care. The Penal Code gives the court a good deal of discretion in selecting an appropriate sentence. The court is guided in its choice of disposition by the nature of the offense and the presentence report on the offender. Thus, the court selects a sanction that will assure general obedience to the law and assist in the offender's readjustment to society. A central principle of the sanctioning rationale is to avoid the imposition of a prison sentence, if possible.

Organization of the National Prison and Probation Administration

The 1970s were marked by attempts to reform the correctional system. A government committee was formed in 1971 to examine the prison and probation services, and a year later it presented several proposals to the Riksdag. Four ideas were singled out as being central to the reform movement. One stressed the importance of noninstitutional treatment as the most effective form of sanctioning. This principle was supported by studies that suggested that institutionalization would merely reinforce an offender's criminal tendencies. Probation and day-fines were identified as the principal alternatives to imprisonment.

Another idea emphasized the need to coordinate institutional and noninstitutional treatment more closely. From an administrative point of view, this has been achieved by creating the position of regional directors who coordinate both institutional and noninstitutional treatment in their regions. Moreover, probation officers are more involved with the treatment programs of those sent to remand and local correctional institutions.

The notion that prisoners should serve their sentences in an institution located near their families was another significant principle behind the reform effort. This idea is based on a belief that the success of any treatment program could be enhanced if a prisoner is permitted easy access to his or her family, friends, and local employment contacts.

Finally, emphasis was placed on the belief that inmates should utilize facilities that are available to the rest of society. This idea enhanced the importance of inmate furloughs. Inmates are able to participate in educational and job-training programs and to seek medical and social welfare assistance in the community, rather than having these programs imported on a limited basis to the institutional setting. Each of these ideas has had a significant impact on the manner in which the national correctional system is organized, administered, and implemented. Figure 3.3 illustrates the organizational structure of the prison and probation service.

Figure 3.3

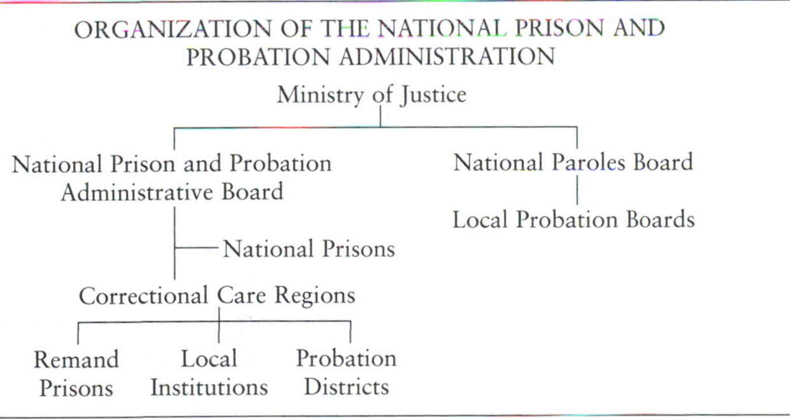

Ministry of Justice The Ministry of Justice has the ultimate responsibility of administering the correctional system. The minister of justice appoints members to central and local boards that administer and monitor the various components of the system. He or she also introduces legislative proposals to the Riksdag and administrative directives to the cabinet that are designed to improve the efficiency of the correctional system.

National Prison and Probation Administrative Board The board of the National Prison and Probation Administration is the central agency entrusted with the duty of administering correctional services in Sweden. The board is composed of laypersons appointed by the government. The chief officer is the director general of administration. In addition to members from the Riksdag and representatives of prison and probation officers, other board members include representatives from the National Welfare Board, the Central Labor Unions, and the National Labor Administration, as well as a director from private industry. The staff is divided into the Department of Treatment and Security and the Department of Work and Training. Other divisions deal with planning, personnel, and finance.

National Paroles Board The National Paroles Board is composed of five members. The chair and vice chair are judges from the Supreme Court or courts of appeal. The board is empowered to make parole decisions for all inmates sentenced to more than two years' imprisonment; they also hear parole appeals from decisions made by local probation boards.

Local Probation Boards There are 30 local probation boards that are responsible for probation and parole decisions in their respective districts. Each board is composed of five members. The chair must be a lawyer (usually a judge from a district court), while the other members are laypersons. If an inmate violates a probation or parole order, the board has the power to initiate proceedings against the person. A board's decision in such matters may be reviewed on appeal. If a parolee is inclined to appeal, the issue is reviewed by the National Paroles Board, whereas the court of appeal for the region handles reviews of probationers.

Correctional Care Regions The country is divided into six correctional care regions. Each region is administered by a director who is a professional probation officer. The responsibility of the director is to supervise the remand prisons, the local institutions, and any various non-institutional care programs in the region. The director does not supervise the national prisons located in the region. If a district court within the region sentences a person to imprisonment, the regional director determines where the person would serve the sentence.

The exception to this rule involves people sentenced to a term of imprisonment of four or more years. These inmates are considered long-term prisoners. Once sentenced to a long-term period of incarceration, they are sent to a reception center (Kumla prison for men or Hinseberg prison for women). After an assessment is made of the inmate's propensity to violence and of the type of treatment regimen that would be most suited to him or her, the National Prison and Probation Administration determines where the prisoner would be sent during the initial phase of incarceration.

Imprisonment Before the various types of correctional institutions are explained, it is important to offer some general comments about the sanction of imprisonment and the nature of the facilities utilized. According to the Penal Code, a person sentenced to imprisonment receives either a fixed term or a life sentence. A fixed term can range from 14 days to 10 years. If a person is convicted of several crimes and at least one warrants a prison sentence, a formula is used to determine a fixed term of incarceration that would not exceed 16 years.

A life sentence is rare and is usually commuted to a determinate sentence of between 15 and 20 years. The National Paroles Board generally issues a conditional release after one-half to two-thirds of a determinate sentence has been served. Thus, a person sentenced to life imprisonment can expect to spend seven to 10 years in prison.

There was a downward trend in prison incarcerations throughout the 1970s until 1982, when it began to rise again. Since that time, it has declined again. For example, 16,098 people were incarcerated in prison in 1988, while 13,836 were imprisoned in 1992 (National Prison and Probation Administration, 1994). Since the turn of the century, the yearly average is around 9,500 (Ministry of Justice, 2004). For the American reader who is accustomed to hearing about lengthy prison terms, these figures can be misleading. In Sweden every attempt is made not to incarcerate convicted offenders; if incarceration is necessary, the term should be for a short period of time. With that in mind, the number of people incarcerated in prison on any one day is about 4,000.

Inmates sentenced in 2007 were convicted of 13,973 crimes. Of that total, 7,430 were crimes against the Penal Code. These include crimes against the person (2,989), crimes against property (3,373), crimes against the public (325), and crimes against the state (743). In addition to offenses listed in the Penal Code, people were incarcerated for violations against the Road Traffic Offences Act (3,914), Narcotics Drugs (Punishment) Act (1,645), Taxes Offences Act (229), and other statutes (755). Of the adults sentenced to a term of incarceration, 17 percent received a sentence of no more than one month, and 15 percent received a sentence of more than six months but less than 12 months. Thirteen percent received a term of more than two years. Of these, 16 received a life sentence (National Council for Crime Prevention, 2008). Both the length of time prescribed in the Penal Code and the actual time served illustrate the country's commitment to limiting the use of imprisonment as a sanction.

It should be pointed out that Sweden initiated an experiment with electronic monitoring. A pilot program was started in 1994 for people sentenced to less than two months of imprisonment and who agreed to refrain from alcohol or other drugs (Svensson, 1995). Because of the positive results from the initial study, it was extended and expanded to include the entire country and those sentenced to up to three months of imprisonment (Ministry of Justice, 1997). In 1999, electronic monitoring became a permanent method of dealing with sanctions that call for a short term of imprisonment. People sentenced to imprisonment for a term of three months or less may apply for intensive supervision. In order to be eligible, the offender must have a residence, a telephone, and be employed for 20 to 40 hours a week. A contact person at the place of employment monitors the person during his or her working hours. The probation service makes frequent visits to assure that the person is not abusing alcohol or other drugs. If a person violates the terms of the intensive supervision, it ceases and the offender serves the remainder of the sentence in prison.

Types of Institutions At the present time, there are 56 prisons in Sweden, of which six are utilized by women prisoners. All of these institutions are categorized into one of three types of correctional facilities: (1) remand prisons, (2) local institutions, and (3) national institutions. Each is designed for a specific purpose and is intended for a particular type of offender. The remand prisons are designed primarily to hold people who have been detained or have been arrested and are awaiting trial. The purposes of these facilities are similar to some of the objectives of jails in the United States. The limited number of remand facilities has led to the creation of remand wings in some other correctional institutions. Legislation mandates that the local probation service provide detained and arrested people with the same treatment and assistance that is available to prisoners housed in these facilities. Because a period of remand is fairly short, little is actually accomplished. However, if a person is eventually convicted and sentenced to a period of incarceration, these preliminary contacts may assist in determining the appropriate institution in which the person will serve the sentence.

The local institutions are used primarily to house people sentenced to less than one year of imprisonment. Local institutions are small, generally handling about 40 inmates, and there is roughly an equal number of open and closed facilities. Because security is not emphasized at these facilities, inmates who are in need of close supervision because of the nature of their crimes are not sent to local institutions. The primary purpose of a local institution is to keep inmates as close to their family as is reasonably possible. Moreover, through the help of probation officers, every effort is made to facilitate the transition back to freedom. Local institutions also enhance the effectiveness of furloughs, work-release programs, and study-release programs because of their proximity to family, employment, and educational opportunities. Inmates who are serving a longer sentence at a national institution are usually transferred to a local facility toward the end of their term in order to prepare them for release. Thus, probation officers work closely with local institutions to prepare for an inmate's release.

Finally, there are national correctional institutions. Unlike the remand and local facilities that are administered by a regional director, these institutions are the direct responsibility of the National Prison and Probation Administration. These facilities are designed to house people who have been sentenced to more than one year in prison. Given the clientele that they serve, approximately three-quarters of these facilities are closed institutions. In comparison to other industrialized countries, these prisons are fairly small. The largest is Kumla, which has a capacity for 206 inmates.

It is possible that offenders sentenced to less than one year of imprisonment may find themselves sent to a national institution. Such decisions are made if a national prison can better accommodate an inmate with the kind of treatment required. Inmates may also be housed in this type of facility if they cannot cope in the more open environment of a local institution. There are a few high-security institutions among the national facilities. These institutions house offenders who are considered dangerous or likely to attempt an escape.

Until recently, each inmate was provided with a separate cell or room. Complaints about prison overcrowding, which are common in many countries, were once nonexistent in Sweden. However, separate quarters are no longer possible because the daily prison population has increased. This has led in some instances to placing two inmates in a cell or turning common living areas into sleeping areas. Some of the new open prisons designed for short-term inmates (especially those incarcerated for drunk driving) are designed to accommodate more than one person to a cell (Svensson, 1995). It has been suggested that three factors have led to the increase in the prison population: (1) parole is more restrictive, (2) short-term imprisonment is an important sanction for drunk driving, and (3) sentences for recidivists have been increased (Jareborg, 1994). In order to address the problem of overcrowding, the National Prison and Probation Administration announced plans to expand the prison capacity by 1,000 beds (Von Hofer, 2003).

Nevertheless, the high standards of cleanliness and humaneness reflected in Sweden's correctional facilities are often praised by outsiders. Knut Sveri put that adulation in perspective, however: "It (prison conditions) is only a reflection of the general high standard of living in the Swedish society in general. A country without any slum-districts cannot let their prisoners live under slum-conditions."

Act on Correctional Treatment in Institutions (1974)

The Act on Correctional Treatment in Institutions (along with more recent amendments to it) offers a fairly thorough understanding of the government's attempt to assure a humane environment for the incarcerated offender. The general provisions of the act state the government's intent to assure that

> [c]orrectional treatment in an institution shall be so designed as to promote the adjustment of the inmate in society and to counteract the detrimental effects of deprivation of liberty. Insofar as this can be achieved without detriment to the need to protect the public, treatment should be directed from the outset towards measures which prepare the inmate for conditions outside the institution.

Thus, the system is designed to enhance an inmate's ability to return to society with a minimum amount of adverse side effects. Obviously, the method is not always successful. But in the difficult world of building more effective and humane correctional models, one cannot accuse Sweden of failing to commit to this goal, for a central theme of the act is that "[i]nmates shall be treated with respect for their human dignity. They shall be treated with understanding for the special difficulties connected with a stay in an institution."

Before some of the more salient features of the act are described, it is important to mention a significant factor that was instrumental in initiating these reforms. A number of intellectuals and ex-offenders formed a group in 1966 known as the Association for More Humane Treatment of Prisoners. This group is more popularly known by the acronym KRUM. This kind of association was not novel to Sweden, for there had already been reform groups established in Norway and Denmark. KRUM started out with a moderate program for change. Members were quite active in counseling and assisting inmates and ex-offenders in any way that they could. Moreover, they were committed to a correctional system that was based on a treatment model.

By the early 1970s, however, KRUM had changed its ideological posture. It assisted in the organization of inmates into vocal groups that demanded change through hunger and work strikes. Two of the principal demands called for less security within institutions and an expansion of work, educational, and recreational programs. KRUM's ultimate goal was to eliminate the sanction of imprisonment from the Penal Code. One should not be left with the impression that reform would not have occurred without KRUM, but it played a significant role in articulating the concerns of inmates and in educating the public and the politicians on the need for reform in the correctional system.

The Act on Correctional Treatment changed the regimen of Swedish correctional facilities in a number of ways. For example, it required inmates to be involved in some form of work, study, or training. The Act stipulates that

> to facilitate his adjustment in society, an inmate of a local institution [and if just cause is given for inmates in national

> institutions] may be permitted to work, to study, or to participate in vocational training or other specially arranged activities outside the institution during working hours. Special efforts are to be made at such institutions to promote these kinds of activities.

Efforts are made, therefore, to find a suitable job or course of study that will enhance an inmate's prospects once released from custody. The person receives a remuneration for any of the above assignments. Even those who are unable to work because of some medical disability are given a remuneration that enables them to purchase personal items. Of the earnings received, 10 percent is placed in a savings account and is returned when the person is released or during a furlough (a short-term leave from the institution).

While the goal of providing a work or study program is designed to reduce the likelihood that the inmate will recidivate, the availability of meaningful work that may contribute to a reduction in reoffending is unfortunately limited. This situation is compounded by other factors. People who have served time and have had previous problems with education and employment are more likely to reoffend (Nilsson, 2003). Moreover, approximately 50 percent of offenders sentenced to more than two months of imprisonment are suffering from some type of substance abuse. Thus, they have issues that must be addressed above and beyond a work ethic and marketable skills.

Whereas solitary confinement has traditionally been used to punish inmates who violate prison rules, this is not the purpose in Sweden. The Act explains the context in which solitary confinement can be used:

> An inmate may be kept separate from other inmates if this is necessary having regard to national security, a present danger to the safety of life or of health of the inmate himself or of others, or of serious damage to institution property or to prevent the inmate exerting a detrimental influence over other inmates.
>
> An inmate who ... has been placed in a closed institution may be kept separate from other inmates if there is reason to fear that he is planning to escape or others are planning to attempt to set him free, and separation is necessary in order to prevent such a plan being carried out.
>
> Decisions under the previous two paragraphs shall be reviewed as often as there are grounds, and in any case at least once a month.

The law also states that the decision to isolate an inmate should be investigated, and the opinion of a physician should be obtained.

In addition to the types of situations cited above, a person can be sent to solitary confinement in the following circumstances:

> An inmate who behaves violently, or who is so affected by alcoholic beverages or other intoxicants or stimulants that it is to be feared he will create a disturbance at the institution, may be temporarily kept separate from other inmates, as long as it is deemed necessary to subdue the violent behavior or until the intoxication has come to an end.
>
> Where other means prove inadequate to control violent behavior on the part of an inmate he may be put under physical restraint if this is unavoidably necessary for security reasons.

Once again, a physician is consulted concerning these decisions.

If solitary confinement is not an acceptable method of sanctioning a recalcitrant inmate, what are considered acceptable alternatives? The Act calls for three types of action when an inmate violates prison rules. One is simply a warning. Another is to cite a specific period of time that does not count toward the inmate's sentence. For a single offense, the maximum time cannot exceed 10 days, and the total amount of extra time for all offenses is limited to 45 days. A final option is to transfer the inmate to another institution.

Disciplinary cases are handled by the prison governor, with the results confirmed by the national prison administration. When a transfer to another prison is recommended as an appropriate form of discipline, it is determined at the regional level. It is a common feature of Swedish society that a person can appeal a decision to a higher level within the bureaucracy; this is also true of the prison system. An inmate subjected to disciplinary sanctions can appeal both internally and externally. Internal appeals are usually the responsibility of the prison governor or the regional director, but some cases involve the national prison administration.

External appeals are made either to one of the administrative courts of appeal that handles prison cases or to the parliamentary ombudsman who is responsible for criminal justice issues. If a case is presented to the administrative court of appeal, a three-judge panel would entertain the case. Moreover, the determination of the issue would be based solely on written arguments. It has been suggested that of the roughly 600 appeals considered annually, approximately 1 to 2 percent are successful. The other method is to petition the parliamentary ombudsman, who handles about 40 prison complaints a year. As was the case with the administrative court of appeal, the ombudsman often upholds the decision of the prison administration (Douglas, 1984).

Another issue that has been resolved somewhat by the implementation of the Act on Correctional Treatment is the ability of inmates to negotiate grievances with prison authorities. For a number of years, this had been an issue raised by KRUM and inmates on strike. Inmate councils are the mechanisms used to air problems, but they are not very effective in practice because of the high turnover rate in the institutions. Moreover, no attempt has been made to establish institutional councils that would include prison management, guards, and inmates with the purpose of collective participation in formulating prison policy.

Probably the most important and creative change has been the extent to which furlough schemes have been utilized in the system. Furloughs have been a part of Sweden's approach to corrections since the 1930s, but the idea has been expanded considerably over the past two decades. A central proposition of the Act on Correctional Treatment was to facilitate an inmate's transition back to society. Various kinds of furloughs are designed to enhance that goal. Work and study furloughs are in effect when an inmate is allowed to leave an institution during the day to work, study, or participate in a vocational training program.

The act also empowers correctional authorities to grant furloughs for leisure-time activities. Participation in a club, attendance at a sporting event, or other types of entertainment are considered part of an inmate's adjustment program. Medical furloughs are granted if the person can receive better care in a public hospital. Sojourns are also available for inmates who would benefit from programs offered at various treatment clinics in the community.

Short-term and release furloughs also are regular features of this scheme. Short-term furloughs may be granted for either a number of hours or a number of days. They are primarily designed to enable inmates to maintain ties with their family. Release furloughs are available for those inmates who are eligible for parole. These are used as a transitional feature between institutionalization and the granting of parole. Approximately 48,000 furloughs are granted annually and, of these, about 5 percent are abused in some way. Examples of abuse usually include returning late, arriving under the influence of alcohol or other drugs, or not returning at all.

There are other significant characteristics of the Act. For example, inmates are allowed conjugal visits. Although correspondence may be scrutinized, it is not censored (with the possible exception of high-security risks). Telephones are readily available. There are no prohibitions on an inmate's choice of reading matter; in fact, each institution subscribes to a number of newspapers and popular magazines. Moreover, legal reference materials are available in each institution and an inmate can borrow books from the local public library. This last feature is a useful illustration of the country's general attitude toward prison inmates. Offenders have the same rights to general social services as do law-abiding citizens. Thus, a variety of groups, such as health and social services, local education councils, housing and employment bureaus, and cultural institutions, work in conjunction with correctional administrators to meet the needs of inmates.

Regimens The Act on Correctional Treatment in Institutions has been described as an enlightened approach for establishing a more humane environment and just treatment of incarcerated offenders. To illustrate the accuracy of this characterization, three methods of applying this approach have been singled out for closer scrutiny. By examining these, one can develop a sense of the range of facilities available and how they comply with the intent of the Act.

In 1965, a new high-security prison opened in Kumla. It was designed and built at a time when the notion that larger institutions would be more cost-effective was popular in Swedish penology. Originally designed to hold more than 435 inmates, Kumla has a 21-foot wall around it. The emphasis on security was augmented further by an extensive television and radar monitoring system. Like other closed prisons, Kumla maintained a policy of random searches of inmates at any time and any place. In addition to living blocks for regular prisoners, who have a good deal of mobility in the institution, Kumla also has two special blocks. One contains a hospital, psychiatric ward, temporary detention unit, and disciplinary section. The other is designed for inmates who are deemed unsuitable for the regular living blocks. This includes dangerous offenders who are most likely to attempt an escape.

As a result of protests from KRUM and changes in attitude toward prisons, Kumla has undergone a number of changes. It has been redesigned to hold 206 inmates and employs a staff of almost 300. The high ratio of staff to inmates is common throughout the system. All inmates in Kumla are serving long sentences by Swedish standards (that is, one or more years). Inmates have been either sent directly to the institution or transferred there after it was determined that they were a security risk. Inmates are either employed in one of the traditional prison workshops or participate in one of the full-time educational programs. These programs range from elementary school to the university level and are run by teachers from the area's educational institutions. Furloughs and conjugal visits of up to three hours in length are available. Finally, with the exception of those individuals identified as high-security risks, inmates are granted sojourns to the local community in order to participate in cultural and sporting events.

Another example is the open national prison at Tillberga. This institution illustrates one side of a recurring debate that addresses whether goods produced in prison industries should be sold in an open or closed market. In most countries that have powerful labor unions, legislation has been passed to prevent the sale of goods on the open market. Opponents of this policy argue that it hinders the correctional institution from becoming more cost-effective. Since 1972, Sweden has been experimenting with a free market scheme at Tillberga. There are approximately 80 inmates at the facility; of these, about 40 are employed in the construction of prefabricated houses, which are sold on the open market by a state-owned company. All workers are members of the construction union and are paid the free market wages negotiated by the union. The union agreed to this idea as long as three conditions were met: (1) the inmates would be paid the same wages as other building-trade members, (2) the houses would be sold at the same price as private companies, and (3) the housing market remained strong.

One caveat is in order, however. The inmates are paid only 70 percent of the wages that their counterparts receive from private firms. Behind this discrepancy is the fact that inmates are not subject to the national income tax, which takes about 30 percent of a factory worker's wage. Inmate workers do not pay taxes because of a conflict between two laws. One law states that all tax returns are a matter of public record; the other states that inmates have a right to privacy. Thus, to avoid a violation of either law, the inmates receive a lower wage.

It should be pointed out that Sweden's privacy law assists inmates in another way. Unless an offender is a well-known person, Swedish newspapers cannot publish the names of people accused or convicted of crimes. Moreover, employers cannot ask a potential employee if they have served a prison term.

It has been pointed out that many of Sweden's incarcerated offenders are not attracted to the Tillberga scheme (Serrill, 1977). One reason is that the work is hard, but another reason frequently cited is that the inmate is given only 25 percent of his or her wage to spend. The rest is used to pay for food, support the inmate's family, and pay any debts. The remaining sum is placed in a savings account that the inmate receives upon release. The money a Tillberga inmate receives to spend while incarcerated is actually less than that awarded inmates in other institutions, for the latter receive all of the money remunerated for their work. Despite these problems, the authorities appear to be pleased with the scheme and have introduced it at Skogome, a closed national institution. Inmates at Skogome work in either a laundry or clothing industry.

Finally, although Sweden appears committed to utilizing more open facilities and decreasing the amount of restrictions in closed institutions, they are faced with a serious issue of managing inmates who suffer from problems with alcohol or other drugs. It is in this context that the drug treatment programs at the Osteraker national prison for men and the Hinseberg national prison for women deserve consideration. Before these programs are described, however, it is important to explain briefly the country's approach to drug abuse.

For years, the principal drug in Sweden has been alcohol, and that remains the case today. Like much of the Western world, concern for narcotic abuse became a significant issue in the mid-1960s. The country's first piece of penal legislation directed at this problem was the Narcotic Drugs Act of 1968. In a span of just five years, this legislation was revised three times. The principal reason for these revisions was to increase the severity of sanctions. Today, the maximum penalty is a 10-year prison sentence.

Correspondingly, criminal justice authorities developed an enforcement strategy to fit not only this legislation but also the prevailing philosophy toward correctional care. Throughout the 1970s, emphasis was directed at drug traffickers, while the abuser was offered treatment instead of prosecution and punishment. That policy changed in 1980. Law enforcement had been fairly successful in curbing drug traffickers, as there was an apparent decline in serious drug offenses. This led the Director of Public Prosecutions to call upon law enforcement to shift their efforts to abusers. As such, arrests and sanctions, which already had the force of law but were simply not utilized because of prosecutorial discretion, were now imposed on people found guilty of less serious drug offenses. This change in policy led to a decline in the number of drug addicts treated in psychiatric care facilities and to an increase in those being sentenced to prison (Svensson, 1986).

Another impetus for the change in policy was legislation passed in 1982. The Social Services Act emphasized the voluntary treatment of people abusing alcohol and other substances. This was essentially a proactive approach directed at young people. At the same time, the Compulsory Care of Alcohol and Drug Abusers Act and the Compulsory Care of Young Persons Act also came into effect. These were reactive approaches directed at serious abusers. In the former case, adult abusers could be taken into custody for up to four months for compulsory treatment. In the latter case, young people up to the age of 20 could be taken into custody for social care for up to six months.

The two compulsory care acts were superseded with the passage of the Act on the Treatment of Alcoholics and Drug Misusers, which went into effect in 1989. While this legislation acknowledges that treatment should be based on a person's willingness to seek help, it contends that there are times when a person is unwilling to do so. In the belief that they are seriously endangering their health and possibly inflicting harm on others, a county court with the assistance of the local social welfare board can order coercive treatment. Section 3 of the Act defines coercive treatment as an attempt "to motivate the misuser so that he can be presumed to be able voluntarily to collaborate in continued treatment and accept support to discontinue his misuse."

Under this legislation, a person can be taken into immediate custody for coercive treatment in either a treatment home or in a hospital. According to Section 20 of the Act, the period of treatment would cease "as soon as the purpose of the treatment is achieved and at the latest when treatment has been undertaken for six months." People subjected to this treatment are provided with certain procedural rights. For example, they are permitted to review the documents that were used by the authorities to issue such an order. Moreover, they have the right to make a written statement to the court, to request an oral hearing in court, and to utilize the services of a public defender at the court's discretion.

Compared to the previous decade, this strategy shifted the emphasis to incarceration either in a prison, a psychiatric facility, a treatment home, or a hospital. According to the Prison and Parole Service, roughly two of every three prison inmates has a drug abuse problem and one out of every two have been sentenced for an alcohol-related offense. In the Swedish context, this is significant—especially if one considers that the total prison population on any day is approximately 4,000 inmates. It is this fact that brings the treatment programs at the Osteraker national prison for men and the Hinseberg national prison for women to our attention.

While drug treatment programs are available at several prisons, the program at Osteraker is considered the most comprehensive (Pettersson, Sundin-Osborne, and Bishop, 1987). It was initiated in 1978 and has space for 50 participants. Special areas of the prison have been earmarked for the program, and there is a close working relationship between treatment staff and participants. Although the treatment staff is autonomous within the prison, they coordinate their efforts with prison officials.

Inmates must apply for entry to the program, which lasts a minimum of eight months. Once an inmate is accepted into the program, a treatment plan is designed for his needs. Rules prohibit unruly behavior and drug use, and inmates must agree to daily monitoring through urine tests. The principal components of the program include role playing, work training, study, and social skills. Thus, it is similar to therapeutic techniques employed elsewhere, but it has been tailored for use within the prison setting.

Because inmates must volunteer for the program, it is recognized that personal motivation is an important factor in measuring the program's success. In a preliminary examination of the Osteraker program, the following information was identified. During the two-year period of the study, 133 inmates were accepted into the program. Of these, 70 completed it, while 63 dropped out. Of the total population of the group, 80 percent had been in prison before. Of these, 55 had violated the Drug Act, 45 had been convicted of theft, and 10 had been sentenced for a violent crime. In addition, two-thirds of the population were under 30 years of age.

Following release from the Osteraker program, recidivism rates were examined. Recidivism was defined as receiving a sentence to imprisonment or a probation order within two years following conditional release from the program. Of those completing the program, 32 participants (46%) did not recidivate, three (4%) were placed on probation, and 35 (50%) were sentenced to prison. Of those not completing the program, 10 participants (16%) did not recidivate, four (7%) received probation, and 47 (77%) were imprisoned again.

While the program at Osteraker emphasizes drug treatment, the program for women at Hinseberg focuses on achieving a drug-free environment (Bishop, Sundin-Osborne, and Pettersson, 1988). Like Osteraker's, the Hinseberg program was initiated in 1978. With this program, the women did not have access to professional drug therapy as was the case at Osteraker. On the other hand, the women did have access to other inmates who were not in the program during work and study periods, which was not the case at Osteraker.

Part of the impetus for the program was the recognition that when an inmate arrived at the institution, she had been held in a detention facility for one to two months. The time spent in detention was often the longest period that the inmate was drug-free, and many wanted to continue their period of incarceration in such an environment. The program's principal objective was to maintain a drug-free environment. Therefore, two special drug-free wings were established at the prison.

The program can accommodate 20 inmates at a time. They are selected by the prison staff based on the desire to remain drug-free and a willingness to submit to urine tests and participate in special activities. The activities consist of work, study, physical training, and leisure activities. There are also group discussion sessions and individual treatment programs. In addition, a prison staff member is assigned to each woman in the program to assist in achieving individual goals and addressing any problems.

A study was conducted to determine the short-term and long-term effects of the program (Bishop, Sundin-Osborne, and Pettersson, 1988). The study included 80 inmates who had entered the program after January 1979 and left by December 1981. One of the women had two stays in the program. Of the 81 stays, 42 were completed according to the program, while 39 were interrupted. Of the interrupted cases, 14 were at the request of the inmate, while the others were the result of some violation of the program's rules. The study concluded that the goal of achieving a drug-free environment was very successful, as urine tests found only four inmates testing positive once, and only one testing positive twice. Researchers further discovered that successful participants tended to have completed elementary school, had a record of employment, and did not have a history of injecting drugs.

In a two-year follow-up study, the researchers found that 50 percent of the women who completed the program remained drug-free and 24 percent of the dropouts remained drug-free. One-half of the 80 participants did recidivate and were sentenced to either prison or probation. Of those sent to prison, more than one-half had dropped out of the program; they tended to be the participants who used alcohol or other drugs excessively.

The researchers concluded that the program was a total success for 25 percent of the participants. They based this assessment on three criteria: (1) the absence of drug use, (2) the absence of recidivism, and (3) a positive attitude toward their occupations. Occupations included work, school, vocational training, job programs, drug treatment, and child care.

The researchers further held that the program has had some positive benefits for the entire prison. Each inmate is assigned a prison staff member as a contact person who will assist in building better social relationships. There has been a shift in emphasis within the total prison to assure a drug-free environment.

Parole Parole is an important component in a correctional system that prides itself on providing treatment for offenders in both an institutional setting and upon release. The Penal Code states: "[a] person serving imprisonment for a fixed term shall, except as otherwise provided ... be paroled after having served one-half of the term. However, parole may not be granted before at least two months have been served." Presently, inmates serving more than two months but less than two years are paroled after serving one-half of their sentence. These decisions are determined by local probation boards. The National Paroles Board is empowered to make parole decisions for inmates serving more than two years in a national institution.

When an inmate is eligible for parole, a probation officer is assigned to the case. The officer visits the inmate in prison and begins to make appropriate contacts in the community. This could involve notifying family or arranging a place of residence and employment. Various studies, however, have suggested that many prisoners do not believe that officers have assisted them in reintegration.

During the term of parole, a parolee is expected to maintain contact with a probation officer, to secure a residence, and to seek employment. If a court orders a parolee to provide compensation for a crime, the person is expected to comply to the best of their ability. If a parole board believes a person should be subject to special directives in order to enhance the prospects of rehabilitation, it may order what it deems necessary. Such directives may include residing at a specific place for a period of time (which cannot exceed one year), securing an appointment in a job training program, seeking medical care, or participating in a treatment program. A board can issue a warning if a parolee fails to abide by the directives of the release; in extreme cases, it can have the parole order revoked.

Noninstitutional Sanctions

The central principle of Sweden's sanctioning rationale is to avoid, if possible, the imposition of a prison sentence. This effort has led to an increased utilization of noninstitutional approaches and a greater emphasis placed on nonpunitive programs. What follows is a description of these noninstitutional methods.

A conditional sentence is a form of probation in which the offender is not supervised by a probation officer. It is imposed upon people who have committed an offense that is punishable by imprisonment but whose prognosis is such that they are unlikely to commit another crime. This sanction serves as a conditional warning to refrain from criminal activity; it is imposed for a period of two years. Although offenders retain their liberty under this scheme, a conditional sentence can be accompanied by other orders. For example, a person could be enjoined to provide compensation for damages and a day-fine could be imposed. Offenders also may be given a warning if they fail to comply with court orders. The order may be altered somewhat, or the sentence could be revoked and a new sanction imposed.

A probation order is another noninstitutional sanction that can be imposed on offenders who have committed an imprisonable offense. It differs from a conditional sentence in that the person is placed under supervision. Moreover, as part of a probation order, an offender can be sentenced to a short term of imprisonment that does not exceed three months. Probation orders are imposed for a period of three years. If it is determined that a person no longer requires supervision, the order can be revoked after one year.

Although offenders retain their liberty while under supervision, they can be subject to other court orders. Like the person who has been conditionally sentenced, a probationer can be enjoined to provide compensation for damages and a day-fine can accompany the probation order. Local probation boards can issue special directives to probationers. These directives usually include maintaining contact with a probation officer and notifying the officer of their place of residence, employment, or schooling. Failure to comply with a court's order or a probation board's directive may lead to a warning, an alteration in the order or directive, or the revocation of the order and the imposition of another sanction.

Since the passage of the Act on Correctional Treatment, the use of probation orders has increased considerably, with approximately 6,500 people placed on probation each year. This has led to an expansion in the number of professional probation officers assigned to the 30 probation districts. This system is actually dependent upon the use of lay supervisors who are paid a token remuneration for their work. Professional probation officers train and supervise the lay supervisors and then assign them to probationers.

The use of probation has not escaped criticism, however, especially among offenders who claim that lay supervisors and probation officers have been ineffective in assisting them. In 1972, an experiment was introduced at Sundsvall, a parole and probation district in the north of Sweden (Kuhlhorn, 1975). The experiment involved increasing resources for the

Sundsvall district in the hope that recidivism rates would decline. More staff and facilities were made available to probationers, and a person was assigned on a full-time basis to assist in securing employment for the clients. Unfortunately, the amount of contact between the supervisor and the probationer did not increase. The results of the evaluation concluded that there was not a significant reduction among the Sundsvall clients' rate of recidivism, abuse of alcohol, or work habits, compared to other probation districts that did not receive additional resources. Despite these findings, correctional authorities remain committed to the idea that probation has the potential of being a more effective and suitable sanction than imprisonment.

If it is determined that an adult convicted of a criminal offense is in need of psychiatric care because he or she suffers from a mental disease, feeble-mindedness, or some other mental problem, a court may order that he or she be surrendered to special care. This could involve care in a mental hospital or treatment through an open psychiatric care facility.

Another type of probation, contract treatment, was established in 1988. It is a special form of probation that is designed for crimes related to alcohol or other drugs. The offender must agree to participate in a treatment program as an alternative to imprisonment. If the participant fails to comply with the treatment order of the court, the contract is terminated and the offender is sent to prison.

Community service is another form of probation. Initially, this started as a pilot project in five districts and has now spread throughout the country. It entails performing unpaid work of between 40 and 240 hours for nonprofit associations and organizations. While mainly utilized by younger offenders, it is not limited to that age group.

The final type of noninstitutional sanction is a fine. Fines are used extensively in Sweden's sentencing scheme and have been employed for more than 50 years. Fines serve a useful alternative to imprisonment and probation when these sanctions are considered inappropriate, but they also can be imposed on offenders in addition to one of the other sanctions.

There are three types of fines. A traditional fine is used in cases involving petty offenses, such as some traffic offenses or drunken and disorderly behavior. Traditional fines are based on the seriousness of the offense and range from 100 to 2,000 kronor (5,000 kronor if more than one offense has occurred). A corporate fine can be imposed for a crime committed in the course of a business transaction. Although rarely used, a corporate fine can range from 10,000 to 3,000,000 kronor. It should be noted that penalties for parking violations are not regarded as fines, but they are monetary in nature and fixed by a schedule issued by the Office of the Prosecutor-General. The charges range from 75 to 300 kronor.

It is the day-fine, however, that has received the greatest attention from students of comparative sanctioning methods. The idea behind a day-fine is to consider two factors before imposing the actual sanction. First, the number of day-fines fluctuates according to the gravity of the offense and can range between 30 and 150 days. If an offender is sentenced for several offenses in which a day-fine is appropriate, the maximum number is raised to 200. Second, the amount of a day-fine is determined by the per diem income of the offender; therefore, the monetary value of a day-fine varies according to the economic circumstances of the offender. The amount can vary from 450 to 1,000 kronor. Thus, the largest day-fine that is imposed for one offense is 150,000 kronor (150 × 1,000) or 200,000 kronor (200 × 1,000) for multiple offenses.

It has been pointed out that the imposition of day-fines rarely reaches the maximum limits allowed. One reason for this is that approximately 70 percent of the day-fines are determined by prosecutors. The fact that prosecutors cannot independently impose more than a 100-day day-fine considerably reduces the number of people sanctioned to the maximum penalty under this scheme (Thornstedt, 1986). In any case in which a day-fine is deemed an appropriate sanction, both prosecutors and courts consider an offender's total economic circumstances before determining the actual day-fine. For example, they review a person's financial liabilities in addition to his or her salary.

People can be granted extensions on the payment of any fine, or they can establish an installment plan to pay it off. If a person fails to pay a fine and collection is determined harmful to the offender or their dependents, the authorities may cease collection if it is determined that it is not in the public interest. Failure to pay a fine may be converted to a sentence of imprisonment for a term of 14 to 90 days, but this is rare. Of the roughly 300,000 fines imposed each year, approximately 40 cases are converted to a period of imprisonment (Thornstedt, 1986).

Critical Issues

The National Council for Crime Prevention issued a report in the late 1970s titled "A New Penal System," which expressed the views of one of the Council's advisory committees (National Council for Crime Prevention, 1978). Although some of the ideas presented were not new, the document served as a useful guide to what many in Sweden saw as the critical issues facing their correctional system. It should be pointed out that some of the concerns raised in the report had already been addressed. Youth imprisonment and internment sanctions, for example, were abolished, and the minimum term of imprisonment had been lowered from one month to 14 days.

The committee's principal concern, however, centered on the deprivation of an offender's liberty. It pointed out that the logic behind incapacitating an offender was based largely on a belief that this was an effective method of preventing the commission of other crimes by an individual. The committee was critical of this logic on two counts: (1) The theory was based on the assumption that it was possible to predict future behavior. While the committee recognized the ability to identify high-risk groups, it argued that it was not possible to predict individual behavior. (2) The other problem was the ethical consideration that too many offenders were being incapacitated for what they might potentially do in the future rather than for their actual crime. In light of this reasoning and the unlikely abolition of imprisonment as a sanction, the committee recommended lowering the rate of imprisonment.

In the late 1980s, another government committee began to explore the possibility of reducing the length of sentences for most crimes. The rationale for this idea was based on two concerns. Under current conditions, most inmates were not serving a significant portion of their sentence. There was a concern that, as the public became aware of this fact, they would lose confidence in the justice system. The other concern involved the sentencing practices of some judges. Judges who opposed the current method of early release might sentence people to longer periods of imprisonment in order to assure a period of incarceration that was originally intended. In addition, the committee had recommended that all inmates be released automatically after serving two-thirds of their sentence. If adopted, this proposal would eliminate the need for the National Paroles Board (Martinsson, 1987).

The committee that helped draft the 1978 report also suggested that a clear line be drawn to distinguish between punishment and treatment and that the choice of punishment be based solely on the crime. This latter issue was resolved, in part, with the annulment of Chapter 1, Section 7, of the Penal Code, which stated "that the sanction shall serve to foster the sentenced offender's rehabilitation in society." With regard to the issue of treatment, the committee was of the opinion that treatment be determined by the offender's social and medical needs, but only with the individual's willingness to participate in a program. They maintained that forcing inmates into programs was simply another form of state coercion that perpetuated the negative and alienated attitudes of inmates.

The Social Services Act of 1982 appeared to comply with that philosophy, as it emphasized the voluntary treatment of people suffering from alcohol and other drug dependency. However, two other pieces of legislation passed in that year—the Compulsory Care of Alcohol and Drug Abusers Act and the Compulsory Care of Young Persons Act—mandated the surrender to care of those people seriously endangered by substance abuse. That position was strengthened further in 1989 with the passage of the Act on the Treatment of Alcoholics and Drug Misusers. As was indicated earlier, this legislation authorized the use of coercive treatment. In light of these kinds of legislation, some people benefited from Sweden's attempt to expand its goal of more humane care, while others were being forced to participate, irrespective of the humane care provided.

Presently, a central goal of the Swedish correctional system remains the establishment of as humane a prison regimen as possible. While treatment is an important component of the regimen, it is no longer the rationale for imposing a prison sanction. Quite simply, the sanction is used to isolate people what have been found guilty of serious criminal behavior.

Finally, brief mention should be made of how the goal of maintaining a humane prison regimen relates to the country's broad social policy of enhancing equality for women. Women represent a very small proportion of the prison population. As such, there are only six prisons specifically set aside for their use throughout the country. Given the size of the country, this organizational fact often makes it difficult for the inmates to maintain close and frequent contact with friends and relatives. While female inmates share some of the social-psychological problems with their male counterparts, such as substance abuse, a poor work ethic, and failed personal relationships, their psychological problems are often compounded further if they have children placed in a care facility.

In 1998, the National Prison and Probation Administration established a set of principles that are designed to address the specific needs of the female inmate population. They include:

1. Women sentenced to imprisonment shall be placed in prisons intended only for women or in wings that are separated from those housing male prisoners.
2. Women's needs and issues should be addressed in a woman-focused environment that is safe, trusting and supportive.
3. Hospital and psychiatric facilities suitable for women shall be provided.
4. Women whose sentences include expulsion orders shall be dealt with taking their special circumstances into account.
5. Visiting apartments shall be provided.
6. Visiting rooms adapted to the needs of children of different ages shall be provided at all prisons housing women.
7. Programme activities and premises shall be designed taking into account the special needs of women prisoners.
8. Staff shall be trained to deal with crime from a gender perspective (Ministry of Justice, 2000).

It should be noted that some of these guidelines are applicable to prisons housing men.

Juvenile Justice

Despite the high standard of living and the significant amount of resources that have been earmarked for their welfare state, Sweden has not been spared the rise in crime among juveniles that has plagued so many industrialized countries. According to one source, the crime rate has increased 400 percent among the entire population since World War II. Crime among young people in the 18- to 20-year-old group has risen 500 percent, while the rate for juveniles between 15 and 17 increased 700 percent (Sarnecki, nd).

Property offenses and theft—especially of vehicles—are considered the more serious problems, but in recent years concern has been directed at the level of violent crime among juveniles (Von Hofer, 2000). Both victim and self-report surveys indicate that youthful perpetrators are often between the ages of 15 and 17, and that the most frequent offenders are in the 16- to 17-year-old age group (Dolmen, 1990). Moreover, as with adults, juvenile criminal activity is frequently linked to alcohol consumption and, in more recent years, abuse of other drugs.

Drug use escalated significantly among young people in the 1990s. One study indicated that the level of drug use among people in the ninth grade had tripled in the decade, and the heavy use of drugs by people under 20 years of age had also tripled. As a result, the police doubled the number of officers who focus their attention on this problem. This led to a quadrupling of drug convictions for people between 15 an 20 years of age. The likelihood of a prison sentence for those convicted has also increased (Tham, 2005). The Swedish model would emphasize rehabilitation during the period of incarceration.

Of particular concern is the degree to which specific crimes, such as burglary, robbery, and theft, are concentrated in urban areas where the opportunities for delinquent behavior are greater and the social control links are weaker (Wikstrom, 1990). As one might expect, the highest crime rates are found in the greater metropolitan areas of Stockholm, Götenburg, and Malmö, where approximately 185 crimes per 1,000 inhabitants were reported in 1988. Illustrative of the increased opportunities for delinquent behavior is the fact that in 1950 there were about 250,000 automobiles throughout the country, and only a few thousand were stolen that year, whereas in 1990, there were approximately 3.4 million cars, of which 60,000 were stolen per year (National Council for Crime Prevention, 1990).

Swedish authorities maintain that juvenile crime continues to increase, but available data on juveniles charged or convicted indicates that there was a decrease during the first half of the 1980s. This discrepancy is largely linked to law enforcement's manner of dealing with Sweden's age of criminal responsibility, which is 15. The police rarely interrogate or investigate offenses that are assumed to have been committed by a juvenile under this age. Delinquent acts of children under the age of 15 are the responsibility of the local social welfare agency. These offenses are not recorded in the police registry.

One expert has suggested that this policy has led police to lose interest in certain kinds of petty juvenile crime that they believe to be committed by juveniles under 15. In light of this, a large number of instances of petty theft or destruction of property reported to police are never cleared by them. Thus, while the number of juveniles charged by police may have declined, it is believed that the number of offenses committed by juveniles continues to rise (Sveri, 1986).

A change in the law in the mid-1980s enabled law enforcement to alter its policy regarding involvement in offenses allegedly committed by young people under 15 years of age. The age presently used as the benchmark is 12. This change should lead to a reduction in the inconsistencies of determining the level of criminal activity among juveniles. This modification in the law will be discussed in greater detail later in the chapter.

The National Council for Crime Prevention has focused a good deal of attention on the nature of juvenile delinquency among boys (Sarnecki, 1985, 1986). From this research, they have offered the following profile of the problem. Approximately 80 to 90 percent of young boys violate some criminal law, and they usually commit the offense as part of a group. Most commit only one or a few minor crimes, such as the destruction of property or a petty theft. A few, however, commit several offenses, some of which are serious.

This behavior is viewed as part of the socialization process of young boys when joining a group. The criminal acts are actually committed more out of an interest in fun than with any specific intention to cause harm. It also was discovered that a group or gang will often dissolve after a short period of time. This significantly reduces the likelihood that members of the gang will continue their delinquent behavior.

There are occasions, however, when a gang's criminal behavior is quite active. In such instances, the gangs will recruit younger members who eventually take over the leadership of the group and perpetuate its delinquent activity. Members of these more active gangs are a particular concern, especially those boys who are suspected of committing more than two crimes before the age of 15. From what has been gleaned from the available data, these boys are more likely to continue their criminal behavior into adulthood. They are also more apt to have a serious problem with drug abuse.

The council's research, along with that of others, has profiled the social background of the juveniles who continue an active career of delinquent behavior into adulthood. The findings offered no real surprises. Prime candidates for delinquent behavior as juveniles have been children coming from homes where parent-child relationships are poor, discipline is lax, the father is an alcoholic, and the financial circumstances are not promising. In addition, these children often had trouble making adjustments at school and lacked proper leisure-time activities (Sarnecki, 1989).

The juvenile justice system's approach to delinquent behavior is characterized by a dual philosophy. First, it is committed to a social and medical treatment model. As such, the intervention of the traditional components of the criminal justice system has been deemphasized. For example, the Social Services Act of 1982 emphasizes the voluntary treatment of people who abuse alcohol and other substances. This is essentially a proactive approach coordinated by social service agencies and is specifically directed at young people.

There has been some criticism of this general approach over the past 20 years, in light of what researchers have learned about the utility of the treatment model and the ever-rising crime rate among juveniles. Some changes have already been introduced to address these concerns. As discussed, the Compulsory Care of Young Persons Act went into effect in 1982 and has been revised on occasion. It calls for a reactive approach directed at serious abusers of alcohol and other drugs. Under its provisions, young people up to the age of 20 can be ordered into custody for social care for up to six months.

The law authorizes the police to become more actively involved with juvenile delinquents at an earlier age. In the past, police became involved with cases involving delinquents who had reached the age of 15. In light of the number of offenses allegedly committed by young people under this age limit, the new benchmark for police involvement is 12 years of age. Although it is unlikely that there will be a dramatic shift away from the treatment policy, these changes suggest that an attempt is being made to alter the balance. Voluntary treatment outside the formal justice system but within the social service community is continued and encouraged when possible, but compulsory care within the social service context (as well as earlier involvement with agents of the justice system) is also acknowledged as a crucial ingredient in addressing juvenile delinquency.

The purpose of this section is to examine Sweden's juvenile justice system. What follows is a brief description of the method of processing juvenile offenders, an explanation of the sanctions imposed, and an assessment of some of the critical issues confronting juvenile justice in Sweden.

Social Boards

Before the personnel and jurisdiction of the local social boards are described, it is important to explain how juveniles are classified according to their age and level of criminal responsibility.

Responsibility of Juveniles In Sweden, the age of criminal responsibility is 15. Therefore, if a young person below this age commits a crime, he or she cannot be subject to prosecution or a penal sanction. Although police can investigate offenses committed by juveniles between the ages of 12 and 15, a prosecutor often heads the investigation if the case is of a serious nature. Moreover, social welfare authorities have the right to request the suspension of an investigation involving a person under the age of 15. Police rarely investigate offenses committed by young people under the age of 12, because that is usually the sole responsibility of the social welfare agency within the child's district. Police may investigate and interrogate a person under 12 if special circumstances warrant it. Acceptable special circumstances include that the offense is considered serious or that adults are among the suspects in the case. Attempting to determine guilt, however, is not considered a special circumstance. The Code of Judicial Procedure calls for the parents or guardians of children under 15 to be present at an interrogation, providing that this does not deter the investigation.

Although juveniles between the ages of 15 and 20 can be prosecuted and sentenced, this is rarely done—especially if the suspect is under 18. The prosecutor decides whether it is appropriate to bring charges against the person. When the offender is under 18, the prosecutor usually turns the matter over to the local social board. This is also frequently done in cases involving people under age 20, but if the crime is serious, the prosecutor can bring charges against the juvenile. The court has the authority to reduce the sentence. Fines, probation, or a suspended sentence are frequently handed down in such circumstances. In exceptional cases, a person under age 18 can be sentenced to imprisonment, but one can never be sentenced to life imprisonment. Moreover, offenders under the age of 21 who are sentenced to a correctional facility may receive a more lenient sanction than that normally prescribed by the Penal Code.

Personnel Sweden does not have a separate court in its judicial hierarchy that specializes in juvenile cases. Should the prosecutor decide to charge a person who has reached the age of criminal responsibility, the offender would be tried in a regular trial court. This, however, seldom occurs. The body that functions like a juvenile court is the local social board. Each municipality throughout Sweden has a child welfare agency that is designed to handle both nondelinquent and delinquent children in need of specialized care. Within this administrative mechanism is the social board, which is composed of five members. These members are elected by the municipal council and serve a four-year term. The board usually includes a minister, a school teacher, a person trained in law, and other people who are interested in juveniles. Board members are not paid a salary, but they do receive reimbursement for some of their expenses. The board determines what type of measures will be taken against a juvenile who is brought before it. It receives a good deal of assistance in its work from professional social workers assigned to the child welfare agency.

Jurisdiction of the Board Social boards have both criminal and civil jurisdiction for people under 21 years of age. As was mentioned above, the prosecutor may order a person who is at least 15 to stand trial in a regular court. Although this has been rare in the past, especially for people under 18, this attitude may be changing. Prosecutors are no longer offering wholesale dismissals of charges. Moreover, boards are not routinely recommending a waiver of prosecution in order to let the board determine the outcome of the case. The civil jurisdiction involves care proceedings in cases in which the child is neglected or the parents or guardians cannot control the child's behavior.

Procedures The procedures of the board are informal. The board is not concerned with establishing the offender's guilt but rather with determining an appropriate treatment. This treatment should guarantee a protective upbringing for a child and enhance the likelihood that the child's social outlook will change. The Social Services Act of 1982 requires that a board's decision to place a child in custody be reviewed by an administrative court of appeal. On those rare occasions when a child is bound over for trial in a regular court, regular trial procedures are followed. Parents or guardians are required to attend all proceedings.

Disposition

The kind of disposition available to authorities in a case involving a juvenile is dependent upon which authority initially handles the matter. There are two types of options available if the case is dealt with by a social board. The first option is usually referred to as a preventive or voluntary measure. These measures are designed to aid the child or the family through social or financial assistance. For example, a social worker may be appointed to offer guidance to both the child and the family, or the family may be in need of financial assistance to help meet the needs of the child. The other option is frequently referred to as a protective or compulsory measure. The board endeavors to limit the application of these to more difficult cases. In most of these cases, preventive measures have already been tried but have failed. The most common protective measure is to place the child in a family home (previously called a foster home). Another option is to place the juvenile in a children's home. These homes are normally designed for six to eight children. The more recalcitrant child will be sent to a reformatory, which can usually accommodate 20 to 30 juveniles. A board does not specify the amount of time that a child will be placed in protective custody, but the custody cannot continue beyond the person's twentieth birthday. Reformatories, however well intended they may be, can have the same adverse effects as a correctional facility. Thus, while at a reformatory school, the child is given extended leaves. The reformatory philosophy is not unlike that found in adult correctional institutions; the goal is to minimize the amount of time an offender must spend institutionalized. Because a protective custody decision is made without the child's or the parents' consent, both offender and family have a right to appeal the board's decision to an administrative court of appeal.

As is the case with adult offenders, the prosecutor has a good deal of discretion in juvenile cases when the evidence is sufficient to prosecute. There are essentially three options. First, a prosecutor may decide to waive prosecution. This is often done. A waiver means that no further action will be taken against the offender, but the crime will be recorded in the police registry. In such instances, the offender must admit guilt in order to secure a waiver. If a juvenile continues to commit delinquent acts, a prosecutor can revoke the waiver. Second, a prosecutor can determine an appropriate sanction. The ability to dispose of a case in this manner is determined by three criteria: the offense must be minor, the juvenile must admit guilt, and the juvenile must agree to the sanction. Summary punishments are issued only in the form of a day-fine. The third option is for a prosecutor to bind a juvenile over to court for trial.

When processed through the regular court, a juvenile can receive many of the sanctions that are appropriate for adult offenders. Although imprisonment is a legally valid sanction for young people above the age of 15, it is rarely used. Usually a fine, probation, or suspended sentence is imposed. The Penal Code further states that offenders under the age of 21 can receive a milder sanction from what the code prescribes for adults who commit the same offense.

In 1987, there were 20,346 juveniles between 18 and 20 years of age whose cases were handled by either prosecutors or courts. Of these, 1 percent received care under the Social Services Act, 9 percent had the prosecution waived, 52 percent were fined by the prosecutor, 10 percent received a suspended sentence, 5 percent were placed on probation, 17 percent were fined, and 6 percent were sentenced to a term of imprisonment. Also in that year there were 14,817 young people between 15 and 17 years of age whose cases were handled by either prosecutors or courts. Of these, 4 percent received care under the Social Services Act, 45 percent had the prosecution waived, 38 percent were fined by the prosecutor, 1 percent received a suspended sentence, 1 percent were placed on probation, 11 percent were fined, and 0.2 percent were sentenced to a term of imprisonment (Sarnecki, 1989).

Critical Issues

It was pointed out earlier that the juvenile justice system of Sweden is characterized by a dual philosophy: commitment to a social and medical treatment model and to the absence of intervention by traditional components of the criminal justice system. It is these two goals that have been the subject of much criticism in recent years.

Treatment Criticism of treatment is based on two concerns. The first questions the effectiveness of the model. This concern, which is similar to that directed at adult treatment schemes, tends to be supported by research studies. One study discovered that 75 percent of delinquent boys who are continually involved in criminal activity maintain that pattern of deviancy for a number of years (Sarnecki, nd). This suggests that the efficacy of the treatment model is highly suspect, especially for the delinquent group that has the greatest need for treatment. Despite such findings, Sweden's policy toward delinquents has not been to implement harsher measures. In fact, the opposite appears to be true, for the government abolished the sanction of youth imprisonment.

The other criticism is the lack of cooperation among various agencies that have a role in the care of juveniles. Although social welfare agencies have the principal responsibility for juveniles, other agencies have a significant amount of contact with them. Schools, alcohol- and other drug-treatment programs, and local recreational departments are all involved with young people and attempt to assist in resolving their problems. Each of these agencies brings a different philosophical perspective to the problem. While this is not necessarily bad, it does lend itself to a fragmented approach to the problem. Because each agency is generally a part of a separate government hierarchy, the inevitable bureaucratic problems may prove insoluble unless the bureaucracy is streamlined. To some extent, inroads have been made to resolve part of this problem. The Social Services Act of 1982 mandates that each municipality establish a social welfare committee that is ultimately responsible for all social services.

Intervention Another major criticism with respect to the current ideology toward juveniles is the lack of intervention by traditional components of the criminal justice system. The primary purpose of this policy is to reduce the stigma of deviant behavior and to avoid labeling a child delinquent. The implementation of this philosophy is evident in the traditional procedural guidelines. For example, the police often are not involved in a thorough investigation of delinquent acts, for this has been considered the responsibility of the social welfare agency in the district. Moreover, the prosecutor must decide if an individual above the age of 15 should be bound over for trial in a regular court rather than have a local social board handle the matter. The prosecutor often defers to the social board. Finally, courts often impose noninstitutional sentences, and all sanctions, whether institutional or noninstitutional, tend to be milder than those imposed on adults.

What the critics are concerned about is the coupling of this noninterventionist ideology with the treatment model. They claim that the system's unwillingness to display society's objection to juvenile deviant behavior may encourage the perpetuation of the irresponsible behavior. The critics are not suggesting that harsher measures, such as punishment, be imposed. They are strongly inclined, however, to favor a method in which the juvenile will be made aware of society's disapproval of their actions.

The validity of this criticism has been recognized by the government in recent years. As indicated earlier, police can now become more actively involved in delinquency cases when the offender is 12 years of age or older. Until 1985, when the law was changed, police were expected to refrain from involvement unless the offender was at least 15.

In 1990, a parliamentary committee was formed to examine the responsibilities accorded the social service system and those of the criminal justice system as it relates to juveniles. At issue was the goal of improving the coordination and cooperation between the two. Known as the Swedish Committee on Juvenile Delinquency, it focused its attention on two issues: the sanctions imposed on juvenile delinquents and the methods of intervention with juveniles. The Committee presented its report to the Riksdag in 1993 (Swedish Committee on Juvenile Delinquency, 1993).

The Committee maintained that the penal system should be guided by four principles. First, the system should be based on humanitarianism, which would be illustrated by controlling the coercive aspects of punishments and by reducing the time between the commission of a crime and the imposition of a punishment. Second, sanctions should be predictable, which means the penalty would be fixed and the consequences of a criminal action would be known in advance. Third, the sanction should be proportional to the crime, which would control for severity of the sanction. Finally, sanctions should be perceived as fair, which would involve issues of proportionality as well as equality before the law. Although the Committee argued that these principles could be applicable both to adults and juveniles, it maintained that they should guide the sanctioning of juveniles.

In order to achieve these principles, the Committee acknowledged the need for greater cooperation among the police, prosecutors, and social service agencies. The Committee recommended that the sanctioning of juveniles be limited to: fines, conditional sentence, probation, imprisonment, and a new sanction called "special supervision." Under the current sanctioning scheme, the order for care within the social service system would be abolished. The recommendation to eliminate this sanction was based on two factors: (1) the sanction is not compatible with the aforementioned principles, namely that care orders are based on the personal conditions of the juvenile; and (2) such orders are issued by local social boards. The Committee also recommended that only courts determine a sanction that is based on criminal behavior.

It is assumed that probation and conditional sentences would replace the care orders. The sanction of special supervision is designed to acknowledge the Committee's view that imprisonment is not a suitable sanction for juveniles but that there is a need to deprive some juveniles of their liberty. A juvenile sentenced to special supervision would be assigned to a facility that presently handles care orders. The long-range plan, however, is the eventual abolition of imprisonment as a sanction for juveniles. The Committee's report is presently a series of recommendations that as yet do not have the force of law.

No doubt part of the reason for not implementing these recommendations has been the significant increase in drug abuse among juveniles. For some drug abusers and those involved in other socially destructive behavior, the care order removes the young person from the environment that has placed them at risk. Finally, in 1999 a Youth Community Service Order was introduced that essentially parallels the community service order for adults, that is, performing unpaid work for a nonprofit association for between 40 and 240 hours.

Diversion Sweden's juvenile justice system has recognized the potential value of the creation of diversion programs. Diversion attempts to direct the juvenile away from the formal adjudication process. Its principal goal is to prevent juveniles from being labeled delinquent. From a broad perspective, diversion programs are designed for both nondelinquent and delinquent youths. It already has been illustrated that prosecutors, courts, social boards, and juvenile caseworkers participate in achieving this goal. It is important to realize that the police are also actively involved in such endeavors.

Probably the most publicized method of police involvement in diversion is the unit known as the social police. Though some of the unit's work is not solely directed at juveniles, the social police unit is considered the principal method by which police can improve their relationship with young people. They also hope to divert some youths from getting caught up in the justice system. The idea for a social police unit has been around since the late 1950s, but it was not until the police were nationalized that the idea was implemented throughout Sweden. The social police are plainclothes officers who patrol streets accompanied by interested social workers. The purpose of this mixed patrol is to identify people who are in need of assistance. The police officer's daily contact with the public helps to keep the local social board informed of incidents that may need their intervention.

The social police have another function. They are usually called on to teach law and justice classes in schools. In addition to explaining the legal system, they participate in pedestrian and road traffic safety instruction and assist in the educational programs on alcohol and other drug abuse. Finally, they have been active in initiating and participating in recreational programs at schools. Although one cannot measure the extent to which this kind of involvement has deterred juveniles from committing crime, it is generally accepted that these kinds of liaisons have encouraged a positive relationship and understanding between police and young people.

Summary

This chapter has offered an introduction to the Swedish criminal justice system. The major components of the system—the police, judiciary, law, corrections, and juvenile justice—were surveyed, along with an overview of the political system. The organization and administration were described; the various roles of the practitioners were explained; the legal process was examined; and some of the critical issues facing the system were assessed.

Sweden is noted for being an exceptionally stable and industrially prosperous country. Part of that success is attributed to the government's ability to seek compromise and to reach a consensus that is beneficial to a large number of the citizenry. This process is illustrated by the manner in which the government and the Riksdag thoroughly analyze an issue that will have a significant long-term impact on the social system prior to enacting legislation. This style has important implications for the justice system, and the person who is given the greatest responsibility for directing those efforts is the minister of justice. This ministry is concerned with criminal justice legislation, the police, criminal procedure, criminal courts, prisons, and probation.

To the American observer, Sweden's justice system has resolved a number of problems that are frequently raised in the United States. For example, the police have been consolidated into a number of efficient forces; there is a separate entry scheme for police commissioners; and new recruits are exposed to a broad range of police work, including criminal investigation. Judges and prosecutors are given special training for their responsibilities. Moreover, there is extensive utilization of laypersons working in the system. The most significant contribution that the Swedes have made to criminal justice is the development of a humane and just sentencing philosophy. Not just a theory, it has been translated into an action model with broad support.

Concepts to Know

Meiji Restoration
the Occupation
Diet
National Police Agency
public safety commissions
kobans
Kidotai
boryokudan
Ministry of Justice
suspension of criminal proceedings
Supreme Court
public procurators
legal support centers
saiban-in
Legal Training and Research Institute
jokoku appeals
National Offenders Rehabilitation Commission
bosozoku
family court

Chapter IV

JAPAN

Introduction

Japan is an island country located off the eastern coast of the Eurasian continent. It is generally considered a small country, in part because its geographical proximity to China and Russia dwarfs its size. However, compared to western European countries, Japan's 145,856 square miles make it larger than England or Italy. In terms of the United States, it is slightly smaller than the state of California. Japan's population of more than 127 million is more than twice that found in England, and they are among the world's most literate people. Because the terrain is very mountainous and the habitable land limited, it is one of the most densely populated regions in the world.

Although the climate is conducive to farming, less than 15 percent of the land is fertile enough for agriculture. Fishing has long been a significant source of income, but the attention Japan receives regarding its economy generally centers on its industrial production. Before the middle of the nineteenth century, Japan was one of the most isolated countries in the world, and this insular position was by design. The political leadership realized, however, that it could no longer maintain that posture completely. As a result, the leaders made a conscious decision to industrialize. Although the country is not rich in mineral deposits, Japan has emerged as an industrial giant since World War II. Japan is unique in that it is the only nonWestern country that has become completely industrialized, exporting a wide range of products that include motor vehicles, electronic equipment, and mechanical tools.

Like the Scandinavians, the Japanese have remained one of the most homogenous of the advanced peoples in the world. More than 99 percent of the population is Japanese, and the largest minority group is Korean. The Japanese have a common history, language, and race. The dominant religions are Shintoism and Buddhism, but these are viewed more as features of Japanese custom than as beliefs that attract devoted followers. It has been estimated that between 70 and 80 percent of the people do not practice any religion. The homogenous qualities of the Japanese are enhanced further by their insular society and entrepreneurial spirit. This may appear somewhat contradictory from a Western perspective, but it is an example of a curious blending of the country's traditions with modern pragmatism.

The Japanese recognized the value of expanding their trade routes and introducing industrialization to an economy that for centuries had been based on feudal principles. Because of their commitment to this change, the Japanese are recognized today for a competitive spirit that had long been associated with capitalist countries in the West. However, it is a group competitiveness rather than an individual competitiveness that has dominated the Japanese psyche. This style is rooted in the traditional cohesiveness of a society marked by a sense of conformity and uniformity. This explains, in part, why greater attention is focused upon the group rather than the individual. It has been suggested that the reliance upon the group is illustrated in a number of ways (Reischauer, 1977). In the world of business, for example, a person is valued more as a member of a team rather than for individual contributions. As a result, the Japanese are competitive in the business world but not very creative. Emphasis on the group stifles the individual initiative that has traditionally been considered the source of creativity and originality. The group characteristic is also evident in the political arena, as emphasis is placed on reaching consensus opinions through decisions made in committee. At a more personal level, parental authority and familial ties are also stronger in Japan than in Western society, although this is beginning to change.

Edwin Reischauer (1977) argued that the group mentality is evident in yet another context. Individuals in Japan generally are not guilt-ridden when they do something wrong, because the culture does not condition people to feel that they have in some way sinned. This is partially attributable to the lack of a dominant Christian heritage. The sense of belonging to a group has a significant impact, however. When committing a wrong, a member is more apt to feel a sense of shame because of violating the norms of the group or society. Thus, deviant behavior is considered a rejection of the social norms to which individuals are expected to conform—norms that are a part of the country's tradition.

Because of an absence of the Judeo-Christian heritage, deviants are neither held in contempt by society nor condemned by the agents of the administration of justice. The Japanese are more likely to display a sense of pity toward the transgressor, and this is accompanied by more lenient judgments imposed on the person.

GOVERNMENT

By the late 1860s, the Tokugawa Shogunate, which represented the last vestiges of Japanese feudalism, was overthrown. In 1868, the imperial family was returned to a new position of reverence. This event is referred to as the Meiji Restoration. The date is usually cited as the beginning of extensive contact with the West. It has been suggested that this contact led to a transformation in the economic system that has enabled Japan to emerge as an industrial giant. At about this time, the Japanese were introduced to Western political principles, and in 1889, Japan adopted its first constitution.

The Constitution

People have a tendency to associate the establishment of a constitutional form of government with the modernization of a country's political system. With our historical hindsight, however, we tend to view Japan's Meiji Constitution as more of a transitional document toward modernity. Although the political ideas of the West were introduced in the document, they had to be justified and placed in the context of Japanese tradition. The form of the Meiji Constitution followed Western tradition. It was noted for the establishment of executive, legislative, and judicial branches of government; the development of cabinet government with a prime minister; the creation of a bicameral legislature; and the emergence of a sophisticated government bureaucracy. However, the similarities to Western tradition end there, for in substance, the political powers were not separated by a system of checks and balances. The emperor became, at least in name, an absolute sovereign, and the state ruled supreme over the citizenry. The authoritarian nature of the system led to a militaristic posturing both at home and abroad that did not end until the Japanese defeat in World War II.

The close of World War II brought the next major political change since the Meiji Restoration. As victors in battle, the United States controlled the postwar reconstruction of Japan. The period between 1945 and 1952 is known as the Occupation. As a part of that control, a new constitution was introduced in 1947. The Preamble to the document states:

> We, the Japanese people, acting through our duly elected representatives in the National Diet, determined that we shall secure for ourselves and our posterity the fruits of peaceful cooperation with all nations and the blessings of liberty throughout this land, and resolve that never again shall we be visited with the horrors of war through the action of government, do proclaim that sovereign power resides with the people and do firmly establish this Constitution.

Thus, both the country's future prospects and recent past are acknowledged at the beginning of the document. The Showa Constitution is truly an Anglo-American document modeled after the British parliamentary system. The emperor's status is limited to a symbolic function, and political power rests in the legislative branch. The constitution established a cabinet form of government with a prime minister and created a new judicial system.

Moreover, Chapter III of the Showa Constitution is devoted to the rights and duties of the people. Many of the articles in this section are similar to the constitutional or statutory pronouncements found in the United States. Articles 31 through 39 are of particular interest because they establish many of the rights that are espoused in the Fourth, Fifth, Sixth, and Eighth Amendments of the United States Constitution. To illustrate, article 31 states: "No person shall be deprived of life or liberty, nor shall any other criminal penalty be imposed, except according to procedures established by law." Article 32 proclaims: "No person shall be denied the right of access to the courts." Article 33 includes the statement: "No person shall be apprehended except upon warrant issued by a competent judicial officer which specifies the offense with which the person is charged, ..."; while article 34 indicates: "No person shall be arrested or detained without being at once informed of the charges against him or without the immediate privilege of counsel. ..." Article 35 proclaims, in part: "The right of all persons to be secure in their homes, papers and effects against entries, searches and seizures shall not be impaired except upon warrant issued for adequate cause." Article 36 states that "cruel punishments are absolutely forbidden," while article 37 indicates that "in all criminal cases the accused shall enjoy the right to a speedy and public trial by an impartial tribunal." Article 38 points out that "No person shall be compelled to testify against himself ..."; while article 39 addresses the matter of double jeopardy, among other things. Clearly, the Japanese constitution embraces the principles associated with the rule of law. In recent years, questions have been raised about the agents of the justice system actually complying with these principles. Those questions will be covered in the subsections of this chapter.

The Diet

Legislative authority rests with the Diet, which is a bicameral parliament consisting of a House of Representatives and a House of Councillors. The House of Councillors is the upper chamber; it includes 252 members who are elected to six-year terms. Candidates for election must be at least 30 years of age. The House of Representatives is the lower chamber. Like other parliamentary democracies, this chamber is the larger one. It has 512 members elected to four-year terms and is considered the more powerful of the two. Candidates for election must be at least 25 years of age. The House of Representatives elects the prime minister and controls the budget. Each of the houses has a committee system that was originally modeled after the American approach. The manner in which the system works is actually more in line with that found in Sweden. The government bureaucracy does most of the work in the preparation of legislation, which is then introduced to the Diet by the cabinet. It should be noted that all Japanese citizens who have attained the age of 20 are eligible to vote.

The Cabinet

Although the Showa Constitution states that "the highest organ of state power" is the Diet, it is the cabinet that holds the political initiative. The prime minister selects the people to serve in the cabinet, and the majority must be members of the Diet. The cabinet is collectively responsible to the Diet. It numbers approximately 20 people, of which about one-third are ministers without portfolio, who administer subministry departments. The other ministers head specific ministries, the most important being finance, foreign affairs, and international trade and industry.

Prime Minister

The political position of the Japanese prime minister is similar to that in England and Sweden. The prime minister is elected by members of the Diet. The person selected is always a member of the House of Representatives. This individual is the leader of the government (or administration) and of his or her political party. The prime minister selects the people to serve in the cabinet and functions like a chair of the board for that body. The prime minister and other cabinet ministers are responsible for developing and defending their government policy in the Diet. They can appear in either chamber to explain the government's position on a specific issue.

As in the British system, the Japanese House of Representatives can pass a no-confidence resolution forcing the prime minister and the associated government to resign.

Political Parties

It was not until the Meiji Restoration that political parties were introduced in Japan. Reischauer (1977) indicated that the Japanese, just as the Chinese, had long opposed the party concept. He pointed out that during the premodern period the notion of a political party was interpreted to mean disharmony and, on occasion, was associated with subversive activities. This attitude was tempered somewhat during the late Tokugawa Shogunate (the period before the Meiji Restoration) when political factions established rivalries within the bureaucracy.

Today, the Japanese maintain a multiparty system. Since 1955, the Liberal Democratic Party has usually held a majority in the Diet and has thus ruled the country. The party attracts a fairly wide following from a number of sources, but tends to be labeled conservative in its overall position on policy issues. What precipitated the party's brief loss of power was a series of corruption scandals that emerged in 1989 and implicated many party leaders. In addition, it was unable to introduce fundamental political reform, in large part because of infighting within its ranks (Yokoyama, 2005).

The closest rival to the Liberal Democratic Party in garnering votes has often been the Socialist Party. This party changed its name in 1991 to the Social Democratic Party and also reversed its previous positions of support for disarmament and opposition to nuclear power. The other traditional parties are fairly small in terms of candidates being elected to the Diet. These parties include the Clean Government Party, the Democratic Party, the Communist Party, and the Conservative New Party.

The Emperor

The restoration of the imperial family in 1868 did not lead to the emperor actually assuming authority. Instead, the political leaders behind the restoration wanted the emperor to reign rather than rule. He was to serve as a symbol of national unity, whereas civilian politicians were responsible for governing the country. The fact that the Emperor Meiji was a boy when he assumed the throne made the system easier to implement. He was succeeded by Taisho (1912–26), who was mentally incapable of asserting his position, even if he had so desired. Finally, many Japanese scholars are of the opinion that Emperor Showa (1926–89) had never aspired to be anything but a symbol for his country.

At the end of World War II, the new constitution changed the doctrine of imperial sovereignty spelled out in the Meiji Constitution to the principle of popular sovereignty. Article I of the Showa Constitution states that "[t]he Emperor shall be the symbol of the State and of the unity of the people, deriving his position from the will of the people with whom resides sovereign power." Thus, the emperor has a position comparable to that of the heads of the few remaining royal families in Europe; he is a figurehead. With his ascension to the throne in 1989, Emperor Akihito announced his firm support for democratic principles and the rule of law. Moreover, opinion polls indicate that the people continue to express a deep attachment to the imperial family and its symbolic role.

Administration

Government administration is carried out at three levels: national, county, and local. The national administration is conducted by governmental ministries and a large bureaucracy. The Japanese system is in line with European systems in that most of the power and control rests with the central administration. Following the war and during the American occupation, attempts were made to decentralize the national government's authority. For example, control of the police and the educational systems were placed at the local level in an attempt to introduce home rule in Japan. The size of the country and its history of modeling procedures along the lines of European governments combined to lead to the abandonment of this scheme. Thus, the Japanese have returned to a system in which the national government dominates the political decision-making process.

In the realm of criminal justice administration, the police are ultimately responsible to the prime minister. The correctional system and some aspects of the legal profession are regulated by the Ministry of Justice. The justices of the Japanese Supreme Court are initially appointed by the prime minister; they, in turn, nominate judges to the lower courts. During the occupation, the Americans introduced the concept of judicial review on the constitutionality of legislation. In comparison to American courts, however, the Japanese justices rarely wield this authority.

The other two forms of government are found at the county and local levels. Japan has long been divided into prefectures. These are similar in size to American and British counties, and they function along the lines of French departments. There are 47 prefectures in Japan, each having an elected assembly and a governor as the chief administrative officer. The local administration includes cities, towns, and villages. These units also have elected assemblies and mayors. Most of the work at the prefectural and local levels involve the implementation of national policy. It has been suggested, however, that this trend may be shifting slightly, for the local units are beginning to address local and regional concerns about the environment and the quality of life (Reischauer, 1977). Nevertheless, national issues and priorities continue to take precedence over local concerns.

Police

Historians of the Japanese police generally divide the evolution of that system into five distinct phases. In many respects, the history of the police (at least before the Meiji Restoration) mirrors the events that occurred in Europe. During the first phase, which encompassed the period between 700 to 1603, Japan had a dual police system composed of both public and private forces. The central government's ministries of War, Justice, and Popular Affairs retained police and judicial responsibilities (Ames, 1981; Hall and Beardsley, 1965). It was the army, however, that initially served as a professional police force. With the advent of feudalism, the method of maintaining order was decentralized. The shogunate increasingly turned to the samurai to provide law enforcement during peacetime. These forces were assisted in their endeavors by mutual self-help groups composed of family households. Mandated by the Taiho Code, this system was strikingly similar in operation to that of the English tithing system.

The second phase occurred between the years 1603 and 1868. This time, known as the Tokugawa period, was marked by efforts to centralize governmental authority and to assure a degree of political stability. While the self-help groups of the previous era continued to exist, this period is noted for developing a centralized law enforcement system similar to that which would emerge in eighteenth-century France. For example, a secret police force was created and given the responsibilities of identifying corruption in government and spying on those who opposed Tokugawa rule (Ames, 1981). In addition, magistrates were also established throughout the countryside and were given the tripartite authority to serve as chiefs of police for their regions and as prosecutors and judges in criminal cases. They were assisted in their police functions by mounted and foot patrols and by a detective unit.

The period between the Meiji Restoration (1868) and the close of World War II (1945) marked the third phase in the evolution of the Japanese police. Until 1868, the development of law enforcement techniques were largely indigenous to the country (although strikingly similar to those occurring in Europe). As the Japanese began to remove their self-imposed barriers of isolation, they borrowed organizational and administrative techniques from the West. The transformation was made easier by the fact that the evolution of Japan's police system coincided with that which was taking place in Europe.

In 1872, Kawaji Toshiyoshi was sent abroad to study European police systems; the measures that he recommended for adoption in Japan were largely borrowed from the French and German systems. A Home Ministry was created to control the police system throughout the country. It was operational at the prefectural level of government. Although the police retained quasi-judicial functions, especially those involving minor criminal matters, judicial responsibilities were largely given to the new Ministry of Justice. The police were given the authority to regulate a wider range of social activities, along the lines of the French model. Duties not related to law enforcement included the issuance of licenses and the regulation of a significant number of public health issues.

Thus, the Meiji period introduced a highly centralized police force. During the first half of the twentieth century, this police force became more powerful and increasingly militaristic in approaching its law enforcement and order maintenance tasks. As a result, heavy-handed tactics were employed to govern the citizenry, tactics that today would not be tolerated because they would be in violation of a person's constitutional rights.

The fourth phase (1945–1954) was highlighted by changes brought about by the American occupation following the war. This brief period was marked by two kinds of reforms that were both substantive and organizational in nature. With the adoption of the new constitution, the authority of the police was harnessed by the constitutional rights given to citizens. The other reform involved the adoption of an American style of decentralized autonomous police forces. The Home Ministry was abolished with this change, and approximately 1,600 independent forces were created to serve the various towns and cities of Japan. Public safety commissions were established to assure that citizens had greater control of their local police force.

The fifth and final phase in the evolution of the Japanese police commenced with the Diet's approval of the Police Law in 1954. This legislation abandoned the decentralized scheme, which had proved both financially and functionally ineffective. That law is the basis for the current police system. To a large extent, it is a return to a highly centralized national police service.

Organization and Administration of the National Police Agency

Although the Japanese have established a national police force, there are a number of significant differences between the current system and the old centralized force that emerged following the Meiji Restoration. The police retain a degree of local autonomy because they are organized into individual units at the prefectural level. In terms of financial considerations and efficiency of operations, this scheme is much more cost-effective than the pre-1954 system, which had independent police forces. The Japanese have retained the public safety commissions that oversee the supervision of the various forces, but the actual control of the police rests with the National Police Agency, which coordinates the nationwide law enforcement system (see Figure 4.1).

Figure 4.1

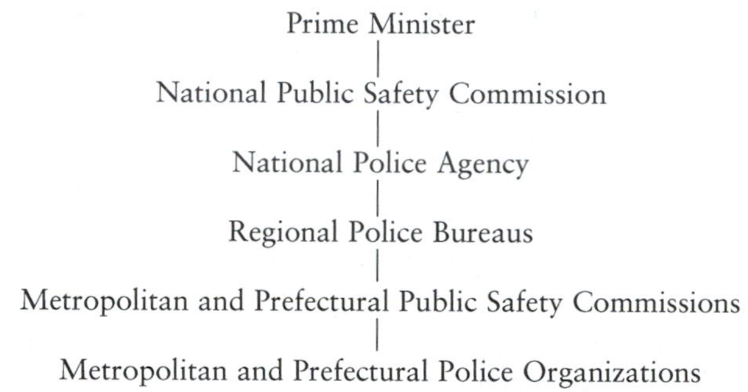

National Public Safety Commission In countries that have a national police force, usually either the minister of justice, interior, or home affairs is assigned the task of serving as the government's advocate in the legislature on issues pertaining to law enforcement. Japan had such a system before the American occupation. The minister of home affairs was the civilian politician ultimately responsible for the police. However, the ministry of home affairs was abolished at the end of the war because of the manner in which it managed police activities. This left the police under the direct control of the prime minister. Because of the nature of the office, the prime minister appoints one of the cabinet ministers, without portfolio, to be the civilian politician directly accountable for the national police, although the minister is not singly charged with this authority. The Police Law mandates that the National Public Safety Commission, which is under the jurisdiction of the prime minister, be responsible for the administration of the police. This arrangement is designed to achieve a degree of political neutrality for the police.

The National Public Safety Commission is composed of six people. The chair, who is a nonvoting member unless there is a tie vote, is the cabinet minister designated by the prime minister to oversee law enforcement issues. The other members are appointed by the prime minister with the consent of both houses of the Diet. The appointment is a five-year renewable term. Excluded from serving on the commission are people who in the previous five years have served in either the police or prosecutor service. In another attempt to ensure a degree of political neutrality, only two members of the commission can belong to the same political party.

The commission has extensive responsibilities regarding the establishment of basic policy throughout the police system. According to the Police Law, these include matters involving: the budget, planning and research, police operations, national emergencies, traffic control, training, communications, criminal identification files, criminal statistics, equipment, personnel, administration, inspection, and the Imperial Guard. The actual implementation of these duties is the responsibility of the National Police Agency. It coordinates this work with the various public safety commissions in the prefectures.

It has been suggested that the authority of the various public safety commissions is negligible (Ames, 1981; Hill, 2003; Yokoyama, 2001). They appear to suffer from many of the same problems that have been attributed to local police authorities existing in England; that is, commission members tend to display a good deal of deference to the authority and opinions of police administrators. As a result, the members do not provide a significant substantive check on the power of the police. Thus, the responsibility for the police actually rests with the National Police Agency.

National Police Agency The National Police Agency is responsible for the control and coordination of the prefectural police forces. The agency is under the direction of the commissioner general, who is appointed (and can be dismissed) by the National Public Safety Commission with the prime minister's approval. In addition to a secretariat, the National Police Agency is divided into the following bureaus: administration, criminal investigation, traffic, security, communications, and safety. The agency is also responsible for the National Research Institute of Police Science, the National Police Academy, and the Imperial Guard. Given the extensive supervisory role of the agency, it is actually more involved than the National Public Safety Commission in the active administration of the police throughout Japan. There are approximately 1,600 police officers and 5,000 civilian personnel assigned to the National Police Agency. In addition, the Imperial Guard consists of a force of about 900.

To illustrate how the National Police Agency both controls and coordinates police work at the prefectural level, one need only consider the role played by the National Research Institute of Police Science. The Institute has essentially three goals. The first is to conduct research on crime and to develop better techniques either to prevent crime or to assist police in their investigation of crime. The second is to promote the use of the scientific method in criminal investigations and their own analysis of criminal evidence. The third goal is to assist in training people at the prefectural level in forensic science techniques. The Institute has a broad range of disciplines represented among its staff members that include: anthropology, biology, chemistry, engineering, medicine, pharmacology, physics, psychology, and sociology. The staff work in one of the departments that are part of the Institute. These include forensic science, crime and delinquency, traffic control and safety, identification, and training.

The National Police Academy is designed to educate and train senior police officers as they assume leadership positions either at the national level or in a prefectural police force. The Academy also provides advanced training in specialized areas of police work. These areas include: community policing, criminal investigation, traffic enforcement, security policing, physical training, and instructor training. Also at the Academy are a series of institutes and centers, which include: the Highest Training Institute for Investigation Leaders, the International Research and Training Institute for Criminal Investigation, the Police Policy Research Center, the Police Info-Communications Research Center, the Police Info-Communications Academy, and the Research and Training Center for Financial Crime Investigation.

Brief mention should be made of the Imperial Guard. The Guard provides escorts for the Emperor, Empress, and members of the imperial family. It is also responsible for the security of the Imperial Palace and any other Imperial facility.

With the increase in high-tech crime involving computers and telecommunications systems, the Japanese government, like other industrialized nations, has recently directed its attention to this international problem. One part of the strategy is to pass new legislation such as the Unauthorized Computer Access Law (1999). Another is to improve the enforcement side of the effort. The National Police Agency is in the process of developing a National Center that will address the current problems of high-tech crime and new threats of cyberterrorism. The objectives of the Center are to provide technical assistance to prefectural police, to assist and support international investigations of high-tech crimes, to investigate cases of high-tech crimes or offer analysis of evidence related to such crimes, and to establish a collaborative relationship with various companies associated with the telecommunications industry.

To assist the National Police Agency in its work with the prefectural police forces, seven regional police bureaus have been established. With the exception of the metropolitan area of Tokyo and the Hokkaido prefecture, which are accorded a special status, these bureaus coordinate police activities in their respective regions. Each bureau is specifically responsible for conducting a regional training school and supervising the region's communications center.

Prefectural Police Each of the nation's prefectures has its own autonomous police force that performs law enforcement and order maintenance responsibilities. The 47 prefectural police forces employ approximately 245,000 officers, of which 10,800 are women. While each of the prefectures determines its own policies and procedures, because the National Police Agency does not possess the legal standing to authorize a national uniform system of rules, the agency can suggest or guide the prefectures in the establishment of local policies and procedures. Encroachment on the autonomy of the prefectural forces also occurs in other ways. For example, part of the expense for maintaining each force is defrayed by the national treasury. All senior police officers above the rank of senior superintendent are considered officers of the national government and employed by the National Police Agency. These officers are sent by the agency to administer the prefectural forces. Their appointment is made through the National Public Safety Commission with the approval of the local public safety commission. Finally, the costs of maintaining the training facilities, communications network, criminal identification files, crime statistics, equipment, special escorts, and special nationwide investigations are the responsibility of the national government.

Each prefecture has an elected governor. A public safety commission for the prefecture is appointed by and accountable to the governor. The commission oversees the administration of the police. In prefectures containing large metropolitan areas, the commission consists of five members; three-member commissions are found in areas that are not as densely populated. The duties of the prefectural commissions are similar to those of the National Public Safety Commission.

The Metropolitan Police Force of Tokyo is headed by a superintendent general, while the prefectural forces are administered by directors. Appointment to these positions comes from the National Public Safety Commission with the approval of the local Public Safety Commission. In the case of the superintendent general for the Metropolitan Police Force of Tokyo, the appointment also must have the consent of the prime minister. The Metropolitan Police Department consists of more than 42,000 officers; approximately 3,000 of these are women.

It should be noted that Japan has had to confront terrorist activities within its borders as well as acts against Japanese citizens abroad for almost 30 years. As such, the Metropolitan Police and some of the prefectural forces have established special assault teams that deal with hijackings, hostage incidents, and other emergency cases. In light of the activities of the Aum Shinrikyo (Supreme Truth) cult, namely, the placing of nerve gas in a Tokyo subway in 1995, the work of these special assault teams has been enhanced to include the prevention and investigation of terrorist acts that utilize or threaten to employ biological, chemical, and nuclear substances. The Metropolitan Police have also created a Mobile Rescue Unit and a Water Rescue Unit to assist with operations at disaster areas and accident scenes.

There are several police stations within each prefecture that serve as the principal operational units of the police. Each station is further subdivided into police boxes. A police box is more popularly referred to as a *koban*. In the late nineteenth century in Tokyo, kobanshos were established at major intersections and other significant locations. A *kobansho* was a specific place where a police officer stood watch. Over time a box was built at some of the kobansho locations to protect the officers from the weather. Today, there are approximately 6,500 kobans situated in the urban areas of the country, and about 20 percent of the Japanese police are assigned to them. In rural areas, a *chuzaisho* (a residential police substation) may be operated by a single officer. There are more than 7,500 chuzaishos. Because the officer is on duty 24 hours a day, living accommodations for the officer's family are included in the chuzaisho.

The size and location of the koban will determine how many officers are assigned to it. All newly recruited officers will spend time at a koban following their initial training. A number of officers who have additional training in community policing are also deployed at kobans, so that the officers represent a diversified age group. The duties of officers assigned to a koban include: standing watch either outside or inside the koban, patrolling their neighborhood, and visiting homes or businesses often about a crime prevention matter. When the police emergency call number is used, the command center dispatches officers from the koban to the scene.

Depending on the size of the area the koban is serving, officers may patrol on foot, bicycle, motorcycle, or small patrol cars. One of the principal purposes of a koban in densely populated urban areas was to provide aid or assistance to people. As such, kobans have a reception area to assist local residents or strangers. The types of issues that they address include: taking a crime report, mediating a dispute, counseling a person, receiving lost property, and providing directions for people.

In recent years it has been difficult to guarantee that a koban would always have at least one officer on the premises at all times. As a result, retired officers were recruited to volunteer as police box counselors. Presently, there are more than 3,000 counselors assigned to kobans throughout the country. They perform non–law enforcement duties, such as consulting citizens, receiving lost property, and giving directions. At the chuzaishos an officer lives with his family on the premises. When the officer is out on patrol, his wife often assists local people. Although not an employee of the police, the wife receives a monthly allowance from the prefectural police in recognition of her contribution.

Duties and Legal Status

Article 2 of the Police Law explains the general duties and legal position of the Japanese police. It states that the "[r]esponsibilities and duties of the police are to protect the life, body and property of an individual, and to take charge of preventing, suppressing and investigating of crimes, as well as apprehension of suspects, traffic control and other affairs concerning the maintenance of public safety and order." It was pointed out earlier that the Showa Constitution contains many of the individual guarantees found in the Constitution of the United States. In the Penal Code, Chapter 25 (crimes of official corruption) and Chapter 31 (crimes of arrest and confinement) illustrate the extent to which the police are subject to the criminal law. If the police are accused of a crime, the public procurator's office conducts the investigation and prosecutes the case, if deemed necessary.

The Japanese police are involved in the host of law enforcement activities necessary for a society that is both urbanized and industrialized. The police are concerned with preventive patrol, traffic enforcement, criminal investigation, juvenile delinquency, and organized crime. They carry firearms, but their policy on the use of weapons is similar to that found in Sweden. With the exception of traffic officers, the weapon is carried only while the officer is on duty. Weapons are stored at the police station at all other times. The frequency of incidents in which firearms are utilized in the line of duty are indeed small compared to the extent to which they are used in the United States. Although the police are authorized to use deadly force if necessary, there is a strong tendency to utilize nonlethal methods when a suspect must be subdued. The reluctance to use such force is essentially a product of the police organizational culture, as they remain conscious of the negative image they generated during the pre-war years. Moreover, the country's strict gun law prohibits citizens from owning most types of guns. Nevertheless, the police are confronted with the problem of the smuggling of handguns into the country. The most common methods include smuggling through imported cars, fishing boats, sea and air cargo, and hand luggage.

Brief mention should be made of the security police, who are responsible for counterintelligence and the surveillance of political extremists. A select group of these officers provide security for domestic and foreign dignitaries. The security police are also responsible for crowd control at holiday events and festivals. Within the security police is a unit called the Kidotai or riot police. The Kidotai are organized into units within the prefectures throughout Japan. Members of the Kidotai are selected from the ranks of the regular police. The criteria for selection include physical strength, command of the martial arts, and ability to cope in stressful situations. The recruits are in their twenties and live a military-style existence while serving in the Kidotai. They generally serve a three-year term with the unit before returning to the regular force. A term served with the Kidotai often enhances the officer's chances of promotion within the police service.

People in the West often associate riots with racial or ethnic minority groups. Although there are some ethnic minorities in Japan, their numbers are insignificant. In a country that is as homogenous as Japan, the groups that cause confrontations with the Kidotai are ideological in nature. The Japanese police perceive minorities as being those people on either the extreme right or left of the political spectrum. An especially fascinating item to the Western observer is the fact that the Kidotai do not arm themselves with guns when called upon to quell a riot. Once again, Japan's strict gun law is the reason for this policy. The Kidotai do not see the need for such weaponry in this kind of confrontation. They are provided, however, with a good deal of up-to-date technical equipment to assist them.

The Police and the Public

Throughout the 1960s, 1970s, and 1980s, Japan had been the only country in the industrialized world that did not register a significant increase in the number of nontraffic offenses reported to the police. In some years, it reported either a decrease or no change. Since 1991, however, there has been an increase in reported crime. Of particular concern are offenses referred to as felonious crimes, including homicide, robbery, arson, and rape. Increases also have been noted in two other categories: violent crimes and larceny crimes. Violent crimes include unlawful assembly with dangerous weapons, assault, bodily injury, intimidation, and extortion; while larceny crimes consist of burglary, vehicle thefts, and larceny.

Part of the increase in crime is attributed to the justice system's efforts to address problems associated with organized crime. For many years, the authorities viewed organized crime, referred to as *boryokudan*, as operating solely outside the mainstream of society. Following the devastation of World War II, the government was not in a position to direct limited resources at this issue. As Japan's economy developed so did the boryokudan. It is alleged in some respects that the boryokudan aided the police in their efforts to maintain order by keeping foreign organized crime elements out of the country. In addition, some developed a cooperative relationship with the police by exchanging information and identifying suspects in ongoing criminal investigations (Hill, 2003; Huang and Vaughn, 1992; Katzenstein, 1996).

By 1990, it was acknowledged that boryokudan were responsible for a significant number of crimes committed with weapons, particularly guns. It was also recognized that some of these gangs were moving into legitimate businesses. The Law Concerning Prevention of Unjust Acts by Boryokudan went into effect in 1992 and was amended in 1993. This legislation has not only enabled the police to crack down on the traditional illegal activities of gang members but also has made it possible for the tax authorities to investigate the gangs for unlawful income (Sinnosuke, 1992). In light of the problems raised by boryokudan, critics have argued that this legislation is not as aggressive as it could be when compared to organized crime legislation in England or the United States (Hill, 2003).

The police have also pointed out that there has been a significant increase in the number of foreign visitors, which more than doubled between 1982 and 1992. The police have expressed concern over the number of drug-related arrests of these visitors. They also have indicated an increase in the number of crimes committed by foreign nationals from Asian countries who are working in Japan. Moreover, there is a recognition that international crime organizations have contributed to this increase in crime (National Police Agency, 1995).

Recently, over a two-year period (2003–2004), there was a decrease in reported crime. When compared to other industrialized countries, Japan continues to enjoy a fairly low crime rate. When one compares the number of reported cases of major offenses, Japan's rate remains remarkably low. In 2003, the United States reported 11,816,782 major cases; the United Kingdom had 5,934,577; and France had 3,974,694. Japan reported 2,790,444. For the year 2004, a total of 3,427,606 penal code offenses were reported in Japan. Larceny was the most common offense at 1,981,574 (60% of the total). Larceny includes such offenses as burglary, pickpocketing, snatching, and auto theft. Larceny was followed by professional negligence in traffic accidents, with 864,569 cases, which was followed by 226,059 cases of destruction of objects. In 2004, there were 1,419 homicides, 7,295 robberies, 35,937 bodily injuries, 23,691 assaults, 2,176 rapes, and 9,184 indecent assaults (White Paper on Crime, 2005).

Western scholars who have studied the Japanese police have described an organization that utilizes a good deal of discretion and maintains a highly cooperative posture with the citizenry (Ames, 1981; Bayley, 1976; Fenwick, 1983b; Fenwick, 1985). In turn, the police had elicited from the people a sense of trust and public support. Opposition to the police by way of open hostility was generally limited to extreme political groups.

According to David Bayley and Charles Fenwick, this positive relationship between the police and the public was partially attributable to the traditional submissiveness that the Japanese showed to authority figures. They further suggested that neither the police nor the public perceived the police as mere agents of the law; instead, they viewed the police as moral authority figures. Despite this significant position, the police usually avoided asserting their authority in a formal manner. They preferred to maintain a more informal presence if possible.

American scholars have suggested that both the position of authority and the style of policing was reflected in an almost total lack of concern for several issues that have been perpetual points of tension in other countries. For example, it was believed that the job of the police officer was not as stressful in Japan as in other countries. Because they already had the public's support, the police were not forced to justify their position to a hostile citizenry. Although stress can be attributed to other factors, at least the Japanese police did not have to cope with that particular stressor.

Police corruption was rare in Japan. According to Bayley, when it did occur, an individual rather than a group is accused of criminality. This was attributed both to the position that the police held in society and to their team approach to policing. As has been indicated in Japan, the team approach to any enterprise is valued more than an individual's contribution. Allegiance to the group and its goals are taken very seriously. With that team mentality present in law enforcement, the opportunities for group corruption were reduced significantly.

Police brutality was also almost nonexistent in Japan, and there was no movement to impose a civilian review mechanism on the police, as was the case in a number of other countries. Civilian supervision of the police was already available both formally and informally, and it was considered adequate. The human rights bureau of the Ministry of Justice had the authority to review human rights violations, including police misconduct. Bayley discovered that few complaints against the police were filed with the bureau, and those that were had been declining in number. The prefectural legislators and the Public Safety Commission also acted as a check on the police. In addition, Bayley pointed out that defense attorneys and the news media actively scrutinized the tactics of the police. Each group supported the contention that brutality was not a problem. When it did occur, newspapers freely reported such cases, as they did other instances of professional misconduct.

Finally, in an effort to augment their own internal commitment to assuring integrity within the law enforcement community, the National Police Agency established a committee on the prevention of misconduct and the development of police integrity. As a result of that committee's work, the agency issued a new code of ethics for police in 1986. The code reiterated the important qualities expected of police officers: honesty, courtesy, impartiality, respect for human rights, and a sense of professional pride and mission.

This favorable image of the Japanese police has been popularized by the writings of American scholars, endorsed by other components of the justice system, and supported by the attitudes of the general public. One should not be left with the impression, however, that the Japanese police have not been the subject of some criticism. In more recent years, a good deal of criticism has been directed at the police. It began with a small group of Japanese scholars and members of the Joint Committee of the Three Tokyo Bar Associations who had become highly critical of some law enforcement practices. The criticisms were not directed solely at the police; they included concerns about some procedures at the pretrial stage that the police were responsible for implementing and that appeared to be endorsed by procurators and judges (Futaba, nd; The Joint Committee of the Three Tokyo Bar Associations, 1989).

These critical issues centered on the investigative tactics of the police—tactics that helped to explain their high clearance rates (Miyazawa, 1992). For example, under the Code of Criminal Procedure, the police have fairly broad powers to arrest people without a warrant. Once arrested, the person is often detained for questioning for up to 23 days. People can be rearrested on other charges in order to continue the detention; these warrants are readily issued by the courts, who tend to defer to the judgment of the police investigators. The accused also has no right to legal counsel during questioning. Once indicted, access to counsel can be and often is restricted by the police; moreover, written communications between counsel and the accused can be censored. In addition, there is no system of court-appointed counsel until after the indictment is issued, and suspects who maintain their innocence are usually refused bail.

The process is further facilitated by the policy of using police holding cells as substitute prisons. Unlike the regular detention facilities maintained by the Ministry of Justice, the substitute prisons are administered by the police. Over the years, the police have encouraged the government to provide more funding for the construction of such facilities, and successive governments have supported this request. There are presently more than 1,000 substitute prisons throughout Japan.

The use of extended detention in these substitute prisons, coupled with the broad procedural powers accorded the police, has led detectives to focus almost exclusively on extracting confessions from the accused rather than building cases based on other kinds of evidence. Critics maintain that the circumstances of detention lead police to employ unjust treatment and sometimes illegal tactics during interrogation. In support of this contention, critics have identified instances in which people have elicited false confessions. They point out further that the United Nations Human Rights Committee recently expressed concern about possible violations of human rights in this context.

While critics of the status quo are concerned about the situation, they readily admit that all of the blame cannot be leveled at law enforcement. Procurators tend to support police tactics, and judges take a passive attitude when it comes to pretrial procedures, often deferring to the procurator. This leaves defense counsel to scrutinize and criticize police tactics. However, as few lawyers specialize in criminal law, they lack strength in numbers. Finally, political parties either support the system or have not raised the issue in any political forum because the general public has not displayed much interest in the issue.

These criticisms do not necessarily mean that American scholars have projected an inaccurate image of Japanese police. What the critics are suggesting is that there has been a shift to some extent in the goals of law enforcement. Presently, the police organization appears to emphasize law enforcement rather than order maintenance and social service objectives. The critics allege that this change began to occur in the 1980s. Thus, some of the generalizations about Japanese police by American scholars may be dated as they pertain to certain contexts or particular areas of the country. This is especially the case when applied to prefectures that have a higher incidence of criminal activity.

Finally, it was already public knowledge that some conservative politicians, especially those associated with the ruling Liberal Democratic Party, were linked to prominent leaders within the Japanese organized crime community. In the 1990s, there emerged a series of revelations about police corruption and abuse, of which some were associated with organized crime (Hill, 2003; Katzenstein, 1996; Yokoyama, 2004b). This was a period when the Japanese people were becoming highly critical of their government and financial institutions as the country remained in an extended period of recession. Revelations about several cases of police corruption coupled with cases of theft, sexual offenses, bribery, violence while drunk, and driving while under the influence added to the negative image of the police.

In 1983, the public was asked to rate the major institutions in Japanese society. The police ranked higher than the government, business, and the press (Katsenstein, 1996). It is important to point out that the vast majority of police in Japan are honest professionals. This is illustrated by the fact that in 2000 only 546 officers received a disciplinary penalty out of roughly 267,000 officers (Yokoyama, 2004b). Unfortunately, the cases mentioned above have led to a decline in the public's trust of the police. One indicator noted by the National Police Agency was that people's willingness to report crimes and suspects fell from 61.6 percent in 1969 to 49.9 percent in 2000 (White Paper on Police, 2000). Recently, the National Police Agency reported that among 2,454 detectives, 79 percent were having a difficult time getting witnesses, suspects, and others to cooperate in criminal investigations (White Paper on Police, 2008). The police are making a concerted effort to recapture the very positive image that the public had of them throughout the 1960s, 1970s, and 1980s. Two areas of attention include recruitment and training and crime prevention.

Recruitment and Training Japan's recruitment scheme is similar to that found on the continent of Europe. A recruit can enter the service as either a police officer or an assistant inspector. Both are required to pass a national qualifying examination. The successful candidates then must complete a physical exam, an aptitude test, and a series of personal interviews. Those recruited to the rank of police officer must have completed high school; at present approximately 80 percent are university graduates. Candidates for the rank of assistant inspector must have a college degree and must have passed an advanced civil service examination. As a whole, the police are better educated than the rest of the population.

During the evaluation process, the personal and family history of the recruit is scrutinized extensively in order to screen out candidates who fail to meet the predetermined profile of a successful officer. Among the issues considered in the background check that can lead to disqualification are: a criminal history, a history of mental illness, identification with left-wing political groups, associating with extreme religious groups, and possessing a "tainted" background because of a prior association with a former outcast class in Japanese society (Ames, 1981). These apply to both the candidate and family members. Obviously, some of these factors would be considered a violation of a candidate's civil rights if applied in the United States.

The candidates for police officer are recruited and trained at police schools in the prefectures. The program is regulated by the National Police Agency. High school graduates spend 10 months at the school, while college graduates complete the training in six months. Recruits study law, police procedures, sociology, psychology, history, literature, and the martial arts. Thus, the program contains a general educational component as well as technical training. After completing this initial training, the recruit (a high school graduate for eight months, a college graduate for seven months) will participate in some on-the-job training at a koban. A senior officer at the koban will train the recruit on the importance of community policing. The recruit then returns to the academy (a high school graduate for three months, a college graduate for two months) for additional training. Once a person becomes a police officer, there are opportunities for in-service training which facilitates promotional opportunities. Some young officers are even given the opportunity to participate in training programs in Europe and the United States.

People who have been recruited to the rank of assistant inspector spend six months in training at the National Police Academy, where the program is designed to groom future police executives. There is also an extensive system of special training to enhance officers' skills in particular aspects of police work. In-service courses, which prepare officers for promotional examinations, are also offered. These are run by regional police schools. Bayley concluded from his study that the typical police officer is young, male, married, a high school graduate, of marginal middle-class background, and, in general, raised outside the larger metropolitan areas of Japan.

The minimum age for recruiting a male candidate is 19, whereas the age established for females is 20. Although female recruits are empowered with all the authority of a police officer, their responsibilities usually have been limited to such areas as traffic, juvenile, and communications functions. This attitude is beginning to change as female officers are being assigned a wider range of police duties, including that of criminal investigation.

In 1991, the National Police Agency embarked on a new policy designed to alter the rank structure of the police within six years. Prior to the implementation of this policy, 80 percent of the police were at the rank of police officer or police sergeant. The goal has been to increase the number of officers above the rank of police sergeant to 40 percent of the total force, with the specific objective of doubling the number at the assistant inspector rank. This policy has two objectives. First, there is a recognition that the current crime problem requires that officers have a combination of breadth of experience and knowledge as well as depth of expertise and specialization. Second, there is a need to recognize and reward people based on merit. The goal, therefore, is not to create a larger desk bureaucracy within the police establishment; rather, the aim is to recognize excellence and reward it, while keeping the officers in the field so that they can continue to excel at what they do best (Leishman, 1993).

Crime Prevention According to Walter L. Ames, the Japanese police have established two approaches to crime prevention. One is in the form of a public relations campaign that enhances the public's image of the police. For example, information about crime prevention techniques is published and distributed by the police. Special programs also have been developed to curb the illegal use of drugs and to reduce traffic accidents.

The other approach, creating a dialogue between the police and the public, is implemented through voluntary citizen support groups. The Japanese have had a long tradition of citizen participation in law enforcement. This is reflected by the neighborhood associations in which every household is represented. Within the neighborhood associations, there are crime prevention and traffic safety associations. The crime prevention associations assist the police in advising residents on household security techniques. The traffic safety associations conduct campaigns to reduce traffic accidents. There are also hundreds of specialized associations that reflect crime prevention needs and strategies of businesses. Banks, department stores, bars, and restaurants are examples of some businesses that have developed their own particular crime prevention associations with the cooperation of the police.

Probably the most important feature of the Japanese crime prevention program is the existence of police boxes, or *kobans*. Kobans, which are scattered throughout the urban areas, function along the lines of the mini-police stations that have become popular in some cities in the United States. Kobans serve two principal functions: (1) they offer information to those in need of assistance, and (2) they are the first line of defense in the system's attempt to maintain law and order, because it is the officers assigned to the kobans who provide the basic street patrols. As Bayley (1976) has pointed out, these are the officers who physically demonstrate the existence of police authority, resolve minor problems, and enhance the public's trust in the law enforcement community.

The kobans reflect a neighborhood-centered policing function. By patrolling a specific area over an extended period of time, they become particularly conscious of the needs and concerns of their immediate community. Their knowledge and understanding of the area is enhanced further by a survey conducted by koban officers twice a year. While conducting the survey, it is common for the officers to advise the residents on various crime prevention techniques. The officers collect a host of information about the neighborhood through the survey. The names, ages, and employment of each resident are recorded, and the ownership of cars and their license numbers are routinely taken down. Additionally, the police inquire about any suspicious behavior or illegal activities in the area. Although people are not required to answer these questions, most cooperate willingly. Any information gathered remains at the koban to assist the officers in their work; it is not passed on to a government agency.

Bayley pointed out that the survey serves another purpose. In the course of their duties, most police come in contact only with the criminal or deviant elements of society. In the process of the survey, however, the police are more frequently in contact with law-abiding citizens. In the long run, it is a healthy experience for the officer and it also serves to reinforce the public's positive image of the police.

Because of the increase in crime, the police have recently issued some new policy guidelines to address these concerns. They include a concerted effort to reduce street crimes by supplying more crime prevention information to the public, by increasing the number of officers assigned to kobans, and by enhancing the officers street patrol activities. Because juveniles commit 70 percent of the street crime, particular attention is focused on them. Efforts are also being initiated to improve the manner in which major crimes are investigated. A greater emphasis is being placed on the collection of forensic evidence rather than securing a confession from a suspect. Both Japanese gangs and foreign gangs are being targeted, and information is being shared among government agencies, such as the Immigration Bureau, and with other governments, such as the Ministry of Public Security of the People's Republic of China (Police Policy Research Center, 2006).

In addition to these initiatives, police focus a good deal of attention on traffic safety education for children and senior citizens, as well as motorcyclists, who have been a particular concern for some time now in

Japan. The police also have a significant presence in most schools for purposes of providing crime prevention and drug education lessons and in offering guidance to juveniles. Finally, the police have targeted fraud and other business offenses, child abuse, and stalking in both the pre-cyber form and when these offenses are facilitated by the Internet.

Judiciary

When compared to the traditions of Western countries, the histories of both the Japanese court system and legal profession are fairly brief. The reason for this centers around the fact that until the Meiji Restoration, the Japanese had neither a court hierarchy nor a legal profession, at least not in the sense that those terms had been utilized for centuries in other countries. Prior to the Restoration, the Japanese followed the Chinese tradition of including judicial matters within the purview of government administrators. In fact, attempts were first made to conciliate disputes privately before turning the matter over to a court. When a case could not be resolved informally, it was usually handled by a local administrator of the shogunate, who also served as a magistrate. Serious matters were resolved at the headquarters of the shogunate. Because the parties in both civil and criminal cases were not permitted legal representation, there had been no need for a legal profession.

With the demise of the Tokugawa Era and the advent of Meiji, a significant change occurred that was based upon the introduction of the principle of the separation of powers. Japan's first judicial code was introduced in 1872. It not only established a court hierarchy, but also created the legal offices of judge and procurator, which, in theory, were not a part of the executive branch of government. The application of the separation of powers in the Western tradition was incomplete, however. This was to be expected in a country that was embracing Western legal concepts, yet lacked the historic traditions and understanding essential to making the new system work. As a result, the minister of justice (a member of the executive branch) sat as the chief judge in the Ministry of Justice Court, the highest court in the land. The minister of justice also had the authority to appoint and dismiss judges and procurators. Because the country did not have a trained judiciary, the minister usually appointed government administrators to serve as judges in the local courts. Thus, the old ways had not been totally abandoned.

Nevertheless, changes in the courts and legal profession were in the offing during the two decades that preceded the adoption of the Meiji Constitution of 1889. For example, the minister of justice ceased taking an active role in the Ministry of Justice Court by 1875. In fact, the name of the highest court was changed to the Great Council of the Judicature.

However, the minister continued to control the appointment and dismissal of judges and procurators. In 1884, a regulation mandated that judges pass an examination prior to their appointment to a court. Procurators were subject to the same regulation by 1886. In that same year, judges were assured a greater degree of independence, because they could no longer be removed without just cause.

For centuries, the Japanese had not recognized the need to have legal counsel representing clients in court. With the acceptance of Western legal ideas, this attitude was to change, albeit rather slowly. Litigants in civil matters could employ the services of counsel by 1872, and this was extended to criminal cases in 1880. Scholars who have examined the history of the Japanese bar have pointed out that the advocates were not accorded special standing in the courts; they were more or less treated like the litigants. Moreover, little was done to regulate the profession. It was not until 1876 that the Ministry of Justice required the passing of an examination to practice law. In 1880, advocates were organized into associations that were responsible to the district procurator. Finally, people began to attend universities to acquire formal legal training.

From the Meiji Restoration until the adoption of Japan's first Constitution in 1889, the Japanese modeled their legal reforms along the lines of the French system. This tradition ended, however, with the drafting of a constitution. Because the Japanese found the Prussian system of an absolute monarchy more fitting to their needs, the Meiji Constitution and the subsequent reforms in the legal system were modeled after the German system. In terms of the manner in which the legal system would operate, the changes were not all that significant. Both the German and the French systems were part of the Romano-Germanic legal tradition that dominated the continent of Europe.

Between the adoption of the Meiji Constitution and the end of World War II, the Japanese judiciary matured into a highly professional body. Part of this success was attributed to the constitutional guarantee of judicial tenure. Another was the marked improvement with which the credentials of judges and procurators were scrutinized. The Attorneys Law of 1893 enhanced the professional status of the Japanese bar and established new admissions standards. Finally, the minister of justice took an active role in regulating the profession.

With the creation of a new constitution during the Occupation, the judiciary was subject to considerable reform. These changes largely reflected the Anglo-American legal background of the occupation forces. Most experts identify three salient reforms that are attributed to the new Showa Constitution. The courts were assured complete independence and autonomy; they would have the power of judicial review over legislative acts, which had been prohibited under the old constitution; and they would adjudicate all litigation, including administrative matters, between the state and a citizen. Special administrative courts handled such cases under the Meiji Constitution, as is the tradition in Romano-Germanic law countries, but these courts were abandoned with the passage of the Showa Constitution.

Although the Japanese established a modern judicial system, there remained deeply rooted in the social context of the country some reluctance to use the system as it was intended (or at least as perceived by people from the West). Central to understanding this attitude is the influence of Confucian natural law on Japanese culture. Two beliefs from this doctrine help to illustrate the basis for the Japanese attitudes to the judiciary: (1) the belief that people do not possess rights but rather have a duty to be loyal to their superiors, and (2) the belief that one should strive to attain individual and collective harmony in society.

In an attempt to follow the Confucian philosophy, procedural rules were devised throughout the Tokugawa Shogunate and the Meiji Era so that conciliation and mediation might resolve a dispute before it was brought to a court of law. The notion of going to court to litigate was considered anathema. Litigation implied that a person had a claim of recourse as a right and threatened to disrupt the social harmony by eventually declaring a winner and a loser in the suit. The loser would feel a sense of shame that would disrupt his or her personal social harmony. Both of these notions were at cross-purposes with the Confucian natural-law doctrine.

The idea of social class, as defined by Japanese law, has been abolished, and people have acquired several rights with the Showa Constitution. Nevertheless, social status remains important in Japan, and people still prefer to have disputes mediated rather than litigated. This helps to justify the amount of time courts spend functioning as conciliators in disputes. It also explains the large number of cases from the lower courts (approximately 50 percent) that are either withdrawn or end in a compromise (See, 1982). It has been suggested, however, that the apparent lack of litigiousness among the Japanese is more a product of institutional constraints (the limited number of people who are permitted to pursue a career as a judge, procurator, or attorney) than of deference to Confucian philosophical principles (Berat, 1992).

More recently, those institutional constraints have led to a good deal of comment and study on the state of the judiciary. As mentioned above in the section on police, throughout the 1990s the Japanese people were becoming highly critical of their government and other institutions in their modern society. Both the extended period in which the country had been in recession and the move toward a more global economy had placed a significant strain on the country's rather small legal profession. As a result, the Japanese business community joined the disgruntled citizenry in demanding reform of the judicial system. To illustrate the issue of the size of the profession for such an advanced industrialized and urbanized society and by way of comparison, Japan had 20,730 legal professionals in 1999. In that same year, the United States had about 941,000; England and Wales had approximately 83,000; and France had around 36,000 (Justice System Reform Council, 2001).

Even before the recession, critics of the status quo, which included a number of the local bar associations, had suggested that there was a need for comprehensive judicial reform. They pointed out that before the end of World War II the judiciary was viewed as part of the bureaucracy designed to control the people. With the introduction of democracy following the war, one of the goals was to introduce the principle of separation of powers in government and, with it, the establishment of an independent judiciary. Critics maintained that the judiciary remained too bureaucratic. Because of the limited number of judges, procurators, and attorneys, people were restricted in their access to the justice system. As such, the judiciary was considered remote and not terribly user-friendly. Suggestions to improve the judiciary and the justice system had been far-ranging. They included appointing practicing attorneys to serve as judges and procurators, reforming the bar examination, and protecting human rights. Concerns that had been directed specifically at the criminal justice system focused on providing a better criminal defense, protecting the rights of the detained, and abolishing the death penalty.

The Justice System Reform Council was created in 1999 with a mandate to consider measures for judicial reform in the context of defining the role of the judiciary for the twenty-first century. The council was composed of 13 people who were appointed by the government with the approval of the Diet. According to the enabling legislation that created the council, six of the members had experience either practicing law or as legal scholars. The other seven members were expected to come from other fields. The objective of this was to enhance the likelihood that the public's views were expressed and considered during the deliberations of the council.

After its creation, the council collected information from a variety of sources about the state of the judiciary and the administration of justice. In an initial report, they concluded that "the administration of justice is hard to understand and difficult for the people to utilize." Obviously, a central goal of the council was to make the justice system more open to the public. Among the issues raised in this initial report were: a recognition not only of the shortage of lawyers but also their uneven distribution throughout the country; the need to reexamine the system of legal education and training; the necessity to improve the legal aid system; a review of criminal procedures to assure that they are in compliance with human rights guarantees; the value of providing information to the public about the administration of justice and also the use and role of alternative dispute resolution programs; and finally, in terms of making the public more knowledgeable about the administration of justice, whether the use of lay judges or the jury should be utilized as in civil and common law countries (The Justice System Reform Council, 1999).

The council issued its final report, *Recommendations of the Justice System Reform Council for a Justice System to Support Japan in the 21st Century* (hereafter RC21), in June of 2001. The report explains the reasons for the government creating the council, which were:

> [for] clarifying the role to be played by justice in Japanese society in the 21st century and examining and deliberating fundamental measures necessary for the realization of a justice system that is easy for the people to utilize, participation by the people in the justice system, achievement of a legal profession as it should be and strengthening the functions thereof, and other reforms of the justice system, as well as improvements in the infrastructure of that system.

The report went on to state that there were three pillars or basic policies to this effort at reforming the justice system and contributing to a more free and just society. The first of these addressed the need to meet the public's expectations by which "the justice system shall be made easier to use, easier to understand, and more reliable." The second pillar focused on the legal profession and its support of the justice system through improving both the quality and quantity of the profession. The third pillar cited the need to improve the public trust in the justice system. This could be achieved by permitting the public to participate in legal proceedings and provide their views in other forums. The report contained a very comprehensive plan for revising the country's judicial system. Proposals were put forward that would change both the civil and criminal justice systems. All of the suggestions alluded to above in its initial 1999 report were included and expanded upon in the final report. What has been somewhat surprising is the speed with which the government accepted the recommendations and introduced enabling legislation to move ahead with a plan.

Organization and Administration of the Courts

Japan has a four-tiered hierarchy with five courts responsible for all litigation (see Figure 4.2). The family courts deal with juvenile delinquency cases and will be examined in the section devoted to juvenile justice. Before the court system is described, brief mention should be made of the responsibilities of the Ministry of Justice.

Figure 4.2

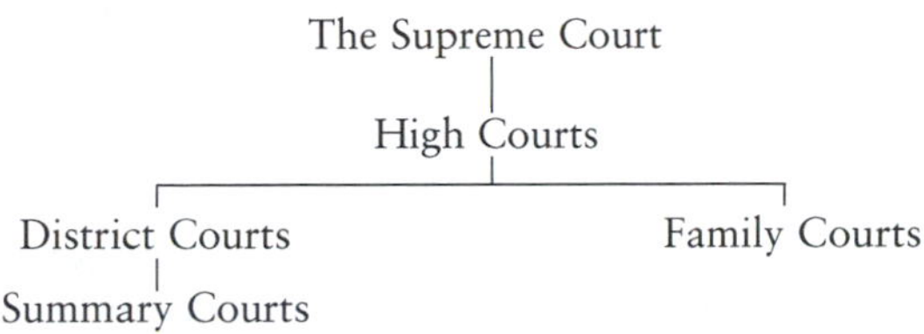

Ministry of Justice The Ministry of Justice is a cabinet-level department headed by the minister of justice, who is appointed by the prime minister. Before the adoption of the Showa Constitution, the ministry was afforded a good deal of authority over the courts, judiciary, and other members of the legal profession. The adoption of the new constitution altered the ministry's authority considerably. The principal reason for this change was the inclusion of the principle of the separation of powers in the Showa Constitution. Modeled after the American system, the Japanese made a clear distinction between the duties and responsibilities of the executive, legislative, and judicial branches of government.

The ministry is divided into seven bureaus: the criminal affairs and civil affairs bureaus are responsible respectively for the research and preparation of bills involving the criminal and civil law; the correction bureau coordinates the prison system and issues involving prisoners; the rehabilitation bureau handles matters pertaining to released inmates and offenders on probation; the litigation bureau serves as the legal department for government agencies and represents the government in court; the immigration bureau processes people entering and leaving the country; and the civil liberties bureau is ultimately responsible for the investigation of allegations of civil rights violations. Most staff members within the ministry are public procurators.

Also under the organizational control of the ministry is the Public Security Intelligence Agency. This agency was created in 1952 with the passage of the Subversive Activities Prevention Law. The purpose of the legislation was to assure the protection and further development of democratic principles in the country by controlling organizations that might attempt violent subversive activities. As such, the agency conducts investigations into groups that are suspected of threatening public security. Because such circumstances are not always limited to internal threats, the agency collects information on international matters that might influence subversive groups within the country. In addition to its headquarters, the Public Security Intelligence Agency is divided into eight regional bureaus throughout the country. There are also field offices in each of the 47 prefectures.

The Supreme Court The Supreme Court has judicial and administrative responsibilities. These are explained in both the Showa Constitution and the Court Organization Law. The court's judicial responsibilities are limited to issues involving constitutional interpretation. The court, which consists of a chief justice and 14 associate justices, hears cases as either a grand bench or a petty bench. A grand bench includes all 15 members of the court and must sit when an issue involves a new constitutional ruling or a new precedent is set. According to Supreme Court rules, nine justices constitute a quorum, and eight justices must concur for a law to be declared unconstitutional.

The court is also divided into three petty benches, which deal with all other cases brought to its attention. A petty bench includes five justices. A minimum of three must be present to hear a case. The court usually reaches its decision by examining only documentary evidence when hearing a case; however, it does permit oral arguments. Opinions of the court are written, and each justice is afforded the opportunity to express personal views on the case.

It should be noted that the Japanese Supreme Court has ruled only six times on the unconstitutionality of statutes (Bolz, 1980; Itoh, 1990). A number of scholars have mentioned various reasons for the court's reluctance to utilize its review powers in this manner. Among the factors frequently mentioned are the court's conservative outlook, the political system's emphasis on the Diet's supremacy as lawmaker, and the inexperience of the legal profession in dealing with constitutional matters because of its long association with the Romano-Germanic legal tradition.

The court has tended to declare unconstitutional only those cases in which the government's discretionary authority points to an extremely unreasonable or arbitrary action. Of the six cases that declared a law unconstitutional, the court considered all of them violations of civil liberties. Two involved equality issues, two addressed property rights, one dealt with due process, and one focused on a freedom of occupation issue. It is also interesting to note that after the court declared a law unconstitutional, it did not provide a policy remedy to rectify the situation. It assumed that politicians and government bureaucrats would correct the wrong by amending the statute and providing appropriate policy guidelines (Itoh, 1990). This is in keeping with the Romano-Germanic tradition that it is the responsibility of the legislature to make or rescind a law and not that of the courts.

The administrative responsibilities of the Supreme Court include the regulation of attorneys (through rule making), the public procurators (by the same method), the internal discipline of the courts, and the administration of all other judicial issues. When the court exercises its administrative responsibilities, it sits in a grand bench session. Finally, the Supreme Court is responsible for three research and training institutes:

one specializes in the training of members for the legal profession, another prepares people to work as court clerks, and the third trains family court investigators.

High Courts There are eight high courts that serve as the intermediate courts of appeal. Each court has a president and a number of other judges who entertain appeals from district, family, and summary courts. When hearing an appeal, three judges sit to decide the case, and one is designated to be the presiding judge. On occasion, judges from either district or family courts may be called upon to supplement the judges of a high court.

As a rule, a case on appeal does not have to be heard in its entirety, because the judges are interested only in the issue that is being questioned. Because of the nature of the issues contested, however, the court often reviews the entire case. The written opinion of the court contains only the majority view, which is signed by all the judges. Unlike the Supreme Court, high courts do not record dissenting opinions. A high court decision can be appealed further to the Supreme Court if the matter involves a constitutional issue. High courts also act as courts of first instance when a person is charged with insurrection or sedition. In such cases, five judges sit to hear the case.

District Courts There are 50 district courts, and these are the principal courts of first instance. Each of the 47 prefectures has one district court, with the exception of Hokkaido. (Hokkaido's size has warranted the establishment of three additional district courts). District courts handle both civil and criminal cases. If the matter is relatively simple, a single judge sits to hear the case. In more complex cases, a three-judge panel handles the issue. Criminal cases that must be heard in this collegial format include offenses for which the defendant could receive a sentence of death, life imprisonment, or imprisonment for one year or more. There are some exceptions to this rule, and they tend to involve robbery cases. District court judges also sit in panels of three to hear civil cases on appeal from summary courts.

Family Courts As it pertains to criminal justice, the role of the family courts is limited to juvenile delinquency cases. As such, family courts will be highlighted in the section on juvenile justice. Brief mention is made here because of its unique position and history in the judicial hierarchy of Japan. Family courts are the only courts in the system that specialize in particular kinds of cases, namely juvenile and family matters. There are 50 family courts that are equal to but independent of the district courts.

The family courts were created in 1949 as a result of the new Constitution. Article 24 established the idea of "equal rights of husband and wife" in marriage. It also states that "laws shall be enacted from the standpoint of individual dignity and the essential equality of the sexes."

In both tradition and law, Japanese family life had been dominated by the male head of the household. The introduction of equality in family law through the Constitution necessitated a change in existing laws. This resulted in a new court—the family court—being authorized to handle domestic and juvenile matters.

Summary Courts There are 438 summary courts. These courts handle minor matters that do not warrant a formal trial. Summary court judges hear civil issues in which the value of the action is less than 900,000 yen. They also offer conciliation proceedings if the issue is a civil law matter. In such instances, a conciliation committee handles the issue. The committee consists of a summary court judge and two conciliation commissioners who assist the parties in resolving their dispute.

The criminal jurisdiction of the summary courts involves cases in which the sanction is either a fine or a lighter penalty, or involves a minor offense, such as theft. If the court concludes that the sanction should be greater than that which it has the power to impose, the court must transfer the case to a district court. Approximately one-half of the judges serving in the summary courts are not trained lawyers but have held legal positions such as court clerks for a number of years.

The Legal Profession

As it relates to the criminal justice system, Japan's legal profession is divided principally into three groups: judges, public procurators, and attorneys. Members of each group have been professionally trained in the law. Most have received a law degree from a university. All have passed the national bar examination and have continued their studies at the Legal Training and Research Institute for an additional 18 months. It is the legal profession and how they are educated that received a good deal of attention in the RC21 report. A number of these recommendations are noted in this section of the chapter.

As mentioned earlier, the size of the Japanese legal profession is small compared to that in other industrial countries with similar populations. At least three reasons are frequently cited for the small size of the Japanese legal profession. First, the Japanese have never been a highly litigious people. Since the medieval period, they have preferred to resolve disputes through private conciliation. As was pointed out earlier, however, this attitude appears to be changing. It also has been suggested that after a civil case reaches the trial stage, the process is often continuously drawn out in the hope that the litigants will settle the issue out of court (Thompson, 1985).

Second, there has been a failure rate of more than 98 percent for applicants who take the national bar examination. One should not conclude from this figure that the educational system is inferior, however. The high failure rate on the bar examination was planned for several reasons. The Legal Training and Research Institute could only accommodate between 450 to 500 new candidates each year. All of the students at the institute receive a subsistence stipend for the two years during which they are in attendance. For years, the government claimed that extra funding was not available to support more students. As was discussed earlier, critics of this system have maintained that this policy discouraged litigation indirectly by controlling the number of people who were authorized to assist litigants. The Ministry of Justice changed its policy as a result of this criticism. It admitted 600 new candidates in 1992 and planned to raise that to 700 in 1993. Critics maintain that while it is a step in the right direction, this figure remains inadequate. Some have even questioned the extent to which the government controls the training of the legal community (Berat, 1992; Leonard, 1992).

Finally, Japanese attorneys do not have a monopoly in what Westerners generally consider the practice of law. For example, they are not widely employed as corporate counsel. That elite position is reserved for people who have studied law at a university and have entered the business world. Generally, they have neither passed the bar examination nor studied at the Legal Training and Research Institute. Tax and patent work are also handled by specialists who have studied law but not passed the bar examination.

The size of the legal profession is about to change considerably as a result of the recommendations of RC21. First, the system and methods of legal education are undergoing significant changes that will be explained shortly. Second, the RC21 recommended, and the government accepted, the goal of having 1,500 applicants pass the existing national bar examination in 2004 and set a higher goal of 3,000 applicants passing a new national bar examination by around 2010. These changes are being made as a result of the basic policies in the RC21 report that were alluded to earlier: the need to increase the size of the legal profession in order for it to support the justice system more effectively and to provide the public with greater access to the legal profession. There is already some improvement in this regard, while in 1999, there were 20,730 legal professionals; by 2007, there were 24,302 attorneys, of which 3,423 were women (Japan Federation of Bar Association). The long-term goal of the government is to increase the number of legal professionals to 50,000 by 2018.

Judges For the most part, Japanese judges represent a separate tier in the legal profession. Once a student has passed the national bar examination, he or she spends the next 18 months in training at the Legal Training and Research Institute. When a person graduates from the institute, he or she can apply for a career as either a judge or public procurator. Individuals selecting a career as a judge are appointed to a court and classified as assistant judges. After 10 years, the assistant judge is raised to the status of judge.

The appointment procedures and requirements for serving on different courts vary according to the Court Organization Law. The justices of the Supreme Court, for example, are formally appointed by the cabinet, with the exception of the chief justice, who is appointed by the emperor on the recommendation of the cabinet. Justices of the Supreme Court must be at least 40 years of age and can serve the court until their seventieth birthday. Most justices, however, are not appointed until they are about 60 years old.

One notable provision in the law is the manner in which the composition of the court is decided. Before the end of World War II, the Japanese adhered to the Romano-Germanic tradition of a career judiciary. Following the war and as a result of the Anglo-American influence, it was decided that this tradition fostered a narrow legal background that was not conducive to handling the significant changes in the constitutional status of the judiciary—especially the responsibility for judicial review. The goal, therefore, was to assure that the court's members would possess both breadth and depth of vision when interpreting the law. This call for a more balanced background from members on the court led to a change in the criteria for selection. Though the Supreme Court judges must meet the previously mentioned requirements, now at least 10 members are chosen from among high court and district court judges who have 10 or more years of experience. Judges from the summary courts, public procurators, attorneys, or law professors who have 20 or more years of experience also can be selected to serve on the Supreme Court. Candidates for the remaining five positions must be at least 40 years of age and possess some knowledge of law.

Judges for all of the lower courts are formally appointed by the cabinet upon the recommendation of the Supreme Court. Specifically, it is the personnel bureau of the court that prepares the list of names. As such, it is the judiciary that makes judicial appointments through consultation with senior judges and the careful screening of candidates. It has been suggested that Japan's judiciary is an autonomous bureaucracy that has the trust of both the politicians and the public in how it selects and promotes its members (Haley, 1998).

High courts and district courts judges can serve until their sixty-fifth birthday. Many started their careers as assistant judges and then were elevated to regular status after 10 years. Summary court judges do not have the same status as high or district court judges. Many had careers earlier in life either as clerks or administrative assistants to a court, or they were career judges or procurators who had reached mandatory retirement age but had an interest to continue to work. Unlike regular judges and procurators, the retirement age for a summary court judge extends to their seventieth birthday.

According to Article 76 of the Showa Constitution, "judges shall be independent in the exercise of their conscience and shall be bound only by this Constitution and the Laws." Judges can be removed, however, if they are declared incompetent because of a mental or physical disorder. They also can be removed by public impeachment, a process handled by members from both houses of the Diet.

The approach taken by Japanese judges toward interpreting the law reflects both their Romano-Germanic tradition and their more recent association with Anglo-American principles. From the Meiji Restoration to the end of World War II, the influence was almost completely that of the Romano-Germanic tradition. That tradition viewed judges as enforcers of the law that had been passed by legislators, who, in turn, were elected by the people. Thus, there was no room for judicial creativity in establishing precedents. The court decision was to be arrived at deductively through either a literal or logical interpretation of a code or statute. The intent of the legislative mandate reigned supreme.

By the turn of the century, two factors altered this perspective of the role of the judge. It was discovered that the codes were not always capable of resolving legal issues. This was especially true of the complex civil and commercial cases that became more prevalent as Japan increased its industrialization efforts. In addition, after World War I, some Japanese legal scholars were exposed to free-law theories from France and Germany. The free-law movement attacked the narrow deductive reasoning of civil law jurisprudence; its scholars were influenced by American legal realism. Increased attention was drawn to the need to decide cases based upon the facts of the individual case. It was argued that this would lead to a more equitable interpretation of the law. The adoption of an American form of constitutionalism after World War II enhanced this movement further. Although the principle of *stare decisis* does not exist in Japan, Japanese judges have adopted the practice of following judicial precedent when rendering a decision.

The impact of the RC21 report on judges is somewhat limited and subtle. The report suggests that more lawyers should be appointed judges and that assistant judges should have a more diversified experience as a legal professional beyond that of serving as a judge. As such, a system has been established that enables assistant judges to work as practicing lawyers for a temporary period of time.

Public Procurators The position of public procurator represents another career path in the legal profession. Public procurators have long displayed a great affinity to the judges in the court system. Several things account for this attitude. One is the fact that, before the war, procurators and judges were both considered components of the judiciary. Reflecting the long-standing influence of the Romano-Germanic tradition in Japan, this relationship is displayed in a number of ways. For example, procurators are trained, like judges, at the Legal Training and Research Institute. They practice a good deal of discretion in their work, as do judges. They are members of the civil service bureaucracy, and they hold offices that correspond to the court hierarchy.

At the top of the procuratorial bureaucracy is the Supreme Public Procurator's Office. This office supervises all of the other procurator offices. There is one procurator office located in each of the courts. The procurator general administers the entire system and is, along with the other members of the upper echelons of the procurator service, appointed by the cabinet. The other procurators are selected by the procurator general.

The purpose of the procurator is to prosecute criminal cases and to determine how a case will be disposed. Although the police conduct most of the criminal investigations, the procurator has the authority to investigate, arrest, and detain suspects. This is similar to the role of prosecutors in other countries that have a criminal justice system modeled after the Romano-Germanic tradition. Although the procurator's office is afforded much independence and is perceived as a part of the judiciary, it is nonetheless part of the executive branch of government. The minister of justice has a certain amount of control over procurators but does not control the actual investigation and disposition of cases. There is one exception to this rule: the minister can control the procurator's investigation through the procurator general. Although this authority is rarely utilized, it has become a controversial political issue when actually employed by the minister.

Because he or she has been afforded a good deal of discretionary authority, a procurator determines how a case will be disposed. Even when the evidence establishes guilt, the procurator may suspend the prosecution. For example, approximately 35 percent of the nontraffic offenses for 1985 in which the evidence established guilt were suspended from prosecution. This included about 5 percent of the homicide and robbery cases and approximately 50 percent of theft charges. The rationale offered for this policy of suspension is that it contributes to the rehabilitation of the offender. The Japanese government views this as an important feature of their criminal policy (Ito, 1986). Ten years later, the percentages had not shifted significantly. Almost 38 percent of the nontraffic offenses for 1995 were suspended from prosecution. The suspension rate for homicide was 4.3 percent and for robbery it was 6.5 percent. Finally, more than 41 percent of the larceny cases were suspended (Kurata and Hamai, 1998).

It is important to point out that this discretionary authority is associated more with the office of procurator than with an individual procurator. To illustrate, there are published guidelines and standards for charging offenders; decisions are often reached by consulting with superiors within the office; there is an annual audit of case dispositions; and the annual personnel review of a procurator's work will undoubtedly influence the manner in which a person exercises his or her discretionary authority. Ultimately, the objectives of the procuratorial bureaucracy are to be consistent and to prevent mistakes (Haley, 1998).

Procurators are expected to be impartial in determining how a case will be disposed; to promote this, they are protected from arbitrary dismissal. Procurators can be removed from office if they are either physically or mentally disabled, or removal can be used as a form of disciplinary action. When needed, a special committee is assigned the task of implementing dismissal. Under the direct authority of the prime minister, the committee is composed of 11 members: six selected from the Diet and five chosen from various walks of life. With the exception of the procurator general, who retires at 65, procurators must retire at 63.

It should be noted that like judges the RC21 report recommended that procurators have a more diversified legal background. The objective is to afford the procurator an opportunity to have a greater understanding of the public's views and in turn improve the public's trust in the office of the procurator. The government has created a system that allows procurators to work temporarily with public-interest groups, with private enterprises, or as a practicing lawyer.

Attorneys Attorneys represent the third branch of the legal profession. Like judges and procurators, attorneys must pass the national bar examination and participate in two years of additional study at the Legal Training and Research Institute. All attorneys are registered with the Federation of Bar Associations and one of the 52 local bar associations. Each prefecture has at least one bar association. The profession is assured its independence under the Lawyer Law, which also empowers the Federation of Bar Associations with the ultimate authority in the regulation and discipline of the profession's membership.

In Japan, an accused can either hire a private attorney or utilize the services of a court-appointed lawyer. As has been mentioned, the number of practicing Japanese attorneys is small compared to that found in other industrialized societies. Most attorneys practice alone, and they tend to specialize in representing people in court rather than working as office lawyers. For years, attorneys were considered second-class citizens within the legal profession. Although these prejudicial barriers have decreased since the end of World War II, they continue to exist to some extent.

In light of the RC21 report, the work of defense attorneys has been impacted considerably. Two criticisms have been directed at Japan's criminal procedure. First, a suspect does not receive the services of a court-appointed lawyer until after he or she is indicted. Second, trials are not conducted in a cohesive fashion. It is not uncommon for a trial to go on for years, because the court calendar is not set up to hear a case over consecutive days. As such, there is no attempt to assure the defendant a speedy trial, although article 37 of the Showa Constitution provides them with that right.

To help rectify these and other problems, a legal support center will be established across the country in at least each of the 50 district courts. The centers will essentially provide five services. The first three are not directly related to criminal justice. They include: providing general legal aid to people who are unable to pay for the services of an attorney, providing legal services in general to areas of the country that have a shortage of lawyers, and providing consulting services that are designed to mediate disputes.

The two services that directly relate to criminal justice are: the establishment of a court-appointed defense attorney system for both suspects and defendants, and the provision of assistance to crime victims in the form of lawyers and organizations that specialize in victim support. The court-appointed defense attorney system is designed to permit a suspect to seek the advice of a lawyer before an indictment is handed down. It is also designed, along with other changes, to facilitate the ability to proceed with the trial process.

Saiban-in

The jury was introduced into the Japanese justice system in 1923 with the Jury Law. Juries were required in cases in which the defendant could receive the death sentence or life imprisonment. Defendants could also demand a jury trial if the sanction would lead to a term of at least three years in prison. At the time, jurors were selected from male taxpayers who were at least 30 years of age. For a number of reasons, among them the fact that a court was not bound by a jury's decision, the jury gradually fell into disuse. The Jury Law was suspended officially in 1943, and for some time there was no movement to reintroduce its use. Some scholars reexamined the prospects for using juries, in light of the growth in both product liability cases as well as the acquittals of some death row inmates after they had been granted new trials (Foote, 1992; Lempert, 1992).

Once again, the RC21 report rejuvenated a serious discussion regarding increasing citizen involvement in the justice system. One of the three pillars shaping the reform effort was to enhance the public's trust in the justice system by having citizens participate in a meaningful way in legal proceedings. While the Japanese are not reintroducing the jury, the Diet passed the Lay Assessors Act (2001), which called for the implementation of the *saiban-in* system by May 2009. The saiban-in system is designed to accomplish three objectives: (1) to improve the public's understanding of and support for the justice system by having them participate in the trial process; (2) to facilitate the objective of assuring speedy trials because of the citizens' involvement; and (3) to make the proceedings and rulings more intelligible through the public's participation in the process.

Presently, the plan calls for utilizing saiban-in (lay assessors) for serious cases in which there is a considerable public interest. This would obviously include trials in which the defendant is accused of murder. The Ministry of Justice has outlined how the system will work. Once a year in December, the names of people above the age of 20 within the jurisdiction of a district court and who are eligible to vote would be selected randomly. These people are notified that they might be called upon to serve as a lay assessor in the coming year.

When a serious case arises in the district, another random selection would occur from the pool of candidates. The people selected would complete a questionnaire. Each candidate would then be interviewed privately by the judge, procurator, and defense lawyer(s). Once all the interviews are completed, the aforementioned legal professionals would meet privately to determine which candidates should serve as a lay assessor for the case in question. Both the procurator and defense can eliminate four candidates from serving, and they do not have to offer a reason for their decision. If the trial court consists of three judges, then six saiban-in will be selected. If the trial court consists of one judge, then only four saiban-in will be selected. The judges and the saiban-in are considered a panel. As a panel, they hear witnesses and examine evidence as a group. They will also decide if the defendant is guilty or not guilty and determine the nature of the sentence if the defendant is found guilty. Finally, a lay assessor will serve for only one case.

Like other systems that include citizen participation in the trial process, there are ways in which a person can be excused from serving in the saiban-in system. They include people who are: at least 70 years of age or older, suffering from illness or injury, raising or caring for a family member, or would suffer financial difficulty by serving. People can also be disqualified if they are in some way connected to the case or are unlikely to consider the case objectively. In addition, some people cannot serve because of their occupation. This includes: members of the legal profession, law professors, police and military officers, members of the Diet, and governors and mayors.

The Ministry of Justice and the Supreme Court have spent a good deal of time preparing for this innovation. There was a need to orient the legal profession to the changes, in part because it impacts procedures in a criminal trial. Courtrooms had to be reconfigured to accommodate the lay assessors, who will sit alongside the judges. Even more important was the need to educate the public about the saiban-in system, for one of the original reasons for this innovation was to improve the public's understanding of the justice system and to have them participate in the process.

To illustrate how the public has been informed about the innovation, in addition to several newspaper articles, the Ministry of Justice has made mock trials available in which citizens can receive a hands-on practical orientation to the new process. Some mock trials have even taken place in high schools to enable young people to become aware of the change. Among those who have either participated or observed a mock trial, most have found it an educational experience. In spite of these efforts, it is uncertain if the people will embrace this change with any degree of enthusiasm. The Asahi newspaper sent a questionnaire on the saiban-in system to 3,000 people in December of 2008. It received responses from 1,830. When asked whether they support the saiban-in system, 34 percent said yes and 52 percent said no. When asked if they would like to participate in a criminal trial as a lay assessor, 22 percent responded positively and 76 percent did not wish to participate. When asked if the public's confidence in the criminal trial process would increase with the introduction of the saiban-in, 20 percent thought it would increase, 52 percent did not anticipate a change, and 10 percent thought confidence would decrease. Finally, when asked if the new system would be accepted widely in the country, only 26 percent responded in the affirmative, while 50 percent did not think it would be accepted (*Asahi Shinbun*, 2009).

Legal Education

The most significant recommendation of the RC21 report was the dramatic suggestion to reform the country's system and method of legal education. These reforms began to be introduced in 2004. In order to appreciate the new system, it is useful first to understand the one being abandoned. The Japanese approach to legal education closely resembled that found on the continent of Europe. Although it was not required, most aspiring legal practitioners first entered a university and completed the undergraduate degree requirements in about four years. The future legal practitioner usually specialized in a law curriculum while at the university, but this was not required. In fact, many who studied law as an undergraduate had no intention of practicing law. The study of law had long been the academic discipline of choice for people pursuing careers in government and business. The candidate for a university law degree spent the first two years taking general liberal arts courses and devoted the final two years to legal studies. This involved instruction in the basic legal principles found in the Constitution, the Civil Code, the Code of Civil Procedure, the Commercial Law, the Penal Code, and the Code of Criminal Procedure. The method of instruction was lecture, in which little effort was made to introduce the student to how the law was applied in practice. Thus, as was the case in France, the exposure of the university student to the law was limited to a theoretical orientation of the subject.

Those who aspired to a career in the legal profession (judges, public procurators, or attorneys) had to pass the national bar examination. A passing grade on this test enabled a candidate to enter the Legal Training and Research Institute, which offered the clinical training necessary to begin a career in the legal profession. For a long time, the bar examination had been characterized as "something of an endurance contest" (McMahon, 1974). To illustrate, less than 2 percent passed the test between 1974 and 1984. From 1985 through 1997, the percentage that passed was more than 2 percent, with the exception of one year. During this period, the percentage went above 3 percent for three consecutive years (1993 to 1995).

Changes had been introduced to the examination, the most recent having been adopted in 2000. The first part of the examination tested general knowledge and academic skills. If a candidate had obtained a liberal arts degree from a university, he or she was exempt from taking that part of the examination. The second part of the examination consisted of three components. It included a multiple-choice test on the Constitution of Japan and the Civil and Penal Codes. There was also an essay component that covered six areas: the Constitution of Japan, the Civil Code, the Code of Civil Procedure, the Commercial Law, the Code of Criminal Procedure, and the Penal Code. The third component of the examination, the oral test, covered the aforementioned branches of the law, with the exception of the Commercial Law. A person who passed the examination entered the institute as an apprentice.

The Legal Training and Research Institute offered the apprentice clinical training in law. The teaching staff was selected by the Supreme Court and was composed of judges, procurators, and attorneys. The candidates spent 18 months in training: three months of classroom instruction, 12 months of field training, and an additional three months of final training. Irrespective of career aspirations to either judge, procurator, or attorney, each apprentice received the same training at the institute. Fifty sites had been identified nationally for the field training; they included courts, offices of public procurators, and various bar associations. It has been suggested that this method of training fostered a sense of unity and mutual understanding within the legal profession, for each candidate was oriented to the work and responsibilities of all the principal members of the courtroom group. Therefore, all apprentices were given a systems view of the court process. It was argued that this led to greater cooperation and coordination of policies among the courtroom work group, which in turn enhanced the goal of achieving a more efficient and effective administration of criminal justice (Shikita, 1981).

Although the method of legal instruction was usually praised, the high failure rate among people who took the national bar examination was a principal point of concern among critics. As mentioned earlier, the high failure rate was planned. All who participated in the process knew that only roughly 2 percent would pass. While there had not been any attempt to radically change the system, efforts had been successful at introducing some incremental amendments to the process. The Japanese preferred to maintain a highly elite group of legal professionals, and they believed that a rigorous bar examination ensured that goal.

The RC21 report recommended the development of a new method of legal training through the creation of law schools. The reason for this recommendation was that the law faculties at the universities were not in the business of training students to become legal practitioners; rather, they were introducing students to the law through their lectures. Students were being prepared with a certain level of knowledge about law that would enable them to find employment in a variety of occupations. Moreover, the focus of that education was not designed to prepare a person for the national bar examination.

Law schools will provide a professional graduate training for people planning a career in law. This training will bridge the gap between the theoretical education received from law faculties at universities and the practical knowledge needed to function as a legal professional. In law schools the objective is to train people to think critically about the law. The Socratic method, rather than lectures, will be employed to enhance the students acquiring the appropriate method of legal analysis for a legal professional. In addition, law school training will in part be directed at the national bar examination, which should facilitate the government's goal of increasing the number of people who pass the test. Finally, although the RC21 report did not specifically refer to clinical legal education, a number of law schools recognize that this should be a component of their curriculum if they are indeed going to train people as legal professionals.

By 2005, 74 new law schools had been approved. Some are found at public and private universities that already had a faculty of law. These faculty had been accustomed to teaching law primarily to undergraduate students. Other law schools are new ventures at both public and private educational institutions. This new system was introduced in 2004. As such, the first cohort of students will be graduating soon.

Presently, people who wish to pursue a career in law can still seek an undergraduate degree from a faculty of law at a university. Upon graduation, they must secure a position in a law school. When they complete this three-year program, they take the national bar examination. This examination was revised recently and is based on the curriculum of the law schools. It has been administered twice, and the results are mixed. In 2006, 48 percent (1,009) of the 2,091 applicants passed. In 2007, however, just 40 percent (1851) of the 4,607 applicants were successful. It has been suggested that the recent proliferation of law schools has contributed to lowering the quality of law school students. It should be noted that the Legal Training and Research Institute will continue to exist for the practical training of people planning on careers as judges, procurators, and attorneys.

LAW

Japan's criminal law and procedure has evolved through four fairly distinct periods. The first phase existed from ancient times until approximately the twelfth century. This phase was marked by early attempts at the codification of law, specifically the Code of 702 (Taiho) and the Code of 718 (Yo-ro). Both were modeled after Sui and T'ang Codes of China. These early codes required that the injured party in a criminal case level a complaint against the accused. The person's guilt was then determined by either a confession or the testimony of witnesses. Torture was permissible for securing a confession, and there was also a system of appeals (Dando, 1965). Although these procedural nuances were similar to those emerging in the West, historians have concluded that these developments were separate, indigenous creations.

The second phase occurred during what is characterized as the medieval period of Japanese history. It started before the twelfth century and ended with the Meiji Restoration in 1868 and was marked by the emergence of Japanese feudalism. Feudalism destroyed the notion of centralization and, with it, the early legal codes. Feudal codes that emphasized an inquisitorial method for determining fault and encouraged the frequent use of torture were introduced. While physical evidence is of value at a trial, torture was employed principally to elicit a confession. Once again, there were similarities with procedural developments in the West, but these were also indigenous creations.

The restoration of the Meiji in 1868 is usually cited as the beginning of the third phase in the evolution of Japanese law. The restoration was noted for its extensive borrowing from Western continental legal thought. At first, the restoration led to a revival in the use of the old Chinese-style codes, with the abandonment of the feudal codes. It was quickly discovered, however, that these codes were too dated to meet the needs of a society that was entering the modern era. The Japanese began to borrow heavily from the French, largely because the Napoleonic Code had received worldwide attention. However, toward the end of the nineteenth century, a more absolute and militaristic attitude emerged in Japan. This led to yet another shift in the search for a Western model to emulate. Japan turned to German legal scholarship for inspiration in adopting its

Meiji Constitution of 1889 and assistance with implementing other reforms in their codified legal system. This association with German legal thought lasted until the end of World War II.

The fourth phase began with the American occupation following the war. As has already been indicated, the adoption of the Showa Constitution in 1946 led to some significant changes in criminal law and criminal procedure. The largest number of changes were in the Penal Code, which had been in force since 1908. The Penal Code was only partially revised with regard to the sanctioning and treatment of offenders. New classifications of crime were added as more sophisticated kinds of deviant behavior associated with modern society emerged. A total revision of the Code has been considered, and a draft for a new penal code has been written, but as yet, it has not been approved by the Diet. According to Yoshio Suzuki (1977), the 1908 Code has retained its usefulness because of the document's flexibility. The definitions of various crimes are written in fairly general terms, leading to a more extensive use of judicial interpretation. In addition, the court's discretion for imposing a sentence is quite broad. Although many of the codes involving criminal justice reflect the Romano-Germanic tradition, the procedures have become more adversarial in nature, reflecting the increased Anglo-American influence.

Criminal Law

The Showa Constitution is quite clear on how the Japanese criminal justice system is regulated. The Diet is responsible for enacting laws, although the initiative in this process is generally controlled by the cabinet. Article 31 of the Constitution states that "no person shall be deprived of life or liberty, nor shall any other criminal penalty be imposed, except according to procedure established by law." Thus, the legal norms of nullum crimen sine lege and nulle poena lege, which were absent from the Meiji Constitution, were incorporated into the Showa Constitution. While Article 77 invests the Supreme Court with certain rule-making authority, Article 76 also states that all judges are bound by constitutional law and other laws. The Diet, therefore, is preeminent in enacting criminal legislation.

It has been suggested that the criminal law should be viewed as a tri-part system: the Penal Code, the Code of Criminal Procedure, and the Prison Law (Dando, 1965). Each law is interrelated with the others in the totality of the criminal justice process. The Penal Code defines the crimes and the types of punishment. The Code of Criminal Procedure assures that legal standards will be followed in determining guilt or innocence and in the execution of the sentence. Finally, the Prison Law governs the policies related to the nature of commitment and confinement to a correctional facility.

All crimes appear either in the Penal Code or in a supplementary statute. The general wording of the code gives judges extensive authority to interpret the law. This has led the judiciary to establish precedents based on the case-law method, always relating precedent to the interpretation of a specific written law. Japanese judges, therefore, employ the practice of following judicial precedents when rendering decisions, but they have not officially adopted the principle of *stare decisis*.

The most important source of the criminal law is the Penal Code, which went into force in 1908 and since has been revised to some extent. The code is divided into two books or parts. The first book covers general provisions. These illustrate an absence of any gradation of offenses. The Japanese, therefore, have not established a formal distinction between felonies and misdemeanors. They have recognized the existence of minor violations, however. These are regulated by the Minor Offense Law (1948).

The code recognizes the importance of the mental state of the offender. Only people who have acted with criminal intent can be punished, unless "special provisions to the contrary exist." Thus, some negligent crimes are punishable. Ignorance of the law is not a defense, but the penalty can be reduced if the circumstances warrant such a consideration. Provisions also exist to avoid punishing offenders who are mentally deranged and to reduce sanctions for those who are "weak-minded." The code establishes the age of criminal responsibility at 14. Offenders who have not attained the age of 20 are generally treated under the rules of the Juvenile Law. Finally, a sanction can be reduced if a person admits guilt before the offense is brought to the attention of the authorities.

The code also explains the types of sanctions available. These include: death, imprisonment with compulsory labor, imprisonment without compulsory labor, detention, fine, and confiscation.

The second book of the code lists the major crimes and elements that constitute each offense. The crimes are not grouped into categories, such as "crimes against the person" and "crimes against property," as is the case with modern codes. Because the code is worded in a fairly general manner, distinctions are not made with regard to the gravity of the offense. For example, the crime of homicide is defined as "a person who kills another." There is no distinction or consideration for degrees of intent or malice, as is made by differentiations between first-degree and second-degree murder and manslaughter. This further enhances the discretionary authority of the judiciary.

Criminal Procedure

A scholar comparing the criminal procedural systems of the United States and Japan offered these summary generalizations that should prove useful in this section of the chapter. First, the American system places procedural fairness at the center of the process, whereas the Japanese system is more focused on achieving the correct decision. Second, the approach to sentencing an offender in the United States is more punitive, while the principal objective of the Japanese is rehabilitation. Finally, there is less public trust of agents of the justice system in the United States, whereas in Japan the public tends to trust their public officials (Goodman, 2003).

This examination of Japan's criminal procedure is divided into two categories. The first involves the pretrial process, including an examination of police powers and other issues pertinent to the preliminary investigation. The second category is concerned with the trial process, consisting of the hearing and the appellate review. The Code of Criminal Procedure, in force since 1949, explains the aforementioned procedures.

Suspension of Criminal Proceedings In examining the pretrial process of the preliminary investigation, it is important to recognize that the Japanese suspend criminal proceedings in a number of cases. It is not imperative that all people accused of a crime have their day in court. The significance of the suspension rests with both the underlying philosophy behind the Japanese procedure and the official authorities who are permitted to make such a decision. It should also be noted that plea bargaining is illegal in Japan.

It was pointed out by Reischauer (1977) that the Japanese place a good deal of emphasis on the importance of belonging to a group. A person is valued more as a member of a team rather than for his or her individual contributions. Because of this kind of social posturing, cooperation and conformity are highly prized attributes. In addition, the Japanese have never embraced the Judeo-Christian heritage that has long encouraged criminal offenders to feel a sense of guilt because they have "sinned."

In light of these cultural attitudes, deviant and criminal behavior is viewed quite differently in Japan than in most Western countries. People who are unwilling to conform are pitied rather than held in contempt and condemned. The offender is more likely to feel a sense of shame because he or she has violated the cultural norms of the group rather than a sense of guilt because he or she has in some way sinned. Because the emphasis is placed on pity for the transgressor rather than condemnation, the deviant is usually handled with leniency by the agents of the administration of justice.

The manner and extent to which the formal adjudication process is avoided is a principal difference between Japanese and Western systems of justice. Both the police and the public procurators employ this kind of discretion quite frequently. It should be pointed out that law enforcement's use of this discretion is neither codified nor established as part of a written policy (Bayley, 1976a). It is more or less a custom—long exercised by the police and familiar to the public—that has acquired the stamp of legitimacy. This type of discretion is exercised in cases involving minor theft, fraud, buying stolen goods, and gambling. These cases, however, must be reported to the procurator for approval. In other cases of minor violations, such as public drunkenness, the officer may simply warn the offender or demand that a formal written apology be made as an alternative to arresting the person or issuing a citation.

David Bayley has identified at least five factors that usually influence the officer's willingness to avoid the formal sanctioning process. These factors include: (1) the public's tolerance of the deviant act in a particular location; (2) the officer's acceptance of such behavior; (3) police priorities regarding law enforcement; (4) the effect that the officer's option to utilize discretion will have on the future behavior of the offender; and (5) the sincerity of the offender's contrition. This last factor is considered very important. Bayley has pointed out that an offender's apology is a sign that the person will not commit the offense again. The acceptance of the apology not only holds the person to that promise but is also a sign that the offender has been forgiven.

Even more significant, however, is the extent to which the public procurator can suspend the prosecution of a case. Unlike the police, the procurator's use of this kind of discretion is explained in the Code of Criminal Procedure. Article 248 states: "In case it is unnecessary to prosecute according to the character, age and environment of an offender, the weight and conditions of an offense as well as the circumstances after the offense, the public prosecution may not be instituted."

The Japanese custom of allowing procurators to suspend prosecutions has been in existence for more than 90 years (Satsumae, 1978). The initial arguments offered for utilizing the scheme were that it would free the courts from handling trivial matters. It is even used today to resolve serious offenses, because the law does not limit the applicability of this authority. Offenses such as robbery, rape, and homicide have been handled by suspended prosecutions. Another cogent argument put forth for utilizing suspended prosecution is that it might prove more effective in rehabilitating the offender because the offender would avoid the stigma of being formally processed through the justice system.

The application of the suspension scheme has been attributed to five major factors. One is the quasi-judicial nature of the procurator's office, which is common in countries with a Romano-Germanic tradition. Another is the public's faith in the procurator's use of discretion. This kind of trust and the deference that is paid to the procurator is common for most agents of the Japanese justice system, because they are perceived as moral authority figures as well as agents of the law. The procurator is also vested with broad powers to investigate alleged criminal activity. From another perspective, the willingness to forgive has long been a feature of Japanese custom. Finally, there is a traditional belief that the family is capable of assuring and regulating the conduct of its members. The importance of belonging to a group is again evident (Satsumae, 1978).

The suspension of prosecution is devoid of any court involvement. The offender is usually required to write a letter of apology and make a promise to avoid further criminal activity. The apology often includes compensation to the victim or the family. The offender's family might also be alerted and advised on how to assist the person in leading a more law-abiding lifestyle. Takeshi Satsumae (1978) has pointed out that the procurator will occasionally place the offender in the custody of his or her family or employer, who, in turn, is requested to promise in writing to supervise the offender. Although the effectiveness of the suspension of prosecution scheme has not been studied extensively, the Japanese appear to be pleased with its results.

Finally, it should be pointed out that the system has established three mechanisms to assure that there is not an abuse of authority by the procurator. Within the procurator's office, there are guidelines stating that if a procurator elects to suspend prosecution in a case, reasons must be given in writing and the decision must be reviewed by a senior member of the staff. There are also 207 inquest committees throughout the country. A committee consists of 11 citizens who were selected at random from the voter registration rolls. They have the authority to receive complaints about suspended prosecutions, investigate the matter, and recommend a change in the procurator's initial decision. Although the procurator is not bound by the committee's decision, Satsumae is of the opinion that it serves as an informal check on procuratorial discretion. The RC21 report suggested that an inquest committee's recommendations to a procurator should be legally binding. This recommendation reflected two general themes of the report: agents of the justice system should listen to public opinion, and the public should participate in the administration of justice. Finally, the concept known as "analogical institution of prosecution" enables the court to conduct its own hearing into a suspended prosecution when it is alleged that procuratorial authority has been abused in this regard. The court initiates such hearings when it receives a complaint, and it either can agree with the suspension or order a trial. Thus far, courts have overwhelmingly sided with the procurator's initial decision. In those instances in which a trial is ordered, the court would select an attorney to assume the duties of the public procurator.

The suspension of the formal adjudication process by the police and the procurators assists in clarifying a number of points about the Japanese criminal justice system. It is a graphic illustration of why the police are portrayed as a source of both legal and moral authority. The judicious use of cautioning people rather than issuing citations or arresting offenders undoubtedly enhances the public's perception of the police. Suspensions of prosecutions also illustrate the extensive authority that has been mandated to the public procurators. Moreover, suspensions by either the police or procurators offer a clear example of the interrelatedness of the Japanese criminal justice system. Judges are not solely empowered to adjudicate criminal acts, because the police and procurators share in that responsibility. This has led to the perception that there is a greater degree of cooperation between the various components of the system.

Preliminary Investigation Once it has been determined that a crime has been committed, a preliminary investigation is undertaken to determine who committed the act or who can be reasonably suspected of being involved in the crime. Preliminary investigations are usually conducted by police detectives. The procurator can issue instructions regarding the course of an investigation. After receiving the police report, the procurator can elect to conduct another investigation into the matter. If the decision is to prosecute rather than to suspend the prosecution, the procurator files an indictment that names the offender, cites the facts in the case, and identifies the nature of the offense.

Power to Arrest and Detain Although most of the rules pertaining to arrest and detention are codified in the Code of Criminal Procedure, the Constitution does address itself to this issue. Article 31 states that "[n]o person shall be deprived of life or liberty, nor shall any other criminal penalty be imposed, except according to procedure established by law." Article 33 contains the provisions that "[n]o persons shall be apprehended except upon warrant issued by a competent judicial officer which specifies the offense with which the person is charged, unless he is apprehended, the offense being committed." Finally, Article 34 states that "[n]o person shall be arrested or detained without being at once informed of the charges against him or without the immediate privilege of counsel; nor shall he be detained without adequate cause; and upon demand of any person such cause must be immediately shown in open court in his presence and the presence of his counsel." As was stated in the section on police, some critics question the extent to which some agents of the justice system comply with these provisions.

The power to arrest involves two sets of circumstances: arrests with a warrant and arrests without a warrant. Most arrests are made by the police who have obtained a warrant from a judge. There is one condition, however. If the offense is punishable by a fine of under 100,000 yen, penal detention, or a minor fine, the accused cannot be arrested unless he or she is found to have no fixed residence or has failed to appear before a procurator when requested to do so. A flagrant offender also can be arrested without a warrant. Flagrant offenders are people who are caught in the act of committing a crime or have been determined within reason to have just committed a crime. The Code of Criminal Procedure also calls for emergency arrests. There are cases in which the police or the procurator have the authority to arrest a suspect without a warrant. This occurs when police have reasonable grounds to believe that a suspect has committed a crime that is punishable by death or imprisonment for more than three years, but they are unable to secure a warrant from a judge.

When the police arrest a person, they must inform the suspect of the reason for the arrest and of the suspect's right to counsel. The suspect is also given an opportunity to provide an explanation for the alleged behavior. If the police believe that detention is not necessary, the suspect can be released. Decisions to detain a suspect must be made within 48 hours of arrest. The suspect, along with the police report, must be sent to the procurator's office. The procurator has an additional 24 hours to determine whether the suspect should be released or detained. With regard to the suspect's right to counsel, the Code of Criminal Procedure makes a distinction between a suspect and a defendant. A suspect is not entitled to the services of a state-appointed counsel. This situation has changed slightly with the creation by local bar associations of a lawyer-on-duty scheme. Under this scheme, an indigent suspect can consult with counsel for an initial visit free of charge. If a detained person's status remains that of a suspect, rather than a defendant, they would be charged a fee for any subsequent meetings with a lawyer.

Before 72 hours have elapsed from the initial arrest, a judge must authorize the continuance of a detention. The judge receives such requests from the procurator. If the grounds are reasonable to hold the person, the judge issues a warrant of detention. Reasonableness is based on the belief that the suspect indeed committed the offense and either has no fixed residence, may destroy evidence, or may flee the jurisdiction. Arguments for or against the detention are heard in court with counsel present. One can apply to a higher court to rescind the initial warrant of detention. The propriety of the warrant is determined by a three-judge panel. If the warrant is upheld, the suspect can be detained for up to 10 days, and extensions can be granted for an additional 10 days if requested by the procurator. Thus, a person could be detained for up to 23 days while the police and procurator continue to investigate the matter. One should realize that approximately 90 percent of all offenders are not detained to guarantee their appearance in court.

The police have the authority to stop and question people on the street if they believe them to be suspects or witnesses, or to have some knowledge of a crime. They also can stop and question people who they believe are about to commit a crime. The police may detain the person at the scene for purposes of questioning or may request that the person accompany them to a police station or koban. The person must freely agree to accompany the police, however. Police who are found guilty of abusing this authority are subject to criminal prosecution. If the person is injured in the course of a detention, a civil suit can be filed for damages.

Power to Search and Seize The laws governing searches and seizures are contained principally in the Constitution and the Code of Criminal Procedure. Article 35 of the Constitution states, in part, that "[t]he right of all persons to be secure in their homes, papers and effects against entries, searches and seizures shall not be impaired except upon warrant issued for adequate cause and particularly describing the place to be searched and things to be seized. ..." The Constitution further states that only a judge can issue a warrant to search. There are exceptions to this rule, however. When an arrest is of a flagrant offender or when an emergency arrest is undertaken without a warrant, the investigating officers have the authority to search for and seize evidence.

Public procurators and police investigators have the authority to conduct search and seizure, and specific procedures have been established for when this is carried out. For example, a search cannot be conducted in a private home before sunrise or after sunset unless a judge orders a nighttime search. Warrants are to indicate the persons, places, and things to be searched and seized. Upon arrival at the premise to be searched, the investigating officer must present identification and show the occupant of the premise the search warrant. The search is to be conducted in the presence of the occupant or a witness if the occupant is absent. The police are permitted to frisk a person for the purpose of discovering weapons.

Some judges in lower courts have excluded evidence seized during an irregular search (Suzuki, 1978b). In 1978, the Supreme Court acknowledged the application of an exclusionary rule in serious cases. Thus, evidence seized in an illegal or improper manner may be excluded from the trial. Under the Penal Code, police are subject to criminal prosecution if they have abused their authority in such a manner. In addition, a victim of police abuse may bring a civil suit for damages.

The reader should be apprised of the fact that an accused person has the right to remain silent. Article 38 of the Constitution states, in part, that a "[c]onfession made under compulsion, torture or threat, or after prolonged arrest or detention shall not be admitted in evidence." Moreover, a person cannot be convicted of a charge when the only proof is the suspect's confession.

Bail The Code of Criminal Procedure also has established rules pertaining to the issuance of bail. Bail can be requested by the accused, the accused's counsel, or relatives of the accused. The judge grants bail but may seek the opinion of the procurator before approving the request. Bail is paid in money or negotiable securities, and the court can permit any person to post the bail. The court has the authority to revoke bail, while the public procurator may only recommend this action to the court. Upon a revocation, the court can confiscate all or part of the bail.

Various categories of suspects are excluded from bail consideration, for example, people who are charged with a crime that could lead to imprisonment for more than a year, recidivists who have served lengthy prison terms, and offenders who habitually commit offenses. If the authorities believe a suspect might destroy evidence or harm a witness, the suspect is excluded from the privilege of bail. Suspects whose name or residence is unknown are also declared ineligible.

The Trial Following World War II, the Japanese clearly established the principles of an adversarial trial emulating the Anglo-American legal system. Trials are open to the public, and both the prosecution and defense counsel have the opportunity to present their case orally.

The standard trial procedure for the main hearing is as follows:

1. The public procurator reads the information explaining the criminal charges.
2. The judge then advises the defendant of the right to remain silent and of the right to refuse to answer questions. The accused or the accused's counsel also has the opportunity to make a statement. In the course of such a statement, the defendant usually admits or denies guilt. If the accused admits guilt, the trial simply moves to an examination of the evidence before the imposition of a sentence. About 95 percent of the defendants in Japanese courts plead guilty.
3. If the defendant does not admit guilt, the public procurator is afforded the opportunity to make an opening statement and present an outline of the case.
4. The evidence is introduced and examined. Included are real evidence, documents, and witnesses. The witnesses are examined and cross-examined at this time. The defendant has the opportunity to introduce evidence designed to refute the procurator's case.
5. The procurator then introduces the accused's prior arrest record, if there was one. Statements supportive of the accused's character are presented by the defense counsel.
6. The defendant is then questioned by the procurator, defense counsel, and the court; however, he or she has the right to remain silent.
7. Closing arguments are made by the procurator.
8. Closing arguments are presented by the defense counsel.
9. The court then concludes the fact-finding phase of the trial and announces a date at which a judgment will be rendered. If the case is fairly simple, an immediate judgment might be announced.

Minor cases are heard in a summary court and the proceedings found there are rather informal. No public hearing is held; rather, the procurator offers the documentary and real evidence in the matter to the court. In a summary proceeding of this kind, a sanction cannot exceed 500,000 yen. If the sanction is not mutually agreeable to both sides, a formal trial is initiated. A formal trial in a summary court follows the same steps as presented above.

Once the trial is concluded with the court passing judgment, the parties have an opportunity to appeal the decision to a higher court. Criminal appeals from both the summary and district courts are entertained in a high court. The Supreme Court has the principal responsibility of handling appeals involving constitutional issues. In the Japanese system, the appeals process is open to the public procurator, the accused, or anyone else to whom the court has rendered a judgment.

The Code of Criminal Procedure has established three kinds of appeals. *Kokoku* appeals are made against court rulings during the course of a trial but prior to the rendering of a judgment. *Koso* appeals are made against the judgment of either a district court, family court, or summary court. The appeal can be based on a point of law or some factual discrepancy. The appellate court can affirm the original judgment, or it can reverse it and remand the case either to the original trial court or another trial court. The new trial court cannot render a decision that is contrary to the appellate court's judgment in the appeal. Finally, although most issues involving interpretations of the law are resolved through koso appeals, there are some exceptions. Questions of constitutional interpretation, errors pertaining to precedents already established by the Supreme Court, and any other issues that involve a significant question of legal interpretation are resolved through *jokoku* appeals. Jokoku appeals are heard by the Supreme Court.

Critical Issues

Speedy Trials Criminal trials in Japan had not been held on consecutive days until a verdict was reached. The judge determined when the court met. In light of the significant workload of the courts, some trials continued for years. This procedure raised questions about the system's commitment to article 37 of the Showa Constitution and its proclamation that people have a right to a speedy trial.

The RC21 report has addressed this problem in several ways. One, which has been mentioned and has implications for the speedy trial issue, is that the growth in the size of the legal profession will result in more judges, procurators, and defense attorneys. This alone should aid in resolving the problem over time. A second change resulting from the RC21 report is that suspects will now have the right of access to a lawyer.

In the past, a suspect could not see a court-appointed attorney until after the indictment had been handed down. A third change, which is associated with the court-appointed attorney scheme, is the establishment of legal support centers throughout the country. The fact that these centers will provide legal aid and mediation services should reduce the volume of cases that are litigated in court.

Finally, another new feature that was recommended in the RC21 report was the introduction of a new procedure before the start of a trial. In order to improve the efficiency and effectiveness of the trial process, it was recommended that a "preparatory procedure" be introduced and presided over by the court. The purpose of the procedure would be to resolve contested issues between the procurator and defense, especially those involving evidentiary matters, that have frequently contributed to impeding the flow of a trial. The ultimate goal is to expand the disclosure of evidence before the trial commences. This recommendation was adopted, and the Code of Criminal Procedure was revised to require its use in all trials involving serious crimes. In addition, once a trial begins, it is expected to meet daily; thus, expediting the trial process.

Crime Victims Throughout this chapter, we have noted the importance the Japanese place on the group versus the individual, which places a good deal of value on cooperation and conformity with community norms. It was further pointed out in this section that the suspension of prosecution is devoid of any court involvement. In that context, what is being sought is usually a letter of apology from the offender, the promise to avoid further criminal behavior, and sometimes compensation to the victim or the victim's family. Much of this is done informally by the offender or his or her family through an attorney in conjunction with an attorney for the victim or his or her family. The procurator is aware of this, but it is not part of formal judicial process (Haley, 1998). Finally, it was noted at trial that the vast majority of offenders who reach the trial stage admit guilt. In such an environment, questions are raised about the extent to which the justice system directs any attention to the victims of crime.

In many justice systems throughout the world, the plight of crime victims has been acknowledged in the formal judicial process in only roughly the past 25 to 30 years. Because the Japanese system has often relied upon an informal process, it has been criticized for lagging behind other advanced countries in looking out for the rights and welfare of the victims. However, it should be pointed out that the Japanese system has not totally ignored the victims of crime. For example, the Crime Victims Benefit Payment Law was introduced in 1981 and is specifically designed for the family of a deceased victim of a random murder or victims of unprovoked acts of violence. The victim makes application to the Prefectural Public Safety Commission in the area, and the Commission determines the eligibility of the applicant and the amount of the compensation. The national government has set aside funds to support this scheme. It is interesting to note that a victim is excluded from these benefits if he or she is not a Japanese national or does not reside in Japan.

Nevertheless, the Ministry of Justice has acknowledged that it needs to do more in aiding victims of crime. In recent years, the ministry conducted a series of surveys in an effort to understand the problem and establish a strategy to address it (Hamai et al., 2000). With regard to the issues of apology and compensation, it was discovered that 48 percent of the offenders apologized. When the issue involved professional negligence that resulted in death or bodily injury, the percentage was higher at 60 to 79 percent. For homicide and larceny, however, the percentage was considerably lower at 25 and 35 percent. Information about the victim's feelings toward the offender were also collected. Of those who would never forgive the offender, the percentage was 64, and this rose to 84 percent for rape victims and 91 percent for families of homicide victims. Only 16 percent were of the opinion that they could forgive the offender.

The victims were also asked what was the most important thing that an offender could do to atone for his crime. The most popular response at 34 percent was that the offender should reintegrate themselves back into society through rehabilitation. This was followed by: obey the court order, 22 percent; provide compensation, 14 percent; apologize, 12 percent; and get a pardon from the victim or the victim's family, 7 percent.

What the ministry learned from these survey results was the extent to which crime victims and their families suffer—not only from the direct impact of the event but also the subsequent damage that was caused in part by the criminal justice process and, most importantly, the long-term mental suffering that impacts the victims emotional well-being and life beyond the specific damage caused by the crime. Because the information was such a revelation, the ministry plans to conduct victimization surveys each year.

The results from such surveys have assisted the initiative to provide more assistance to crime victims. In 2001, the Crime Victims Benefit Payment Law was amended to enable expanded benefits to crime victims and their families. Survivor benefits are determined by the age and income of the victim. Disability benefits are determined by the severity of the injuries. Benefits are also available for medical expenses beyond that covered by the victims health insurance. Finally, the family of a deceased victim can claim medical expenses incurred prior to the death of the victim.

The National Police Agency had taken the lead on support for crime victims. It initiated several measures that are being implemented across the country at the prefectural police level. Once a crime occurs, the police: provide a brochure for crime victims, assign crisis intervention officers and counselors to help victims of serious crimes, promote counseling to crime victims that is provided by the police, assign female officers to investigate sex crimes and install a hot line for counseling. After the investigation is completed, the police establish a victim support network and provide a victim liaison on the case. Finally, the police are developing networks with administrative agencies and medical institutions to aid the victims. They are also assisting in the establishment of private victim support organizations.

The Ministry of Justice has also become more actively involved in the support for crime victims. Recently, legislation was introduced that would allow victims to recover the cost of damage to property. The legal support centers that were created as a result of the RC21 report will also be involved in providing information and support to crime victims, in particular the access to an attorney who is familiar with victim rights.

Capital Punishment The United States and Japan are the only highly advanced industrialized countries that have retained capital punishment. The Japanese Penal Code lists 13 crimes that identify the death penalty as an appropriate sanction, and an additional five are cited in other statutes. Since 1967, capital punishment has been limited to murder, death caused in a robbery, and death caused by explosives. The method employed to carry out the sentence is hanging. While the United Nations, Amnesty International, and other human rights organizations have called for the abolition of the death penalty throughout the world, the Japanese government has consistently rejected this position.

Opposition to capital punishment within Japan began to receive notoriety in the early 1980s. What led to this development was a 1975 Supreme Court decision that made it easier to seek retrials. Essentially, the court indicated that it would grant retrials if new evidence came to light that, along with existing evidence, led to a conclusion that reasonable doubt exists. As a result of this ruling, four men who had been on death row for years (each on separate murder convictions) sought and were granted retrials. In each case, the person had originally confessed to the crime but had recanted and claimed innocence either before or during the original trial. Each had maintained his innocence since the first trial.

The retrials were granted between 1983 and 1989, and each man was found not guilty. It was revealed that the police had acted inappropriately during their investigations, and the actions of the procurators and judges were also the subject of criticism. The notoriety of these cases was based not so much on exposing the inappropriate behavior of members of the justice system as on the fact that these crimes were committed between 1948 and 1955. As a result, these men had been on death row for 34, 33, 31, and 27 years, respectively. Proponents of capital punishment contend that the circumstances surrounding such cases would not occur today. When these cases were adjudicated, Japan was still suffering from the social upheavals caused by World War II (Foote, 1992).

Another concern voiced by opponents of capital punishment is the nature of the process, specifically the length of time it takes to carry out the sentence and the secrecy surrounding it. It often takes 20 years to carry out a death sentence in Japan, given the various appeals and clemency hearings that are available. Critics argue that an appellate process that takes so long to complete is inhumane. Once the appeals are exhausted, the minister of justice must sign the execution order, which can lead to further delays. Once the order is signed, however, the execution is carried out within five days. It is interesting to note that the actual execution is shrouded in secrecy, so much so that the inmate is not told in advance, and the family of the offender is informed of the execution after it has occurred. Critics maintain that this also is inhumane, but the authorities argue that they are protecting the privacy of the family.

Prompting some criticism of the sanction was the fact that death penalty abolitionists had apparently been hoping that the various human rights organizations were having an impact on their government. In 1993, however, seven prisoners were executed. This was an unusually large number, topped only by 12 people executed in 1976. From 1979 to 1989, the death sentence was carried out on one person per year. No one was executed from 1990 to 1992, which is attributed to the fact that the justice minister was a Buddhist. From 1993 through 2000, 33 people were executed, for an average of about five executions per year. In addition, the defense attorney for one of the people executed in 1993 argued that his client was mentally unstable when the sanction was handed down, and the doctor at the detention center who examined his client indicated that the client was unstable at the time of the execution. According to the Penal Code, these are grounds to stay the execution (Dean, 1994). Nevertheless, a survey was conducted by the government in 1994 to assess public attitudes about capital punishment. Approximately 13.5 percent supported abolition of the sanction, while almost 74 percent favored its retention. Surveys by the media in more recent years have reported results that are similar to those of the government (Kurata and Hamai, 1998).

It has been suggested that the abolition of the death penalty will come to Japan only with a revision of the Penal Code, because the nature of the Japanese judiciary is such that it will not act independently of the legislative branch (George, 1990). The abolitionists recognize the difficulties that they face in gaining converts to their cause. One observer suggested that a compromise might be reached by substituting capital punishment with the sanction of life imprisonment without parole (Kikuta, 1993). Nevertheless, a 2004 government opinion poll found that 81.4 percent supported the death penalty, while only 6 percent were opposed to it. The poll noted that supporters were of the opinion that only capital punishment could provide closure for families of the victims. Supporters also maintained that the punishment had a deterrent effect.

Corrections

It should come as no surprise that Japan's correctional system has evolved in a manner not unlike that of their police, judiciary, and law. The Penal Code of 1908 and other legal measures related to corrections were initially influenced by French and German ideas from the mid-nineteenth century through the early twentieth century. Much of this legislation remains in force today, albeit with some modifications. In addition, the American occupation had many effects on the correctional system, the introduction of probation and parole being most notable. Finally, a clearly distinct juvenile justice system also was created following the war.

The significant influence of Western ideas on corrections must be placed in the Japanese context. Although the form the correctional community has taken appears strikingly Western, the substance of the system must be viewed and understood within the social and cultural framework of Japan. The purpose of this section is to offer a brief explanation of the sentencing philosophy, a description of the organization and administration of the correctional system, an examination of both the institutional and noninstitutional forms of sanctioning, and the identification of some of the critical issues confronting the correctional system.

Sentencing Philosophy

The traditional objectives behind sanctioning an offender are retribution, deterrence, isolation, and rehabilitation. Most countries emphasize one or more of these objectives as a rationale for their sentencing philosophy. In that regard, Japan is no different than the others. However, both practitioners within the Japanese justice system and foreign observers of it are in agreement that the Japanese tend to emphasize retribution and rehabilitation.

Before these two objectives are examined, it is important to mention why there is a greater impetus directed at them than at deterrence and isolation. Japanese and foreign commentators are fond of pointing out the homogeneity of Japan's population and the social cohesiveness of the people, as illustrated by the importance placed on group associations. It is within this context that the Japanese sentencing philosophy must be understood.

In determining how to proceed with the disposition of an offender, the paramount concern for the Japanese is how the decision will benefit society. This goal is strikingly different from that found in many countries, which claim, at least in theory, that their principal concern is for the individual offender. Of course, the Japanese are still concerned about the individual, just as justice systems that appear to concentrate their efforts on the offender are also interested in the societal benefits that result from their decisions.

This helps to explain two features of the Japanese criminal justice system: (1) agents of the justice system are not viewed only as enforcers of the law but also as guardians of society's morals (a good deal of deference is paid to them as dispensers of this authority); and (2) broad discretionary power is accorded these agents. It is an accepted practice for the police to decide whether a minor infraction of the law should be resolved through a formal citation or an apology. It is legally permissible for the procurator to decide if a criminal, irrespective of the nature of the offense, should be prosecuted or have the prosecution suspended. Those offenders who are formally adjudicated may have their sentence modified by the judge exercising powers of discretion. These extensive discretionary powers are accepted by the public because the public displays a great deal of faith in the agents of their criminal justice system. This faith is based on a belief that in each case, the agent's judgment will be guided by the interests that best serve society.

Returning to the twin objectives of retribution and rehabilitation, the Japanese base the specific sentence on the gravity of the offense and the degree of culpability of the offender. The offender's character, personality, age, and environmental history (criminal, familial, and educational background) are also taken into consideration. It should be pointed out that this kind of information is usually provided to the court by the procurator and defense counsel, rather than by a professional who has a specific expertise in the social or behavior sciences. All of the above-mentioned criteria are used, however, in determining the extent to which retribution and rehabilitation will be sought in the sentencing process.

According to Tadahiro Tanizawa (1979), the principal rationale for the imposition of a formal sanction is retribution. However, Yoshio Suzuki (1978a) has pointed out that this should not be misconstrued as a Japanese revival of the old talionic law. Rather, it is simply an acknowledgment that the need to satisfy vengeance is deeply rooted in any society. The victim, as well as society, wants to be assured that justice is done. Retribution either achieves or enhances the prospects of that realization. The actual application of retribution is considerably different, however, from the old notion of "an eye for an eye, a tooth for a tooth."

Nevertheless, for the Japanese offender who is not a professional criminal, the sanction can be as psychologically painful as some of the earlier forms of corporal punishment. Retribution is achieved through disgrace. This is specifically brought about by alienating the offender from the group—that coveted association that often ensures and fosters a person's identity. Imprisonment is the ultimate form of alienation from the group and rejection by society. The long-standing impact that this is intended to achieve explains, in part, why prison sentences in Japan are fairly short.

Another reason for the brief length of most sentences is associated with the second major objective for sanctioning, that is, rehabilitation. Tanizawa (1979), among others, has indicated that a lenient sentence, whether or not it includes incarceration, is meant to encourage the rehabilitation process. The goal is to impress upon the offender the court's generosity, thus leading the offender to desire rehabilitation. The Japanese seem to understand, possibly better than most cultures, that the chances of success are greater within the community than in an institutional setting. Once again, this is based on the importance placed on maintaining close ties with a group. If membership in a group provides emotional sustenance to the noncriminal, it is assumed that such an association for a criminal offender can only strengthen the efforts to rehabilitate oneself.

Organization and Administration of Corrections

Ministry of Justice The Ministry of Justice is a cabinet-level department headed by the minister of justice, who is appointed by the prime minister. Like the rest of the Japanese criminal justice system, Japanese corrections is controlled by the national government. As mentioned earlier, the ministry is divided into seven bureaus, of which two—the Correction Bureau and the Rehabilitation Bureau—are concerned with all matters pertaining to correctional administration.

Correction Bureau The Correction Bureau is responsible for the administration of adult prisons as well as facilities for juvenile delinquents. The chief administrative officer of the bureau is the director general. The director general's staff is divided into six divisions. The general affairs division is responsible for such issues as planning, budgeting, inspections, staff training and welfare, and the drafting of regulations and policy. The treatment division handles the admission and release of prisoners, along with the daily security needs of the correctional facilities. The industry division is concerned with issues related to prison labor and vocational training. The medical care and classification division is responsible for such issues as the feeding, sanitation, and medical needs of the inmates, along with classification and parole procedures. The education division addresses all academic training, welfare concerns, and recreational needs. Finally, the counselor's office is responsible for drafting and amending changes in the laws and regulations that impact on the services provided by the correctional system.

The director and staff are assisted in their work by eight regional headquarters. The regional centers are designed to coordinate the management of the various correctional institutions in their respective geographical areas. Their duties range from administrative concerns, inspection of facilities, and dealing with personnel issues involving the staff, to supervisory responsibilities such as the classification and transfer of inmates and the coordination of prison industries (see Figure 4.3).

The Japanese have developed a fairly elaborate scheme for classifying offenders as they enter the prison system. The scheme is employed to determine the placement of inmates either in a particular correctional facility or in a specific section within an institution. The first method of classification takes into consideration the gender, nationality, and age of the offender, as well as type of sentence. The Japanese have established correctional facilities that are specifically designed for different populations: females, foreigners, people sentenced to imprisonment without compulsory labor, inmates serving a term of more than eight years, adults under the age of 26, and juveniles. The second classification issue takes into consideration the degree of criminal tendency. Under this scheme, inmates are categorized as either having or not having advanced criminal tendencies. A third method of classification identifies those inmates who have either a mental or physical disability. Finally, inmates are categorized according to their treatment needs.

Figure 4.3

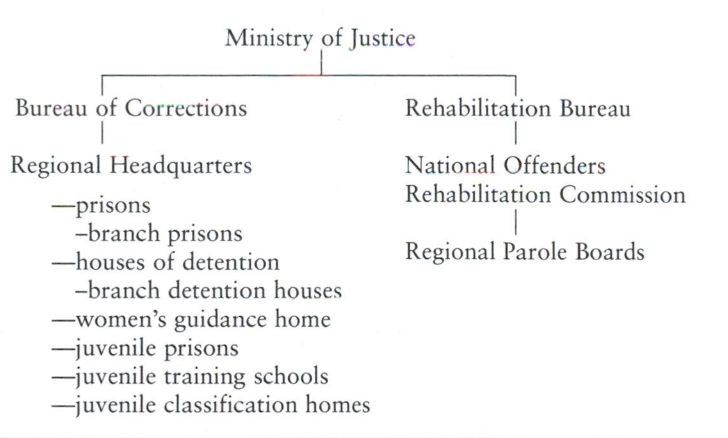

Imprisonment Before the regimen of the correctional institutions is explained, it is important to offer some general comments about the sanction of imprisonment in Japan. According to the Penal Code, an offender sentenced to a term of incarceration receives either a sanction of imprisonment with compulsory labor, imprisonment without compulsory labor, or penal detention. Imprisonment with compulsory labor and imprisonment without compulsory labor are either for a fixed term or for life. The fixed terms range from one month to 15 years; however, they can be increased to 20 years when circumstances warrant such an extension. The only difference between imprisonment with compulsory labor and imprisonment without compulsory labor is that the former requires the performance of some type of work. Although imprisonment without compulsory labor does not require a work assignment, most inmates request one. The sanction of penal detention requires the offender to serve a term of between one and 29 days in a house of detention.

An examination of the data provided by the Ministry of Justice on people sentenced to prison since World War II indicates that there has been a dramatic decline. In 1950, there were 83,492 people sentenced to a period of incarceration, creating a total prison population of 103,204 in that year. Of those sentenced, approximately 71 percent were guilty of some form of theft. Japanese criminologists attribute the high level of this particular crime to the fact that the country was in a state of social chaos and economic collapse during the years immediately following the war. People convicted of war crimes are also included in these totals. In 2004, the average daily population in penal institutions was 75,289. Of that number, 11,686 were awaiting trial.

Several reasons are offered for the small number of offenders sentenced to prison. One is that the rate of nontraffic offenses either continues to decline or remains stable. Another is that judges prefer to sanction the offender with a fine, if at all possible, or to a minimum term of deprivation. Fines are the most popular form of sentence. It is estimated that approximately 97 percent of all sanctions involve a fine. Finally, about 60 percent of all prison sentences imposed are granted a suspension of execution by the judge. Offenders who are sentenced for up to three years of imprisonment can have the sentence suspended if they meet one of two criteria: (1) the person has never been sentenced to imprisonment before, or (2) a period of five years has elapsed since a prison term has been imposed.

In addition to the small number of offenders sentenced to prison, it is interesting to note the length of the terms of incarceration imposed by the courts. For example, the White Paper on Crime reported that of the people sentenced to imprisonment in 2004, those sentenced to less than six months made up 4.4 percent of the total, while those sentenced to at least six months but less than one year represented 14.9 percent of the total. Those receiving a sentence of more than one but less than two years made up 41.4 percent, while 31.3 percent of the total received a term of more than two but less than three years. Thus, only 8 percent received a sentence of more than three years. Of these, only 423 were sentenced to a term of more than 10 years. All of those were found guilty of homicide, rape, or robbery resulting in death or bodily injury.

Although greater attention was directed at the issue of capital punishment earlier, brief mention should be made here of the apparent support for the death penalty in Japan. While the Japanese tend to favor its retention, they also expect its use to be restricted. The Penal Code permits the death sentence for particularly heinous crimes, such as murder or murder in the course of committing a robbery. Hanging is the only method employed to execute the sentence.

Types of Institutions Compared to other countries, the number of offenders sentenced to incarceration in Japan might be small and the length of sentences fairly short, but several scholars have pointed out that Japanese prisons impose a good deal of discipline on inmates. It has been suggested that "leniency is extended to those who confess, demonstrate remorse, accept their accountability by compensation to any victims" but that it "stops at the prison door" (Haley, 1998). The justification for the rigorous discipline imposed on inmates is that it is designed to correct behavior rather than to punish the person. This approach is considered a central feature in the Japanese rehabilitative process. The discipline is reflected in the very detailed daily schedule that inmates follow. There are a number of rules, which range from general rules (e.g., how inmates are expected to speak and act toward others), to rules within the cell (e.g., when a person is permitted to lie down), to an extensive array of work rules. All correspondence is censored and may not even be delivered. Moreover, inmates do not have access to telephones.

The Japanese have established two types of adult correctional facilities: prisons and houses of detention. There are 59 prisons and five branch prisons, and there are seven detention houses and 110 branch detention houses. There is also a women's guidance home, which is utilized for the purpose of rehabilitating prostitutes. The purpose of this facility is to provide social and vocational guidance along with medical and psychological treatment. The houses of detention are used either to hold suspects or defendants awaiting trial or to incarcerate offenders sentenced to penal detention for committing minor crimes. There are also three medical prisons designed to house inmates who are not capable, either physically or psychologically, of serving their sentence in a regular prison. Finally, six of the prisons are designated for women.

As mentioned above, the purpose of the adult prison is to aid in the rehabilitation of the offender. In order to enhance the prospects of that, the convicted offender is first sent to one of the eight regional classification centers. While at the center, the inmate is oriented to prison life and given a series of aptitude tests to assist the authorities in determining the institution that might best serve the inmate's needs. A host of other actors also are taken into consideration, including age, gender, nationality, criminal record, type of sentence, mental stability, and any physical handicaps.

Sentences to imprisonment (either with or without labor) are subject to a progressive system. In operation since 1934, the progressive system is a scheme involving four grades or steps in an inmate's period of detention. Inmates begin their term in the fourth grade. When they display self-discipline and a willingness to accept and cooperate with the rehabilitative regimen, they are advanced to the other grades. First-grade inmates enjoy more privileges and a greater degree of self-government. There is also a greater likelihood that they will be released on parole. It should also be pointed out that a number of the prisons are open facilities.

Most sentences mandate that inmates perform some kind of compulsory labor. In light of this fact, it has been pointed out that much of the Japanese prison system is organized along the lines of a factory system (Clifford, 1976). Among the types of work found in a prison are: woodwork, metalwork, tailoring and printing. An appropriately qualified inmate could be assigned a job in industry. With the absence of restrictions imposed by Japanese trade unions, the prisons are able to negotiate contracts with the private sector to produce goods. While some products are manufactured within a prison, it is not uncommon to send crews of inmates out of an institution to work. This is primarily limited to farming. All profits from such contracts are transferred to the national treasury. Other inmates are assigned maintenance tasks around the prison, such as kitchen, janitorial, or physical plant repair duty. Finally, a few inmates are selected for vocational training. This enables them to learn a skill while in prison, apply that skill in a prison industry, and find employment upon release from the institution. Although inmates are awarded some financial remuneration for their work, it is not considered a wage. It is regarded as a gratuity designed to encourage the inmate to work. Some of this money is saved for the prisoners and returned to them upon their release from prison, while the rest can be used to buy necessities or help support their families.

The prison regimen also includes educational programs that are generally designed for younger inmates. For example, inmates who have not completed the nine years of compulsory education or who need remedial assistance are required to attend classes. Correspondence courses are also provided, including high school classes and vocational education courses, of which some have been approved by the Ministry of Education. Moreover, vocational training is provided in the prisons. The participants of such programs have their regular work hours reduced so they can participate. Those who complete a vocational or technical program and then pass the appropriate national examination are eligible to receive a license or certificate issued by the Ministry of Labor. This enhances the inmate's opportunities for employment upon release.

The Japanese have had remarkable success in maintaining the internal security and order within the prison system. Article 60 of the Prison Law explains the 12 types of disciplinary measures that can be taken against an inmate. These include: a simple reprimand, a suspension of various kinds of privileges, such as reading and writing, a reduction in food for up to seven days, a suspension of exercise for up to five days, and solitary confinement for up to two months. By way of illustration, in 1991, there was one escape, one case of an inmate seriously assaulting another inmate, and no instances of an inmate killing an officer or another inmate (Yokoyama, 1994).

Rehabilitation Bureau Whereas the Corrections Bureau is responsible to the Ministry of Justice for the penal institutions of Japan, the Rehabilitation Bureau is the central bureaucracy within the ministry that is concerned with the release and oversight of inmates from a correctional facility. The facilities include prisons, juvenile training schools, and women's guidance homes. It is recognized that inmates often require a transition phase in their movement from a total lack of freedom to the exercise of responsible freedom. Parole serves the purpose of testing an inmate's ability to cope with this responsibility. The Bureau is also responsible for monitoring the progress of those adults who received a suspended sentence and those juveniles who have been placed on probation.

The National Offenders Rehabilitation Commission has an important role to play in this process, and it is accountable to the ministry through the Rehabilitation Bureau. The commission is composed of five people who are appointed by the minister of justice with the approval of the Diet. According to the Offenders Prevention and Rehabilitation Law (1949), the commission is mandated two responsibilities. It makes recommendations to the Ministry of Justice regarding pardons, reductions, and remissions of sentences, as well as the restoration of inmates' rights. It also oversees the eight regional parole boards that determine who is eligible for parole. These boards are located in each of the cities that have one of the high courts. A board is composed of three to 12 members; at least three members are needed to render a parole decision.

According to the Penal Code, inmates sentenced to a fixed term are eligible for parole after they have served one-third of their sentence. Inmates condemned to a life sentence are considered for parole after serving 10 years. Approximately 60 percent of all inmates are granted parole, but the favorable decision usually comes after they have served more than one-half of their original sentence. While on release, inmates are supervised by a probation officer who is expected to offer aid and guidance. Among the most notable problems associated with the Japanese parole system is the fact that most prison sentences are relatively short. As a result, the length of time on parole is equally short. It has been argued that there is simply not enough time to assist the parolee in any meaningful way before the termination of the conditional release. The other major concern focuses on the apparent passivity displayed by members of the parole boards. They tend to rely upon the opinions expressed by the superintendents of the correctional facilities rather than actively attempt to collect their own data and formulate their own opinions based on a particular case (Horii, 1973).

It has been suggested recently that there might be support in the Diet to add a new sanction, life without parole. This idea has emerged because of the soon-to-be-introduced saiban-in system, which was discusses previously in the section on the judiciary. At issue is the concern that lay assessors might be reluctant to impose the death penalty and thus be left with the next most severe sanction, life with the possibility of parole after 10 years. While technically eligible after 10 years, most inmates sentenced to life serve between 20 and 30 years in prison. There appears to be support in the Diet to add life without parole to the list of penal sanctions, but it has not been introduced at this time.

Noninstitutional Sanctions

The role that the police and procurators play in diverting offenders from the formal adjudication process can be considered a form of noninstitutional sentencing. Like many progressive countries, Japan recognizes the value of utilizing noninstitutional sanctions when sentencing its offenders. They realize that if rehabilitation is truly a goal of the sentencing philosophy, then it is more likely to succeed if the offender is kept in the community and is able to benefit from the positive influences of a group. This is especially noteworthy in Japan, where the family remains an important source of that group support.

The suspension of a sentence can be granted under two kinds of circumstances. According to the Penal Code, a person sentenced to imprisonment for not more than three years or fined less than 200,000 yen can have the sentence suspended for a period of one to five years, depending upon the offender's sentencing history. A person who is sentenced to imprisonment for not more than a year and who has previously received a suspended sentence of imprisonment is also eligible for a suspended sentence. In the former case, the court can order the suspension with or without supervision, while in the latter case, the court orders the suspension with supervision. Thus, a suspension of sentence with supervision is the Japanese version of a probation order.

The Japanese utilize the suspended sentence in approximately 50 percent of the cases that go to trial. In each of the 50 cities containing district courts, there is a probation office that is under the jurisdiction of the Ministry of Justice. Each probation office employs full-time probation officers and volunteer probation officers who assist offenders on probation or parole. The Japanese have long emphasized the importance of the community's role in reducing crime; the extensive use of volunteer probation officers is one example of that tradition. Presently, there are about 49,000 volunteers working in this area.

As was previously indicated, approximately 97 percent of the sentences involve a fine. A regular fine ranges from 4,000 yen and up, but the amount can be reduced to below the 4,000 yen figure. A minor fine ranges from 20 to 4,000 yen. If a person is unable to pay either a regular or a minor fine, he or she may be detained at a workhouse for a period of time. The amount of time is determined by the court and is based on the amount of the fine.

A final aspect of Japan's correctional system is the aftercare program. Although the government is responsible for this program, Japan's system of aftercare is dependent on the help of voluntary organizations to provide halfway houses. The system is available on a voluntary basis to specific kinds of offenders and is designed to enhance their prospects of reintegration into society. The scheme specifically assists inmates released without parole supervision, parolees who have completed their term of parole, offenders who have received a suspended sentence without probation, and people released by the procurator's suspension of their case. The type of care provided includes food, lodging, clothing, medical care, counseling, and employment or welfare assistance.

Critical Issues

It should be noted that the Japanese correctional system is not devoid of problems. The government is mindful of several concerns and speaks fairly openly about them in their official reports. Some scholars also have commented on these issues (Archambeault and Fenwick, 1988; Johnson and Hasegawa, 1987; Yokoyama, 1994). Among the problems mentioned is the fact that the law regulating the prison system came into effect in 1908. As such, it contains serious defects with regard to modernizing the management of the correctional system. In particular, this involves timely issues related to rights versus restrictions that are placed on inmates. Examples include the implementation of visitation privileges and work release programs. While some modifications have occurred, attempts at revision are usually slow because of the political consequences.

In 1995, Human Rights Watch/Asia issued a highly critical report on the conditions in Japanese prisons. While it acknowledged that Japanese prisons are clean and that inmates are provided clean clothes and an adequate diet, it focused much of its attention on the rigid enforcement of prison rules and the restraints placed on human contact. To illustrate, many prisoners live in single cells that are very small and sparsely furnished. The lighting in the cells is controlled from outside by guards and is only dimmed at night. All forms of communication with the outside world are controlled. For example, correspondence is read and may be censored, and if the censors are not familiar with the language, the materials may never be delivered. Legal visits are usually curtailed, and when they do occur, they are monitored by guards. The amount of time inmates are permitted to exercise outside is restricted usually to three times a week and usually for less than 30 minutes. Prisoners are told how and when to sleep; they are told how they must sit in the cell, especially during inspection; they are told when and where they can write; and they are taught how to march when they are permitted to leave their cells. Finally, the most common method of punishment for a violation of any prison rule is to spend up to two months in solitary confinement. Human Rights Watch acknowledged that the existence of rules in the course of regulating behavior is a common feature of Japanese society. As early as primary school, numerous rules have been established to control the behavior of students. Recently, the educational system has become a bit more flexible with regard to the importance of rules. This has not happened in the prison system. As such, prison policies appear for some critics to be devoid of any notion that prisoners have rights.

Another problem involves the age of most prisons. Many are older facilities that are in need of either reconstruction or demolition. The problem with tearing down an old facility is that it would have to be replaced with a new one—at a staggering cost. Economics is not the only consideration, however. Citizens are sensitive to the prospect of having such an institution located near them. If an existing facility is demolished and a new facility is constructed in a different location, the prison staff would have to relocate. This would require selling their residence, possibly moving to a remote area of the country and placing their children in a school system inferior to the one that they left in a more urban setting. Because the Japanese place such a high premium on a quality educational program for their children, this could have a serious effect on prison staff morale.

Although the Japanese have established a fairly progressive system for recruiting, screening, and training correctional officers, a specific point of concern involves the nature of a recent demographic change that has been occurring among prison staff. At issue is the large number of staff presently retiring from the correctional service. This mass exiting from the workforce was to be expected; its roots date back to the close of the war when prison authorities had to recruit a large number of people to work within the system.

These numbers are now at retirement age and are being replaced by younger people. This might be considered a blessing in some countries, particularly by those who consider it an excellent opportunity to reduce the generation gap between the staff and the inmates. That is not the case in Japan, however, because the prison population is aging. Therefore, the system is employing staff who are younger than the bulk of the inmates. Although the younger officers are capable of maintaining prison discipline and security, it is feared that they will not be as successful at counseling inmates. In this instance, a reversal of the generation gap works to a disadvantage in maintaining or implementing various rehabilitation programs for long-term prisoners.

In recent years, Japan has become a popular place for tourists. Although most visitors are law-abiding, those who throw caution to the wind may find themselves placed in prison. This creates a host of problems for the inmates and their keepers. The most obvious is the language barrier. There are additional problems, however, that include such issues as dietary needs, sleeping accommodations, and correspondence from home. The Japanese have designated three prisons to receive foreign inmates. Some staff can speak other languages at these facilities; Western-style meals are prepared; beds have replaced the traditional Japanese sleeping mat; and showers have been installed instead of the traditional bathing pools. Problems with correspondence and reading materials remain, however. Chapter 9 of the Prison Law requires the censorship of all such materials, and the prison system is simply unable to provide inmates with a free translation service. The absence of correspondence from the outside obviously compounds the unsettling experience of the foreign inmate.

Another management and supervisory concern for the prison system is the growing number of inmates who are members of either organized crime syndicates or gangs. These inmates represent a significant part of the total prison population. Their numbers are estimated at more than 25 percent. Because they have been ingrained in their own subculture, these career criminals reject any effort to cooperate with the system's rehabilitation programs. They also pose a constant threat to the maintenance of security within the prison.

Finally, as is the case with most prison systems, the Japanese are confronted with the problem of drug abuse inside the prisons. While the number of stimulant-drug offenders entering the prison system has increased significantly for both sexes, of particular alarm to the Japanese is the greater increase of such abuse among women. For the most part, the problems mentioned here are not unique to Japan; they can be found in almost any modern correctional system in the world today.

JUVENILE JUSTICE

Among modern industrialized countries with a comparable population, the low level of criminality in Japan is enviable. Both Japanese experts and foreign observers have identified a number of reasons for this. They usually include: the homogeneity of the population, the emphasis directed at family solidarity, the importance placed on the cultural trait of respect for authority, the extent to which transgressions of society's norms are translated into a stigma of shame toward the violator, the low rate of unemployment, the stringent controls on firearms and drugs, the overall efficiency of law enforcement, the fact that the geographical size of the country reduces the likelihood of easy escape from the police, and the extent to which the public cooperates with agents of the criminal justice system. For the most part, these are social structural characteristics of the society.

Since the end of World War II, the degree of criminality among people under the age of 20 has undergone three distinct phases in which delinquent activity increased to serious proportions (Saito, 1993; Yokoyama, 1986). The level of juvenile crime reached its first peak in 1951. This was attributed largely to the aftermath of the war. The war not only had placed the country in a social and economic state of chaos, but also left a large number of poor and orphaned children who turned to crime in order to survive their personal economic hardships.

The second peak occurred in 1964. As was the case in many industrialized countries, this increase was attributed to the large postwar baby boom generation reaching the delinquency-prone years. Of particular concern at that time was the rise in crimes of violence, intimidation, and injury. In 1965, the level of serious crime started a steady decline.

The third phase reached its peak around 1981. While violent offenses continued to decline, there were significant increases in theft, especially shoplifting, theft of bicycles, and cases of embezzlement. In Japanese law, embezzlement includes the unauthorized borrowing of an unattended bicycle. The number of young people arrested on drug abuse charges was also escalating. Abuse included using stimulants, sniffing glue, and inhaling paint thinner. Another type of concern was the emergence of the bosozoku, which are reckless driving gangs consisting of a large number of school dropouts.

What was particularly distressing to the authorities was the emergence of a new profile of the juvenile offender. More offenders were coming from middle-class families. A large number were junior high school students or dropouts from school. They were also younger than the typical offender of previous years; in addition, there was a significant increase in the number of female offenders.

At the height of this new phase, the police augmented their efforts toward curtailing these problems. The nature of that particular strategy will be discussed later in this section. What is important at this point are the explanations offered for the emergence of these problems (Fenwick, 1983a; Tokuoka and Cohen, 1987; Yoder, 2004). At the top of the list was the changing nature of the Japanese family. The rapid industrialization of the country caused a shift from extended families to nuclear families. As a result, the degree of quality in parent-child relationships declined. More mothers entered the work force, fathers were at work for longer hours and away from home more, and the divorce rate increased. This problem was not limited to the family though. Industrialization also led to demographic shifts in housing patterns, which had an adverse effect on the constitution of the community. Children were no longer spending their entire formative years in the same community. As a result, other adults in the community ceased to function as surrogate parents if and when the need arose. The diminished role played by family and community in insulating young people from delinquent behavior is an issue familiar to students of the United States justice system.

Another factor was the emergence of a highly competitive school system. Traditionally, the Japanese teacher played a vital role in dispensing moral education. Although this remains true to some extent, the role of the teacher has shifted principally to imparting academic knowledge. The pressure for academic excellence has hindered the low achievers, enhancing the likelihood that they become alienated from the system and eventually drop out of the process.

Finally, industrialization has led to the expansion of a highly skilled work force. This has placed in jeopardy the opportunity for some unskilled workers to participate in, and benefit from, the country's economic expansion. This problem is especially acute among young workers who have dropped out of school. They have already experienced one form of isolation in the educational system and may avoid the threat of economic isolation by turning to illegitimate modes of economic enterprise.

The breakdown in the role of family, community, school, and work in assisting and augmenting the Japanese method of structural integration led some of these isolated young people to turn to delinquent peer groups, which they relied on for purposes of socialization. Therefore, the traditional social structure conditions and processes that had explained the decline in crime among the adult population are presently in a state of flux and have lost some cogency among the younger generation.

The rate of juvenile crime declined until 1994, at which point it started to increase again. According to the report, "White Paper on Crime, 2005," the number of juveniles who committed Penal Code violations in 2004 totaled 193,076, down 5.2 percent from the previous year. Of these crimes, 54.7 percent were larceny offenses and 27.6 percent involved embezzlement (which includes converting lost property), amounting to 82.3 percent of the total. In 2004, the number of robbery offenses were 1,301.

Of particular concern is the continued level of violent offenses committed by bosozoku groups, which are motorcycle and customized car gangs that have existed for a long time in Japan. The gangs are primarily made up of males between the ages of 17 and 20. Criminologists have suggested that membership in these gangs usually lasts about two years (Kersten, 1993). What has alarmed the police in recent years is the relationship between the increase in violence among bosozoku members and the apparent influence that boryokudan groups (organized crime) are having on some of these gangs.

Part of the recent increase in delinquency rates, however, is attributed to first-time offenders or juveniles who did not have a prior record. The Research Department of the Ministry of Justice conducted a survey of juvenile offenders in the hope of seeking an explanation for this development. For a large percentage of the Japanese population, poverty and economic hardship are almost nonexistent. In light of these circumstances, what motivates juveniles to commit larceny, extortion, and embezzlement offenses? The survey found that more than 50 percent were motivated by greed, while between 20 and 39 percent considered their actions to be a form of amusement. With regard to offenses involving assault, more offenders indicated that they were motivated by violent emotion rather than by a grudge or revenge. The researchers who analyzed the data identified four trends or characteristics among these juvenile delinquents: diminished moral standards, fragile support groups, limited self-control, and a tendency toward impulsive behavior (Research Department, 2000).

It should be noted that in the late 1990s and after the turn of the century there have been a few horrific murder cases in which both the victim and perpetrator were at or younger than 14 years of age. In light of the public outrage, the government moved to amend the Juvenile Law in 2000. The amendments lowered the minimum age (from 16 to 14) in which a juvenile can be tried in an adult criminal court, ordered the family court to refer all juvenile murder suspects who are at least 16 years of age to the procurator, and emphasized the importance of parental responsibility for children. For the first time since the Juvenile Law was enacted in 1948, there was a shift in policy as to how a juvenile offender who commits a serious crime would be handled. There would be punitive consequences for such offenders (Fenwick, in Muncie and Goldson, 2006).

Family Court

Before the personnel and jurisdiction of the family court are examined, it is important to explain how juveniles are classified according to their age and level of criminal responsibility.

Responsibility of Juveniles The term *juvenile* refers to anyone under the age of 20. The Juvenile Law (1948), which established the procedures for handling juveniles committed to trial, created a categorization scheme for making distinctions among juveniles who are labeled delinquent. A "juvenile offender" is a person between the ages of 14 and 20 who has committed a criminal offense cited in the Penal Code or some other statute. A "lawbreaking child" is a juvenile under the age of 14 who has committed a criminal offense. A "pre-offense juvenile" is a young person considered to be susceptible to committing criminal acts. Incorrigibles, runaways, and young people prone to harmful behavior are examples of this last category. Harmful behavior could include such actions as loitering at midnight or smoking.

Personnel The Japanese have established the family court to handle juvenile matters. In cases involving juveniles, the police are usually the first to respond. They send all cases pertaining to lawbreaking children and pre-offense juveniles directly to this court or to a child guidance center. If the matter involves a juvenile offender, the police refer the case to the public procurator. The procurator, out of necessity, may conduct a second investigation to determine whether charges are warranted. The procurator does not have the power to suspend a prosecution, as is the case with adult offenders; he or she must turn the matter over to the family court judge. The judge in a juvenile case, therefore, is accorded a good deal of discretionary authority in determining how juvenile cases are disposed.

In addition to the judge, family court probation officers offer an invaluable service. Trained in the social and behavioral sciences, the probation officers administer psychological and aptitude tests to the juveniles; interview the young offender and members of the family; and investigate the juvenile's family, social, educational, employment, and criminal history. They prepare a profile on the juvenile that is used by the judge when determining an appropriate manner for handling a case.

Jurisdiction of the Family Court The family court has original jurisdiction over all matters pertaining to family or juvenile cases. In the court hierarchy, the family court is considered an equal to district courts. Its jurisdiction is totally independent from that of district courts. Appellate reviews from family courts are entertained in high courts. Although family courts have principal jurisdiction over juvenile cases, a judge can send a case back to the public procurator for criminal prosecution in an adult court, if the person could be sentenced to death or imprisonment if found guilty.

Procedures The procedures of the family court are usually quite informal. In many cases, the court is not overly concerned with establishing the offender's guilt, but rather with determining an appropriate format for treatment. The process adheres to the principle of *parens patriae* (in which the court takes the position of guardian), and the hearings are not open to the public. In addition, the media is forbidden from publishing articles or photographs of juveniles processed in a family court. Cases involving juveniles that have been transferred to a district court are more formal, but they also retain the principle of *parens patriae* as the case proceeds and a decision is rendered.

Disposition

According to the Juvenile Law, the purpose of the juvenile justice system is "the sound upbringing of juveniles, to carry out the protective dispositions relating to the character correction and environmental adjustment of delinquent juveniles, and to take special measures with respect to the criminal cases of juveniles and adults who are harmful to the welfare of juveniles." The thrust of the juvenile system, therefore, is to protect, educate, and rehabilitate the young offender. This is reflected in the kinds of dispositions that are available to the judge.

To illustrate, the family courts handled about 231,973 cases in 2004. Of those cases involving a non-traffic offense, almost 84 percent were dismissed either without a hearing or after the hearing (White Paper on Crime, 2005). The most important consideration offered for adopting this strategy is the desire to avoid labeling the young person as a delinquent. If at all possible, the court also prefers to keep the child at home in the hope that the family and other institutions traditionally associated with exerting a positive influence on a young person's behavior (such as schools) can be utilized to the fullest extent possible. Once again, the importance that the Japanese place on the group is reflected here.

Beyond an outright dismissal of a case or a referral to the public procurator for prosecution in a district court, the family court has five alternatives remaining. The juvenile could be placed on probation. In 2004, 4,575 non-traffic offenses were handled in this manner. There are about 50,000 volunteer probation officers who assist the professional officers. One of the greatest concerns among Japanese experts is the failure of younger volunteers to come forward and serve as probation officers for juveniles. There are a number of older volunteers, but what is needed presently are younger people who could help bridge the generation gap and serve as realistic role models. Unfortunately, the average age of the volunteer is rising rather than falling. In 1953, it was 53 years of age, while in 1994 it was 62 (Winterdyk, 1997).

A second possibility is that the court will issue a conditional probation. Under this order, the delinquent is placed in the custody of a family court probation officer. This order enables the court to study the conduct of the juvenile more closely before deciding to issue a regular probation or a protective custody measure.

A third type of disposition is a court order that requires the juvenile and his or her parents to avail themselves of the services provided at a child guidance center. There are a number of these centers located throughout Japan; they are under the direction of the Ministry of Health and Welfare. These centers are staffed by child specialists in medicine, psychology, and social work. Their goal is to assist the child and the parents through counseling and therapy.

Commitment to a home to support the independence of children is another alternative. It is granted to children under the age of 18 who have committed delinquent acts or who have been neglected. The governor of a prefecture also can impose such an order with the parents' consent. Although the juvenile delinquent is usually sent to a home under an indeterminate sentence, he or she is released after having completed junior high school studies. The purpose of the home is to provide both an educational and a protective environment for these children.

The fifth alternative is to send the juvenile to one of the Ministry of Justice's juvenile training schools. In recent years, between 2 and 2.5 percent of all juvenile cases end in a disposition to a training school. The purpose of these schools is to offer rehabilitation, along with regular school and vocational courses. The schools are divided into four categories, each designed to handle a particular type of juvenile offender. Primary juvenile training schools house young offenders between the ages of 14 and 16 who have no serious psychological or physical defects. Middle juvenile training schools handle offenders between the ages of 16 and 20 who have no mental impairments or physical handicaps. Advanced juvenile training schools are designed to handle juveniles above the age of 16 who have established serious criminal tendencies. Finally, medical juvenile training schools are responsible for delinquents above the age of 14 who suffer from either a mental or a physical handicap. Juveniles who are sent to these facilities are given an indeterminate sentence but usually are released after two years. Some of the training schools have been converted to short-term facilities in which juveniles serve a term of less than six months.

Finally, juveniles who have been found guilty in a district court and sentenced to a term of imprisonment are sent to a juvenile prison. There are eight of these facilities, and while they emphasize a work regimen, it is in the form of academic or vocational training. There has been a marked decline in the number of young people sent to juvenile prison. Over the course of the past decade, less than 100 juveniles per year have received a sentence of incarceration. Part of the reason for this low figure is that juveniles cannot be sentenced to a term of imprisonment unless they are at least 16 years of age.

Critical Issues

When cases of juvenile delinquency increased during the early 1980s, the police augmented their efforts at curtailing the problem. They essentially instituted proactive strategies designed to prevent juveniles from becoming delinquent. This involved the police exercising broad discretionary authority to determine what constituted potentially "bad" behavior and who fit the profile of a predelinquent. For example, smoking, drinking, and hanging around public places late at night were considered "bad" behaviors. Police began to issue warnings to these predelinquent juveniles and monitored their activities. They reported such instances of improper behavior to parents, schools, and employers in the hope that these people would assist the police in guiding the juvenile to avoid such behavior.

Criticism of this strategy developed, with three concerns in particular receiving a good deal of attention (Fukuda, 1988; Yajima, 1988; Yokoyama, 1989). The first involves a policy issue. Should the police be permitted to exercise such broad discretionary authority in defining what constitutes "bad" predelinquent behavior when the law governing juveniles does not even define what constitutes delinquent behavior? The police are of the opinion that this authority falls under their legal responsibility to provide public security. Critics maintain that the exercise of this discretion is too broad. After all, the Juvenile Law places the exercise of discretion in delinquency cases with the family court and not with other agents of the justice system.

The second criticism raises the whole issue of whether it is prudent to label so many juveniles as predelinquent. While admitting that some juveniles might benefit from this strategy, critics point out that too many juveniles are being subjected to this strategy and labeled predelinquent. For example, of all the cases of police intervention with juveniles in 1985, it has been suggested that 84 percent involved predelinquents (Fukuda, 1988).

The third concern addresses a basic legal issue that can be understood only in its historical context. Before the war, children had few legal protections and were subject to abuse by the authorities. The postwar Constitution provided all Japanese citizens with basic rights, and the tone of specific juvenile justice legislation passed after the war was a reaction to the abuse suffered by juveniles during the pre-war period. For example, the Juvenile Law (1948) states that the purpose of the juvenile justice system is for the welfare of the individual. This process should involve protection, education, and rehabilitation. Some critics alleged that the police may be going too far in their tactics directed at predelinquents and in the process are endangering the juvenile's constitutional and legal rights (Yokoyama, 1992).

Summary

This chapter has offered an introduction to the Japanese criminal justice system. The major components of the system—the police, judiciary, law, corrections, and juvenile justice—were surveyed, along with an overview of the country's political system. A brief history of some of the components of the system was presented; the organization and administration were described; the various roles of the practitioners were explained; the legal process was examined; and reference was made to some of the areas of concern within the system.

To the American observer, Japan's justice system displays many Anglo-American characteristics resulting from the postwar influence. Nevertheless, the system still retains many of the Romano-Germanic legal traditions that have had an impact for a far longer period of time. An interesting feature of the system is the extent to which deference is shown to agents of all components of the system. This is largely based on the fact that the public views the agents of the administration of justice as enforcers of both law and social morality. Because this attitude is so pervasive, there appears to be a great degree of cooperation between the various components. One is left with the impression that the Japanese are sincerely attempting to make the criminal justice system function as a system rather than as a series of dysfunctional components.

For some time now, the Japanese have been able to mix the ancient traditions of their culture with the modern innovations of an industrialized society. They have borrowed Western ideas judiciously and have uniquely blended them to fit their Eastern mores. Although these attitudes may change in time, thus far they have had a profound and positive effect on their criminal justice system.

Concepts to Know

Marxism-Leninism

Mikhail Gorbachev

democratization

Constitution of the Russian Federation

president of the Russian Federation

Committee for State Security (KGB)

propiska

Constitutional Court of the Russian Federation

Judicial Department

procuracy

defense counsel

justices of the peace

jury

material definition of crime

measures of restraint

plea bargain

Ministry of Internal Affairs (MVD)

commission on juvenile affairs

Chapter V

Introduction

The longest-running social science experiment of the twentieth century officially ended on December 25, 1991, with the resignation of Mikhail Gorbachev as president of the Soviet Union. From the Bolshevik Revolution of 1917 until Gorbachev's resignation, the rulers of the Soviet Union had attempted to create a communist society that would be the envy of the world. Support for this goal was continual for more than 70 years, but the sense of purpose and direction began to unravel during the late 1980s. The principal cause for this shift in opinion was Gorbachev's alternative rationale for achieving socialism. Although his ideas were a radical departure from some of the basic tenets of Leninism, Gorbachev generally favored implementing them incrementally. Nevertheless, disaffection with these ideas became quite pronounced among devoted communists, which led to the attempted coup of August 1991. This was followed by Gorbachev's resignation and the formal dissolution of the country by year's end.

The Soviet Union had been comprised of 15 republics: Armenia, Azerbaijan, Byelorussia, Estonia, Georgia, Kazakhstan, Kirghizistan, Latvia, Lithuania, Moldavia, Russia, Tadzhikistan, Turkmenistan, Ukraine, and Uzbekistan. Russia was not only the largest republic in terms of territory and population, but it also dominated the policies of the Soviet Union—so much so that the words Russian and Soviet were often used interchangeably when referring to the foreign and domestic policies of the Soviet Union. Today, Russia is the largest country in the world, almost twice the size of the United States. It encompasses more than 6.5 million square miles that stretch from eastern Europe through the northern half of Asia. The population of about 142 million has become more urban over the past 50 years. In fact, it has reached about 80 percent of the population—almost an exact reversal of the urban and rural ratio at the time of the 1917 Revolution.

Russia is a federation consisting of six categories of administrative units. These include: 21 republics, six territories, 49 provinces, two federal cities, one autonomous province, and 10 autonomous regions. Among these administrative units, the republics have the greatest claim to self-government. Although Russians comprise more than 80 percent of the country's population, there are some 126 nationalities with distinct racial, linguistic, and religious preferences. The nature of the federation's administrative units, coupled with the number of ethnic groups, has led some commentators to suggest that Russia might eventually follow the path of the Soviet Union and be divided into still smaller units.

Before the Bolshevik Revolution, Russia was characterized as a large, authoritarian, backward rural nation. After the Revolution, especially as a result of Joseph Stalin's reign, it emerged as a large, authoritarian, backward, industrialized nation. Believed to be one of the richest countries in the world, it has extensive holdings in oil, natural gas, and coal. While Russia is considered one of the few countries with the capability of becoming self-sufficient, this is unlikely to happen in the foreseeable future. Today, the principal industries are steel, machinery, machine tools, vehicles, and chemicals. Under the Soviet regime, centralized planning was emphasized and individual creativity was essentially discouraged. The one exception to this rule related to the vast defense industry. In recent years, attempts have been made to shift this industry to civilian use. Shortfalls continue to occur among the agricultural yields, and the extensive natural resources remain largely untapped because of deficient applications of technology. Thus, although the country is a highly industrialized society by world standards, it is not an advanced society. In addition, the industrial sector is becoming antiquated and less efficient. A large part of these circumstances are the result of unstable economic conditions.

To state that a country is industrialized as well as backward is rather paradoxical. Yet, Russia is just that—a paradox. Western scholars, journalists, politicians, and travelers have described it in this way for more than a century. For example, despite the fact the Soviet leaders heralded the establishment of socialist democracy, there were numerous indications that it was a totalitarian regime. The people often perceived themselves as strong, powerful, and morally superior, but they displayed an unqualified submissiveness to their leaders as well as a sense of inferiority to the accomplishments of the West. Their communist ideology called for the elimination of the exploitation of humankind; however, their political and economic institutions fostered a rampant form of corruption that infiltrated all aspects of life. The Soviets claimed to establish a land of the proletariat, yet they were extremely conscious of rank. Their historically significant revolution was designed to overthrow the tsar's chains of oppression, but these were merely supplanted by the chains of the Communist Party. The party devoted a good deal of time and energy to publicizing its ideological principles to a people who were largely nonpolitical. The Soviet Constitution proclaimed free speech, free press, and free assembly, but institutional censorship and self-censorship were quite common, and the Committee for State Security watched over all assemblies. Finally, the Soviets spoke of the benefits of collective agriculture, but an estimated one-third of the agricultural output was grown on private plots.

Despite these paradoxes, there has been a pronounced, deep love of country on the part of the Russian people. This quality is different from that of other countries, because the Russian love of country has been frequently tested, often to extraordinary limits. Throughout its history, Russia has been vulnerable to attacks from Asiatic tribes to the east and from Europe to the west. The last time this occurred was during World War II, when 20 million citizens died in defense of the motherland.

Protection from Russia's enemies—real or imagined—was a central feature of the country's foreign and domestic policies. It took two forms. One form of protection was security from the world beyond the borders. This was achieved by building a strong military establishment that was second only to China's in size, by creating satellite zones that served as a buffer to the motherland, and by supporting or encouraging dissension in other parts of the world in the hope that these events would keep the enemy preoccupied.

The size of the military has been reduced because the leadership realized that it contributed to the economic woes of the country. Events in eastern Europe led to a dismantling of the buffer zone that was established following World War II. While some of the popular commentary in the West viewed this as weakening Russia, that was not necessarily a correct assessment. Eastern Europe had been an economic drain for several years, as well as a source of insecurity from dissenting parties in the buffer zone countries. Today, some Russians view the former republics of the Soviet Union (characterized as the "near abroad") as a new buffer zone.

The second protectionist approach focused on assuring security from within the country. With some 126 nationalities inhabiting Russia, there had been a great fear that internal dissent might arise. The Communist Party's own history was a witness to that political reality. Since its inception, the party's all-powerful Committee for State Security served to deter internal dissent. Since the creation of the Russian Federation, these fears have been realized as ethnic unrest continues to erupt. A good deal of attention has been devoted to events in Chechnya in particular.

Originally, the Soviet government was able to implement this security policy because the people were essentially patriotic and nonpolitical. Throughout their history, the Russian people came to respect power and authority. Whereas most citizens in democratic countries show deference to their law, Russian citizens display a similar regard for authority. Because such awe of power and authority generally leads to conformity, freedom—at least as United States citizens understand it—had no place in Soviet society. American concepts of law and freedom are based on historical events. The Renaissance, Reformation, and Enlightenment were instrumental in the evolutionary development of such ideas; however, these periods of intellectual change were essentially absent from Russian history.

The most pronounced theme running throughout Russian history has been the presence of totalitarian authority. Such authority has been all the Russians have known, be it a Mongol-Tatar khan, a Russian tsar, or a Communist Party leader. This factor assists in explaining some of the significant implications for the Russian political process and its criminal justice system. It also suggests that hope for dramatic changes in the region should be tempered by a recognition of that history.

The events in Russia since 1991 have focused almost exclusively on the leadership's attempt to transform the old order to a new order. Central to this change has been a shift from a socialist economy to a free market economy. In this context, students of comparative criminal justice should be aware of three important observations.

Since the initial focus of change has been directed at the economic system, most of the political energy has been directed at achieving that goal. This has taken two forms: (1) changes directed specifically at the economy, and (2) reforms of the political system that control the economic infrastructure. As a result, there has been only limited incremental changes introduced in the criminal justice system.

The changes that have occurred in the justice system were introduced in the form of legislation or policy. This does not mean, however, that these intended changes have actually occurred in practice. The difficulty of implementing new policy is not unique to Russia. All organizations (or perhaps, more specifically, the people employed by them), irrespective of political ideology, have some degree of difficulty accepting most kinds of change in the status quo.

What compounds the problems for the reformers in Russia are the profound changes that are central to political and social institutions. The magnitude of the changes has implications for a person's ability to cope. To illustrate, two scenarios are presented here. One form of coping is directed at employees of the justice system. The vast majority of people working in the Russian criminal justice system are the same people who were employed in the Soviet system. They—more than most Russian citizens—were apt to support the communist cause, because the nature of their jobs was to enforce law and maintain order. While many may feel betrayed by their leaders and disillusioned with the current situation, in all likelihood, many also would be more reluctant to embrace the new order. As such, they might thwart change by looking nostalgically at the old order and seeking a return to it.

The other kind of coping problem is directed more at the ordinary citizen, but could also apply to some employees of the justice system. At issue is the psychological impact that the dissolution of the Soviet Union has had on its citizens in general. According to Richard Pipes, the collapse of the Soviet empire "has dealt a heavy blow ... to the self-esteem of Russians" (Isham, 1995). This climate of self-doubt has manifested itself in several ways. For example, there is a reluctance in some cases to accept the new legal order and in other cases to reject the ethical basis for the new market economy. The inability to develop a consensus on legal and ethical issues of this kind fosters instability. In addition, the absence of a sense of internal unity has led to an unstable balance of authority within the administration of government. It has been pointed out by more than one commentator that this kind of situation only enhances a nihilistic attitude toward the state and its agents.

A second observation of which students of comparative criminal justice should be aware is that whenever a country undertakes a massive transformation in its view of the social order, disorder inevitably occurs. The movement from a socialist economy to a free market system is an example of a massive transformation in the social order. Hence, a good deal of disorder can be expected. Every two steps taken forward toward a free market economy will undoubtedly be followed by one, and sometimes two, steps backward. Change of this magnitude seldom, if ever, occurs in a straight, constant, upward curve. This point has been illustrated well by the attempted coup in August 1991 by hard-line communists, the armed uprising of October 1993, the election of ultra-nationalist legislators in December 1993, the ongoing battle to keep the republic of Chechnya within the Russian Federation, the Communist Party's comeback in the parliamentary elections of 1995, and since 2000, president and now prime minister Vladimir Putin's authoritarian efforts to consolidate more power under his leadership.

A final observation is that the leaders of the movement to transform the Soviet system were all products of the old order. They will rely upon agents of the criminal justice system for the retention of a degree of order. Despite the fact that the leadership is attempting to move the country to a new social order, they may condone or encourage the use of law enforcement and order maintenance methods that have proved effective in the past. This fact also suggests why significant change in the justice system will not be forthcoming during the early stages of the transformation to a new social order. Thus, while people in the West might be encouraged by reforms adopted in Russia, they should realize that lasting change will only occur gradually over an extended period of time.

Government

Social systems and their governments are supported—and in some cases held together—by a belief or value system that offers direction and a sense of purpose. The United States, for example, holds that all people are created equal and are worthy of equal protection and due process of law. Russia is presently in the process of changing its social system and hence is altering its belief and value system. Obviously, this process will take a good deal of time. In this context, time is not estimated by months or a limited number of years but rather is measured in terms of at least a generation or more. As has been mentioned, the central feature of this transformation from the old order to a new order has to do with adopting a different set of economic principles that are embraced by society. This process has a profound impact on the political and economic infrastructure of the country. In the Russian context, this transformation has enhanced the status of law because the application of legal principles is vital to the successful implementation of the changes. The role that law plays in this process is not limited to economics, however. Its enhanced stature is utilized in other political and social context, including criminal justice.

Because Russia has been in a state of flux and is uncertain about its immediate future and long-term prospects, it is important to consider the events that have been unfolding in the country since 1991 in the context of the ideology that gave the Soviet Union its direction and purpose throughout much of this century. Unlike the beliefs that hold other social systems together, the Soviet value system was much more ambitious. Referred to as Marxism-Leninism, it was both a normative and descriptive theory that purported to explain social interaction and to prescribe the means of changing it. When one takes into consideration the historical and cultural characteristics of the country and its people, it should come as no surprise that the Marxist-Leninist philosophy became the official ideology of the government. What follows is a brief summary of the evolution of the communist ideology in the Soviet Union. It is designed to provide the reader with an outline of the ideology of the old order so that one can better understand the significance of the decision to abandon it for a new order.

Communism

Marx The central contribution of Karl Marx (1818–1883) to the development of the communist ideology was his belief in the role that economic factors played in political and social change. The production and distribution of wealth and the kinds of property relationships that developed had a considerable influence on the social consciousness of humankind. Historically, this was the case under slavery, serfdom, and capitalism, and it would also be true under socialism and communism. This economic interpretation of history was central to understanding society.

For Marx, the principal factor that causes dynamism in the historical dialectic is the class struggle. This struggle is carried on by two conflicting classes: those who own the land and the means of production and those who work in order to subsist. In a capitalist society, class antagonism exists between the proletariat (or urban workers) and the bourgeoisie (or capitalist producers). Marx viewed capitalism as an economic system that exploited the masses. He felt that there would come a time when the proletariat would rise up in revolution and eliminate the bourgeoisie. Socialism would then be established to replace the capitalist system. With this change, the class struggle would cease to exist. Since the bourgeoisie used the state for the sole purpose of controlling other classes, it would become obsolete and wither away. All of this would be but a prelude to the creation of the ideal communist society in which prosperity would abound for all. Orthodox Marxists were of the opinion that the proletariat revolution would occur in a highly industrialized society. They felt that in a country such as England, the revolution could even occur peacefully.

Lenin At the beginning of the twentieth century, Russia was not industrialized. It was an agrarian society having a small proletariat incapable of overthrowing the bourgeoisie. In light of these facts, it was the theoretical contributions of Vladimir Ilich Lenin (1870–1924) that made the revolution possible in Russia. Many of his ideas remained the guiding force in Russia until the emergence of Mikhail Gorbachev. Among Lenin's principal ideas was a belief that the socialist revolution could occur in Russia if the proletariat united with the numerically superior peasantry. From his perspective, it was imperative that the proletariat be led by an elite, militant, and highly disciplined organization. This group would become the Communist Party, whose single purpose was to unite the masses to lead the revolution. Because of the need for unity of purpose, there could be no room for divisions within the party. Lenin referred to this principle as democratic centralism: all authority would rest with the party executive.

Lenin saw the revolution and the deterioration of the state occurring in two phases. The first stage was labeled socialism. During this phase, the state would continue to exist; it would appear on the surface to characterize a bourgeois society, but there would be a significant difference. Under socialism, suppression would be in the hands of the majority rather than the minority. The masses would systematically suppress the oppressors of the old regime, and the means of economic production would be socialized. Although equality would not exist in the workplace, at least exploitation would be eliminated. In addition, in order to assure the success of the revolutionary movement, aspects of bourgeois law would have to be retained because of the need for control. The second stage would see the withering away of the state and law, as well as the emergence of equality for all workers. At that point in time, the ideal communist society would be established.

Stalin In his critique of Lenin's democratic centralism, Leon Trotsky was fearful that a dictator might emerge from the powerful executive of the Communist Party envisioned by Lenin as necessary for a successful revolution. Until his death, Joseph Stalin (1879–1953) proved Trotsky acutely prophetic. Some have argued that Stalin was necessary in order for socialism to have succeeded in Russia. When Lenin died in 1924, the revolutionary movement was in disarray and an agrarian economic base existed in the country. Stalin changed that by converting the country into a powerful and increasingly modern industrialized state. He accomplished this feat through summary executions, mass imprisonment of suspected enemies, and an extensive system of forced labor camps. Just as credit is given to Lenin for creating a viable revolutionary formula for Marxism in Russia, Stalin is acknowledged for transforming the country into a powerful giant among states. His methods, however, have been criticized from within the Soviet Union since his death.

Gorbachev Not since Lenin had a Soviet leader made such a significant theoretical contribution to communist ideology as Mikhail Gorbachev (1931–). His theory consisted of an alternative rationale for achieving socialism that radically departed from some of the basic tenets of Leninism and offered a method designed to realize that objective. There were essentially two factors that motivated Gorbachev to depart from standard interpretations of the communist ideology. First, he was highly critical of the manner in which Lenin's democratic centralism was adopted, that is, the extent to which power was allocated exclusively with the Communist Party. Second, Gorbachev wanted to dispel the myth that the Soviet Union had entered into a mature form of socialism. Lenin had argued that the socialist revolution would occur in two phases. The first stage was referred to as socialism. Although the state would continue to exist, it would be transformed through the elimination of the exploitation of the masses. The second stage would be marked by the withering away of the state and law, and the emergence of an ideal communist society in which equality would exist for all. During Leonid Brezhnev's regime, this myth implied that, because they had entered a mature form of socialism, the Soviets were on the road to achieving the ideal communist society. Gorbachev felt that nothing could be further from the truth.

Gorbachev's theoretical contribution was an attempt to resuscitate the communist ideology toward the establishment of a truly socialist society. His prescription for what was ailing the Soviet Union was based on three concepts: *glasnost* (openness), *perestroika* (restructuring), and democratization. Each of these ideas was interrelated. For example, democratization could not be achieved without glasnost, and perestroika could not be realized without democratization. Gorbachev acknowledged that what had caused the inertia in the Soviet economy was a bloated bureaucracy. This phenomenon was not limited to the Communist Party (although Gorbachev largely placed blame on it); it was also evident in the national, republic, and local levels of government as well as in the state-run economic system. Various bureaucracies had looked after their own interests for years and had largely ignored the interests of the people. According to Gorbachev, the people must be free in order for socialism to succeed, and this could be achieved only if the interests of all were represented in society's decision-making processes. The policy of glasnost (openness) was the starting point, for it was the means by which the inefficiencies in public life were criticized. Gorbachev's views on what was wrong with Soviet society served as a practical illustration of glasnost. Actually changing the status quo would be achieved through perestroika (restructuring), but perestroika could not be realized without democratization. When Gorbachev spoke of democratization, he was referring to democratic socialism. For Gorbachev, democracy must be socialistic, and socialism must be democratic. Here he remained true to his ideological roots, while also transforming that ideology into a viable theory for the present.

In order to achieve democratization, several changes were necessary in the Soviet system. These changes corresponded to three major issues. First, a democratic society is governed by the rule of law. Law assures rights and freedoms for individuals and controls the potential abuse of power and authority of the leadership. Thus, constitutional reform was necessary to establish a socialist style of checks and balances. There was also a need for an independent judiciary that was not tied to the dictates of the Communist Party. Reforms that addressed some of these issues were introduced and adopted during Gorbachev's tenure in power. Second, democratization should lead to both equality of social justice and equality of opportunity. The latter was designed to encourage and assure individual initiative and enterprise—something that had been largely absent in the Soviet Union and was sorely needed for its economy. Gorbachev faced the difficulty of squaring individual interests with the more traditional collective interests of socialism. Third, democratization would inevitably lead to a plurality of ideas. In the political context, this would lead to the abandonment of a single-party system and the establishment of a multiple-party system. While Gorbachev was in power, legislation had been adopted to enable this to happen, but it was only realized after the dissolution of the Soviet Union. According to Gorbachev, democratization would strengthen, rather than weaken, the Communist Party.

This democratic style of governance would lead to the realization of the strategy of perestroika, because democratic styles of management would be introduced in all aspects of life. This restructuring would enable the introduction of efficient methods of planning and development in the economic sectors of society. Further, it followed that perestroika would eventually lead to the resolution of the country's economic woes. In light of the political developments in the Soviet Union, a case could be made that the policy of glasnost and the strategy of perestroika succeeded beyond the wildest dreams of its proponents, in particular those of Gorbachev. While some people in Russia remain supportive of communism, it is not suggested here that Russia might return to this system, irrespective of the fact that the efforts to establish a new order have been painful for people and disruptive for society at large. What is possible is that Russia might grow weary of its efforts to chart a course toward democracy and abandon such a course in favor of an ideology that in the end is as repressive as that found under the communist system.

Democratization

When discussing domestic political events in the Russian Federation, the Western press has often used the terms "democracy" and "democratization" interchangeably. This is an inaccurate use of those terms and a flawed portrayal of reality. In this context, democracy should be used to explain a fact. It literally means "government by the people," and it has been used to make distinctions among different types of governments, such as government by a few (aristocracy) or government by one (monarchy or dictator). Democratization, on the other hand, is a process in which proponents of democracy are aspiring to establish that form of government but as yet have not achieved that goal (Berman, 1992; Iakovlev, 1990; Juviler, 1990).

The central feature of democratization is a recognition of the importance of government by rule of law. Gorbachev recognized the significance of this, for he saw law as the vehicle for assuring rights and freedoms and for checking potential abuses of power and authority. From the time of Gorbachev to the leadership of the Russian Federation, Russia has been establishing the legal foundations for a democratic system of government. Legislation has been passed that is designed to assure basic political rights that are fundamental to the creation of a democratic state. These rights include: freedom of expression, freedom of assembly, freedom of association, freedom of speech, and freedom of the press. Although these efforts are concrete illustrations that the proponents of democratization are having some success, the Russian Federation is still a considerable distance from reaching the ultimate goal of an established democracy. In addition (as mentioned in the previous section), the fact that legislation has been passed does not necessarily mean that it has been implemented in practice, enforced by Russian standards, or is being complied with in a manner deemed appropriate by the West.

From a Western perspective, one of the most important concepts associated with the rule of law is due process of rights and the concomitant notion of an independent judiciary. Although legal documents of the former Soviet Union spoke of rights for citizens, in practice, they did not mirror reality. Rights were vested in the state, not in people. As such, it will take time for the Russian Federation to pass a sufficient amount of legislation that addresses due process issues. It will require even more time to enable it to function in a manner that meets an objective Russian standard. Even when this occurs, it may not have reached an appropriate standard from a Western perspective. Moreover, a state that proclaims to be subject to its own laws must guarantee its citizens an independent judiciary. While efforts are under way to move in this direction, this has not been realized at this time in the Russian Federation.

Throughout Vladimir Putin's tenure as president from 2000 to 2008, there were growing concerns that Russia was returning to a highly centralized authoritarian state. Some have argued that there is a need to impose order at the expense of liberty in order to salvage a degree of liberty, which most Russians had found alien to their personal experience. A good deal of criticism has been directed at the government's increased control of the media (*Amnesty International Report*, 2008). Protests by opposing political parties or other groups are frequently stopped by police, and such incidents are not reported in the media. It is alleged that some journalists who have been critical of the government were sent to psychiatric hospitals. This strategy can have an obvious chilling effect on the press in light of the use of such hospitals to curb dissent during the Soviet era.

The extent to which corruption is widespread is another concern that threatens to undermine democratization. It is important to note that corruption did not emerge during Putin's tenure as president. It was rampant during the Soviet era and continues to flourish in both the private and public sectors. It exists in the economic, judicial, political, and social life of Russians and is viewed as normal. To illustrate the degree of the problem, Transparency International issued a Corruption Perception Index for 2007. The Index provides for most countries a score of between 1 and 10, with 10 being the highest in the confidence range. The score is based on the views of country analysts and businesspersons. Russia received a score of 2.3. By way of comparison, the other countries that have a chapter devoted to them in this book received the following scores: United Kingdom, 8.4; France, 7.3; Sweden, 9.3; Japan, 7.5; and China, 3.5. The United States received a score of 7.2 (Transparency International, 2008). While the Russian public is not oblivious to the issue of corruption, because they are frequently confronted with it in their daily lives, they accept it as a normal pattern of behavior. The principal focus for most Russians is simply to improve their standard of living.

Constitution

The Constitution of the Russian Federation was adopted on December 12, 1993, the same day it was approved by the voters. The document consists of nine chapters and 137 articles. It explains how the state functions, what the rights of citizens are, and how the government is organized and administered. The document has been referred to as the "Yeltsin" Constitution because former President Boris Yeltsin was the force behind delineating its legal principles and assuring its subsequent approval. Chapter 1 consists of basic provisions for the establishment of the constitutional system for the country. For example, Article 1 states: "The Russian Federation/Russia is a democratic and federal state based on the rule of law, with a republican form of government." Articles 10 and 11 clarify in general terms the organization of the central government by indicating that the three branches of government—executive, legislative, and judicial—are separate and independent from each other.

Although constitutions of the former Soviet Union spoke of citizens' rights, in reality, rights were vested in the state and citizens were accorded a series of obligations. With this constitution, the roles are reversed. For example, Article 2 declares: "Human beings and their rights and liberties are the supreme values. The recognition, observance and protection of human and civil rights and liberties is the obligation of the state." Article 7 states: "The Russian Federation is a social state whose policy is aimed at creating conditions that ensure a dignified life for human beings and their free development." Other articles in this chapter recognize diversity of ideas and religious beliefs, guarantee freedom in economic endeavors, and acknowledge private forms of ownership.

While Chapter 1 acknowledged the importance of human rights, Chapter 2 provides a list of specific rights and liberties that were deemed significant enough to include in the constitution. These rights are divided into 47 categories. Articles 20 through 25 identify some of the rights that are of particular interest to students of criminal justice. They state:

> Article 20. Everyone has the right to life. Pending its abolition, capital punishment may be established by federal law as an exceptional measure of punishment for especially grave crimes against human life, provided that the accused is given the right to have his case considered in a trial by jury.
>
> Article 21. Human dignity is protected by the state. There can be no basis for its derogation. No one may be subjected to torture, violence or other treatment or punishment that is cruel or degrading to human dignity. No one may be subjected, without his or her voluntary agreement, to medical, scientific, or other experiments.

> Article 22. Everyone has the right to freedom and personal inviolability. Arresting persons, taking them into custody and keeping them in custody are permitted only on the basis of a court decision. A person may not be subjected to detention for more than 48 hours before a court decision is rendered.
>
> Article 23. Everyone has the right to inviolability of personal life, personal and family privacy, and the protection of his or her honor and good name. Everyone has the right to confidentiality of correspondence, telephone conversations and postal, telegraph and other communications. Restriction of this right is permitted only on the basis of a court decision.
>
> Article 24. The gathering, storing, use and dissemination of information about a person's private life without his or her consent are not permitted. Bodies of state power and bodies of local self-government, as well as their officials, must provide everyone with an opportunity to become familiar with documents and materials directly affecting his or her rights and liberties, unless stipulated otherwise by law.
>
> Article 25. Dwelling quarters are inviolable. No one has the right to enter dwelling quarters against the will of the residents, except in cases established by federal law or on the basis of a court decision.

These articles illustrate some of the constitutional concerns that have implications for both citizens and agents of the Russian criminal justice system. In addition, other issues that deal with criminal justice in general and criminal procedure in particular are also addressed in this chapter of the constitution. They will be discussed in the section on law.

Chapter 3 is devoted to a wide range of issues that are significant for a federated system of governance. For example, distinctions are made regarding those issues that are solely the responsibility of the federation and those that are shared jointly between the federation and members of the federation. Of particular significance is Article 76, which illustrates the newfound importance placed on the rule of law. The article states, in part:

> Federal laws may not be at variance with federal constitutional laws.
>
> Laws and other normative legal acts of the members of the Russian Federation may not be at variance with federal laws. … If there is a contradiction between a federal law and another act issued in the Russian Federation, the federal law prevails.

The other chapters of the constitution deal with various branches or levels of government and are described below.

President

The president of the Russian Federation is elected to a six-year term by direct universal suffrage. He or she is limited to holding the position for two consecutive terms. The president is the head of state, which gives him or her the constitutional authority to represent the Russian Federation within the country and in the international community. The president is responsible for the formulation of domestic and foreign policy and serves as the head of the Security Council of the Federation and the Supreme Commander in Chief of the Russian Federated Armed Forces.

The constitution authorizes the president to appoint the chair of the government (or administration) of the Russian Federation, with the consent of the State Duma; to preside over meetings of the government; and to make decisions on dismissing the government. The president is responsible for presenting judicial candidates to the Constitutional Court and to the Supreme Court and a candidate for the position of Procurator General of the Federation. These candidates must then receive the approval of the Council of the Federation. The president also has the authority to issue directives and decrees that are binding throughout the federation, as long as they comply with constitutional and federation law.

As was alluded to earlier, the Constitution of the Russian Federation has been criticized within Russia because it extends significant powers to the president. Further illustrating the level of authority granted the office is Article 80, which states, in part, that:

> The President of the Russian Federation is the guarantor of the Constitution of the Russian Federation and of human and civil rights and liberties. In accordance with procedures established by the Constitution of the Russian Federation, he takes measures to protect the sovereignty of the Russian Federation, its independence and its state integrity, and he ensures the coordinated functioning and interaction of all bodies of state power.

Clearly, significant powers are vested in the office of president, but this is not unusual by Russian standards. The political history of Russia has been dominated by strong, powerful leaders for centuries. In the Soviet context, Mikhail Gorbachev amended the Constitution of the USSR (Union of Soviet Socialist Republics) in 1990 to enhance the role of president. Until that time, the office had been largely ceremonial. Gorbachev's purpose was to use the office to support his efforts at perestroika. In fact, amending the constitution to strengthen the presidency was a practical example of perestroika. Moreover, because the Russian people do not have a point of reference in their history with participatory forms of governance, Boris Yeltsin may have actually enhanced the likelihood that the country will remain on a path toward a democratic system by vesting significant authority in the office of the president. Only history will tell if the presidential authority is used to avert chaos or to cause it. As alluded to earlier, Vladimir Putin's efforts to centralize more power under his presidency has raised concerns among those proponents of democratization and rule of law.

Prime Minister

Article 110 of the constitution states: "Executive power in the Russian Federation is exercised by the government of the Russian Federation." The government includes a prime minister (chair of the government) and other federal ministers. The prime minister is appointed by the president with the consent of the State Duma. The principal responsibilities of the prime minister, in coordination with other federal ministers, is to establish and organize the work of the government. The government can be dissolved under the following circumstances: if it relinquishes its authority when a new president is elected; if it tenders its resignation, which can be accepted or rejected by the president; if the president decides to dismiss the government; or if the State Duma indicates its displeasure with the government through a no-confidence vote.

Federal Assembly

The Federal Assembly is a bicameral parliament that consists of the Council of the Federation and the State Duma. The members of each chamber elect a chair and a vice-chair who preside over their respective chambers. The State Duma is composed of 450 deputies who are elected to a term of four years and serve as full-time legislators. The administrative responsibilities of the Duma include: consenting to the president's selection of a prime minister, determining issues of confidence in the government, and bringing charges against the president with the intention of removing him or her from office.

Once legislation is adopted by the Duma, it is sent to the Council of the Federation for that chamber's consideration. The Council is composed of 178 members. Each of the 89 local administrative units that form the Russian Federation send two representatives to this chamber. One representative is selected from the ranks of the legislative branch of the administrative unit, while the other representative is a member of the executive branch of the local unit. All legislation that deals with financial issues, international treaties, the country's borders, or matters of war and peace must be entertained by the Council. Approval from the Council for all other legislation can occur either by a simple majority vote or by default if the Council fails to entertain the matter within 14 days of receiving it. The constitution assigns several other duties to the Council. These include: confirming presidential decrees on such sensitive issues as the imposition of martial law or the introduction of a state of emergency, determining the use of federation troops outside the boundaries of the Russian Federation, appointing judges to the Constitutional Court and the Supreme Court, and removing the president from office.

Political Parties

At the beginning of this section, it was suggested that the development of the communist ideology gave the Soviet Union direction and purpose throughout much of this century. The Communist Party has played a significant role in the politics of the Soviet Union. Unlike political parties in many Western countries, the Communist Party of the Soviet Union (CPSU) possessed a number of unique characteristics. Most significant was the fact that it was the real source of power and authority within the country. Another was the special purpose that it bestowed on itself. Whereas most political parties exist in the hope of winning elections, the CPSU's original purpose was to foment revolution and to achieve power through force rather than the ballot box. Subsequent to the formation of the Soviet Union, the party's primary goals were to maintain power and to determine and implement its policy for the future of the socialist state. This was fairly easy to achieve because the CPSU was either the dominant party or, for many years, the only political party in the Soviet Union. Membership in the party was kept small intentionally. In a country of more than 285 million inhabitants, party membership was approximately 16.5 million. This coincided with Lenin's belief that only a small number of committed, disciplined revolutionaries were capable of directing the country through the various stages of revolution, socialism, and communism.

In considering the state of political parties in Russia today, we return to the context of the country's efforts at democratization. Basic political rights are fundamental to the creation of a democratic state. Freedom of expression, assembly, and association establish a climate of opinion that in turn encourages a diversity of ideas. Support for this position has been included in the Constitution of the Russian Federation. Article 13 states: "Ideological diversity is recognized in the Russian Federation. No state or mandatory ideology may be established. Political diversity and a multiparty system are recognized in the Russian Federation."

Following the dissolution of the Soviet Union, a number of political parties emerged in Russia, which suggested the people were embracing the concept of political diversity. At the time, it could have been argued that there were actually too many parties. To illustrate, of the 43 parties that competed for seats in the parliamentary election of December 1995, 33 of them each received less than 3 percent of the vote. Recently, the number of political parties that have attracted the attention of voters in a significant way have diminished considerably.

United Russia is the political party that has supported the administration of Putin. In the parliamentary elections to the Duma in December of 2007, it received 64.3 percent of the vote for 315 seats in the 450 seat Duma. The Communist Party is the only group that could be considered an opposition party in parliament. It espouses a socialist agenda that emphasizes moderate reform, including more public-sector spending and less privatization. It holds 57 seats in the Duma, having garnered 11.6 percent of the vote. The Liberal Democratic Party and the Fair Russia Party are the only other parties of note, and both have supported Putin. They received 8.1 percent and 7.7 percent, respectively, of the parliamentary vote, for 40 and 38 seats in the Duma. In March of 2008, Dmitry Medvedev became president of Russia. Like Putin, and with his endorsement, he ran as an independent but with the support of the United Russia Party. He received 71.5 percent of the vote, while his opponent from the Communist Party garnered 17.9 percent.

Administration

The administration of the government of the Russian Federation is carried out by a combination of ministries, committees, and other federal agencies. Some of the ministries and federal agencies are directly subordinate to the president because of constitutional or legislative provisions. These include the Ministries of Defense, Internal Affairs, and Foreign Affairs. The other federal agencies that report directly to the president are: Chief Security Guard Administration, Foreign Intelligence Service, Government Liaison and Information, Border Service, Counterintelligence Service, Television and Radio Service, and Archives Service. Oversight of the other federal government units would fall to the prime minister. This would include Ministries of Agriculture and Food, Economics, Education, Fuel and Power, Justice, and Transportation. In addition, there is a host of other federal committees and departments.

As is the case in any large country, local governments serve a useful purpose. They usually provide many of the basic services to the citizenry, including schools, hospitals, recreational facilities, and distribution centers for goods, as well as other social services. The Constitution of the Russian Federation addresses this issue to some extent. For example, Article 131 states: "Local self-government is exercised in urban and rural communities and other geographical areas with regard for historical and other local traditions. The population independently determines the structure of the bodies of local self-government." In addition, Article 132 indicates: "Bodies of local self-government independently manage municipal property; draw up, confirm and fulfill the local budget; establish local taxes and fees; safeguard public order; and alone resolve other questions of local significance." In a country whose history has known only authoritarian rule and whose political perspective had been dominated by a single view of its social destiny (a revolutionary one at that), the Russian Federation has recognized the importance of self-governance by including it in its strategy of democratization.

POLICE

A government that espouses principles associated with democracy is expected to adhere to the rule of law. Under such a system of government, people are vested with legal rights, and the state through its agents is obliged to protect the people in the exercise of those rights. Usually, the police are the initial government agents called upon to assure adherence to these democratic principles.

The basic principles associated with the governance of the Soviet Union were the reverse of those found in a democratic system. Government was not based on the rule of law but on the dictates of the Communist Party. The state was vested with all rights, while the people were subservient to the obligations of the state. Under this system, police considered themselves above the law, and people generally conformed to this arrangement because they tended to defer to authority.

During the Soviet era, three kinds of police systems were established: state security, militia, and ancillary forces. To a large extent, the government of the Russian Federation has had a difficult time reconciling or adapting these police systems to the democratization movement. In particular, basic issues of organization and policy have been in a state of flux. What follows is a description of the organization and administration of the three kinds of police systems established during the period of the Soviet Union, and how each system has attempted to adapt since the establishment of the Russian Federation (see Figure 5.1).

Figure 5.1

ORGANIZATION OF THE POLICE OF THE RUSSIAN FEDERATION

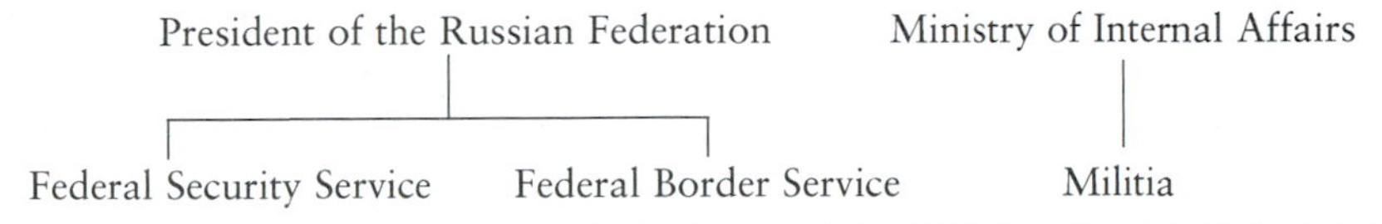

Organization and Administration of State Security

The history of the Soviet police began almost immediately after the October Revolution of 1917, when the principal law enforcement organizations were established. The method of organization goes a long way toward explaining the administrative history of these forces. In December 1917, the Council of People's Commissars created the Extraordinary Commission for Combating Counter-Revolution and Sabotage (known by the Russian acronym Cheka). It was the new government's first state security force and, as the name suggests, it was charged with eliminating all acts of counter-revolution and sabotage. The Cheka quickly acquired the power to impose summary executions on opponents of the regime. For example, it is estimated that the Cheka executed 50,000 people during the Civil War. Thus, the Cheka became the investigative arm as well as the executioner of the Party and revolutionary government.

This kind of police force was not new to Russia. As early as 1565, Tsar Ivan (the Terrible) had established the Oprichnina, a political police force known for its reign of terror. Subsequent Russian tsars adopted similar forces. It is generally assumed, however, that the Cheka was more effective than its predecessors. This is partly attributable to the use of Cheka agents posted throughout the country and the utilization of other local law enforcement personnel to assist in achieving the Cheka's objectives.

The evolution of the state security force has been marked by changes in both the organization's accountability to a higher government authority and the significant role it played in the development of Soviet society. The Cheka allegedly was created because of the extraordinary conditions that existed at the time, such as the founding of a revolutionary government and the fact that the country was in a state of civil war. The Cheka was disbanded in February 1922 because of the infamous reputation it had acquired and because the times no longer warranted such an institution. Undoubtedly, some of the party faithful sincerely wanted the organization abolished, but in reality, a state security police continued to exist. The agency was renamed periodically as the central government was reorganized. The last time this happened was in 1954, when the Committee for State Security (KGB) was created and made accountable to the Council of Ministers of the USSR.

Thus, from the early development of the Soviet state, the government saw the need to create a security force that was distinct from a regular law enforcement corps. In terms of organization and responsibility, the state security force and the regular force were generally kept separate. On occasion, however, they were merged under one government unit. Two explanations have been offered for this change. One has focused on the pretext that party leaders were attempting to curb the often unwieldy power of the state security force. It was thought that amalgamation would achieve that end, but it seldom lasted for long. There was always an extraordinary event—either internal or external—to justify the party leadership's desire to strengthen the state security unit. After all, since its inception, the state security force viewed itself as the "Sword and Shield of the Party." The other explanation suggested that the mergers occurred when the party needed a mechanism that would instill greater fear into the lives of the average citizen. It was felt that the state security force would be in a better position to achieve that end if it was administratively merged with the regular forces.

The KGB remained the state security force until the demise of the USSR. It was a centralized force whose geographical jurisdiction stretched across the USSR and beyond. Its central office was located in the Lubyanka building in Moscow at No. 2 Dzerzhinsky Square. The Lubyanka building had been the headquarters of the Cheka; Felix Dzerzhinsky was that organization's founder.

For Americans to comprehend the power and authority of the KGB, they would have to envision a merger of the FBI, the CIA, the National Security Agency, and the Secret Service, and then grant that consolidated agency the authority to implement on a regular basis policies and programs that are above the law. This authority had been afforded the KGB. One should not get the impression that the KGB was beyond control though, for the party leadership was careful to monitor the actions of the organization. The leadership remembered Lavrenti Beria's attempt to make the unit a force unto itself. Moreover, the leaders of the KGB were loyal party members who remembered that Beria was arrested and executed for attempting to implement his scheme.

Despite the party's diligence in monitoring the actions of the KGB, its ability to accomplish that goal was hampered somewhat during the 1960s, 1970s, and 1980s. In the past, particularly during Stalin's time, state security agents were essentially characterized as thugs. During these three decades, however, the people recruited to perform this work were highly educated and sophisticated individuals. They had been trained in the business of developing new methods to avoid detection. As a result, it would be folly for the party leadership to assume that they were kept apprised of all the activities of the KGB, especially those activities directed at them.

In order to understand how the KGB was organized, one must first appreciate its mission. The organization's basic purpose was to maintain and extend the power of the Communist Party throughout the world. Among the principal means used to achieve that end was the carrying out of espionage, subversion, and terrorist acts in capitalist and third-world countries. It also attempted to control the communist parties and governments in the various satellite countries that existed along the borders of the Soviet Union. This was achieved by infiltrating the party and influencing its policies.

The KGB was also actively involved in the surveillance of its own people in an attempt to isolate and check the growth of anticommunist feelings among them. It was assisted in this endeavor by an extensive network of informers strategically situated in all walks of life. A subtle pall of terrorism hung over every Soviet citizen, because most had a relative or friend (or knew someone) who had been exiled or liquidated for anti-Soviet behavior in the past. For the estimated 10,000 politically active dissidents, the pall was not subtle. Rather, the fear was a constant in their lives. Gorbachev attempted to alleviate this fear when he expressed the desire to permit the establishment of a multiparty political system. This view was given legal force with the passage of the Law on Public Association (1990), which declared free association to be an inalienable human and civil right.

According to experts, the KGB was organized into several directorates (Barron, 1974, 1985; Corson and Crowley, 1986; Hingley, 1970; Levytsky, 1970; Myagkov, 1976). The first chief directorate was responsible for monitoring espionage and subversion outside the Soviet Union. It trained and planted KGB agents in foreign countries; it obtained sensitive information, often of a defensive nature, from Western countries; and it recruited foreigners into the KGB service.

Of more interest to the student of foreign criminal justice systems was the second chief directorate. It was divided into a number of departments, of which several were designed to monitor and control the lives of the Soviet people. In many respects, this was the most important unit within the KGB. It investigated and attempted to curb the large network of black marketeers as well as the corruption and waste that existed in the government. It also protected the vast industrial complex and sensitive research centers of the country. Other departments within this unit specialized in spying on tourists, foreign students, and foreign journalists. It was not uncommon for the KGB to try to recruit foreign students and journalists as KGB agents.

While Nikita Khrushchev was in power, he attempted to offer the appearance that the party was willing to permit the expression of unorthodox views. As a result of this change in policy and the subsequent attempts at free artistic expression, the leaders concluded that it was getting out of hand: there appeared more open displays of dissent from within the country than had originally been anticipated. In 1969, the party hierarchy approved the creation of the fifth chief directorate. Its primary responsibility was to eliminate dissent. Within this directorate, various departments suppressed literary works, nationalism among the various ethnic groups, and the practice of religion. This directorate was abolished during the Gorbachev era, in part because of its excesses. Another reason was that its mission was at cross-purposes with glasnost and democratization. For example, the Law on Freedom of Conscience (1990) enabled the free expression of religious beliefs, and the Law on Public Association (1990) permitted the free association of individuals with various groups.

The purpose of the eighth chief directorate was to monitor and decipher foreign communications. This was accomplished through the use of spy satellites and communications equipment located in Soviet embassies around the world. This unit was also responsible for maintaining the security of the Soviet communications systems within the country.

The unnumbered Border Guards directorate dated back to 1918, when Lenin formed a border guard unit within the Cheka. Because it was composed of land, sea, and air troops who guarded the Soviet borders, it had both a law enforcement and a military function. It kept undesirables out of the country, while also preventing people from illegally leaving. When Sino-Soviet relations soured in the 1960s, the troops from this unit fought the Chinese along their common border. These troops were assisted in their work by support brigades composed of civilians living in towns and villages near the borders. The number of checkpoints along the Soviet borders had been increasing under Gorbachev, allegedly in an attempt to curtail the smuggling of contraband. Among the more significant concerns was the emergence of illegal narcotics.

Finally, a new directorate was created for the protection of the Soviet constitutional system. It had three specific tasks. One was to prevent foreign groups from engaging in anti-Soviet actions that were designed to overthrow the Soviet state. Another was to curtail terrorist attacks within the country. It had been alleged that more than 1,500 persons were identified as being involved in terrorist activities during the 1970s and 1980s. The directorate's third purpose was to address the problem of organized crime, which had been identified as a growing problem throughout the country.

Information about the KGB became more readily available to the public because of Gorbachev's efforts at glasnost and the attempted coup in August 1991. As a result, the people of the Soviet Union began to learn what many had suspected for a long time: the KGB had truly extensive authority and exceptional power throughout the country, and it was utilized not only against ordinary people but also against high-ranking Soviet officials. The KGB was in a strategic position to implement this activity because it had a monopoly over the government's communications system, which facilitated their efforts at surveillance and enhanced the likelihood of assuring total secrecy. They were also charged with protecting the president and the borders of the USSR.

In an attempt to deflect criticism during the autumn of 1991, KGB officials argued that the state security force should only be responsible for intelligence, counterintelligence, and, possibly, a few crimes, and the militia should be the principal law enforcement system dealing with crimes against individuals and property. The willingness to placate the rise of public opinion against the KGB came too late, though. In October 1991, the KGB was replaced with three separate organizations: a central intelligence service, an inter-republic counterintelligence service, and a state border service. It was assumed that the central intelligence service would be responsible for information dealing with foreign, military, and economic issues. The inter-republic counterintelligence service would handle domestic intelligence. The state border service would continue to guard the borders but would be established as an agency independent from the other intelligence-gathering services. At the time of the dissolution of the KGB, it was also suggested that a definition be provided to explain what constitutes state security in light of the fact that no law existed on the subject in the new political context.

The collapse of the Soviet Union in December 1991 caused the creation of the Russian Federation. Presently, attempts are being made to adapt a Soviet-styled state security service within the context of a Russian commitment to democratization. The principal concerns influencing the debate have centered on basic issues of policy and organization.

One of the key policy issues is the extent of the authority that should be granted to the new state security service. Specifically, there is concern that the security service has attempted to reclaim its former absolute power. To illustrate, requests have been made since 1992 to permit eavesdropping on telephone conversations, opening correspondence, and performing secret searches without a warrant. In addition, it has been suggested that public and private organizations should be required to permit the installation of bugging devices and the hiring of agents as employees. Critics of these requests point out that this is an attempt to establish a police state once again, but this time it would have a legal basis. An important organizational issue has focused on whether the border guards should be a separate entity or a subordinate unit within the security service.

At the beginning of 1994, a new state security service was created: the Federal Counterintelligence Service (FCS). Although the head of the FCS is a director, the service is actually administered by a committee of 11 people. The president of the Federation appoints the director and exercises control over the activity of the FCS. Unlike most governmental agencies that usually report to a ministry, the service reports directly to the president.

The principal duties of the FCS are to prevent intelligence-gathering and subversive activities by foreign special services, to combat terrorism and trafficking in arms and drugs, to detect the more dangerous armed groups in the country, and to provide the president with information on threats to the security of the Russian Federation. It was also decreed that the border troops would be a separate service. Moreover, the FCS was deprived of several responsibilities that were usually associated with the Soviet security service. For example, investigative duties were assigned to procurators and the Lefortovo prison was placed under the authority of the Ministry of Internal Affairs.

This arrangement of the Federal Counterintelligence Service did not last long, for the government had been arguing for a number of years that there was an enhanced need to combat dangerous crime. To address these concerns, changes were introduced at the end of 1994 and the beginning of 1995 that had an impact on both the operational policy and the organization of the state security service. First, the Federal Counterintelligence Service (FCS) had its name changed to the Federal Security Service (FSS). The principal duties of the FSS are: counterintelligence, intelligence, and combating corruption and organized crime. These duties reflect how the FSS is organized. Among the principal directorates of the FSS, the Investigation Directorate is responsible for the illegal trafficking in weapons, drugs, organized crime, and corruption. The Directorate for Economic Counterintelligence is responsible for combating attempts at undermining Russia's new but weak economic system and the fragile infrastructure that was introduced and designed to facilitate the move from a socialist economy to a market economy. The Military Counterintelligence Directorate is concerned with the protection of Russian military and state secrets. Finally, Directorate T is responsible for counter-terrorism. Some of their efforts are directed at organized crime.

Under the reorganization plans that led to the establishment of the FSS, the authority of the Russian state security service was expanded. Critics of this plan argued that the security service was taking on many of the attributes of the KGB. Of considerable concern was the fact that various investigative functions had been returned to the FSS. In addition, Lefortovo prison is utilized as a pretrial detention center for the FSS. Finally, the FSS is no longer subject to the oversight of the Procurator's Office.

To illustrate the nature of the critics concerns, agents of the FSS can enter and search a premise without a warrant if they are of the opinion a crime is in progress or a citizen might be at risk. They are expected to notify the procurator of these activities within 24 hours. FSS agents are also permitted to open mail, tap telephones, and monitor other forms of communication without a court order if they are of the opinion that this is an emergency or the country's security is threatened. Security issues are not limited to military or political concerns, but also include economic and environmental matters. While a judge must be notified of these activities within 24 hours, concerns have been raised that the law does not adequately explain or define the terms emergency or security.

Since the demise of the Soviet Union, the Border Guards, originally a part of the KGB, have retained an independent status. At one point in 1992, plans were under way to restore the Border Guards to a subordinate position with the state security service, but they have been able to retain their independence as the Federal Border Service (FBS). The FBS has been accorded the rank of a ministry, and it upholds the commitment of protecting state borders that now link the Russian Federation with a number of states. It has also devoted a good deal of attention to the illegal drug trade.

Organization and Administration of the Militia

The militia was the other police force established during the early years of the developing Soviet state. It was created on November 10, 1917, and was mandated as the principal force for securing law and order for the new socialist government. The militia was empowered to perform the more traditional tasks of police work (that is, law enforcement and order maintenance in the usual sense in which those words are used). It was responsible to the People's Commissariat of Internal Affairs (NKVD). Although the militia performed traditional police tasks, its authority extended beyond those parameters as understood in the West. For example, because the state had a monopoly over the means of production, there was an acute need for economic regulation and control. The militia played an influential role in that regard. The militia was designed as the principal regular police force in the Soviet Union, whereas the Cheka was styled as the first state security force. Compared to the state security force, the history of the militia was fairly uneventful.

From its inception, the militia had always been accountable to a government unit or ministry. When the Soviet Union ceased to exist, the Ministry of Internal Affairs (MVD) was responsible for the administration of the militia. The chair of the MVD was a member of the Council of Ministers of the USSR. For more than two decades before the demise of the country, the Soviets had a serious crime problem, similar to that found in capitalist countries. A more candid attitude toward these concerns had emerged and resulted in an attempt to strengthen and improve the quality of the militia. In fact, it was suggested that the MVD had become a very powerful ministry in light of its broad range of law enforcement responsibilities (Juviler, 1976). Moreover, some experts were of the opinion that a significant agency rivalry had developed between the MVD and the KGB.

The militia supposedly followed the principle of democratic centralism from its inception. This means it had a dual accountability: one to the Ministry of Internal Affairs for the USSR and one to the local soviet district in which the militia carried out its responsibilities. The militia, therefore, was both centrally and locally supervised in accordance with Soviet law. The unity of this dual accountability was achieved by having divisional inspectors of the militia appointed to executive committees of the local soviets. During the waning years of the Soviet Union, the executive committees of the local soviets increased their efforts at overseeing both the effectiveness and efficiency of the local militia. Of particular concern were issues involving public order, crime prevention, traffic safety, and the reduction of the number of instances in which people were avoiding socially useful work (Gabrichidze, 1986–87).

The individual militia units found throughout the Soviet Union were each divided into four major departments. The size of the territory policed determined the size of the unit and the strength of each department. Both uniformed and plainclothes officers were assigned to these departments. While each department had a general responsibility for crime prevention, each was assigned a specific task in order to achieve that goal.

One of the most important departments was criminal investigation. This department investigated crimes that had been committed and those that were suspected of being planned. Within the department was a child welfare office responsible for juvenile offenders and neglected young people, which worked in conjunction with the local soviet community councils on juvenile crime prevention. Members of a criminal investigation department were given an additional responsibility that in other countries is normally assigned to probation and parole officers: they attempted to find employment for inmates who had been released from prison.

The department for combating the misappropriation of socialist property was involved with economic and technical crimes. It was concerned with theft, bribery, and speculation in trade and industrial production. Department employees were not only concerned with detecting such crime, they also advised the managers of industrial complexes on ways to prevent such criminal activity. Members of this department watched for people who were living beyond their means. This was relatively easy to discover, because the militia or the KGB were likely to either have someone in the personnel department of the organization or have legal access to the person's employment and salary record. Moreover, the department was assisted in its work by the Voluntary

People's Guard. This organization aided the militia by monitoring the activities of fellow workers or residents in housing complexes.

The passport department was another important component of the militia. The Soviet Union had an internal passport system designed to monitor the movements of its citizens. All citizens who had reached the age of 16 had an internal passport. The document contained the individual's name, birth date, place of birth, nationality, marital status, number of children (if any), military service record, place of work, recent photograph, and any other pertinent information. The passport also included the propiska, a stamp indicating the specific location where the person had a legal right to reside.

These passports restricted the movement of people by indicating where a person was supposed to be residing and where he or she was employed. The passport system enabled the government to control where people lived and worked; it also served as a useful tool for police seeking leads about the lifestyle of a person suspected of anti-Soviet behavior. If a person was stopped far from his or her official place of residence without a pass, he or she became a suspect. The passport system also was used to determine whether a person was employed or was avoiding "useful work" (useful work was a constitutional duty of all Soviet citizens).

The state automobile inspection and traffic control department was another significant division within the militia. Involved in the prevention of traffic accidents through public education programs, this department was particularly concerned about reckless drivers—especially drunk drivers. Excessive alcohol consumption was considered a significant national problem and that point was brought home frequently by the number of alcohol-related traffic offenses. The department also was involved (in conjunction with the producers of automobiles) with improving the quality of motor vehicles (Karpets, 1977).

During the Gorbachev era, the Ministry of Internal Affairs announced several initiatives designed to improve either the efficiency or effectiveness of the police in general and the militia in particular. It suggested that there was a need for laws governing the rights and duties of the police. In addition, efforts were under way to improve operational equipment, particularly in the area of criminal investigation. Finally, there were discussions regarding organizational changes. It was suggested that the local militia be accountable solely to the Ministry of Internal Affairs for their republic. These local forces would be responsible for the more typical duties of law enforcement and order maintenance. A centralized national unit would remain and be responsible for major investigations; it would retain its dual subordination to the local and national government. A third unit would consist of regional task forces designed to address concerns such as organized crime, illegal drugs, and terrorism.

With the dissolution of the USSR, each of the former republics retained a militia force. In the Russian Federation, efforts have been directed at improving the effectiveness of the force, with particular attention to combating street crime. Several strategies have been employed to achieve this goal. First, the militia has recruited and trained more officers. Second, because the quota of conscripts to the army has been reduced, young men can serve their compulsory duty by assisting the militia. Third, officers have been shifted from units that had a more-than-adequate staff, such as the motor vehicle inspectorate. Finally, the militia has been relieved of some order maintenance duties. For example, referring alcoholics to treatment has been assigned to the Ministry of Public Health, although the militia continues to remove them from the streets. The Ministry of Social Protection has assumed responsibility for placement centers for children. The militia also has been relieved of the duty to help people who have been released from prison find employment and housing. Finally, the duty to install and operate traffic signals has been assigned to local administrations.

During the waning years of the Gorbachev era and since the dissolution of the Soviet Union, the militia has been the subject of reform efforts. In 1991, legislation, "On the Militia," was passed that was designed to make the mission of the organization more transparent to the public. In 1996, a strategy was developed to reform the militia as it grappled with increased levels of crime and attempted to participate in the development of a democratic state and embrace the principles of the rule of law. Unfortunately, the militia has been one of the major disappointments at achieving reform, and some of the failure is not of its own making. There is a large-scale turnover within the militia among those who have the education, training, or skills to move into the more lucrative private sector. This is largely the result of poor working conditions, shortages of equipment, low pay, and limited career prospects of advancement.

While efforts have been made to introduce ideas about democratic policing and human rights concepts, they have not been very effective at this initial stage. These problems should not come as a significant surprise to those familiar with the difficulty of attempting to change the culture of an organization. This is especially the case in this context when the goal is to move an organization from a highly authoritarian approach to one that is based on democratic and rule-of-law principles. The militia have been accused of human rights abuses. A number of officers have not accepted the rule-of-law principles. Petty bribes and large-scale corruption have been identified as serious problems confronting the militia. Obviously, low pay and an indifference to the rule of law contribute to these problems. Unfortunately, this situation leads to a lack of trust from the public (see Beck and Robertson, in Pridemore, 2005).

Organization and Administration of Ancillary Forces

Soviet citizens were encouraged to mind other people's business; one overt expression of this attitude was the extent to which the Soviet Union had implemented a series of ancillary police forces. They represented a third type of law enforcement system. As was spelled out in their Constitution, the Soviets had a penchant for stressing that citizen duties included: protecting socialist property from theft and waste, defending the country, and promoting social order. The ancillary forces illustrated how these duties were translated into action, and they made a significant impact on law enforcement in the Soviet Union.

Volunteer guards were organized by workers, collective farmers, students, pensioners, and other groups. They were directed by the local soviet executive committee. Membership was limited to people who were at least 18 years old and who had been accepted by the guards. Ideally, the scheme was supposed to attract those people who were already model Soviet citizens. The volunteers were expected to perform their work within the limits of socialist law.

A statute updating the duties of the Voluntary People's Guard was approved in 1974. These duties included "protecting public order, reporting or delivering alleged violators to the authorities, and assisting agents of the justice system." The rural executives exemplified another type of ancillary force that has operated in villages since 1924. They consisted of people appointed by the local soviets who assisted the local militia in crime prevention, transporting people under arrest, guarding government property, and supervising health and fire safety. Housing administrators also assisted the militia, as they were the caretakers and watchers of government housing projects. One of their principal tasks was to maintain a register of all residents, which was turned over to the militia.

Finally, Soviet youth groups often provided the militia with auxiliary forces. This was primarily limited to the Komsomol (Young Communist League). Members of this group, ranging in age from 15 to 27, aspired to membership in the CPSU. Membership in Komsomol was limited to people who had been sponsored by other Komsomol members or members of the Communist Party. There were, however, two additional youth groups that accepted virtually all children. The Youth Octobrists accepted seven to 10 year olds, while the Pioneers was a group designed for children ranging in age from 10 to 15. All of these groups emphasized party doctrine and the importance of collective responsibility to the socialist society. In addition to this extensive auxiliary system, the KGB and the militia—like police throughout the world—relied upon an extensive network of informers who may or may not have been associated with one of these ancillary groups. Most of these ancillary groups ceased to exist with the collapse of the Soviet Union. Even before 1991, young people's interest in joining the various youth groups was declining.

One area in which police volunteers may emerge without ties to a political party is in the large municipal areas of the Russian Federation. To illustrate, Moscow has established a new law enforcement organization called Volunteer Police Aides. This group is organized on a volunteer basis by people who live in the city, have reached the age of 18, and do not have a criminal record. Although these police aides will be under the authority of the mayor of Moscow, the goal is to have them work in close contact with law enforcement agencies. According to the municipal resolution that created the volunteer police aides, these aides are supposed to assist police in combating crime, help keep order on the city streets, offer crime prevention seminars for citizens, and perform some of the functions that formerly were the responsibility of the militia. While they do not have the power to search, seize, or arrest, they do have the right to check documents, write up reports, and send lawbreakers to the appropriate agencies.

Legal Status

It has already been pointed out that the Soviet state placed the rule of law in a subordinate position to politics, which was determined by the Communist Party. The Party was ultimately responsible for establishing the policy and directives for the various law enforcement systems. Each force, in its own way, was concerned with assuring obedience to the collective social rights and obligations of the citizenry. The extrajudicial powers afforded the police, particularly the state security force, enabled them to perform their responsibilities and claim that it was being accomplished within the context of the Constitution of the USSR and the laws of the Soviet state.

The Soviets permitted violations of a person's civil rights—something that is generally viewed as unacceptable in the West—if it would achieve obedience to the collective social rights and obligations. Until the waning years of its existence, this was not perceived as a significant issue inside the Soviet Union. One reason was that people respected and showed deference to power and authority. In addition, throughout their history, the Soviet people had been conditioned to expect the police to serve as the guardians of communist orthodoxy. When a person's rights were violated, it was supposedly done with the intent of furthering the socialist cause—the preeminent goal to which all citizens were expected to subscribe (at least nominally). Thus, whatever process could further the Marxist-Leninist ideology was ultimately deemed politically and legally acceptable.

The legal status of the police, at least in theory, has changed dramatically in the Russian Federation. The democratization movement has drawn attention to the importance of government by rule of law. The leadership of the Russian Federation is attempting to establish the legal foundations for a democratic system of government. The Constitution of the Russian Federation, which was adopted in 1993, is an illustration of that effort. What remains to be seen over time is the application of the theory in practice so that the police are conditioned to carry out their law enforcement and order maintenance duties within the law.

The Police and the Public

The militia remains the principal regular police force responsible for daily law enforcement and order maintenance tasks. During the Soviet era, it suffered from a serious degree of inefficiency. Some of the reasons are familiar to people in the West. For example, part of the inefficiency was the result of having multiple law enforcement agencies that had overlapping or shared jurisdictions that were often hampered by bureaucratic infighting and a failure to coordinate information. Budgetary allocations favored the KGB over the militia, which prevented the militia from having a reasonable assurance that equipment such as automobiles and radios would work. It also kept them from having access to basic technology, such as computers. This lack of access hindered the militia in implementing modern proactive and reactive policing strategies.

In many cases, members of the militia had attempted originally to join the KGB. The militia was then their second choice, in the hope that they might still be able to improve their standard of living. In a country in which citizens were constantly confronted with shortages in basic necessities, the situation had a profound impact on the choices people made. Few recruits were guided by the idealistic desire to improve the socialist system or possibly even an interest in police work.

In light of the economic crisis that continues to confront Russia, budgetary problems persist for the militia and have had an adverse impact on its effectiveness as the principal law enforcement agency for the country. Their equipment is often old (weapons and transport), in short supply (ammunition and transport), or nonexistent (handcuffs and flak jackets). They are no longer provided with special subsidized housing. Their wages are low and often not paid in a timely manner. Obviously, this situation has had an adverse impact on the morale of the officers and is not conducive to attracting the kind of new recruit that the militia seeks as it attempts to change its image.

Under the Soviet system, police considered themselves above the law. People generally conformed to this arrangement because they had long paid deference to authority. With the advent of the Russian Federation, the people became vested with legal rights and the police became obliged to protect the people in the exercise of those rights. While this change in basic principles of governance should have a considerable impact over time on the relationships between the police and the public, one cannot expect it to happen immediately. For example, the significant increase in crime has caused officials to approve search and seizure strategies for law enforcement that infringe on some of these new legal rights. Segments of the population appear to support this strategy. As one Moscow shopkeeper put it, "the state used to protect us from harm, but it also kept us under control. Now, we have the freedom to be insecure" (Handelman, 1995). Some people have become weary of this kind of insecurity, especially in light of all the other kinds of uncertainties that people must confront on a daily basis.

In view of these facts, the relations between the police and the public are presented in the context of three issues: (1) recruitment and training, (2) crime prevention, and (3) the public perception of the police. Much of this information relates to the militia rather than to the Federal Security Service, because information is more readily available on the former. In addition, it should be pointed out that several of the crime prevention efforts were initiated during the Soviet regime and were considered worthy of continuation under the new political arrangement.

Recruitment and Training Bureaucratic infighting and the lack of technological sophistication contributed to low morale in the militia. This was compounded by inefficiency in the recruitment and training process. By the late 1980s and throughout the 1990s, opportunities within the militia were not improving as they were in other ventures. As such, officers began to leave the service. This could not have happened at a more inopportune time, as crime in general and organized crime in particular had begun to flourish.

The Russian Federation's Ministry of Internal Affairs has attempted to address some of these concerns, particularly in the area of recruitment and training. The militia recruits people between 18 and 35 years of age who have completed a high school education and are physically fit. In the past, a significant proportion of recruits came from rural areas in the hope of securing a stable job and an improved standard of living. This will no doubt continue in the immediate future, especially with the elimination of the internal passport system. The recruit is also expected to have completed compulsory military service, although some are permitted to have their service in the militia count as their compulsory service. Background checks on a recruit's character and criminal history are mandatory, as is a psychological test.

Under the new structure, Russians are experiencing a new freedom of movement. Today, a recruit can apply anywhere in the country for a position with the militia. There is an expectation that in time there will be a good deal of flexibility in transferring to another part of the country. In addition, the militia are beginning to recruit some female officers for patrol, although most of them are assigned to work in an office or to specialize in working with juveniles.

The profile of a militia officer emphasizes three characteristics: to be versed in law, to be skilled at patrol work, and to possess the qualities of a "military man" (Morn and Sergevnin, 1994). These characteristics have implications for the recruitment and training of militia officers. In the past, an emphasis was placed on military traits, whereas today attempts are made to balance the attributes of each characteristic.

The Ministry of Internal Affairs has established more than 60 regional training centers that train militia recruits and persons planning a career as a correctional officer. Basic training for the militia recruit is usually four to six months. This is followed by another four-month probationary period that combines training and working at a police department. Basic training attempts to combine a mix of theory, technology, and practical education. This includes an elementary introduction to the study of ethics, history, Russian society, administrative law, criminal law, criminal procedure, criminology, and forensic medicine. In addition, a somewhat more concentrated effort at training is devoted to first aid, arrest procedures, self-defense, police driving, firearms, and physical training. Once basic training is completed, the recruit spends six months working on the streets under the guidance of a field training officer.

Militia officers who aspire to a rank above that of first lieutenant must continue their training at one of the 17 militia colleges. This is a two-year program that includes four areas of study. The social studies component includes courses on philosophy, history, economics, politics, social science, and basic law. The law component deals with such topics as administrative law, financial law, family law, criminal investigation, criminal procedure, correctional labor law, corrective labor psychology, court psychology, forensic science, and medicine. The skills component of the training focuses on police driving, criminal investigative photography, forensic science, self-defense, and firearms. A final component deals with military training. This explains why some recruits are able to fulfill their compulsory military obligation by entering the militia. This two-year program also provides students with some basic practical training by having them spend time at local militia offices. The successful graduate of the militia college begins a career as a second lieutenant.

There are also 17 militia universities. The militia university is a four-year program that is similar to the militia college, but has a greater emphasis on theory. The successful graduate of the university also begins a career as a second lieutenant but can be considered for promotion to the rank of colonel because of this university training.

Finally, those officers who aspire to the highest ranks within the militia must gain entrance to the Academy of the Ministry of Internal Affairs.

A candidate must be recommended to the Academy. This usually occurs if the person has been recommended to a high-level administrative post within the militia or if the person is completing a doctorate degree from a university and is likely to be hired by one of the militia colleges or universities. At the Academy, the emphasis is placed on the study of administration and management. The successful graduate is eligible for promotion within the militia to the rank of general.

While Russia has established an extensive training program for officers who aspire to various levels of promotion within the militia, a good deal of criticism has been directed at this scheme. For example, some of the training appears to be redundant, and it has been suggested that this could be reduced by abolishing the militia colleges. Another concern is that more attention should be devoted to ethical and legal topics in light of the country's move from a police state to one that is in the process of democratization. Finally, it has been suggested that the vast social and economic changes in the Russian Federation should lead to an overall evaluation of the relevance of the various training programs (Morn and Sergevnin, 1994).

Crime Prevention Until 1989, the Soviet media did not publish crime statistics because the government did not divulge them. One reason frequently given for the absence of such information was the belief that by publishing such statistics the CPSU would be perceived as having failed in its efforts to create a socialist society. After all, Soviet citizens had been led to believe that crime was a product of the capitalist economic system. It follows from this line of thinking that money would not be forthcoming to support criminal justice in general and crime prevention techniques in particular because crime would diminish naturally as socialism reached its mature form. Even if the government had been willing to release the information, it probably would have been inaccurate. The size of the country, the poor communications network, and the unwillingness of local officials to admit the existence of a high level of criminality were cited as distorting factors (Zeldes, 1981).

Although local officials remained reluctant to discuss the level of crime with citizens of a particular community, senior government officials began to express their frank concerns to the nation as a whole. During his brief tenure as general secretary, Yuri Andropov initiated extensive investigations into corruption on the part of government officials. Gorbachev's policies of glasnost and perestroika further heightened both the identification of instances of corruption in government and the public's awareness of the role of law enforcement in combating it. The process of investigating inefficiency in government and industry uncovered cases of white-collar crime. Moreover, Soviet law enforcement personnel, which had long been suspected of corruption, had their image tarnished by the number of officers dismissed on corruption charges. For example, 161,000 officers under the jurisdiction of the Ministry of Internal Affairs were dismissed between 1983 and 1985 (Dobek and Laird, 1990). The number of dismissed officers continued to rise. One expert on the Soviet Union suggested that approximately 15 percent of the militia had been dismissed as a result of this anti-corruption campaign (Shelley, 1990b).

Gorbachev's policies led to the publication of Soviet crime statistics for the first time. Data from the period between 1985 and 1989 illustrate why government officials were concerned about the level of crime throughout the Soviet Union. During that period, the number of registered crimes increased by 18 percent (from 2,083,501 to 2,461,692). Specifically, murders and attempted murders increased by 15 percent, serious bodily injury by 34 percent, robbery by 82 percent, and crimes committed by gangs by 20 percent. In 1991, the last year that the Soviet Union existed, the number of registered crimes was 3,102,748, which represented an 11 percent increase over the previous year (Serio, 1992).

After Gorbachev assumed the position of general secretary, he attempted to address the problem of alcohol abuse, a major contributor to a number of social ills, including crime. For several years, the government had undertaken campaigns to curb alcohol consumption, but Gorbachev enhanced the campaign. Alcohol was considered a key factor in the poor productivity of Soviet industries, it was a major cause of traffic accidents, and it was cited as the principal cause of hooliganism. "Hooliganism" was a term used to describe a number of offenses, such as disorderly conduct, vandalism, and minor assaults.

The minister of internal affairs for the Soviet Union also commented on the nature of the crime problem (Fedorchuk, 1985–86). Among the concerns cited were the ineffectiveness of attempts at reducing embezzlement and theft of state and public property. He pointed out that the level of juvenile crime was increasing. Such a trend, however, may be partly explained by improved efforts of law enforcement in concentrating on juvenile delinquency, which in turn caused an increase in recorded crimes committed by juveniles. The minister also addressed the perennial problem of alcohol abuse by noting that 43 percent of all crimes were linked to drunkenness. In some cases, such as those of hooliganism and vandalism, the percentage rose to between 70 and 80 percent. Moreover, two-thirds of all murders and serious assaults were related to alcohol abuse.

Authorities in the Russian Federation continued to report increases in the level of criminal activity. For example, there was an 18 percent increase in the amount of crime recorded from 1990 through 1991. In that comparison, robberies rose by about 33 percent, while thefts grew by approximately 50 percent. The level of crime continued to be a very serious problem throughout 1992. For example, premeditated murders increased by 40 percent, and assaults and robberies rose by 60 percent over the 1991 figures.

Within the Russian Federation, illegal drug abuse is joining alcohol consumption as a serious problem. Black markets are flourishing in narcotics, tobacco products, and weapons. Counterfeiting is also widespread, and there is a growing concern over the theft and resale of cultural and art items. The degree of concern about crime has increased significantly among citizens. When asked in 1991 if the army and police should jointly patrol the streets of Moscow, 46.3 percent of the respondents said yes. One year later, 53.3 percent of the respondents agreed with the idea. In an opinion poll conducted in 1993, people indicated that they wanted tougher legislation and measures against criminals. Moreover, in a series of surveys on crime in Russia, Izvestia reported that people were as worried about the level of crime as they were about inflation and the rise in prices of consumer goods.

In 1992, the government identified 4,000 organized crime groups, of which 1,000 had interregional or international connections. Recently, a good deal of attention has been directed at the issue of organized crime in Russia (Handelman, 1995; Oleinik, 2003; Smith, 1996; Wodel in Pridemore, 2005; Williams, 1997). It is interesting to note that an organized criminal underworld with codes of honor and rituals, not unlike that of the mafia, existed in Russia long before the Bolshevik Revolution in 1917. Throughout the Soviet era, organized crime was an important force in the black market economy, and the leaders of these criminal enterprises frequently directed their operations from prison. Government bureaucrats, including those associated with criminal justice agencies, were aware of this relationship and allowed it to flourish. In some cases, particularly during those years leading up to the demise of the Soviet Union, bureaucrats participated in black-market enterprises.

It has been suggested that with the collapse of communism and the dissolution of the Soviet Union, organized crime was poised to fill a void. For example, amidst the insecurity and disorder confronting Russia, organized crime has been able to impose order in some sectors of the society where government agencies have failed. In addition, while organized crime in the West is usually involved with the supply of illicit goods and services, that kind of association is sometimes blurred in Russia. In the context of Soviet law, organized crime was involved in a variety of business enterprises that were deemed illegal, such as extortion and creating a competitive open market within the economy. While extortion remains illegal, the techniques for developing a market economy are considered legal for the most part. At issue is the lack of clarity in law as to which practices are legal or illegal. Under these circumstances, both the legal and illegal prospects for organized crime are enhanced further. This situation impedes and frustrates the crime prevention efforts of law enforcement. It has been suggested that the ascendancy of organized crime and the pervasive impact it has had on social and economic conditions throughout the country has disturbed the public more than many of the other problems that they are confronting.

In a report issued in 1997, the Ministry of Internal Affairs offered its assessment of the crime problem in the country. One of the most significant issues confronting the government is the inability to collect revenues to which it is entitled. The number of companies that are not paying taxes has been a serious concern for some time, and these numbers continue to increase. This problem is facilitated to some extent by the serious problem of corruption at both the central and local levels of government. The ministry also points out that banks have been crippled by embezzlement, bribes, and various fraudulent practices, as have pension funds and the insurance industry. Another problem is the amount of counterfeit currency, both domestic and foreign, and various state securities that are in circulation. It has been suggested by some Russian scholars that the nature and degree to which some of these economic crimes have proliferated was due in part to the lack of experience among senior government officials in understanding how market economies function.

In light of the economic hardships confronting so many people, the ministry acknowledges that more people are involved in illegal activities. For example, 1,618,000 people were charged with a criminal offense in 1996; of these, 1.25 million were first-time offenders. The vast majority of offenders were guilty of theft, with residential burglaries the most common crime. This led to further expansion in the private security industry. The government is also concerned with the large quantities of firearms and explosive devices that are in circulation. Finally, public indifference to law and order is reflected in the level of alcohol and other drug abuse. The problem of alcohol consumption has been a long-standing problem in Russia and was mentioned earlier. The ministry presently estimates that more than 36 percent of the people charged with a crime were under the influence of alcohol, while 15 percent were under the influence of another type of drug or toxic substance (see Gavrilova et al. and Paoli, in Pridemore, 2005). The consumption of narcotics by injection has led to a serious public health problem in Russia. The World Health Organization estimates that three out of every four Russians infected with HIV/AIDS is a narcotic addict between 17 and 30 years of age (see Butler, in Pridemore, 2005).

Public Perceptions of Police Like crime statistics, accurate information about the extent to which Soviet citizens had official contact with police also has been lacking. It was suggested that the average citizen did not have much personal contact (if any) with the KGB, because most citizens were not involved in the overthrow of their government. People in the West were sometimes given a distorted view of the extent to which the KGB intruded on people's lives. A political dissident had some justifiable fears, but most Soviet citizens were nonpolitical. The KGB, however, did maintain a vigilant watch over people through the dossiers they possessed on them.

KGB contact with the general public was minimal outside the confines of the job. KGB agents lived in separate apartment complexes and had privileges of shopping at special government stores. The manner in which KGB agents were afforded better living accommodations and other perquisites reflected just one aspect of the rank-conscious class structure evident in the Soviet Union. Citizens were more apt to have contact with members of the militia or the Voluntary People's Guard, for these were the forces that were principally responsible for daily law enforcement and order maintenance efforts.

Because the communist ideology had been the official doctrine of the state for most of the century, people reacted in different ways when it collapsed. Some felt a sense of loss, others felt relief, and yet others still felt a good deal of apathy toward politics. Irrespective of one's view of communism and the collapse of the Soviet Union, it was inevitable that many would be frustrated with their current circumstances. While the world learns through the media of the many incidents of instability at the national political level, there are countless circumstances of instability on an individualized personal level. One commentator has suggested that, above all, in Russia, there is a lack of the legal, ethical, and psychological bases necessary for the establishment of new market relations. Until a fundamental change occurs, the sense of loss and feelings of instability are likely to continue (see Ivanov, in Isham, 1995).

There is also widespread skepticism of the government's ability to deal with such issues as poverty, welfare, and crime. According to one commentator, the absence of a strong centralized authority, to which Russian citizens had long been accustomed, has created two differing perceptions. The absence of authority has expanded the amount of freedom experienced by citizens, though this is often falsely attributed to democracy. On the other hand, the level of violence that has been occurring in Russia can also be attributed to the absence of a strong centralized government (see Dragunskii, in Isham, 1995).

It has been suggested that a dislike of state authority, either because of what it once was or because of what it has become, impacts on how all state employees are perceived by the public. Presently, law enforcement officers have one of the lowest ratings among the public-sector agencies (see Filatov and Vorontsova, in Isham, 1995). It is generally assumed that part of the reason for this low rating is the rather ineffective record of police at controlling crime. In addition, growing cynicism on the part of law enforcement officers has led some to be corrupted by the very organized crime elements that they are expected to pursue.

Judiciary

When a state proclaims that it is subject to its own laws, it usually supports the validity of that proclamation by guaranteeing an impartial and independent judiciary. The Russian Federation is in the throes of transforming its judicial machinery so that it can assure its citizens that the state is, indeed, subject to its own laws. As is the case with so much of the Russian justice system, the judiciary is undergoing incremental reforms. In some instances, significant change has been introduced; in others, the proposed reforms remain largely on the drawing board. In those instances in which reform has been introduced, a word of caution is in order: the introduction of reform does not necessarily mean that it will be implemented in a timely manner—or, perhaps, at all.

Throughout the era of the Soviet Union, the basic principles associated with the administration of justice were the reverse of those found in a democratic society. Just as the Soviet police were subject to the dictates of the Communist Party, members of the judiciary were also expected to comply with the wishes of the party and the state. Thus, the notion of an impartial and independent judiciary was essentially absent.

It should be noted that during the Soviet era, the judicial structure retained many of the characteristics that were in place before the Bolshevik Revolution of 1917. These characteristics were similar to those found in the Romano-Germanic law countries on the continent of Europe. The reasons for these similarities were twofold. First, although Russia was characterized as a backward country until the twentieth century, there were enlightened tsars who occasionally attempted to modernize the state administrative apparatus. From at least the sixteenth century into the eighteenth century, a number of tsars borrowed legal principles and administrative mechanisms from the West. The French model was the one that was principally emulated. Thus, a Russian version of the Romano-Germanic legal system and its accompanying judicial mechanisms were in place before the 1917 Revolution.

Admittedly, the composition and purpose of the judiciary changed following the Revolution, but in a number of respects, its form was strikingly similar to what had evolved on the continent of western Europe. In some respects, this became even more pronounced after the end of World War II. As a result, some legal scholars questioned treating the socialist legal system as a separate legal family. They argued, not without justification, that socialist law was merely an aberration of the Romano-Germanic law family. Other legal scholars maintained that the Soviet legal system was a distinct family and should be treated as such. What made it distinct was not its form but rather the substance of the law and the purpose of its legal mechanisms.

The importance of substance versus form was first illustrated during the early days of the Revolution. The leaders of the revolutionary movement had not developed a precise plan to replace the existing judicial system. Most scholars attribute this to the fact that the revolutionaries were caught off guard by the success they achieved in Russia. It should be remembered that Marx had not envisioned the socialist revolution occurring in a country with such an underdeveloped economic base. He was convinced that the revolution would first occur in an established capitalist country.

Lenin, therefore, failed to address a basic issue that confronts most revolutionary leaders: that of not having devised a clear plan for replacing the status quo, in this case the existing governmental mechanisms of the tsar. Lenin was not without some guidance, though. Marx and Engels had explained the role that the legal system would play in a socialist society, and the leaders of the Revolution moved quickly to transform those views into action by establishing a new court system.

For example, the People's Commissars issued a decree in November 1917 that abolished all of the courts and legal institutions that had existed under the tsar and created the people's courts. One judge and two assessors would sit in a newly established people's court to hear both civil and criminal cases in which the accused could be sentenced to as much as two years of imprisonment. Both judges and assessors were to be elected by the people of the district they served. The decree also called for the abolition of government investigators, prosecutors, and private attorneys. The judge was to conduct the preliminary investigation until a new legal system was established with appropriate administrative mechanisms. Any citizen could serve as a prosecutor or counsel for the defense.

In December of the same year, the revolutionary tribunal was created. It was responsible for more serious criminal offenses and for crimes against the state. Opponents of the revolutionary government found themselves before this tribunal, which was composed of a chair and six assessors elected by the people. The tribunal had the power to establish investigating commissions that were composed of people elected by local soviets. Each commission was empowered to issue orders regarding searches, seizures, and arrests. Although any police force could carry out the wishes of an investigating commission, the Cheka served as the tribunal's principal investigative arm. Moreover, all citizens were eligible to serve as prosecutor or defense counsel before revolutionary tribunals.

Although piecemeal changes in the court system were introduced through decrees issued by the People's Commissars after 1917, the most significant changes occurred with the enactment of the Statute on the Judiciary of the RSFSR (Russian Socialist Federative Soviet Republic) in 1922. This legislation established a unified judicial system throughout the federation. A court hierarchy was created with people's courts, provincial courts, and the Supreme Court of the RSFSR. The Supreme Court was given the responsibility of supervising the other courts. With this legislation, the revolutionary tribunals were eliminated, and their authority was largely transferred to the provincial courts. There were two exceptions to this plan: separate military tribunals and military-transport tribunals were retained and were given the authority to hear crimes that threatened the military and transport systems, respectively.

Statutes also appeared in 1922 regulating the bar and the procurator's office, which had been decimated as a result of the events of 1917. During this period, new legal codes were enacted dealing with civil law, criminal law, and criminal procedure. With the passage of the 1924 Constitution of the USSR, much of the previously adopted legislation was elaborated further. Thus, by the mid-1920s, the new Soviet legality was created, with judicial institutions designed to assure the success of the new social order. Serious setbacks to the furtherance of the Soviet legal system were to occur during the period of Stalin's regime, especially during the purge trials of the 1930s. Since Stalin's death, the Soviet leadership and legal profession attempted to resurrect a socialist version of legality with legitimate mechanisms to administer the system. With the advent of Gorbachev's leadership, an even greater impetus was directed at reforming the legal system to achieve his vision of democratic socialism.

The Soviet Union had a four-tiered court hierarchy responsible for handling civil and criminal litigation. The courts were regulated by the 1977 Constitution of the USSR, the Code of Criminal Procedure, the Law on the Status of Judges in the USSR, and various statutes passed by the Supreme Soviet. The highest court in the Soviet Union was the Supreme Court of the USSR. The work of the court was performed in two ways. Four times a year, the court held plenary sessions. A plenum had a responsibility to consider: (1) protests of decisions from divisions within the USSR Supreme Court or union republic Supreme Courts, (2) interpretations of USSR law, and (3) disputes among the judicial agencies of the union republics. Thus, a plenum was concerned principally with an examination of judicial patterns that were emerging in the Soviet court system.

When the court was not addressing itself to issues at plenary sessions, its members were divided into three judicial divisions or collegia: (1) the collegium on civil cases, (2) the collegium on criminal cases, and (3) the military collegium. As a collegium, the court handled two kinds of matters. For exceptionally significant cases, it would occasionally serve as a court of first instance; under these circumstances, the court was composed of a judge from the court and two people's assessors. In addition, the court entertained judicial protests from the chair of the Supreme Court of the USSR, the procurator general of the USSR, or their deputies. These protests were limited to decisions handed down in the Supreme

Courts of the Union Republics that were considered contrary to all-union legislation or were in some way at odds with the interests of the particular union republic. In such cases, the bench consisted of three judges from the Supreme Court of the USSR.

As was indicated earlier, the Soviet Union was a federated country composed primarily of 15 union republics. Each republic had a Supreme Court that in many respects mirrored the organization of the Supreme Court of the USSR. The regional courts were the next tier in the hierarchy and consisted of courts of first instance and courts of appeal. As courts of first instance, they handled more complex civil cases and more serious criminal cases. As a court of first instance, a judge and two assessors would hear these cases. The appellate jurisdiction was limited to decisions, judgments, and rulings from the people's courts that had not as yet entered into legal force. People's courts were sometimes called district courts or city courts. These courts consisted of judges and assessors who were elected by a superior soviet of people's deputies. Judges were elected to a 10-year term and assessors to a five-year term; both were renewable. The vast majority of cases of first instance were handled by the people's courts.

Organization and Administration of the Courts

With the creation of the Russian Federation, the authorities have attempted to establish a new judicial system. For longer than a decade, significant attempts have been made to establish an independent judiciary that conforms to the rule of law and democratic principles. This is an important undertaking, because throughout the Soviet period most people did not trust the courts. Judges were viewed as an extension of the law enforcement community, who were concerned about maintaining the interests of the Soviet state rather than the administration of justice. The Russian Federation has a five-tiered court hierarchy responsible for handling civil and criminal litigation (see Figure 5.2). The courts are regulated primarily by the Constitution of the Russian Federation, the Code of Criminal Procedure, and the 1996 Federal Constitutional Law on the Judicial System of the Russian Federation.

Constitutional Court of the Russian Federation When a country is ruled by the dictates of a single political party that is considered above the law, as was the case with the Soviet Union, issues of constitutionality are irrelevant. The Constitution of the USSR authorized the procurator general to oversee the utilization of laws with the objective of assuring that they were executed properly and fairly. The Constitution, however, did not grant the procuracy the authority to rule on the constitutionality of laws and decrees.

Figure 5.2

ORGANIZATION OF THE COURTS OF THE RUSSIAN FEDERATION

Constitutional Court of the Russian Federation
|
Supreme Court of the Russian Federation
|
Regional Courts
|
District Courts
|
Justices of the Peace Courts

During Gorbachev's tenure, it was acknowledged that unconstitutional laws had been approved throughout the history of the Soviet Union. To rectify the problem, a Constitutional Supervision Committee was created to review draft legislation and to indicate whether it conformed to constitutional provisions. The need to have a mechanism in place for purposes of constitutional review was acknowledged early in the Russian Federation. As a result, the Constitution of the Russian Federation authorizes the Constitutional Court of the Russian Federation to be the supreme judicial body of constitutional oversight in Russia.

The Constitutional Court has several responsibilities. It handles cases concerning conformity with the constitution. These include federal laws and acts, laws and acts of members of the Federation, and domestic and international treaties. It resolves judicial disputes between two or more federal bodies, between a federal body and a member of the Federation, and between members of the Federation. Generally, these cases are entertained following a request from either the president, the Council of the Federation, the State Duma, one-fifth of the members from either chamber, the government of the Russian Federation, the Supreme Court of the Russian Federation, or other bodies of executive or legislative authority. The court also considers complaints from citizens if the issue involves an allegation that a person's constitutional rights and liberties were violated.

The court consists of 19 judges. Depending on the nature of an issue, the court may sit in plenary session. If the matter involves an interpretation of the Constitution, a majority decision requires two-thirds of all the judges on the court with no abstentions. When not in plenary session, the court is divided into two chambers in order to handled the other business brought before it. The judges are nominated by the president of the Russian Federation and appointed by the Council of the Federation for a 12-year term. Members of the court must be at least 40 years of age; they retire at 70.

Supreme Court of the Russian Federation According to the Russian Constitution, the Supreme Court of the Russian Federation has the ultimate judicial responsibility for civil, criminal, administrative, and other cases from general jurisdiction courts. At least once a month, the Presidium of the court will meet to decide, among other things, cases heard by way of supervision. Judicial supervision involves entertaining either an appeal or a protest against a judgment of an inferior court before the lower court's decision enters into legal force, or if it does have legal force, it is not being appealed by way of cassation.

Most of the work of the court is conducted in the three judicial divisions: civil, criminal, or military. For exceptionally significant cases, usually when important interests of state are at issue, the court may occasionally serve as a court of first instance. Under this circumstance, the court would consist of a judge and a jury, but on occasion, a panel of three judges might hear a case. Usually, the court handles appeals by way of cassation from regional courts. In these cases, the court consists of three judges. The judges of the Supreme Court are nominated by the president of the Federation and appointed by the Council of the Federation. Finally, the court is composed of 13 judges who can serve until the mandatory retirement age of sixty-five.

Attached to the Supreme Court is the Judicial Department, which is a federal agency responsible for the administration of the Russian court system. It assumed this responsibility in 1998 when a federal law removed court administration from the duties of the Ministry of Justice. This is a practical example of protecting the independence of the judiciary. The Judicial Department deals with all organizational issues that impact the court below that of the Supreme Court. It is responsible for the oversight of a number of personnel matters, such as the selection and training of judicial candidates, working with law institutes, and raising the qualifications of judges and other court personnel. It also maintains court records and issues statistical reports. Finally, the Judicial Department is responsible for the maintenance of court buildings and the purchase of supplies and equipment for the courts.

Regional Courts For our purposes, the courts at the regional level are referred to as regional courts, but one should be apprised of the fact that not all of these courts are officially referred to by this title. Some of these middle-tier courts are called courts of autonomous territories and supreme courts of autonomous republics. Such names explain the nature of the locality served. Moreover, some of the principal cities (such as Moscow and St. Petersburg) have city courts that enjoy the jurisdictional status of a regional court. These courts are divided into civil and criminal divisions. Regional courts include judges, who are nominated by the president of the Federation, and may include a jury depending on the nature of a case at trial.

Regional court jurisdiction includes original and appellate cases. As courts of first instance, regional courts handle the more complex civil cases and the more serious criminal cases that are not considered appropriate for the district courts. A judge and a jury or a panel of three judges hear these cases. The appellate jurisdiction is limited to decisions, judgments, and rulings from the district courts that have not as yet entered into legal force. A panel of three judges entertains such appeals.

District Courts District courts, which used to be referred to as people's courts until 1996, are primarily courts of first instance. With regard to criminal cases, they handle the more serious offenses in which a defendant could receive a term of imprisonment of more than three years. At a criminal trial, the court would include a single judge and a jury.

The district courts also hear appeals from justices of the peace courts. In this context, the appellate procedures are different from what one would expect of a court with appellate responsibilities. Once a case is appealed, a single district court judge retries the case. Thus, the matter is not returned to the justices of the peace court for a reconsideration of the matter.

Justices of the Peace Courts Justices of the peace courts were first introduced into Russia in 1864 but were abolished following the Russian Revolution in 1917. Throughout the 1990s, when there was a good deal of talk about judicial reform, it was suggested that justices of the peace courts be reintroduced in order to alleviate the backlog of cases in the district courts. This was also considered by some as another example of the introducing democratization to Russia. Justices of the peace courts were gradually introduced throughout Russia from 2001 to 2003. From an organizational perspective, these courts are unique in that administrative support is supplied partially by the regional government rather than solely from the federal government. The regional administrative support includes the recruitment and training of the justices, providing court staff, and maintaining court rooms. The federal government provides a budget to cover the salaries of the justices and many of the court personnel.

The jurisdiction of the courts includes three general areas of Russian law. Civil cases include simple divorce issues that do not involve disputes over property or children, some property cases, disputes over land, and some labor disputes. Criminal cases encompass those offenses in which the maximum punishment is less than three years imprisonment. Finally, certain federal administrative law cases have been assigned to these courts. For purposes of criminal justice, the most prominent issues include: petty hooliganism, public drunkenness, and serious traffic violations of a noncriminal nature.

When the court sits, it consists of one justice of the peace. Thus far, many of the criminal cases have involved personal accusations, consumer fraud, and hooliganism. One study has indicated that the personal accusation cases are often successfully mediated by the justice. Less than 3 percent of those found guilty are incarcerated. When a person appeals the decision of the justices of the peace court, the matter is retried in a district court. The aforementioned study found that only 1.5 percent of the verdicts were overturned, and only .8 percent of the sentences were altered on appeal (Solomon, 2003).

Legal Profession

As it pertains to the criminal justice system, the Russian legal profession is divided into three distinct groups: (1) judges, (2) procurators, and (3) defense attorneys. By and large, members of each group are professionally trained in the law. Although jurors serve an important purpose in the judicial process, they are distinct from the legal profession. Their role will be discussed separately.

Before the status of the three professional legal groups are presented in their Russian context, some general comments about the Soviet legal profession are in order. As of 1988, the number of practicing attorneys in the Soviet Union was approximately 25,000; this was small in relation to the population of the country and in contrast with other industrialized countries (Schroeder, 1990). The history of the legal profession since the 1917 Revolution provides an explanation for the status of lawyers in the Soviet context. It should be remembered that the official view of the Revolution was that law, and therefore the legal profession, would ultimately become superfluous in a socialist society. It was expected that they would wither away in time. This attitude was illustrated by the fact that early decrees stated that anyone could serve in a judicial capacity, irrespective of their legal training. Although some jurists who had been trained in law before the Revolution were utilized by the government, the tendency was to recruit people who had not been exposed to the prerevolutionary law school curriculum. Thus, people who were interested in studying law were discouraged from doing so because it was uncertain that such training would enhance their careers. Moreover, the traditional method of studying law came to an abrupt halt with the abolition of university law departments.

With the passage of the 1936 Constitution, the Soviet leaders reversed themselves by opting for a view of law different from that of their predecessors. Stalin, among others, saw law as serving a vital role in assuring the stability of socialist society. As a result, legal education became respectable; by the late 1950s, it had reached new heights in terms of the number of people enrolled in university law departments and legal institutes. An important characteristic of the Soviet legal profession was the fact that most members worked for the state. This was obviously the case among procurators and judges, but it was equally true among professional defense attorneys. They belonged to professional bar associations that were controlled by the Ministry of Justice.

Despite this kind of control, the legal profession was not without some political clout. Donald Barry and Harold Berman have indicated that the CPSU was influenced by public opinion. Professional organizations, such as the Soviet bar, were in a significant position to offer meaningful advice regarding party policy (1968). With the law elevated to a respectable status, a principal concern of the bar had been to enhance the status of the profession, especially through improvements in the educational system. Their goal was to improve their chances of influencing party policy.

It should be pointed out that the legal profession did not hold exclusive rights to representing people in courts. People not trained in law retained the right to participate in trials. Some experts suggested that the maintenance of this policy was an implicit example of the party leadership's belief that in time a professional class of lawyers would not be necessary, as their purpose would wither away with the state. Thus, though the Soviet bar was attempting to become a more influential voice in party policy, at least as it pertained to law and the legal profession, the party was keeping its options open by controlling the extent to which it would allow the bar to become a strong lobbyist for its causes.

With Gorbachev's efforts at democratization and perestroika, the legal profession improved its standing considerably. The introduction of economic change required the skills of lawyers. For example, changes in the law of property significantly increased the number of cases brought to court. With the introduction of new regulations governing cooperatives in 1988, legal cooperatives emerged that were not controlled by the Soviet bar (Schroeder, 1990).

Judges Gorbachev's attempts at redefining the communist ideology led to significant discussions about reforming the judiciary. The impetus for this reform was based on his view of democratic socialism. One of his goals was the establishment of a socialist style of checks and balances within government, and a specific feature of that goal was the creation of an independent judiciary. In order to appreciate what Gorbachev was attempting to achieve, it is important to consider the state of the judiciary (in terms of both the official position and actual perceptions of people) in the Soviet Union.

Judges were elected, they performed a collegial task, and they were independent and subject to the law. According to the Soviet Constitution, all judges were elected by specific groups. Moreover, all citizens who had attained the age of 25 were eligible for election as judge. A long-standing criticism from both within and outside the Soviet Union was directed at the lack of credentials held by many people's court judges. According to M. Cherif Bassiouni and V.M. Savitski, this concern was largely resolved

(1979). Citing a 1976 article in Pravda, they pointed out that 95 percent of the people's judges had a university education (a considerable improvement since 1960, when only 71 percent had achieved that distinction). A formal legal education was finally imposed as a prerequisite for election (though a majority had already pursued advanced legal studies before this requirement was introduced). Those without formal legal training had to take a law course to assure their competency.

A second characteristic of the Soviet judiciary was the collegial manner in which they performed their tasks. Whether it was hearing a first-instance case or an appeal, a single judge did not decide an issue. A judge was always assisted in the process by either other judges or lay assessors. This characteristic was not unlike the principle of shared responsibility found in countries utilizing juries or lay judges.

A third characteristic was the independence of judges. Soviet legal writers had often criticized the manner in which some judges were appointed to their positions in the West. They maintained that it was flawed logic to assume that such judges would display a greater sense of equity because of their purported independent status. They argued that this kind of permanency of tenure instead would lead to arbitrary actions, because the judges would endow themselves with a perception of superiority. Moreover, as members of the bourgeoisie, judges would tend to perpetuate and protect the interests of the property class. In a country that claimed the elimination of class as one of its goals, this was an unacceptable method of judicial selection. From their point of view, election was the only way to assure a true sense of independence in the administration of law.

Associated with judicial independence was the principle that judges were subject only to the law. This principle implied that judges should not be exposed to excessive political pressure, because this would hinder their judicial objectivity. This principle is found in constitutional documents of most countries and was present in the Soviet Constitution. One must keep in mind, however, that the principle had not been honored in practice. The CPSU was not only the ultimate interpreter of the law, but it also controlled who was placed on the ballot for election as a judge.

From a Western perspective, these factors raised serious questions about the extent to which judges were allowed to interpret the law freely and independently. In the waning years of the Soviet Union, these concerns were discussed openly. The Soviets began to admit that too many judges deferred to the judgment of others, especially procurators and their investigators, and that judicial decisions had often been designed to conform more to the dictates of the Communist Party and the whims of local party officials than to the written law. In addition, the method of determining judicial effectiveness was not unlike that used for police and procurators, because part of a judge's mandate was to reduce crime. As a result, judges were evaluated on the basis of the number of convictions and acquittals in their court. This kind of posturing resulted in defendants not being acquitted of charges that either lacked sufficient evidence or were based on illegally obtained evidence, which helped to explain the 99.7 percent conviction rate of criminal cases in Soviet courts (Dobek and Laird, 1990). These concerns, which were acknowledged by government officials, severely hampered attempts at judicial objectivity and led to charges of accusatory bias on the part of judges.

Finally, in countries that view the rule of law as a basic and decisive feature of the social fabric, citizens tend to regard the position of judges as prestigious because they are considered society's guardians and interpreters of the law. This was not the case in the Soviet Union. Law had never played a significant role in Russia, and the Marxist ideology alleged that law would eventually wither away. As such, its value in the Soviet political and social context was limited and viewed as temporary. Moreover, the CPSU was the actual guardian of the law and the ultimate interpreter of the role that it and the judiciary would play in society (Ginsburgs, 1985).

While discussions continued on ways to improve the Soviet judiciary, the Law on the Status of Judges in the USSR (1989) was designed to establish its independence. The new law consolidated the rules governing the judiciary, which were scattered throughout various pieces of legislation and policy. It attempted to improve the standards of quality among judges that were often lax or totally absent. For example, judicial appointments would now call for a higher level of legal education, along with the passing of a qualifying examination. The law also established a mechanism for judicial oversight, with the creation of qualifications collegia. Members of the collegia were judges elected to a five-year term by the conference of judges for the region served by the collegia. Finally, Article 3 of the law stated that "judges and people's assessors are independent and subordinate only to law." This was designed to address the problem of party interference within the judicial process.

With the establishment of the Russian Federation, the judiciary was confronted with several problems. The approval of a new Constitution in 1993 helped to clarify some judicial issues. Chapter 7 of the Constitution is devoted to the judicial branch. It addresses such basic principles as judicial independence, authority, and autonomy. The Constitution states:

> Article 118. In the Russian Federation, justice is administered only by the courts. Judicial authority is exercised through constitutional, civil, administrative and criminal proceedings. The judicial system ... is established by the Constitution of the Russian Federation and federal constitutional law. The creation of extraordinary courts is not permitted.
>
> Article 120. Judges are independent and are subordinate only to the Constitution ... and federal law.

> Article 121. Judges are not subject to removal from office. The powers of a judge may be terminated or suspended only on grounds and according to procedures established by federal law.
>
> Article 122. Judges have immunity. Criminal charges may not be brought against a judge except according to procedures determined by federal law.
>
> Article 124. Courts are financed solely from the federal budget, and this financing must make possible the full and independent administration of justice in accordance with federal law.

The Russian Constitution established some basic principles about judicial independence, authority, and autonomy. These principles are significantly different from those espoused in the Constitution of the former Soviet Union and are similar to those found in Western countries.

In light of Soviet history, a central point of discussion remained the independence of the judiciary, specifically what independence would mean in the Russian context. In crafting the 1992 Law on the Status of Judges of the Russian Federation, the authorities used the 1989 Law on the Status of Judges in the USSR as a starting point. The 1992 law has been amended. With regard to the matter of independence, Article 2 of the law states, "Judicial power is self-dependent and acts independently of legislative and executive power." Article 4 further points out, "Judges are independent and submit only to the Constitution of the Russian Federation and to the Law. They are not accountable to anybody in their activities which deal with the administration of justice."

Despite these positive steps, a practical problem confronts the Russian Federation. There is a serious shortage of qualified judges. Some judges resigned with the collapse of the Soviet Union, others were asked to step down because of their judicial conduct, and some left to pursue other careers. For those judges who stayed, a process was not immediately in place to replace them as their judicial terms expired. Some judges were re-elected by the now defunct people's soviets to terms of five or 10 years and, in some instances, for life. There also are cases in which judges have continued to serve on the basis of the previous electoral mandate.

Many judgeships have been left vacant, however. It was estimated in 1994 that there were about 1,400 judges in the Russian Federation. As such, the lower courts were understaffed by approximately 1,500 judges. There were severe shortages in the higher courts, too. In some regions of the country, the shortage of judges amounted to more than 20 percent. There are also parts of the country where the judicial branch is close to paralysis. In some instances, people's assessors were functioning as judges; in other cases, people who had no legal background or training were serving as judges. Finally, during this rather chaotic situation, some parts of the country attempted to alleviate the problem by electing justices of the peace who had been mandated to handle minor civil and criminal matters so that the understaffed courts could focus on more significant cases.

In an attempt to improve the quality of candidates for judicial appointment, the Law on the Status of Judges of the Russian Federation lists the basic requirements. A candidate must be a Russian citizen who is at least 25 years of age. The person is expected to have received a higher legal education and had experience within the legal profession for at least five years. A candidate must also pass a qualifying examination which is administered by the Ministry of Justice. Based on a candidate's background, the results of the qualifying examination, and what specific judicial office is being sought, the Qualifying Collegium of Judges offers a recommendation to the office of the president of the Russian Federation. The president in turn offers his or her recommendation to the Council of the Federation. The Council is legally charged with making judicial appointments.

The newly created justices of the peace must meet many of the criteria established for Russian judges. The age, education, and work experience within the legal profession are the same. The qualifying examination and recommendation for appointment is the responsibility of judges from the region in which the person would serve. The rules for selecting a justice of the peace offer a good deal of latitude. They can be appointed or elected by the regional legislature or they can be elected directly by the people. Thus far, regions prefer to appoint rather than elect the justices. Finally, the justices serve a specific term in office that cannot exceed five years. The specific term is determined by local law. Once the term of appointment expires, the justice can seek another term in office.

In an effort to further improve the quality of the judiciary, the Russian Academy of Justice was founded in 1998 by the Supreme Court of the Russian Federation and the Supreme Arbitrazh Court of the Russian Federation. The Academy of Justice was established for two purposes: to provide training for new judges and continuing education for members of the judiciary and to conduct research on court organization and issues that impact the judiciary. The *arbitrazh* courts constitute a separate system of federal courts with its own procedural code. Arbitrazh courts specialize in matters that deal with a wide array of contractual issues, such as right of ownership, changes in a contract, performance of obligations, loans, bank accounts, and bankruptcy.

Recent commentary on the judiciary has been somewhat mixed. On the one hand, it has been suggested that the levels of incompetence and corruption are exaggerated. The arbitrazh system was singled out as effective when dealing with disputes between businesses. Moreover, the number of people seeking the assistance of courts to resolve disputes has increased from 1 million under Yeltsin to 6 million during Putin's tenure (Sakwa, 2008). On the other hand, Transparency International found that a Russian survey reported that more than 78 percent of the respondents did not expect to find justice in the courts. Part of the problem deals with "the unofficial expenditures" to some courts or bribes. Comments from senior judges appear to support this public perception that corruption is clearly prevalent at the trial court level (Transparency International, 2007). Recommendations to address this problem have included: public awareness campaigns to educate people about the role of judges, regular review of judicial salaries with the goal of achieving near-parity with the private sector, examination of existing penalties for corruption within the judiciary, and randomizing the allocation of trial cases to judges.

Procurators The Office of the Soviet Procurator was originally established in 1922. It was a unique institution as compared with prosecutor's offices found in Western criminal justice systems. Experts have characterized it as a highly centralized agency that embraces a unity of purpose and is assured a good deal of independence.

The procurator general of the USSR was appointed by, and accountable to, the Supreme Soviet of the USSR. Subordinate to the procurator general were three principal deputies, each responsible for the coordination of a group of departments. Included among these major units were: general supervision; office of investigation; supervision and review of civil cases; supervision and review of criminal cases; supervision of the affairs of minors; supervision of the MVD; supervision of the KGB; supervision of the prisons; and supervision of the control and inspection department (Smith, 1978).

The procurator general was ultimately charged with the appointment of other procurators throughout the USSR, who served renewable five-year terms. The office represented a highly centralized system that assured a strict interpretation and observance of socialist law by all governmental and nongovernmental organizations, officials, and citizens. Unlike other components of the legal profession, the procuracy was clearly dominated by party members (one estimate placed it at 83 percent). It also tended to be a male bastion (Butler, 1988).

The Statute on Procuracy Supervision in the USSR explained the principal tasks of the procurators. Tasks included supervision of the execution of laws, the activities of preliminary criminal investigations, the legality and justification of judgments, the execution of judgments, and the places of confinement. Although the procuracy performed the role of the prosecutor in criminal cases, the office had a much greater role and authoritative scope than the prosecutors of other countries. Indeed, the procuracy served a powerful and influential role throughout all phases of the administration of justice in the Soviet Union. In addition to being highly centralized and unified in purpose, the procuracy retained an independent status. It was accountable solely to the Supreme Soviet.

This further enhanced its position of authority among the various government units at the national, republic, provincial, and local levels.

It had been suggested for some time that Soviet criminal procedure was biased in favor of the prosecution because procurators were responsible for investigating the charges. To rectify this injustice and to assure greater objectivity, it was suggested that the investigation function be removed from the procurator's office and placed with the Ministry of Justice. Although this approach was not introduced, it would have mirrored the method employed by countries adhering to Romano-Germanic procedural principles.

The Soviet procuracy was late in responding to Gorbachev's reform agenda. Initially, it was thought that the procuracy might lose its authoritative position and jeopardize its future role in the criminal justice system (Smith, 1992). Although the legislative and executive branches of the Russian Federation had intended to curtail its powers, the procuracy remains the most powerful component of the Russian justice system. The other branches of government concluded that the procuracy was the only office capable of guaranteeing that law and order would be maintained while also acknowledging the importance of due process rights (Smith, 1996).

As a result, reference to the procuracy in the new Russian Constitution assures that it will remain a powerful organization with significant breadth and depth of authority in the justice system. For example, Article 129 of the Constitution states: "[the] Procurator's Office constitutes a single centralized system in which lower-ranking procurators are subordinate to higher-ranking procurators and to the Russian Federation Procurator General." The 1995 Law on the Procuracy, which has been amended several times, also explains in greater detail the responsibilities of the office, which illustrates why the procuracy is considered such a powerful organization within the justice system.

The procuracy essentially has two kinds of responsibilities. One of these is a supervisory function that is applied within four different forms or contexts. The first of these, and the most important, is a general supervisory authority over the execution of laws throughout the federation. Essentially, the procuracy provides oversight of the Russian bureaucracy and citizenry, ensuring that they are in compliance with the law. The ultimate goal is to assure that the law is executed and thus interpreted in a uniform fashion. A second supervisory function involves providing protection to the rights and freedoms of the citizenry by advising people of their rights, offering recommendations to prevent further violations, and initiating legal proceedings against offenders. A third supervisory function focuses exclusively on the preliminary investigation into a criminal matter. Specific concern is directed at assuring that any search and seizure of evidence, any arrest or detention of a suspect, and all legal requirements leading to a prosecution are in compliance with the law.

A final supervisory function of the procuracy involves oversight of all correctional facilities. This would include both institutions that detain people awaiting trial and those used for confining people to a period of incarceration after trial. In addition to these supervisory functions, other units within the procuracy are responsible for prosecuting criminal cases. Some of these personnel are involved in either coordinating or conducting the preliminary investigation into alleged criminal conduct, while others focus their attention on prosecuting cases in court (Butler, 1999).

The procurator general is nominated by the president of the Russian Federation and appointed by the Council of the Federation to serve a five-year term. All the other procurators are appointed by the procurator general, and the entire procuracy is organized by and subject to the procedures of federal law. The basic requirements to become a procurator are somewhat similar to those of candidates for judicial appointment that were mentioned earlier. A candidate for the procuracy must be a Russian citizen who is at least 25 years of age. The person is expected to have received a higher legal education and serve a six-month probationary period. It is interesting to note that people who work for the procuracy today cannot be involved with an organization that pursues a political agenda. This policy is in stark contrast to the Soviet era, when procurators and the investigative staff often followed or enforced the dictates of the Communist Party.

The Office of the Procurator General includes the Research Institute, which has existed for more than 30 years. The mandate of the Institute is to research and disseminate information about law, order, and crime. Because of the dramatic changes that have occurred in Russia since 1991, the Institute has spent a good deal of time directing its efforts at defining and clarifying the role of the procuracy as it relates to its mandated issues of law, order, and crime, as well as to internal organizational issues of administration and management (Skuratov, 1994).

Defense Counsel Following the Russian Revolution and with the enactment of the 1917 Decree of the People's Commissars on the Courts, the long-accepted notion that there should be a profession of practicing attorneys came to an abrupt end. Private attorneys were viewed as yet another product of a bourgeois society. In 1918, special collegia were formed for people who agreed to act as either prosecutors or defense counsel. Two years later, that system was abolished, as prosecutors were separated from defense attorneys. Under the new system, lists of people willing to serve as legal representatives were made available, but there were no regulations requiring that the people have formal legal training. By 1922, however, defense attorneys were organized into collegia or bar associations. In order to join a collegium, the candidate had to complete a legal education program and must have practiced for two years. Although this remained the basic requirement for admittance to the Soviet bar, it did not mean that the person had completed a five-year course of study at a university law department.

Bar associations (collegia of advocates) were organized throughout the country at the town, regional, and republic levels. There were 157 such collegia in the Soviet Union before the nation's demise. Although these associations claimed to be independent social organizations, the organization and work of the membership was regulated by the state through specific statutes that pertained to their functions. Moreover, the collegia were ultimately controlled by the ministries of justice at both the republic and national levels.

For years, lawyers for the defense were confronted with an image problem fostered by the attitudes of judges and procurators. People who supported a change in the standing of judges also suggested that the status of defense lawyers must improve. One suggestion was to establish a national bar association that would supersede in some respects the 157 local bar associations. It was alleged that a national association would provide the bar with a greater political voice and in turn strengthen the quality and quantity of counsel for the defense.

The status of defense counsel gradually improved in the years after World War II. Article 158 of the Soviet Constitution gave the accused a right to defense counsel. It was estimated in 1988 that counsel appeared in court for about 70 percent of the criminal cases and was present for approximately one-third of the preliminary investigations (Butler, 1988). In addition to defending a person in a criminal case or serving as an advocate for their interests in a civil matter, Soviet attorneys performed other tasks that were similar to those undertaken by lawyers in the West. For example, they advised clients on legal matters and drew up legal documents.

Soviet citizens in need of legal assistance could select their own defense counsel or allow the local legal aid bureau to assist in selecting an attorney. Over the years, Western scholars had been highly critical of the apparent limits imposed on counsel when defending criminal defendants. They took issue with the purported extent to which an attorney was free to provide counsel to a client. For example, a client in a political trial was not free to select an attorney of his or her choice because only a small number of lawyers had been cleared by the state to defend such clients (Kaminskaya, 1982; Subtelny, 1984).

Prior to 1958, defense counsel was not involved in any case until the matter came to trial. Until recently, the task of defending a client was initiated after the completion of the preliminary investigation conducted by the procurator, KGB, or militia. Peter Juviler, among others, pointed out that on occasion the accused either was not told by the investigator of their right to legal assistance or had been discouraged from availing themselves of that right (1976). Moreover, Juviler argued that once counsel was appointed, it was not uncommon for investigators to attempt to block counsel's access to the client before the trial. As a result of the democratization efforts during Gorbachev's era, the law was changed to permit access to defense counsel for suspects, the accused, and defendants at the time of their detention, arrest, or the filing of charges.

Also of great interest to students of the common law system was the fact that Soviet defense attorneys did not conduct their own investigation into the case. In the Soviet system, it was the responsibility of the procurator to collect the evidence and identify witnesses, for it was assumed from the outset that the procurator would conduct an objective investigation. This method was characteristic of other countries influenced by the Romano-Germanic tradition. Defense counsel, however, could request that the procurator interrogate a particular witness. The vast resources at the disposal of the procurator were supposed to be used to uncover all relevant facts in a case. Thus, information that may lead to the accused's exoneration was as significant as that which might incriminate the person. This method further enhanced the Soviet argument that defense attorneys need not be actively involved in the preliminary investigation.

The assumption that the procurator would perform an objective investigation was proven false and became the subject of a good deal of criticism in the Soviet Union. Since 1970, counsel had been permitted to participate in the investigation with the approval of the procurator. However, according to Juviler, this type of waiver was rare. Another suggestion from proponents of democratization recommended that defense counsel be permitted to participate in the collection of evidence (as is the case in countries that adhere to Romano-Germanic legal principles). It was felt that such a change would improve the quality and objectivity of criminal investigations.

In the past, Soviet authorities argued that an active involvement by defense counsel at the investigatory stage would inevitably lead to two investigations. The procurator would begin to lose objectivity and become an advocate for the state's actions, which was not the purpose—at least in theory. Moreover, the cost of a defense investigation would create an unnecessary burden on the accused and deprive some citizens of counsel. From the Soviet perspective, this was unacceptable, for it would destroy one of the purposes of socialist democracy.

During the Gorbachev era, two strategies were employed to improve the status of defense counsel. One involved reducing the supervisory authority of the Ministry of Justice over the various local bar associations. For some, the goal was to establish a national bar association. In 1989, proponents of a national association managed to create the Union of Advocates, a voluntary association. With the dissolution of the Soviet Union and other subsequent changes, it was not clear if the Union of Advocates would eventually gain supervisory authority over its profession or reach a compromise with the Ministry of Justice over its role in the Russian Federation. Early indications suggested that the Ministry of Justice might be reasserting its authority (Burrage, 1993; Huskey, 1990). The other strategy was to enhance the role of defense counsel in protecting the interests of their clients in criminal cases. The ultimate goal was to establish a level playing field by developing procedures that were more adversarial in nature. This would involve accepting the notion of the presumption of innocence of the accused and according defense counsel equal rights with those of the procurator.

Although nothing concrete happened during the Gorbachev era to establish a more equitable system of procedure, the new Constitution of the Russian Federation offers hope that significant change might be in the offing. Article 48 states: "Everyone is guaranteed the right to receive qualified legal assistance ... Everyone who is detained, put in custody or charged with committing a crime has the right to avail himself or herself of the assistance of a lawyer (defender) from the time he or she is detained, put in custody or charged." Article 49 indicates: "Everyone accused of committing a crime is presumed innocent until his or her guilt has been proved according to the procedure stipulated by federal law and established by a court verdict that has entered into force. An accused person is not obligated to prove his or her innocence." Finally, Article 50 points out: "No one may be convicted more than once for the same crime. During the judicial process, the use of evidence obtained by violating federal law is not permitted. Everyone who is convicted of a crime has the right to a review of the verdict by a superior court according to the procedure established by federal law, as well as the right to request clemency or a lighter penalty."

The Russian Constitution acknowledged various rights of the accused, but the procurator still retained a significant amount of power. In fact, some of the informal practices of the Soviet period that benefited the procurator continued to be utilized (Jordon, 2005; Solomon, in Pridemore, 2005). Although it is still too early to assess its impact, the recently adopted 2001 Code of Criminal Procedure has been heralded as another illustration of Russia's embrace of the principles of the rule of law. Various features of the Code are practical examples of a procedural shift away from the inquisitorial method to an adversarial approach. This, of course, enhances the position of defense counsel. Among the rights that counsel has gained are: to meet privately with a client, to collect evidence independently of the procurator, to identify defense witnesses, to invite professional experts to testify on behalf of the defense, to be present for all procedural actions involving a client's case, to examine and make copies of the government's documents after the investigation, and to file appeals regarding pretrial or trial procedures.

It was mentioned earlier that there were 157 collegia of advocates at the time of the dissolution of the Soviet Union. In 2002, there were

47,000 advocates registered with one of the 145 collegia of advocates or one of the 50 "alternative" collegia throughout the Russian Federation. Each collegia is an independent self-governing professional association (Butler, 2003). It is also important to note that the 2002 Federal Law on Advocate Activity was designed to establish a national framework for the profession. One product of this legislation is the Federal Chamber of Advocates of the Russian Federation. The Chamber's mandate is to represent the interest of advocates.

Jury

Trial by jury was first introduced into Russia in 1864, but it was abolished with the 1917 Revolution. During the period of the Soviet Union, a trial court included a professional judge and two people's assessors. In all Soviet courts, assessors were elected to a five-year term. People's court assessors were elected by the people the court served. Assessors serving in superior courts were elected by the corresponding soviet of people's deputies. Any Soviet citizen who was at least 25 years of age was eligible for election. The work of an assessor was not a full-time responsibility; assessors heard cases for approximately two weeks out of the year. It was not a requirement to have any understanding of the law, and most assessors did not. Once elected, assessors were given an information handbook and were expected to attend lectures by jurists. These measures were designed to supplement their minimal understanding of the law.

Because of the limited amount of time actually served in court, assessors did not become very knowledgeable about either the substantive or procedural nuances of the law. Thus, they were dependent on the advice and counsel of the professional judge. The purpose of people's assessors was not unlike that of lay judges in Sweden and jurors in England and France. They assured civilian participation in the administration of justice. From the official Soviet point of view, this was an important responsibility, but it appeared to be a cosmetic exercise in actual practice. Nevertheless, it served as another illustration of socialist democracy in action.

People's assessors continued to be utilized in the courts of the Russian Federation until fairly recently. As was pointed out earlier, people's assessors had functioned as judges in those regions of the country that do not have a sufficient number of professional judges to serve the needs of the area. Although assessors were viewed originally as assuring civilian participation in the administration of justice, the Russian Federation has introduced jury trials into the system on a limited basis. As a result, issues are likely to be raised regarding the necessity or desirability of having two distinct approaches for assuring citizen involvement in the judicial process.

When in 1992 the Ministry of Justice proposed the establishment of jury trials, there was some opposition to the idea, especially from the procurator general. Nevertheless, legislation was adopted in 1993 to introduce the jury on an experimental basis for certain types of cases in nine regions of the country. Support for its use was reaffirmed with the new Constitution of the Russian Federation. Article 123 states: "In instances stipulated by federal law, judicial proceedings are conducted with the participation of jurors." By 2003, the experiment was extended to the other 69 regions of the country. Further guidelines for the use of the jury are found in the 2001 Code of Criminal Procedure.

Essentially, the procedure allows the defendant, if he or she has been accused of a specific kind of crime, to choose between a jury trial or a traditional trial. The list of crimes that fall under this category include: murder, kidnapping, rape with aggravating circumstances, child trafficking, gangsterism, large-scale bribery, treason, terrorist acts, calls for violent change in the constitutional system, and some other select crimes against the state.

Any Russian citizen who lives in the district where a trial will take place can serve as a juror. A juror must be at least 25 years of age, legally competent to serve, and without a criminal record. Twelve people are selected by the procurator and defense counsel after having their names drawn from a list of 30 to 40 eligible to serve. Potential jurors are questioned by the procurator and defense counsel and a written challenge can be submitted to the judge objecting to the possible selection of a juror.

As is the case in English trials, the Russian jury sits separately from the judge in the courtroom. This is unique to recent Russian experience, because when people's assessors were used, they sat on either side of the judge. Like common law countries that employ a jury, the Russian jury decides matters of fact, while the judge determines issues of law that arise during the trial. The responsibility of the jury is to determine if the accused is guilty or not guilty of the charges. Russian juries are expected to return unanimous verdicts during the first three hours of deliberations. Majority verdicts are permitted after that time. A not-guilty verdict is adopted if at least six jurors cast such a vote. If the jury finds the accused guilty, they can request that the judge show leniency at sentencing or they may decline to make such a request.

Legal Education

There were three approaches to acquiring a legal education in the Soviet Union. The most desirous method was selection as a day student in one of Russia's 48 law departments that were associated with a university. Day students were selected from the people who scored the highest on a competitive entrance examination. They participated in a five-year program and were given books, tuition, and a stipend for living expenses.

Night students, whose numbers had been equal or larger than day students, were individuals who had not scored as high on the entrance examination but had been accepted to the school. They participated in a six-year program and worked full-time at a job during the day. Finally, there was an extensive system of legal correspondence courses available for people who wanted to study law, even though they had not qualified for a law school position. As is the case in the United States and other countries that offer similar programs, this course of study was not held in high regard, because such programs lacked the academic rigor of a full-time course. Nevertheless, correspondence courses served a useful purpose in producing people knowledgeable in law, for the demand for lawyers had been outweighed by the numbers produced by law departments.

The system of legal education in the Soviet Union resembled that established on the continent of Europe, at least in terms of the range of nonlegal subjects offered. This was because Soviet law students had not already acquired the equivalent of an undergraduate college education. The typical first-year law student was 20 years old, had completed 10 years of formal education, and had worked the previous two years.

The curriculum was planned by authorities within the central government bureaucracy. The plan consisted of three groups of courses. The first group consisted of ideological courses. These courses, taken at the beginning of the program, included: basic principles of scientific communism, history of the Communist Party of the USSR, and Marxist-Leninist philosophy. In addition, all students studied a modern foreign language (English, German, and French were most popular) as well as Latin. The second group included courses dealing with the culture and history of the law. Among the courses prescribed at this phase were: Roman law, theory of state and law, history of political science, history of state and law of foreign countries, history of state and law of the USSR, government and law of bourgeois countries and countries liberated from colonial dependency, logic, court statistics, and accounting. The third category included more specialized law courses such as: administrative law, finance law, civil and family law, civil procedure, criminal investigation, criminal law, criminal procedure, collective farm law, land law, labor law, social insurance law, international law, criminology, corrective labor law, court psychology, and forensic medicine and psychiatry.

The course format included lectures and a seminar component in the more advanced classes. Starting with the second-year students, approximately five weeks out of the year were spent in practical training in a court or government law department. Fifth-year students spent most of their time in practical training and in writing a thesis to be defended at the end of the year. Upon graduation, about 50 percent of the students joined the staffs of political agencies such as the MVD, KGB, procuracy, and courts; these were the most prized positions. About 25 percent entered practice as an advocate; approximately 20 percent became legal counsel for various institutes, industrial enterprises, and collective farms; and 5 percent continued their studies (Juviler, 1976).

The student desiring to continue legal studies at the graduate level was required to gain admittance to one of the four law institutes. These institutes trained future legal scholars and law professors but were not associated with the law departments of universities. The placement was quite competitive for the limited number of positions available. Candidates in the law institutes were required to complete two years of practical work before they were permitted to apply. Anyone meeting the entrance criteria was eligible, but only those invited to apply stood a serious chance of being accepted. In addition to training legal scholars, the institute's staff produced legal treatises on Soviet law. Students spent a good deal of time assisting the staff in the preparation of these works. The rest of their time was spent in the research and writing of a thesis. Once a thesis was successfully defended, the student was awarded the degree of candidate of legal science. The student could remain at a law institute to continue a career of scholarly research or return to a university to teach.

Because of the heavy teaching assignments in Soviet law departments, the teaching faculty were not noted for their scholarly research (as is the case with law faculties in the West). Most scholarship was produced by the staffs of law institutes. Graduates of the institutes usually were awarded a doctorate degree for their contributions to the enhancement of Soviet legal knowledge. This was awarded approximately five to 10 years after receiving the degree of candidate of legal science. To achieve that distinction, the thesis must be defended before the faculty of a law institute other than the one attended by the writer.

Since the demise of the Soviet Union, two observations have been reported with regard to legal education in the Russian Federation. First, the ideological courses have been removed from the required courses of the law school curriculum. They have been replaced by courses designed to assist students in understanding the role of law in a market economy, such as banking, commercial law, and taxation. Some courses have also been introduced to retrain lawyers who initially studied law during the Soviet era. Second, interest in the study of law has increased significantly in the country. Although this may be initially attributed to the change in economic system and the opportunities the market offers to people trained in law, it should eventually benefit the justice system as the quality and quantity of lawyers interested in public law issues increase over time.

In light of the increased interest in the study of law, existing law schools have expanded their programs, and new law schools have been created to handle the demand. The five-year undergraduate degree is still designed to produce specialists in a branch of law. Because of the political and economic changes in Russia, the law graduate has a variety of career opportunities in the private sector that did not exist for previous generations of Soviet lawyers.

Law

The essential idea behind the democratization movement has been a recognition of the significance (indeed the necessity) of government by rule of law. The leadership of the Russian Federation has acknowledged its importance by indicating in Article 1 of their new Constitution that "[t]he Russian Federation is a democratic and federal state based on the rule of law, with a republican form of government." This acknowledgment is a first step, because throughout the history of the Soviet Union, government was ruled by ideology—specifically that of the Communist Party. Moreover, as has been indicated elsewhere, creating law does not in itself assure that it will be implemented or enforced.

As it relates to the criminal justice system, the rule of law is often associated with issues such as due process, presumption of innocence, and rules of evidence. What follows is a presentation of the changing nature of such issues, first in the context of the Soviet Union and then considered under the circumstances found in the Russian Federation. Of particular interest is the impact on criminal law and criminal procedure as the country moves from a set of assumptions based on government by rule of ideology to a government based on the rule of law.

The history of socialist law began in November 1917 when the Bolsheviks assumed power in Russia and established a new order that was intended to lead to the emergence of a communist society. In that society, both the state and law were to disappear as a result of becoming superfluous in a communist society. The Soviet leadership, however, never claimed to have established a communist society.

Since 1917, they had been in the process of creating a socialist state in the Soviet Union. The purpose of a socialist state was to prepare for the emergence of a communist society. According to Soviet jurists, all law was used to exploit the masses. However, they held that socialist law was unique. In fact, they argued that there were only two kinds of law: nonsocialist law and socialist law. Nonsocialist law was more maturely developed in capitalist countries; its purpose was to assure the protection of private interest through the exploitation of the masses. Socialist law was dominated by the doctrines of Marxism-Leninism; its purpose was to establish a collective interest by exploiting conformity in accordance with the goals of the Communist Party. Soviet society was considered imperfect because of its dependence on the use of coercion to achieve some of its ends. Nevertheless, Soviet leaders contended that their use of law was far superior to that found in capitalist countries.

Although the history of socialist law began in 1917, the Bolshevik break with the past was not a total rejection of previous practices. Admittedly, the substance of law changed drastically, causing socialist law to become a distinct legal family, but much of its form could be traced back to the Romano-Germanic tradition. The importance placed on codifying the law, the retention of many of the formal judicial organizations, and the rules of pretrial procedure were noticeably similar to those found in Romano-Germanic countries.

With the advent of Gorbachev's leadership and his attempts at redefining communist ideology, the reform of law was raised to a new status. The impetus for this reform was based on Gorbachev's views of democratic socialism. To summarize, democratic socialism required governance through the rule of law. Law assured individual rights and freedoms and was designed to control the potential abuse of power by the authorities. In order to achieve this form of democracy within the Soviet Union, constitutional and other legal reforms were necessary. Reforms had already been introduced in the judiciary. Efforts were also under way to change substantive and procedural law.

From a Western perspective, the history of socialist criminal law was marked by a lack of clarity, while criminal procedure suffered from arbitrary enforcement. Both were products of the Bolshevik leaders' failure to create an orderly plan to replace the law of the tsarist regime that they had abolished. Some efforts at codification were undertaken following the adoption of the 1918 Constitution, but it was not until the early 1920s that an extensive attempt to systematize the law was commenced in earnest. In 1922, The Criminal Code of the RSFSR (Russian Socialist Federative Soviet Republic)—the largest of the 15 republics—was adopted. Its purpose was to unify the criminal law and to check the indiscriminate practices of revolutionary tribunals and the Cheka. It also served as a model code for the other union republics.

Although the code systematized the law to some extent, it did not really clarify its limits. In the general section of the code, two principles were introduced establishing both the uniqueness of socialist criminal law and perpetuating its vague and arbitrary characteristics. One of those principles was the material definition of crime; it was expressed in Articles 6 and 7 of the code:

> A crime is any socially dangerous act or omission which threatens the foundations of the Soviet structure and that system of law which has been established by the Workers' and Peasants' Government for a period of transition to a Communist structure.
>
> A person is dangerous if he commits acts which are injurious to the community, or if his the established laws of the community.

The Soviets, therefore, established a principle stating that acts or omissions that were criminal did not have to be specifically described in the code. Rather, any act or omission that was deemed "socially dangerous" was a crime. Thus, the code lacked a specific definition of crime. Such an approach was alien to the Western method of codification. It also assured the continuance of broad discretionary powers for the investigative arms of the Soviet criminal justice system.

The second principle, known as the principle of analogy, was a logical extension of the first. It was found in Article 10 of the code:

> In the case where the Criminal Code makes no direct reference to particular forms of crime, punishment or other measures of social protection are applied in accordance with those Articles of the Criminal Code which deal with crimes most closely approximating, in gravity and in kind, to the crimes actually committed, and in conformity with the regulations laid down in the General Section of the Present Code …

With such a principle in force, a formal criteria for criminal liability was absent from the code. Defenders of the principle alleged that the revolutionary nature of the time warranted the use of this concept. However, it further enhanced the elastic interpretation the courts and investigative agents could apply to an accused's criminal conduct.

The codes were revised again in 1926, but the principles of material definition and analogy remained intact. In fact, they were more harshly interpreted throughout Stalin's regime, especially during the purges of the 1930s. Stalin's measures led a number of prominent scholars to criticize these principles. They were abolished when the Soviet leadership attempted to divorce itself from the methods of Stalin in the late 1950s. Although attempts were made to reduce the ambiguity of the law and to modify its severe application, the leadership did not totally abandon Stalin's methods. Critics contend that despite the fact that the principle of analogy was rescinded, it remained effective in spirit. In fact, it has been suggested by some scholars that everything was prohibited in the Soviet Union unless a law stated otherwise.

Finally, one of the most persistent causes for ambiguity in socialist law was the number of government branches with authority to enact law. Although this problem had existed since 1917, it was illustrated by the current guidelines established under the 1977 Constitution. These were essentially the same rules that existed under the 1936 Constitution, so they had been a part of the legislative process for some time. Unlike a common law country that finds its sources of law in legislation, judicial decisions, and custom, the socialist legal system more closely subscribed to the continental legal system's method of legal sources. The supreme law-making authority was vested in the popularly elected legislative bodies. In the Soviet Union, this included the Supreme Soviets of the 15 republics as well as the ultimate legislative authority, the Supreme Soviet of the USSR. Moreover, the doctrine of separation of powers had been absent from the Soviet political system. Both the judiciary and the executive were ultimately accountable to the legislative branch.

At this point in this discussion, it would appear that the Soviet Union had a highly efficient and orderly lawmaking system. However, although law was enacted by the Supreme Soviet and the various union republics, the Constitution authorized other government branches to legislate as well. The Supreme Soviet could issue decrees and acts; the Presidium of the Supreme Soviet could amend legislation, issue edicts, and adopt resolutions; the Council of Ministers could issue decrees and resolutions; and the various local units of state administration could adopt and execute decisions and orders. There was concern that many of these units of government did not publish their decrees or resolutions. For example, it had been suggested that 80 percent of the acts issued by the Council of Ministers were not published (Dobek and Laird, 1990). Thus, the people were left unaware of acts (by commission or omission) that violated established policy.

The number of agencies empowered to legislate and the amount of legislation enacted had created a serious dilemma. This situation was compounded further when the legislation was not published. This problem had existed since 1917. Despite Soviet attempts to reduce the ambiguity through codification, it persisted. The situation created difficulties for agencies responsible for interpreting and enforcing the law. For the Soviet criminal justice system, this overwhelming amount of legislation merely added to the ambiguity of the law and the arbitrary fashion with which it was administered.

In the 1980s, the Soviets attempted to address the issues of ambiguity and arbitrariness in their legal system. For example, the Institute of State and Law of the USSR Academy of Sciences produced a document called the "Theoretical Model of a Criminal Code (General Part)" in 1985. It was used as a point of departure in the debates about revising the criminal law, and in 1990, it was instrumental in the draft and adoption of amendments to the Fundamentals of Criminal Legislation of the USSR. In the course of these discussions, it became obvious that a more liberal sentencing policy would likely receive the most immediate benefit from these efforts at reform (Butler, 1988).

In another development, the Law of Appeals went into effect in 1988. It provided citizens with a right of appeal when they thought that the actions of an official of the government had in some way violated their rights. This legislation was expected to curtail the arbitrary actions of bureaucrats—particularly those involved with employment and housing law. According to Soviet legal experts, the law would not have a significant impact on agents of the criminal justice system because provisions in the act limited the actions that could be taken against members of the KGB, and complaints against the Ministry of Internal Affairs appeared to be excluded from the legislation (Quigley, 1988a). Nevertheless, these developments suggested that a new climate of opinion was emerging in the Soviet Union, and if it was permitted to continue, additional legislation might be forthcoming that would specifically address concerns related to arbitrary actions of agents of the criminal justice system.

Criminal Law

In an attempt to revise the criminal law, the Supreme Soviet of the USSR adopted several new laws in 1958. These included: the Fundamentals of the Criminal Legislation of the USSR and the Union Republics, the Law on Criminal Responsibility for Crimes against the State, the Law on Criminal Responsibility for Military Crimes, and the Fundamentals of Criminal Procedure of the USSR and the Union Republics. The Fundamentals served as a binding model, with each Soviet republic establishing its own laws. The intent behind these reforms was to clarify the laws and to eliminate the arbitrary fashion with which they were previously enforced. In short, it was an attempt to de-Stalinize the Soviet criminal justice system. In addition, each union republic was required to amend its existing laws to conform with the new basic principles established by the Supreme Soviet and to enact new criminal codes and codes of criminal procedure. This was largely accomplished during the early 1960s.

With the collapse of the Soviet Union, the government of the Russian Federation adopted the Criminal Code of the RSFSR as its own and then proceeded to make incremental amendments to it. Much of this effort had been directed at eliminating issues that were based on ideology rather than the rule of law. To illustrate, a person in the Soviet Union could be imprisoned for involvement in a commercial activity. Today, the Russian leadership wants its citizens involved in commercial activities in order to strengthen its market economy. Thus, one of the obvious changes in the criminal code was that it was no longer a crime to be involved in a commercial venture. It also should be pointed out that the change in economic system resulted in several new types of economic crime. They included: violating securities procedures, false business activities, violating antimonopoly laws, divulging commercial secrets, and violating the tax laws.

One of the more troublesome issues with the adoption of the old Criminal Code was the retention of the general definition of crime. The Russians insist on retaining the old Soviet term "socially dangerous act" in the definition (Finckenauer, 1995; Van Den Berg, 1992). From a Western perspective, we expect our criminal laws to meet objective standards that are rational, certain, and impartial. By meeting these standards, there is a greater likelihood that people will be treated fairly and equally. Including the concept of "socially dangerous" lends itself to arbitrary, capricious, and discriminatory interpretations of a person's actions. The history of criminal justice in the Soviet Union offers numerous illustrations of arbitrary investigations and questionable convictions. The concern then is that the Russians are apt to continue such practices, which has led one scholar to suggest that "the rule of law in Russia is, as of yet, an illusory goal" (Finckenauer, 1995).

In 1996, a new Criminal Code of the Russian Federation was introduced. It replaced the Criminal Code of the RSFSR that was originally enacted in 1960 and amended after the demise of the Soviet Union. The new Criminal Code of the Russian Federation took effect in 1997 and was amended in 1998. It is divided into two parts: the general part and the special part. The entire code is subdivided further into 12 sections, 34 chapters, and 360 articles. The general part is subdivided into six sections that are titled: (1) criminal law, (2) crime, (3) punishment, (4) relieving from criminal responsibility and punishment, (5) criminal responsibility of minors, and (6) compulsory measures of medical character.

The principal purpose of the Soviet criminal law was to protect the socialist political and economic system, along with the socialist legal order. The purpose of the 1996 Criminal Code is strikingly different, and the tasks are spelled out in Article 2: "protection of the rights and freedoms of man and citizen, ownership, public order and public security, the environment, and the constitutional system of the Russian Federation against criminal infringements, ensuring the peace and security of mankind, and also the prevention of crimes."

While "socially dangerous act" has been retained in the definition of crime, critics of the term, when employed in the Soviet context, should note that it is not being used as it had been in the past. Moreover, other principles and standards have been introduced into the new Code that are designed to prevent arbitrary, capricious, or discriminatory investigations that could lead to questionable convictions. To illustrate, Article 1 states: "Criminal legislation of the Russian Federation shall consist of the present Code. New laws providing for criminal responsibility shall be subject to inclusion in the present Code." Thus, the Code is supposed to be an all-inclusive document. Article 3 points out that "[t]he criminality of an act, and also the punishability thereof and other criminal-law consequences, shall be determined only by the present Code. The application of a criminal law by analogy shall not be permitted." In addition to the principle of legality, the new Code includes other principles that are designed to differentiate this Code from the codes of the Soviet era. Article 4 speaks to the principle of equality of all persons before the law; Article 5 addresses the principle of guilt, that is, the need of the authorities to establish guilt; Article 6 is devoted to the principle of justness, which is concerned with determining an appropriate level of punishment; and Article 7 is concerned with the principle of humanity, which prohibits the assessing of sanctions that cause either physical suffering or are demeaning to an individual.

The issues of intent and negligence are considered under Articles 25 and 26, respectively. Article 25 states:

> An act committed with direct or indirect intent shall be deemed to be a crime committed intentionally.
>
> A crime shall be deemed to be committed with direct intent if the person was aware of the social danger of his actions (or failure to act), foresaw the possibility or inevitability of the ensuing of socially dangerous consequences and wished the ensuing thereof. A crime shall be deemed to be committed with indirect intent if the person was aware of the social danger of his actions (or failure to act), foresaw the possibility of the ensuing of socially dangerous consequences, did not wish them, but consciously permitted these consequences or was indifferent to them

Article 26 explains negligence:

> An act committed through thoughtlessness or carelessness shall be deemed to be a crime committed through negligence. A crime shall be deemed to be committed through thoughtlessness if the person foresaw the possibility of the ensuing of socially dangerous consequences of his actions (or failure to act) but without sufficient grounds arrogantly counted on the prevention of these consequences.
>
> A crime shall be deemed to be committed through negligence if the person did not foresee the possibility of the ensuing of the socially dangerous consequences of his actions (or failure to act), although with necessary attentiveness and prudence these consequences should and could have been foreseen.

Two factors influence criminal responsibility: age and mental capacity. People who have reached 16 years of age are subject to criminal responsibility. While people under the age of 16 are generally not subject to criminal responsibility, there are a number of exceptions made to this rule. Young people who have attained the age of 14 and have committed certain serious crimes may be prosecuted. The crimes for which a young person may be prosecuted include: homicide; intentional causing of grave harm to health; intentional causing of average gravity of harm to health; stealing a person; rape; forcible actions of sexual nature; open stealing; assault with intent to rob; extortion; unlawful taking possession of an automobile or other means of transport without the purpose of stealing; intentional destruction or damaging of property under aggravating circumstances; terrorism; taking a hostage; knowingly making a false communication concerning an act of terrorism; hooliganism under aggravating circumstances; vandalism; stealing or extortion of a weapon, ammunition, explosive substances, or explosive devices; stealing or extortion of narcotic means or psychotropic substances; and the destruction of transport or railways into unfitness.

By way of clarification, it should be noted that the term *hooliganism* refers to a specific criminal offense that existed under Soviet law and has been retained with the new Russian law. According to Article 213, hooliganism is defined as: "the flagrant violation of public order expressed by a clear disrespect for society accompanied by the application of force to citizens or by the threat of the application thereof, and likewise by the destruction or damaging of another's property ..." It has long been one of the most common types of offenses committed in the country.

The other factor that determines a person's criminal responsibility involves mental capacity. People who are in a state of nonimputability (that is, not aware of the character and consequences of their actions because they suffer from chronic or temporary mental disturbance, feeble-mindedness, or other mental illnesses) are not subject to criminal responsibility. Article 21, however, states that "compulsory measures of a medical character provided for by the Code may be assigned by a court to a person who has committed a socially dangerous act in a state of nonimputability ..." This could possibly lead to the person's commitment to a general or special psychiatric hospital. The use of psychiatric hospitals in the Soviet Union had been a topic of intense dispute, because political dissidents often found themselves sent to such facilities. At issue in those cases was the criteria used to determine mental illness, derangement, or deficiency. For example, critics of the Soviet system alleged that the desire to emigrate to Israel should not have been grounds for such a commitment, but such a criterion was used for that purpose in the past. It should also be noted that defendants who commit crimes while in a state of intoxication are not free from criminal responsibility. According to Article 23, the state of intoxication can be caused by alcohol, narcotics, or other stupefying substances.

The general part of the code also contains a section on punishments. The code lists three purposes for punishment that include: restoring social justness, reforming the convicted person, and preventing the commission of a new crime. As was the case during the Soviet era, the Russians make a distinction between punishments that are considered either basic or supplementary measures. These were identified in Article 45:

> Obligatory tasks, correctional tasks, limitation in military service, limitation of freedom, arrest, confinement in a disciplinary military unit, deprivation of freedom for a determined period, deprivation of freedom for life, and the death penalty shall be applied only as basic types of punishments.

> A fine and deprivation of a right to occupy determined posts or to engage in a determined activity shall be applied either as basic or as supplementary types of punishments.
>
> Deprivation of a special, military or honorary title, class rank, and State awards, and also confiscation of property, shall be applied only as supplementary types of punishments.

Notably absent from this list of punishments are the sanctions of exile and banishment. These sanctions were utilized for a number of years during the Soviet regime; both were eliminated shortly before the collapse of the Soviet Union.

The death penalty is considered an acceptable sanction in exceptional cases and those instances include: homicide, infringement on the life of a State or public official, and genocide. The method of carrying out the sanction is through shooting a bullet in the back of the head. It is interesting to note that the code prohibits carrying out the death penalty on women, people who committed the crime before reaching the age of 18, and men who have attained the age of 65 at the time of sentencing. In addition, through the pardon process, a death sentence can be replaced by a sentence of deprivation of freedom for life or deprivation of freedom for 25 years. Finally, the Russian Federation suspended the use of capital punishment in 1997 (Mikhlin, 1999).

The special part of the 1996 Criminal Code is subdivided into six sections that represent the major crime categories: (1) crimes against the person, (2) crimes in sphere of economy, (3) crimes against public security and public order, (4) crimes against the state, (5) crimes against military service, and (6) crimes against peace and security of mankind. Each crime is listed under one of these categories with the specific elements that constitute the offense and the type of sanction that may be imposed. To illustrate, Article 162, the crime of assault with intent to rob, states: "Assault with intent to rob, that is, an attack for the purpose of stealing another's property committed with the application of force dangerous for life or health, or with the threat of the application of such force shall be punished by deprivation of freedom for a term of from three up to eight years with or without confiscation of property." This article also includes subsections devoted to when this offense is committed either by a group of persons or by an organized group. In those instances, the sanction of deprivation of freedom ranges from seven to 12 years and from eight to 15 years, respectively.

Russia is clearly a country in transition, moving from one set of political ideals and economic principles to a profoundly different set of ideals and principles. The 1996 Criminal Code of the Russian Federation illustrates that fact well, for it is similar to criminal codes found in Western democratic countries. Many similarities have to do with Russia's attempt to establish a market economy. Some parts of the code, however, are unique to the country's experience. They reflect either the Soviet past or the current transitional phase that the country is and will continue to confront for the foreseeable future.

Criminal Procedure

When the Code of Criminal Procedure of the RSFSR was introduced in October of 1960, it was designed (like the criminal code) to de-Stalinize the Soviet criminal justice system. It is worthwhile to note some of the basic or fundamental principles that were expressed in the code. Among the more important principles, Article 2 stated that no innocent person would be prosecuted or convicted. Unfortunately, the application of this principle was largely ignored in practice—an allegation that has been supported by critics both in and out of government. Article 13 assured that only the courts would administer justice, suggesting that counter-revolutionary trials would no longer be handled by military tribunals. Article 16 proclaimed that judges and people's assessors were independent and subordinate only to the law. The principle of judicial independence must be viewed within the context of Soviet ideology, for the article also stated that court decisions were made "in conformity with socialist legal consciousness," which was determined by the CPSU.

Article 14 stated that the administration of justice was based on equality of all citizens before the law and courts. Nationality, race, religion, and social or economic status were not supposed to affect the outcome of the case. Soviet jurists had been fond of claiming that this principle was frequently violated in capitalist countries. This was one of the reasons frequently offered for the superiority of socialist law over capitalist law. Article 17 assured that judicial proceedings would be conducted "in the language of the majority of the local population." This was considered an important principle because of the number of ethnic groups that resided in the Soviet Union. The right to a public trial was granted under Article 18. There were some exceptions to this rule, however. For example, trials involving state secrets were not open to the public, and the court could decide to conduct closed trials if the defendant was under 16 years of age or when the case involved a sex crime.

Finally, the Soviets maintained that there was an implied presumption of innocence in their law. Whether the presumption truly existed has been a hotly debated issue among both Soviet jurists and Western experts on socialist law. If one accepts—at least in theory—the role of the procurator, a case could be made for the existence of this principle. Although the presumption of innocence was implied in a number of articles in the code and in other pieces of Soviet legislation, Article 20 was often cited as an important illustration of this sentiment. It proclaimed that "a thorough, complete and objective analysis of the circumstances of the case" was an obligation of the procurator, the investigators, and the court. A number of critics argued that this was not the case, and they pointed to countless examples of accusatory bias by judges and procurators to prove their point. Much of the bias was the result of the Soviet procedure's focus on the "objective truth" of the case, that is the factual guilt of the accused. This procedure did not make a distinction between factual guilt and legal guilt, which is an important feature of the adversarial process. As such, courts frequently permitted the procurator to conduct supplementary investigations into a case after the trial had started.

Though the code was designed, in part, to de-Stalinize the Soviet criminal justice system, experts on the earlier codes argued that the procedural codes were not substantially different from the codes in force during Stalin's regime. Obviously, the hope was that Soviet citizens would be assured legal protection as a result of these procedural guarantees. A number of Western experts believed that the average Soviet citizen was protected, but they were quick to point out that this was not the case for political dissidents. Critics of the Soviet system contended that procedural abuses continued despite attempts at reform, but that the abuse was not nearly as blatant nor as harsh.

Upon the dissolution of the Soviet Union, Russia continued to use the Code of Criminal Procedure of the RSFSR in an amended form as the Code of Criminal Procedure of the Russian Federation. There was a healthy skepticism regarding the ability or willingness of agents of the Russian justice system to comply with the new procedural protections. Of course, the Russian Federation's new Constitution assured a commitment to a number of fundamental procedural rights that were designed for people involved in the justice process. Article 15 states: "Bodies of state power, bodies of local self-government, officials, citizens and associations of citizens, must observe the Constitution of the Russian Federation and the laws." Article 46 proclaims: "Everyone is guaranteed judicial protection of his or her rights and liberties." Article 49 indicates: "Everyone accused of committing a crime is presumed innocent until his or her guilt has been proved according to the procedure stipulated by federal law and established by a court verdict that has entered into force. An accused person is not obligated to prove his or her innocence." Finally, Article 50 assures: "No one may be convicted more than once for the same crime." Some of these constitutional rights were strikingly similar to the protections enunciated in the old Code of Criminal Procedure of the RSFSR. As a result, there was some uncertainty as to whether the agents of the justice system would display a deference toward these constitutional rights. At issue was whether the agents of the justice system had accepted the principle of government by rule of law.

While a new Criminal Code was approved in 1996, the initial attempts were unsuccessful at drafting a new Code of Criminal Procedure. Some commentators were concerned that the office of the procurator retained too much authority. Critics argued that the new code should enhance the independence of the judiciary and strengthen the role of defense counsel in the process (American Bar Association Central and East European Law Initiative, 1996). Finally, on July 1, 2002, and after having been amended four times, the 2001 Code of Criminal Procedure of the Russian Federation went into effect.

The new Code is significant because it introduces several changes to the criminal procedural process that did not exist in the old Soviet code. As such, a new approach to criminal procedure has been introduced with this Code. Chapter 2 of the Code is devoted to explaining the philosophical principles that are the foundation for the rules that guide the procedural changes. The purpose of the criminal court proceedings is to protect the rights of people and organizations who are victims of crime and to protect the rights and freedoms of people who have been unlawfully accused or convicted of an offense. The principle of legality states that any violation of the procedural norms of the Code by a court, procurator, investigator, or body of inquiry in gathering evidence would lead to that evidence being declared inadmissable. Other principles point out that justice will be administered only by a court and that the procedures employed in the court will be of an adversarial nature. Thus, the court is independent of the procurator, and the accused will be represented by counsel in many circumstances. With the declaration of the presumption of innocence, the burden of proof in clearly placed on the procurator. A number of principles speak to: prohibiting violations to the honor and dignity of participants in a criminal proceeding, protecting people from illegal arrest and detention, protecting peoples rights and freedoms, prohibiting illegal searches and seizures, guaranteeing the right of a defense, and the right of appeal against procedural actions or decisions of the trial court. The two most prominent changes are judicial supervision at the pretrial stage, which still employs an inquisitorial approach while also enhancing the independence of the judiciary, and an adversarial process during the trial.

An examination of criminal procedural issues is divided into two categories. The first involves the pretrial process, which includes police and procurator powers, along with other issues pertinent to the preliminary investigation. The second category is concerned with the trial process. It consists of the main hearing as well as appellate reviews.

Preliminary Investigation Once a complaint has been received by the police or procurator, a decision to initiate a case has to be made. Even before that, a written report is entered into the record that confirms the complaint was received by the appropriate authority. Anonymous complaints are not grounds for starting an investigation. The decision to proceed must be made within 72 hours of receiving the complaint, but the period can be extended by a procurator for up to 10 days. Either an investigator with the consent of a procurator or the procurator will issue a decree to initiate an inquiry into the matter. After a decree has been approved, a preliminary investigation begins. Either an investigator from the procurator's office or the militia usually conducts the investigation. The procurator, however, is mandated at all times to supervise the entire process. If a decree is issued that refuses to initiate an inquiry, obviously with reasons for such a decision, an appeal can be made to the procurator or to the court. The Code also permits a private accusation, which enables the victim of a crime to initiate a prosecution through an application to the court.

The preliminary investigation should normally be completed within two months, with a possible extension of up to six months. Further extensions are possible depending on the complexity of the case. It should also be noted that during this investigative stage the Code now permits defense counsel or the suspect and a victim or a civil plaintiff the right to interrogate witnesses, to conduct their own investigation, and to collect evidence that they may deem pertinent to the case.

There are a number of legal issues—most importantly, the rights of the accused—that are of great concern during a preliminary investigation. These will be examined presently. For the moment, though, assume that the preliminary investigation has been completed. At this stage of the process, a decision must be reached either to indict the defendant or to terminate the case based on the evidence collected. The procurator scrutinizes the investigator's recommendation in all instances. If the investigator recommends the issuance of an indictment, the procurator can concur and prosecute the case or vacate the recommendation and terminate the case. If the investigating officer favors terminating the case, the procurator will either concur or decide to indict the defendant. In all cases, the ultimate decision rests with the procurator.

Articles 24 through 28 of the Code explain the reasons for terminating a criminal prosecution. Among the more obvious reasons for refusing to initiate a prosecution are: the absence of a crime, the absence of evidence, the expiration of the time to initiate a prosecution for the specific offense, and the death of the suspect or the accused. Other reasons for declining to prosecute include: if the parties have reconciled and the incident was a first-time offense that is considered of average gravity and if the accused is no longer considered socially dangerous. Finally, a prosecution might be halted in connection with article 75 of the Criminal Code of the Russian Federation. Article 75 states in part:

> A person who committed a crime for the first time of average gravity may be relieved from criminal responsibility if after the commission of the crime he voluntarily acknowledged his guilt, facilitated the eliciting of the crime, compensated the damage caused or otherwise made amends for the harm caused as a result of the crime.

If an indictment is sought in the case, the next phase of the process is a trial in a court of first instance. Before that process is described, however, it is important to examine some of the procedural issues involving the rights of the accused during the preliminary investigation.

Power to Detain According to the Code The investigators have the right to detain a person suspected of committing a crime for which punishment may be assigned in the form of deprivation of freedom, only if one of the following grounds exists: if the person is caught committing the crime or immediately after committing it; if the person is identified by eyewitnesses; and if the person has traces of the crime on him or her or at his or her place of residence. Other reasons for detaining a person include when information suggests that the person is a suspect and he or she either attempts to flee, has no permanent address, or his or her identity cannot be established.

Following such a detention, the procurator must be notified within 12 hours. Within 48 hours, the procurator must either approve the confinement or order the person's release. The Constitution of the Russian Federation lends further credence to this policy, for Article 22 states "[a] person may not be subjected to detention for more than 48 hours before a court decision is rendered." Once a person is detained, he or she has the right to see counsel, and this must be honored within the first 24 hours of detention.

Before a suspect is interrogated, the suspect must be informed of his or her rights, which include the right to know what crime(s) he or she is accused of committing, and the opportunity to offer explanations, submit petitions, and appeal from the actions and decisions of the person conducting the investigation. If the suspect is being detained, he or she must be interrogated within the first 24 hours of detention, and defense counsel has the right to be present during this initial interrogation.

If sufficient evidence has been collected, the investigating officer may issue a decree to prosecute the suspect as the accused. Once the accusation is presented, the investigator is "obliged to explain to an accused his rights." These rights are explained in the Code, which states, in part:

> The accused shall have the right: to know what he is accused of and to give explanations concerning the accusation presented to him; to present evidence; to submit petitions; to become acquainted with all the materials of the case upon completion of the preliminary investigation or inquiry; to have defense counsel; to participate in the judicial examination in the court of first instance; to submit challenges; and to appeal from the actions and decisions of the person conducting the inquiry, the investigator, procurator and court.

It is important to point out that under Soviet procedure the accused was not permitted assistance of counsel until after a formal charge had been submitted. The Constitution of the Russian Federation, however, changed this timetable to benefit the accused. Article 48 states: "Everyone who is detained, put in custody or charged with committing a crime has the right to avail himself or herself of the assistance of a lawyer from the time he or she is detained, put in custody or charged." Although a suspect has a right to counsel, many do not have representation during this initial phase of the process. Often, the person cannot afford to pay for this service and the authorities have a difficult time finding counsel that is available and willing to take on the case at this initial stage. This is unfortunate, because it is at this phase in the process that a suspect often needs counsel the most to protect his or her rights.

Power to Search and Seize Article 12 of the basic principles of the Code focuses on the inviolability of the living quarters. It states in part that "[a]n examination of the living quarters shall be carried out only with the consent of the persons residing in them, or on the ground of a court decision ..." Searches may be permitted:

> If an investigator has sufficient grounds to suppose that the instruments of a crime, or articles or valuables criminally acquired, or other articles or documents which may be of significance for the case, are on some premises or in any other place or are in someone's possession, he shall conduct a search to find and remove them.
>
> A search may also be conducted for finding wanted persons, as well as corpses.
>
> A search shall be conducted in accordance with a reasoned decree of the investigator and only with the sanction of a procurator. In instances not permitting delay, a search may be conducted without the sanction of a procurator, but the procurator must be informed subsequently within one day of the search.

Witnesses should be present during searches and seizures. The accused, an adult member of the family, or a representative of the manager of an apartment complex may serve as witness to the investigation. Moreover, only items pertinent to the investigation may be seized. Article 13 of the basic principles addresses the issue of privacy. "Restrictions of the citizen's right to the privacy of the correspondence, of the telephone and other talks, of the postal, telegraph and other communications shall be admissible only on the ground of a court decision."

Searches of persons are subject to the same regulations as searches of objects. In addition, a personal search may be conducted during detention or confinement or in any other place if there is sufficient cause to believe a person is concealing information that is pertinent to the case. Personal searches are conducted in the presence of witnesses of the same gender. These policies have essentially been reiterated in

Chapter 2 of the Constitution of the Russian Federation dealing with human and civil rights and liberties.

Measures of Restraint In order to assure cooperation throughout the preliminary investigation and trial, the investigator, procurator, or court can impose measures of restraint upon the accused. A number of factors are taken into consideration when selecting a measure. These include the seriousness of the accusation as well as the accused's criminal history, personality, employment status, age, state of health, family situation, and other circumstances.

Several options available to the authorities are categorized as measures of restraint. For example, an accused's written promise not to depart from his or her residence without the investigator's approval may be a sufficient restraint in some cases. Personal surety is another method. This is a signed promise from a minimum of two people who are willing to ensure the good conduct of the accused. Surety of a social organization is similar to a personal surety. The difference is that the restraint is ensured by a social organization with whom the accused is associated. Confinement under guard is yet another method. The standard term of confinement cannot exceed two months, but extensions are permitted in exceptional cases. Finally, bail (in the form of money or valuables that are deposited with the court) is a method of restraint. When people evade the authorities while on bail, the money is turned over to the state.

Defense Counsel Out of all the members of the Russian courtroom work group, defense counsel has the potential for the most significant role expansion. In the Soviet system, defense counsel's involvement was permitted only after the preliminary investigation was completed. Thus, until counsel was selected, the procurator was the sole guardian of the accused's rights. During the last few years under the Soviet system, this policy was superseded by a law that permitted suspects, the accused, and defendants access to counsel at the time of their detention, arrest, or the filing of charges. Some experts have alleged that under the Soviet system, the primary role of defense counsel was to attempt to mitigate the accused's responsibility based on the circumstances of the case. In addition, the accused could choose to refuse the assistance of counsel.

In the Russian Federation, a person now has a constitutional right to assistance of counsel. Article 48 states: "Everyone is guaranteed the right to receive qualified assistance. In cases stipulated by law, legal assistance is provided free of charge. Everyone who is detained, put in custody or charged with committing a crime has the right to avail himself or herself of the assistance of a lawyer (defender) from the time he or she is detained, put in custody or charged." It is this constitutional right that provides the basis for the potential expansion of defense counsel's role in the courtroom work group. With the new Code of Criminal Procedure, the role of defense counsel has been enhanced further.

According to Article 49 of the code, the accused has a right to counsel at various stages in the procedural process. These include: the moment a criminal case is instituted; the moment a person is detained; the moment a person is declared a suspect; the moment a person's rights and freedoms are procedurally infringed upon; and the moment a ruling orders a person to trial.

The accused has the right to refuse the use of counsel, but he or she must state this request in writing. There were some occasions when the utilization of defense counsel is required. These are cited in Article 51 of the code and include cases in which: the suspect has not refused the use of counsel; the suspect is underage; the suspect cannot exercise his or her rights because of a physical or psychological defect; the suspect does not have a command of the language in which the case is being conducted; the suspect is accused of an offense in which the punishment is a form of deprivation of freedom of at least 15 years or harsher; or the suspect is scheduled to have a jury trial.

There are also several rights and duties given to defense counsel. These include: meeting with the accused; collecting and presenting evidence; employing specialists to assist with the defense; being present when the accusation is brought; taking part in the interrogation of the accused, as well as other investigative actions; acquainting oneself with the materials of the case and copying the necessary information; entering petitions; taking part in the judicial proceedings of the case; and lodging complaints against actions and decisions of the investigators, procurators, and the court.

The Civil Plaintiff People who have suffered a material loss as a result of a crime can bring a civil suit against the accused, and it can be entertained by the court, along with the criminal case. A victim who brings a separate civil suit by way of civil proceedings and has had that civil suit dismissed cannot then jointly introduce the same suit with the criminal case. If a civil suit is not brought, the court can compensate the victim for material losses on its own initiative.

Concern for victims of crime was also entertained in the Constitution of the Russian Federation. Article 52 states: "The rights of victims of crimes and of abuse of power are protected by law. The state ensures the victims access to the judicial system and compensation for damages incurred." Article 53 further indicates: "Everyone has the right to reimbursement by the state for damages incurred through illegal actions (or inaction) by bodies of state power or their officials."

The Trial Once a procurator decides to refer a case to trial, the court (in an administrative session) must make a preliminary determination regarding the case. The composition of the court in an administrative session is a single judge. Both procurator and defense counsel are eligible to present their positions at this session. While in an administrative session, the court entertains various petitions from the participants in the case. It also resolves various questions that pertain to the trial. The judge can refer the case for a preliminary hearing or bind the case over for trial to the appropriate jurisdiction. The judge has 30 days in which to make a decision if the accused is not in custody and 14 days if the person is in custody.

If the case is to be bound over for trial, the judge determines the type of trial and location, whether the accused needs counsel for his or her defense, and whether measures of restraint should be applied or altered. The trial should begin within 14 days of this decision; unless it is a jury trial, in which case the trial should begin within 30 days.

A preliminary hearing is conducted by a single judge at the request of one of the parties in a criminal proceeding. It is held to entertain requests that evidence be excluded, to request time to obtain additional evidence, and to interview witnesses. The judge rules on the admissibility of the evidence, and in such instances, the procurator may amend the accusation. This, in turn, may influence which court has jurisdiction and determine the type of trial that is appropriate for the case. The judge may bind the case over for trial, return the matter to the procurator for further consideration, suspend the proceedings, or terminate the case.

Having concluded the preliminary phase of the trial, the main hearing or judicial examination is ready to begin. Under the 2001 Code of Criminal Procedure, the various roles of the courtroom workgroup have changed to reflect the adversarial nature of the trial process. The judge now has a neutral passive role, while both the procurator and defense counsel have a more active role. Emphasis is also placed on the openness of the procedural process, with the court's judgment based on the evidence presented at trial. While closed trials or sessions of trials are still permitted, they are limited to cases involving state or other secrets protected by federal law, an accused under the age of 16, or crimes of a sexual nature or other crimes that demean the victim.

What follows are the various steps in a standard trial:

1. The procurator explains the accusation and identifies the precise offenses cited in the Criminal Code. The judge inquiries if the accused understands the charges that have been brought against him. The judge asks if the accused wishes to enter a plea or if he wishes to make a statement regarding the accusation.

2. The procurator then submits evidence to the court, and it is cross-examined by the defense. Defense counsel submits evidence to the court, and it is cross-examined by the procurator.

3. If the accused agrees to give testimony, he may do so at any stage of the trial with the approval of the judge. The

accused would be first questioned by defense counsel and any other participants of the defense, if more than one defendant was being tried. The procurator would then question the accused which would be followed by counsel for any civil plaintiff. The judge may reject any leading or irrelevant questions put to the accused. Once the counsel for each side has finished questioning the accused, the judge may ask questions of the defendant.

4. If the victim gives testimony, this may also occur at any stage of the trial with the approval of the judge. The victim would be first questioned by the procurator and counsel for any civil plaintiff. Defense counsel or multi-counsels would then pose questions to the victim. Again, the judge may reject any leading or irrelevant questions put to the victim. Finally, the judge may put questions to the victim. While being questioned, the victim may use notes and read from documents to elaborate on their testimony.

5. Then, witnesses in the case are interrogated. Each witness is questioned first by the party that called them as a witness. The judge may ask questions after both sides have completed their interrogation of the witness. While being questioned, the witnesses may use notes and read from documents to elaborate on their testimony. In addition to being kept separate from other witnesses, they are not permitted in the courtroom until called to testify. Witnesses must remain in the courtroom after the completion of their interrogation until the judicial investigation is completed, unless the judge grants them permission to leave early.

6. Next, the expert witnesses who provided testimony during the preliminary investigation are interrogated. They do so when either petitioned by one of the parties in the case or at the request of the judge. The interrogation questions are submitted in advance to the expert in order to give the person time to prepare their answers. Initially, the questions are read out in court in order to solicit the views of the parties to the case. This may lead to questions being amended or rejected by the judge. If expert witnesses contradict one another, the judge may seek the opinion of another expert.

7. Material evidence may be introduced for examine at any point in the trial at the request of one of the parties. Once the evidence has been examined, the judge asks the parties if they wish to add anything to this judicial investigation. The judge would rule on any requests. Once any actions are completed the judge would declare the judicial investigation completed.

8. The trial then moves to the oral argument or pleading phase. Oral arguments are speeches presented by the procurator, defense counsel, defendant, victim. and participants in any civil issues being aired during the trial. While the court determines the sequence of these speeches, the rules call for the accuser being heard first and the defendant always being heard last. The speaker may not be interrupted as long as the presentation does not digress from the issues raised in the case. These speeches may only refer to evidence that has already been introduced during the judicial investigation.

9. Following the oral arguments, the participants are allowed to rebut. Defense counsel and defendant always have the right to the last rebuttal.

10. The defendant is then permitted to make a final statement, at which time no questions may be put to him or her.

11. Before the court retires to consider the case, the major participants have the right to propose in writing their views as to how the court should resolve the standard questions raised during the trial (see Item 12). The court is not bound to entertain these proposals.

12. The judge then retires to a conference room to consider the case. The court is mandated to return a judgment that is both legal and well-reasoned. Chances of the court reaching such a judgment are enhanced by the court discussing and responding to a series of questions. The questions posed include: Did the criminal act take place? Did the act contain the elements of a crime as described in the Criminal Code of the Russian Federation? Did the accused commit such an act? Is the accused guilty of committing the crime? Is the accused subject to punishment for the crime committed by him or her? Exactly which punishment must be assigned to the accused and are there either mitigating or aggravating circumstances? Are there grounds for finding guilt but not imposing a punishment? To what type of correctional facility should the prisoner be sent? Is the civil suit subject to satisfaction? Is the material loss subject to compensation? On whom and in what amount must court costs be imposed? What will be the measure of restraint with respect to the prisoner? While considering these questions, the court may decide to reopen the judicial investigatory phase of the trial to clarify points of interest.

13. The court must then reach a judgment either to convict or acquit. A judgment to convict must be based upon a reasoned evaluation of the information presented during the judicial investigation. Acquittals are permissible if: the event of a crime is not established; the elements of a crime are not in the act of the accused; and participation of the accused in the commission of the crime is not proved.

    If a civil suit was entered jointly in the criminal case, its outcome also is determined at this time.

14. The court returns to the courtroom to render its judgment. All people in the room are required to stand when the judgment is announced. If the defendant has been found guilty, the sentence is passed.

When a case is heard by a three-judge panel, the questions raised in the aforementioned item 12 of the trial process are determined by a simple majority vote. Any member of the court may explain in writing his or her dissent from the majority opinion. This dissent is not revealed when the judgment of the court is announced, but is included in the case file. Thus, the dissent may be considered if the case is appealed or subjected to judicial review.

In 2002, the Russians introduced a special proceeding, which is a form of plea bargaining. In the event the accused admits guilt to the charges leveled against him or her and if the parties to the case agree, a judgment can be issued by the court without a trial. In such cases, the sanction for the offense cannot exceed five years of imprisonment. The procedure calls for the court to certify that the accused understands the consequences of his or her decision to plead guilty and that it is being made voluntarily. If the court or another party to the case is not satisfied, the trial would proceed.

The jury trial was introduced in 1993 on an experimental basis in nine regions of the country. Support for its use was reaffirmed with the new Constitution of the Russian Federation. Article 123 states: "In instances stipulated by federal law, judicial proceedings are conducted with the participation of jurors." By 2003, the experiment was extended to the other 69 regions of the country. Guidelines for the use of the jury are found in the 2001 Code of Criminal Procedure. The procedure allows the defendant, if he or she has been accused of a specific kind of crime, to choose between a jury trial or a traditional trial. The list of crimes that fall under this category include: murder, kidnapping, rape with aggravating circumstances, child trafficking, gangsterism, large-scale bribery, treason, terrorist acts, calls for violent change in the constitutional system, and some other select crimes against the state.

Any Russian citizen who lives in the district where a trial will take place can serve as a juror. A juror must be at least 25 years of age, legally competent to serve, and without a criminal record. Twelve people are selected by the procurator and defense counsel after having their names drawn from a list of 30 to 40 eligible to serve. In addition to the 12 jurors, two alternates are also selected. Potential jurors are questioned by the procurator and defense counsel, and a written challenge can be submitted to the judge objecting to the possible selection of a juror.

At trial the Russian jury sits separately from the judge in the courtroom. The responsibility of the Russian jury is to decide matters of fact, while the judge determines issues of law that arise during the trial. The opening procedures of a jury trial are slightly different from those of a non-jury trial that are explained above. At the beginning of a jury trial the procurator and then the defense counsel provide an introductory statement that essentially outlines the case that they are about to present. Russian jurors are permitted to ask questions of the accused, victim, and witnesses during the course of the trial. They submit their questions in written form through the jury foreman to the judge. The judge may reject questions that are deemed irrelevant. In addition, information about the accused's prior criminal record cannot be introduced, as it might prejudice the jury.

According to Article 334 of the 2001 Code of Criminal Procedure, the responsibility of the jury is to determine three questions: (1) did a criminal act take place? (2) did the accused commit the criminal act? and (3) is the accused guilty or not guilty of the charges? Before the jury commences their deliberations, the judge will provide them with a list of written questions that they must answer in the course of their deliberations. The parties to the case are able to examine and comment on the questions before they are presented to the jury. The defense is permitted to put questions to the jury that deal with the factual circumstances of the case that the judge must include in his or her list of questions. After receiving the questions but before leaving the courtroom, the judge sums up the case for the jurors by reviewing the accusation, the evidence, and the positions of procurator and defense. The judge further explains the rules surrounding the evaluation of the evidence and the important principle of the presumption of innocence. Russian juries are expected to return unanimous verdicts during the first three hours of deliberations. Majority verdicts are permitted after that time. A not-guilty verdict is adopted if at least six jurors cast such a vote. If a jury finds the accused guilty, they can request that the judge show leniency at sentencing or they may decline to make such a request. If a jury finds the accused guilty, but the judge is of the opinion that the person is innocent, the judge may dissolve the jury and send the case back to a new preliminary hearing.

After the jury has submitted their verdict to the judge, they are dismissed. The trial would then continue with the matters involving any civil litigation that may be attached to the trial. For example, funeral expenses, medical costs, or other damages that might be at issue would be entertained only the judge.

Once the trial (traditional or jury) in a court of first instance is completed, the next stage in the criminal process involves any possible appeals. The court that heard the case is responsible for informing participants of this right. The procurator and defense counsel have the right to appeal the judgment of the court by way of cassation. Those involved in the civil suit may also do the same, so long as it involves the judgment of the civil suit. The procurator, through the cassation process, has a professional obligation to protest any illegal or unfounded judgment.

When a cassation has been filed, the original judgment of the court of first instance is suspended. The cassation is entertained by the court at the next level in the court hierarchy. Actually, when an appeal is made against the judgment of a justice of the peace, there is an automatic retrial in the district court. All courts hearing cassation appeals must do so within 10 days of receipt of the petition. There is one exception, however, in that the Supreme Court has a 20-day period.

Cassation is not an entire review of the case. Its purpose is to verify the legality of the original decision. There are four reasons for vacating or altering the judgment of the trial court: the judgment of the court is not based on the factual circumstances of the case; the procedural rights of the accused as spelled out in the Code of Criminal Procedure were violated; the Criminal Code was misinterpreted; or the punishment is unjust. Cassation sessions are open to the public. The major participants in the original trial are eligible to participate in the appeal. A panel of three judges hears the cassation petition. The court hearing the appeal may return one of four decisions: to uphold the original judgment, to vacate the judgment and refer the case for new investigation or a new judicial consideration, to vacate the judgment and terminate the case, or to change the judgment. When the court changes the original judgment, it cannot increase the punishment or issue a sanction for a more serious crime. The court can only reduce the original punishment for the original offense or sentence the defendant to a less serious offense. After the cassational judgment is rendered, the case is returned to the court of first instance for execution. This is done within five days of the cassational court's ruling.

Once the cassational judgment has been rendered, the overwhelming majority of cases are considered final. Nevertheless, there is one final method by which a judgment can be protested. This is referred to as judicial supervision. A judicial supervision is considered only after a judgment has taken legal effect. A supervision can be initiated only by the chair of a court that ranks above the court that rendered the judgment or by a procurator who is above the rank of the procurator who participated in the protested judgment. Judicial supervisions are initiated to check illegal procedures or unfounded judgments. The court may return one of five decisions when considering a judicial supervision: (1) uphold the judgment; (2) vacate the judgment and all subsequent judicial rulings and decrees, and terminate proceedings in the case or transfer it for new investigation or new judicial consideration; (3) vacate the cassational ruling as well as subsequent judicial rulings and decrees (if any have been rendered) and transfer the case for new cassational consideration; (4) vacate the rulings and decrees rendered by way of judicial supervision, leaving the judgment of the court and cassational ruling either unchanged or changed; or (5) change the judgment, ruling, or decree of the court. As in the cassational proceedings, a panel of three judges renders the judgment. Russian procedure also provides for the reopening of a case if new evidence is discovered.

Corrections

The Russian people have been subjected to authoritarian governments throughout their history, whether it was the capricious and at times benevolent direction of the tsars or the planned and calculated leadership of the Communist Party. In both cases, the majority of Russian citizens displayed a good deal of respect for the power and authority imposed by their leaders. This attitude has been attributed to the fact that the Russian people are essentially patriotic and nonpolitical. This created a conformist attitude toward the state by the citizenry. Since 1917, deference was paid to the authority of the CPSU because the party was the principal interpreter of Marxism-Leninism, the ideology upon which the Soviet socialist system was based.

Irrespective of the country, there tends to be general agreement as to the purpose of a correctional system. It is designed and responsible for those individuals who have been sanctioned for failing to abide by society's norms as articulated by law. It has been pointed out that the Soviet Union placed a greater emphasis on ideology than on law, while the Russian Federation is attempting to establish a society based on the rule of law. Thus, the present dilemma facing Russia is that of transforming the basis for the correctional system to a set of legal principles. Considering the history and present circumstances, a good deal of progress has been made in this endeavor.

The correctional system of the Soviet Union had been established primarily to handle two types of norm violators. There were those people who had violated "traditional" dictates of Soviet criminal law. The term "traditional" is defined here as crimes that are found in all countries; that is, offenses described either as street crime or white-collar crime. The other norm violators were political prisoners, referred to by Amnesty International as "the prisoners of conscience." Depending on how one wants to interpret this category, most countries are likely to have some people who are depicted as "prisoners of conscience" or who view themselves as such. The Soviet Union appeared to have more political prisoners than would be found in most other countries. This was largely attributed to two factors. The first was the unwavering faith of the Soviet leadership in the Marxist-Leninist philosophy and the desire to have all citizens conform to its dictates. The other factor was the leadership's ongoing policy objective of assuring the country's internal and external security. Soviet corrections served as an important mechanism in the government's attempts to enhance and assure security within the country.

Some experts were of the opinion that the introduction of glasnost would lead to a reduction of the number of people labeled political prisoners. They based this view on the fact that Gorbachev had made it known that he was committed to strengthening socialist legality. This was translated to mean that he favored ensuring greater social justice by providing citizens with more rights and legal safeguards. There were at least two tangible signs that this was occurring. In 1985, the Institute of State and Law of the USSR Academy of Sciences drafted for circulation and discussion the "Theoretical Model of a Criminal Code (General Part)," and in 1990, amendments were introduced to the Fundamentals of Criminal Legislation of the USSR.

It was stated earlier that correctional systems are designed and responsible for those people who have been sanctioned for failing to abide by society's norms as articulated by law. However, law in the Soviet Union was not considered a guiding force behind the correctional system; rather, the system sought direction from the dictates of Communist ideology. Both the rationale and method of sanctioning an offender were tied to the ideology, as were the administrative goals and management objectives of the correctional system. With the establishment of the Russian Federation, efforts have continued to build on those initially introduced by Gorbachev to strengthen the role of law in society—including changes in the correctional system. In several instances, legislation has been adopted to rectify some of the long-standing concerns, while in other instances the lack of funding precludes implementation.

Sentencing Philosophy

The general part of the 1996 Criminal Code contains a section on punishment. Article 43 is devoted to the concept and purposes of punishment.

> Punishment is the measure of State coercion assigned by judgment of a court. Punishment shall be applied to a person deemed to be guilty of the commission of a crime and shall consist of the deprivation or limitation of rights and freedoms of this person provided for by the present Code. Punishment shall be applied for the purpose of restoring social justness, and also for the purpose of reforming the convicted person and preventing the commission of new crimes.

As was the case during the Soviet era, Russia ascribes to multiple-purpose objectives for sanctioning, which include such standard rationales as deterrence and rehabilitation.

The Soviet efforts to achieve the sentencing rationales of deterrence and rehabilitation were clouded by the allegations that physical suffering was very much in evidence when a person was sentenced during the Soviet era, in particular when the sanction included a term of deprivation of freedom. Mindful of these criticisms, a draft of the Fundamentals of Criminal Legislation that was undertaken during the Gorbachev era suggested that the purpose of sanctioning should include deterrence and rehabilitation rather than punishment. This view has essentially been introduced into the Russian Federation with the 1996 Criminal Code.

By way of illustration and alluded to earlier in the section on law, the new code is guided by a series of principles. One is legality; that is, an act can be deemed criminal only if it is addressed by the present code. Another is equality, or the proposition that all people are equal before the law. A third principle is that guilt must be established in order to hold a person criminally responsible. A fourth principle is justness; that is, the punishment must correspond to or fit the crime. The last principle is that of humanity, which is specifically concerned with the purpose of sanctions and punishment. Article 7 of the code in which the principle is spelled out states: "Criminal legislation of the Russian Federation shall ensure the security of man. Punishment and other measures of a criminal-law character applicable to a person who has committed a crime may not have as their purpose the causing of physical sufferings or the demeaning of human dignity." While acknowledging that these principles will be significant and useful only if they are interpreted correctly and implemented in practice throughout the various stages of the judicial process, they do offer a new standard for administering justice in Russia.

With regard to the underlying philosophy behind Russian sentencing, it is useful to consider the fourth principle of justness to a greater extent. This principle is spelled out in Article 6 of the code. "Punishment and other measures of a criminal-law character applicable to a person who has committed a crime must be just, that is, correspond to the character and degree of social danger of the crime, the circumstances of committing it, and the personality of the guilty person." It goes on to state that "No one may bear criminal responsibility twice for one and the same crime." The central issue here is that judges are asked to consider the nature of the crime and the personality of the offender, which would include mitigating circumstances and aggravating punishment.

Among the circumstances that might mitigate the punishment are: being a first-time offender; the age of the offender; pregnancy; being responsible for young children; being prompted by arduous living conditions or compassion; physical or mental compulsion; unlawful behavior of victim; rendering assistance to the victim; and acknowledgment of guilt. The circumstances that might aggravate the punishment include: being a repeat offender; grave consequences of the crime; degree of participation; use of a weapon; degree of cruelty; prior collusion or being in an organized criminal group; the victim having been young, pregnant, defenseless, or helpless; and the offense having been motivated by hate based on nationality, race, or religion. Some of these factors were available and utilized by judges during the Soviet era.

As mentioned earlier in the section on law, the Russians make a distinction between punishments that are considered basic and those considered supplementary measures. The sanctions that can be imposed only as a basic measure include: obligatory tasks, correctional tasks, limitation in military service, limitation of freedom, arrest, confinement in a disciplinary military unit, deprivation of freedom for a determined period, deprivation of freedom for life, and the death penalty. Two sanctions can be assessed as either basic or supplementary punishments; they include: a fine and the deprivation of a right to occupy a determined post or to engage in a determined activity. Finally, a few punishments can be issued only as a supplementary measure; they include (1) the confiscation of property, or (2) the deprivation of a special, military, or honorary title; class rank; or State award. These sanctions will be explained in greater detail throughout this section of the chapter.

Of particular interest to students of comparative correctional institutions is the degree to which they differ under the administration of the Russian Federation from that of the Soviet era. A central feature of the Soviet correctional system was the tripartite rationale for sanctioning. It was based on the need to reform or reeducate the offender to the goals and purposes of socialist society and legality, to assure that the offender performed a useful service or socially significant labor while they were being punished, and to enhance the possibility that the person would comply with the law in the future and not commit new crimes. Various regimes had been developed to impress upon the individual the state's commitment to establishing an orderly society with which all citizens were expected to comply. From the Soviet point of view, it was the task of reeducation that was—at least theoretically—the most significant rationale for sanctioning and thus central to each type of sentence.

The extent to which Soviet corrections was shrouded in secrecy resulted in Western accounts being largely limited to those of Soviet émigrés who had personally experienced a term in a correctional facility. Because these people were often convicted of political crimes, and given the Soviet attitude toward such offenders, their prison regimen was harsher than that to which an ordinary street criminal might be subject. Both the regimen and the sincerity of the Soviet commitment to rehabilitation became highly suspect in light of these émigré accounts—at least in terms of the Western perspective.

As was suggested earlier, the purpose of sentencing in the Russian Federation has focused on deterrence and rehabilitation. It is important to note that in the Russian Federation rehabilitation is used in two contexts. On the one hand, the traditional use of the term refers to programs within correctional settings and more recently to the diversion of people from custodial to noncustodial sentences. On the other hand, rehabilitation has a special significance for former political prisoners. In the Russian context, it also means the restoration of a person's rights, standing, and reputation, which were destroyed because the person was persecuted and labeled a criminal within the framework of the Soviet criminal justice system (Moskal'Kova, 1992). Although much effort has been made to correct this past injustice, there remain political prisoners who have not yet had their names and reputations restored.

The principles behind the 1996 Criminal Code are designed to offer a new standard in which to administer justice. Part of that new standard should be the transformation of the old correctional system of the Soviet Union to a more humane approach under the Russian Federation. While the legal principles mentioned above are clearly a start in the right direction, the state of corrections in Russia is presently in a crisis mode. The nature of that crisis is incorporated into a description of the organization and administration of the correctional system.

Organization and Administration of the Correctional System

Ministry of Internal Affairs The organization and administration of the correctional system of the Russian Federation was initially the responsibility of the Ministry of Internal Affairs, as it had been under the Soviet Union. In late 1998, that authority was transferred to the Ministry of Justice. Although one can hope that a change in administration might facilitate an improvement in the state of corrections in Russia, it does not appear likely. Part of this has to do with external factors that are beyond the control of any ministry responsible for administering corrections. The central problem has been a lack of adequate government funding to support corrections. Given the breadth and depth of the economic crisis confronting the country, this should come as no surprise. Another significant problem is the number of people who are either being sentenced to a period of incarceration or are being held awaiting trial. This is a reflection of the increased crime rate throughout the country. The abysmal economy is a contributing factor to these circumstances, as is the manner in which government bureaucracies function in the country. A key feature of these bureaucracies, which is a holdover from the Soviet era, is an overreliance on centralized decisionmaking. There is also a crisis in both the quality and quantity of personnel working in the field of corrections. All of this makes one skeptical that the state of corrections will soon improve in the Russian Federation.

In light of the fact that the Ministry of Internal Affairs had long been responsible for the central planning and policy development of the correctional system during both the Soviet era and the initial years of the Russian Federation, it is useful to review its tenure as that authority. The ministry has long been an important part of the government. As pointed out earlier, this ministry was also accountable for the militia (the regular police force) during the Soviet era, and it has retained that responsibility today. When it was responsible for Soviet corrections, it had an even more powerful role. As a ministry, it could issue legal orders, and as a member of the Council of Ministers, it could participate in the passage of legal decrees that influenced the administration of the correctional system. Because most legislation affecting corrections was seldom published for public consumption, this kind of law-making authority was quite significant. The actual implementation and administration of the correctional system was handled through the offices of the ministry at the union republic or regional level. The ministry's original arbitrary legal authority was curbed significantly during the Russian Federation's attempts to administer its institutions according to rules of law.

Because penal statistics were considered state secrets, Western experts were unable to acquire an accurate assessment of the number of penal institutions or inmates in the Soviet Union. Amnesty International, however, had identified at least 330 facilities in the course of their defense of Soviet political prisoners (1975). They indicated further that more than one-half of these institutions were located in the RSFSR, the largest of the Soviet Union's 15 republics. As a result of the dramatic changes during and since the demise of the Soviet Union, information about the justice system of the Russian Federation is not considered a state secret.

Scholars have suggested that statistical data from Russia should not be interpreted as precise numbers but rather as approximations to be considered along with other information (King, 1994). It is in that spirit that the following data is offered. In 1991, the Ministry of Internal Affairs of the USSR reported holding 765,000 convicted prisoners in its various prison facilities and 200,000 people were also being held in detention, which meant that they had either not gone to trial or were awaiting their sentence. In 1992, the Ministry of the Interior for the Russian Federation reported 600,000 convicts incarcerated and another 150,000 awaiting either a trial or their sentence. In recent years, Amnesty International has reported that there are approximately one million people incarcerated in Russian correctional facilities; of these, hundreds of thousands have not been sentenced but are awaiting trial. A more recent study indicated that the prison population peaked at more than one million in 2000. Since that time, the population declined, rose again, and has begun a steady decline, measuring about 865,000 in 2003 (see King and Piacentini, in Pridemore, 2005).

With regard to the number of facilities in operation, the Ministry of the Interior reported in 1992 that it utilized 981 facilities for its prison population. Of these, 922 are for adults and 59 are for young offenders. Among the adult institutions, 30 are for female inmates. Of the 59 facilities for young offenders, three are designated for female offenders. The facilities for the prison population are designated as colony settlements, educational labor colonies for juveniles, hospitals, labor colonies, prisons, and remand prisons (or jails).

Imprisonment Before the various types of correctional institutions are explained, it is important to offer some general comments about the sanction of imprisonment in the former Soviet Union and in the Russian Federation. Imprisonment had been frequently utilized in the Soviet Union. It was estimated that one-half of all convictions—for approximately .5 million people annually—involved deprivation of freedom (Juviler, 1976). More recently, it was suggested that as late as 1983, between 70 and 80 percent of the defendants in people's courts were sentenced to a term of imprisonment. High rates of incarceration were the order of the day and had always been so under the Soviet regime because the prison population was a significant feature in the Soviet economy. Recently, Nils Christie reminded us that the prison colonies "were among the best functioning parts of the old economy. Here was a captive work force, sober, well-ordered, working in two shifts in factories inside the same fence" (Christie, 2000). By 1988, however, the percentage of sentences to incarceration had dropped to about 30 percent (Butler, 1988). This change in policy was attributed both to glasnost and to the policy of strengthening socialist legality.

It should be noted that the term "imprisonment" is not used by Russians when describing forms of punishment in general and periods of incarceration in particular. Presently, an offender in the Russian Federation can be sentenced to a term of imprisonment or incarceration in one of three ways. The term "arrest" is used in the 1996 Criminal Code to describe a period of confinement from one to six months. This sanction cannot be imposed on people who have not reached the age of 16, or on women who are pregnant or have children up to the age of eight.

Deprivation of freedom for a determined period is another sanction associated with incarceration. The term ranges from six months to 20 years. The type of facility that an offender would be sent to would depend on the nature of the crime and aggravating and mitigating circumstances associated with the offense. The facility could be a prison, correctional labor colony, or colony-settlement. It has been reported that the average length of a sentence imposed by a Russian court is five and one-half years and that the actual time served is about three years (King, 1994).

The final sentence to a term of incarceration is deprivation of freedom for life. As Article 57 of code indicates, this is a sanction imposed as an alternative to the death penalty for "especially grave crimes infringing life." The code goes on to state that this form of deprivation of freedom "shall not be assigned to women, and also to persons who have committed a crime in age of up to eighteen years, and men who have attained at the moment of the rendering of judgment by the court sixty-five years of age."

During the waning years of the Soviet Union, Gorbachev's policy of democratization and his strategy of perestroika had a significant impact on the correctional system. The goal was basically to humanize some criminal legislation. These efforts were also assisted by the human rights movement within the country. Of particular interest to that movement was the issue of capital punishment. While the government advocated eliminating it for most economic crimes, human rights groups favored the total abolition of the sanction.

In public opinion polls taken in the late 1980s, it was suggested that 80 to 85 percent of the population opposed the complete elimination of the death penalty. When readers of *Moskovskiye novosti* were asked if they favored the abolition of capital punishment, approximately nine out of 10 opposed the idea on the grounds that they felt the death penalty deterred murders. Although the deterrent effect had not been studied in the Soviet Union, Soviet officials and scholars pointed out that they were familiar with the studies and debate in the United States. Many scholars and officials were convinced that the reform of socialist legality would inevitably lead to a reduction in the number of offenses punishable by death.

According to official records, 25,000 people were executed between 1962 and 1994. While 76 people were executed in the Soviet Union in 1990, only three people suffered this fate in Russia in 1993 and four in 1994. The president of Russia established a committee on clemency, which commuted death sentences to life imprisonment. This usually meant a 15-year sentence in a labor camp. In 1994, 150 people had their sentence commuted. It appears that those who failed to have their sentence commuted were convicted of serial murders.

The Russian government has altered the use of the death penalty. Article 20 of the Constitution of the Russian Federation states: "Everyone has a right to life. Pending its abolition, capital punishment may be established by federal law as an exceptional measure of punishment for especially grave crimes against human life, provided the accused is given the right to have his case considered in a trial by jury." As mentioned earlier, the death penalty, according to the 1996 Criminal Code, is considered an acceptable sanction in exceptional cases and those instances include: homicide, infringement on the life of a State or public official, and genocide. It is interesting to note that Article 59 of the code, which deals with the death penalty, prohibits carrying out the sanction on women, people who committed the crime before reaching the age of 18, and men who have attained the age of 65 at the time of sentencing. In addition, a petition through the clemency process can replace a death sentence with a sentence of deprivation of freedom for life or deprivation of freedom for 25 years. Finally, it should be noted that the Russian Federation suspended the use of capital punishment in 1997. While several notable politicians have expressed their opposition to the sanction and legislation has been introduced to abolish it, this has not happened as yet.

Figure 5.3

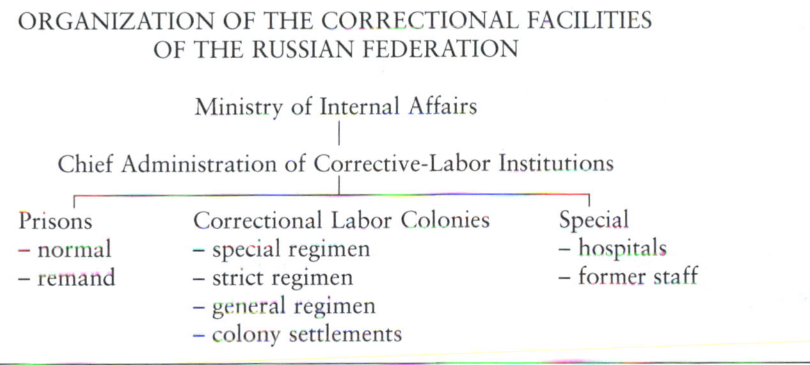

Types of Institutions The Russian Federation has continued the Soviet practice of having two basic types of correctional facilities: prisons and correctional labor colonies (see Figure 5.3). According to the Principles of Correctional Labor Legislation, offenders are sentenced to prison when they have committed "heinous crimes" or are considered "particularly dangerous recidivists." It should be noted that a remand prison is primarily used to hold offenders who are awaiting trial. Thus, its population and some of the management problems associated with that population are like those found in countries that use jails for similar purposes.

There is a multiple classification scheme for correctional labor colonies. The general regimen is designed for most first-time offenders and offenders sentenced to less than three years. The strict regimen is reserved for people convicted of particularly dangerous crimes against the state or who have previously served a term of deprivation of freedom. The special regimen is designed for offenders deemed particularly dangerous recidivists or persons for whom the death penalty has been replaced by deprivation of freedom.

Colony settlements are open institutions that are utilized for two kinds of offenders. Inmates who have displayed significant progress toward rehabilitation while in a correctional labor colony are transferred to colony settlements. In addition, people who have been found guilty of an act of negligence, rather than of specific intent, are usually sent to a colony settlement.

While the Soviets had not considered psychiatric hospitals part of their correctional system, the use of such hospitals for the rehabilitation of criminal offenders attracted an unusual amount of international concern. On the surface, the Soviet Criminal Code appeared to espouse a fairly modern and humanitarian view toward criminal offenders suffering from some form of mental illness. Article 11 of the general part of the code stated that a "person shall not be subject to criminal responsibility who at the time of committing a socially dangerous act is in a state of non-imputability." According to various articles in the code, the court had the authority to commit a person to compulsory treatment in either a general or a special psychiatric hospital. In addition to the offender's mental condition, the court was expected to take into consideration "the character of the socially dangerous act" and "the special danger" that the offender's actions represented toward society.

At issue was the lack of procedural protections in the Soviet use of such facilities. Three principal concerns were expressed by professionals in the West, as well as by some members of the psychiatric profession in Russia. These concerns centered on the type of offenders sent to these hospitals, the arbitrary procedural safeguards that were spelled out in the code, and the lack of written regulations protecting the offender's rights as a patient. In 1975, Amnesty International published a report, "Prisoners of Conscience in the USSR," which offered one of the more extensive assessments of these concerns. Probably the most serious allegations leveled at the Soviets regarding their use of psychiatric hospitals had been the confinement of political and religious nonconformists (Slovenko, 1983). Amnesty International, among others, documented a number of cases in which people who did not follow the Communist Party's line or who attempted to express their religious convictions in a manner that was deemed unacceptable by the authorities, found themselves labeled insane and thus subject to treatment in a psychiatric institution.

In addition to this concern was the ever-present fear that abuse by design or negligence was possible in these highly secretive facilities. It is important to stress that this issue had been raised not only by critics from the West but also by those within the country. Two pieces of legislation were passed during Gorbachev's tenure that were designed to reduce the confinement of political and religious nonconformists. The Law on Public Associations (1990) and the Law on Freedom of Conscience (1990) acknowledged political and religious freedoms of expression.

Another concern regarding the use of psychiatric hospitals concerned the arbitrary, and at times contradictory, procedural safeguards granted a person declared mentally ill. For example, Article 188 of the Procedural Code stated that "[i]f a suspect is referred to a forensic medical institution in connection with an expert examination, he shall be granted the rights established by Articles 184 and 185 of the present Code." Article 185 guaranteed the rights to:

1. challenge the expert;
2. request the assignment of an expert from among persons indicated by him or her;
3. present additional questions in order to obtain the opinion of an expert concerning them;
4. be present, with the permission of the investigator, at the expert examination and give explanation to the expert; and
5. become acquainted with the opinion of the expert.

However, Article 184 stated that a "decree to assign a forensic psychiatric expert examination and the opinion of the experts shall not be announced to the accused if his mental state makes this impossible." Thus, the rights established under Article 185 could—and allegedly had been—disregarded as a result of the statement in Article 184. A final procedural concern in such cases was the declaration cited in Article 407 that a judge may exclude a person diagnosed as mentally ill from attending the court hearing. Although this rule may have had some validity for a person who truly was diagnosed insane, serious questions arose regarding the person's rights if the diagnosis was based on political or religious convictions.

Finally, Amnesty International alleged that there was no code guaranteeing the rights of people sent to psychiatric hospitals, nor were there regulations explaining the conditions under which they would be detained. Amnesty International had already claimed that inmates' rights were violated in prisons and labor colonies that purportedly had legal protections. They were concerned, based partly on cases they had collected, that there existed serious human rights violations in Soviet psychiatric facilities. Their examples focused on political and religious dissidents.

In an attempt to dispel some of the international concern over this issue and to strengthen socialist legality, the Soviets ratified a new law in 1988: the Statute on Conditions and Procedures for the Provision of Psychiatric Assistance. This legislation called for the Ministry of Internal Affairs and the Ministry of Public Health to determine appropriate medical care and assigned to public health agencies the responsibility for establishing procedures for retaining a person in a mental institution. It also assured that a person in need of psychiatric assistance would be guaranteed a legal defense with assistance of counsel and that the procuracy would be responsible for supervising the issuance of such an order. In addition, a person deemed in need of psychiatric assistance could appeal the decision to either a higher public health agency or directly to a court. A final feature of the new legislation was a criminal penalty for medical personnel who assigned a person known to be healthy to a mental institution. They could receive a sentence of either deprivation of freedom or of corrective labor for up to two years; they could also be deprived of the right to hold certain positions or engage in certain activities for one to three years. The Russian Federation has essentially turned its psychiatric hospitals over to the Ministry of Public Health.

Regimens Our knowledge of the regimen in Soviet correctional facilities is based largely on information obtained from émigrés who at one time were incarcerated in these institutions. Many were political prisoners, and it was assumed that they were subjected to harsher treatment than most inmates. Nevertheless, they frequently found themselves serving their time alongside regular or nonpolitical prisoners (Anonymous, 1986; Feldbrugge, 1986).

Amnesty International's report, "Prisoners of Conscience," offered a useful synthesis of the conditions that existed in Soviet correctional institutions. The information presented in the report came as no surprise to students of Soviet government and society. Books and articles had already appeared that graphically illustrated the conditions in Soviet correctional institutions. The most notable were the literary works of Aleksandr Solzhenitsyn. Nevertheless, Amnesty International's report served as a useful updated synthesis on the conditions.

Among the concerns raised in the report were the manner in which prisoners were generally maintained and the methods adopted to assure the achievement of the goal of reeducation. Apparently, these were two significant factors that distinguished the regimens in Soviet prisons as well as the various correctional labor colonies. In terms of general maintenance, Amnesty International alleged that the quality and quantity of food distributed to Soviet inmates was a serious concern. They also contended that food was often rotten and the daily consumption of calories was below the level required for active people, according to the World Health Organization. Soviet inmates were very active because of the hard labor that was an integral part of the regimen. Moreover, it had been reported that food parcels sent from family and friends rarely reached the inmates. In addition, the quantities of food decreased with the severity of the institutional regimen. This was of particular concern to Amnesty International, considering that the harsher regimens imposed a more strenuous form of labor that required more calories in the diet, rather than less.

The other major concern about general maintenance was the quality of medical care. Inmates on a low-calorie diet lost weight, which was often a contributing cause to their reduced work output. This in turn resulted in smaller portions of food being distributed as a form of punishment, which could cause malnutrition and serious medical problems for inmates. Amnesty International alleged that a common complaint among prisoners was poor medical care. This included inadequate medical facilities and equipment, as well as inexperienced doctors and unqualified medical assistants (the latter were sometimes drawn from the ranks of the inmate population).

Article 7 of the Principles of Correctional Labor Legislation identified four principal means by which the reeducation of inmates was achieved. They included "the regimen under which sentence is served, socially useful labor, political education, and general and vocational education." Amnesty International, among others, offered some comments and criticisms on these methods. They were generally concerned about the compulsory nature of prisoners' participation in the rehabilitation program and the lack of correctional personnel who were truly qualified to evaluate the inmate's progress toward reeducation. Most correctional personnel were guards who had been recruited and trained by the Ministry of Internal Affairs. It had been suggested that many of the guards were unsuccessful police candidates who were seconded into this alternative career path. This had implications for their approach and commitment to their job as well as their methods of treating inmates.

According to the Soviet Constitution, all people had a duty to work. This tenet, which was an integral part of the Marxist-Leninist collective philosophy, was extended to the laws and rules regulating correctional facilities. Inmates were paid for their work based on its quality and quantity but were required to reimburse the institution for their food and clothing. The most significant concerns expressed by critics of the Soviet's work requirements were the inadequate diet provided for inmates who must perform strenuous physical labor and the lack of safety precautions provided for inmates who were often assigned dangerous work.

Political education also was considered a principal means of reeducation. Apparently, the Soviets did not make serious attempts at the reeducation of political prisoners. It has been suggested that this was largely the result of inadequate instructors for the political education classes. It was not uncommon for a young, uneducated guard to conduct such sessions. This could lead to some rather awkward situations if the class was attended by highly educated dissidents who possessed a superior understanding of Marxism-Leninism.

Finally, general and vocational education programs were suspect. Corrective labor regulations mandated that inmates who had not attained a grade school education be given access to one, and a high school program should be offered whenever feasible. There was no information available as to the success of these programs. Vocational education was considered a failure, however, because inmates generally left correctional institutions without gaining appreciable employment skills.

On the surface, Soviet correctional facilities had many of the same goals as Western penal institutions. Rehabilitation, work, and education were integral components of the correctional regimen—at least in theory. However, critics of this system were bothered by the methods employed to achieve these goals. Without regard for moral principles, it was relatively easy to conclude that the Soviet system was at least more cost-efficient than the systems found in the West. Indicators suggested, however, that the system was not more effective than those adopted in the West; recidivism, a principal index of effectiveness, was apparently quite high in the Soviet Union.

The concerns expressed about the regimens in Soviet correctional facilities were similar to those expressed in the West. They had been expounded upon by Soviet émigrés, Soviet writers in Russia, and Soviet scholars in the West. These concerns were already familiar to students of American corrections. Many of the Soviet correctional facilities were old. The correctional personnel were often undertrained and frequently they were people who had been rejected from service in the regular police forces. As a result, their commitment to and motivation for their profession was questionable. Although inmates were expected to perform useful labor while incarcerated, few actually acquired a marketable skill that could benefit them upon release.

Confinement in an institution often led to serious problems for inmates and staff. Isolation could completely destroy the inmate's previous ties with society. In recent years, this had been exacerbated by the passage of more liberal divorce laws. Inmates also became frustrated by the hopelessness of their situation. This could lead either to violence within the institution or to dangerous passivity (which aided the guards while the person was incarcerated but had negative consequences for the individual upon release). Moreover, the Soviets' acknowledgment of high rates of recidivism had implications for the rehabilitative programs devised for inmates.

Finally, inmates experienced additional frustrations upon release. These included the dissolution of marriages and the deprivation of residence permits where their families were located. Although local soviet committees were expected to assist the offender in finding employment, it was not uncommon for them to be less than enthusiastic about placing former inmates in jobs within their districts. These kinds of frustrations often led former inmates to return to criminal activity, eventually increasing the recidivism rate further.

On the eve of the collapse of the Soviet Union, officials of the Ministry of Internal Affairs acknowledged that the conditions in some prisons were becoming more violent. Of particular concern was the increase in the number of assaults on prison guards. Ministry officials attributed this situation to three factors: (1) more violent forms of criminal behavior had escalated throughout the country; (2) a greater proportion of the prison population consisted of violent criminals; and (3) the greater proportion of violent inmates was also attributed to a decrease in the number of white-collar criminals sentenced to these institutions. This last factor was the result of a change in policy introduced as part of a reform effort to humanize the correctional system.

The principal concern expressed about Soviet prisons was the need to humanize the conditions under which inmates must live. The leadership of the Russian Federation indicated a desire to improve the system. During strikes and riots, inmates demanded that the conditions be brought up to international standards. While the Russian leadership is probably sincere in its desire to change several correctional policies, there is a basic fact of life in Russia that will either prevent or retard the implementation of strategies to correct some of the more serious problems: the fact that the entire country is in the throes of transforming its former centralized planned economic system to a market economy. Because so many law-abiding citizens are having a difficult time feeding and clothing themselves and their families during this period of transition, it is highly unlikely that funding will be provided to assist with the reformation of the prison system.

As a result, it is assumed that inmates will continue to be crowded into very old facilities. Many of these institutions are well over 100 years old and have not been modernized to even early twentieth-century standards. The staff will also remain undertrained. In fact, there have been instances over the past few years in which there was no money to pay the staff. In these circumstances, it follows that there is also no money to pay the inmates who are working in labor colonies.

The diet of the inmates remains poor. In the past, this was part of the planned prison policy, by which an inmate's normal intake of food was reduced as a disciplinary measure. Today, the poor diet is attributed to the fact there is limited funding to purchase food for the prison system. This translates into meager food rations for the inmates. In recent years, prison officials have enhanced the ability of inmates to receive food packages from outside the system. They have also increased the number of visits an inmate can receive. Conjugal visits, limited to family members, have long been permitted in Russian prisons.

It has been pointed out that the health of people entering prison is often in a deteriorated state. Prison only accelerates this problem, which has led to a high incidence of tuberculosis (Mikhlin and King, in Matthews and Francis, 1996). In recent years, the concern over this problem has been heightened by the fact that a multiresistant form of tuberculosis has been identified among inmates. Amnesty International, among others, has been reporting on this problem for several years. In its 2001 annual report (which covers the year 2000), Amnesty International reported that 100,000 inmates suffer from tuberculosis and approximately 10,000 die each year. It has also been suggested that about 30,000 inmates have the multiresistant form of the disease (Christie, 2000). The alarming rate at which tuberculosis has contaminated the prison population is a serious concern. What is even more alarming are the predictions that it will spread rapidly throughout the general population as inmates with the disease are released from prison and infect others. In addition to these problems, the Russians have finally come to terms with the fact that illegal drug abuse and HIV/AIDS has become a serious concern in the general population and in particular with its prison population (see Butler, King, and Piacentini, in Pridemore, 2005).

Unlike some correctional systems in the world, Soviet—and now Russian—inmates work at real jobs in correctional labor colonies. They are paid wages similar to those outside the prison. In recent years, some industries even permitted paid annual leaves. However, the change in the economic system has created havoc in some of the Russian correctional labor colonies. In a centralized planned economy, the raw materials needed to produce goods in the prison industries were provided by the state. The goods produced in the labor colonies were then sold and distributed by the state. Under this system, the prison industries were not confronted with competition. Presently, some labor colonies are finding it impossible to compete in a market economy. Because they are no longer being subsidized by the state, many industries are idle. This situation has further enhanced the tensions associated within the Russian correctional system.

One study has indicated that some prison colonies have increased their efforts to barter with the local community. Bartering helps maintain the social welfare needs of both the prisoners and the staff of the facility. Moreover, it benefits the local community by often assisting local farmers or a light industrial venture. Of course, one concern is that successful bartering arrangements could lead to an economically self-sufficient prison that might in turn lead to the exploitation of the prison population (Piacentini, 2004).

It should be pointed out that several policies have been introduced in recent years in an attempt to humanize the correctional system. For example, inmates are no longer required to have their heads shaved; they can wear athletic clothing and running shoes; they can use their own bedding from home; they are permitted to wear watches; and restrictions have been lifted on purchases from prison stores, that is, assuming the store is able to stock items (which has been difficult).

It should also be noted that Russian prisons are housing more dangerous inmates than in the past. Most of the political prisoners of old have been released. Many white-collar criminals and petty criminals are diverted to other forms of sanction. It has been suggested by some accounts that more than 40 percent of the prison population consists of people convicted of murder, rape, or robbery. In addition, almost 45 percent are considered very dangerous, and many of these are mentally disturbed. The living conditions are already in a serious state of disrepair. If the living conditions remain the same or deteriorate further because of a lack of funding, the threat of violence and riot will inevitably escalate.

Finally, it is important to offer a further note on the living conditions of the various facilities. While the conditions listed below are common throughout the correctional system, the remand prisons, which hold people who are awaiting trial, are in a considerable state of neglect. It is important to remember that of the one million people incarcerated in correctional facilities, hundreds of thousands are being held in remand prisons. These are some of the older facilities within the correctional system. Various groups, among them Amnesty International, have commented on the overcrowded conditions. Rooms that were designed for 20 people now hold five times that number. The cells are pest-infested and lack adequate lighting and ventilation. Because of the severe overcrowding, there is a lack of beds and bedding. As such, people sleep in shifts. Food is inadequate and medical care infrequent. In addition to tuberculosis, a number of inmates suffer from various kinds of skin disease. Through grants of amnesty, the government has released some people from these appalling conditions in recent years. For the most part, these people had been sentenced or were awaiting trial for minor offenses. Unfortunately, because of the crime problem, the overcrowded space of the beneficiary of an amnesty is quickly filled by a new arrival awaiting trial.

Parole Inmates who were considered model prisoners were eligible for parole after they had served at least one-half of their sentence. In the past, this type of release was not available to certain types of offenders, but in 1977 parole opportunities were expanded. Although the number of offenses that were deemed outside the parole scheme were reduced, new candidates were required to serve up to three-fourths of their sentence.

The 1977 legislation also created another type of conditional release that differed from the regular parole regulations. Under this scheme inmates could be released early, provided that they secured employment in the community as a method of furthering their socialization process. Requests for parole or conditional release usually were made by the administrators of the correctional facility. The actual granting of such a release was made by the court.

At the beginning of 1988, another change was introduced in the form of an experiment at 52 correctional labor colonies. A scheme was devised in which model inmates who produced beyond the norm of their work assignment would have days subtracted from their sentence. For example, three days would count as four, two as three, and in exceptional cases, one as two. Under this scheme the model inmates still had to serve at least one-third of their sentence, but they could then either be released or serve the rest of their sentence under an easier regimen. Authorities maintained that this was a practical illustration of perestroika being adopted in the correctional system.

One might expect that a society priding itself on its collective work ethic would endeavor to find employment for inmates eligible for release. However, experts have indicated that the local executive committees responsible for work placement were frequently slow and at times unresponsive to the needs of parolees. Thus, the Soviet parole scheme suffered from the same impediment found in the West, that is, the public's unwillingness to assist in the reintegration of the ex-offender.

Parole remains an option in the Russian Federation. The opportunities for parole have been expanded for first-time offenders, older inmates, inmates with disabilities, and inmates who had served in the defense of the country. According to the 1996 Criminal Code, a court determines if the original period of incarceration can be reduced and not have an adverse impact on an inmate's efforts at reform. A person deprived of their freedom must serve a minimum of six months of their sentence. Other than that stipulation, Article 79 states that a convicted person must serve "(a) not less than half of the term of punishment assigned for a crime of minor or average gravity; (b) not less than two-thirds of the term of punishment assigned for a grave crime; (c) not less than three-quarters of the term of punishment assigned for an especially grave crime." If granted, the court can place some standard restrictions on the individual. These include: not changing one's residence or place of employment or study without informing the authorities; avoiding certain places; when appropriate, undergoing treatment for such conditions as alcoholism or substance abuse; and providing material support for one's family.

Noninstitutional Sanctions

For those offenders not sentenced to a term of deprivation of freedom, there are several noninstitutional sanctions available. In some cases, a person serving time in prison or in a correctional labor colony may also receive a noninstitutional sanction. Usually, the offender meets the obligations of the noninstitutional sentence upon release from a correctional facility.

The 1996 Criminal Code introduced a new noninstitutional sanction called obligatory tasks. A more familiar term to describe this sanction is community service. A convicted person performs work during his or her free time through an agency of local government. The amount of time that a person must complete is between 60 and 240 hours. Offenders are not permitted to perform more than four hours of community service per day.

Correctional tasks make up another sanction that is served at the offender's regular place of employment. The sanction can be imposed for a term of two months to two years. The court further orders that part of the wages of the offender be deducted and paid to the state. The amount can range from 5 to 20 percent of the person's gross pay. In addition, the time served while working under this sanction is not included when determining the person's eligibility for vacation time, benefits, salary raises, and job seniority. An offender who displays exemplary work habits may gain some of these benefits back if the local organization petitions the court to do so.

Confiscation of property entails the transfer of all or part of the offender's property to the state. Only items that are not deemed necessities for the offender and his or her dependents are included in this sentence. This sanction is limited to crimes against the state and certain kinds of mercenary crimes identified in the special part of the Criminal Code.

Limitation of freedom involves sentencing a person to a half-way house. There is a degree of confinement, but the person is not isolated from society. It is a sanction designed for the first-time offender. If the person was convicted of an intentional crime, the terms of the sentence would be between one and three years. If the person was convicted of a crime through negligence, the terms of the sentence would be between one and five years.

Fines are designated for specific offenses under the special part of the Criminal Code. In imposing this penalty, the court considers both the gravity of the offense and the offender's ability to pay. Deprivation of the right to occupy certain offices or to engage in certain activities may be imposed for a period of one to five years. This form of sanctioning implies that the offender's environment is a factor that has encouraged or enabled the person to commit a specific type of crime.

If a person is convicted of a particularly serious crime, the court can also consider the personal history of the individual and deprive them of special, military, or honorary titles; class rank; or a State award that they had previously earned. With regard to the military, the Criminal Code provides two sanctions that specifically address military service. Limitations in military service authorizes a deduction of 20 percent in military maintenance of convicted service personnel. This deduction is paid to the state for a period of between three months and two years. In addition, the person cannot be promoted in office or rank during this time period. Another military sanction is confinement in a disciplinary military unit for a period of between three months and two years.

JUVENILE JUSTICE

In the past, the Soviets placed a good deal of blame for their crime problems on bourgeois influences. Both before and after the 1917 Revolution, they argued that there were whole generations tainted by capitalism and that these people passed on those beliefs, motives, and drives to their children. Hence, crime existed because the remnants of capitalism were too pronounced to be eradicated in such a short period of time. Moreover, a number of historical events—largely beyond the control of the authorities—further enhanced the prospects for the commission of delinquent acts. Famines in the early 1920s, late 1920s, and early 1930s caused a large number of people—especially orphans—to move to urban centers. The large number of orphans was largely the result of World War I, the civil war in Russia, and the Great Depression. World War II not only increased the orphan population but also was a factor in the post-war baby boom, which occurred in most countries and has been identified as a variable in the rise of juvenile crime in the early 1960s.

Despite the fact that most Russians had never lived in a capitalist society, the Soviets did not totally abandon their claim that their problems of crime could be attributed to capitalistic influences. For several years, they alleged that the West had waged a form of psychological war on their young people by exposing them to Western decadence. Identified as the principal sources of this type of attack were foreign news and entertainment broadcasts and the availability of Western literature and material goods on the extensive Soviet black market. Although the Soviets continued to blame capitalist influences for their level of crime, they gradually admitted that there were factors indigenous to the Soviet regime that contributed to the crime and delinquency problems. They had to make this admission in light of the fact that only Soviet citizens in their mid-seventies and older were born before the Revolution and, therefore, could possibly have been exposed directly to capitalist influences.

Given this line of reasoning, it should come as no surprise that a number of Soviets believed that the underlying causes of crime were social. Two developments in particular had been identified as contributing factors since the end of World War II. They were the extensive developments throughout the country toward urbanization and industrialization, and the resulting dislocation, alienation, and disintegration of the family. In recent years, a third factor (an outgrowth of the other two) also troubled the Soviet leadership. It was that young people experienced a relatively peaceful and comfortable lifestyle. Whereas war and deprivation tempered the expectations of previous generations of Soviet citizens, the new generation of young people were impatient with the degree and tempo of change, and their expectations for consumer goods and leisure time had been enhanced further by parents deferring their own personal gratification for that of their children. The Soviet leadership recognized that if glasnost and perestroika were going to have any long-term impact, it was the youth of the country that would have to play a pivotal role in its success. As a result, the initiatives for many social policies and programs were specifically directed at this group. It naturally followed that a concern for juvenile delinquency was an ever-present and prominent feature of this total agenda (McClellan, 1987).

Among some Soviet researchers, it was believed that people between the ages of 14 and 18 commit 8 to 15 percent of all crime. If one considered that one-third to one-half of all juvenile cases were dropped or handled by a commission of juvenile affairs (and thus never reached a court), the total number of delinquents was probably between 15 and 20 percent. Moreover, it was estimated that 9 to 20 percent of juveniles recidivated and that, among the adult recidivists, 60 percent started their criminal careers as juveniles (McClellan, 1987).

Both Soviet and Western experts on the Soviet system were basically in agreement as to the indigenous causes for juvenile delinquency in Russia. As was the case with adult offenders, a significant percentage of delinquent acts were committed while the perpetrator was under the influence of alcohol. The Central Committee of the CPSU passed a resolution in 1985 that attempted to grapple with this problem. One of the specific goals was to reduce drastically the production of alcoholic beverages. Another was to curtail the distribution of such beverages by reducing the number of off-license establishments, curtailing the hours of sale, and restricting sale to people over the age of 21. A final goal was to change the drinking habits and patterns of people by increasing the fines both for public intoxication and for driving while under the influence. In addition, adults who encouraged minors to drink alcohol were subject to prosecution. The media became involved in the educational campaign to discourage young people from drinking alcohol. Finally, rehabilitation centers were established at locations that facilitated the continuation of a person's employment (Partanen, 1987).

In recent years, the government had also acknowledged that it underestimated the problem of abuse of other drugs as well. While they claimed that it did not reach the epidemic proportions found in some countries of the world, they recognized that they were not exempt from this dangerous trend. Moreover, they estimated that 80 percent of the hemp and poppies used to manufacture illicit drugs for use within the country were grown in the Soviet Union. While it was illegal to use and sell drugs, senior government officials had tried to emphasize a policy of treating the drug user as a victim of a sickness rather than as a criminal (Anonymous, 1988). In line with that reasoning, the Statute on Educational-Treatment Facilities for Those Ill with Drug Addiction was passed in 1986. In addition to the Ministry of Internal Affairs and the procuracy, healthcare and educational officials have a central role to play in the organization and administration of these facilities (Levitsky, 1988).

Also recognized as a principal cause of delinquency was the deterioration of the home and family environment. Some children were abused by parents suffering from alcoholism, and in a society in which most adults work, the young were often left unattended. Because people had achieved a degree of mobility, the days had long passed when a grandparent or other relative might live with the family and care for the children. As a result, there was a new initiative to provide family counseling services—especially in urban areas.

Although unemployment was extremely low in the Soviet Union, it was not unusual to find people underemployed. Moreover, children who dropped out of school had difficulty finding a job that would ensure self-sufficiency. Underemployment, however, was only part of the problem. Soviet authorities claimed that about two-thirds of all delinquent acts were committed by people who were employed or in school and that such crimes were generally committed during the offender's leisure time. Thus, the government suggested that greater efforts be directed at initiating more leisure activities. An effort was under way to establish more facilities for this purpose.

The authorities also blamed part of the delinquency problem on deficiencies in the Soviet educational system. Many delinquent youths had a history of problems in school or had simply dropped out. Part of the criticism was leveled at teachers who failed to encourage the students, but the authorities focused much of their attention on the lack of stimulation in the home—a factor that had been shown to have a significant impact on both the child's interest and willingness to learn. The Soviets commenced a thorough reform of their school system in 1984. Plans called for extending the number of mandatory years of schooling from 10 to 11 years, as well as building more schools and vocational training centers. Raising teachers' salaries by 40 to 50 percent was part of the reform, along with recruiting new people to the profession. Curriculum revision was another important component of the reform efforts. This included the introduction of a universal vocational training component; classes in technical areas, such as computers, to meet the needs of the modern workplace; and an expansion of offerings in college preparatory courses (McClellan, 1987). The Soviets had also been committed to improving citizens' understanding of law for several years. Because it had been recognized that many juveniles failed to understand the consequences of their delinquent actions, legal education became a significant component in the regular school system and in special educational program for juveniles convicted of criminal behavior.

Finally, peer pressure was recognized as another cause of juvenile crime. The Soviets argued that in the Soviet Union this took a form different from that found in the West. Whereas capitalist countries were noted for their organized gangs of delinquents, the Soviets alleged that they did not have that kind of problem. Although gangs of youths often committed offenses, they did not do so as a formally organized group. The emergence of gangs was more spontaneous in that the participants had only a casual relationship with one another.

All of the aforementioned causes for juvenile delinquency in the Soviet Union have been further enhanced in the Russian Federation. From the earliest days of the country, the social structure has been in disarray, with the demise of the socialist system and the initial development of an economy based on market forces. The Ministry of Internal Affairs has contended that the nature and dimensions of juvenile crime are associated with the moral well-being of the country. At a time when the social system has been turned upside down, many young people are confronted with a lack of standards and a disrespect for authority. The economic problems confronting the country are similar to those facing most Russian families. As a result, there is a good deal of resentment. For some, it is a resentment directed at the old order; others are bitter about the new rules.

There are several notable concerns that have been identified by the authorities. For example, there has been an increase in the number of juveniles leaving school, a significant rise in the number of homeless children on the streets of urban areas, and an increase in the number of children being reared in children's homes and single-parent families.

The authorities also have identified a growing trend for criminal enterprises to utilize juveniles. To illustrate, young people are being used to fence stolen goods, to sell illegal drugs and weapons, and to participate in various extortion schemes. In addition, juvenile gangs are largely responsible for the proliferation of robberies, burglaries, and auto thefts. Of particular concern is the number of juvenile gangs that are assuming the attributes of professional criminal operations.

According to the Ministry of Internal Affairs, the number of juvenile offenders in 1994 increased by 50 percent over the course of the previous five years. It also was reported that juvenile crime is increasing at a rate 15 percent higher than that of adult crime, and every third person involved in a group-related crime is a juvenile. Of the most serious crimes, such as murder and serious injury, juveniles commit one out of every six offenses. The Ministry also has indicated that they have identified about 360,000 problem teenagers throughout the country. They have been quick to acknowledge that the real number of potential juvenile offenders is significantly greater than the number registered. In 1997, the Ministry issued a report on crime data collected for the previous year. They concluded that juvenile delinquency is "an exceptionally dangerous phenomenon," and pointed out that 80 percent of the crimes committed by juveniles are felonies. The prospects of seeing these statistics reduced are not promising. Of particular concern, cited by the Ministry, is the fact that so many young people are neglected or left unsupervised. They become easy targets for organized crime in its efforts to identify new recruits.

In 1999, legislation was passed that is designed to emphasize a more protective rather than a punitive approach to juveniles. It is designed to restrict the role of the militia in dealing with juvenile offenders and to enhance the role and responsibility of social welfare agencies. The law also calls for the establishment of two kinds of temporary shelters: for youths who are simply homeless and for juvenile offenders. For the juvenile offenders, these institutions are both opened and closed facilities.

Juvenile Adjudication Process

One of the factors mentioned in Soviet studies on delinquency was the failure of some juveniles to understand the consequences of their actions (Minkovsky, 1976). Before the adjudication process for juveniles is described, it is important to explain the age of criminal responsibility for juveniles in the Russian Federation.

Age of Responsibility Although the age of criminal responsibility varies with the kind of offense, young people who have reached 16 years of age are subject to criminal responsibility according to the Criminal Code. While people under the age of 16 are generally not subject to criminal responsibility, there are a number of exceptions made to this rule. Young people who have attained the age of 14 and have committed certain serious crimes may be prosecuted. The crimes for which a young person may be prosecuted include: homicide; intentional causing of grave harm to health; intentional causing of average gravity of harm to health; stealing a person; rape; forcible actions of sexual nature; open stealing; assault with intent to rob; extortion; unlawful taking possession of an automobile or other means of transport without the purpose of stealing; intentional destruction or damaging of property under aggravating circumstances; terrorism; taking a hostage; knowingly making a false communication concerning an act of terrorism; hooliganism under aggravating circumstances; vandalism; stealing or extortion of a weapon, ammunition, explosive substances, or explosive devices; stealing or extortion of narcotic means or psychotropic substances; and the destruction of transport or railways into unfitness. As mentioned earlier in the section on law, hooliganism refers to violations of public disorder that are associated with threats to people and the destruction or damage to property. It is an offense that existed under Soviet law and has been retained in the 1996 Criminal Code.

According to the Code of Criminal Procedure, it is imperative that a preliminary investigation be conducted in cases involving juveniles. Although a police investigator is likely to conduct the investigation, a procurator controls the actual inquiry. Whereas early representation of defense counsel is a recent development for adults, it has long been provided for juveniles, specifically, as soon as an accusation has been presented. Juveniles awaiting trial are usually released into the custody of their parents or guardians. In exceptional cases, they may be detained, but assurances must be given that the confined juvenile will not associate with adults or with minors who have already been convicted. The nature of the offense in addition to the person's arrest record and behavior are the principal factors used to determine if the juvenile should be prohibited from release into custody.

Personnel The Russians have not established a single court in their judicial hierarchy to handle juvenile cases. Instead, they have developed a dual tracking system. If the offense is serious and the age of the offender warrants such a procedure as stated in the code, the juvenile may be required to appear before a justice of the peace or in a district court.

In all other cases, the procurator turns the matter over to a commission on juvenile affairs. These commissions have been in existence since 1918. Although they are not technically considered a judicial body, they provide a number of judicial functions. Members of a commission are appointed by local officials for a two-year term. Members come from a variety of walks of life, such as jurists, police, teachers, trade union members, factory workers, and housing representatives. Their selection is based on their interest in juvenile affairs.

Jurisdiction The law considers a young person under the age of 18 to be a minor. Either a justices of the peace court or a district court can adjudicate those cases in which the offender is at least 14 and the offense is considered very serious in nature. As previously indicated, these crimes are identified in the code. A commission on juvenile affairs handles cases for less serious offenses committed by young people above the age of 14 as well as for all crimes committed by juveniles younger than 14.

The responsibility of a commission on juvenile affairs is not limited to handling individual cases of delinquency. The commissions play a significant role in general approaches to delinquency prevention: in supervising various institutions that are responsible for young people, such as the police, special vocational schools, and corrective labor settlements for minors; in the organization of programs to prevent child neglect; and in the protection of the rights of all minors. All of this requires a good deal of coordination between various government authorities who are specifically responsible for the maintenance, supervision, and protection of young people, and those citizens who are willing to voluntarily assist in the work of delinquency prevention.

Procedures The procedures in a justices of the peace court or a district court are similar to those in force when an adult stands trial, but if the person is under 16 the court may prevent the public from attending the hearing, as long as it states its reasons. The child's parents are not required to attend. Under Russian law, however, parents can be interrogated as witnesses during trials. In addition, representatives from the offender's school or place of employment must be notified of the proceedings and may attend the hearing and offer testimony.

At a criminal trial, a juvenile above the age of 14 is financially liable for damages caused in the commission of an offense. Thus, juveniles are treated like adults. Because many young people are unable to pay damages, their parents are liable because they are viewed as sureties. Moreover, parents can be fined by the court for failing to supervise their children properly.

The procedures of a commission on juvenile affairs are more informal than a trial. They are not as concerned with establishing the legal guilt of the juvenile as they are with determining a specific preventive measure that will assure that the conditions leading up to the offense will be eliminated.

Disposition

Both the justices of the peace courts or the district courts and the commissions on juvenile affairs have the authority to impose a sanction on a juvenile found guilty of a criminal offense. Because the Russians view the underlying causes of crime as social in nature, their rationale for sentencing an offender is based on the dual purpose of rehabilitation and deterrence. Rehabilitation is designed to reeducate the offender to the "correct views" and "proper habits" of a citizen. The Russians also adhere to the notions of specific and general deterrence. Specific deterrence is directed at the individual offender through reeducation and the elimination of the conditions that cause such deviant attitudes. General deterrence is designed to encourage crime prevention measures throughout society. Furthermore, in the course of imposing a sentence on a young person, Article 89 of the Criminal Code calls upon the sanctioning authority to consider "the conditions of his life and nurturing, level of mental development, other peculiarities of the personality, and also the influence of older persons."

When sanctioning a juvenile, the sentencing authority utilizes a number of penalties that are available for the adult offender. There are some exceptions, however. The death penalty, for example, cannot be imposed on an offender who committed the offense before the age of 18. Deprivation of freedom is an acceptable sanction, but the maximum sentence cannot exceed 10 years for a person under 18.

It is estimated that more than one-half of the juveniles found guilty in a court are sentenced to a term of deprivation of freedom with the time being served in an educational colony. As was the case with the adult system, there are various kinds of regimens in these colonies, but all emphasize manual labor. Few juveniles receive the maximum sentence to an educational colony. It has been suggested that the average term is approximately three years. Few inmates serve that full term, though; they are usually released on parole after having served less than one year.

There are other common methods of sanctioning a juvenile, and some of these are somewhat abbreviated versions of sentences that can be imposed on adult offenders. The term "arrest" is used in the 1996 Criminal Code to describe a short period of confinement. In the case of young people, it can be imposed only on those who have reached the age of 16. The period of confinement is from one to four months.

A fine can serve as a method of punishment as long as the young person has the means, either through earnings or property, to pay the fine. Obligatory tasks or community service can be imposed for a period of 40 to 160 hours. Correctional tasks is another sanction that can be imposed on a young offender for a period of no more than one year. In this instance, the court can order that part of the wages of the offender be deducted and paid to the state. The amount can range from 5 to 20 percent of the person's gross pay. In addition, the time served while working under this sanction is not included when determining the person's eligibility for vacation time, benefits, salary raises, and job seniority. It should also be pointed out that most first-time offenders receive a suspended sentence.

SUMMARY

This chapter has offered an introduction to the criminal justice system of the Russian Federation. The major components of the system—the police, judiciary, law, corrections, and juvenile justice—were described, and an overview of the political system was presented. A brief history of some of the components of the system was presented; the organization and administration were described; the various roles of the practitioners were explained; the legal process was examined; and reference was made to some of the areas of concern within the system.

The dissolution of the Soviet Union and the establishment of the Russian Federation has obviously had a profound impact on the region. Since 1991, every event in Russia has served as an illustration of the leadership's attempt to transform the old order into a new order. The old order was dominated by the Marxist-Leninist philosophy, which encouraged governance based on ideological principles and established a highly centralized planned economic system. Presently, the country is in a state of transition. At times, that transition can best be characterized as democratization—the process by which proponents of democracy aspire to establish a democratic form of government but as yet have not achieved their goal. At other times, the country has appeared to be in a chaotic state. This is largely the result of either the inability or lack of will to introduce the measures necessary to establish a free market economy. While both situations impact criminal justice, it is chaos that has troubling implications for the criminal justice system—the principal source for law enforcement and order maintenance in a civil society.

For the most part, the leadership and people of the Russian Federation are grappling with two central features of the democratization process. One is the establishment of a market economy, which is having a striking impact on all people throughout the country. The other key feature is a recognition of the importance of government by rule of law. It is this feature that is having such a profound impact on the country's criminal justice system.

What students of comparative criminal justice should be aware of is that such a massive transformation in the social order will inevitably cause a good deal of disorder. The country has already witnessed examples of this, and these cases have had an impact on the justice system. Thus, people in the West can and should be encouraged by reforms adopted in the Russian Federation, but they should also realize that lasting change will only occur gradually over an extended period of time. Five years, 10 years, or even 50 years is not a long time in the establishment of a new order for a country with such an extensive history.

Concepts to Know

Kuomintang
Cultural Revolution
Deng Xiaoping
National People's Congress
Standing Committee
the "mass line"
Ministry of Public Security
residents' committees
adjudication committees
Supreme People's Court
Basic People's Courts
procuratorate
people's assessor
Confucians
Legalists
compulsory measures
administrative regulations
labor camps
death penalty
bang-jiao

Chapter VI

Introduction

China is an ancient country that has one of the oldest civilizations on earth. Its written history is almost 4,000 years old, and throughout much of its existence, its cultural traditions have had a profound impact on the entire East Asian region. China occupies much of the mainland of East Asia and shares land borders with 14 countries (Afghanistan, Bhutan, India, Kazakhstan, Kirgizstan, Laos, Mongolia, Myanmar, Nepal, North Korea, Pakistan, Russia, Tajikistan, and Vietnam). With a geographical area of about 3.7 million square miles, China is slightly larger than the United States. Among the countries of the world, only Russia and Canada are larger in area. Unlike the United States, where almost 20 percent of the land is utilized for agriculture, China cultivates around 10 percent of its land on a permanent basis.

Because of rugged and inhospitable geographical conditions, particularly in the western regions, large areas of China are uninhabited. As a result, approximately two-thirds of the population live along the east coast, which represents about one-fifth of the land. China has long held the distinction of having the world's largest population at more than 1.3 billion. This figure is greater than the combined populations of Europe, Russia, and the United States. More than 90 percent of the people belong to the Han ethnic group. All of the other ethnic minorities represent less than 1 percent of the population, with the exception of the Zhuang minority at 1.4 percent of the total population.

Approximately 50 percent of the labor force is employed in agriculture and forestry, with industrial and commercial ventures employing another 23 percent. Iron, steel, and textiles are among the more prominent industries. In 1978, Chinese leaders initiated a program to modernize agriculture, industry, science and technology, and national defense. Their goal was to achieve a fairly advanced industrialized country by the year 2000. This program was prompted, in part, by the fact that the standard of living had been in a considerable state of decline since the 1950s.

Throughout China's more recent political history under communism, the state essentially owned the industrial enterprises and commercial ventures of the country. Because people were guaranteed life-long employment, concerns about workforce productivity had been negligible. As a result, most enterprises were largely overstaffed and highly inefficient. In this context, if China was serious about modernizing its economy, there was a need to make dramatic changes in attitudes about employment and to make considerable alterations of basic workplace values.

Through a series of reform initiatives, for example, the dismantling of the communal system in agricultural communities and promoting self-management in state-owned enterprises, China has been transformed from a centralized planned economy to one that has embraced market-oriented principles. The central feature of this transformation has been to encourage and enable individual initiatives in a host of economic ventures that has fostered an entrepreneurial spirit that is unique to the Chinese experience. In spite of these efforts, the state-owned enterprises continue to employ approximately 40 percent of the urban workforce. Even in this realm, there is an effort to improve the efficiency of the state-owned enterprises by the elimination of a guarantee of life-long employment. As a result, it is estimated that between 45 and 60 million people in urban areas have been laid off (see Madsen, in Lin and Hu, 2003).

China has been a peasant-based society throughout its history. One of the programs initiated by the Communists was to universalize primary education. Although some success has been achieved, roughly 20 percent of the rural population remains illiterate or semiliterate. While approximately 70 percent of the primary-school students continue their studies in middle school, only one-third of China's young people remain in school beyond the ninth grade. In order for China to achieve the status of an advanced society, it must establish higher educational standards and develop better training for its people. Although a considerable amount of work remains, a good deal of effort has already been directed at the science and technology, banking and insurance, education, transportation, and communication sectors.

In recent years, much of the attention directed at China has focused on three factors. First, China is the only remaining major country in the world that continues to embrace Communism. Some suggest that this has had adverse implications for the country's internal political stability and economic growth. While it is prudent to take note of this warning, it is important to remember that China had one of the longest traditions of autocratic rule before the Communists took over. Second, China is attempting to introduce modern economic principles without granting the democratic political freedoms that are usually associated with modernization. This has led to a good deal of commentary on the long-term prospects of China's modernization efforts. Third, China has opted throughout its history to turn inward for extended periods of time and not associate with much of the rest of the world. From 1949 until 1978, China essentially adopted an isolationist policy toward the West. Since 1978, it has reversed that tendency. At that time, the country acknowledged the need to acquire information and technology from the West in order to undertake the task of modernization. As a result, China's significance on the world stage in general—and its prominence in the East Asian region in particular—has grown considerably.

Government

On October 10, 1911, the Qing dynasty was overthrown. With this, the 4,000-year-old tradition of dynastic rule in China formally came to an end. Throughout much of the dynastic period, feudalism determined the methods of social and economic interaction. As a result, China had not been exposed to many of the political, social, or economic ideas that are generally considered modern. Through foreign assaults and occupation, external ideas were sometimes introduced or imposed on the country, especially during the nineteenth century, but the results often had adverse consequences.

From 1912 to 1949, the Chinese people were subjected to much violent turmoil. Long-standing tensions with Japan erupted on more than one occasion even before the start of World War II. There was also a good deal of internal dissension as China attempted to establish a new political identity. The era of warlordism engulfed the country from 1916 to 1927, as independent armies attempted to gain control of large regions of the country. The most important internal conflict, however, was waged by the Kuomintang (or Nationalist Party) and the Chinese Communist Party. The Kuomintang was a political faction that espoused the republican views and democratic ideals of Sun Yat-sen, who founded this faction in 1905 as the Alliance Society and who became the provisional president of the Republic of China in 1912. The Chinese Communist Party was formally established in 1921. This occurred two years after Vladimir Ilich Lenin founded the Comintern to coordinate efforts at expanding communist movements throughout the world.

Following the Japanese defeat in World War II, the Kuomintang and Communists renewed their rivalry for political control of China. By late 1949, the Communists had defeated the Nationalists. Those that remained loyal to the Kuomintang fled with its leader, Chiang Kai-shek, to Taiwan. On October 1, 1949, Mao Zedong, the leader of the Communists, established the People's Republic of China. Thus, the Communists assumed control throughout the country and proceeded to create their new social order.

Communist Ideology

Marxism The central concept in Karl Marx's (1818–1883) approach to the study of history and society was the role that economic factors played in political and social change. The manner in which wealth was produced and distributed and the establishment of various types of property relationships had a significant influence on humankind's social consciousness. For Marx, this economic interpretation of history was true under slavery, serfdom, and capitalism, and it would also be true with socialism and communism.

The most significant feature of Marx's view was the class struggle. This struggle is carried on by two distinct classes: those who own the land and the means of production and those who work in order to subsist. Marx viewed capitalism as an economic system that exploited the masses and encouraged class antagonism between the *proletariat* (urban workers) and the *bourgeoisie* (capitalist producers). He was of the opinion that in a highly industrialized society the proletariat at some point would revolt and eliminate the bourgeoisie. Socialism would then replace capitalism as the economic system of choice. Under these circumstances, the class struggle would be eliminated and the state would cease to exist, because it was simply a tool of the bourgeoisie used to control other social classes. Eventually, an ideal communist society would be created and all would prosper.

Leninism Marxist ideology was developed further with the theoretical contributions of Vladimir Ilich Lenin (1870–1924), who made the revolution possible in Russia. At the time, Russia was not an industrialized country but an agrarian society. Lenin was convinced that the proletariat revolution could occur in a country such as Russia if the proletariat united with the numerically superior peasantry. Lenin was also of the opinion that the bourgeoisie could be overthrown only if the proletariat was led by an elite, militant, disciplined organization. This group would become the Communist Party. Because of the need for unity of purpose, there could be no room for divisions within the party. Lenin referred to this principle as democratic centralism, that is, all authority would rest with the party executive.

From Lenin's perspective, the revolution would occur in two stages. The first was the socialist stage in which the state would continue to exist. On the surface, it would appear that the bourgeois society continued to exist, but, in fact, there would be a significant difference. Suppression would be in the hands of the majority rather than the minority; the means of economic production would be socialized; and exploitation in the workplace would be eliminated. During the second stage, the state would wither away and there would be no need for law. The ideal communist society would be established and equality would exist for all workers.

Mao Zedong Thought From the initial efforts to create a Communist Party in China, Mao Zedong (1893–1976) was actively involved in organizing students to work among the peasants. Mao accepted Marx's idea that society progresses from one stage to another and Lenin's views on the feasibility of staging a revolution in a nonindustrialized country. Mao's major contribution to the enhancement of communist ideology was his ability to adapt communist principles to the realities of the Chinese political environment. The most distinct and important feature of Mao's thought was to base the revolution on the mass support of the peasants. As such, he offered a different strategic perspective from that espoused by traditional Marxism, which emphasized the importance of the urban industrial proletariat. He also established an army controlled by the Communist Party that had the support of the peasants and recruited peasants into its ranks.

A central component of Mao's thought and a pragmatic feature of his strategic policy initiative was the importance placed on the mass mobilization of people as an essential ingredient to creating a socialist society. During his tenure in power, he implemented several programs that illustrate this objective. Two of his most famous initiatives were the Great Leap Forward and the Cultural Revolution.

The Great Leap Forward was introduced in 1958. It was based on the notion of mobilizing people into communes for purposes of social transformation and as a strategy designed to increase industrial and agricultural production. To illustrate, an agricultural commune might consist of approximately 5,000 households. Because private property no longer existed, individual income was based on the total production of the commune. The commune was responsible for all administrative and service needs of its members, such as nurseries, schools, and care for the elderly. The communal system was imposed on factories and other commercial enterprises as well. It was also employed as a method of managing large projects that were introduced to improve the country's infrastructure. For example, many students and soldiers worked in communal settings to reclaim land and build dams.

The Great Leap Forward was an attempt to maximize agricultural and industrial production through mass mobilization. It enabled the

Communists to eliminate any remnants of private property and to impose the notion of socialist ownership. The principal criticisms directed at this initiative involved the manner in which decisions were made in a communal setting. In agriculture and industry, planning often lacked logical procedures and rational processes. Goals that were far too ambitious and devoid of quality concerns were established to maximize production. In addition, skilled managers were replaced by Communist Party cadres who played crucial roles in communal decisionmaking but lacked the necessary technical expertise. The results of the Great Leap Forward were that several failures occurred in industrial settings and serious famine plagued various regions of the country.

The Cultural Revolution occurred between 1966 and 1976. It was Mao's radical attempt to reform the Communist Party. He called for the destruction of what he characterized as old thought, old culture, old customs and old habits. Once again, Mao mobilized the masses, in particular young people, to join an effort to establish a socialist program that emphasized self-reliance.

The establishment of an independent socialist agenda was prompted by a worsening of relations between China and the Soviet Union, which had influenced China's Communist Party since its inception in 1921. Mao also was dissatisfied with the Party's efforts at achieving his agenda. He wanted his ideas to guide the Chinese people in all aspects of their lives. Moreover, he believed that revolution was necessary and that the class struggle was continuous. Support for the ongoing revolution and class struggle would enable society to move beyond socialism to communism.

Mao organized young people into Red Guard units that were instrumental in attacking the four "olds"—thought, culture, customs, and habits. This campaign, which reached its most intense and destructive phase from 1966 through 1968, affected all levels of society. Economic and social institutions were disrupted throughout the country, and the political system was weakened to a considerable degree. The chaotic conditions created by the Cultural Revolution enhanced significantly the responsibilities of the People's Liberation Army. With the police and other components of the justice system under attack, the military assumed responsibility for maintaining law and order. As the Revolution continued, the breadth and depth of the military's involvement in civilian and political issues increased considerably.

Members of the political leadership eventually recognized that the revolution was an impediment to the socialist movement. They emerged from the disorder to counter the Red Guards and the Maoist radical agenda. Gradually, the central political leadership of the country was able to moderate the more radical wing of the Cultural Revolution. Mao's death in 1976 was instrumental in bringing closure to the Cultural Revolution.

Deng's Influence At the time of Mao's death, key members within the leadership of the Communist Party had begun to focus attention on modernization through economic development. In order to implement such an agenda, efforts would first have to be made to break with the Maoist past, while acknowledging Mao's achievements. As a result, Mao was praised for his role in establishing the Chinese Communist Party and for his leadership in carrying out the revolution in China. What was being abandoned by the leadership was Mao's revolutionary visions and methods for developing a socialist society. His emphasis on the class struggle and anti-intellectualism, his method of economic development through the communal system, and his isolationist attitude toward the rest of the world were all being abandoned in order to implement a new vision for China and its role in the world.

The principal architect of the new vision was Deng Xiaoping (1904–1997). His goal was to modernize China in four key areas: agriculture, industry, national defense, and science and technology. These became known as the "Four Modernizations." In order to achieve these goals, it was imperative to abandon the country's isolationist policy and establish an open-door policy, especially with the West. Such a policy would enable China to acquire the necessary knowledge and technology in its pursuit of creating a modern economy or, as Deng often defined it, a "socialism with Chinese characteristics."

Because of the chaos imposed upon the country by the Cultural Revolution and its immediate aftermath, a good deal of effort also had to be directed at strengthening government functions and procedures. Deng set out to rectify these deficiencies in a variety of ways. Four are singled out here for illustration. First, because of his long tenure both in and out of politics, Deng realized that whomever controlled the military also controlled the country. As a result, he proceeded to establish a strong military that was under the direction of the Communist Party. Second, Deng recognized the need to identify and groom new leaders for the future. He not only recruited a future generation of leaders but he also ended the long-standing practice of life-long tenure in party and government positions. This change in policy would enhance the likelihood that Deng's efforts at modernization would continue after he was gone from the scene. Third, Deng acknowledged that too much authority and control was centralized at the top of the party and government and that this was stifling creative efforts at introducing change in society and the economy. In light of this, he granted more authority to local people's governmental units. This was designed to assure that the new and future group of leaders could experiment with pragmatic approaches to socialist modernization. The most practical application of this change in policy occurred in 1979 when four cities in southern China were permitted to develop as special economic zones (SEZs). Finally, China's legal code was weak and its judiciary was without authority or independent status. In order to demonstrate to the world that China was attempting to establish a society that acknowledged the importance of the rule of law, specific legal initiatives became an important priority on Deng's reform agenda. Several administrative procedures and codes of law—among them a new criminal code—were introduced, and a new Constitution was ratified in 1982.

Deng's ultimate goal was to raise the standard of living of the Chinese people, which had been declining since the 1950s, by modernizing the country. In that regard, capitalist methods were employed to achieve those economic ends. Deng reconciled this apparent contradiction in a socialist country and explained his pragmatic approach to economics by his now-famous maxim: "It doesn't matter whether the cat is black or white, as long as it catches mice."

A degree of freedom extended to various sectors in the country led to changes in society and the economy and facilitated the movement toward modernization. Extending that degree of freedom to politics, however, was never part of the agenda. Unlike Mao, who encouraged revolution to achieve his objectives, Deng emphasized order and stability and adherence to party discipline and its leadership. This, in part, explains the 1989 tragedy at Tiananmen Square, in which a number of student protestors were killed in a confrontation with the People's Liberation Army.

There tends to be agreement among scholars and commentators that the Tiananmen Square incident can only be understood in the context of the democratic reform movement that was occurring in the Soviet Union and developing in eastern and central Europe. Unfortunately, the Tiananmen demonstrators clearly misread the Chinese leadership's agenda for the country. In the aftermath of the tragedy, the leadership, including Deng Xiaoping, were willing to face international vilification to maintain political control.

By way of comparison, it is interesting to note that the Soviet Union and China—the two major communist countries in the world at the time—took two different approaches to reform. The Soviet Union, under the leadership of Mikhail Gorbachev, focused much of its attention on political reform. Moreover, the basis or motivation for the reform would come from the central administration with the principal architect being Gorbachev and his three concepts of glasnost (openness), perestroika (restructuring), and democratization. Glasnost meant that the inefficiencies of public life would be open for criticism; perestroika called for a reorganization of the Soviet system so that it might be transformed into a more efficient form of socialism and enhance the well-being of the people; democratization was essential if perestroika was to be realized. Democratization referred to democratic socialism and was designed to embrace constitutional reform that included a socialist style of checks and balances and an independent judiciary. Democratization would also lead to a plurality of political ideas, which would inevitably lead to the abandonment of a single-party political system. Gorbachev's dream for the Soviet Union ended with its demise.

As indicated above, the People's Republic of China under the leadership of Deng Xiaoping focused most of its attention on economic reform. Whereas the idea for the Soviet reform effort came from the top of the political hierarchy and was implemented from the central administration, China's idea for reform also came from the top of the political hierarchy, but it was initiated at the grassroots level, with many of its attempts flourishing beyond people's expectations. Thus, Deng's dream has been very successful. The fact that China did not address political reform simultaneously with economic reform has probably benefited its economic successes in the short run. If the Chinese leaders continue to avoid significant political reform, however, it could prove detrimental in the long run to a stable political, economic, and social system.

Jiang's Contribution Deng Xiaoping anointed Jiang Zemin (1926–) as his successor. Jiang was elected general secretary of the Chinese Communist Party by the Communist Party Congress in 1989 and served until 2002. He was also elected president of the People's Republic of China by the National People's Congress in 1993 and served until 2003. While it is too early to evaluate Jiang's lasting contribution to China in general and to communist ideology in particular, he argued that the Communist Party had a very important role to play in the transformation of Chinese society to a socialist market-economy. In describing the role of the party, he coined the term "Three Represents," which meant that the Chinese Communist Party represented society's most productive economic forces, represented society's most advanced culture, and represented the interests of all the people. Thus, the party was being defined as the organization that was at the center of the economic, cultural, and social changes that were designed to benefit all Chinese citizens. Clearly, the party was no longer the revolutionary party of Mao Zedong. It was no longer solely concerned about the proletariat, that is, the workers and peasants of Marx, Lenin, and Mao. It was the party of the broad masses of people irrespective of their social-economic status in the changing Chinese society.

By abandoning its association with Mao's revolutionary zeal, Jiang adhered to and reinforced Deng Xiaoping's view that in order to transform China's economic system there had to be order and stability throughout the country. The party through its adherence to party discipline would lead this transformation. By doing so, it would no longer be viewed as a revolutionary party but rather as the ruling party. From the perspective of Deng, Jiang, and other leaders in the party, this new role for the party would assure its dominant role in China and prevent its demise or near demise as has been the case in other socialist countries that are in the process of transforming their economic system.

During Jiang's tenure, he focused a good deal of his attention on three domestic issues that were initiated by Deng. First, he helped expand the developing socialist market economy by encouraging individual initiatives in various economic ventures that have fostered a new entrepreneurial spirit in China. He also began to scale back on the number of state-owned enterprises that had long been a drain on the economy. Second, he has reduced the size of the central government and given more responsibility to the provinces, regions, municipalities, and local administrative divisions. Finally, he has strengthened the legal system. Among the most important pieces of legislation passed are: the administrative litigation law, civil procedure law, a revised criminal procedure law, and a new criminal code. While the legal profession was almost nonexistent at the time of Mao's death, it is now estimated that there are more than 100,000 lawyers in the country. This was made possible by the reopening of old law schools and the establishment of a number of new law schools and legal institutes.

Communist Party

Unlike most countries that have political parties competing with one another for the right to set the political agenda of the country, China has but one recognized political party: the Chinese Communist Party (CCP). This is in keeping with a socialist tradition initiated in the former Soviet Union. Lenin indicated that the success of the proletariat revolution hinged in part on the establishment of an elite, militant, disciplined organization that would lead the revolution. That organization was the Communist Party. As indicated earlier, Mao Zedong followed that tradition by utilizing the CCP to establish the People's Republic of China in 1949.

The principal requirements for membership in the CCP are accepting the party's agenda and a willingness to work for its programs. Candidates for membership must be at least 18 years of age. Presently, there are approximately 66 million party members who come from all walks of life.

In order to understand and appreciate the political agenda of the CCP, it is instructive to turn to the Constitution of the Chinese Communist Party for some insight. In the section titled "General Program," which is similar to a preamble, the party indicates that its ultimate goal is to create a communist social system and that it will be guided in this endeavor by adhering to Marxism-Leninism and Mao Zedong thought. By adhering to a Marxist interpretation of history, it states further that "the inevitable replacement of capitalism by socialism is an irreversible general trend in the history of social development." Although an ideological victory is projected for the long term, the party acknowledges frankly that the country is only "in the initial stage of socialism. This is an impassable stage for economically and culturally backward China in the drive for socialist modernization, which may take up to a hundred years. Socialist construction in our country must proceed from its own conditions and follows the road of socialism with Chinese characteristics."

Throughout the 1980s, when attempts to modernize China's economy were introduced, there was a good deal of discussion about reforming the CCP, because it was recognized as contributing in a significant way to the creation and perpetuation of a highly centralized, bureaucratized, and rigid political system. A lively debate within the Party hierarchy followed in which it was suggested that the CCP should reduce its extensive involvement in the daily operations of government. In addition, the CCP was urged to function in a more democratic manner and be held accountable to other organizations within society. With the demise of communist regimes in eastern and central Europe and the impact that democratic reforms had on the former Soviet Union, the Chinese leadership concluded that political control should be enhanced rather than reduced. The argument was also put forth that centralized political authority was necessary in order to facilitate efforts at modernizing the economy.

Several scholars from the West have indicated that this issue will undoubtedly be revisited. The central government is finding it difficult to wield its authority over the entire country, thus raising questions about the viability of its power. Moreover, the legitimacy of the CCP as the sole political party within the country has come under greater criticism (Lubman, 1996).

Over the course of the past decade, the political culture has changed significantly in terms of the relationship between the state and society. Economic growth has led to the rise of materialism and individualism among the citizenry who have been successful with the market economy. Both young and old feel alienated politically from either the ideology of the CCP or its policies (Ding, 2001). The efforts of Deng and Jiang to improve the economy have led to a considerable number of protests. While in 1993 the government acknowledged 8,700 demonstrations, that number rose to 87,000 in 2005. These protests are essentially local in nature and directed at local officials. The people are objecting to a wide range of issues, including: employment concerns, health and safety issues, illegal land sales, local tax increases, and environmental concerns. For the most part, these demonstrations have focused on single issues. As such, there has not emerged a regional, let alone a national, effort to challenge the CCP (Perry and Selden, 2000). It has been suggested that demonstrations of this kind are actually beneficial to the central government, as they alert the government to problems at the grassroots level. This, in turn, can lead to positive reforms initiated by the central government and is a practical illustration of how the Communist Party represents the interest of the people (see Perry, in O'Brien, 2008).

Probably the most significant issue that has fostered the sense of alienation and the growth in protests has been the level of corruption that appears widespread throughout society, in particular that related to official corruption. Scholars have noted that there was corruption before the post-Mao era and the rise of a market economy. Local party officials were involved in a number of illicit activities that included bribery, embezzlement, and extortion. Such abuses continue to this day and have proliferated with the market economy because of the growth in opportunities in both the public and private sectors.

From time to time, the government has initiated strike-hard campaigns against particular crime problems, and this has included corrupt government officials. Strike-hard campaigns are coordinated efforts by the government and agents of the criminal justice system to focus a good deal of attention and resources for a specific period of time on a particular crime problem. There have been three strike-hard campaigns. The first was initiated in 1983 and ended in 1987. It made a very broad sweep of all types of criminal activity. The second campaign from 1996 to 1997 and the third campaign from 2001 to 2003 were more focused. They were directed at such groups as drug dealers, pornographers, and organized crime. All campaigns are noted for the objective of quickly and severely punishing criminals. As a result, there has been an increase in the number of people sentenced to death (Liang, 2008). In the course of such campaigns against corruption, government officials have been arrested, tried, and convicted. Some have received fines or a prison sentence, and on occasion, they have been sentenced to death.

In spite of these efforts, corruption persists. Part of the problem is that local authorities have increased their power, and the central government has not been successful at establishing an effective oversight mechanism (Lu, 2000). The continued inability of the government to control or address the corruption problem in any meaningful way could be a central factor that prompts change in the single-party political system of China. As one scholar has pointed out, the democratic alternative offers at least two methods of addressing corruption: a media that can expose such problems and an electoral process that enables the removal of such officials (Sun, 2004).

Presently, the administration of the CCP more or less parallels that of government, for the party is organized at the local, county, provincial, and national levels. Brief mention is made of the party structure at the national level. In theory, the National Party Congress is at the top of the hierarchy. It is composed of almost 2,000 delegates who are elected by party members from local, county, and provincial units. The responsibilities of the National Party Congress include: revising the constitution of the Party, discussing major policy issues, entertaining various reports from the party executive, and approving the selection of people for various committees.

Because the Congress only meets once every five years, the Central Committee is responsible for the functions of the Congress when it is not in session. The composition of the Central Committee is determined by the National Party Congress. Presently, the Committee consists of about 190 members; their term of office is five years. The Central Committee holds at least one plenary session a year. One of the principal responsibilities of this committee is to select people who will administer and manage the daily activities of the CCP.

The real power within the CCP resides in the Politburo, the Standing Committee of the Politburo, and the Secretariat. The members of these groups are selected by the Central Committee. The Secretariat is responsible for the daily management of the CCP. The Politburo and the Standing Committee of the Politburo focus their attention on national and international issues. The most important person within the CCP is the General Secretary, who administers the work of the Secretariat and convenes the meetings of the Politburo and the Standing Committee of the Politburo.

The Constitution

Since the fall of the Qing dynasty in 1911 and the end of imperial rule, political leaders in China have recognized the significant role that a written constitution can play in legitimizing the status and agenda of government. It is very important to point out, however, that the Chinese do not view their constitution in the same context as do people in the West. The basis for this difference is found in history. Traditionally, law was viewed in China as the command of a superior to assure uniformity and conformity. Although the superior could opt to adhere to the law for the sake of consistency, this was not required. Thus, the superior was not bound by the law, and if he deviated from it, his subordinate could not seek redress from a higher authority.

In light of this tradition, the Constitution of the People's Republic of China should not be viewed as a list of rights designed to curtail the power of the central government. For example, Article 5 states, in part: "No organization or individual may enjoy the privilege of being above the Constitution and the law." In spite of this statement, the Chinese leadership has not uniformly adhered to this principle, thus continuing the tradition from previous eras. Rights are listed in the document, but they are mentioned more as a statement of the government's policy orientation.

The present Constitution of the People's Republic of China was adopted in 1982 and has been amended since that time. It is the fourth constitution promulgated since the country was founded in 1949. Although the constitution displays a continuity with its earlier versions of 1954, 1975, and 1978, it also reflects a change in the government's policy orientation since the days of Mao Zedong. For example, the preamble states, in part:

> Our country will be in the primary stage of socialism for a long period of time. The basic task before the nation is the concentration of efforts on socialist modernization construction along the road of building socialism with Chinese characteristics. Under the leadership of the Communist Party of China and the guidance of Marxism-Leninism, Mao Zedong Thought and Deng Xiaoping Theory, the Chinese people of all ethnic groups will continue to adhere to the people's democratic dictatorship and follow the socialist road, and to uphold reform and opening to the outside world, steadily improve socialist institutions, develop a socialist market economy, promote socialist democracy, improve the socialist legal system, and work hard and self-reliantly to modernize industry, agriculture, national defense, and science and technology step by step to build China into a strong and prosperous, culturally advanced, democratic socialist nation.

This is clearly an affirmation of the policies introduced by Deng Xiaoping, in particular, the attention directed at modernization through economic development.

The constitution is divided into four chapters and consists of 138 articles. While the preamble makes reference to the leadership role of the Chinese Communist Party (CCP), Chapter 1 indicates the pervasive nature of that power. It states that China "is a socialist state under the people's democratic dictatorship." While Article 2 proclaims that "all power in the PRC belongs to the people," Article 3 indicates that "the state organs of the PRC apply the principle of democratic centralism," or all power rests with the leadership of the CCP.

Many of the articles in Chapter 1 (there are 32 in total) indicate the breadth and depth of the state's involvement in the lives of the citizenry. Among the more prominent issues are: the economy, education and training, health care, social services, and national defense. Article 6 is indicative of the socialist view, it states:

> The basis of the socialist economic system of the PRC is socialist public ownership of the means of production, namely, ownership by the whole people and collective ownership by the working people.
>
> The system of socialist public ownership supersedes the system of exploitation of man by man; it applies the principle of "from each according to his ability, to each according to his work."

These are classic socialist phrases that one would expect of a country aspiring to establish a communist society. In 1999, Article 6 was amended with the addition of the following sentence.

> In the primary stage of socialism, the state upholds the basic economic system with the dominance of the public ownership and the simultaneous development of an economy of diverse forms of ownership, and upholds the distribution system with the dominance of distribution according to work and the coexistence of diverse modes of distribution.

Obviously, this was an acknowledgment of the impact of that market-oriented principles were having on the Chinese economy.

For students of criminal justice, Article 5 is worth mentioning in particular. It states:

> The People's Republic of China exercises the rule of law, building a socialist country governed according to law.
>
> The state upholds the uniformity and dignity of the socialist legal system.
>
> No law or administrative or local rules and regulations shall contravene the Constitution.
>
> All state organs, the armed forces, all political parties and public organizations, and all enterprises and undertakings must abide by the Constitution and the law. All acts in violation of the Constitution and the law must be looked into.
>
> No organization or individual may enjoy the privilege of being above the Constitution and the law.

As was suggested earlier, the Chinese leadership has not been uniformly bound by the law. In recent years, however, the enforcement of this provision has escalated to some extent. This has sparked discussion about the possible enhanced status of law throughout Chinese society. It should be noted that Article 5 was amended in 1999 with the addition of the first sentence and its mention of the rule of law. While adding this term rule of law suggests a possible change in the political dynamics of the country, this has either not reached fruition or is simply not the case. As was mentioned in the introductory chapter, a central feature of the rule of law is the idea that the exercise of state power must be regulated by law. In light of the Chinese Communist Party's role in the governance of the country and the continued adherence to Lenin's principle of democratic centralism, it is more accurate to describe China as a country ruled by law. In this context law is a tool employed by the state usually to control or direct others without establishing a mechanism that can restrain the state from its exercise of such power (Peerenboom, 2002).

Constitutions of socialist countries usually include a section on rights and duties of citizens. In this regard, China is no exception, as Chapter 2 addresses issues such as freedom of speech, press, assembly, and religious belief; the right to rest, to social insurance, and to medical and health service; the duty to safeguard the country's interests, perform military service, and pay taxes; and the right and duty to work and to receive education. Article 48 proclaims that women enjoy equal rights in all aspects of life. Finally, Article 53 indicates that citizens "must abide by the Constitution and the law, keep state secrets, protect public property, and observe labor discipline and public order and respect social ethics."

It might be useful at this point to interject a few comments about the group known as Falun Gong. Various human rights groups, along with the Western media, have portrayed Falun Gong as a spiritual movement that has been deprived by the Chinese government of the constitutional protection of religious freedom. The Chinese government does not accept this characterization of the group; it views Falun Gong as a dangerous cult that is not accorded such constitutional protection. The central feature of Falun Gong is not a particular religious belief, as that term is usually employed, rather it is the practice of *qigong*. Qigong consists of a series of five exercises, of which the fifth involves sitting in the lotus position and meditating. The objective is to regulate *qi*, a nonphysical energy or life force that circulates throughout the body. Through channeling and harmonizing the qi, a person is attempting either to prevent or cure illness.

Theories of qi have long been a feature of traditional Chinese medicine. As such, most Chinese do not consider qigong to be associated with religion; rather, it is viewed as a health practice. The religious connection is made by some in part because Falun Gong means Dharma wheel practice. The Dharma wheel refers to the cycles of birth and death and is associated with the teachings of Buddha.

Many of the followers of Falun Gong in China have reached middle age or beyond. It has been suggested that these people have been attracted to this practice because the ideological failure of communism has left a void in their lives. Some commentators have argued that the government's attempts to eliminate the movement are not directed so much at its practice of qigong but because the government is alarmed at Falun Gong's organizational abilities and considers it a possible threat to the Communist regime (Madsen, 2000).

Some legal issues found in the Chinese Constitution are of particular interest to students of criminal justice, and they can be found in Chapter 2 of the document. The full text of those articles are cited here.

> Article 37. The freedom of person of citizens of the PRC is inviolable.
>
> No citizen may be arrested except with the approval or by decision of a people's procuratorate or by decision of a people's court, and arrests must be made by a public security organ.
>
> Unlawful deprivation or restriction of citizens' freedom of person by detention or other means is prohibited; and unlawful search of the person of citizens is prohibited.

> Article 38. The personal dignity of citizens of the PRC is inviolable. Insult, libel, false charge, or frame-up directed against citizens by any means is prohibited.
>
> Article 39. The home of citizens of the PRC is inviolable. Unlawful search of, or intrusion into, a citizen's home is prohibited.
>
> Article 40. The freedom and privacy of correspondence of citizens of the PRC are protected by law. No organization or individual may, on any ground, infringe upon the freedom and privacy of citizens' correspondence except in cases where, to meet the needs of state security or of investigation into criminal offenses, public security or procuratorial organs are permitted to censor correspondence in accordance with procedures prescribed by law.

It is important to reiterate, especially as it relates to citizens' rights to freedom from oppressive or intrusive actions of the government, that the Constitution of the People's Republic of China should not be viewed as a list of rights designed to curtail the power of the central government. Rather, it is a statement of the government's orientation toward public policy. References to other portions of the Constitution are made below, as the structure of government is explained.

The National People's Congress

In theory, state power in China is unitary rather than separated. While the Chinese government is composed of a number of units, all owe their authority and receive guidance from a single source of state power: the people's congress. The National People's Congress is the ultimate source of state power; it is also the principal legislative body in China. Its members are referred to as deputies, and they are elected to five-year terms from either a province, autonomous region, or municipality. It is interesting to note that a portion of the deputies are elected from branches of the armed forces. There are almost 3,000 deputies in the National People's Congress.

The Congress is accorded several duties. Their legislative authority includes amending and enforcing the Constitution and enacting and amending statutes. The deputies elect the president and vice president of the People's Republic of China, the chair of the Central Military Commission, the president of the Supreme Court, and the procurator general. They confirm the choice of premier, who is nominated by the president of the People's Republic of China, as well as other ministers of state who are nominated by the premier. The Congress also approves the budget and nationwide plans for economic and social development.

Finally, they have the authority to remove from office the president and vice president of the People's Republic of China, the premier and other ministers, the chair of the Central Military Commission, the president of the Supreme Court, and the procurator general.

According to the Constitution, the Congress must meet at least once a year and may be called into extraordinary sessions at other times. Because the Congress meets for such a limited time, it wields little power. Its primary purpose is to endorse the legislation and policy initiatives of the central administration.

The Standing Committee

The National People's Congress elects from among its members the deputies who serve on the Standing Committee. Presently, there are about 135 people, which includes many of the leading government officials and influential members of the Chinese Communist Party. The Standing Committee is the legislative body that functions throughout the year; it also sets the agenda and presides over the National People's Congress when it is in session. The Standing Committee retains its authority until a new congress is elected.

In light of the fact that the Standing Committee is a full-time legislative body, it has been given an extensive list of responsibilities. It interprets the Constitution and other statutes and enforces the Constitution. It also can enact and amend statutes when the National People's Congress is not in session, but this authority is limited. The Committee supervises the State Council, the Central Military Commission, the Supreme People's Court, and the Supreme People's Procuratorate. The Standing Committee can annul various rules, regulations, decisions, and orders at both the national and provincial levels. It also appoints and can remove senior members of the judiciary and procuratorate. When the National People's Congress is not in session, the Standing Committee can approve the appointment of ministers to the State Council and members to the Central Military Commission. Finally, if the National People's Congress is not in session, the Standing Committee can decide to ratify or abrogate treaties, to enforce martial law, and to declare war.

President of the People's Republic of China

Throughout the history of socialist states that have aspired to adopt the principles of Marxism-Leninism, the Communist Party and the state have been interrelated with the dominant position accorded the party. To illustrate, the role of the president of the People's Republic of China is limited to that of head of state. Based upon decisions made by others, specifically the National People's Congress and its Standing Committee, the president promulgates statutes, appoints and removes key government officials, declares martial law, and proclaims a state of war.

In order for a person to be eligible to serve in this office, he or she must be a citizen and have reached the age of 45. The president serves a five-year term, which corresponds to the term of the National People's Congress. A person can be elected to the office for no more than two consecutive terms.

The State Council

According to the constitution, the State Council is the principal unit of state power; it is the executive body for state administration. The premier is ultimately responsible for the State Council, which includes several vice premiers, state councilors, and ministers. Because the Council includes so many government units, the premier is assisted by vice premiers and state councilors in the coordination of the Council's work. The ministers are specifically responsible for either a government ministry or commission. Once again, the term of office for members of the State Council corresponds with that of the National People's Congress. In addition, the premier, vice premiers, and state councilors are limited to serving in these capacities for no more than two consecutive terms.

For people who have lived only in a capitalist society in which government shares with the private sector the authority and responsibility to create a viable social system, it can be difficult to comprehend the totality of government authority under a socialist state that aspires to create a communist society. A listing of the various ministries, commissions, and organizations that are part of the State Council should assist the reader in appreciating the breadth and depth to which the Chinese government is the principal administrator and regulator of people's lives. The ministries include: agriculture, chemical industry, civil affairs, coal industry, communications, construction, culture, electronic industry, finance, foreign affairs, foreign trade and economic cooperation, forestry, geology and mineral resources, internal trade, justice, labor, machinery industry, metallurgical industry, national defense, personnel, posts and telecommunications, power industry, public health, public security, radio, film and television, railways, state security, supervision, water resources, auditor general, and the People's Bank of China. The commissions consist of: science, technology, and industry for national defense; state economics and trade; state education; state family planning; state nationalities affairs; state physical culture and sports; state planning; state restructuring of the economic system; and state science and technology. Other organizations that fall directly under the authority of the State Council are: civil aviation administration of China, counselors' office, general administration of customs, government offices administration bureau, national tourism administration, state administration for industry and commerce, state administration of taxation, state environmental protection bureau, state land administration, state legislative affairs bureau, state press and publications administration, state religious affairs bureau, and state statistical bureau.

In 1999, the government announced plans to streamline the bureaucracy. The objective is to consolidate groups of ministries and commissions that have similar functions or categories of responsibility into single ministries. The purpose is to make the government bureaucracy smaller but more efficient. This effort is also designed to facilitate the development of the market economy that the government is committed to establishing. Once the consolidation is completed, the State Council will consist of 29 ministries and commissions. The ministries include: agriculture, civil affairs, communications, construction, culture, education, finance, foreign affairs, foreign trade and economic cooperation, health, information industry, justice, labor and social security, land and resources, national defense, personnel, public security, railways, science and technology, state security, supervision, and water resources, along with the National Audit Office and the People's Bank of China. The commissions consist of: development planning, economic and trade, science, technology and industry for national defense, ethnic affairs, and family planning.

Administration

When one considers the size of China in terms of both its geography and population, it is essential that the administration of government be carried out at multiple levels within the political hierarchy. As a result, the administrative divisions below the central government include: 23 provinces (Taiwan is considered a province), five autonomous regions, and four municipalities (Beijing, Chongqing, Shanghai, and Tianjin) under the central government; 115 prefectures; 1,894 counties; 476 cities; and 650 districts. At the county level and above, there are people's congresses and standing committees. It should be pointed out that deputies to people's congresses at the county level are elected directly by the people. Presently, the government is considering expanding direct elections at other levels in the government. The people's congresses are supposed to make government more responsive to the needs of the local people, while the standing committees are expected to facilitate the policies and programs of the central government at the local level. In addition, the day-to-day administration at the local level is handled by governors, mayors, and heads of counties.

The role of local administration has been an important issue in domestic politics for almost 25 years. The post-Mao leaders realized that the centralized state planning process often inhibited economic growth. As such, some of the planning process has devolved to regional, provincial, and local administrative units in order to enhance the opportunities for the new market-oriented ventures.

Staffing government administration at all levels is also being reformed. The cadre system, which was based on family and personal relationships, is being replaced by a civil service system familiar to the West. Competitive examinations and a regularized system of rules and norms determine the selection process. The selection of a more competent civil service has led to the introduction of a more competitive wage scale. It is hoped that this will help reduce the degree of corruption among government officials throughout the country, which has been an issue of significant concern for some time.

While a number of issues mentioned in this section are useful in helping to understand China's approach to criminal justice, none is more important than how law has been viewed in the establishment and development of the People's Republic of China. People from the West take for granted that a country's legal system profoundly influences the criminal justice system, for it is law that is at the heart of the justice process. In the case of China, however, the context is significantly different. Law and the various components of the criminal justice system have been viewed in a strikingly different fashion.

It is important to remember that when the People's Republic of China was established in 1949 the leaders of the Communist Party abolished the laws that had been established by the Kuomintang Party during the period of the Republic of China (1912–1949). The Communists intended to create a new government that would be based on a socialist legal system. While some law was passed during the early years of the new government, most notably the 1954 Constitution of the People's Republic of China, a good deal of legislation languished in draft form (for example, criminal law and criminal procedural law). The activities of the Cultural Revolution (1966–1976) halted all efforts to enact legislation and even attacked those components of the justice system that were responsible for maintaining law and order.

The attitude toward law changed markedly following the death of Mao Zedong and the emergence of Deng Xiaoping as leader. Since the late 1970s, law has been viewed as a vehicle that could enhance and stabilize the country's efforts at creating a socialist democracy. With the enactment of a criminal law and a criminal procedural law in 1979, the People's Republic of China established the first criminal justice legal standard in its 30-year history.

Finally, in studying the Chinese justice system, it is important to remember that China has essentially two kinds of justice systems. One is the formal system, which is the creation of the government and will be the principal focus of attention in this chapter. The other is the informal system, which is essentially part of the cultural tradition of the country that dates back to ancient times. It is reflected in communities taking an active role in assuring that social order is maintained locally and in the preference of citizens to utilize mediation rather than allow the courts to resolve disputes.

Police

As was suggested earlier, the considerable interest in China over the last two decades of the twentieth century was prompted by its emergence from a period of prolonged, self-imposed isolation from the rest of the world and the establishment of an open-door policy, in particular toward the West. This change in attitude was initiated by the government's desire to modernize the country through economic development. Over the course of the initial phase of this economic transformation, the country witnessed a significant increase in crime. Initially, the increase was most pronounced in the special economic zones that were established by the government to experiment with and promote economic development, but the problem has since spread to other parts of the country as well.

Crime statistics collected by the police are frequently flawed irrespective of the country being studied. Victim surveys often illustrate that crime is a more serious and common problem than the police data suggest. In the Chinese context, the problem of under-recording crime has long been associated with the lack of transparency in the methods employed in collecting the data. More recently it has also been associated with the social and organizational pressures that the police have had to confront as a result of the changes in the economy (Yu and Zhang, 1999). With this caution in mind, one scholar cited data from the Institute of Public Security, which is part of the Ministry of Public Security. It estimated that the national crime rate had risen 7.3 percent between 1978 and 1982, that it had grown 11.5 percent between 1984 and 1988, and that it had increased to 45.1 percent between 1989 and 1991 (Dai, 1994). Another study, also based on official data, suggested that the overall crime rate increased by 160 percent between 1980 and 1990 (Ma, 1997).

More recently, the Ministry of Public Security provided nationwide data on criminal cases that were reported. The number of cases reported to the police in 2000 was 3,637,307. This figure rose to 4,337,036 in 2002 and continued to increase to 4,718,122 by 2004 (Ministry of Public Security, 2005). In 2007, the number of cases reached 4,807,517, which was an increase from 4,653,265 reported in 2006 (Ministry of Public

Security, 2008). Scholars have argued for some time now that the increased level of crime across China can be attributed directly to the inequalities that have emerged as a result of the economic reforms. This has led to serious disparities of income that were unheard of until Deng Xiaoping introduced his economic reform initiative (see Cao and Dai, in Liu, Zhang, and Messner, 1994; Friday, 1998).

Data from the ministry appear to support this position. In 2007, the largest volume of cases among the most serious offenses was for the most part associated with crimes against property: theft (3,268,670), burglary (1,063,201), auto theft (611,696), and robbery (292,549). Crimes against the person tend to attract the headlines in the Western media and cause the most alarm among the public. In 2007, the number of these offenses reported in China was very small: homicide (16,119), rape (31,883), and assault (167,207). Of these three, only assault has increased from the 2004 figures, while homicide and rape have declined.

It is important to keep in mind that the total rate of crime in China is not reflected in the official published rates. One reason was mentioned briefly in the introduction, which pointed out that China has an informal justice system in addition to the formal system. The informal system is part of the country's cultural tradition that dates back to ancient times. The informal system encourages people to settle disputes privately, in part because the Chinese have historically tended to avoid formal legal procedures. In addition, neighborhood committees established with the Communist regime frequently served as a mechanism to reduce conflicts between neighbors and domestic tensions between parents or parents and children.

A final reason for examining the official crime statistics with caution is that there is a group of offenses for which data is collected but does not become part of the statistics on criminal cases. These are the public order offenses that are handled exclusively by the police. Although now written as administrative regulations, this is also part of the informal justice system. It allows the police to arrest, detain, try, and impose sanctions on people who have committed public order violations. Thus, there is no formal prosecution or trial.

More will be said about police powers and the administrative regulations in other sections of this chapter. For our present purposes, it is important to note that public order cases include: disturbing the peace, gang fights, carrying a weapon or explosives, minor assault, minor thefts, vandalism, prostitution, gambling offenses, and not complying with the household registration system. In 2000, the nationwide total of public order cases reported was 4,437,417. In 2004, this figure rose to 6,647,724, and in 2007, it had reached 8,709,398. Among the most frequently reported public order offenses were: battering other persons (2,544,082), minor theft (2,025,560), and disturbing the peace (446,846).

When crime has increased in the West, the police have often been criticized for allowing the situation to arise in the first place, and they have been blamed for not expeditiously bringing the problem under control. The Chinese police have not escaped the same criticism. For their part, the police have made concerted efforts to address the problem, particularly in the special economic zones. For example, they have initiated campaigns that target criminal gangs; they have been especially attentive to the security needs of foreign businesses; and they have enhanced border security (Zhihua, 1993). In spite of these efforts, however, there appears to be a general agreement that the police need to adapt, both organizationally and individually, to the social and economic circumstances that are changing the country in such a dramatic fashion. To appreciate the dilemma confronting law enforcement in this regard, it is useful to consider briefly the recent historical development of the police.

Throughout its history, China has experienced periods of order and profound periods of disorder. Each period has obviously had an impact on how the state defined public security, how society perceived the need for social order, and how the police implemented their law enforcement and order maintenance functions. During the twentieth century, periods of order have been marked by the state's attempt to stress the significant role of law in the maintenance of political, social, and economic order. Periods of disorder have been noted for an absence of law and the ascendance of ideology serving a dominant role in state governance.

To illustrate, at the conclusion of World War II, China was subjected to civil war between two rival factions for control of the country. The Kuomintang (or Nationalist Party) espoused the democratic ideals that helped establish the Republic of China in 1912, while the Chinese Communist Party sought to introduce a socialist agenda that was based on the principles of Marx and Lenin. Throughout the civil war (1945–1949), the Communists established large base areas that were beyond the control of the Kuomintang. Amid the disorder of civil war, the Communists developed a system of government at the base areas that included creating laws and establishing a system of police.

Policing tended to be the responsibility of three groups. Public security forces were responsible for basic police functions in the secure base areas. Militia groups monitored the border regions of the territories occupied by the Communists. Finally, the Communists could turn to the People's Liberation Army (PLA), which was the military wing of the Chinese Communist Party, as an additional method of assuring public order. It is important to note that the public security forces established at base areas were primarily composed of people recruited from either the PLA or militia groups.

Another significant issue that emerged at this time and had implications for public security was the importance that Mao Zedong placed on the "mass line." The mass line was a theoretical perspective espoused by Mao that was based on the premise that the role of bureaucratic elites in government decisionmaking should be reduced significantly and at times replaced by the direct involvement of the people. Thus, government officials, as servants of the people, should be guided by the public because the people are the true supervisors of the officials. For this perspective to work in any practical manner, officials had to collect and interpret the views of the people and then synthesize them into a coherent policy.

The mass line is an important concept for understanding how China approached public security, particularly under Mao's leadership. During periods of order, the police were able for the most part to control the mass line process by determining what the wishes of the people were. In times of disorder, however, the mass line enhanced considerably the notion of an arbitrary "popular" justice at the expense of a more predictable "bureaucratic" form of justice. As a result, more excessive applications of the mass line often perpetuated imbalance and increased disorder in the country. Mao considered this a positive feature of his approach to establishing a communist society (see Bracey, in Troyer, Clark, and Rojek, 1989; Brewer et al., 1996).

Following the Communists' victory over the Kuomintang in 1949, the People's Republic of China was established. During the following four years, there was a good deal of turmoil throughout the country. Supporters of the Kuomintang attempted to resist the new government. Groups that were not necessarily opposed to the Communists rioted in protest over some of the policies the government was attempting to implement. China's involvement in the Korean War caused others to raise doubts about the permanency of the Communist government.

Because of the level of dissent and the degree of disturbance, the public security forces continued to rely on the assistance and support of the militia and the PLA. This period of disorder prevented the public security forces from establishing an organizational structure for police that was independent from other government entities. It also inhibited the development of policies for an effective and efficient management of the police organization. Moreover, the mass line played a prominent role at the time in compounding the problems of order maintenance. As the Communists exercised their newly won political power, they used the mass line to determine those who were criminals and those who were counterrevolutionaries.

From a law enforcement perspective, the period between 1954 and 1966 was characterized as fairly stable and orderly. Of course, there were some exceptions. For example, the Anti-Rightist Campaign (1957–1958) disrupted the lives of China's intellectuals, and the Great Leap Forward (1958–1960) created economic disorder and chaos in the lives of large sectors of the population. Nevertheless, several factors helped to foster a somewhat tranquil time for the police. They included a considerable reduction in internal dissent, an end to the Korean War, and the introduction of the First Five-Year Economic Plan (1953), which was designed not only to improve the economy but also to assure social stability.

For criminal justice in general and policing in particular, this period was marked by the government acknowledging the significant role that the codification of law could have in establishing a stable society. The aim was to create standard predictable policies and practices. To illustrate, the first constitution of the People's Republic of China was approved in 1954. It would influence the creation and application of police procedures. With regard to criminal procedures in general, a clear division of responsibility was emerging among police, procurators, and the courts. While the Communist Party wielded the ultimate authority, an attempt was made to establish order within a legal context, rather than permit ideological whims of the moment to control the development of policies.

In light of the emergence of these formal standards, there was less emphasis placed on the role of the informal mass line approach for assuring justice. In addition, there was a recognition not only of the importance placed on recruiting people to perform public security work but also in training them. Thus, an effort was made to establish a professional group of public security officers. As a result, the PLA's role in law enforcement and order maintenance declined significantly during this period.

This time of relative calm ended with the inception of the Cultural Revolution (1966–1976), one of the most horrendous periods in recent Chinese history. As mentioned earlier, the Cultural Revolution was Mao Zedong's radical attempt to reform the Chinese Communist Party. He wanted to destroy old ideas, customs, and habits. His method of achieving this was to create a state of disorder throughout the country by mobilizing young activists, known as Red Guards, to support revolution and the class struggle within Chinese society.

During the early phase of the Revolution (1966–1969), which is generally considered the most destructive of the whole period, government officials were attacked, relieved of their duties, and sent to work on farms or in factories. The goal was to eradicate their bourgeois attitudes through manual labor. Senior police officials were among the government officials attacked and exiled; police stations and courts were taken over by the Red Guards. Law and order was replaced by ideology and disorder, which was reflected in a total allegiance to Mao Zedong and his pronouncements. Local police were placed under even closer scrutiny by local Communist Party officials and the significance of the mass line was renewed, which further eroded the sense of order.

The Cultural Revolution caused chaos within the ranks of the Communist Party and throughout various levels of government, in part because veteran government officials were sent to the countryside to perform manual labor. The state of disorder escalated further because some of the activities of the Red Guards were not unlike those of gangs of street thugs. By 1967, it was clear that something had to be done to address the problem. Mao Zedong called upon the People's Liberation Army (PLA) to reinstate some sense of order. They provided this kind of service until the end of the Cultural Revolution, at which time they resumed their military role on a full-time basis.

The Cultural Revolution came to an end in 1976 with the death of Mao Zedong. The "Gang of Four," the principal leaders of the Cultural Revolution, were arrested and subsequently tried and convicted for many of the atrocities committed during the Revolution. With Deng Xiaoping's ascendance to power, China embarked upon a new era that was considerably different from the previous period of turmoil. Deng's goal was to modernize Chinese society by abandoning its isolationist policy and opening its doors to the West so it could acquire the requisite knowledge and technology to transform China into a modern country.

In order to achieve his objective, Deng recognized the need to establish a stable society. He began by making distinctions between the role of the Communist Party and that of the state. Although ideology was important to perpetuate the communist cause, it was being displaced from the center stage by pragmatic views regarding how best to modernize Chinese society. Deng further admitted that the rule of law had a central role to play in the modernization process, and he introduced initiatives to reform China's legal system. He also acknowledged the importance of maintaining good public order. As such, the police were brought back, with their responsibilities enhanced and their expertise acknowledged as playing a vital role in assuring the success of China's transformation into a modern society.

As a result of Deng's initiative, the police have entered a phase in which law and order have superseded ideology and disorder. Moreover, the police have had to adapt to the changing social and economic circumstances of the country. One practical example of this was the passage of The Police Law 1995, which explains the organization, duties, and authority of the principal police agencies in China. The distinctions of authority among the principal police agencies and the specialized police forces is another illustration that stability and order are being achieved through the maintenance of distinct organizations with expertise in and responsibility for specific aspects of policing. In addition, since the late 1970s, the police have had to become more accountable to procurators when detaining people for serious crimes. In cases of less serious offenses, however, the police are given a good deal of authority that is independent from the formal legal system.

Organization and Administration of the Chinese Police

The Chinese have established five distinct police organizations. They include public security, state security, judicial police for the people's procurator, judicial police in the people's courts, and prison police. The public security police receive the greatest focus of attention in this chapter because the breadth and depth of their law enforcement and order maintenance responsibilities mirrors that found in traditional police forces throughout the world. From an organizational perspective, one of the more interesting features about the Chinese police is that they are administered at times by more than one government authority. For example, some police forces are responsible to more than one government ministry, while other police forces may be accountable to directives from both central and local governments.

Ministry of Public Security The Ministry of Public Security is one of the most important ministries within the State Council. It is headed by a civilian politician. The Ministry is ultimately responsible for approximately 1.4 million police personnel, of which roughly one-half are armed. Police responsibilities were reorganized in 1984 to improve efficiency and effectiveness. At the time, the Ministry of Public Security was charged with law and order, traffic safety, and fire control. The Ministry's responsibilities have been refined further under the Police Law 1995. By examining the operational divisions in the organizational chart (see Figure 6.1), the reader is provided some understanding of the breadth of the responsibilities assigned to the Ministry of Public Security.

The uniformed patrol division provides basic police services. These officers are found throughout the country and are most visible in large and medium-size cities. These patrol units are used to maintain daily public order, to assist with crime prevention measures, to control parades and demonstrations, and to supervise certain businesses and industries in order to control and prevent specific kinds of criminal activities. The businesses singled out for such attention include: car rental companies, hotels, pawn shops, printing companies, and scrap metal dealers. While uniformed police patrol on foot, they also have mobile patrol units that improve the response time to certain calls. This has become more important as China has introduced a 110 emergency phone-call service.

The criminal investigation division is responsible for the investigation of all serious crimes. These units have long been responsive to needs such as pursuing fugitives and eliminating criminal gangs. In light of the rapid development of the economy, these units have had to increase attention to types of criminal behavior that were not as prevalent before the social and economic changes. Theft has become a particular problem, including bank robberies, car thefts, and various kinds of fraud. Recently,

Figure 6.1

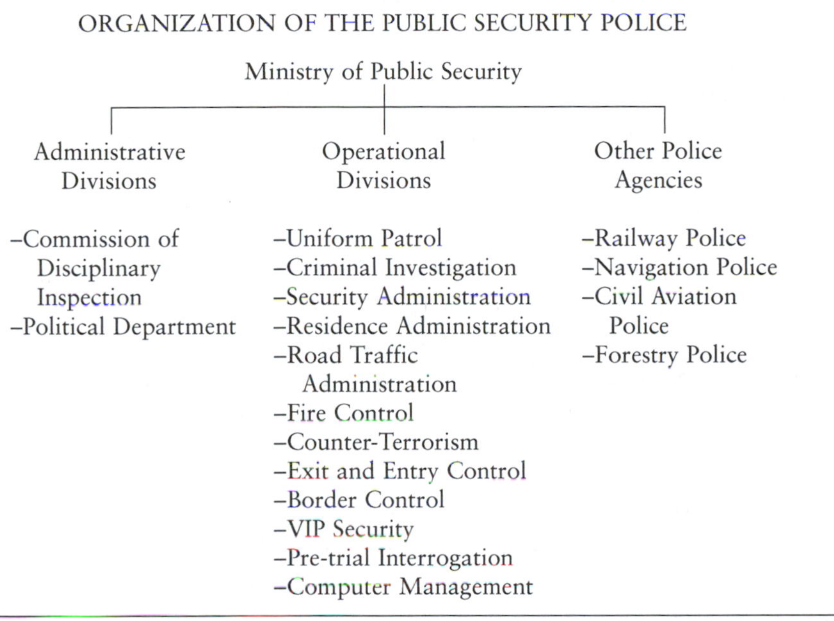

public security agencies throughout the country have targeted counterfeiters, underground banks, and tax-related criminal activities. Also receiving special attention are smugglers in general and drug traffickers in particular.

Security administration is involved with a host of preventive policing issues. One mandate is directed at combating economic crime. This has taken the form of providing security at financial institutions and other state enterprises involved with the economy. The security police also address the law enforcement and order maintenance needs of various cultural and educational institutions. Finally, security police are responsible for establishing Community Service Commissions (CSCs). The CSCs are groups composed of citizens who assist police in crime, fire, and accident prevention. More will be said about the role of CSCs later in this section.

The residence administration division is responsible for maintaining the household registration system. This system has been in place for a long time as a method of taking the census. It was designed to control the population by requiring that people stay in the place where their household registration is held. Under this scheme, everyone is expected to register their place of residence with the local police. Neighborhood committees, an earlier version of the CSCs, assisted police in monitoring the registration system. For many years, this system assisted the police in controlling the activities of criminals, in particular, criminal gangs. It also prevented people in rural areas from moving to urban areas.

In light of the recent economic changes that China has experienced, many people who lived in rural areas have started to move to urban areas in search of employment. As a result, a transient or floating unregistered population has developed that complicates the work of police involved with residence administration. Estimates of the size of the floating population have ranged from 50 million to 100 million people. Obviously, a transient population of this size poses social instability concerns for the government. The household registration system and the neighborhood committees were central features of the Chinese approach to maintaining public order and security. With this traditional approach breaking down, the government adopted reforms that targeted the problem of the floating population in particular. Personal identification cards were introduced that enabled people moving from rural to urban areas to secure temporary residence permits legitimately. Landlords and employers of these people are expected to assist public security agencies with monitoring this population.

Road traffic administration has become a particularly acute concern in recent years. Before the introduction of policies to modernize the economy, the principal methods of transportation in urban areas of China were public transportation, bicycles, or walking. While these modes of transportation remain important, improved economic conditions have created a significant growth in the taxi industry and the number of privately owned automobiles. This has led, in turn, to a significant increase in the number of traffic accidents. The road traffic administration has attempted to address some of the issues associated with this problem. They have standardized the enforcement of traffic laws to assure a uniform policy; they have improved the quality of traffic signals to reduce congestion and the quantity of road markings to improve safety; and they have introduced a campaign to encourage the public to adhere to traffic laws. In recent years, they have focused attention on overloaded commercial vehicles, because of the dangers they pose on the highways. They have also become more aggressive at suspending or revoking the driver's licenses of habitual violators of the traffic laws. In addition, more examiners are now available to train and assess the skills of people seeking a driver's license.

Public security police are also responsible for fire control. The police fire brigade is responsible for fire supervision, firefighting, and rescue in times of disaster. They oversee the construction of high-rise buildings, hotels, markets, places for public entertainment, and warehouses storing dangerous materials in order to assure that they are up to code. They also inspect these facilities in order to ensure that they adhere to fire prevention laws and participate in campaigns to improve fire safety.

The exit and entry control division is responsible for matters related to immigration and the issuance of passports and visas. In recent years, methods have been introduced to streamline the process for Chinese citizens attempting to go abroad and for foreigners seeking to enter the country as visitors.

The border control division has an important role to play in the overall security needs of the country. China shares land borders with 14 countries and has an extensive coastline along the Yellow Sea, East China Sea, and South China Sea. The border control inspects all vehicles, vessels, planes, and trains that enter Chinese territory. They also guard the borders, frontiers, and coastlines and develop specific operations to target illegal activities, such as drug and gun trafficking. Other illegal operations dealt with include smuggling CDs, car parts, and cigarettes. The border control also responds to emergency calls from fishermen.

The counter-terrorism division has been upgraded in recent years. There has been a concerted effort to improve the capabilities to prevent terrorist incidents and the capacity to respond in an effective manner within the country. Moreover, China is participating in efforts to establish cooperative ventures in dealing with this problem throughout the international community.

The VIP Security Bureau is responsible for the protection of officials of the Chinese Communist Party and the government, as well as for the security needs of foreign guests. The Bureau also handles security matters for significant meetings and important international conferences.

The Pre-trial Interrogation Bureau has two general kinds of responsibilities. The Chinese Procedural Code limits to 24 hours the length of time a person can be held in custody prior to the start of an interrogation; it also indicates that a decision to arrest a person who is being detained must be made within three days. In these circumstances, the Pre-trial Interrogation Bureau is concerned with determining if the criminal case is of sufficient quality to bind it over to a procurator. The Bureau is also responsible for the welfare of those detained in police custody.

In addition to developing the computer network utilized by the police, the Computer Management Bureau is charged with the security of computer information systems throughout the country. In recent years, they have made advances with improving information security protection. They have apprised the public of the need to protect themselves from Internet fraud. China's cyber police have focused a good deal of attention on pornographic web sites, Internet fraud, and Internet businesses. Within the Bureau is the China Criminal Information Center (CCIC), which stores information about criminals, stolen cars, and firearms.

Finally, there are four more police forces with specialized law enforcement tasks. Railway Police handle security matters at railway stations and on trains, with special attention to passenger trains. The Navigation Police are responsible for the security of coastal areas and inland waterways. The Civil Aviation Police handle security at airports and airline companies; they are also charged with other security issues related to civil aviation, such as the transportation of dangerous objects.

The Forestry Police are concerned with protecting forests and wildlife. What is somewhat unique about these four police forces is that they are not only accountable to the Ministry of Public Security but also to other ministries: respectively, the Ministry of Railway, the Ministry of Transportation, the Civil Aviation Administration of China, and the Ministry of Forestry.

Public security police exist throughout the country and are organized accordingly. There are public security departments found in provinces and autonomous regions. Public security bureaus are established in municipalities that come under the direct control of the central government. Public security bureaus are also found in prefectures and counties, while sub-bureaus are created in urban districts. Bureaus are further divided into police stations and substations. The size of a geographical area, the population density, and the diverse characteristics of a specific area being policed determine the extent to which the various operational divisions would be a part of a local public security police agency. It is important to note that the public security police are financed by the local governments for the most part. Inadequate funding has often led the local security police to enter into money-making enterprises. The public security police are not unique in this regard. The People's Liberation Army has been involved in money-making ventures for a number of years.

Other Police Organizations As was mentioned above, there are five kinds of police organizations in China. The extensive responsibilities of the public security agencies have been explained. Prior to 1983, the Ministry of Public Security was responsible for collecting various kinds of intelligence, but in that year the duties of foreign and domestic intelligence were transferred to the newly created Ministry of State Security and its police organization. State security police constitute an armed force with a special mandate to prevent conspiracy, espionage, and sabotage. They are also responsible for the protection of government buildings, embassies, and other facilities deemed important by the government. State security police are found in provinces, autonomous regions, municipalities that are under the direct control of the central government, and other areas that require this kind of enforcement capability.

The judicial police work either for the people's procurators or in the people's courts. They function as security guards, they serve legal papers authorized by a procurator or a court, and they are responsible for assisting in the execution of court orders. This includes the administration of the death penalty. The judicial police for the people's procurators are ultimately responsible to the Supreme People's Procurator, while the judicial police in the people's courts are accountable to the Supreme People's Court. Finally, prison police are responsible for guarding people serving time in prison. The prison police are accountable to the Ministry of

Justice, because the Chinese correctional system is the responsibility of that ministry.

Residents' Committees Under a political system that espouses the principles of communism, the social structure is designed, at least in theory, to include the participation of the citizens. The ultimate authority rests with the Communist Party, but a basic social objective of communism is to encourage citizen involvement in his or her community. The People's Republic of China adhered to this idea from the start. Committees were formed in residential neighborhoods, at factories and schools, within occupational units, and throughout the countryside among various rural production teams.

One of the primary purposes of the residents' committees was to assist police in maintaining public order. Thus, local public security units coordinated the work of their local citizens' committees. In reference to their mandate to assist with the maintenance of public order, these committees were assigned specific responsibilities. Responsibilities included: to mediate disputes, to patrol streets, to assist with traffic control, to inspect the sanitation conditions of neighborhood residences, to distribute information about health and community issues, to organize political meetings, and to educate people about crime prevention and the legal system.

This committee system served as the conduit in which the mass line was able to function at the grass-roots level. During periods of disorder, when ideology supplanted any attempt at the rule of law, people were often abused under this system. Neighborhood watch became neighborhood surveillance. During periods of order, when law has a role to play in regulating society, the system has assisted police in solving crimes.

Many of the neighborhood committees have been composed of retired people who serve as the eyes and ears of police. They monitor the activities of residents, observe visitors or strangers in the neighborhood, and assist police with maintaining the household registration system. As such, this method is often characterized as a form of community policing that has existed in China since the early 1950s. The Community Service Commissions (CSCs) (mentioned earlier in the context of the role of the security administration division of the Ministry of Public Security) are simply the latest version of China's efforts to organize citizens for practical involvement in public security matters.

One of the serious problems confronting China in general and its criminal justice system in particular is that the old social infrastructure that was based on Communist ideology has been weakened considerably by the move toward a market economy. In the past, people were willing to perform their social duty, such as serving on a neighborhood committee to assist the local public security officers with maintaining social order. Today, this attitude is not as prevalent, especially among the younger generations. People have embraced the work ethic of the market economy: they want to make money, and they are interested in their individual welfare. As such, there has been a decline in the number of people willing to perform their social duty. With regard to public security, the police have had to become more personally proactive in matters of public order and security.

Police Accountability In recent years, the government has acknowledged a concern for the degree of corruption among government officials throughout the country. While this concern has existed for some time, only recently has a strategy been adopted to help rectify some forms of the problem. For example, a new civil service system is being introduced that is based on rules and regulations, competitive entrance and promotional examinations, and a competitive wage scale. It is hoped that this kind of strategy will improve the level of accountability among government employees.

Given the nature of basic police work, there is always a concern about potential police abuse of power, especially with the infringement of citizens' rights. Like other police forces around the world, the police of China have not escaped this charge. Since the introduction of economic reforms, there has also developed a more pronounced concern about police corruption, particularly regarding an increase in the number of opportunities for such behavior and the monetary value associated with the criminal enterprise. The government has acknowledged that corruption is a problem, particularly with officials of the criminal justice system. Moreover, the citizens are aware of the problem to varying degrees. Corruption among the police tends to occur in three ways: some officers develop an arrangement with organized crime; individual officers may be bribed by suspects; and some officers use their position of authority to demand gifts.

The Police Law 1995 introduced a four-pronged approach designed to inhibit police abuse and corruption in its various forms. While some of these methods existed before the passage of this legislation, greater attention is presently being directed at police accountability. Under this new scheme, the police are subject to four different kinds of supervision. Procurator supervision is primarily concerned with assuring that the police perform their functions within the law. Three of the most common situations in which this kind of supervision is performed are: determining the legality of an arrest, deciding if sufficient grounds exist to prosecute a case, and overseeing the investigation of cases for possible abuse.

Another form of accountability is provided through the Ministry of Supervision. This kind of ministry is common in a country that only recognizes the legitimacy of one political party, in this case the Communist Party. It has administrative supervisory authority over all government agencies; therefore, it is not limited to police. While its primary responsibility is to monitor agencies to determine if they are in compliance with laws and regulations in the performance of their duties, it can provide direction and influence in areas of political ideology, policy, and personnel matters. It also can receive complaints from citizens and conduct investigations into allegations of misconduct.

A third form of supervision is internal to the police organization. Within each police bureau at the prefectural level, there is an internal supervisory committee that is responsible for ensuring that the bureau is in compliance with all laws and regulations and that the officers comply with the law in the exercise of their duties. Like the Ministry of Supervision, this type of committee enables the local Communist Party to provide direction and influence in areas of ideology, policy and personnel. This internal supervisory committee is also responsible for receiving citizen complaints about alleged police abuse. In such instances, the committee has the authority to investigate the matter and to impose sanctions upon officers found guilty of misconduct.

A final method of monitoring the police is citizen supervision. This is a practical illustration of the continued use of the mass line policy in present-day China. Essentially, citizen supervision takes one of three forms. Citizens have the right to make recommendations to public security agencies, which is clearly in keeping with the intent of the mass line policy. Second, citizens can file complaints against the police through the procurator, the Ministry of Supervision, or the internal supervisory committee at the local public security agency. Although rarely used, a final example of citizen supervision is that citizens can bring lawsuits against the police. Two of the more common methods are through the Administrative Litigation Law 1989, which enables citizens to sue a government agency, and through the State Compensation Law 1994, which permits citizens to seek monetary damages for losses suffered as a result of police misconduct. In the event a citizen is awarded damages by a court, it is the responsibility of the police to reimburse the citizen. Ideally, the damages should be paid by the offending officer. The manner in which this law is enforced encourages public security agencies to demand that officers comply with the various laws and regulations in the exercise of their duties (Ma, 1997).

Police Functions

The primary duties and powers of the police are explained in the Police Law 1995. Article 6 of the legislation specifically lists the variety of duties and notes that they are to be carried out according to law. The responsibilities include:

(1) to prevent, stop and investigate illegal and criminal activities;

(2) to maintain public order and stop acts that endanger public order;

(3) to ensure traffic safety, maintain traffic order and deal with traffic accidents;

(4) to organize and carry out fire prevention and control and supervise routine fire protection;

(5) to control firearms and ammunition, and keep under surveillance knives, inflammables, explosives, deadly poisons, radioactive materials and other dangerous articles;

(6) to administer special trades and professions as provided by laws and regulations;

(7) to serve as bodyguards for persons specially designated by the State and protect important places and installations;

(8) to keep under control assemblies, processions and demonstrations;

(9) to administer affairs of household registration, citizens' nationality, and entry into and exit from the territory, and handle matters concerning aliens' residence and travel within the territory of China;

(10) to maintain public order along the border (frontier) areas;

(11) to execute criminal punishments with respect to criminals sentenced to public surveillance, criminal detention, or deprived of political rights and criminals serving sentences outside prison, and to exercise supervision over and inspection of criminals who are granted suspension of execution or parole;

(12) to supervise and administer the work of protecting the computer information system;

(13) to guide and supervise the work of security in State organs, public organizations, enterprises, institutions, and major construction projects; and guide mass organizations such as public security committees in their work of maintaining public order and preventing crime; and

(14) other duties as stipulated by laws and regulations.

Legal Status

The Constitution of the People's Republic of China and the Criminal Procedure Law of the People's Republic of China are two of the principal sources that explain the legal status of police. The constitution has been discussed in this chapter in the section on government, while the Criminal Procedure Law will be explained in some detail in the section on law. The legal status of police, however, is also gleaned from other sources, particularly from regulations and other laws, such as the Police Law 1995. When enacted, these regulations and laws are expected to be in compliance with the constitution.

According to the Regulations of Police of the People's Republic of China, the police are charged with two types of responsibilities. One is enforcing laws against criminal activities. This essentially involves the prevention, enforcement, and investigation of serious crimes or felony offenses. In these instances, the police utilize their regular police powers of arrest and detention as explained in the Criminal Procedural Law. The adjudication and correctional process would include a procurator and court.

The other type of responsibility is referred to as the enforcement of laws concerning administrative affairs. These laws address less serious behavior that would often be classified in the West as ranging from gross misdemeanors to ordinance violations. What is striking about this responsibility is that a procurator and court are not involved in the adjudication or correctional process. The Security Administration Punishment Act, which was initially enacted in 1957 and has since been amended, authorizes police not only to apprehend but also to adjudicate the case. Obviously, the discretionary authority of police is enhanced considerably in such cases, as is the potential for abuse of authority.

As was mentioned previously, the police undergo four kinds of supervision designed to control or reduce police abuse. Another feature that has gained considerable popularity is the establishment of a legal affairs unit within many of the public security agencies across the country. The growth of such units is an indication that the government is attempting to place greater emphasis on the importance of the rule of law. The units tend to focus their attention on three specific objectives. The first is training their officers in understanding the rule of law and the changes that occur with the passage of various legal regulations. The second is to provide guidance in difficult or dubious cases in order to improve the quality of cases brought to a procurator. The final objective is an attempt to educate citizens about the renewed importance that has been placed on the rule of law within society.

The Police and the Public

The tradition of policing in China since 1949 can be characterized as a cooperative participatory endeavor on the part of the public security agencies and various groups within society. The groups include different levels of local government and the many committees formed in residential neighborhoods, at factories and schools, within occupational units, and throughout the countryside among the various rural production teams. All have had a role to play in assisting police with the maintenance of public order.

Over the years, especially during periods of order when the significance of the rule of law has been stressed, neighborhood committees work very closely with local public security officers to improve crime prevention, public safety, and an understanding of the role of law in society. In fact, these committees are often in a position to act in ways that police are legally prohibited from pursuing. This includes entering and searching private areas and property, as well as questioning people about personal matters. During periods of disorder in which ideology dominated government policy, police were often feared and the system of committees was usually distrusted. In such circumstances, the neighborhood committees that looked out for one another for crime prevention purposes often became neighborhood surveillance committees in the cause of ideological purity.

It should also be pointed out that, irrespective of whether the country was experiencing a period of order or disorder, the system of policing in China has not been noted for its professionalism. For many years, there were no formal standards for recruiting or training officers; there were no regulations imposed to control police in the exercise of their authority; and there were no credible methods, either internal or external, to assure police accountability.

The consequences of this inaction have been acknowledged only in recent years. For example, a 1988 survey of Beijing residents examined the prestige associated with different occupations and found that police were rated lower in China than in Japan, Taiwan, or the United States. This was attributed at least in part to the role that police played in events such as the Cultural Revolution. People who were too young to remember the periods of disorder in China's recent past offered a more positive view of the police (see Bracey, in Troyer, Clark, and Rojek, 1989). A national survey in the late 1990s suggested that the public view the police in a positive manner and have expressed confidence in them (Ma, 1997). The change in the results of these kinds of surveys can be attributed in large part to the concerted effort to professionalize the Chinese police service. This strategy was first initiated in the late 1970s, at the same time the country started its program to modernize its economy.

In recent years, there has been a concerted effort to improve the overall quality of the security forces throughout the country. First, a new code dealing with the organization and management of the public security agencies had been drafted. Second, there has been a campaign to standardize the recruitment and training of officers. This standardization process has been extended to include the design of uniforms, types of police vehicles, and uniformity in the appearance of police stations.

Third, there is a serious effort to improve service to the public, which includes protecting the legal and human rights of people. This is being accomplished through three strategies. One is the selection and training across the country of effective police spokespersons. This is designed to enhance public awareness. Another strategy is the dissemination of information on laws, public safety, traffic safety, fire safety, and drug-prevention programs. These efforts improve the public's understanding and support for the police. The third strategy is to utilize the discipline inspection departments to conduct more planned and unplanned inspections of police stations. These inspection departments also receive and investigate citizen complaints. A final effort to improve the overall quality of the security forces involves a campaign to eliminate corruption within the public security agencies. What follows are two illustrations of China's attempt to professionalize its police. One deals with recruitment and training; the other addresses efforts at crime prevention.

Recruitment and Training For many years, the source of police recruits was primarily the People's Liberation Army (PLA). Moreover, there was a minimal amount of training because it was assumed that the military experience was sufficient to prepare a person for police work. During the Cultural Revolution, all institutes and colleges that trained police were closed, on orders from Mao Zedong.

In the late 1970s, the training academies were reopened, and the curricula were revised to prepare people to function as professional police officers in a society that was attempting to become more modern through economic development. The Ministry of Public Security is given the responsibility to plan, coordinate, oversee, and inspect all police training facilities throughout the country. Course offerings vary, depending upon the purpose of the particular education or training program, but may include: Chinese literature, foreign languages, public speaking, political theory, political economy, psychology, history of the Chinese Communist Party, police science, criminal investigation, security, communications, legal principles, constitutional law, criminal law and procedure, weapons training, driving police vehicles, physical training, boxing, and drill (Bracey, in Troyer, Clark, and Rojek, 1989).

Today, candidates who wish to join the public security police as a basic uniformed officer must be at least 18 years of age, be of good character, be in excellent physical condition, and be a high school graduate. In recent years, college graduates with no work experience and those with work experience and a particular skill have been recruited. In order to apply for important leadership positions within public security, a candidate must have practical experience in police work, hold a college degree, possess the requisite knowledge in law, have both administrative talent and managerial skills, and have successfully completed training at a police college or university.

There are almost 300 educational institutions for police throughout China. Police universities and institutes offer undergraduate college courses, two-year training programs, correspondence courses, and night courses. Graduates of police universities and institutes either work in public security departments throughout the country or are employed in research institutes or police universities. Professional training colleges offer a course of study that lasts three years. Graduates receive a college diploma and are then assigned to work in a public security department. These colleges also offer a two-year program for in-service officers. Police administration colleges also offer a two-year program for in-service officers who are under 40 years of age, and secondary police schools offer a two-year course of training that leads to a secondary school diploma. Police schools are training schools that offer short-term programs for in-service officers. Finally, the armed police command schools train junior command officers and technical personnel for the armed police through programs that take two years to complete. The command schools also offer short-term training courses for other officers in the armed police (Zikang, 1993).

The leaders of the Chinese justice system have long appreciated the value of science and technology in the work of public security agencies. In more recent years, they have begun to embrace the importance of law and rules of procedure. One of the most important educational institutions that combines the study of forensic science and law is the China Criminal Police University in Shenyang. Students and officers come from across China to study in one of the many specialized programs dealing with criminal investigation. Among the investigative programs offered are: computer crime, commercial crime, document examination, financial crime, forensic chemistry, forensic medicine, and the science of narcotics.

Special institutes also have been established to promote the use of science and technology in police work. These efforts include the production of equipment to carry out scientific investigations associated with criminal investigations, crime prevention, fire supervision, and road traffic control. There are also research institutes across the country that assist public security officers at the local level. The emphasis placed on the importance of science and technology has enabled public security police to improve the national police communications network, the national police computer-based information system, the national criminal evidence and identification network, and the urban traffic control systems (Yuzhen, 1993).

Crime Prevention As was mentioned earlier, the crime rate in China has escalated significantly. Much of this change is attributed to the pursuit of a new economic policy throughout the country and the transformation that this has caused within society. The public security police are attempting to address this problem by rethinking and evaluating their methods of policing. In some instances, they are introducing new approaches to law enforcement and order maintenance.

One of the most basic methods of policing is patrol. This was one of the police strategies made subject to evaluation. Much has been said about the role that the neighborhood committees have played in patrolling residences in the name of crime prevention. Many scholars have suggested that this Chinese method of community policing was often the only kind of patrol that was performed on a regular basis or in a routine manner. Foot or bicycle patrols by public security police were carried out infrequently. With the increase in crime, the police discovered that they had depended too much on these committees for patrol. The police were practicing a form of reactive policing, in which they waited for an event to occur or a request for assistance before they mobilized themselves into action.

In the 1980s, the police introduced a more proactive strategy toward patrol, especially in urban areas, which was designed to maintain order and social stability and to reduce crime in the long run. The police have learned several things after shifting from a reactive to a proactive method of patrol. First, the reaction time in arriving at crime scenes has been reduced. Second, the street environment in reference to order maintenance has improved significantly, which has had a positive impact on crime prevention efforts. Third, police officers find themselves assisting people in a number of situations that have brought the police closer to the citizens and further enhanced the citizens' sense of security. Finally, a new or renewed sense of awareness that public security means serving the community has led police to make a more concerted effort to improve their image as professionals (Qinzhang, 1993).

The Chinese have acknowledged that drug abuse is becoming a serious problem in their country and that it is a factor in the increase in various kinds of crime. A White Paper on Narcotics Control illustrated this concern by pointing out that the number of registered addicts rose dramatically from 148,000 in 1991 to 681,000 in 1999. By 2003, that figure had reached one million (Chang, 2004). The government established a three-pronged strategy to address the problem. The first stage has involved a massive publicity campaign that educates people about the danger of drugs. Second, a legislative strategy has enhanced the penalties for drug-related crimes. Finally, attention is directed at the rehabilitation of both criminal and noncriminal drug users (Li, 1998). For their part, public security agencies in general and some of the more specialized operational divisions discussed earlier are making joint efforts to intercept illegal drugs entering the country. The government is also attempting to curb illegal poppy and marijuana cultivation within the country.

In 1990, the government established the National Narcotics Control Commission. From the start, the Chinese have viewed drug abuse from a systems perspective. It was never considered the sole responsibility of the Ministry of Public Security. As a result, local government agencies and public health officials are involved in the compulsory treatment and education programs that are imposed on drug abusers. In the early 1990s, more than 250 drug treatment centers had been established across the country, but these were not sufficient to handle the volume of drug abusers. Moreover, it was estimated that 80 percent of addicts who enter and complete a treatment program are unsuccessful at controlling their addiction upon release (Fang, 1993). The number of treatment facilities has risen dramatically since that time. There are now 746 compulsory rehabilitation centers and 168 treatment and reeducation-through-labor centers (White Paper on Narcotics Control, 2001).

There are several current strategies directed at China's drug problem in which public security police are playing an active role. They include: the allocation of more resources to the specialized public security squads that deal with the drug problem; the identification and elimination of distribution centers and underground markets for illegal drugs; the tightening of controls on legal drugs that may be used or altered for illegal use; the imposition of tougher import and export regulations on chemicals that are used to manufacture drugs; the registration of all drug addicts at the provincial level; the development of an improved anti-drug education campaign throughout the country; and the continued strengthening of international cooperation for the control of illegal drugs (Chang, 2004; Fang, 1993).

According to the White Paper on Narcotics Control, the anti-drug campaign that was implemented by the National Narcotics Control Commission in 1997 has brought significant results in solving major drug cases and the arrest of drug traffickers. Between 1991 and 1999, more than 800,000 drug cases were solved and tons of heroin, opium, marijuana, and methamphetamine confiscated. In 2007, 267,790 drug cases were reported. Presently, the National Narcotics Control Commission has established an anti-drug education campaign specifically directed at young people. It is a comprehensive effort that begins in primary schools and continues through colleges and universities.

Another concern focuses on economic crime. As China attempts to create its market economy, there is a need to establish a modern financial system that includes laws and regulations designed to facilitate the development of legitimate businesses. A central feature of this effort is the creation of a security infrastructure for the emerging financial institutions that is vigilant in both a proactive and reactive manner to the many forms that economic crimes may take. While financial fraud is an international problem, it is particularly troubling to the Chinese who have not, until recently, been accustomed to dealing with bank, credit card, insurance, and securities fraud; counterfeit checks; faulty contracts, drafts, deposit receipts, and mortgage loans; and various scams, such as pyramid schemes.

In 2007, the number of fraud cases rose significantly to 239,698 from the 127,884 reported in 2006. A final issue that has attracted a good deal of attention from the police is road traffic accidents. While it is not so much a crime-prevention issue, it is an order-maintenance concern of significant proportions. As was pointed out earlier, the number of motor vehicles has increased considerably in China, especially during this current phase of economic development. The increase in vehicles has led to a rise in the number of traffic accidents. Over the course of a 15-year period beginning in 1978—the start of the modernization movement—and ending in 1992, there were a total of 2,866,828 traffic accidents that resulted in 568,709 deaths and 1,850,936 injuries (Zhengchang, 1993).

Chinese officials have identified several reasons for the number of accidents. First, most people do not have an understanding of the traffic laws, and this includes pedestrians. Second, many drivers have not developed the requisite basic skills to drive successfully. Of particular concern are transportation companies that employ drivers who lack these basic skills. Third, the increase in road traffic has outpaced the development of roads and other issues related to the transportation infrastructure, such as improving existing roads and the production and distribution of better road signs. Finally, the traffic management and accident prevention system that is in place often cannot keep pace with the rapidly changing nature of the problem, especially in urban areas. This is coupled with a shortage of equipment, funds, and human resources needed to address the problem in a comprehensive manner.

In 1986, the government authorized the Ministry of Public Security to assume responsibility for national road traffic control. While the traffic police have attempted to address the problems and have undertaken some successful initiatives, limited resources hinder their efforts as the problem continues to grow. Specifically, it is estimated that the number of motor vehicles will increase annually at a rate of 15 percent. Moreover, it is expected that the number of motor vehicles will exceed 20 million and bicycles will increase to 400 million by the end of the century (Zhengchang, 1993).

In recent years, the Ministry of Public Security has identified several objectives that it is attempting to implement in order to prevent and reduce traffic accidents. They include: conducting research into the prevention of accidents, assessing in a comprehensive manner the present traffic engineering management system, educating people about traffic safety, enforcing and improving traffic laws and regulations, reducing major accidents by the identification and control of dangerous sections of roads, and increasing the number of officers assigned to the traffic police. As a result of these efforts, traffic safety has improved significantly by establishing uniform traffic laws, improving both the quality and quantity of traffic signals and road markings, upgrading roads to handle the volume of traffic, and educating the public with brochures about traffic safety. These efforts have led to a significant reduction in serious traffic accidents. In 2008, there were 265,204 traffic accidents that resulted in 73,484 deaths and 304,919 injuries (Ministry of Public Security, 2009). This is a significant improvement over the earlier data mentioned above. The 2008 decline is in part attributed to a traffic safety campaign initiated before and during the Beijing Olympics.

Judiciary

Although China has a long tradition that dates back to ancient times, the role of law in the development of the country and its civilization is clearly lacking in prominence when compared with that found in the West. The concept of law and the manner in which it has emerged in China will be the subject of the next section of this chapter. What is of interest at this time is a consideration of how justice is administered in China. A brief introduction is provided, regarding the manner in which a judicial system was established and operated in a country that was not dependent upon law as the principal method of regulating society.

The period between the Xia Dynasty of 2205–1766 BCE and the Qing Dynasty of 1644–1911 CE is referred to as imperial China. Over that extremely long period, successive emperors established an elaborate, and often quite sophisticated, hierarchy of institutions that were responsible for the administration of government. From both a geographical and an organizational perspective, the bottom of this administrative hierarchy consisted of districts followed by departments, prefectures, provinces, and, finally, the central administration. Government bureaucrats were found at each level of the hierarchy. At the district level, the head of local government was the magistrate. One of the magistrate's many administrative responsibilities was dispensing justice, and this was done in his capacity as police chief, prosecutor, and judge.

It is important to remember that the purpose of justice in this context was to assert the authority and power of the emperor by punishing people who violated the order of the state. The person accused of violating the good order was placed at a significant disadvantage. To illustrate, the accused was presumed guilty rather than innocent. Defense attorneys did not exist. Torture was an acceptable method of extracting confessions. Further, judges occasionally applied the penal code by analogy. This meant that a penalty could be imposed for an act that was not specifically prohibited in the code but was analogous to an act that was prohibited.

In imperial China, all government officials, including magistrates at the district level, belonged to a single civil service. They were appointed and promoted by the central government. Most entered the civil service first by pursuing an education and, second, by passing a series of examinations. Although magistrates were educated individuals, they were not trained in law. Because magistrates had to prepare cases for trial and submit legal reports to higher authorities, they employed legal secretaries to assist them in their judicial work.

Although people functioned as legal advisers during the imperial era, it was not until the late Qing dynasty that they began to study law formally. The first people to do this usually pursued their legal studies abroad. To illustrate the lack of interest in pursuing a career in law, it is estimated that during the first half of the twentieth century, there were only a few thousand lawyers in China. Many limited the practice of law to the major port cities of the country. While a few bar associations were founded in some large cities, they were not very successful at improving the standing of lawyers in comparison with other professionals.

It is important to remind the reader that for centuries China has had two kinds of justice systems. One is a formal system created by government that is bureaucratic, hierarchical, and designed to enforce and interpret a codified set of laws and regulations. The other kind of justice system is informal and based on the country's cultural traditions that date back to ancient times. It is essentially administered at the local grassroots level and is extrajudicial in nature. Originally, this informal system had its basis in Confucian thought. Such a system was directed by a set of broad moral principals. These principals, in turn, led to the establishment of socially approved norms and values that required enforcement.

One could characterize this informal system as an early form of the alternative dispute resolution technique that has recently become popular in the West. Because China has been a peasant society for most of its history, the vast majority of its people had little need for a formal legal system in their daily lives. Conflicts continued to be resolved as they had for centuries—through an informal justice system. One of the principal changes that took place in the informal justice system after the Communists assumed power was that the socially approved norms and values that were enforced were based on the ideology of the Communist Party rather than the teachings of Confucius.

When the People's Republic of China was founded in 1949, one of the first things that the victorious Communist Party did was abolish the laws enacted under the Kuomintang and eliminate the legal system and profession designed to make those laws operational. The government essentially relied on an informal system for the administration of justice that was based on the political ideology of the Chinese Communist Party. The purpose was to eliminate bourgeois elements, counterrevolutionaries, and other unsavory vestiges of the previous regime. Thus, the period from 1949 to 1953 marked a time when a good deal of political consolidation and economic transformation was going on throughout the country. It is interesting to note that many of the characteristics of this period were strikingly similar to those experienced in the Soviet Union following the October Revolution of 1917.

Following the introduction in 1953 of the first Five-Year Plan that was designed to develop the country's national economy, the Chinese turned their attention to establishing a more formal legal system. They essentially modeled many of their efforts after the justice system that was operating in the Soviet Union. A particularly eventful year in the creation of this new justice system was 1954. In that year, the first Constitution of the People's Republic of China was approved. Other pieces of legislation that were enacted at that time were: the Organic Law for the People's Courts of the People's Republic of China, the Organic Law of People's Procuratorates of the People's Republic of China, and Regulations for Arrest and Detention. Plans were also initiated to draft a criminal code and a procedural code. Neither code, however, came to fruition during this period.

The effort to establish a more formal legal system for the administration of justice began to unravel with the Anti-Rightist Campaign (1957–1958) and then during the Cultural Revolution (1966–1976). Many party leaders were skeptical about importing the Soviet judicial model because of cultural and political differences. Some legal critics were concerned that the Soviet model was too Western. The Soviet codes were, after all, basically the civil law system of the West, which had incorporated socialist ideology as interpreted during Joseph Stalin's tenure in power. Moreover, the Soviets had started to revise their own criminal and procedural codes as part of their de-Stalinization campaign. The adoption of these revisions made the Soviet codes appear even more Western, which simply heightened the alarm of some of the Chinese critics. The critics, for example, considered ideas such as legality, equality before the law, and an independent judiciary as bourgeois concepts that should be rejected.

Finally, Mao Zedong clearly preferred an informal method for the administration of justice over that of a more formal system. During his long tenure as leader (1949–1976), he permitted the adoption of or experimentation with a formal method for the administration of justice, but for only a relatively brief period of time. For the most part, Mao favored the role of party policy over that of law in regulating society. As a result of his position, law was either abolished or ignored. The judicial system was seriously injured during the Anti-Rightist Campaign and virtually destroyed during the Cultural Revolution. This was accomplished by attacking the legal profession and exiling judges, procurators, and lawyers to the countryside.

Following Mao's death, the Chinese again commenced to experiment with a formal method for administering justice. The 1978 Constitution of the People's Republic of China reintroduced some basic rights in the administration of justice. For example, the accused had a right to a defense and an open trial; the procuratorate was reestablished, and police had to receive approval from a court or a procurator to arrest a suspect. The 1982 Constitution expanded individual rights further.

In 1979, the National People's Congress approved the Criminal Law of the People's Republic of China and the Criminal Procedure Law of the People's Republic of China. Both went into effect in 1980. Thus, the creation of criminal and procedural codes, which were initially discussed and drafted 25 years earlier, finally placed China's justice system on a legal footing. Since that time, a number of other laws have been enacted and decisions adopted that further illustrate the newfound importance of law in the governance of the country.

Legislation was also approved that established a judicial system throughout the country. Three pieces of legislation were of particular significance. The Organic Law of the People's Courts of the People's Republic of China (1980) and the Organic Law of the People's Procuratorates of the People's Republic of China (1980) created a court hierarchy and a system of prosecutors. The Organic Law of the Local People's Congresses and Local People's Governments of the People's Republic of China (1980) was also significant. It applied the principle of dual leadership, which had a long-standing tradition in the People's Republic of China. Essentially, the principle states that local courts and procurators are not only accountable to a court or procurator that is at a higher level within their respective organizational hierarchies, but also to the local people's congress and its standing committee. The congresses and standing committees have the authority to elect, appoint, and remove from office members of the judiciary.

Organization and Administration of the Courts

The Chinese courts are organized into two categories: people's courts and special people's courts. The people's courts consist of a four-tiered hierarchy, with five courts or tribunals responsible for the bulk of cases associated with the administration of criminal justice (see Figure 6.2). Before the court system is explained, it is important to mention briefly the responsibilities of the Ministry of Justice as they pertain to courts and judicial personnel.

Ministry of Justice The Ministry of Justice has had a checkered history since the founding of the People's Republic of China. Throughout much of the 1950s, the ministry was responsible for the administration of courts. In 1959, the ministry was abolished as a result of the Anti-Rightist Campaign (1957–1958). Many judges, procurators, and other people trained in law were sent to the countryside for purposes of rehabilitation. This also happened during the Cultural Revolution (1966–1976). With the demise of the ministry, the Supreme People's Court assumed responsibility for the administration of the courts.

Figure 6.2

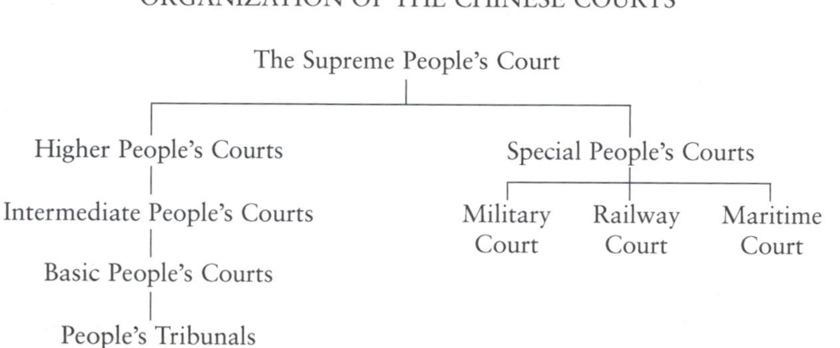

With the government acknowledging the important role that law would play in the development of contemporary Chinese society, the Ministry of Justice was reestablished in 1979. Its principal responsibilities include: training legal personnel, improving legal education, supervising lawyers, overseeing the mediation system, conducting legal research, compiling laws and decrees, publishing materials on law, and disseminating legal information to the public.

In reference to the Chinese courts the principal pieces of legislation governing the judicial authority of the courts are the Constitution of the People's Republic of China and the Organic Law of the People's Courts of the People's Republic of China. Several principles that relate to the courts are enunciated in Section VII of the Constitution of the People's Republic of China. They include: (1) judicial proceedings are conducted in a manner designed to assure that all people are equal before the law; (2) trials are open to the public, unless special circumstances warrant a closed trial (such as cases involving state secrets and crimes committed by a minor); (3) an accused has a right to a defense; (4) the courts' judicial power is exercised independently and not subject to the interference of other institutions or individuals; and (5) citizens of all nationalities have a right to use their own spoken or written languages in court.

The Organic Law of the People's Courts not only reiterates these constitutional principles but also offers additional provisions that explain the general administration of the court system. First, the courts have adopted a collegial system toward the administration of justice. This means that first-instance cases are tried before a panel of judges or a panel of judges and people's assessors. Only in minor criminal cases does the law provide for a trial before a single judge. In all appellate matters, the court would be composed of a three- to five-judge panel. Second, judgments and orders at first instance from a local people's court can be appealed to the next court in the hierarchy and a procurator can present a protest to the next court in the hierarchy. The appellate judgment or orders from the second instance court are final. Third, cases involving the death sentence must be approved by the Supreme People's Court or a court that has been authorized by the Supreme People's Court to handle such matters. Fourth, if a court judgment or order is legally effective but an error in fact or law is subsequently determined, the Supreme People's Court may review the case or authorize a retrial in a lower court. If a procurator discovers a definite error, the procurator can lodge a protest, which can also trigger a rehearing of the case. Fifth, if a trial court decides that the procurator has initiated a prosecution in which the evidence is insufficient or not clear or that there are other possible illegalities, the court can return the case to the procurator for further investigation. Finally, a member of a judicial panel can be asked to withdraw from a case if a party in the case is of the opinion that the member of the panel may have an interest in the case or cannot be impartial. The president of the court decides if the member must withdraw from the case.

The Organic Law also indicates an established and ongoing method of monitoring and influencing the work of courts on a regular basis. Article 11 states: "people's courts at all levels set up adjudication committees which practice democratic centralism. The task of the adjudication committees is to sum up judicial experience and to discuss important or difficult cases and other issues relating to the judicial work." Thus, adjudication committees are often the most important decision-making authority within a court. The committee is composed of the president and vice presidents of the court, heads and deputy heads of various divisions, as well as some additional judges. While chief procurators are invited to attend the meetings of adjudication committees, they do not have the right to vote.

Adjudication committees have the authority to decide individual cases and are often given the responsibility of handling particularly difficult cases. They can override the decision of a judge and direct the judge to determine a case in a specific manner. It should be pointed out that this specific kind of influence is not unique to China. It is a natural feature of a judicial system that operates within a communist political context, and it has been common in other countries that have subscribed to the communist ideology in the recent past. While many legal scholars oppose the use of such committees, it has been suggested that in light of questions surrounding the competence of some trial judges and concerns over corruption at the trial level, adjudication committees might serve a useful purpose for the near future (Peerenboom, 2008).

The Supreme People's Court The Supreme People's Court is not only the highest court in the judicial hierarchy, but it is also constitutionally responsible for the administration of all lower courts. The court is organized into seven permanent divisions. These include two criminal divisions and single divisions for administrative, civil, communications and transport, complaints and petitions, and economic matters. Other divisions can be created if necessary.

The Supreme People's Court is accountable to the National People's Congress and to the Standing Committee. The President of the Supreme People's Court is elected by the National People's Congress to a five-year term that can be renewed once. The vice presidents, chief judges of divisions, associate chief judges, and judges are appointed by the Standing Committee and can be removed by that committee.

It is important to note that the Supreme People's Court does not have the authority to invalidate a law that has been passed by the National People's Congress. The court is responsible for the following kinds of judicial matters: first-instance cases assigned by law or decree to its jurisdiction or cases that the court decides to hear (which are extremely rare); cases on appeal or protest from higher people's courts or special people's courts; cases of protest from the Supreme People's Procurator; and the approval of death penalty cases. It is interesting to note that the court has been called upon to assist in the drafting of legislation for the National People's Congress.

The Higher People's Courts There are 30 Higher People's Courts, and they are found in provinces, autonomous regions, and municipalities that are directly under the central government. These courts are organized into three permanent divisions—civil, criminal, and economic; other divisions can be established if needed. These courts handle the following kinds of judicial matters: first-instance cases originally assigned by law or decree or cases transferred from a lower court, appeals of and protests against judgments and orders from lower courts, and protests lodged by a procurator.

While the Higher People's Courts are supervised by the Supreme People's Court, they are also accountable to the appropriate people's congress in the geographical region in which they are located. For example, if a Higher People's Court handles judicial matters for a specific province, then it is accountable to the people's congress of that province. The presidents of Higher People's Courts are elected by the local people's congress. The other judges are appointed by the standing committee of the local people's congress; they can also be removed by this standing committee.

The Intermediate People's Courts The Intermediate People's Courts are found in prefectures and municipalities that are under the direct control of either a province, autonomous region, or the central government. There are 381 Intermediate People's Courts; these courts each contain civil, criminal, and economic divisions and can establish other divisions if necessary. The courts handle the following kinds of judicial matters: first-instance cases assigned by law or decree or cases transferred from a lower court, appeals of and protests against judgments and orders from lower courts, and protests lodged by a procurator. The Criminal Procedure Law (1996) is quite specific on the kinds of first-instance cases assigned to intermediate people's courts. They include: state security endangerment cases, criminal cases punishable by life imprisonment or the death penalty, and criminal cases involving foreign nationals.

The Intermediate People's Courts are ultimately responsible to the Supreme People's Court, but they are also accountable to the people's congress in the local prefecture or municipality. The presidents of intermediate people's courts are elected by the local prefectural or municipal congress. The other judges assigned to the court are appointed and removed by the standing committee of the local people's congress.

The Basic People's Courts The Basic People's Courts are generally responsible for a county, municipality, or municipal district. There are approximately 3,000 of these courts, and they may also be organized into the three traditional divisions—civil, criminal, and economic. These courts essentially handle the typical or ordinary criminal cases. If a court is of the opinion that it is about to preside over a significant criminal or civil case, it can request that the case be transferred to a court at a higher level. Basic people's courts can establish people's tribunals in rural areas, and they serve as a branch of the basic people's court. More than 18,000 tribunals have been established throughout the country. Basic people's courts are also authorized to handle minor criminal matters informally, to settle civil disputes, and to coordinate people's mediation committees.

As was the case with other courts in the hierarchy, the president of a basic people's court is elected by the local people's congress. All the other judges associated with the court are appointed and can be removed by the standing committee of the local people's congress.

Special People's Courts Both the Constitution and the Organic Law authorize the creation of special people's courts. It is the responsibility of the Standing Committee of the National People's Congress to establish such courts. Presently, these include military courts, railway courts, and maritime courts. The military courts are a fairly closed system within the People's Liberation Army and are essentially responsible for handling criminal cases of military personnel. The railway courts are responsible for criminal cases involving the railway system and economic disputes pertaining to railways. The maritime courts deal exclusively with maritime law and maritime trade matters.

The Legal Profession

In the first half of the 1950s, there were approximately 3,000 lawyers throughout China. They were organized into 800 legal advisory offices and were considered legal workers for the state. With the Anti-Rightist Campaign and then the Cultural Revolution, the legal profession ceased to exist (Leng and Chiu, 1985).

The government reestablished the legal profession in 1982. Initially, the Provisional Regulations of the Peoples Republic of China on Lawyers explained the responsibilities and qualifications of lawyers. Chinese lawyers were viewed as legal workers for the state. The requirements for practicing law in China were: Chinese citizenship, support for the socialism system, having the political rights that enable a person to elect or be elected to various positions within government or society, and possessing the requisite educational qualifications. At the time, a person's political connections were more important than formal education. Moreover, there was no requirement to pass a bar examination. Although bar associations were established, they did not have any authority to regulate the profession; that was the responsibility of the government.

Under these circumstances, the legal profession was viewed essentially as a tool of the government. The Lawyers Law of 1996 was passed to change that perception and to illustrate a modest degree of independence from the government for the profession. Lawyers were no longer considered legal workers for the state, but rather as professionals providing legal services to society. In some areas of legal practice, lawyers are asserting their professional rights and obligations. This implies a degree of independence from government control. Unfortunately, lawyers who practice criminal law often remain constrained by procurators and police from exercising any significant level of professional independence (Peerenboom, 2002).

Throughout the 1980s and early 1990s, it was acknowledged that the minimal educational requirements to practice law were having an adverse impact on the legal profession. People were complaining about the level of incompetence and degree of unethical behavior. As a result, a greater emphasis was placed on enhancing and enforcing the educational requirements of graduating from a university law department or a political-legal institute and by being employed in judicial work for at least two years. Another way of satisfying the educational requirement was to have graduated from a higher education institute; have an understanding of law in a particular area of expertise, such as economics or business; or have some formal training in law. In 2001, the Lawyers Law was amended to require that a person have a college degree as a basic prerequisite to sit for the bar examination.

To practice law a person's qualifications are scrutinized at the provincial level of government. It is the judicial department of a province that issues the certificate that enables a person to practice law. The person must then register with the Ministry of Justice. Once approved, lawyers are expected to uphold the socialist legal system by protecting not only the rights of an individual client but also by providing a service to society.

According to legislation approved by the National People's Congress, lawyers are responsible for performing a number of tasks that include: acting as legal advisors to state agencies and groups, serving as agents to litigants in civil suits, defending people accused of crime, taking part in litigation for a party who has initiated a private prosecution or an injured party involved in a public prosecution, furnishing legal advice in nonlitigious matters, acting on behalf of a party involved in mediation or arbitration, answering questions on law, and drafting documents related to legal issues.

The growth in the legal profession has been significant. In 1981, there were about 4,800 lawyers in the country, and this increased to 12,000 by 1983. By 1990, it was estimated that the profession had increased further to 34,000 (Gelatt, 1991; Leng and Chiu, 1985). It should be pointed out that approximately one-half of these people are considered part-time lawyers. Part-time lawyers are people who are employed full-time as law teachers or legal researchers. The educational institutions in which they are employed have established legal consultancy offices. They are available to consult on legal questions and do not charge fees. By 1998, the profession had experienced another significant growth spurt with more than 110,000 lawyers registered (Peerenboom, 2002).

Judges Prior to 1979, the legal system was either weak or nonexistent in the People's Republic of China. Throughout most of the period, law was viewed in a negative context, and the judiciary was without any real authority in light of the political climate. Courts tended to focus almost exclusively on criminal matters, with many cases being decided on the basis of party policy rather than law. As a result, judges were selected on the basis of their political qualifications rather than an understanding of or training in law. From 1949 to 1979, particularly during periods of crisis, military officers were frequently recruited to serve as judges throughout the court hierarchy. They were selected because of their proven political allegiance.

Since the early 1980s, the government has stressed the importance of law in economic development. The leaders acknowledge the need to develop a socialist legal system and a judiciary that can deal with technical legal issues. The government made a concerted effort to introduce significant incremental changes in the judiciary. For example, according to Article 34 of the Organic Law of the People's Courts (1980) "citizens who have the right to vote and to stand for election and have reached the age of 23 are eligible to be elected presidents of people's courts or appointed vice-presidents of people's courts, chief judges or associate chief judges of divisions, judges or assistant judges; but people who have ever been deprived of political rights are excluded." Added to these criteria in 1983 was that "judicial personnel of people's courts must have an adequate knowledge of the law."

In 1995, the Judges Law of the People's Republic of China took effect. Article 9 of the Judges Law lists the qualifications that a judge must possess:

> (1) to be of the nationality of the People's Republic of China;
>
> (2) to have reached the age of 23;
>
> (3) to endorse the Constitution of the People's Republic of China;
>
> (4) to have fine political and professional quality and to be good in conduct;
>
> (5) to be in good health; and
>
> (6) to have worked for at least two years in the case of graduates from law specialties of colleges or universities or from non-law specialties of colleges or universities but possessing the professional knowledge of law; or to have worked for at least one year in the case of Bachelor of Law; those who have Master's Degree of Law or Doctor's Degree of Law may be not subject to the above mentioned requirements for the number of years set for work. The judicial personnel who do not possess the qualifications as provided by sub-paragraph (6) of the preceding paragraph prior to the implementation of this Law shall receive training so as to meet the qualifications as provided by the Law within a prescribed time limit. The specific measures shall be laid down by the Supreme People's Court.

These qualifications illustrate the attempts that the government has made to enhance the quality of candidates for the judiciary.

To facilitate the efforts at educating judges and other court personnel, the government commissioned law institutes and law departments of universities to provide training in basic legal subjects. It was reported that 17 percent of all judges had received some law training at a university by 1987 and that this figure had risen to 66 percent by 1993. The significant jump was apparently due to a large number of judges completing a three-year night school program in law. Advanced training is also now available for senior judges and those judges who have completed a university education (Finder, 1993). The availability of such training will continue in light of the aforementioned judicial requirements that are spelled out in the Judges Law 1995.

Irrespective of these efforts to improve the qualifications of the judiciary, there continues to be a shortage of technically competent judges. To illustrate, only 5 percent of judges had a bachelor's degree in law in

1995. By 2000, 19 percent of presidents and vice presidents and 15 percent of the other judges of the basic people's courts had a bachelor's degree. The degree, however, was not necessarily in law (Peerenboom, 2002). According to Transparency International, 51 percent of judges had a college degree by 2007 (Transparency International, 2007).

The Judges Law has been amended to enhance judicial qualifications. All new judges must have a bachelor's degree in law or a bachelor's degree and knowledge of law. In addition, two years of legal work experience is required. Judges are also required to take a national examination. After passing the examination, the judicial candidates participate in three months of training before assuming their duties as a judge.

In reference to selecting people for judicial appointments, presidents of the people's court at a specific level within the court hierarchy are elected by the corresponding people's congress. For example, the President of the Supreme People's Court is elected by the National People's Congress, while the president of a basic people's court that is serving a municipality is elected by the people's congress for that municipality. Thus, presidents of courts at all levels are selected because of their political career rather than a career or significant knowledge in the law.

The term of office of a court president is five years, the same as that of deputies serving in a people's congress. A people's congress also has the authority to remove from office a president that they elected. All of the other judges that are working within a specific court are appointed by the corresponding standing committee of that particular court. To illustrate, the judges working in an intermediate people's court for a prefecture would have received their appointment through the standing committee for that prefecture. Standing committees also have the authority to remove a judge from office. At all levels within the judicial hierarchy, people's courts can appoint assistant judges to aid the regular judges with their work and may grant them the authority to function as a judge for a period of time. These assistant judges also can be removed from service by the court.

In 2001, new efforts were initiated to improve further the selection of judges. Presidents of the basic people's courts were to be selected based on merit associated with their judicial work. Presiding judges of trial courts would be selected on a competitive basis. All judges were also expected to improve the quality and quantity of their work. Moreover, in 1998 a five-year plan was announced that required all existing judges to meet the new educational and work product standards. Failure to comply could lead to termination or a transfer to another type of position within the court system.

In addition to improving the educational standards of judges, the other major problem is the level of corruption associated with the judiciary. The major cause for this corruption is associated with inadequate salaries that are less than those paid to lawyers and in some cases below that of police officers. While judges are supposed to receive raises, many local governments have failed to implement the increases. While the principal form of judicial corruption is associated with bribery, there remains the problem of government interference, especially local party officials abusing their authority. To address this problem, the Supreme Court issued a code of ethics for judges in 2003. The following year the procuratorate focused increased attention on corruption enterprises involving law enforcement and judicial personnel. It has also been suggested that the judicial process should be made more transparent by permitting the general public to observe trials (Transparency International, 2007).

Procuratorate Within the context of the judicial system and possibly beyond it, the procuratorate is one of the most powerful components within the criminal justice system of the People's Republic of China. The procuratorate is governed essentially by two pieces of law: the Constitution of the People's Republic of China and the Public Procurators Law of the People's Republic of China 1995. According to the constitution, the procuratorate is responsible for "legal supervision," and it exercises this authority "independently and are not subject to interference by administrative organs, public organizations, or individuals."

As is the case with other components of the government, the procuratorate is a large hierarchical bureaucracy in which various levels correspond to many administrative divisions of the central government. The Supreme People's Procuratorate is at the top of the organizational pyramid. This is followed by people's procuratorates established in provinces, autonomous regions, and municipalities directly under the control of the central government. Branches of these procuratorates are located in provinces, autonomous regions, municipalities directly under the control of the central government, autonomous prefectures, cities under the control of provincial governments, counties, cities, autonomous counties, and municipal districts. In some instances, a procuratorate might be established for an industrial, mining, or agricultural area or a forestry zone. In order to become a public procurator, a person must possess the requisite qualifications that are spelled out in the Procurators Law 1995. The qualifications are identical to those of a judge (listed above).

Like the courts, the procuratorate is influenced in a special manner by the political system through the existence of procuratorial committees. According to Article 3 of the 1980 Organic Law of the People's Procuratorate, "people's procuratorates at all levels shall each set up a procuratorial committee. The procuratorial committee shall apply the system of democratic centralism and, under the direction of the chief procurator, hold discussions and make decisions on important cases and other major issues." As was the case with the courts, this committee system is not unique to China. It is a natural feature of a judicial system that is operating within the communist political context, and it was common in other countries that subscribed to the ideology of communism in the recent past.

While the constitutional purpose of the procuratorate is "legal supervision," the breadth and depth of this responsibility is explained in greater detail in the Procurators Law 1995. According to Article 6, the functions of the public procurator are: "(1) to supervise the enforcement of laws according to law; (2) to make public prosecution on behalf of the State; (3) to investigate criminal cases directly accepted by the People's Procuratorates as provided by law; and (4) other functions and duties as provided by law." Article 7 also states that "Chief procurators, deputy chief procurators and members of procuratorial committees shall, in addition to the procuratorial functions and duties, perform other functions and duties commensurate with their posts."

Article 8 goes on at to explain specific obligations associated with the procuratorate. These include:

> (1) to strictly observe the Constitution and law;
>
> (2) to take facts as the basis and law as the criterion, to enforce laws impartially and not to bend law for personal gain when exercising their functions and duties;
>
> (3) to safeguard the State interests and public interests, and to safeguard the lawful rights and interests of citizens, legal persons and other organizations;
>
> (4) to be honest and clean, faithful in the discharge of their duties, and to abide by discipline;
>
> (5) to keep State secrets and the secrets of procuratorial work; and
>
> (6) to accept legal supervision and supervision by the masses.

This list reflects the government's attempt to retain its commitment to its socialist legal principles while also acknowledging the importance of principles associated with the rule of law. Throughout the Chinese criminal justice system, the power and authority of the procuratorate is considerable.

As was indicated earlier, the procuratorate is a large bureaucracy. At the top of the organizational pyramid is the Procurator-General, who administers the Supreme People's Procuratorate. The Procurator-General is elected and removed by the National People's Congress. The deputy procurators-general, members of the procuratorial committee, and other procurators are all appointed and removed by the Standing Committee of the National People's Congress upon the recommendation of the Procurator-General. The chief procurators at the provincial, regional, and municipal levels are elected and removed by the corresponding people's congresses. The term of office for a chief procurator is the same as that for deputies of the local people's congress. The deputy procurators and procurators are appointed and removed by the standing committee of the people's congress for the province, region, or municipality.

Defense Counsel A defendant has the right either to defend himself or herself or to entrust that responsibility to another. Legal representation can be provided by a lawyer, by an organization of which the defendant is a member, or by the defendant's relatives, guardians, or friends. The principal objective of defense counsel is to prove that the defendant is innocent. As is the case in most trials, especially following civil law procedures, the defense will present an argument that emphasizes the mitigating or extenuating circumstances of the defendant's responsibility, in the hope of securing a reduced sentence.

In order to practice law in China and use the professional title of lawyer, a person must acquire both the educational qualifications and a certificate of practice. Article 6 of the Lawyers Law 1996 explains the options that a person has to obtain the educational qualifications which could be met with "three years legal education in an institution of higher learning, or higher qualification or attained an equivalent professional level, or has acquired an undergraduate education in another major in an institution of higher learning, or higher qualification, and has passed the examination for qualification as a lawyer." The practice certificate is granted once the person shows proof that they passed the examination for qualification as a lawyer, that they served a year in training with a law firm, and that they are of good character and conduct.

Until recently, any attempt at serious legal representation of a defendant in China was highly unlikely because of procedural law prohibitions. The Chinese Criminal Procedure Law formerly stated:

> After a people's court has decided to open a court session, it shall proceed with the following work ... to deliver to the defendant a copy of the bill of prosecution of the people's procuratorate no later than seven days before the opening of the court session and inform the defendant that he may appoint a defender or, when necessary, designate a defender for him.

This seven-day rule excluded the defense from any involvement in the investigative stage of a case. It also severely limited the amount of time that a defense could be prepared for a defendant before the trial started. In fact, it was reported that in 30 percent of the cases, the trial had already started before a lawyer received notice (Chenguang and Xianchu, 1997).

The Chinese procedural system was essentially adopted from the former Soviet Union; it is, therefore, based on the civil or inquisitorial legal tradition. For students of the common law or adversarial tradition, it is important to note that in the civil law context, a defense attorney does not conduct an independent investigation into a client's case. In the civil law system, the investigative stage in a criminal case is the responsibility of the procurator. This includes the collection of evidence and the identification and interviewing of witnesses. Under this method, it is assumed at the outset that the procurator will carry out an objective investigation. Unfortunately, serious questions have been raised about the extent to which procurators have been objective in their investigations.

While the defense does not conduct an independent investigation, the defense in many civil law countries has been permitted to influence the final investigative report. For example, the defense is permitted to request the inclusion of certain kinds of evidence that are favorable to a defendant. The defense might also suggest to the procurator that a specific line of questioning be put to particular witnesses during the investigative phase. This line of questioning might influence the decision to send the case to trial or at least alter the nature of the charges against a defendant.

The revised Criminal Procedure Law (1996) has attempted to correct several of the concerns mentioned above. The time frame in which a suspect may have access to a lawyer has been advanced considerably. According to Article 96, the accused can now consult with a lawyer "after the criminal suspect is interrogated by an investigative organ for the first time or from the day on which compulsory measures are adopted against him ...." The rights of the lawyer have also been expanded at this initial stage in the process. Article 96 states in part that a suspect "may appoint a lawyer to provide him with legal advice and to file petitions and complaints on his behalf. If the crime suspect is arrested, the appointed lawyer may apply on his behalf for obtaining a guarantor pending trial." Article 96 also indicates:

> The appointed lawyer shall have the right to find out from the investigation organ about the crime suspected of, and may meet with the criminal suspect in custody to enquire about the case. When the lawyer meets with the criminal suspect in custody, the investigation organ may, in light of the seriousness of the crime and where it deems it necessary, send its people to be present at the meeting. If a case involves State secrets, before the lawyer meets with the criminal suspect, he shall have to obtain the approval of the investigation organ.

Although these changes in rights of Chinese defense lawyers are clearly improvements over the previous procedural law, significant restrictions still exist.

The initial stage in the legal process represents the time when a defense counsel's client is a mere suspect and possibly one of many. As a result of recent procedural amendments, once the procurator decides to examine a case and a specific suspect with the objective of initiating a prosecution, the defense counsel of that suspect is extended some additional rights. For example, Article 36 states: "Defence lawyers may, from the date on which the People's Procuratorate begins to examine a case for prosecution, consult, extract and duplicate the judicial documents pertaining to the current case and the technical verification material, and may meet and correspond with the criminal suspect in custody." Thus, defense counsel begins to have access to the evidence at the investigatory stage of the process.

Article 37 points out that: "Defence lawyers may, with the consent of the witnesses or other units and individuals concerned, collect information pertaining to the current case from them and they may apply to the People's Procuratorate or the People's Court for the collection and obtaining of evidence, or request the People's Court to inform the witnesses to appear in court and give testimony." The article goes on to state that: "With the permission of the People's Procuratorate or People's Court and with the consent of the victim, his near relatives, or witnesses provided by the victim, defence lawyers may collect information pertaining to the current case from them." Some of these provisions are in keeping with modern versions of civil procedural methods found in democratic countries, but it has been suggested that some adversarial elements may be entering into the Chinese procedural system. The initial view is that these provisions, if actually implemented, could enhance defense counsels' efforts and place a greater burden on the procurator to prove guilt.

These amendments to the Criminal Procedure Law presuppose that the defendant has identified a person to serve as defense counsel. What about the defendant who has not entrusted his or her defense to counsel because of indigence, ignorance, or some other reason? The law addresses these circumstances in Article 34:

> If a case is to be brought in court by a public procurator and the defendant involved has not entrusted anyone to be his defender due to financial difficulties or other reasons, the People's Court may designate a lawyer that is obligated to provide legal aid to serve as a defender.
>
> If the defendant is blind, deaf or mute, or if he is a minor, and thus has not entrusted anyone to be his defender, the People's Court shall designate a lawyer that is obligated to provide legal aid to serve as a defender.
>
> If there is the possibility that the defendant may be sentenced to death and yet he has not entrusted anyone to be his defender, the People's Court shall designate a lawyer that is obligated to provide legal aid to serve as a defender.

According to this article, an indigent defendant "may" be given legal counsel, whereas a defendant who has a physical disability, is a minor, or is facing the death penalty "shall" be granted counsel. These defendants would not have benefited from the expanded rights associated with Articles 36, 37, and 96 of the amended Criminal Procedure Law (1996).

People's Assessors The Organic Law of the People's Courts explains the requirements and duties for serving as a people's assessor. People who have voting rights and have reached the age of 23 are eligible to elect and be elected to serve as a people's assessor. If a person has been deprived of their political rights, they are excluded from serving. While serving as an assessor, a person continues to receive their wages from their place of employment. If a person is not employed, they would receive a stipend for their services.

A typical first-instance case heard in either a basic or intermediate people's court would utilize two assessors. Generally, one assessor would be elected from the neighborhood in which the defendant lives, while the other would be elected from the defendant's place of employment. From the Chinese perspective, the use of assessors has two objectives that are central to the communist philosophy. People's assessors are another illustration of the mass line in practice; that is, courts should consider the views of ordinary citizens when conducting judicial business. The other objective is to educate citizens about the work of courts. When assessors return to their neighborhood or work unit, they are expected to talk about their experience with the legal process. While the law indicates that assessors enjoy the same rights as judges, deference tends to be paid to the judge who has some degree of judicial experience.

Legal Education

From the founding of the People's Republic of China in 1949 to the beginning of the Cultural Revolution in 1966, approximately 19,000 students had studied law in China. During that period, there were only six universities that had law departments and four political-legal institutes that provided legal training (Leng and Chiu, 1985). All of these institutions for legal study were forced to close during the Cultural Revolution. In 1977, one year following the conclusion of the Cultural Revolution, two institutions reopened. By the middle of the 1980s, there were 29 law departments or law schools established; this figure rose to more than 80 by the middle of the 1990s (Chenguang and Xianchu, 1997; Leng and Chiu, 1985). According to a 2008 white paper issued by the State Council entitled China's Efforts and Achievements in Promoting the Rule of Law, China has now established its legal education system that will build a modern socialist country. At the end of 2006, there were 603 institutions of higher learning offering a bachelor's degree in law,

333 authorized to provide a master's program, and 29 entitled to offer doctorates in law.

In China, legal education is the responsibility of both the Ministry of Justice and the Ministry of Education. In light of the growing importance that is being placed on law in the transformation of the society, law has become an important field of study. Students study it in high school and can pursue a two-year course in college. There are also short-term training courses in law.

The most prestigious places to study law are in a law department that is associated with a university or at a political-legal institute. Students must take a national examination to enter either type of legal training. Both offer undergraduate and graduate programs. Undergraduate programs last four years, while graduate programs are usually three years. An undergraduate program consists of the following kinds of courses: Marxism and Leninism, history of the Communist Party, political theory, political philosophy, political economy, logic, foreign language, theories of law and the state, Chinese legal history, foreign legal history, administrative law, civil law and procedure, constitutional law, criminal investigation, criminal law and procedure, economic law, marriage law, and public and private international law.

The political-legal institutes are designed for people who want a practical orientation to the law. Institutes also offer courses in evidence, investigation, and forensic medicine. While law departments have a more academic orientation, most graduates enter a practical career in law by working for courts, procurators, or public security. As part of their legal education, students of both law departments and legal institutes are required to participate in some clinical training with either a judicial department (court or procurator) or a public security agency.

In 1986, the Ministry of Justice introduced a national bar examination to determine if candidates were qualified to practice law. The examination is offered twice a year. In order to be eligible to take the exam, a person must complete their legal education program and have completed two years of either judicial or other legal work.

Critical Issues

Defense Counsel Although changes in the Criminal Procedure Law, as it relates to the expanded role of defense counsel, are welcome, there is a degree of skepticism on the part of some comparative scholars. One concern focuses on whether the spirit or only the letter of the law will be followed by agents of the justice system. A natural comparison is drawn in this regard between the recent changes in China's procedures with those that occurred in the Soviet Union. Before 1958, defense counsel in the Soviet Union were not involved in a case until it went to trial.

After that date, the law gradually changed to permit counsel greater access to clients at progressively earlier stages in the investigative process. In the Soviet context, it was not uncommon for investigators either not to tell a suspect of his or her right to legal assistance or to discourage a suspect from exercising that right. In other cases, investigators attempted to block defense counsel's access to clients. When these injustices were occurring, the Soviet police and procurators were extremely powerful. It was difficult to check their authority within the Soviet justice system. At the core of the skepticism are the strikingly similar circumstances of present-day China and the Soviet Union then.

Recently, it as been suggested that while changes in procedures have been introduced in the law to benefit defense counsel, they have not necessarily been implemented in practice. The police and procuratorate have opposed and often resisted adopting many of the amendments to the Criminal Procedure Law. As such, defense counsel have been denied access to their clients and to exculpatory evidence. They have also been prevented from interviewing key witnesses. Because of the increase in crime, the public is not sympathetic to reforms of the criminal law that appear to assist defendants (Peerenboom, 2008).

Another concern from some critics is that the amendments to the Criminal Procedure Law do not go far enough. In reference to the provisions in Article 96, for example, some critics are of the opinion that defense counsel should have access to the client before the first interrogation, rather than after it. In addition, at this stage of the process, defense counsel does not have access to the information the investigators have collected. He or she receives only the information provided by the client. Of particular concern is the fact that the suspect can be denied any privacy when conferring with defense counsel. The authority to decide this issue rests with the organization investigating the case—often a public security agency or a procurator.

Until fairly recently, defendants were not assured assistance from defense counsel unless they had a specific physical disability (blind, deaf, or mute), were a minor, or were facing the death penalty. According to the Lawyers Law 1996, legal aid is now provided to indigent defendants involved in criminal cases. Such aid can also be sought by people in need of legal assistance for other matters, such as workers' compensation, claims for State compensation, and pension disputes for the disabled or families of the deceased. If an indigent defendant is granted assistance, defense counsel is available at the start of the trial. Thus, despite the flaws identified in recent amendments to the Criminal Procedure Law, these defendants do not benefit from the expanded role of defense counsel.

Finally, in cases involving state secrets, a suspect must seek the permission of the investigators not only to secure a lawyer but also to speak with the lawyer. At issue are two concerns. One involves providing a clear definition or legal standard for what constitutes a state secret. The other involves the possible denial of access to legal counsel in a high-profile case. At a time when China is attempting to show that it embraces the rule of law, the use of this procedure would likely raise concerns over the denial of a person's due process rights.

Law

The historical development of law in China was dominated by two schools of thought: Confucian and Legalist. The Confucians were followers of the philosophical and political ideas of Confucius (551–479 BCE). While Confucius acknowledged that positive or written law (*fa*) had a role to play in state governance, he maintained that moral virtue or a moral code (*li*) was far superior. Confucius stated his position clearly in this oft-quoted passage from the Analects:

> Lead the people with governmental measures and regulate them by law (fa) and punishment, and they will avoid wrongdoing but will have no sense of honor and shame. Lead them with virtue and regulate them by the rules of propriety (li), and they will have a sense of shame and, moreover, set themselves right.

The Confucians favored relying upon li as the source for regulating human behavior and social order. The Confucian position was based on the following arguments. Humankind is either basically good or is capable of learning goodness. The study of li shapes a person into an acceptable human being, as li is in conformity with human nature and the cosmic order. When a government is based on li, it operates harmoniously. Because li is unwritten, it has the flexibility to be interpreted to meet the needs of a particular situation.

It is important to stress the context in which these arguments were played out. The early development of li occurred when China was a feudal society. Society was highly stratified, and hierarchical differences were emphasized and considered very important. The emphasis placed on social stratification would continue into the twentieth century, even after the demise of the Qing dynasty in 1911.

The other school of thought was the Legalist perspective. The Legalists were pragmatic government bureaucrats for the most part. Their goal was to expand and secure the authority of the state or empire. For them, law (fa) was a written standard imposed by a superior upon an inferior. It was viewed essentially as a method of controlling people in a highly stratified society within the jurisdictional boundaries of the empire.

The position of the Legalists was based on the following rationale. Humans act out of self-interest. Law is used to control and punish selfish motives. The basis of a stable government can be law, as long as it is impartially applied to all and is publicized. The existence of harsh laws serves to deter people from committing wrong. In the long run, the existence of strict laws will enable society to be free from conflict.

The Legalist position was successful at helping the Qin dynasty (221–206 BCE) establish the first unified empire in China. During the Han dynasty (206 BCE–220 CE), however, the Confucian view was in the ascendancy. Throughout the long imperial period (2205 BCE–1911 CE), both schools of thought would influence how law was perceived and utilized in China, and thus the basis for traditional Chinese law was formed (Bodde and Morris, 1967).

The characteristics of traditional Chinese law distinguish it from legal systems that emerged in the West. The traditional law was developed when the country was a feudal society with a patriarchal system that recognized and protected the hierarchical status of people. Thus, equal rights before the law was not recognized as a viable legal principle. The traditional legal system was founded on totalitarian rather than democratic political principles. Therefore, it followed the dictum of government by rule of humans rather than government by rule of law. The traditional law included an extensive legal code that was primarily devoted to criminal law. In this context, law was meant to be viewed as a vehicle for suppression. Under traditional law, government officials functioned as both administrators and adjudicators of the legal system. Thus, a distinct judicial branch with separate powers was absent. It also followed that there was no need for a separate legal profession. Finally, the specific purpose of the traditional law was to protect the government and its interests rather than those of a private individual.

As China began to open up to the rest of the world during the Qing dynasty, it recognized the need to modernize its legal system. In the middle of the nineteenth century, it sought the assistance of Japanese legal scholars to advise on law reform. Although these efforts were not successful, China was introduced to Western legal concepts. During the second half of the nineteenth century and the first half of the twentieth century, China was exposed to other aspects of the civil law and common law systems. With the founding of the People's Republic of China in 1949, China turned to the Soviet Union and its socialist legal system for guidance in determining the role that law should play in a socialist society. To understand the purpose of law in China today, in particular as it relates to criminal justice, one must be attentive to the manner in which law was perceived and utilized throughout China's past.

Criminal Law

Since the founding of the People's Republic of China in 1949, the country functioned without a codified version of its criminal law until

1980. In that year, the Criminal Law of the People's Republic of China took effect. The law was revised in 1997 to further reflect the country's efforts to establish a society that acknowledged the importance of the rule of law. The Criminal Law is divided into two parts, subdivided into 16 chapters, and consists of 452 articles. The section on general provisions is subdivided into five chapters that include: basic principles and scope of application, crimes, punishments, concrete application of punishments, and other provisions.

Clearly the 1997 law is a more mature form than that of the 1980 version. It attempts to spell out legal principles and has reduced significantly the ideological flourishes found in the 1980 version. To illustrate, Article 1 of the 1980 version of the law stated:

> The Criminal Law of the People's Republic of China, which takes Marxism-Leninism-Mao Zedong Thought as its guide and the Constitution as its basis, is formulated in accordance with the policy of combining punishment with leniency and in light of actual circumstances and the concrete experiences of all of our country's ethnic groups in carrying out the people's democratic dictatorship led by the proletariat and based on the worker-peasant alliance, that is, the dictatorship of the proletariat, and in conducting socialist revolution and socialist construction.

In the 1997 version, Article 1 is free of political commentary. It reads: "In order to punish crimes and protect the people, this Law is enacted on the basis of the Constitution and in light of the concrete experiences and actual circumstances in China's fight against crimes." Moreover, the term "counterrevolutionary crime," which was associated with political crime, has been deleted from the 1997 version. This change may appease some of China's human rights critics, but it does not mean that political crime has been completely eliminated. The word "counterrevolutionary" may have been deleted, but it was replaced with "crimes that endanger national security."

Of particular interest is the definition of crime that is found in Article 13:

> A crime refers to an act that endangers the sovereignty, territorial integrity and security of the State, splits the State, subverts the State power of the people's democratic dictatorship and overthrows the socialist system, undermines the public and economic order, violates State-owned property, property collectively owned by the working people, or property privately owned by citizens, infringes on the citizens' rights of the person, their democratic or other rights, and any other act that endangers society and is subject to punishment according to law. However, if the circumstances are obviously minor and the harm done is not serious, the act shall not be considered a crime.

While the Chinese have specifically described certain kinds of criminal behavior elsewhere in the law, they have retained this rather vague and therefore flexible notion of declaring certain behavior as criminal because it is a danger to society. Critics suggest that this broad definition enables the authorities to conduct arbitrary investigations that can lead to questionable convictions. Some of these concerns may be reduced by the addition of a new principle in the 1997 version of the law. Article 3 states: "For acts that are explicitly defined as criminal acts in law, the offenders shall be convicted and punished in accordance with law; otherwise, they shall not be convicted or punished."

Another change in the 1997 version of the law was the repeal of the principle of analogy, which had long been a part of the Chinese legal tradition. This principle was explained in Article 79 of the 1980 version of the Criminal Law: "Crimes that are not expressly defined in the Special Provisions of this Law may be determined and punished in according to whichever article in the Specific Provisions of this Law that covers the most closely analogous crime, …." This principle inhibited the establishment of formal criteria for criminal liability. It also enabled the authorities to interpret an accused's conduct with a tremendous amount of discretion that enhanced further the likelihood of abuse. In addition to being a part of the Chinese legal tradition, this principle was for many years a standard feature of socialist law; and it was accepted by those countries that subscribed to the socialist legal system. The principle was simply no longer compatible with the China's efforts to acknowledge the importance of the rule of law.

Issues of intent and negligence are also considered in this law. According to Article 14, "an intentional crime refers to an act committed by a person who clearly knows that his act will entail harmful consequences to society but who wishes or allows such consequences to occur, thus constituting a crime." Article 15 states that "a negligent crime refers to an act committed by a person who should have foreseen that his act would possibly entail harmful consequences to society but who fails to do so through his negligence or, having foreseen the consequences, readily believes that they can be avoided, so that the consequences do occur. Criminal responsibility shall be borne for negligent crimes only when the law so provides."

A person is generally responsible for his or her criminal actions upon reaching the age of 16. The law, however, offers some exceptions for young people who attain the age of 14. Article 17 states, in part: "a person who has reached the age of 14 but not the age of 16 commits intentional homicide, intentionally hurts another person so as to cause serious injury or death of the person, or commits rape, robbery, drug-trafficking, arson, explosion or poisoning, he shall bear criminal responsibility."

The law also authorizes assessing a lighter sentence for people between the ages of 14 and 18. If punishment is not given to a young person because he or she has not attained the age of 16, the law calls upon the family to provide appropriate discipline and education needed to correct the behavior. The law further states that, if it becomes necessary, the government might take control of a young person for purposes of rehabilitation.

For those claiming mental incapacity or intoxication, the issue of criminal responsibility is addressed in Article 18. It states:

> If a mental patient causes harmful consequences at a time when he is unable to recognize or control his own conduct, upon verification and confirmation through legal procedure, he shall not bear criminal responsibility, but his family members or guardian shall be ordered to keep him under strict watch and control and arrange for his medical treatment. When necessary, the government may compel him to receive medical treatment.
>
> Any person whose mental illness is of an intermittent nature shall bear criminal responsibility if he commits a crime when he is in a normal mental state.
>
> If a mental patient who has not completely lost the ability of recognizing or controlling his own conduct commits a crime, he shall bear criminal responsibility; however, he may be given a lighter or mitigated punishment. Any intoxicated person who commits a crime shall bear criminal responsibility.

Finally, the General Provisions section includes a chapter on the kinds of punishments that are available. They are grouped as principal and supplementary punishments. The principal punishments consist of: public surveillance, criminal detention, fixed-term imprisonment, life imprisonment, and the death penalty. The supplementary punishments include: fines, deprivation of political rights, and confiscation of property.

The Specific Provisions section consists of a series of chapters devoted to the major crime groups. They include: crimes of endangering national security; crimes of endangering public security; crimes of disrupting the order of the socialist market economy; crimes of producing and marketing fake or substandard commodities; crimes of smuggling; crimes of disrupting the order of administration of companies and enterprises; crimes of disrupting the order of financial administration; crimes of financial fraud; crimes of jeopardizing administration of tax collection; crimes of infringing on intellectual property rights; crimes infringing upon citizens' right of the person and democratic rights; crimes of property violation; crimes of obstructing the administration of public order; crimes of impairing judicial administration; crimes against control of national border; crimes against control of cultural relics; crimes of impairing public health; crimes of impairing the protection of environment and resources; crimes of smuggling, trafficking in, transporting, and manufacturing narcotic drugs; crimes of organizing, forcing, luring, sheltering, or procuring other person to engage in prostitution; crimes of producing, selling, or disseminating pornographic materials; crimes of impairing the interests of national defense; crimes of embezzlement and bribery; crimes of dereliction of duty; and crimes of servicemen's transgression of duties.

This list of the various major crime groups in the 1997 edition of the Criminal Law is significantly different from the categories found in the 1980 edition. Specific chapters devoted to various forms of economic crime and the attention directed at illicit drugs illustrate that China is attempting to grapple with a host of new forms of deviancy that did not exist in the country, at least to any significant degree, only two decades earlier. The emergence of these types of crime are a result of the country's efforts to modernize its economy by embarking on a plan to create a socialist market economy.

Criminal Procedure

For our purposes, the examination of China's criminal procedure is divided into two categories. The first includes the preliminary investigation, which involves an examination of police powers and other pertinent pretrial procedural issues. The second category is concerned with the trial process, which consists of the main hearing and appellate review procedures. The legal document that explains the manner in which these procedures are executed is the Criminal Procedure Law of the People's Republic of China. Like the Criminal Law, the Criminal Procedure Law took effect for the first time in 1980. The law was recently revised with the new version becoming effective in 1997. The law is divided into four parts, subdivided into 17 chapters, and consists of 225 articles.

Chapter One of Part One deals with basic principles. It is useful to draw attention to some of these principles for comparative purposes, because they point out not only substantive philosophical differences but also similarities in which legal ideas and concepts are expressed. For example, Article 1 states: "This Law is enacted in accordance with the Constitution and for the purpose of ensuring correct enforcement of the Criminal Law, punishing crimes, protecting the people, safeguarding State and public security and maintaining socialist public order." This statement highlights a basic distinction between the ideals of the judicial process in China with those found in many democratic countries in the West. The modern judicial process in many Western countries has a tendency either to emphasize or be highly sensitive to protecting individual rights and interests. In China, the judicial process is primarily concerned with the protection of the public interest. The idea of the public interest taking precedent over that of the individual's interest has a long tradition in Chinese history. It has assumed a modern rationale with the establishment of a socialist system of governance in 1949.

This is not to suggest that the position of the individual is ignored by this process. To illustrate, Article 2 indicates:

> The aim of the Criminal Procedure Law of the People's Republic of China is to ensure accurate and timely ascertainment of the facts about crimes, correct application of law, punishment of criminals and protection of the innocent against being investigated for criminal responsibility; to enhance the citizens' awareness of the need to abide by law and to fight vigorously against criminal acts in order to safeguard the socialist legal system, to protect the citizens' personal rights; their property rights, democratic rights and other rights; and to guarantee smooth progress of the cause of the socialist development.

Note that property rights are mentioned for the first time in this new version of the law, reflecting the changing nature of the economic system in the country.

The basic principles also provide several fundamental procedural assurances for citizens involved in the judicial process. Article 3 spells out the division of labor among public security agencies, procuratorates, and courts, and indicates that "Except as otherwise provided by law, no other organs, organizations or individuals shall have the authority to exercise such powers." When conducting a criminal proceeding, it also points out that police, procurators, and courts "must strictly observe this Law and any other relevant stipulations of other laws."

The issue of independence is mentioned rather prominently in the new procedural law. For example, it states at Article 5: "The People's Courts shall exercise judicial power independently in accordance with law, and the People's Procuratorates shall exercise procuratorial power independently in accordance with law, and they shall be free from interference by any administrative organ, public organization or individual." It is important to point out that the use of the word "independent" should not be equated with a form of separation of power. The Organic Law of the People's Courts and the Organic Law of the People's Procuratorates also speak of the independence of these two components of the justice system. Other legislation clearly indicates that courts and procuratorates are similar to other administrative agencies of the state. To illustrate, Article 3 of the Constitution of the People's Republic of China states, in part: "All administrative, judicial, and procuratorial organs of the state are created by the people's congresses to which they are responsible and under whose supervision they operate." Case studies confirm that courts and procurators are subject to the policies of the Chinese Communist Party and the dictates of political authorities.

Here, the principle of dual leadership is more prominent than efforts to allow courts and procurators to function in an independent fashion. Dual leadership means that local courts and procurators are not only accountable to the court or procurator that is at a higher level within their respective organizational hierarchies, but that courts and procurators are also responsible to the local people's congress and its standing committee. As was mentioned in the previous section, local congresses and standing committees have the authority to elect, appoint, and remove from office members of the judiciary.

Some of the rights mentioned in the Constitution of the People's Republic of China are reiterated in Article 11 of the Criminal Procedure Law. For example, a trial is heard in public unless otherwise prohibited by law, and a defendant has a right to a defense. Article 10 states that "the People's Courts shall apply the system whereby the second instance is final." This means that after a case is tried in first instance, there is a right to appeal the case to the next level in the court hierarchy, but this can only be exercised once.

Article 9 addresses the issue of language. Although Mandarin is the official Chinese dialect, local dialects are used in some regions of the country. Moreover, there are various minority ethnic groups living in the country. In an attempt to address potential conflicts over the language of choice in the courtroom, Article 9 states:

> Citizens of all nationalities shall have the right to use their native spoken and written languages in court proceedings. The People's Court, the People's Procuratorates and the public security organs shall provide translations for any party to the court proceedings who is not familiar with the spoken or written language commonly used in the locality.
>
> Where people of a minority nationality live in a concentrated community or where a number of nationalities live together in one area, court hearings shall be conducted in the spoken language commonly used in the locality, and judgments, notices and other documents shall be issued in the written language commonly used in the locality.

Another feature of the newer Criminal Procedure Law that was absent from the 1980 version is found in Article 12: "No person shall be found guilty without being judged as such by a People's Court according to law." Previously, it was often assumed that a suspect was guilty. This perspective had its roots in traditional Chinese law. It is too early to determine if this principle of presuming the person not to be guilty will be taken seriously in the Chinese context. In light of the government's serious attempts and early successes at improving the judiciary's basic educational level and technical sophistication with legal materials, there is probably room for cautious optimism—particularly in cases that are clearly criminal and have nothing to do with political issues.

Preliminary Issues Once a crime is committed or alleged, the matter can be reported to a public security agency, procurator, or court. Following a preliminary examination of the evidence, if it is determined that the matter should be investigated, then a case would be filed. Either a public security agency or procurator would initiate an investigation. If the evidence is insufficient to warrant an investigation, a case would not be filed. The agency receiving the initial report from the complainant would report its decision to the complainant.

In the event that the police are unwilling to file a case, the law offers remedies. Article 87 states:

> Where a People's Procuratorate considers that a case should be filed for investigation by a public security organ but the latter has not done so, or where a victim considers that a case should be filed for investigation by a public security organ but the latter has not done so and the victim has brought the matter to a People's Procuratorate, the People's Procuratorate shall request the public security organ to state the reasons for not filing the case. If the People's Procuratorate considers that the reasons for not filing the case given by the public security organ are untenable, it shall notify the public security organ to file the case, and upon receiving the notification, the public security organ shall file the case.

If none of the agencies of the justice system are inclined to pursue an allegation, the victim can elect a private prosecution. According to Article 88, "the victim shall have the right to bring suit directly to a People's Court. If the victim is dead or has lost his ability of conduct, his legal representatives and near relatives shall have the right to bring suit to a People's Court. The People's Courts shall accept it according to law."

Power to Detain and Arrest According to Article 61 of the Criminal Procedure Law, a public security agency can detain a suspect initially under the following circumstances:

> (1) if he is preparing to commit a crime, is in the process of committing a crime or is discovered immediately after committing a crime;
>
> (2) if he is identified as having committed a crime by a victim or an eyewitness;
>
> (3) if criminal evidence is found on his body or at his residence;
>
> (4) if he attempts to commit suicide or escapes after committing the crime, or he is a fugitive;

(5) if there is likelihood of his destroying or falsifying evidence or tallying confessions;

(6) if he does not tell his true name and address and his identity is unknown; or

(7) if he is strongly suspected of committing crimes from one place to another, repeatedly, or in a gang.

The public security agency is expected to secure a detention warrant from the local procurator. The public security agency is supposed to inform the suspect's family of the reason for the detention and the whereabouts of the person detained. This should be done within 24 hours of the suspect's detention, unless notification would hinder the investigation. Moreover, public security is expected to interrogate the detainee within 24 hours of detention.

In order to arrest a suspect who is not in custody, a public security agency must submit a request for a warrant to the local procurator. The request would include the case file and evidence. In major cases, the procurator might send his or her own personnel to participate with public security in the investigation of the case. If a person is already being detained, public security must submit a request for an arrest to the procurator within three days of the initial detention. According to Article 69, "Under special circumstances, the time limit for submitting a request from examination and approval may be extended by one to four days." Where a person is strongly suspected of committing crimes at multiple scenes or is a member of a criminal gang, the time limit for submitting the request may be extended to 30 days.

The procurator is expected to make a decision regarding a request for an arrest warrant within seven days. In the event it is approved, the public security agency must produce a warrant when making the arrest. The public security agency is expected to notify the suspect's family of the reasons for the arrest and where the person is being held. This should be done within 24 hours of an arrest, unless notification would hinder the investigation.

Generally, the time period in which a suspect may be held during an investigation is not to exceed two months. A one-month extension can be granted if circumstances justify delay. The approval for an extension would come from a procurator at the next level in the procuratorate hierarchy from that of the procurator who is involved in the case.

The recent revisions of the Criminal Procedure Law have expanded the ability to extend the life of an investigation further. For example, Article 126 states:

> [I]f investigation cannot be concluded within the time limit specified in Article 124 of this Law, an extension of two months may be allowed upon approval or decision by the People's

> Procuratorate of a provinces, autonomous region or municipality directly under the Central Government:
>
> (1) grave and complex cases in outlying areas where traffic is most inconvenient;
>
> (2) grave cases that involve criminal gangs;
>
> (3) grave and complex cases that involve people who commit crimes from one place to another; and
>
> (4) grave and complex cases that involve various quarters and from which it is difficult to obtain evidence.

An additional two-month extension of an investigation can be granted under Article 127 if a suspect in one of the aforementioned cases could be sentenced to 10 or more years of imprisonment. After an investigation is completed by a public security agency and if the facts and evidence are sufficient, public security would submit a written recommendation to a procurator to initiate a prosecution.

Interrogation A person should be interrogated within the initial 24-hour period of custody following arrest. The people conducting an investigation should be members of the investigative staff of either the procuratorate or public security agency. The law requires that at least two investigators be present during an interrogation. When the interrogation is completed, Article 95 mandates:

> The record of an interrogation shall be shown to the criminal suspect for checking; if the criminal suspect cannot read, the record shall be read to him. If there are omissions or errors in the record, the criminal suspect may make additions or corrections. When the criminal suspect acknowledges that the record is free from error, he shall sign or affix his seal to it. The investigators shall also sign the record. If the criminal suspect requests to write a personal statement, he shall be permitted to do so. When necessary, the investigators may also ask the criminal suspect to write a personal statement.

One of the significant additions to the revised Criminal Procedure Law is the right of a suspect to secure legal advice from a lawyer following the interrogation. If a suspect is under arrest, the lawyer may apply for bail. According to Article 96, "the appointed lawyer shall have the right to find out from the investigation organ about the crime suspected of, and may meet with the criminal suspect in custody to enquire about the case." The law does not guarantee that a lawyer can meet with a client in private. Instead, it states that if investigators consider it necessary, they can be present when a lawyer meets with a client. Moreover, in cases involving state secrets, a lawyer must seek the permission of investigators in order to meet with a client.

Power to Search and Seize Investigative personnel are authorized to search persons, places, and things of a defendant, as well as other appropriate places. According to Article 110, "Any unit or individual shall have the duty, as required by the People's Procuratorate or the public security organ to hand over material evidence, documentary evidence or audio-visual material which may prove the criminal suspect guilty or innocent." A search should be conducted with a warrant, but this requirement is waived in the event of an emergency.

When a search is conducted, according to Article 112, "the person to be searched or his family members, neighbors or other eyewitnesses shall be present at the scene. Searches of the persons of women shall be conducted by female officers." A record of a search is maintained by the authorities and is signed and sealed by investigative personnel and by the person searched or his or her family members or other eyewitnesses.

According to Article 116, investigators have the authority "to seize the mail or telegrams of a criminal suspect." In the course of an investigation, it might be necessary to conduct a physical examination of victims or defendants. If a defendant refuses to cooperate with an examination, Article 105 authorizes investigators to conduct a compulsory examination when they deem it necessary. Moreover, investigative experiments may be conducted if approved by the director of a public security bureau. In the course of conducting such experiments, Article 108 states: "it shall be forbidden to take any action which is hazardous, humiliating to anyone, or offensive to public morals."

Compulsory Measures If a defendant is awaiting trial but is not in custody, the people's courts, procuratorates, and public security agencies can issue compulsory measures that impose restrictions on the defendant. These generally include: compelling the defendant to appear before one of the aforementioned authorities, securing a guarantor before the trial, or subjecting the person to a residential surveillance. Defendants and suspects under custody have a right to obtain a guarantee or bail to await trial out of custody. The period of a guarantee pending trial cannot exceed 12 months, and a residential surveillance cannot exceed six months. Guarantors must be able to meet certain requirements that include: not being involved in the case, being able to fulfill the guaranty obligation, enjoying political rights and freedoms, and having a stable residence and income.

Defendants awaiting trial out of custody are subject to the following regulations, according to Article 56. They cannot leave the city or county of residence without permission, they must be present in court when summoned, they cannot interfere with witnesses, and they may not destroy evidence or collude with others to devise a consistent account. The article also indicates that if there is a failure to comply with these requirements, "the guaranty money paid shall be confiscated. In addition, in light of specific circumstances, the criminal suspect or defendant shall be ordered to write a statement of repentance, pay guaranty money or provide a guarantor again, or shall be subjected to residential surveillance or arrested."

Guarantors are expected to monitor the activities of the defendant and report any conduct that violates the requirements explained in Article 56. Failure to comply could lead either to a fine or a criminal investigation into their behavior. If the defendant fulfills the obligations, bail would be refunded.

Defendants who are subject to residential surveillance must abide by the following requirements, according to Article 57:

> (1) not to leave his domicile without permission of the executing organ; or if he has no fixed domicile, not to leave the designated residence without permission;
>
> (2) not to meet with others without permission of the executing organ;
>
> (3) to be present in time at a court when summoned;
>
> (4) not to interfere in any form with the witness when the latter gives testimony; and
>
> (5) not to destroy or falsify evidence or tally confessions.

If the original charges against the defendant are serious and the defendant violates the conditions of residential surveillance, he or she may be subject to arrest. The decision to arrest is made by either a procurator or court, with the actual arrest being carried out by a public security agency.

Initiation of a Public Prosecution It is the responsibility of the people's procuratorate to determine if a case should be prosecuted. Once a public security agency has transferred a case to a procurator recommending that a prosecution be undertaken, the procurator is given one month to concur or oppose the recommendation. Additional time may be granted to decide the matter if the case is either significant or complex. During this time, the procurator can interrogate the defendant, interview the victim, speak with defense counsel, and examine the evidence.

The procurator may request a supplementary investigation be undertaken by a public security agency or decide to conduct an investigation on his or her own. According to the law, supplementary investigations should be completed within a month. Moreover, the number of supplementary investigations should be limited to two. If the evidence remains insufficient following a supplementary investigation, the procurator may decide not to initiate a prosecution.

If the evidence is reliable and sufficient, the procurator will usually initiate a prosecution unless the case conforms to Article 15 of the Criminal Procedure Law. According to this article, a prosecution shall not be initiated under the following circumstances:

(1) if an act is obviously minor, causing no serious harm, and is therefore not deemed a crime;

(2) if the limitation period for criminal prosecution has expired;

(3) if an exemption of criminal punishment has been granted in a special amnesty decree;

(4) if the crime is to be handled only upon complaint according to the Criminal Law, but there has been no complaint or the complaint has been withdrawn;

(5) if the criminal suspect or defendant is deceased; or

(6) if other laws provide an exemption from investigation of criminal responsibility.

Article 142 of the Criminal Procedure Law indicates that the procurator has an option not to initiate a prosecution if criminal punishment is not warranted because the issue involves a minor crime. The article also states that while an individual might not be prosecuted, he or she could be subject to administrative punishment and sanction. If that is the case, the procurator would transfer the matter to the appropriate public security agency. Administrative punishments and sanctions will be explained later in this section.

If a procurator decides not to prosecute, this decision must be delivered in writing to the defendant and to his or her work unit. In this case, a defendant in custody would be released immediately. The public security agency that initially requested the prosecution would also receive written notice. The public security agency can request that the procurator reconsider the matter. If this request is rejected, the public security agency could request that a procurator at the next level within the hierarchy of the procuratorate review the matter. The victim must be notified of the procurator's decision not to prosecute. If the victim disagrees with this decision, he or she can petition a procurator at the next level within the hierarchy of the procuratorate to review the case. If the victim's petition is rejected at this higher level, the victim could engage in a private prosecution of the case, which would occur in a people's court.

Trial Once a procurator decides to initiate a prosecution, a trial would be scheduled in a court with the appropriate jurisdiction. The court would determine the composition of the collegial panel hearing the case. Cases of first instance that are heard in basic and intermediate people's courts are conducted by a collegial panel composed of three judges or a judge and two people's assessors. If the nature of the case is such that simplified procedures can be employed, then basic people's courts may utilize a single judge alone. First-instance trials in the higher people's courts or the Supreme People's Court are conducted by a collegial panel composed of three to seven judges or a combination of three to seven judges and people's assessors. While performing their duties, people's assessors enjoy equal rights with the judges.

Trials that are held because of an appeal or protest are conducted by a collegial panel composed of three to five judges. The president of the people's court or the chief judge of a division designates one judge to serve as the presiding judge of the panel. If the president of the court or the chief judge of a division participates, they would serve as the presiding judge.

Judicial decisions are based on majority rule. If a minority opinion exists, it would be entered into the record. The record of the deliberations is signed by all members of the collegial panel. In the event that a panel cannot reach a decision, it would report to the president of the court, who would decide if the case should be submitted to the judicial committee of the court. In such cases, the collegial panel that originally heard the case would execute the decision that was handed down by the judicial committee.

In trials of first instance, in which the case is a public prosecution, the court would first examine the case that was initiated by the procuratorate. If a decision was made to open a court session, several administrative matters would be addressed. These are noted in Article 151 of the Criminal Procedure Law and include:

> (1) to determine the members of the collegial panel;
>
> (2) to deliver to the defendant a copy of the bill of prosecution of the People's Procuratorate no later than ten days before the opening of the court session. If the defendant has not appointed a defender, he shall be informed that he may appoint a defender or, when necessary, designate a lawyer that is obliged to provide legal aid to serve as a defender for him;
>
> (3) to notify the People's Procuratorate of the time and place of the court session three days before the opening of the session;
>
> (4) to summon the parties and notify the defenders, agents ad litem, witnesses, expect witnesses and interpreters, and deliver the summons and notices no later than three days before the opening of the court session; and
>
> (5) to announce, three days before the opening of the session, the subject matter of the case to be heard in public, the name of the defendant and the time and place of the court session.

Although cases of first instance are heard in public, there are exceptions to this general rule that include state secrets or private matters pertaining to individuals. Article 152 also states that "No cases involving crimes committed by minors who have reached the age of 14 but not the age of 16 shall be heard in public. Generally, cases involving crimes committed by minors who have reached the age of 16 but not the age of 18 shall also not be heard in public." When a case is not heard in public, a reason is provided and announced in court.

When a court session opens, the presiding judge determines if all of the parties are present. The judge informs the people of the issue that is being presented in the case. Next, he or she announces the names of the members of the collegial panel, the court clerk, the public procurator, the defender, the expert witnesses, and the interpreter. The presiding judge also advises the parties of their right to ask any member of the collegial panel, the court clerk, the public procurator, any expert witnesses, or the interpreter to withdraw from the case. Finally, the presiding judge informs the defendant of his or her right to a defense.

After these preliminary matters have been attended to, the court is ready to conduct the main hearing of the trial. What follows are the various steps in a standard trial:

1. The procurator reads the bill of prosecution in court.
2. The defendant can make a statement about the charges in the bill of prosecution.
3. The victim can make a statement about the charges in the bill of prosecution.
4. The procurator can interrogate the defendant.
5. With the permission of the presiding judge, the victim, as well as the plaintiff and defender in an incidental civil action, can question the defendant.
6. Judges can interrogate the defendant.
7. With the permission of the presiding judge, witnesses and then expert witnesses are questioned by the procurator, parties, defendants, or defense counsel. The presiding judge may halt the line of questioning if he or she deems it irrelevant to the case. The parties and defendant have the right to request that new witnesses be summoned to the session, that new material evidence be collected, that a new expert evaluation be conducted, or that another inquest be held. The collegial panel would rule on the merits of each request. If the request is granted and the hearing postponed, the procurator would be granted one month to complete the supplementary investigation.

8. Judges can question witnesses and expert witnesses.
9. Procurators and defendants can present material evidence in the court for parties to identify.
10. The records of the testimony of witnesses who are not present in court, the conclusions of the expert witnesses, the records of inquests, and other documents serving as evidence are read out in court. In the event the collegial panel has questions about the evidence presented, it can adjourn the session in order to verify the evidence.
11. The opinions of the procurator, parties, defendant, or defense counsel are heard by the judges. They can debate the quality of the evidence and facts in the case.
12. After the presiding judge has declared the debate concluded, the defendant has a right to present a final statement.
13. The presiding judge announces an adjournment, and the collegial panel begins its deliberations with the goal of making the following decisions:
    a. If the facts are clear, the evidence adequate, and the defendant guilty by law, the court should pronounce a verdict of guilty.
    b. If the defendant is found not guilty by law, the court should pronounce a verdict of not guilty.
    c. If the evidence is insufficient, the defendant cannot be found guilty. The court would pronounce a verdict of not guilty on the grounds of a lack of evidence or that the charges were not substantiated.
14. Judgments are pronounced publicly in court. A written copy of the judgment is delivered to the parties and to the procuratorate that initiated the prosecution. The written judgment is signed by all the members of the collegial panel and the clerk of the court. The judgment indicates the time limit for appealing the decision and the appellate court to which the appeal should be directed.

For a case to proceed as a private prosecution in a trial of first instance, it must meet the following criteria. There must be a complainant; the victim in a minor criminal case must have evidence; the victim's evidence must prove that the defendant violated his or her personal or property rights; the defendant ought to be investigated for criminal responsibility; and the public security agencies or the people's procuratorate must not have investigated the defendant for criminal responsibility.

The people's court can conduct a trial for a private prosecution if the facts of a crime are clear and the evidence is sufficient. In the event the evidence is not adequate to proceed, the court would advise the private procurator to withdraw the prosecution or order its rejection. The court can also conduct a mediation in a case of private prosecution. Before the court pronounces a judgment, the private procurator has the option of arranging a settlement with the defendant or withdrawing the prosecution. Finally, during the course of the proceeding in a private prosecution, the defendant can raise a counterclaim. The rules governing a private prosecution would apply to a counterclaim.

While cases of first instance are heard by collegial panels of judges or judges and people's assessors, some cases are adjudicated by a single judge in the basic people's court. The new Criminal Procedure Law offers greater detail as to when a single judge might preside over such cases and the procedures involved. Cases that can be entertained by a single judge include minor criminal cases in which a private prosecution has been initiated and the victim has evidence of an alleged crime. Publicly prosecuted cases can be handled in this simplified manner, provided they meet the following criteria: (1) the procurator recommends or agrees to the simplified procedure; (2) it is clear that a crime occurred and that the evidence is sufficient; and (3) if found guilty, the defendant's sanction would be limited to either less than three years imprisonment, criminal detention, public surveillance, or a fine.

The simplified procedure calls for a reading of the bill of prosecution, which is followed by the introduction of evidence and a discussion or debate by the parties involved. These cases can be handled rather informally. To illustrate, Article 175 states "the People's Procuratorate may send no procurators to the court. The defendant may present a statement and defend himself regarding the crimes accused in the bill of prosecution. In cases in which the People's Procuratorate sends procurators to the court, the defendant and his defenders may, with permission of the judges, debate with public prosecutor." It is assumed that cases utilizing this simplified method of adjudication will be resolved within 20 days from the date that they were accepted.

Once a trial is completed, the next stage in the process involves filing any possible appeals or protests. Appeals are submitted either in writing or orally to the people's court at the next level in the court hierarchy. Appeals or protests against a judgment must be filed within 10 days, while appeals or protests against an order must be submitted within five days.

The defendant and a private procurator can appeal based on a judgment or order. If a civil action has been part of the adjudication process, a party to the civil action can file an appeal against the judgment or order that deals with the civil action. In the event a procurator identifies an error in the judgment or order, he or she would present a protest to the people's court at the next higher level. A victim who does not accept the judgment or order can request that the procurator file a protest on his or her behalf. The ultimate decision to file such a protest rests with the procurator. It should be pointed out that a protest from a procurator can be withdrawn by the procuratorate at the next level within the hierarchy if it finds the protest inappropriate.

A people's court would form a collegial panel to handle an appeal. The panel would read the file, interrogate the defendant, and listen to the opinions of the parties involved. If the facts in the case are clear, the panel may decide not to hold a hearing. In the event the case is entertained because of a protest from the procurator, then the people's court would hold a hearing.

A court essentially handles an appeal or protest in one of three ways. First, if the original judgment was correct based on the facts, the law and the appropriate punishment, the original judgment would be affirmed by the court and the appeal or protest would be rejected. Second, if there was no error in fact but the problem of the original judgment centered either on an incorrect application of the law or an inappropriate punishment, the court would revise the judgment. According to Article 190 of the Criminal Procedure Law, "a case appealed by a defendant, or his legal representative, defender or near relative, the People's Court of second instance may not increase the criminal punishment on the defendant." This provision does not apply to cases appealed by private procurators or protests lodged by the procuratorate. Third, if the facts in the original judgment are unclear or the evidence insufficient, the court could revise the judgment after the facts are discovered, or it could remand the case for retrial to the people's court that originally tried the case. Finally, according to Article 197 of the procedural law, the appeal process is limited, as "All judgments and orders of second instance and all judgments and orders of the Supreme People's Court are final."

It should be noted that in cases in which the death penalty is imposed there is an automatic review of the sentence. A collegial panel of three judges reviews the case. In the event that an intermediate people's court imposes the death sentence and the defendant does not appeal, then a higher people's court reviews the case. If the higher people's court disagrees with the original sentence, it can try the case or remand it for retrial. If a higher people's court serves as the court of first instance and imposes a death sentence, the Supreme People's Court reviews the case.

Finally, there are procedures designed to reopen a case if new evidence is discovered. According to Article 204, the case would have to conform to one of the following situations in order to secure a retrial:

(1) There is new evidence to prove that the confirmation of the facts in the original judgment or order is definitely wrong;

(2) The evidence upon which the condemnation was made and punishment meted out is unreliable and insufficient; or the major pieces of evidence for supporting the facts of the case contradict each other;

(3) The application of law in making the original judgment or order is definitely incorrect; or

(4) The judges in trying the case committed acts of embezzlement, bribery, or malpractices for personnel gain, or bended the law in making judgment.

If an error in a legally effective judgment or order is brought to the attention of the president of a people's court at any level, the president would refer the matter to the judicial committee of the court. If a people's court at a higher level finds an error in a judgment or order of a people's court at a lower level, it has the authority to try the case itself or to direct a people's court at a lower level to conduct a retrial. If a people's procuratorate at a higher level finds any error in a legally effective judgment or order of a people's court at a lower level, it has the authority to protest the judgment or order.

Administrative Regulations

The preceding description provided a brief orientation to the pretrial, trial, and posttrial phases of the criminal process. It included a consideration of the role of the police and their powers, especially in the investigative process. Most of this process has its basis in the revised Criminal Procedure Law that went into effect in 1997. It is important to caution the reader, however, that this is not the only method by which a person can be found guilty and sanctioned by the authorities.

Reference was made previously to the extrajudicial nature of the Chinese justice system. It was also pointed out that the People's Republic of China was without a formally approved Criminal Law or Criminal Procedure Law until 1980. From 1949 to 1979, the administration of criminal justice was often controlled or dominated by public security agencies. As was mentioned in the section on police, public security agencies were often accorded wide-ranging powers to enforce laws and to maintain public order. They were given the obvious powers to arrest, detain, and investigate suspected criminals. Their authority was expanded further and given legal force with two pieces of legislation. The Act for Security Administration Punishment (1957) enabled public security agencies to impose fines and detain people. The Decision of the State Council Relating to Problems of Reeducation Through Labor (1957) authorized public security to send people to labor camps for up to four years without a trial.

In spite of the fact that the Criminal Law and the Criminal Procedure Law have been enacted, public security agencies retained extensive administrative powers that they acquired in the 1950s. In China, the Criminal Law is limited to the more serious criminal offenses. The less serious offenses against public order are covered by administrative regulations. Thus, public security agencies have the authority to impose administrative punishments on people who violate rules and regulations against less serious forms of public order. This authority is based on the current legislation within the Regulations of the People's Republic of China on Administrative Penalties for Public Security.

The context in which this legislation is available to public security agencies is explained in Article 2 of the Regulations.

> Whoever disturbs social order, endangers public safety, infringes upon a citizen's rights of the person or encroaches upon public or private property, if such an act constitutes a crime according to the Criminal Law of the PRC, shall be investigated for criminal responsibility; if such an act is not serious enough for criminal punishment but should be given administrative penalties for public security, penalties shall be given according to these regulations.

There is a fairly long list of social order offenses that fall under the jurisdiction of this legislation. The general kinds of offenses include: disturbing public order; carrying or manufacturing firearms or dangerous objects; minor assaults; breaking and entering; theft of property in small amounts; purchasing stolen goods; violating drug laws; damaging or destroying property; disturbing the peace; violating fire safety regulations; violating motor vehicle regulations; violating the resident control system; producing narcotics; and cases involving prostitution, pornography, and gambling.

When imposing a sanction on a person who has violated some aspect of the regulations, three kinds of penalties are available to public security agencies. They include: a warning, a fine of up to 2000 yuan, or detention up to a maximum of 15 days. The manner in which a sanction is imposed under the Regulations is as follows. If the violation calls for a warning, a maximum fine of 50 yuan, or a fine above 50 yuan to which the offender does not object, then the matter can be handled immediately by the public security officials. If the violation calls for a fine larger than 50 yuan or a period of detention, then the public security agency would issue a summons to the offender. The offender would be interrogated and evidence collected. The public security agency would issue a written ruling in the matter. If the sanction includes a fine, the regulations call for it to be paid within five days. An offender or a victim has the right to protest the ruling made by the public security agency. Within five days of the initial ruling, the person can petition the public security agency at the next level within the hierarchy. Because such cases are handled through the administrative regulation process, the offender does not have any right of appeal through the regular courts.

Corrections

In the previous section, brief mention was made of the important role that two schools of thought—the Confucians and the Legalists—played in the evolution of law in China. The philosophical position of both schools also influenced Chinese attitudes about the purpose of sanctions and the development of a penal system. The Confucians espoused a belief that humankind was essentially good or capable of becoming good. Thus, humans are malleable and have the capacity to reform their own behavior. The Legalists were of the opinion that harsh laws were necessary in order to deter people from committing wrong, which was likely because humans basically act out of self-interest. For those who transgressed the law, punishment was an appropriate consequence. Throughout the long history of the country, the notions of rehabilitation and punishment played dominant roles in Chinese penology.

From ancient times through most of the imperial age, the "five punishments" were employed as the principal legal sanctions. The first and second punishments were a beating with light bamboo and a beating with heavy bamboo. A beating was administered on the buttocks. The seriousness of the offense determined the number of blows, which were administered in units of 10. The third punishment was penal servitude, which called for the convicted person to be removed from the community and transported to another province where he or she would perform hard labor for a fixed period of time. The range of time was generally one to five years. This sanction also included several blows with heavy bamboo. The fourth sanction was exile for life. The length of the distance that the person was exiled from his or her family and community determined the severity of the sanction. Like people sentenced to a period of penal servitude, those in exile were required to work. It should be noted that there was also a punishment known as military exile. It was initially used to punish soldiers found guilty of crime. They would be sent to a distant military base for a lifetime of military service. Eventually, this form of exile was imposed on civilians as well. The fifth punishment was death, which was administered either by strangulation or decapitation.

It should be pointed out that while prisons existed in China during ancient times, they were not used for imposing punishment in the strict legal sense. Instead, prisons were utilized for holding people who were either being detained before trial or were awaiting the final execution of their sentence. Although a fine could be imposed, and often was, it did not constitute a punishment in its own right. Rather it was considered a substitute punishment. Fines were frequently employed for certain types of offenders, including women, people over 70 years of age, children under 15 years of age, government officials, and a select group of other people. Fines were often used for certain kinds of offenses, in particular accidental injury or death (Bodde and Morris, 1967).

With the demise of the imperial era, contemporary ideas about prisons were introduced in the early twentieth century. When the Chinese Communists introduced a socialist ideology and practices to the country, the influence of the Soviet Union became evident. Nevertheless, the link with the past was not broken. Whereas criminal justice agents of previous eras punished transgressors of the ancient legal order established by the Legalists, agents of the modern justice system punished transgressors of the new legal order that was being created by the Chinese Communist Party.

At the heart of socialist ideology is the goal to transform the very structure of society into a socialist democracy. Within that context, elements of the Confucian philosophy remained evident and in some cases complemented the socialist agenda. For the Confucians, individuals had an obligation to their family and community; they were expected to assist in maintaining social harmony for the good of the cosmic order. With the advent of the People's Republic of China, people were expected to assist in the creation of the dictatorship of the proletariat. Those who declined to support the socialist agenda or attempted to wreak havoc on the social fabric were labeled either deviant or counterrevolutionary.

Sentencing Philosophy

Since ancient times, Chinese penology emphasized rehabilitation and punishment as rationales for sanctioning offenders. These two objectives continue to dominate the approach to sentencing under the government of the People's Republic of China. To understand this policy in action, it is important to appreciate how deviance is perceived and addressed. The primary goal of the Chinese Communist Party is to maintain the present social order and the Party's place as the principal source of power. Any attempt—be it political, social, or economic—to alter the status quo is considered a form of social deviance unless it has been authorized by the Party. This position is clearly stated in Article 2 of the Criminal Law.

> The aim of the Criminal Law of the People's Republic of China is to use criminal punishments to fight against all criminal acts in order to safeguard security of the State, to defend the State power of the people's democratic dictatorship and the socialist system, to protect property owned by the State, and property

> collectively owned by the working people and property privately owned by citizens, to protect citizens' rights of the person and their democratic and other rights, to maintain public and economic order, and to ensure the smooth progress of socialist construction.

Deviant behavior has often been attributed to limited educational opportunities or to an inadequate appreciation of the dangers to the socialist agenda that are posed by nonconformist behavior. As such, a sentence that includes a period of incarceration automatically requires that the offender work, if the person is able. Traditionally, forced labor has been viewed from the Chinese perspective as helping the socialist society with some of its production goals. It is also based on the belief that deviant behavior can be curbed if the offender accepts education and reform through labor. In this context, deviant behavior is distinguished from counterrevolutionary behavior (or endangering state security, the term that recently replaced it). The latter form of behavior is usually associated with political crimes against the socialist system. One generally cannot characterize these offenders as having been deprived of educational opportunities.

In the section of the Criminal Law devoted to sentencing, the issue of leniency is rather prominent. The section begins with Article 61 stating: "a punishment shall be meted out on the basis of the facts, nature and circumstances of the crime, the degree of harm done to society and the relevant provisions of this Law." Article 63, however, authorizes two approaches in which the offender could receive a milder sentence.

> In cases where the circumstances of a crime call for a mitigated punishment under the provisions of this Law, the criminal shall be sentenced to a punishment less than the prescribed punishment.
>
> In cases where circumstances of a crime do not warrant a mitigated punishment under the provisions of this Law, however, in light of the special circumstances of the case, and upon verification and approval of the Supreme People's Court, the criminal may still be sentenced to a punishment less than the prescribed punishment.

These passages were designed to encourage the offender to embrace the rehabilitative regimen that the court imposes at sentencing. Moreover, the development of labor reform institutions and the creation of policies of reeducation through labor were intended not only to punish but also to reform individuals who were at odds with the socialist agenda.

The Chinese have established two categories of sanctions: principal punishments and supplementary punishments. Principal punishments include: public surveillance, criminal detention, fixed-term imprisonment, life imprisonment, and the death penalty. Public surveillance will be discussed in the subsection devoted to noninstitutional sanctions.

Criminal detention is a period of incarceration for not less than one month but no more than six months. Criminal detention centers are similar to jails in that they are found at the local level and are administered by local public security agencies. A fixed-term imprisonment is for a period between six months and 15 years. Fixed-term and life imprisonment are served in correctional facilities that are administered by the Ministry of Justice. Finally, the death penalty can be ordered in two ways. One calls for the immediate execution of the judgment; the other permits a two-year suspension of the sentence. The death penalty will be a topic of discussion in the subsection titled "Critical Issues."

Supplementary punishments consist of: fines, the deprivation of political rights, and the confiscation of property. These sanctions can be imposed independently of the principal punishments. Moreover, an offender could receive a civil compensation order from the court. According to Article 36, "If a victim has suffered economic losses as a result of a crime, the criminal shall, in addition to receiving a criminal punishment according to law, be sentenced to making compensation for the economic losses in the light of the circumstances." The article further states that "a criminal who is liable for civil compensation is sentenced to a fine at the same time but his property is not sufficient to pay both the compensation and the fine, ... he shall, first of all, bear his liability for civil compensation to the victim."

Organization and Administration of the Correctional System

Ministry of Justice A Bureau of Prisons was established in 1949 and placed under the administrative control of the Ministry of Justice. In 1951, however, this responsibility shifted to the Ministry of Public Security. The Ministry of Justice renewed its authority over the correctional system in 1983. The ministry is assisted in this endeavor by other government departments, such as civil affairs, education, labor, and public security. The minister of justice is a member of the State Council. The actual construction of a correctional facility is the responsibility of local government at the provincial and municipal level and is based on need.

Procuratorate Previous sections have pointed out the important role that the procuratorate plays in the administration of criminal justice in China. The authority of the procuratorate does not end with the prosecution of offenders. According to the Organic Law of the People's Procuratorate of the People's Republic of China, the procuratorate exercises "supervision over the execution of judgments and orders in criminal cases and over the activities of prisons, detention houses and organs in charge of reform through labor, to determine whether such execution and activities conform to the law." In the event that the procuratorate identifies an error in the execution of a judgment, it notifies the appropriate agency so the problem can be corrected. If a correctional facility is in violation of a law, it is the responsibility of the procuratorate to inform the facility of the matter and oversee its efforts to comply with the rules and regulations.

Types of Institutions There are four kinds of correctional facilities for adult offenders, but only two of them are the responsibility of the Ministry of Justice (see Figure 6.3). Prisons are used to hold the more dangerous inmates, which include people with a suspended death sentence, a life term, or a fixed term of more than 10 years. These inmates are not considered suitable for work outside a closed facility. Offenders who have been found guilty of endangering state security (the political prisoners) may also be sent to prison. The number of people housed at each prison varies depending on the size of the complex and where the facility is located in the country (Seymour and Anderson, 1999).

Figure 6.3

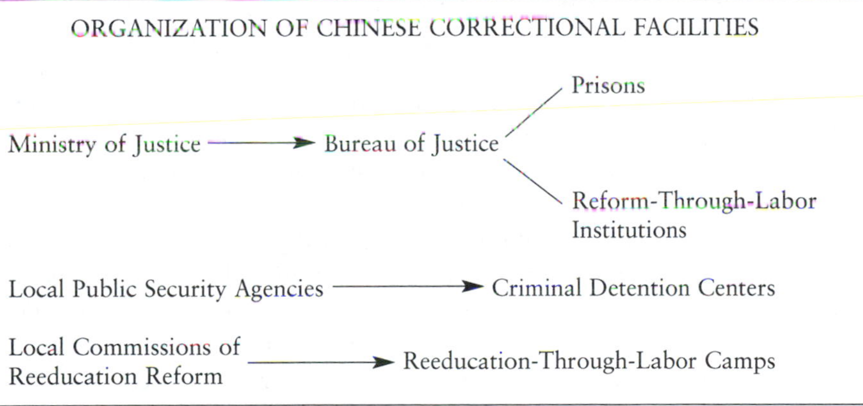

The other type of correctional facility that is the responsibility of the Ministry of Justice is the reform-through-labor institution. These institutions are designed for inmates who are not considered a risk outside the facility and who have been sentenced to at least one year of imprisonment. Political prisoners may also be a part of the population of this kind of institution. Between 3,000 to 5,000 inmates are housed at this type of facility.

Criminal detention centers are the administrative responsibility of local public security agencies. These facilities are similar to jails. They house people who are awaiting the sentence of a court or who have been imprisoned for less than two years. Reeducation-through-labor institutions make up the fourth kind of correctional facility for adults. They are administered jointly at the local level by a commission represented by the department of civil affairs, the department of labor, and the public security agency. The role of these institutions in the Chinese justice system will be explained in the subsection on administrative penalties.

Regimen Correctional facilities are organized for the most part along the lines of the military. Inmates are assigned to a squadron that consists of 10 people. The squadron works, sleeps, eats, and studies together. This approach is based in part on the view that inmates will monitor and control one another. Inmates are permitted short visits once a month from relatives; they also can send letters. Relatives may bring or send food and other items, but this is controlled by the authorities at the facility.

The principal piece of legislation that governs the correctional system is the Act of the People's Republic of China for Reform Through Labor (1954). The purpose of the correctional system is explained in Article 1: "This Act is adopted specially in order to punish all counterrevolutionary and other criminal offenders and to compel them to reform themselves through labor and become new persons." Thus, the two rationales of punishment and rehabilitation are placed in the context of work.

The nature of work performed by inmates is largely dependent on the location of the correctional facility. Agriculture and industry, along with the construction of railways, roads, and irrigation projects, have been utilized since the inception of the system. As was mentioned earlier, this system of forced labor is supposed to help society achieve various production goals, while reducing the cost to the country as a whole. Recently, it has been suggested that the economic output of the various prison industries does not make a significant contribution to the gross domestic product (Seymour and Anderson, 1999).

According to one source, certain general work principles apply to inmates sentenced to incarceration. They include: (1) that all inmates are expected to work, (2) that all inmates must meet or surpass production quotas, (3) that all inmates must obey orders, and (4) that those who fail to maintain or develop a proper work habit will be punished (Wu, 1992). Today, inmates work at least an eight-hour day and possibly longer, depending on the nature of the work or season of the year.

The country's move to a market economy had an adverse impact on the nature of work in prisons. The goods produced in prisons were long considered shoddy, and it was increasingly difficult to find markets for such products. The inmates' skills were often low-level or nonexistent, and the machinery was generally antiquated, which contributed to poor product quality. In addition, the government is no longer providing the raw materials for production. Thus, prisons must purchase the materials on the open market. Prison farms have lost the limited profitability that they once possessed. In addition, the number of jobs is smaller than the number of inmates seeking work. In the past, prisons were often able to assist inmates in securing employment upon release. This is increasingly difficult to accomplish as both the new private sector and the traditional public sector seek more skilled workers (see Dutton and Zhaugrun, in Bakken, 2005).

In the past, the three daily meals were often designed just to keep inmates alive. The diet was poor and reference was made to the similarities between it and that found in the gulag of the former Soviet Union. Breakfast was essentially corn gruel and a piece of salted carrot. Lunch and dinner consisted of cabbage soup, which sometimes included a meager portion of pork fat or vegetables cooked in water. The soup or vegetables would be accompanied by either corn bread or a small portion of steamed rice (Xiguang and McFadden, 1997; Zongren, 1995). It has been suggested that today the food is similar to that available at regular farms and factories. The difference is that the ration is decreased if the inmate fails to maintain an adequate production level (Wu, 1992). Moreover, important sources of protein, such as meat and eggs, are still not included in the regular diet of inmates. Such products are permitted in packages sent from relatives, however.

The daily schedule also calls for a specific period of time for study in the evening. Prisoners are expected to participate in the political education program at the facility. From the 1950s to the mid-1970s, this often consisted of studying the writings of Mao Zedong. Such activities are associated with rehabilitation. In order to become rehabilitated, the inmate must proceed through a three-step process that consists of acknowledging one's guilt for the offense committed; criticizing one's behavior as being antisocialistic, which is a form of repentance; and submitting to authority by obeying the rules and regulations of the correctional facility (Wu, 1992). Each correctional facility has at least one correctional officer who is trained to serve as a political instructor for the camp. It is the political instructor who usually determines if and when an inmate would be permitted an early release from the facility. The decision is generally based on the inmate's participation in the political education program and general work habits.

Under Deng Xiaoping's leadership, and because of the importance placed on economic development, vocational training was introduced in many correctional facilities as a method of not only providing labor but also of enhancing the offender's efforts at becoming a productive member of society upon release. Unfortunately, many of the work skills acquired while incarcerated are not in demand outside the facility. Elementary- and high-school-level programs have also been introduced through the Ministry of Education, and some inmates have participated in correspondence courses with universities (Zhou, 1991).

Parole Inmates have an opportunity to qualify for parole. Those serving a fixed term are generally eligible for release after serving one-half of the sentence. Those incarcerated for life are eligible after completing at least 10 years of the sentence. According to Article 81 of the Criminal Law, "No parole shall be granted to recidivists or criminals who are sentenced to more than 10 years of imprisonment or life imprisonment for crimes of violence such as homicide, explosion, robbery, rape and kidnap."

Eligibility for parole is based on an inmate's expression of repentance and the authorities' view that he or she is not a danger to society. The period of parole for a person serving a fixed term would equal the time not served in a correctional facility, while the period of parole for an inmate serving a life sentence is 10 years. Certain conditions can be placed on an inmate released on parole. They include: observing laws and regulations, submitting to supervision, reporting on one's activities, observing the rules regarding contact with specific individuals, and obtaining permission to leave the immediate jurisdiction or to change one's residence. Failure to abide by these provisions can lead to a revocation of the parole. Inmates on parole are supervised by the local public security agency.

Noninstitutional Sanctions

Public surveillance is the Chinese version of probation; it is imposed on those offenders who do not require a period of incarceration. The terms of the sanction are similar to those imposed on inmates released on parole. The offender also reports to the local public security agency periodically. If an offender is employed, his or her work unit would be informed of the sanction and thereby expected to assist in monitoring the offender's activities. This sanction may be imposed from a period of three months up to two years.

A suspended sentence can be awarded to a defendant sentenced to a criminal detention or to a fixed sentence that does not exceed three years. This is contingent on the person demonstrating a sufficient degree of repentance and is not considered a risk. If the suspension is for a criminal detention, the term of the suspension is between two months and one year. If the suspension is for a fixed sentence, the term is from one to five years. Either the local public security agency or the offender's work unit would monitor the person's behavior while the suspension is in effect.

A fine is another noninstitutional sanction. Article 52 of the Criminal Law states that "The amount of any fine imposed shall be determined according to the circumstances of the crime." Fines can be paid in installments but must be paid within a specific time limit. Depending on the circumstances, the law permits a reduction or cancellation of a fine.

Depriving a person of their political rights refers to several rights. According to Article 54 of the Criminal Law, they include:

> (1) the right to vote and to stand for election;
>
> (2) the rights of freedom of speech, of the press, of assembly, of association, of procession and of demonstration;
>
> (3) the right to hold a position in a State organ; and
>
> (4) the right to hold a leading position in any State-owned company, enterprise, institution or people's organization.

Any person who is convicted of endangering national security or who is found guilty of seriously undermining public order offenses receives this sanction as a supplementary punishment. The period of time in which this sanction is enforced usually ranges from one to five years. If a person is sentenced to life imprisonment, he or she would be deprived of these political rights for life. In the event this sanction is imposed as a supplementary punishment to public surveillance, the time frame in which an offender could be deprived of his or her political rights would correspond to the period of public surveillance. Finally, confiscating an offender's property is limited to personal property. Courts generally honor the requests of creditors before executing this sanction.

Administrative Penalties

It was pointed out in the section on law that public security agencies have been provided with wide-ranging powers to enforce laws and maintain public order. As noted, this authority was given legal force initially in 1957 with two pieces of legislation.

The Act for Security Administration Punishment authorized public security agencies to impose fines and detain people without the benefit of a trial. This legislation is presently referred to as Regulations of the People's Republic of China on Administrative Penalties for Public Security.

The kinds of activities that are subject to these regulations include: disturbing public order, carrying a dangerous weapon, violating safety regulations, minor assaults, breaking and entering, theft, violating traffic regulations, prostitution, gambling, drug violations, and the production and distribution of pornography. When imposing a sanction on a person who has violated some aspect of the regulations, three types of penalties are available to public security agencies. They include: (1) a warning, (2) a fine of up to 2000 yuan, or (3) detention for up to 15 days. The objective of the sanction is to combine education with punishment, which has been a central feature of the Chinese correctional system for some time.

The regulations also call for the confiscation of items used in the commission of these activities. If the actions of an offender cause an injury, the offender is expected to compensate the victim or pay for any medical expenses. According to Article 8 of the regulations, "if the offender is not an able person or is a person of limited ability, unable to compensate for the loss or bear the medical expenses, his guardian shall make the compensation or bear the medical expenses according to law." Public security agencies are authorized to reduce the penalties if the person is between the ages of 14 and 18. Young people under 14 years of age are exempt from punishment but can be issued a reprimand. Moreover, the young person's guardian is expected to impose restrictions on the offender's daily activities.

The other piece of legislation enacted in 1957 was the Decision of the State Council Relating to Problems of Reeducation Through Labor. It was amended in 1979 with Supplementary Regulation on Reeducation Through Labor. The 1957 Decision had two purposes; it was "a measure of a coercive nature for carrying out the education and reform of persons receiving. It is also a method of arranging for their getting employment." The education and reform are carried out at labor camps. Like the previous legislation, the process of determining who needs education and reform is carried out without the benefit of a trial. In addition, like the correctional system, the establishment of labor camps is not the responsibility of the central government. Local government at the provincial or municipal level determines whether there is a need for such a facility.

According to the 1957 Decision, reeducation through labor was designed "to reform into self-supporting new persons those persons with the capacity to labor who loaf, who violate the law and discipline, or who do not engage in proper employment, and in order further to preserve public order and to benefit socialist construction." The legislation identifies the categories of people for which it was intended. They include: people not engaged in honest pursuits; hooligans; people who have committed larceny, fraud, or other acts for which they have not been held criminally liable; violators of public security rules; counterrevolutionaries and antisocialist reactionaries who commit minor offenses and are not held criminally liable, who have been excluded from an agency, organizations, enterprises, or schools, or who are having difficulty making a living; employees of the government or people's organizations who are able but refuse to work; people who jeopardize public order; people who refuse to accept the work assigned to them or the arrangement made for their employment; and people who behave disruptively, obstruct officials, and refuse to correct their behavior.

Under this legislation, public security agencies are authorized to send people to labor camps for a period of one to three years, with the option of adding an additional year if necessary. As mentioned above, local government determines the need to establish a labor camp. The management of a camp is the responsibility of a local commission represented by the departments of civil affairs and labor, along with the public security agency.

The labor camps utilize the same military style of administration as is found in the correctional system. People are organized into squadrons of 10 individuals, and they work, sleep, and eat together. The conditions of the labor camps are also similar to those found in correctional facilities. While at the labor camp, people receive a wage that is based on the work performed. Some money is either deducted to assist in the support of the person's dependents or set aside as a savings account for use upon release from the camp.

Critical Issues

Human Rights China has often been criticized for its record on human rights (Davis, 1995). The violation of those rights has frequently taken place within the context of the criminal justice system. A brief comment is presented here on the issues of rights in general and human rights in particular as they relate to criminal justice in China.

Throughout much of the contemporary Western world, rights and justice tend to focus on the individual's interest. Procedural rules are designed to assure that an individual's rights are protected and that an individual who is caught up in the criminal process will be guaranteed treatment associated with fundamental fairness and justice. It does not always work out that way, but that was the intent in the design of the process.

The Chinese offer a different approach to this issue, because they begin with a distinct set of assumptions. They acknowledge that individuals have rights, and this position has been given legal standing in various laws from the Constitution of the People's Republic of China to other legislation (e.g., the Criminal Procedure Law of the People's Republic of China). Despite this position, the Chinese tend to prioritize the public interest over that of an individual's interest. The roots of this attitude are found in the country's history, and those traditions have simply been modernized with the adoption of a socialist system.

As a result, when a crime is committed in China, the perpetrator is viewed first and foremost as having infringed on the collective human rights of all citizens and the individual rights of the victim. These rights take precedence over the perpetrator's claim to certain rights. Because the perpetrator is either directly or indirectly violating the collective rights of the people, his or her actions are considered a threat to the socialist system and socialist state. It is the responsibility of public security agencies to prevent and punish those who threaten or violate these collective rights. As has been suggested, punishment is accompanied by a regimen designed to educate and rehabilitate the perpetrator. Education orients the perpetrator to an understanding of and appreciation for the regulations and laws of the socialist system. Rehabilitation strongly encourages the perpetrator to acknowledge the error of infringing on the collective rights of the citizenry and the individual rights of the victim.

Over the course of the past decade, the Chinese have become more sensitive to the criticisms leveled against them regarding human rights. They have acknowledged the need to establish guidelines and criteria for enforcing law in order to assure citizens that agents of the justice system are not incorrectly interpreting regulations or laws. The revision of the Criminal Procedure Law is an illustration of this change. Despite these efforts, one should not expect a radical change in this matter in light of the fact that the Chinese view the issue from a different set of assumptions.

Death Penalty China is one of the few major countries in the world that has retained the death penalty. This is the basis for some of the criticism leveled by various human rights groups. Like the United States, there does not appear to be an effective movement to have the sentence abolished. While a country-wide public opinion poll has not been conducted in China on the subject, it is assumed that most people favor the death penalty, especially for violent criminals. This is based on the fact that most Chinese have a strong aversion to chaos, because so many have experienced a good deal of it personally and would prefer a government that assures law and order.

According to the Criminal Law, the death penalty can be imposed only on "criminals who have committed extremely serious crimes." According to the Criminal Law of the People's Republic of China 1997, these crimes include: homicide, arson, explosion, inflicting serious injury or death on people or causing heavy losses of public or private property, sabotage, hijacking an aircraft, some rape cases, some cases of trafficking in human beings, some kidnapping cases, armed robbery, some cases of embezzlement, some drug trafficking, and some cases of impairing the national defense.

In order for the death penalty to be carried out, the offender must have reached the age of 18 at the time of the crime. People, who have reached the age of 16 and have committed "particularly serious" crimes can be sentenced to death with a two-year suspension. As pointed out earlier, the death penalty can be imposed in one of two ways. The court can order the immediate execution of the judgment or permit a two-year suspension of the execution. It is estimated that about one-half of the sentences are ordered with the two-year suspension (Scobell, 1990).

If a person is sentenced to death with a two-year suspension, his or her punishment will be commuted to a life sentence as long as the person does not commit an intentional crime during the period of suspension of the sentence. A panel of three judges from the higher people's court reviews the record and formally approves the change in the sentence. If the person shows signs of repentance and is an excellent worker, the life sentence could be reduced to a 15- to 20-year term. If it is proven that the person committed an intentional crime during the period of suspension, then the death sentence is carried out. The higher people's court, however, must submit the matter to the Supreme People's Court for approval.

When a judgment calls for the immediate execution of the death penalty, it must first be approved by the Supreme People's Court. In the course of reviewing a case, members of the Court do not entertain oral or written arguments from defense counsel, although that has been suggested in recent years. Generally, Court staff meet informally with interested parties in a case (Finder, 1993). Once an order has been granted, the execution occurs within seven days, with a member of the procuratorate supervising the execution.

According to Article 212 of the Criminal Procedure Law, the sentence "shall be executed by such means as shooting or injection." While it is common for people condemned to death to be paraded through the streets on the back of a truck with a sign around them indicating their name, crime, and sentence, the actual execution is not supposed to be held in public. Nevertheless, it has been reported fairly widely that there have been public executions and that they have even appeared on television. Once the sentence has been carried out, the family of the prisoner is notified by the people's court that issued the judgment.

Death penalty statistics are not readily available through the government. Nevertheless, it has been estimated that during the 1980s, at least 10,000 people and possibly as many as 30,000 were executed. The vast majority of these people were categorized as violent criminals who had committed nonpolitical crimes. Many were under 30 years of age (Scobell, 1990).

JUVENILE JUSTICE

Mao Zedong likened deviant behavior to an illness. He maintained that society's response to this social disease should be to seek a cure by emphasizing a rehabilitative approach rather than a strict punitive method. The Chinese have tended to associate the causes of deviance with a general lack of education and an inadequate understanding of the socialist system. Therefore, patterns of bad behavior are a result of degrees of ignorance on the part of individual delinquents. In order to curb deviance, the principal objective has been to place a good deal of emphasis on early intervention strategies (see Bracey, in Troyer, Clark, and Rojek, 1989).

Using the medical analogy further, the Chinese adopted a preventive care system that was designed to combat any social disease that might arise. This explains the important role that informal justice has played in the total justice system. The fact that the local community takes an active role in assuring that social order is maintained illustrates both the informal design and preventive nature of the system. Although somewhat more formal because they have the force of law, administrative regulations and penalties at the disposal of public security agencies are also part of the preventive effort. They are designed specifically to arrest lesser forms of delinquency in order to prevent an escalation to a more serious form of deviance.

As is the case with most countries, China has experienced both upward and downward trends in levels of delinquency. In the relatively brief history of the People's Republic of China, scholars have identified three distinct periods in the study of juvenile crime. Each phase provides context when considering the contemporary issues confronting juvenile justice in China. The first period was between 1949 and 1965. During the early years of this period, crime was considered a very serious problem and was generally associated with the social and political changes brought about by the founding of the People's Republic of China. Most adult offenders were characterized as thieves and gangsters from the old society.

With respect to juvenile delinquency, this period was marked by very low rates of juvenile offenses, with the lowest registered in 1956 at 18 percent of all crime. This percentage rose to 32 percent by 1957 and reached a high of 35 percent in 1965, the last year of this period. It should be pointed out that the general crime rate in the country was in decline during this period. Therefore, while the percentage of juvenile offenses was increasing, the number of juvenile delinquents was decreasing. The fact that juvenile delinquency was not considered a serious problem during this period was attributed to a healthy social mood, patriotic dedication, and a sense of discipline (Daosheng, 1992).

The second period was between 1966 and 1983. This period encompasses the time of the Cultural Revolution (1966–1976) but goes beyond that event to include the country's early efforts at modernization and opening up to the rest of the world. Most scholars contend that the Cultural Revolution created a social climate that caused a considerable growth in crime, particularly during the early 1980s. As mentioned earlier, the Cultural Revolution was a period of general lawlessness. During much of the period, when crime was difficult to categorize and crime statistics were easily distorted, it is estimated that juvenile offenses represented between 40 and 50 percent of all crime. By 1981, it had reached a rate of 61 percent and would rise to 67 percent by 1983, the last year of this period.

Several factors have been identified to explain this significant increase. First, the Cultural Revolution caused social disorder throughout the country. In some cases, it destroyed the family structure or made it dysfunctional. It clearly fostered a large group of troubled, illiterate young people. Second, the proportion of juvenile delinquents among the population of young people was rising, and the proportion of juvenile offenders would become the largest category within the total number of criminal offenders. Third, more serious criminal offenses by juveniles were reported formally to the authorities. Fourth, the number of criminal gangs and gangs of hooligans increased sharply. Fifth, some foreign criminal activity entered the country with the new open-door policy. Sixth, the rate of recidivism increased. Seventh, the initial phase of the economic reform period provided young people with a greater degree of social mobility that had not been experienced in the past and that fostered a change in values. Eighth, social mobility also caused a migration of young people to cities, in search of employment. In many instances, job opportunities were woefully lacking, which led some of the new arrivals to turn to crime as a source of income (Bakken, 1995; Daosheng, 1992).

The third period commenced in 1984 and continues to the present. It is important to point out that the Chinese make a distinction between a juvenile delinquent and a juvenile criminal. The former encompasses the 14-to-25 age group, while the latter refers to people between 18 and 25. As a result of the dramatic increase in juvenile crime, the government initiated a crackdown on crime in 1983. This was known as the "severe blows" campaign. The campaign was directed at the proliferation of gangs, particularly the recruitment of juvenile delinquents. Part of the government's strategy was the arrest, expedited trial, and execution of gang leaders. Officials and scholars in China considered the campaign a success because there was a decline in the rate of juvenile crime in 1984. In 1985, offenders under 18 years of age committed 23.8 percent of all crimes in China. By 1995, that age group was identified as having committed 10.5 percent of all crimes (Guo, 1999). Much of the credit is associated with early intervention techniques mentioned below. In spite of these successes, there are concerns with juvenile drug use and delinquency that is gang-related.

Offenders in the age group between 18 and 25 years remain a concern for the authorities. This group has been identified as committing a large amount of crime, and of particular concern is that these offenses are becoming more serious and violent. A number of factors have been identified to explain this. First, the migration of young people to urban areas in search of employment continues. Second, there has been a significant number of young people dropping out of school in both rural and urban areas. The rationale frequently offered by students for dropping out has been a desire to pursue business opportunities. Third, the inability to find employment or the failure of a business has led some of these young people to turn to crime. A significant number of juvenile offenders have concentrated on burglary, robbery, and other hooligan behavior. Fourth, juvenile offenders have become more violent, as indicated by the increase in the number of murders, rapes, and robberies. Fifth, the increase in youth gangs continues despite the "severe blows" campaign. Finally, juveniles are engaged in more sophisticated types and methods of crime that include forgery, smuggling, and drug offenses.

While there has been legitimate concern about the rise in juvenile delinquency over the past 20 years, it is important to place this anxiety in context. When compared to other countries, China's crime rate remains low (Bakken, 1995; Office of the Fifth Bureau, 1995). Nevertheless, there is growing concern about the increase in crimes of violence (such as robbery), the level of drug use, and evidence that a good deal of juvenile delinquency is gang-related (Guo, 1999).

Juvenile Adjudication Process

Responsibility of Juveniles When categorizing delinquent behavior as juvenile, many countries cease using the term "juvenile" when the offender has reached either age 18 or 21. In China, the term "juvenile delinquent" is associated with people between the ages of 14 and 25. The term "juvenile criminal" refers to people between the ages of 18 and 25.

According to Article 17 of the Criminal Law, "If a person who has reached the age of 16 commits a crime, he shall bear criminal responsibility." Young people between the ages of 14 and 16 who commit serious crimes can also be held criminally responsible. Among the crimes deemed serious are: intentional homicide, rape, robbery, drug trafficking, and arson. Moreover, young people between 14 and 17 years of age receive a lighter sanction at sentencing. The Regulations of the People's Republic of China on Administrative Penalties for Public Security (1987) use the same age brackets when considering issues of responsibility.

Personnel Throughout China's history, most juvenile offenders have been handled either informally or through administrative regulations. As a result, the Chinese did not establish a juvenile court system throughout the country. Those juvenile offenders who required a trial according to the criminal procedure laws were brought before a basic people's court. However, the Chinese did begin to experiment with juvenile courts in Beijing in 1989. By 2000, there were more than 2,500 juvenile courts throughout China. These courts use a combination of judges and people's assessors to hear cases (Dai and Pi, 2004). This innovation had more to do with improving efficiency, though, than with creating a new procedural process for juveniles.

Procedures With a few qualifications, juvenile offenders are treated essentially the same as adults during the pretrial and trial processes. Article 14 of the Criminal Procedure Law states: "In cases where a minor under the age of 18 commits a crime, the criminal suspect and the legal representative of the defendant may be notified to be present at the time of interrogation and trial." An adult defendant is not permitted to see a legal representative until after the initial interrogation. When a person under the age of 18 is a witness, the procedural law allows for legal representation during questioning. At trial, cases are not heard in public if the defendant is 14 or 15 years of age. The rule generally applies to cases involving defendants who have not reached the age of 18, but exceptions can be made for this age group.

Disposition

There are both informal and formal methods for dealing with juvenile delinquents. Officers from local public security agencies frequently admonish juveniles for petty forms of delinquency. There are also two additional informal strategies that may be used to intercede in juvenile matters. While these strategies are informal because they are outside the boundaries of administrative regulations or the criminal law, there is a formal structure to the organization and process.

One of the strategies utilizes the local neighborhood committee. In the section on police, it was mentioned that committees were formed in residential neighborhoods, at factories and schools, within occupational units, and throughout the countryside among various rural production teams. One of the purposes of these committees was to assist police in maintaining public order. Moreover, they are specifically mandated to mediate disputes. If there is tension between a young person and a member of his or her family, a neighbor, or a friend, the neighborhood committee (now commonly referred to as community service commission) might be able to solve or mediate the dispute.

The other informal strategy is the formation of a *bang-jiao*. Bang-jiao is a grassroots effort to prevent or curb delinquent behavior in the immediate community. Its goal is to assist and guide a juvenile and his or her family. A bang-jiao usually includes: the young person's parents; a member of the neighborhood committee; a local public security officer; the head of the person's work group, if the juvenile is or was employed; and the head of the person's school, even if the person is no longer attending. The bang-jiao is available to assist juveniles who have already been in trouble formally with the authorities or are on the brink of doing so. With regard to the former, once the juvenile is released from a period of incarceration, the bang-jiao assists with the rehabilitation process. In reference to the latter, the objective of the bang-jiao is early intervention in order to prevent a minor matter in the juvenile's life from becoming a serious problem that requires the formal involvement of the agents of the justice system (Zhang et al., 1996).

It should also be pointed out that the State Education Commission has established work and study schools. These are special schools designed for juveniles who are habitually truant, disruptive at school, or have committed minor crimes in which the nature of the case and the offender's prospects are such that it would be inappropriate to send the person to a reformatory. The schools follow the regular curriculum, but there is an added focus on the importance of discipline.

The formal methods for dealing with juvenile delinquents are basically explained in the Criminal Law of the People's Republic of China (1997) and the Regulations of the People's Republic of China on Administrative Penalties for Public Security (1987). Juveniles are essentially subject to the same sanctions as adult offenders. The Criminal Law lists as principal punishments: public surveillance, criminal detention, fixed-term imprisonment, life imprisonment, and the death penalty. Supplementary punishments consist of: fines, deprivation of political rights, and the confiscation of property. Under the Administrative Regulations, three kinds of penalties are provided: warning, fine, and detention. The Decision of the State Council Relating to Problems of Reeducation Through Labor provides yet another option of a one- to three-year term at a labor camp.

Each of these sanctions was explained in the previous section on corrections. What is important to emphasize here is the manner in which these sanctions are carried out when the offender is a juvenile. The Criminal Law calls for "a lighter or mitigated punishment" for people between the ages of 14 and 17. In reference to the death penalty, a juvenile must have reached the age of 18 at the time of the crime for that to be considered a viable sanction by a court. If a juvenile commits a "particularly serious" crime and has reached the age of 16, he or she can be sentenced to death with a two-year suspension. As mentioned in the previous section, a two-year suspension usually means that the punishment would be commuted to a life sentence and possibly reduced further to a fixed-term sentence.

In the event that a court does not issue an order calling for a specific sanction, it will assign responsibility to the parent or guardian to impose discipline and provide appropriate educational opportunities. The Administrative Regulations also favor the imposition of lighter sanctions on young offenders. If the young person is unable to compensate the victim for injuries, Article 8 of the Regulations points out that "his guardian shall make the compensation or bear the medical expenses according to law."

Juvenile offenders who have been sentenced to a period of incarceration will generally be sent either to a juvenile reformatory or to a reform-through-labor farm. The reformatories are designed primarily for juveniles between the ages of 14 and 16. These facilities include an educational and work component in the daily regimen. They also impose discipline through drill and other forms of exercise. Each province has a juvenile reformatory, which can handle offenders sentenced to a term of reform through labor or a term of reeducation through labor.

Juveniles over the age of 16 are usually sent to a reform-through-labor farm. The rationale for such facilities is that the offender committed a crime (often for economic gain) but was capable of legitimate work. At the labor farm, the offender is required to perform physical labor with the goal of correcting the delinquent behavior.

On occasion, juvenile offenders will be sent to prison. This occurs if their fixed term of imprisonment is lengthy, they have been sentenced to life imprisonment, or they have received the death penalty with a two-year suspension.

SUMMARY

This chapter has offered an introduction to the criminal justice system of China. The major components of the system—the police, judiciary, law, corrections, and juvenile justice—were surveyed, along with an overview of the political system. A brief history of some of the components of the system were presented; the organization and administration was described; the various roles of the practitioners were explained; the legal process was examined; and reference was made to some of the areas of concern within the system.

China is an ancient country that has one of the oldest civilizations on earth. Throughout much of its history, it has been a peasant-based society. It is one of the largest countries in the world in terms of area, and it has the largest population. From 1949 to 1978, China adopted an isolationist policy toward many of the advanced countries in the world, while it embraced the political principles of communism. Since that time, its significance in the world in general and its prominence in the East Asian region in particular has increased significantly. Presently, China is making an attempt to transform its society to the status of a fairly advanced, industrialized country. What is unique about this venture is that China is the last major country in the world that continues to embrace Communism. Thus, it is attempting to introduce modern economic principles without granting the democratic political freedoms that are usually associated with modernization.

Throughout the twentieth century, China experienced periods of order and profound periods of disorder. The periods of order were marked by the government's attempt to stress the significant role of law in the maintenance of political, social, and economic order. Periods of disorder have been noted for their absence of law and the ascendance of ideology serving a dominant role in state governance.

For students of Western justice systems, the People's Republic of China offers a particularly striking contrast. For example, during the first 30 years of its existence, the country had neither a criminal code nor a criminal procedure code. It has only been in the past two decades that the justice system has been placed on a legal footing. As a result, law and the judiciary have only recently been cited as important to the governance of the country.

In addition, China has maintained two kinds of justice systems that are designed to complement one another. One is the formal system that was established by the government. Much of this chapter was devoted to describing and explaining the features of the formal system. The other system is informal in that it is essentially part of the cultural tradition of the country and its roots can be traced back to ancient times. Although the government did not create the informal system, it clearly influences and controls the manner in which it operates today. The informal system is reflected both in communities taking an active role in assuring that social order is maintained locally and in citizens resolving disputes through mediation rather than relying on courts.

Finally, the authority of public security agencies is enhanced considerably within the formal and informal justice systems. This authority is particularly noteworthy in the informal system, where public security agents can impose fines and detain people without benefit of a trial. Such a policy is permitted, in part, because the Chinese approach the issue of rights from a different perspective. The Chinese tend to prioritize the public interest over that of an individual's interest. As a result, the collective rights of the people are accorded greater deference than the rights of an individual.

Concepts to Know

Prophet Muhammad
The Quran
The Sunna
The Pillars of Islam
Sunni
Shia
ulama
Sharia
Mazalim
Siyasa Sharia
Madhahib
ijma
ijtahad
Hudud
Quesas
Tazir
Muhammad ibn Abd al-Wahhab
Consultative Council
Senior Council of the Ulama
Supreme Judicial Council
Bureau of Investigation and Public Prosecution
Commission for the Promotion of Virtue and the Prevention of Vice
matawain
mujtahid
Ayatollah Ruhollah Khomeini
Faqih
Council of Guardians
basij
Mustafa Kemal Ataturk
Supreme Council of Judges and Public Prosecutors
Constitutional Court

Chapter VII

ISLAMIC LAW

Introduction

In the Introduction to this text it was mentioned that some countries view the purpose and function of law in a different context from that which emerged in the West. For our purposes, Islamic law will illustrate this fact. It is important to point out that Islam is primarily a religion, a belief system that espouses a specific moral code. Islam means submitting to God's will. From its inception, the most important group associated with Islam was the *umma*, the community of believers, and the ultimate goal of Islam was to establish a theocratic society. In such a context, the state is viewed as a vehicle to enhance and foster the revealed religion throughout the community of believers.

Islam is often referred to as one of the three Abrahamic faiths; the other two are Judaism and Christianity. What these three religions have in common is monotheism, the belief in one God. Today, Islam is the second largest religion in the world with more than 1.3 billion followers, while Christianity is the largest with more than 2.1 billion adherents, of which 1.1 billion are Roman Catholic.

The Quran

It should be noted that it was not the intent of the Prophet Muhammad (570?–632) to establish a new religion; rather, his objective was to reform the religion of one God. The Quran clearly states:

> We sent Jesus, son of Mary, in their footsteps, to confirm the Torah that had been sent before him: We gave him the Gospel with guidance, light, and conformation of the Torah already revealed—a guide and lesson for those who take heed of God. So let the followers of the Gospel judge according to what God has sent down in it. Those who do not judge according to what God has revealed are lawbreakers.
>
> We sent to you [Muhammad] the Scriptures with the truth, confirming the Scriptures that came before it, and with final authority over them: so judge between them according to what God has sent down (5:46–48).

Thus, Muslims believe that Muhammad was the last of the great prophets. Those preceding him were Abraham, Moses, and Jesus.

Before proceeding further, it should be noted that when citing the Quran the first number following the quote refers to the chapter, while the number or numbers following the colon indicate the specific verse(s). Also please note that because there is not one standard method of transliteration of Arabic to English, names and terms often have several different spellings. I have attempted to use a simplified form that is free of many diacritical marks. Any quotations, however, are retained in the original form.

As the aforementioned passage indicates, according to the Quran, Muhammad received messages from God through the angel Gabriel. These messages represented God's final revelations to humankind, with the previous noteworthy revelations coming to Moses and Jesus. As a result, Muslims believe that Islam supersedes Judaism and Christianity, for it is the culmination of God's message to humankind.

Muhammad received the revelations over a 23-year period, which represented two distinct phases of the Prophet's life in Mecca and Medina. Initially, Muhammad had tried to introduce the revelations to the people of Mecca, but they were unwilling to believe in the principal feature of his message: that there was one God. As such, he left Mecca, the place of his birth, for Medina. It was there that he would establish the first Islamic government and where he also died in 632.

While the largest number of revelations was received during the initial 12 and one-half years in Mecca, it was during Muhammad's time in Medina that the legal rules and various regulations pertaining to everyday life were revealed. According to the Quran, "We sent it in this way to strengthen your heart [Prophet]; We gave it to you in gradual revelation" (25:32). In light of this approach, the Prophet and his Companions were able to memorize the Quran. The Quran also states: "[Prophet], do not rush your tongue in an attempt to hasten [your memorization of] the Revelation: We shall make sure of its safe collection and recitation. When We have recited it, repeat the recitation and We shall make it clear"

(75:16–18). Because it was largely illiterate at the time, the Arab population found this gradual method of revelation beneficial. During the Prophet Muhammad's life, parts of the Quran were written. It was not until after his death, however, that a single authorized version of the entire text became available.

Thus, the Quran is Islamic scripture; it is the primary source of these revelations or the Word of God. The Quran consists of 114 chapters or *surats* (*surah*, singular) and 6,342 verses or *ayas* (*ayah*, singular). Each chapter has a title, with the longest of the chapters appearing first and the remainder getting progressively shorter in the text. It has been pointed out that the "contents of the Qur'an are not classified subject-wise. The ayat [signs of God] on various topics appear in unexpected places, and no particular order can be ascertained in the sequence of its text" (Kamali, 1989).

Of the 6,342 verses in the Quran, scholars offer differing figures on how many verses deal with legal issues. It ranges from 350 to 500, and many of these are concerned with religious duties, such as prayer and fasting. With regard to the legal verses, it has been suggested that "most of which were revealed in response to problems that were actually encountered. Some were revealed with the aim of repealing objectionable customs such as infanticide, usury, gambling and unlimited polygamy. Others laid down penalties with which to enforce the reforms that the Qur'an had introduced. But on the whole, the Qur'an confirmed and upheld the existing customs and institutions of Arab society and only introduced changes that were deemed necessary"(Kamali, 1989). It was further estimated that approximately 30 verses dealt with crimes and corresponding sanctions, while another 30 pertained to matters of justice, equality, and rights and obligations of people.

In the introduction to his translation of the Quran, which is used in this chapter to cite Quranic verses, M.A.S. Abdel Haleem pointed out:

> The Qur'an was the starting point for all the Islamic sciences: Arabic grammar was developed to serve the Qur'an, the study of Arabic phonetics was pursued in order to determine the exact pronunciation of Qur'anic words, the science of Arabic rhetoric was developed in order to describe the features of the inimitable style of the Qur'an, the art of Arabic calligraphy was cultivated through writing down the Qur'an, the Qur'an is the basis of Islamic law and theology; indeed, as the celebrated fifteenth-century scholar and author Suyuti said, "Everything is based on the Qur'an." The entire religious life of the Muslim world is built around the text of the Qur'an.

Muslims consider the Quran as a moral and ethical blueprint for a civilized society, which is neither unique to nor restricted to the society of believers, that is, the Muslim community. The Quran explains the importance of compassion, fairness, honesty, and justice. While the Quran addresses how a devout Muslim should conduct himself or herself with regard to other people, it is especially concerned with the relationship that a devout Muslim has with God. Moreover, the right to interpret the Quran was not restricted to an elite group. Anyone with a pious disposition and the willingness and aptitude could study the Quran.

The Sunna

While the Quran is the primary source of Islamic scripture, because it reveals the Word of God, another primary source is the Sunna. Sunna means "clear path" or, in this context, established practice. Various approaches have been taken to organize the Sunna. First and foremost, the Sunna consists of three basic methods in which a message was transmitted: verbal, practical, and approved. The verbal method consists of the sayings of the Prophet Muhammad that are called *hadiths*. The practical method includes the actual deeds of the Prophet. The approved method encompasses the actions or sayings of the Companions that the Prophet approved. The Companions were the initial small group who were followers of Muhammad and who referred to themselves as his Companions.

The Quran indicates the importance of the Sunna on several occasions:

> You who believe, obey God and the Messenger, and those in authority among you. If you are in dispute over any matter, refer it to God and the Messenger, if you truly believe in God and the Last Day: (4:59).
>
> By your Lord, they will not be true believers until they let you decide between them in all matters of dispute, and find no resistance in their souls to your decisions, accepting them totally (4:65).
>
> When the true believers are summoned to God and His Messenger in order for him to judge between them, they say, 'We hear and we obey.' These are the ones who will prosper (24:51–52).

What makes the Quran the superior source of Islamic teaching is that it was believed to be received from God, whereas the Sunna was essentially the recollections of witnesses.

The Sunna is a significant source of Islam in its own right for at least three reasons. It reiterates the rules and standards that were already revealed in the Quran, thereby confirming its authenticity. It is a significant aid in explaining or clarifying Quranic verses that are vague or unclear. Finally, it is the source of pronouncements on which the Quran was silent. The rulings from the Sunna, however, could not contradict or oppose a standard that was clearly stated in the Quran. Obviously, it is this last characteristic that makes the Sunna such an important independent source.

The Pillars of Islam

The central beliefs of Islam that unite the umma, the community of believers, and that are prescribed in the Quran are referred to as the Pillars of Islam. The Pillars of Islam are the five practices that devout Muslims are required to follow. Thus, these practices or tenets unite the worldwide community of Islam. The first tenet is the *shahada* (testimony): "There is no god but God, and Muhammad is His messenger." The second tenet is the *salat* (ritual prayer) that is said each day at five different times: dawn, noon, afternoon, sunset, and evening. The third tenet is *sawm* (the obligatory fasting) during the month of Ramadan. Fasting includes refraining from food, drink, and sexual activity from sunrise to sunset during this month. Exceptions are made for people who are old, ill, or traveling. The fourth tenet is the obligation to participate in the *hajj* (pilgrimage) to the Kaba in Mecca at least once in a lifetime. The Kaba is a cube-shaped structure that is the major shrine of Islam. Muslim tradition claims that it was built by Abraham and Ishmael. It contains the Black Stone that Muslims believe was given to Abraham by the angel Gabriel. As such, it is considered the sanctuary of the "House of God." It should also be noted that the pilgrimage is expected of those who are physically and financially able. The fifth tenet is the imposition of the *zakat*. Zakat means purification and is considered a religious obligation. It is a tax on Muslims for the care of the poor (see Aslan, 2006, and Esposito, 2002).

Sunni and Shia

Christianity is divided into several denominations that embrace the basic Christian message. There are differences among the denominations that often deal with biblical interpretations and church governance. Islam is not divided along these same lines, because all devout Muslims adhere to certain core beliefs that include: a belief in God, the Quran as divine revelation, the Prophet Muhammad and his teachings, and the basic tenets found in the Pillars of Islam. It should be noted that there are some differences on theological questions, but those are beyond the scope of our purpose.

The significant division in Islam was over the political and religious leadership of the umma, the community of believers, upon the death of Muhammad. When Muhammad died in 632, his efforts to reform the religion of one God was still in its infancy. Because Muhammad had not designated a successor, the elders of Medina, the seat of his reform movement, selected Abu Bakr as leader. Abu Bakr had excellent credentials in that he was noted for his piety and wisdom and the fact that he was an advisor and father-in-law to Muhammad. Abu Bakr's tenure as *caliph* (successor to Muhammad) lasted only two years. Upon his death, he was succeeded by Umar, who ruled from 634 to 644 and is credited with expanding Islam to additional cities in the region. The third caliph was Uthman, who managed to antagonize a number of people in the Muslim community, which led to his assassination in 656. He was succeeded by the fourth caliph, Ali, who was both a cousin and son-in-law of Muhammad. Some within the Muslim community were angry over Uthman's murder and opposed Ali's selection. This led to Ali's murder in 661.

Two groups emerged over the leadership issues that plagued the umma during its first four decades of existence. Sunni Muslims (from followers of the Sunna of Muhammad) are the main or orthodox branch of Islam. They noted that Muhammad did not name a successor; as a result, they were of the opinion that the most qualified person should be selected as leader or caliph, and the selection should not rely on hereditary succession. From the Sunni perspective, because Muhammad was the last prophet, a caliph's authority would be limited to the political realm and would not be given a theocratic status. Of course, the caliph was expected to be a protector and defender of the Islamic faith. Thus, Sunnis believe that an Islamic government is a civil matter without any religious authority. Sunni Muslims account for about 85 percent of the adherents to the Islamic faith.

Shia Muslims (from the party of Ali) gradually developed a movement that asserted the hereditary succession of Ali's descendants to the position of leader, because they believed that Muslims should be ruled by a male descendant of Muhammad. As such, the people should have no voice in determining the ruler, because it is a prophetic matter. These leaders, who were descendants of Ali, were called *Imams,* and their leadership authority extended to the realms of both religion and politics. As religious leaders, they were considered the interpreters of God's will. Although they did not have the status of a prophet, the speeches and writings of Imams are considered important religious texts. Shias became the largest sect in Islam, and Shia Muslims, known as Shiites, represent about 15 percent of Muslims worldwide.

Within Shia Islam there are divisions that are based on differences over how many Imams succeeded the Prophet Muhammad. Today, the largest of these divisions are known as Twelver Shias. They believe that Muhammad, the twelfth Imam, who was born in 869 and a descendant of the Prophet Muhammad through his son-in-law Ali, went into hiding in the ninth century. Originally, it was thought that this period of seclusion would not last long. As the period of Occultation continued over centuries, there emerged the belief that the Imam Muhammad would return on Judgment Day.

While the Imam was in seclusion, there emerged the belief among the Shia community that the *ulama*, the religious scholars, were the only legitimate authority to offer guidance on governance, for it was the ulama who had undertaken long years of study of the Quran and Sunna. The ulama were not mandated to govern, but they were to offer moral and ethical guidance to the Shia community. The Shia community had its greatest concentration and development in Persia, that is, modern-day Iran. Over time the ulama of the Shia community established a clerical hierarchy. The upper echelons of this hierarchy are senior leaders who are called *ayatollahs* (signs of God) that are noted both for their piety and religious knowledge.

What makes this sect of Islam significant and different from Sunni Islam is that from its inception Islam had not established a church hierarchy or an ordained clergy as those terms are used in a Christian context. Any Muslim could lead a prayer service or preside over a religious ceremony. Today, every mosque has an imam. Here, the term, imam, is used in a different context from that mentioned above. An imam is a respected member of the community who is recognized for his piety and knowledge; he leads the prayer service and provides a Friday sermon (see Alsaif, 2007; Aslan, 2006; Esposito, 2002; Martin, 2003).

It is important to interject here that the ulama is not unique to Shia Islam. The term ulama is associated with all Muslim men of extensive religious learning. They initially studied at a *madrassa*, an informal Islamic religious school. These men went beyond merely memorizing the Quran though. They studied the subject in greater depth and were identified by their community for their religious learning. They became the guardians of the beliefs, values, and practices of the umma. Some became noted as famous theological scholars, while others were noted for their legal scholarship and were referred to as jurists. The elite among the ulama were called upon to serve as judges in important courts, as teachers at the famous schools, and as preachers in the major mosques.

HISTORICAL DEVELOPMENT OF ISLAM

As mentioned in the Preface and Introduction, Islamic law will not be examined in the context of a single country, but rather it will be viewed in the manner in which it has influenced the justice system of a few countries associated with Islam. Three countries have been selected; they are today called: Saudi Arabia, Iran, and Turkey. Each was selected because the overwhelming majority of their populations are Muslim, but also because each has embraced Islam in distinct ways. Some of the distinctions are based on the cultural traditions of each country that predate the arrival of Islam; some are based on when Islam was received and how Islam evolved in the geographical areas that we call Saudi Arabia, Iran, and Turkey. In light of this, a brief sketch is presented of the historical reception of Islam to these three regions.

The Arabian Peninsula

In pre-Islamic times, the Arabian Peninsula was inhabited by Bedouins, whose culture was based on a patriarchal tribal social structure. The various tribes initially created unwritten rules that over time established customary laws for a tribe. A single executive and legislative authority, as we use those terms today, did not exist. As a result, there was no organization for the administration of a central government in general or for criminal justice in particular. Law and order was based on rules established by the tribes.

Much of the region consisted of a vast desert terrain, and its significance to the rest of the known world was limited to that of providing important trade routes, especially when the principal empires in the region—Persian and Byzantium—were at war with one another. During the fourth, fifth, and sixth centuries, however, these empires experienced a period of peaceful coexistence. As a result, the significance of the region for trade routes declined somewhat. With regard to religion, it should be noted that the Zoroastrain faith was dominant in Persia, while Christianity was establishing a strong foothold in Byzantium. Both of these, along with the Jewish faith, were more sophisticated than the primitive pagan practices of the Arab region. Through the various trade routes across the peninsula, Arabs were becoming familiar with these religions.

In or around the year 570, Muhammad was born in the small market town of Mecca. His family were members of the Quraysh tribe. When Muhammad was about 40 years of age, it is said that he began to receive messages from God through the angel Gabriel. For Muhammad these were God's final revelations to humankind. Because of his monotheistic beliefs, he was associated with the prophets of the Jewish and Christian religions. Both of these religions had small communities within the Arabian Peninsula. While Muhammad began to gather around him a small group of followers, most people in the Arabian Peninsula in general and his Quraysh tribe in particular worshipped multiple gods. As such, they rejected his message, which caused him to leave Mecca and move to Medina, an oasis community. In time the people of Mecca would accept Muhammad's message and welcomed him back.

According to one scholar, "Muhammad worked to create a community based on shared religious beliefs, ... which would transcend the traditional social structure based on families, clans, and tribes and would unite disparate groups into a new Arabian society." He further pointed out that the "idea of the family was at the core of the Muslim conception of the individual person and the umma, the community of believers. The family ideals reinforced the concept of individuality by stressing the religious importance of individuals as God's creatures rather than as mere objects in the clan system of society, and by stressing the individual's responsibility for moral relations within the family" (Lapidus, 2002). It is important to note that the Middle East is another region of the world where there is a long cultural tradition in which the group is more important than the individual. This is a very significant cultural feature that impacts personal responsibility in general and issues associated with criminal justice in particular.

While creating his community of believers in Medina, Muhammad established the first Islamic government. It has been pointed out by one scholar that unlike the founder of Christianity, Jesus of Nazareth, who said: "Render therefore unto Caesar the things which are Caesar's; and unto God the things that are God's" (Matthew 22:21), Muhammad was establishing an Islamic state that would be ruled by God's messenger, Muhammad, on behalf of God. Thus, whereas Christianity made a distinction between the functions of the imperium and sacredotium, Muhammad did not acknowledge such a division. His state would be governed by a law found in a new scripture that was designed to supplant the two previous religious testaments revealed by this same God.

That scholar has also pointed out:

> There is thus a crucial difference between the career of Muhammad and those of his predecessors, Moses and Jesus, as portrayed in the writings of their followers. Moses was not permitted to enter the promised land, and died while his people went forward. Jesus was crucified, and Christianity remained a persecuted minority religion for centuries, until a Roman emperor, Constantine, embraced the faith and empowered those who upheld it. Muhammad conquered his promised land, and during his lifetime achieved victory and power in this world, exercising political as well as prophetic authority. As the Apostle of God, he brought and taught a religious revelation. But at the same time, as the head of the Muslim Umma, he promulgated laws, dispensed justice, collected taxes, conducted diplomacy, made war, and made peace. The Umma, which began as a community, had become a state. It would soon become an empire (Lewis, 1996).

Thus, this was a religious reform movement with a difference. Its leader set out to conquer territory and to preach his spiritual message. The spread of Islam throughout the Arabian Peninsula set the stage for a rapid expansion beyond these borders. Islam would extend its reach throughout the Middle East and beyond to include northern Africa and Spain. While this was carried out by conquest and colonization, a number of scholars have indicated that the objective was not to impose this new faith by force, for the Quran clearly states: "There is no compulsion in religion" (2:256).

When Muhammad died in 632, his reform movement was still limited to the Arabian Peninsula. The caliphs that succeeded him continued the military expeditions that he had initiated. By the end of the reign of the second caliph, Umar, Arabs controlled all of the Arabian Peninsula and areas in the Persian and Byzantium empires that are known today as Iran, Iraq, Syria, and Egypt. By the middle of the seventh century, the political climate in the region had been transformed in a unique way, and it was the direct result of God's revelation to Muhammad. As Islam spread through Arab conquest, so also did the Arab language. The Quran was the first book written in Arabic. Arabs were given a heightened status because Islam originated in their region. It should also be noted that it was during the reigns of the first four caliphs that the introduction of Islamic law or Sharia began to develop through the interpretation of the Quran. Finally, many of the early converts to Islam tended to live in urban areas. As their numbers grew, Islamic institutions were established. Among the most notable were the mosque and law court. The emergence of these courts will be discussed below.

The Arab empire that had been created as a result of these military conquests was short-lived, however. Like most empires, it failed because of internal decay, which is frequently precipitated by a combination of internal political, social, and economic factors coupled with an external superior military threat. Through various battles in 749 and 750, the Arab Umayyad dynasty was defeated by the Persian leader, Abu'l-'Abbas, which established the Abbasid Caliphate. With this development the center of political power moved from Medina to Baghdad. Of course, the spiritual center would remain in Mecca, the site of Kaba. Nevertheless, the Arabian Peninsula receded in significance until oil was discovered and it became a significant resource in the twentieth century.

Persia

Persia had a long and famous cultural tradition that extended back to the Achaemenids dynasty that ruled from 559–330 BCE. Among the famous rulers associated with this ancient dynasty were: Cyrus II, Darius I, and Xerxes I. It was the Sasanian Dynasty (224–651 CE) of the Persian Empire that was weakened by prolonged wars with the Byzantine Empire that ultimately led to its defeat by the Arabs. In the 650s, Arab culture was in the ascendancy throughout the region, and many Persians converted to Islam. In spite of this change in faith, Persians retained their language and their long-standing cultural traditions. While they may have embraced Islam, they were not Arabs but Persians. One hundred years after their defeat in 651, the fortunes of war were reversed with the creation of the Abbasid Caliphate. This dynasty would remain in power until 1258.

For our purposes, Persia was important in the development of Islam because of its cultural and intellectual traditions that were enhanced further by the fertilization of Greek and Roman ideas. Two examples, which are intimately related and intertwined at times, will suffice to illustrate both this tradition and its continued significance that has evolved up to the present time. One deals with politics and political theory, while the other example focuses on the long-standing significant place of religion in Persian culture and society.

Ever since the death of the Prophet Muhammad, there was an ongoing debate over who was the legitimate ruler of the umma, the community of believers. Initially, the umma was small and highly localized in Medina. At the time of his death, however, Muhammad had established an Islamic state that was essentially within the boundaries of the Arabian Peninsula. With further military conquests by succeeding caliphs, an Islamic empire had been created that extended well beyond the geographical confines of Arabia. The principal participants in this leadership debate were members of the ulama, the religious scholars. They had long been acknowledged as the only legitimate authority to offer guidance on governance, for it was the ulama who had undertaken long years of study of the Quran and Sunna.

At issue in this leadership debate was not only who should be the legitimate ruler, but also what should be the extent of the leader's authority. One of the more fruitful areas for this debate occurred in Baghdad, a center of intellectual activity. Two of the contributors to this debate were Abu Al-Hasan Al-Mawardi (972–1058) and Abu Hamid Muhammad al-Ghazali (1058–1111). Al-Mawardi had a distinguished career in the service of the Abbasid Caliphate, which began with a judgeship, progressed to Chief Justice at Baghdad, and also led to ambassadorial service. He was noted for making scholarly contributions as a jurist, sociologist, and political scientist. Al-Mawardi favored a powerful caliphate and indicated that support for this position could be found in the Quran: "You who believe, obey God and the Messenger, and those in authority among you" (4:59). The ultimate purpose of the caliphate was to protect the umma and administer justice that was based on Islamic jurisprudence.

In the matter of the extent of the leader's authority, a good deal of tension developed over the authority of the ruler and the specific role of the ulama, who were considered the guardians of Islam. Abu Hamid Muhammad al-Ghazali contributed to this issue. He was a scholar who wrote a number of books on such diverse subjects as theology, philosophy, psychology, science, and jurisprudence. From al-Ghazali's perspective, the caliphate consisted of three parts or duties. First, the caliphate was the appropriate successor to the Prophet as the political leader of the umma. Second, the caliph was also responsible for the administration of government and the military. Finally, the caliph had a duty to guard and defend the faith. Al-Ghazali was of the opinion that each of these responsibilities should be placed in the care of a single person, the caliph. If this was not possible, the caliph should retain the position of successor to the Prophet and the remaining duties should be distributed to others in positions of leadership. The role of the ulama was always that of guardian of the beliefs and practices of Islam. The issue over the amount of power accorded the secular political leaders and the authority granted to the religious leaders of Islam was not resolved in the tenth century, although the debates did help to clarify the issue. As empires emerged and then declined, and as nation states were parceled out of these old empires with populations overwhelmingly Muslim, the issues of power and authority were addressed, and they continue to be addressed in a number of contexts up to the present time.

How this aforementioned political debate specifically played out in Persia and later Iran can be traced in part to the long-standing significant place of religion in Persian culture and society. For our purposes, the significant role of religion for Persia began with Zoroastrianism. Zoroaster (630?–550 BCE) was a Persian religious prophet who taught a form of monotheism. Rather than believing that there were many gods, which was a much more common belief at the time, he maintained that there were two forces in the world. Ahura Mazda is the Creator who represents the powers of light, good, and order. Ahriman is the Destroyer who represents the powers of darkness, evil, and disorder. The concepts of paradise and hell were important features of this religion. People determined their fate regarding the hereafter by the manner in which they responded to the battle between good and evil on earth. A significant feature of Zoroastrian beliefs was social justice, that is, the ultimate goal of humankind's battle against evil was to improve society for all. It was believed that the elimination of disorder and the establishment of order could be achieved by a powerful king ruling in the name of justice. It is important to note that in this context and period of time the administration of justice was a duty of the king and not a right of an individual. Thus, this religion had not only a spiritual dimension but also a social and political mission. The first king of Persia to acknowledge this religion was Darius I (558?–486 BCE). Zoroastrianism had become the dominant faith in Persia during the period of the Sasanian dynasty and served an important role in supporting the role of the king throughout the Persian Empire. It has been suggested that the "Persian theory of kingship was basically religious… [It] had introduced a kind of state Church, which in turn sanctified the royal power, and took an active part in social and political life" (Lewis, 1996).

Shia Islam, which was explained earlier, emerged as a distinct but small sect in the late ninth century and had devout followers throughout the Islamic world. It was in Persia, however, where a significant number of followers were found, and Persia's rich intellectual tradition enabled the nurturing and development of the Shia sect of Islam. It would eventually become the state religion of Iran in 1501, when the Safavid dynasty (1501–1736) established it as such. Thus, it has been suggested that "Islam broke the centuries-old Zoroastrian bond between subject and ruler, faith and state. In its place, Muslims were called to commit to something greater than the state—the Ummah, the community of believers whose only boundaries are faith" (Mackey, 1996).

Over time, there emerged the belief among the Shia community that the ulama, the religious scholars, were the only legitimate authority to offer guidance on governance. As noted earlier, although the ulama were not mandated to govern, they were to offer moral and ethical guidance to the Shia community. Within this community, the ulama established a clerical hierarchy that assumed the legitimate mantle of authority to offer guidance on governance. This clerical hierarchy is a unique feature of Shia Islam, for Sunni Muslims, who represent the largest number of adherents to the Islamic faith, do not subscribe to a clerical hierarchy. The role of religious leaders in the Iranian Revolution of 1979 and the subsequent creation of the Islamic Republic of Iran illustrate the most recent chapter in the debate surrounding the amount of power accorded the secular political leaders and the authority granted to the religious leaders of Islam.

The Ottoman Empire

A noted scholar on the history of the Arab world pointed out:

> By the end of the tenth century there had come into existence an Islamic world, united by a common religious culture expressed in the Arabic language, and by human links which trade, migration and pilgrimage had forged. This world was no longer embodied in a single political unit, however. There were three rulers claiming the title of caliph, in Baghdad, Cairo and Cordoba, and others who were in fact rulers of independent states. This is not surprising. To have kept so many countries, with differing traditions and interests, in a single empire for so long had been a remarkable achievement. It could scarcely have been done without the force of religious conviction, which had formed an effective ruling group in western Arabia, and had then created an alliance of interests between that group and an expanding section of the societies over which it ruled (Hourani, 1991).

By the eleventh century, however, another group, the Turks, was moving across the northern frontiers of the Islamic empire. Turkish military slaves had been used in Islam since the eighth century. Now Turks were migrating into Islamic territory and converting to Islam. One group, led by the Seljuk family, was noted for their military prowess. The leader of the family, Tughrul, assumed the title of sultan following his conquest of Baghdad. This illustrated not only his political right to rule as a king but also was claiming the Islamic right to be the defender of the Islamic faith. It was noted that "Turkish Islam was dedicated from the start to the defence or advancement of the faith and power of Islam, and never lost this militant quality" (Lewis, 1996). To illustrate, it was largely Turkish-led armies that fought the medieval European crusaders who sought to recapture the Christian religious sites in and around Jerusalem. As a result of a number of factors, the caliphate was being eclipsed by the Ottoman sultanate.

The conquests would continue under Ottoman sultans. They conquered Constantinople in 1453, which had been the capital of the Byzantine Empire. They seized Athens in 1458, Damascus in 1516, Cairo in 1517, Baghdad in 1534, and Tripoli in 1551. In 1529, they had reached the outskirts of Vienna and were a threat to that city for more than a century. In light of these developments, it is understandable why devout Muslims would view so many successes as proof that they had a sacred duty to continue to expand their true faith over more regions of the world. While retaining the use of their Turkish language, the Ottomans succeeded in centralizing their administrative governing authority and with expanding the size of the Islamic empire through military expeditions. The Western world had not seen such dominance since the time of the Roman Empire.

Scholars have often commented on the large bureaucratic state that was created and that enabled the Empire to operate for so long. One summarized it in this manner: "Ottoman rule was based upon a mixture of imperial and patrimonial modes of governance" (Sunar, 2004). The sultan was at the top of this governing hierarchy. He relied upon two groups to administer the day-to-day functions of the empire. The military corps already had a long tradition among the Turkish people; the development of a civil service bureaucracy benefited from Persian influences. Of course, the sultan had a fundamental duty to defend and protect the Islamic faith. Because Islam was not organized along the lines of a church with a bureaucracy, the sultan recognized the ulama as a third element in the administration of the empire. They were the official guardians of the beliefs and practices of Islam.

The height of the Ottoman Empire was between the sixteenth and eighteenth centuries. This empire, with its capital in Istanbul, had come to dominate all Arab-speaking countries. It has been suggested that the "Turks consider the Ottoman period to have been a golden age of ethnic harmony and cultural diversity" (Kinzer, 2001). Three languages dominated the Middle East: Arabic, Persian, and Turkish. Each contributed in its way to the administrative, legal, religious, and secular culture of the region. The principal centers of power were Turkey, Iran, and Egypt. It would be the Ottoman Empire that was "the last great expression of the universality of the world of Islam" (Hourani, 1991).

The Ottoman Empire began its decline in the nineteenth century. The decline "was due not so much to internal changes as to their inability to keep pace with the rapid advances of the West in science and technology, in the arts of both war and peace, and in government and commerce" (Lewis, 1996). One example will illustrate the dilemma facing the empire. From its inception, the Ottoman Empire employed three sources of law. First and foremost was Sharia, the Islamic law, derived from the Quran and Sunna. Second were the rules and principles established to address issues that were not explained in the Sharia. The very process of creating these rules, however, was guided by the Quran. A third source of law was official rulings or directives to cope with various social circumstances at a particular time and a specific place in the vast empire. A fourth source of law emerged during the nineteenth century. As a result of the importance of commercial enterprises and the borrowing of scientific and technological advances from the West, the empire sought additional assistance with nagging problems in other areas of governance. Initially, the empire adopted legal ideas from the codes of European countries. By the late nineteenth century and with specific reference to criminal justice, they were adopting a Penal Code (1857) and a Code of Criminal Procedure (1879) that was based on the contemporary legal codes of France.

This has been a very brief sketch of the historical reception of Islam to the regions that we now call Saudi Arabia, Iran, and Turkey. We will return to these three countries later in this chapter in order to examine the role that Islamic law plays in the contemporary context of each country. First, it is important to provide the reader with an orientation to Islamic law in general and its application to issues associated with criminal justice in particular.

SHARIA

Historical Development

The primary objective of the Prophet Muhammad was religious reform and not the transformation of the customary traditions of Arabia (Khadduri, 1961). Those in opposition to Muhammad maintained that he was indeed violating the tenets of the established law. At the time, religion and law were interrelated in Arabia, as was the case in most primitive societies. It was difficult to suggest that one was reforming one without impacting the other. To illustrate, Muhammad claimed he was simply replacing the idols that had been worshipped in the past with the one true God, Allah. Idolatry, however, was part of the customary tradition of Arabia.

During the early formative years of Islam's development, law emerged from the decisions of the Prophet and upon his death by his political successors, the caliphs. As a result of these decisions and a familiarity with the Quran and Sunna, jurisprudential debates arose over the interpretation of law in the Muslim community. From these debates emerged the theory that the Sharia was "the comprehensive and preordained system of God's commands, a system of law having an existence independent of society, not growing out of society but imposed upon society from above"(Coulson, 1969).

Upon the death of the Prophet in 632, the caliphs led a series of military campaigns that significantly expanded the geographical region associated with Islam. These conquests were instrumental in the development of Islamic law. The decrees of the early caliphs introduced answers to some legal problems that confronted them in their new territories. Caliphs could initiate legal rules that were outside the realm of Sharia, for the Quran gave them that authority: "You who believe, obey God and the Messenger, and those in authority among you" (4:59). Issues that tended to deal with a specific local problem, however, were resolved through the customs and legal traditions of the local community.

The caliphs were interested in the introduction of Islamic law, for it was considered both a code of law and a code of morals. Thus, a distinction was not made between the two concepts. The Quran, in particular, is the fundamental vehicle that defines what is appropriate in the Islamic community of believers. Various Quranic verses clearly illustrate what is right and wrong or what is proper or inappropriate. For example, "[T]hey say, 'Trade and usury are the same,' but God has allowed trade and forbidden usury"(2:275–276); "You who believe, intoxicants and gambling, idolatrous practices and [divining with] arrows are repugnant acts" (5:90); and "Do not go near the orphan's property, except with the best [intentions], until he reaches the age of maturity" (17:34).

In Islamic society, religious morality was instilled in people through both religious teachers and preachers but also by public officials, like the Muhtasib, the market inspector, who had some authority to sanction law violators. Islamic law established "the code of life for the Muslim community, covering religious obligations (*ibahat*) as well as social relations (*muamalat*). Thus, law (*fiqh*) plays a more vital role in Islamic society than that played by modern or secular law in western societies"(see Kamel, in Bassiouni, 1982).

For the most part, the caliphs retained the administrative organization that existed in the territories that they conquered. The local chiefs of police and judges that were appointed by the provincial administrator and given the authority to hold a court to adjudicate local disputes were expected to utilize local law or custom to resolve issues. It should be noted that in addition to local customs, some of these new territories had been previously influenced by Roman, Byzantine, and Persian legal ideas. Moreover, because there was no hierarchy of courts from which a local judge could seek guidance, he was left to his own discretion in deciding disputes. Initially, the extent to which Islamic legal norms were integrated into legal decisions was totally dependent on the extent to which the judge understood Islamic law. Even with an understanding of the Quran, the legal verses were still often subject to interpretation when confronting the facts in a specific case. Thus, the judge was still dependent on his discretion. In light of this situation, legal historians of Islam questioned whether the law of the Quran was actually being implemented in these newly conquered territories.

While there were no appellate judges in a court hierarchy, a dissatisfied litigant could appeal a judgment to the head of state. When the sovereign elected to sit as a court himself or through his designate, it was known as the court of *mazalim* (complaints). This was based on the notion that the ruler, whether a caliph or a sultan, had a responsibility to correct any wrong and ultimately to guarantee justice to all his people. In the context of criminal cases, the political authority or the delegate exercised a legal prerogative to resolve an apparent wrong that had occurred in an Islamic court. There were no rules or texts that defined the limits of the jurisdiction of mazalim. Whereas judges in the regular Islamic courts were bound by rules based on Islamic law, mazalim judges were free to exercise their discretion beyond such procedural or evidentiary rules in order to achieve the goal of righting a wrong.

The criminal law was singled out as a facet of law in which the jurisdiction had been essentially delegated to the police by the *wali al-jara'im*, who was the official authorized to handle criminal offenses by the political leader. Thus, criminal law became a particular focus of mazalim jurisdiction. Senior police could hold a court, and they often ignored the procedural rules established by the Sharia. For example, they entertained the use of circumstantial evidence; they heard the testimony of questionable witnesses; they imprisoned suspects; and they extorted confessions. While the police courts could apply the punishments of Hudud offenses (which are explained below), they were not required to do so if the Sharia standards of proof were not met. These highly flexible criminal procedural standards enabled them to use a good deal of discretion when determining an appropriate sanction for the convicted offender (Coulson, 1964). Thus, very early in the development of Islam there was a dual court system. One court was clearly Islamic and was presided over by an Islamic judge that handled a host of legal issues, especially those that related to family law (marriage, divorce, and inheritance). The other court was of local origin and dealt with local issues, often assuming in particular the responsibility for issues associated with criminal offenses.

It has been pointed out that there emerged a tension among the jurists, the Islamic legal scholars, who were the guardians of the ideal interpretation of Sharia and how the law was actually interpreted in practice in the various courts that existed throughout the expanding Islamic territories (Coulson, 1969). At issue was the fact that Sharia represented the ideal order of things for Islam, but the political rulers of Islamic territories had to be concerned with practical matters associated with the community of believers or what we would today call the public interest.

By the eleventh century, the tension began to dissipate. The notion of mazalim courts and judges eventually led to the development of the doctrine of *siyasa* (administrative justice policy). Essentially, siyasa permitted the sovereign a good deal of authority in the administration of justice. It is important to remember that this doctrine was embraced because it was assumed that the sovereign was ideally qualified to serve in his capacity. The most significant qualification was a degree of religious piety and an understanding of God's purpose for the community of believers.

One of the early responsibilities that the political leaders assumed under the doctrine of siyasa and focused on was the development of criminal procedural rules. While a procedural process could conform to cultural and societal norms, it ultimately had to be in compliance with Sharia. The term *siyasa sharia* means an administration of justice policy that is essentially in conformity with Sharia. Therefore, a distinction was made between Sharia and siyasa. Sharia is that blend of both a code of law and a code of morals. Siyasa sharia is the method of introducing practical pragmatic policies for the administration of justice that are in conformity with the spirit of Sharia, especially when Sharia does not provide specific guidance.

Many contemporary scholars maintain that Islamic law has a rich and important history that introduced concepts and principles that would not be achieved in other legal systems for hundreds of years. For example, they maintain that the idea of equal treatment before the law was introduced to Muslim societies at the beginning of the Islamic era. In pre-Islamic Arab society, customary criminal law placed more severe sanctions on the accused if his victim was of a higher social rank, which was obviously associated with wealth and power. With regard to a retributive sanction, an entire tribe might suffer the consequences of the crimes of one of their tribe because of the collective responsibility of the tribe for its members. With the advent of Islam, Muslims were guided by Quranic verses that such societal distinctions were no longer applicable. For example, "People, We created you all from a single man and a single woman, and made you into races and tribes so that you should recognize one another. In God's eyes, the most honoured of you are the ones most mindful of Him: God is all knowing, all aware" (49:13). As such, the laws of Islam did not permit the gradation of sanctions based on the social rank of the perpetrator or the victim.

Madhahib

It has been pointed out that: "The first 150 years of Islam were characterized by an almost untrammeled freedom of juristic reasoning in the solution of problems not specifically regulated by divine revelation" (Coulson, 1969). In the eighth century, however, there emerged conflict in Islamic jurisprudence. The basis for the conflict was the tension between divine revelation from Islamic scriptural sources and human reason associated with legal questions and practical cases. This tension was central to the debates and emergence of Islamic legal theory. From these disagreements emerged an acknowledgment to establish a coherent Islamic legal doctrine that would be found in the Quran and Sunna. There was also a recognition that legal reasoning had to become more consistent and less arbitrary. This would lead to the use of analogical deduction.

Unlike the common law of England, which was originally based on case law decisions of the judiciary, Islamic law was developed by jurists, the legal scholars of Islam. Initially, the term *sunna* was employed to speak in a general way of established practices of the community of believers and those of the Companions. It has been pointed out that the Sunna of the Prophet Muhammad was introduced as legal theory by jurists at the end of the seventh century, and by the end of the eighth century the juristic use of the term Sunna was in reference solely to the Prophet. It should also be noted that originally, hadith was a narration of some act of the Prophet, while Sunna was an example or law that could be deduced from a hadith. Hadith also was used to cite statements attributed to the Companions and their Successors. Eventually, hadith was only used when mentioning an act or saying of the Prophet. As a result, the distinction between Sunna and hadith was eliminated (Kamali, (1989).

Initially, there were many *madhahib* (singular, madhhab) or schools of Islamic law. They existed throughout the expanding territories of Islam and participated in the debates on legal theory. Two of the central features associated with the debates focused on jurisprudential methods. The first of these was the importance and emphasis placed on established doctrines that were gleaned from the Quran and Sunna. The second was a significant reliance on reasoning based on analogical deduction rather than the arbitrary views of judges that were expressed in court decisions.

Historians consider the formative period of the development of Islamic law between the seventh and ninth centuries, and this coincides with the emergence of two major schools of Islamic legal theory in the late eighth century. One school was located in Kufa and was therefore influenced by Persian ideas, while the other school was located at Medina, a significant city in Arabia. In addition to Arab and Persian influences on Islamic legal theory, contact with the Byzantine Empire brought another dimension to the discussions on law. Ultimately, Islamic law was developed through the doctrines of the jurists and appeared in medieval texts. It has been suggested that by the tenth century "the law was cast in a rigid mould from which it did not really emerge until the twentieth century" (Coulson, 1964).

Since the fifteenth century, four legal schools in Sunni Islam have continued to exist. What follows is a brief sketch of these schools. The sketches are followed by some examples of how these schools either agree or disagree when addressing various legal issues.

Hanafi The Hanafi madhhab was founded by Abu-Hanifa (d. 767), who was open to ideas from other legal systems. Given the ongoing territorial spread of Islam at the time and in light of local conditions, this school favored the freedom to recognize supplementary sources of law. This school originated in Kufa, an urban center, and was influenced by Persian ideas. The jurisprudential approach to Sharia of the Hanafi madhhab was adopted by the Abbasid dynasty (750–1258) of Islam. The Hanafi madhhab came to dominate much of the Middle East region. Today, this encompasses Turkey, Syria, Lebanon, Iraq, Jordan, and Egypt in addition to India.

Maliki Medinan scholar Malik ibn-Anas (d. 796) produced the first compendium of Islamic law. His name is associated with the Maliki madhhab. It is noted for adhering closely to the traditions of Arabian tribal society. It also favors recognizing supplementary sources of law in the name of the public interest. The Maliki madhhab is noted for emphasizing a moralistic approach to law, and it is dominant in various regions of Africa.

Shafii Muhammad ibn-Idris ash-Shafi-i (767–820) was noted for his theory of the sources from which law is derived. His treatise, *Risala*, states this theory. According to Shafi-i, there are four principal sources of Islamic law. The first source was obviously the Quran. He interpreted the Quranic verses that commanded devout Muslims to obey God and to obey the Prophet to mean that Muhammad was also a source of law, albeit a secondary source when compared to God. The pronouncement that Muhammad was a lawgiver was an important theme in Shafi-i's treatise. The second source was the Sunna of Muhammad, which displaced the sunnas of local legal schools. Thus, instead of multiple sunnas representing various schools, there was now recognized in this theory a single Sunna, that of Muhammad. The third source was *ijma* or consensus.

Shafi-i rejected the authority of a single school to establish a consensus. From his perspective, a consensus must be reached among the entire community of Islamic scholars. The fourth source was reasoning by *ijtihad* or analogy. This method was employed to resolve issues in which the other sources did not provide an answer; however, the other sources should serve as a guide in the resolution of an issue. This source of Islamic law is considered strikingly significant by today's scholars, because it has enabled Islamic legal scholars to develop new theories of law. This is especially pertinent with the development of modern fields of law. While Shafi'i's theory acknowledged the obvious importance of God's will in law, he enhanced the status of human reason through the resolution of legal issues. The Shafii madhhab dominates southern Arabia, east Africa, and South East Asia.

Hanbali Ahmad ibn-Hanbal (d. 855) collected hadiths into a work titled *Musnad*. He rejected human reason as a source of law and claimed all legal rules could be found in either the Quran or the Sunna of the Prophet. Thus, the followers of this school rejected judicial reasoning by analogy. They were of the opinion that the prophet's Sunna, in particular, was being compromised through the broadening of the sources of Islamic law by the other schools. They strongly favored the traditional approaches or sources of Islamic law and focused on both the legal and moral teachings that could be derived from the Quran. This madhhab did not dominate a region until it was adopted by the Wahhabi movement in the eighteenth century. It then became the official interpreter of Sharia in Saudi Arabia.

There was agreement among the four madhahib regarding the principal tenets of the Islamic faith, the Five Pillars of Islam. There was also a consensus among the schools regarding the political sovereignty in the Islamic state. All supported the doctrine of the Caliphate, that the successor to Muhammad would be the political leader of the Islamic community, and the caliph would assume this position following his election by the qualified representatives of the community of believers. Moreover, his authority would be limited by law. There were differences among the schools, however, when interpreting the actual implementation of certain laws. A few examples that relate to criminal law and procedure should illustrate these differences.

For instance, the Quran states that: "... if anyone repents after his wrongdoing and makes amends, God will accept his repentance: God is most forgiving, most merciful" (5:39). Jurists differed on how this verse should be interpreted. While the Hanifa madhhab maintained that repentance did not eliminate punishment in this life, but only in the hereafter, the Shafii madhhab were of the opinion that repentance meant the elimination of punishment in this life and the hereafter. In reference to the conditions of witnesses, Islamic law established certain standards that potential witnesses were required to meet before they were permitted to testify in court. One of the standards was that the witness must be able to speak. The madhahib had varying opinions on the testimony of people who could not speak or hear. The Malik and Hanbali madhahib accepted the written testimony of a person who could not speak, whereas the Hanafi madhhab rejected the testimony.

On the subject of confessions, the Hanafi madhhab maintained that a valid confession had to occur in court, whereas the Maliki, Shafii, and Hanbali madhahib were of the opinion that a confession was valid outside of court, if there were two witnesses to the testimony. In reference to compensation as a legal punishment, it was considered a payment by the perpetrator, as a ransom for a lost life or an injury received. In cases of murder, however, it was argued by some that if the perpetrator was to undergo the penalty of retribution, the victim's family could not impose upon him a demand for compensation. The Shafii and Hanbali madhahib disagreed with that position and maintained that a murderer was obliged to pay compensation if the victim's family demanded it. On another matter, the Shafii madhhab employed ijtihad to justify inflicting the penalty of stoning for sodomy. The other schools claimed that this was not necessary, because the legal definition of fornication already included sodomy.

Finally, in the matter of wine drinking as an offense, the various madhahib had been in disagreement over whether it should be expanded to include other alcoholic beverages and other drugs. In addition, the Hanafi and Maliki madhahib maintain that the sanction for this offense is 80 lashes, but the Shafii madhhab is of the opinion that the penalty should be 40 lashes. They make this distinction based on the practices of the first Caliph, Abu Bakr, and the fourth Caliph, Ali.

Legal Theory and Shia Islam There is agreement between Sunni Islam and Shia Islam regarding the principal tenets of the Islamic faith, the Five Pillars of Islam. With regard to law, Shia Islam maintains that the Quran established a new legal system. The principal sources of Shia law are the Quran and Sunna. As such, customary law was eliminated, unless it was supported in the Quran. One of the major distinctions between Shia Islam and Sunni Islam is associated with legal sovereignty. Sunni Islam supported the doctrine of the Caliphate, that is, the successor to Muhammad would be the political leader of the Islamic community, and the caliph would assume this position following his election by the qualified representatives of the community of believers. Moreover, his authority would be limited by law. With regard to legal sovereignty, the Shia Imam had supreme authority of the divine lawgiver. The difference politically has been characterized as that between a constitutional form versus an absolute form of government. Finally, a significant difference with Sunni Islam is in the area of inheritance. Whereas Sunni Islam emphasized the customary law of the tribal heirs, that is, the male agnate relatives of the deceased person. The inheritance law in Shia Islam emphasized the immediate family. It was based on the closeness of the deceased to the relationship. Moreover, gender was irrelevant under this legal interpretation. Shia legal theory has been dominant in Iran, India, East Africa, and Iraq.

Sources of Sharia

Islamic law is characterized as a series of standards that are religious and moral in nature and that are designed to establish and to explain appropriate conduct of the believers of Islam. As the Quran proclaims: "Be a community that calls for what is good, urges what is right, and forbids what is wrong: those who do this are the successful ones" (3:104). Thus, Islamic law emphasizes a series of duties rather than focusing on rights, which is often a major concern of legal systems in the West. The principal sources of the Sharia are the Quran and Sunna.

Quran Throughout the Quran there are several verses that provide the devout Muslim with an explanation for the legitimacy of Islamic law. For example, scholars cite: "Authority belongs to God alone, and He orders you to worship none but Him: this is the true faith, though most people do not realize it" (12:40), and "Follow what has been sent down to you from your Lord; do not follow other masters beside Him"(7:3).

By extension, the legitimate authority bestowed on the agents of the theocratic community are also noted. One was specifically directed at Muhammad: "So [Prophet] judge between them according to what God has sent down. Do not follow their whims, and take good care that they do not tempt you away from any of what God has sent down to you" (5:49). Scholars have interpreted that other verses are directed at state leaders and those authorized specifically to adjudicate civil and criminal disputes. To illustrate,

> You who believe, obey God and the Messenger, and those in authority among you (4:59);
>
> Those who do not judge according to what God has sent down are rejecting [God's teachings] (5:44);
>
> Those who do not judge according to what God has revealed are doing grave wrong (5:45); and
>
> Those who do not judge according to what God has revealed are lawbreakers (5:47).

It is important to point out that the Quran is not a constitutional document or legal code. The Quran clearly states: "This [revelation] is a means of insight for people, a source of guidance and mercy for those of sure faith" (45:20). The Quran is a blueprint for establishing a civilized society that speaks to such notions as fairness and compassion. Because it is a source of guidance, many of the legal-oriented verses are presented as general principles in recognition that societal conditions might change. The Quran is specific, however, with regard to issues that are considered immutable (Kamali, 1989). The distinction between general principles and that which is immutable will become clear when explaining the range of crimes and corresponding punishments.

It was mentioned earlier that the Quran consists of 6,342 verses and that scholars often differ over how many verses deal with legal issues. The debate ranges from 350 to 500. Those verses that are clearly legal in nature usually begin with either a command to enhance the security of the Muslim community or a prohibition to prevent acts that are detrimental to the well-being of Islamic society. In order to comprehend the meaning of the legal verses, Muslims relied on the analysis of jurists, scholars of Islamic law.

Sunna *Sunna* or established practice is also considered a scriptural source for Muslims. The Quran states: "accept whatever the Messenger gives you, and abstain from whatever he forbids you" (59:7). The Sunna consists of the spoken words of Muhammad and deeds attributed to him that were reported by authoritative sources. Whereas the Quran is the revealed Word of God, the Sunna is another source that is both sacred and divinely inspired. The Quran proclaims: "Obey God; obey the Messenger" (24:54). Upon Muhammad's death, the significance of the Sunna was enhanced in guiding the Islamic community. It has been suggested: "The Sunna plays its significant role as a source of Islamic law either by complementing the Quran or by interpreting its texts"(Sanad, 1991).

For our purposes, the Sunna can be divided between legal and nonlegal criteria. For the most part, the nonlegal consists of the normal everyday activities of the Prophet that had nothing to do with Islamic law. The legal consists of the verbal, practical, and approved that address or explain some aspect of Islamic law found in the Quran. As mentioned earlier, the verbal are the sayings of the Prophet Muhammad; the practical are the actual deeds of the prophet; and the approved are the actions or sayings of the Companions that the Prophet approved. These legal explanations occurred either in the prophet's capacity as messenger of God, as head of state, or as judge. It should also be noted that reference to the hadiths by the founders of the major legal schools reinforced the importance of the Sunna.

Ijma In the early years (roughly the seventh through the ninth centuries), when Islam was establishing its foundation in various geographical areas, there was a good deal of diversity in interpreting Islamic law. Part of this diversity was associated with differences of opinion regarding interpreting the Quran or the context of the Sunna. Part had to do with accommodating the local customary law and procedural customs of tribunals with the introduction of the Sharia. As a result of this diversity, there gradually emerged another source of Islamic law, *ijma*. Ijma is a general consensus about a legal ruling that is reached among jurists, Islamic legal scholars.

In support of the use of ijma, jurists cited the Quranic verse: "[Believers], you are the best community singled out for people: you order what is right, forbid what is wrong, and believe in God" (3:110). A unanimous general consensus among jurists meant that the ruling was binding. Such a consensus, however, could not conflict with rulings based on the superior sources of Islamic law, namely the Quran and Sunna. The Quran is very clear on this point: "if anyone opposes the Messenger, after guidance has been made clear to him, and follows a path other than that of the believers, We shall leave him on his chosen path—We shall burn him in Hell, an evil destination" (4:115). Thus, although inferior to the Quran and Sunna, ijma became another source of Islamic law, as long as it was consistent with the superior sources of law. Of course, a consensus established at one point in time could be overturned with a new consensus. It has been pointed out that a decision based only on ijma was rare (Sanad, 1991).

Ijtihad A final source of Islamic law is *ijtihad* or legal reasoning by analogy. Ijtihad is the process in which jurists determine a rule based on analogy. It is utilized when a rule conflicts with another rule or when a rule is rather vague and somewhat questionable. Moreover, jurists turn to ijtihad when neither the Quran nor the Sunna has specifically addressed the issue at hand. The ultimate goal of ijtihad is to resolve a conflict or clarify an issue that is in the best interests of the Muslim community. Originally, the use of ijtihad led to contentious debates over its validity. Opponents cited the Quranic verse, "We have missed nothing out of the Record ..." (6:38), to justify their position. Proponents, however, also cited the Quran with a rejoinder: "Learn from this, all of you with insight!" (59:2). Ijtihad eventually won the day and is an especially valuable legal source in modern times, because it is the mechanism that allows Islamic law to evolve with time. To illustrate, originally the Quran forbade the drinking of wine, which was common in ancient times. Over time and through ijtihad, all alcoholic beverages were prohibited. More recent translations of the Quran now refer to intoxicants, which enables the inclusion of illegal drugs. Like ijma, ijtihad is not a totally independent source, because it must be consistent with the superior sources of law, namely the Quran and Sunna.

Basic Assumptions

In order to understand Islamic law, it is important to begin with an understanding of two basic assumptions that Muslims embrace. First, God is the sole source of authority and the lawgiver. The Quran states:

> Judgment is for God alone: He tells the truth, and He is the best of judges (6:57);
>
> Your Lord is God, who created the heavens and earth in six Days, then established Himself on the throne; He makes the night cover the day in swift pursuit; He created the sun, moon, and stars to be subservient to His command; all creation and command belongs to Him (7:54); and
>
> Authority belongs to God alone, and he orders you to worship none but Him: this is the true faith, though most people do not realize it (12:40).

While God is the sovereign lawgiver, "God has made a promise to those among you who believe and do good deeds: He will make them successors to the land, as He did those who came before them; He will empower the religion He had chosen for them; He will grant them security to replace their fear" (24:55). This verse has been interpreted as acknowledging that man is God's trustee on earth and thus has the authority to make law, but it must be in conformity with Sharia. Thus, while God is the lawgiver, man has the authority to be a lawmaker. These passages illustrate the basis for the Islamic theocratic state. Obviously, it differs from the modern political tradition of the West that places sovereignty with the people.

The other basic assumption is the emphasis of both the individual and collective moral duties of Muslims. While many Western societies speak to the importance of individual rights, the Quran focuses on community obligations. One of the most important examples of a collective duty is the call of the community to prayer five times a day, but especially on Friday. "Believers! When the call to prayer is made on the day of congregation, hurry towards the reminder of God and leave off your trading—that is better for you, if only you knew—then when the prayer has ended, disperse in the land and seek out God's bounty" (62:9–10). Another is related to the notion of man as a trustee of God on earth. "It was He who created all that is on earth for you" (2:29). Collectively, man has a duty to care for all of God's creations. He has a particular obligation to help maintain the social order of the community. "The believers are brothers, so make peace between your two brothers and be mindful of God, so that you may be given mercy"(49:10). Finally, man has a collective duty to pursue justice. The Quran states: "You who believe, be steadfast in your devotion to God and bear witness impartially: do not let hatred of others lead you away from justice, but adhere to justice, for that is closer to awareness of God" (5:8). Moreover, "God commands justice, doing good, and generosity towards relatives and He forbids what is shameful, blameworthy, and oppressive" (16:90). The importance of community, an obligation to care for one another and all things created, and a duty to pursue justice are lofty objectives. These are among the general assumptions found in the Quran that explain why scholars have referred to it as "a constitution and an organic law which concerns fundamental rights. These general principles are immutable. But particular provisions may be modified as long as they remain subordinate to the spiritual interest of the community" (see Kamel, in Bassiouni, 1982).

Principles of Islamic Criminal Justice

Islamic law deals with a wide range of legal topics that include: the person, property, the family, and inheritance. For our purposes, we focus only on that which relates to crime and the penal law. The aforementioned verse of the Quran points out that "God commands justice." Three principles are gleaned from the Quran that explain how justice is pursued within the realm of Islamic criminal justice. The first principle is that of criminal responsibility. According to contemporary scholars, "Islam guarantees five essential things to all persons and prevents unwarranted infringement of them by the state. These include: (1) religion, (2) life, (3) mind, (4) posterity, and (5) property" (see Abd-el-Malek al-Saleh, in Bassiouni, 1982). Collectively, this is known as the theory of protected interests. Essentially, these scholars maintain that this theory is designed to allow a person to live his or her life with dignity.

In order to benefit from participating in this arrangement with the state, a person was expected to be individually responsible for their actions. The Quran states: "Each soul is responsible for its own actions; no soul will bear the burden of another" (6:164). Thus, an important condition for imposing a punishment on a person was that they intended to commit a criminal act. With reference to criminal justice, the person is also entitled to a degree of security when accused of a crime. It also states, "Whoever does good does it for his own soul and whoever does evil does it against his own soul"(41:46), and "anyone who does wrong will be requited for it and will find no one to protect or help him against God"(4:123). Therefore, a person is responsible only for acts of commission or omission that he or she committed and is not answerable for crimes committed by others. This is a significant change from the ancient notion of collective tribal responsibility, which was the norm in Arab society. But it is important to point out that the collective responsibility of the family was retained with regard to paying any damages for a crime committed by one of its members.

Moreover, degrees of accountability were recognized, based upon the extent to which one participated in a criminal offense; that is, was the person a principal or an accomplice? If a person had not reached the age of majority, he or she could not be held criminally responsible for his or her actions. Thus, legal penalties could not be imposed on children; however, a judge could reprimand young people who had committed a criminal act. Moreover, people with insufficient mental capacity were not held liable. Islamic scholars maintain that the principle of individual responsibility was established in Islamic law much earlier than in other legal systems.

The second principle deals with legality, specifically the issue of crime and punishment. Throughout the Quran, there are countless examples of God refraining from imposing a punishment until he had first told man through a messenger that a specific behavior was wrong. To illustrate, the Quran states: "No soul will bear another's burden, nor do We punish until We have sent a messenger"(17:15). Moreover, a person cannot be punished for acts that were not criminal at the time they were committed. Islamic scholars cite several Quranic verses to support the origin of this principle. Some verses are general announcements of the important role of the messenger. For example, "They were messengers bearing good news and warning, so that mankind would have no excuse before God, once the messengers had been sent: God is almighty and all wise" (4:165), and "This Qur'an was revealed for me to warn you [people] and everyone it reaches" (6:19). Other verses are a bit more specific and clearly warn that certain conduct will lead to punishment:

> Your Lord would never destroy towns without first raising a messenger in their midst to recite Our messages to them, nor would We destroy towns unless their inhabitants were evildoers (28:59); and

> We have sent you with the Truth as a bearer of good news and warning—every community has been sent a warner. If they call you a liar, their predecessors did the same: messengers came to them with clear signs, scriptures, and enlightening revelation and afterwards I seized the disbelievers—how terrible My punishment was! (35:24–26).

As a result of such guidance, jurists concluded that no person could be accused of a crime or suffer punishment unless it was specified in a law. This concept is now well known and embraced in the modern world.

In the context of Islam, only those offenses expressly cited by God the lawgiver and those legislated by the duly authorized lawmakers of a government have the force of law. Like the principle of criminal responsibility, the principle of legality is designed to protect the security of an individual from arbitrary, capricious, and discriminatory intrusions by the government. It is also designed to curb the possible excesses of a judge at the sanctioning phase of a criminal procedure. "Those who do not judge according to what God has revealed are lawbreakers" (5:47). Thus, judges were expected to impose sanctions that were in compliance with the Quran.

The third principle addresses the nonretroactivity of criminal law, which is associated with the principle of legality. Once again, this is designed to protect the individual who may be a recent adherent to Islam and ignorant of the law. We turn to the Quran for examples. On the subject of marriage, "Do not marry women that your fathers married—with the exception of what is past—this is indeed a shameful thing to do, loathsome and leading to evil"(4:22). On the subject of usury, "Trade and usury are the same, but God has allowed trade and forbidden usury. Whoever on receiving God's warning, stops taking usury may keep his past gains—God will be his judge—but whoever goes back to usury will be an inhabitant of the Fire" (2:276). The prohibition against adultery and the drinking of wine are also noted as behavior that did not constitute a crime in the pre-Islamic period but was now deemed forbidden. In modern times, the principle of nonretroactivity tends to focus more on protecting the individual from the abuse of governmental power.

Crime and Punishment

With regard to punishment, the Quran offers a general guideline: "If you [believers] have to respond to an attack, make your response proportionate" (16:126) and "Let harm be requited by an equal harm, though anyone who forgives and puts things right will have his reward from God Himself—He does not like those who do wrong"(42:40). It is important to interject at this point that the sanctions imposed under Islamic law are also considered religious decisions, because they are either directly or indirectly inspired by religious texts. They often not only speak of a temporal punishment for a crime against the community of believers but also indicate that a punishment will be imposed in the hereafter for the sin against God. To illustrate, "if anyone kills a believer deliberately, the punishment for him is Hell, and there he will remain: God is angry with him, and rejects him, and has prepared a tremendous torment for him" (4:93). For the crime of highway robbery or unlawful rebellion, the perpetrator will experience "a disgrace for them in this world, and then a terrible punishment in the Hereafter," (5:33).

With regard to violations of Islamic law, the Quran alerts all Muslims to the consequences of their actions:

> These are the bounds set by God: God will admit those who obey Him and His Messenger to gardens graced with flowing streams, and there they will stay—that is the supreme triumph! But those who disobey God and His Messenger and overstep His limits will be consigned by God to the Fire, and there they will stay—a humiliating torment awaits them! (4:13–14)

The significance of this religious element should not be ignored or overlooked, for it has been pointed out that for the devout Muslim "each person becomes in effect his own judge, with his faith in God preventing him from indulging in forbidden pursuits and doing injury to the rights of others" (see Salim al-'Awwa, in Bassiounu, 1982). What makes the Islamic legal system unique compared to other legal systems is that it traces its origins to divinely inspired sources. Therefore, with regard to criminal justice there is no distinction between the criminal law and the moral law.

Islamic law recognizes two categories of crime and punishment. Determined crimes and the corresponding sanctions refer to those offenses and punishments that have been specified either by God in the Quran or by the Prophet Muhammad in the Sunna. Discretionary crimes are those not mentioned specifically in the aforementioned sources; however, the Quran and Sunna did offer examples of sanctions that are associated with discretionary crimes. As such, scholars note that there is an important relationship with these discretionary offenses and the original sources of Islamic law. Discretionary crimes are categorized as criminal by an appropriate authority and process within an Islamic state.

Hudud Determined crimes are of two types. The crimes of *hudud* (which means limits), in which a *hadd* punishment is imposed, are associated with threatening the social order and security of the community of believers. Because hudud crimes are specified in the Quran or Sunna, the corresponding punishment is also cited. In such a context, a judge is not permitted to exercise discretionary judicial authority that might contradict the punishment found in the sacred texts.

Hudud offenses include: theft, banditry, and rebellion against a legitimate (political) authority, because they threaten public property and security; adultery and fornication, because they threaten the family structure; defamation, because it threatens a person's reputation; apostasy, because it threatens the religious order of the community; and the drinking of wine, because it threatens the moral conduct of individuals. Scholars of Islamic law suggest that the rationale for the sanctions of hudud offenses were an early version of general and specific deterrence.

The sanctions associated with hudud crimes are harsh and are designed to protect the public interest of Muslim society. To illustrate, the Quran clearly states what the hadd (singular for hudud) punishment is for theft: "Cut off the hands of thieves, whether they are man or woman, as punishment for what they have done—a deterrent from God: God is almighty and wise" (5:38). Over time there was a good deal of discussion among jurists, usually after consulting the Sunna, as to when such a sanction could be imposed for theft. For example, the intention to fraudulently take another's property had to be established. It was concluded that the sanction should not be used for petty theft, which was when the value of the item(s) was less than 20 dirhams. The sanction could only be imposed when the theft occurred in a private area rather than a public space. Finally, the sanction would not be imposed if the theft occurred among members of a family.

Banditry or highway robbery and the endangering of public safety through unlawful rebellion were addressed in one Quranic verse: "Those who wage war against God and His messenger and strive to spread corruption in the land should be punished by death, crucifixion, the amputation of an alternate hand and foot, or banishment from the land: a disgrace for them in this world, and then a terrible punishment in the Hereafter"(5:33). The amputation of the right hand and left foot is often associated with highway robbery. In addition, banishment or exile could also be interpreted to mean imprisonment. Given the variety of punishments mentioned, the Maliki madhhab concluded that the judge would determine the sanction in light of the specific criminal act and the person's involvement in the act. The other Sunni madhahib (Hanafi, Shafii, and Hanabli) developed a rank order of sanctions that was dependent on the gravity of the act committed. Accordingly, "If a bandit kills, he will be subject to execution by sword; If he steals money, his hands and feet will be cut off from opposite sides; If he only threatens the travelers and frightens them without killing or stealing, he will be expelled out of the land (this includes imprisonment); If the bandit kills and steal property at the same time, he will be crucified" (Sanad, 1991). With this system no discretion is extended to the judge. Finally, if an offender repented before being caught and turned himself in, the punishment could be suspended, for it was written: "unless they repent before you overpower them—in that case bear in mind that God is forgiving and merciful" (5:34).

Rebellion against a legitimate political authority was considered a serious offense against the public order. While legal scholars have disagreed over a precise definition, there is agreement that it involves treason or some type of armed rebellion. According to the Quran: "If two groups of the believers fight, you should try to reconcile them; if one of them is oppressing the other, fight the oppressors until they submit to God's command, then make a just and even-handed reconciliation between the two of them: God loves those who are even-handed" (49:9). Early in Muslim society it was determined that rebels who refuse to be reconciled should be put to death. It has been pointed out by scholars, however, that lesser sanctions had been imposed.

Adultery and fornication were both considered crimes against the family structure and public morality. The Quran warns: "And do not go anywhere near adultery: it is an outrage, and an evil path" (17:32). As for other hudud offenses, the punishment was fixed. In such cases, the Quran states: "Strike the adulteress and the adulterer one hundred times. Do not let compassion for them keep you from carrying out God's law—if you believe in God and the Last Day—and ensure that a group of believers witnesses the punishment"(24:2). Some jurists, however, made a distinction between offenders who were single and those who were married. If the offender was single, then the aforementioned punishment was considered appropriate. If, however, the offender was married, the Sunna cited the punishment was death by stoning. Not all jurists adopted this position; some imposed exile for a year in addition to the flogging. Others limited the punishment to flogging in order to comply with the Quran. Whereas hudud offenses generally require the testimony of two men of sound reputation, in matters of adultery and fornication, four witnesses or a confession by the adulterer were required. Finally, it is important to note that any sexual activity less than intercourse was not considered a hadd offense. Other acts would fall under the category of a *tazir* crime, which is explained below. The crimes of adultery and fornication are excellent illustrations in the Islamic context of how the Sharia is both a code of law and a code of morals for the community of believers.

The most common example of defamation cited by Islamic legal scholars is associated with fornication. For those falsely accused, the Quran states: "As for those who accuse chaste women of fornication, and then fail to provide four witnesses, strike them eighty times, and reject their testimony ever afterwards: they are the lawbreakers, except for those who repent later and make amends—God is most forgiving and merciful" (24:4). Only an innocent accused person can file a grievance in such a case.

Apostasy threatens both the public order and the spiritual order of the community in a significant way. As mentioned earlier, Islam is first and foremost a religion. An apostate is a person who once embraced Islam and is now rejecting it. According to the Quran, "If any of you revoke your faith and die as disbelievers, your deeds will come to nothing in this world and the Hereafter, and you will be inhabitants of the Fire, there to remain" (2:217). Moreover, "As for those who believe, then reject the faith, then believe again, then reject the faith again and become increasingly defiant, God will not forgive them, nor will He guide them on any path" (4:137). Obviously, these passages suggest that the punishment for an apostate will occur in the hereafter.

During the formative years of Islam, when the leaders were attempting to establish a theocratic society, a consensus was reached that the sanction for apostasy in this life should be death. Before this sanction is imposed, however, it must be clear that the accused committed an act that illustrates rejection of the Islamic faith. Denying the existence of God or any of the five tenets of the faith (the five Pillars of Islam explained earlier) would be sufficient grounds. In addition, the person must be given an opportunity to repent their actions and return to the Islamic faith. A consensus was not reached among jurists on the length of time a person should be given to recant.

The prohibition against drinking wine has been expanded over the years to include all alcoholic beverages and even the use of illegal drugs. As such, a modern translation of the Quran states, "you who believe, do not come anywhere near the prayer if you are intoxicated, not until you know what you are saying" (4:43). It also admonishes: "With intoxicants and gambling, Satan seeks only to incite enmity and hatred among you, and to stop you remembering God and prayer. Will you not give them up? Obey God, obey the Messenger, and always be on your guard: if you pay no heed, bear in mind that the sole duty of Our Messenger is to deliver the message clearly" (5:91–92). The sanction for this offense is 80 lashes, but the Shafii madhhab is of the opinion that the penalty should be only 40 lashes.

It is important to interject that the Quran points out that: "... if anyone repents after his wrongdoing and makes amends, God will accept his repentance: God is most forgiving, most merciful" (5:39). Jurists differed on how this should be interpreted. The Shafii madhhab was of the opinion that repentance meant the elimination of punishment in this life and the hereafter, whereas the Hanifa madhhab maintained that repentance did not eliminate punishment in this life, but only applied to the hereafter.

It is also important to note that neither the victim nor the state may pardon a person for a hadd crime. Moreover, because hudud crimes threatened the social order and security of the community, the execution of the sanction was carried out in public. For those who object to such severe hudud penalties, such as amputation, proponents maintain that "[t]hose who protest amputation should consider the welfare of society, since the occasional use of that sanction has proven to be an effective deterrent in Islamic societies" (see Mansour, in Bassiouni, 1982).

Moreover, on the subject of theft, Muslims maintain that one of the Pillars of Islam, the five required practices that devout Muslims are required to follow and that unite the worldwide community of Islam, is specifically designed to reduce the need to steal. The *zakat*, which means purification, is a religious tax on Muslims. The purpose of the tax is to help the poor, sick, disabled, and elderly. The beneficiaries of such a tax were not limited to Muslims but included the People of the Book, in particular Christians and Jews. Because Christians and Jews did not pay zakat, they were assessed the *jizya* tax, which not only provided them with a protective status in a Muslim community, but also enabled them to contribute to this community chest for the poor, sick, and elderly.

Finally, scholars of Islamic law offer a final rationale for the use of hudud sanctions. They point out that these are physical penalties over a limited time frame, which inflict severe pain that is designed to prevent the perpetrator from ever forgetting the sanction and to cause the offender to cease his or her criminal lifestyle. In addition, because the sanction occurs over a limited period of time, the perpetrator is able to return to his or her family and assist in their support. Scholars also question the wisdom of relying too much on the use of imprisonment as a sanction. The downside to imprisonment, they maintain, is that imprisonment not only reduces the deterrent effect over a period of time but it also reduces the inmate's sense of responsibility: a sense of responsibility not only for his or her criminal actions but also for the support of his or her family. In other words, the inmate has all of his or her basic needs provided by the state and often the family of the inmate becomes a recipient of welfare. In addition, the precarious state of the inmate's family may lead to delinquency and serious criminal activity among other family members (see Mansuor, in Bassiouni, 1982).

Quesas The other type of determined crimes is *quesas* (which means equality). These offenses are deemed violations against the rights of an individual. As a result, these offenses are associated with retribution and compensation or *diyya* (also known as blood money). In light of the fact that there was no organized system of criminal justice administration during the emergence of Islamic societies, this was viewed as a sound method for imposing a sanction on a criminal while at the same time attempting to preserve the social order. The Quran warns: "You who believe, uphold justice and bear witness to God, even if it is against yourself, your parents, or your close relatives. Whether the person is rich or poor, God can best take care of both. Refrain from following your own desire, so that you can act justly—if you distort or neglect justice, God is fully aware of what you do"(4:135). The rationale for the sanctions of quesas crimes were like those for hudud offenses, that is, an early version of deterrence.

Homicide, assaults, and other offenses associated with the physical security of a person are included among these offenses. With quesas crimes, the punishment was of a retributive nature, equal to the harm suffered by the victim. If the victim waved his or her right to retribution (and in some cases this waiver was not necessary), the offender or the offender's family paid compensation to the victim or the victim's family for the harm caused.

With regard to homicide, the Quran admonishes: "Do not take life, which God has made sacred, except by right: if anyone is killed wrongfully, We have given authority to the defender of his rights, but he should not be excessive in taking life, for he is already aided [by God]" (17:33). The Quran essentially acknowledges two kinds of homicide: intentional and accidental. With regard to intentional homicide and assaults, the Quran continued the Judeo-Christian tradition of *lex talionis* (retaliation): "In the Torah We prescribed for them a life for a life, an eye for an eye, a nose for a nose, an ear for an ear, a tooth for a tooth, an equal wound for a wound: if anyone forgoes this out of charity, it will serve as atonement for his bad deeds"(5:45). What this verse clearly indicates is that murder is punishable by death. The Quran offers additional guidance on this matter. "You who believe, fair retribution is prescribed for you in cases of murder: the free man for the free man, the slave for the slave, the female for the female. But if the culprit is pardoned by his aggrieved brother, this shall be adhered to fairly, and the culprit shall pay what is due in a good way"(2:178). In this verse there is the assurance that *diyya* (blood money or compensation) would be paid, even if the family elected to pardon the murderer and not seek the ultimate form of retribution.

With regard to *lex talionis*, scholars of Islamic law have pointed out that a number of rules were developed by the various legal schools. They included that the retaliatory punishment inflicted cannot be greater than the harm caused by the offender. In the case of murder, the right to decide to inflict the sanction or forego it belonged to the male parents of the victim, that is, the father and then the grandfather. Distinctions were made with the killing of a male versus a female. The family of a female victim was only entitled to diyya, and its value was half what it would be if the victim had been a male. If the victim was an infant, insane, or physically handicapped, the victim or the victim's family was also treated differently, with the sanction less harsh than if the victim were a healthy male.

It is important to keep in mind that these rules were developed in a patriarchal setting, when men were considered the essential economic source for the family in particular and society in general. These rules clearly fail any equality test based on the policies that have emerged in the West. It would be prudent, however, to keep in mind that many of our modern Western policies of equality were primarily introduced during the twentieth century.

In cases of accidental homicide, the Quran states:

> Never should a believer kill another believer, except by mistake. If anyone kills a believer by mistake he must free one Muslim slave and pay compensation to the victim's relatives, unless they charitably forgo it; if the victim belonged to a people at war with you but is a believer, then the compensation is only to free a believing slave; if he belonged to a people with whom you have a treaty, then compensation should be handed over to his relatives, and a believing slave set free (4:92).

In cases associated with assaults and other physical injuries, whether intentional or accidental, reference was again made to the Quranic verse: "In the Torah We prescribed for them a life for a life, an eye for an eye, a nose for a nose, an ear for an ear, a tooth for a tooth, an equal wound for a wound: if anyone forgoes this out of charity, it will serve as atonement for his bad deeds"(5:45). Thus, an equal amount of pain was called for, but a monetary compensation was also expected in those cases that were intentional. It was further determined that only a monetary compensation was required for accidental physical injury.

Although the punishment for quesas crimes is of a retributive nature, equal to that suffered by the victim, scholars of Islamic law have argued that the Quran is supportive of foregoing the retributive sanction and replacing it with a just compensation or diyya. For example, they cited the following Quranic verses: "By an act of mercy from God, you [Prophet] were gentle in your dealings with them—had you been harsh, or hard-hearted, they would have dispersed and left you—so pardon them and ask forgiveness for them. Consult with them about matters, then, when you have decided on a course of action, put your trust in God: God loves those who put their trust in Him" (3:159). Moreover, "God commands you [people] to return things entrusted to you to their rightful owners, and, if you judge between people, to do so with justice: God's instructions to you are excellent, for He hears and sees everything. You who believe, obey God and the Messenger, and those in authority among you. If you are in dispute over any matter, refer it to God and the Messenger, if you truly believe in God and the Last Day: that is better and fairer in the end" (4:58–59). Acts of mercy and forgiveness are reminders that the Quran is a religious text. Some scholars have suggested that replacing the retributive sanction with the diyya is a predecessor to the modern notions of victimology.

With regard to diyya, it is important to note that it is not completely divorced from having a punitive quality. Moreover, the state is involved in the process to assure that the victim or the victim's family receives the compensation from the perpetrator or the perpetrator's family. Debates have occurred among the legal schools as to the responsibility for paying the diyya. As mentioned earlier, one of the fundamental principles of Islamic law from its inception was individual criminal responsibility: "Each soul is responsible for its own actions; no soul will bear the burden of another" (6:164). As a result, why is the family of a criminal required to pay or assist in the payment of diyya? The Quran maintains that there is a collective duty to secure social order and to pursue justice. It was pointed out that "the overriding policy is one of social solidarity by which the family knows that it has responsibility for its members. Such a policy leads to a system of social compliance by having family members exert control over one another because all fear a certain financial responsibility for the deeds of each individual member of the family" (Bassiouni, 1982). It was mentioned earlier in the chapter that the Middle East is another region of the world where there is a long cultural tradition in which the group is more important than the individual. This aforementioned Quranic policy is an illustration of how it impacts personal and group responsibility for issues associated with criminal justice.

Finally, in order to prove a quesas offense, certain evidentiary rules had to be met. For example, some crimes required at least one eyewitness or a confession. The judge had to be assured that the confession was given voluntarily and without coercion. In cases of homicide, two male witnesses were required or one male witness and two female witnesses. In the event there was insufficient evidence to prove a quesas offense, the judge might be able to impose a tazir sanction, which is explained below.

A useful summary of the rules associated with quesas offenses was developed and is cited here.

> 1. The accused must be an adult who is of sound mind and understanding at the time of the act, and the act must have been done intentionally.
> 2. The victim must be a male Muslim or a Dhimmi (Christian or Jew), or according to a majority of writers, a Musta'amin (a non-Christian or non-Jew who has entered the Land of Islam pursuant to a peace treaty or guarantee of safe conduct).
> 3. Only the male blood relative (father or grandfather) in line of ascendancy can claim Quesas in case of the death of the victim. Only the victim can claim it in case of maiming, although some jurists require that the ascendant male parent agree.
> 4. A Muslim or Dhimmi cannot be executed or maimed (based on the equivalency principle) for the killing or maiming of someone not ma'asoum (immune), that is in the case of a Kafir (an idolater, not a Musta'amin), one who has abandoned Islam, or a rebellious Muslim (one who commits the Had crime of rebellion as set forth under Islamic law).
> 5. According to most jurists, the Had crime must be inflicted with the sword (the weapon known in early Islam to be swiftest and least capable of inflicting more pain the necessary).
> 6. The infliction of the Quesas must be in the least painful manner.
> 7. As responsibility is personal, the death of the offender extinguishes all other claims.
> 8. Pardon or forgiveness extinguishes Quesas but not Diyya, according to some jurists, while others say it also extinguishes Diyya.
> 9. If the offender is a minor or is insane there is no Quesas but only Diyya, which a majority of jurists impute to his family. Others say that there also is no Diyya if the aggressor is a minor or insane.

10. Female Muslim victims or their families are only entitled to Diyya, the amount being equivalent to half that of the male. This rule exists by analogy to the rule that the male's inheritance is twice that of a female.

11. Reconciliation is encouraged between the parties even before adjudication, although the collectivity retains the right to impose a Ta'azir penalty.

12. The Diyya is otherwise applicable to all other forms of killing and maiming and to those cases in which the requirements of Quesas are not met. The Diyya does not require that the victim or aggressor be an adult, sane or male. No Diyya is payable for one who is not a ma'asoum (see supra number 4).

13. An exception to Quesas is made in the case of Quesama (oath), that is when fifty members of the community, who are adult, sane and devout Muslims, swear that the accused could not have committed the crime (Bassiouni, 1982).

Once again, it is important to be mindful that these rules were developed in a patriarchal setting, when men were considered the essential and often the sole economic source for the family in particular and society in general. Obviously, these rules fail any equality test based on the policies that have emerged in the West during the modern era.

Tazir Discretionary crimes are referred to as *tazir* offenses. The rationales for hudud or quesas offenses have already been noted as focusing on deterrence. The sanctions associated with tazir crimes are also designed to seek a deterrent effective, but they also claim that the primary purpose is to achieve a corrective or rehabilitative purpose. It has been suggested that both the Quran and Sunna illustrate examples of sanctions that are associated with tazir crimes. Thus, the sanctions for tazir offenses have a basis in the original sources of Islamic law and are not solely determined by the authorities of the Islamic state (see Salim al-'Awwa, in Bassiouni, 1982). It has also been argued, however, that tazir offenses are not determined by religious law. As a result, the sanction is left to the discretion of the judge or some public authority (see Kamel, in Bassiouni, 1982). Strictly speaking, this discretionary authority actually belongs to the sovereign and is delegated to the judge by the sovereign.

When compared to hudud or quesas offenses, it has been pointed out that "[c]rimes of Ta'azir, by contrast, are not subject to the principle of legality in the same manner. Islamic law has not specified all violations subject to Ta'azir to the same extent as for other crimes. However, it considers that regardless of circumstances, all acts that infringe on private or community interests of the public order are subject to Ta'azir" (see Benmelha, in Bassiouni, 1982). Thus, the goal of maintaining the public and moral order of the community of believers, which is a significant theme throughout the Quran, provides a valid though expanded interpretation of the principle of legality.

Tazir offenses are considered less serious because they do not involve physical injury to a victim. It has been suggested that these crimes can be grouped into two categories: (1) offenses against religion, public order, and public morals, and (2) offenses that violate the rights of individuals. Because the Quran does not state a specific sanction, yet the behavior is clearly prohibited, judicial discretion is relied upon to determine an equitable punishment (Khadduri and Liebesney, 1955).

While violations of religious obligations of Muslims are punished in the hereafter, it is generally recognized in Islamic countries that such failure can also lead to a tazir punishment in this life. In reference to public order and morals issues, the Quran admonishes: "You who believe, intoxicants and gambling, idolatrous practices, and [divining with] arrows are repugnant acts—Satan's doing—shun them so that you may prosper"(5:90). Here a judge would determine the sanction that is appropriate and in the process take into consideration the age, gender, and social standing of the person in conjunction with seriousness of the offense. The typical punishments include: flogging, imprisonment, warning, and fines.

Fraud is a good example of a tazir offense that violates an individual. The Quran states: "Do not withhold from people things that are rightly theirs, and do not spread corruption in the land" (11:85) and "Give full measure: do not sell others short. Weigh with correct scales: do not deprive people of what is theirs. Do not spread corruption on earth" (26:181–183). These practical examples clearly indicate that it is wrong to violate the rights of individuals and that there was no physical injury to the victim. Moreover, the Quranic verses are silent on an appropriate sanction. Thus, the judge determines the punishment, while always being guided by the Quran and Sunna.

Sanctions for tazir crimes are divided into two categories. One group consists of traditional sanctions that include corporal punishment, deprivation of liberty, and fines. The corporal punishment sanctions consist of the death penalty and flogging. While the death penalty is normally associated with hudud or quesas crimes, there are a few tazir offenses that can lead to a death sentence. They include espionage and heresy. Both are considered a serious threat to the public and moral order of the community. The logic for employing flogging as a sanction for tazir crimes is the same justification for its use with hudud offenses. The sanction can be imposed quickly, which allows the offender to return to his or her family and place of employment. Thus, the offender and the offender's family do not become a financial burden on the community. Moreover, as a term of imprisonment might lead the offender to become a more dangerous or persistent violator, that concern is eliminated by imposing a corporal punishment. One scholar has pointed out that flogging is usually carried out by using a stick or an unknotted whip. After protecting those parts of the body that might prove fatal to the whipping, the individual lashes are supposed to be administered over the entire body and not limited to one area, such as the back. Jurists disagree on the number strokes an offender should receive, with the range as high as 65 to as low as three (see Benmelha, in Bassiouni, 1982).

Imprisonment was employed when flogging did not appear to work. The period of incarceration could generally range from one day to one year, with the period of time determined by the judge. Islamic law also utilized an indeterminate sentencing scheme. It was reserved for offenders who were recidivists, especially those deemed dangerous. Moreover, other offenders may be sentenced to a term of restricted liberty or probation.

A fine is another form of traditional sanction for tazir crimes. It was introduced with some degree of reluctance on the part of legal scholars. Part of the concern was that judges might utilize the fine too much. While some jurists viewed a fine as a principal penalty, others considered it only as a supplemental sanction. It is interesting to note that when a fine was imposed by a judge, part of the offender's wealth or possessions were confiscated. If the offender was contrite for his or her actions and displayed a rehabilitative change in general behavior, he or she might possibly have the money or possessions returned.

The other category of sanctions for tazir crimes tends to have an educational and moral purpose within the context of Islamic society. For example, an offender could be fired from his or her place of employment if the job and actions were a threat to the public interest; the offender could be summoned to court where a judge would admonish him or her either in public or in private; or the offender could be sent a letter indicating the wrong committed and the expectation that the behavior will cease.

Criminal Procedure

It is important to note that Islamic law or Sharia did not provide a detailed process for criminal procedure in general or the investigative and prosecutorial stages in particular. With regard to the practice of justice, the Quran offers a general principle: "God commands you [people] to return things entrusted to you to their rightful owners, and, if you judge between people, to do so with justice: God's instructions to you are excellent, for He hears and sees everything" (4:58) and "You who believe, be steadfast in your devotion to God and bear witness impartially: do not let hatred of others lead you away from justice, but adhere to justice, for that is closer to awareness of God" (5:8).

The responsibility for developing procedural rules was a delegated authority to the sovereign or ruler. While the process could conform to cultural and societal norms, it ultimately had to be in compliance with Sharia. This delegated authority to a ruler is a feature of *siyasa*, which literally means administrative justice policy. More specifically, the term *siyasa sharia* means an administration of justice policy that is in conformity with Sharia. Therefore, a distinction was made between Sharia and siyasa. Sharia is that blend of both a code of law and a code of morals. Siyasa sharia is the method of introducing practical pragmatic policies for the administration of justice that are in conformity with the spirit of Sharia, especially when Sharia does not provide specific guidance.

Ultimately, the objective was to establish an administrative justice process that was in the best interests of the Muslim community. As such, "Islamic law has adopted rules of criminal procedure based on the principle that justice not only requires the offender to be punished for his guilt but also protects the innocent from punishment for crimes committed by another" (see Abd-el-Malek al-Saleh, in Bassiouni, 1982). Originally, the administration of Islamic criminal justice was delegated to a number of different officials, depending on the region in question. Among the officials delegated this authority was: the Caliphate, the Office of Complaints, the military commander, the governor, the chief of police, and the judge.

It should be noted that this delegated authority has not escaped criticism from some scholars, especially during the second half of the twentieth century. For example, with specific reference to criminal justice, Awad pointed out that:

> many state officials have in the past inflicted unwarranted exemplary penalties on suspects on the assumption that the matter was purely political (or administrative) and not a matter for the Shari'a. They wrongly believed it was their right and duty to regulate such matters without restrictions. Their ignorance of the true meaning of the Shari'a cause grave injustice and impermissible changes in administrative practice and policy (siyasa) which were either falsely attributed to the Shari'a or blatantly substituted for it. They have further claimed that the Shari'a was inadequate and failed to protect the public welfare and thereby replaced it with generalities that contradicted sound Shari'a teachings and precepts (see Awad, in Bassiouni, 1982).

What follows is a general sketch of how a criminal offense might be investigated and prosecuted under the rules and guidelines of Islamic law.

Initiation of a Criminal Action The initiation of a criminal action generally takes one of two forms. If the offense is an act of commission or omission against God, it is considered against the public interest. In such cases, the state would commence the criminal action.

While the victim does not have a right to initiate such an action, he or she does have the right to seek damages. For example, in the case of theft, both the state and the victim have an interest in the case. The state would have the right to seek and inflict a punishment on the guilty party, while the victim would have the right to seek compensation or restitution. If an offense is an act of commission or omission solely against an individual, the criminal action is considered a violation of a private right. As such, the victim would initiate the action. Crimes dealing with assault, defamation, and tazir offenses fall under this category. Once the victim requests that an action be taken, then the agents of the state would assume responsibility for the investigation and prosecution of the matter.

Presumption of Innocence As mentioned earlier, Islamic law embraced the presumption of innocence as a right for all people. Without such a presumption it would generally be difficult in the extreme for people to prove that they had not committed the crimes of which they were accused. As a result, the burden of proof rested with the accuser. Moreover, the evidence produced must lead to a conviction that is based on a certainty of guilt and not based on a mere probability.

An indictment, which was carried out by a specific agency, charged a person with a crime by confronting them with an accusation or in the case of some suspects their arrest and detention for preventive purposes. The indictment limited the rights and freedoms of the accused. This was justified on the grounds that it was in the interests of seeking truth and justice. The person under indictment had a number of rights, however, the most important of which was the right of a defense.

Jurists frequently cited the comment the Prophet Muhammad made to Ali when he named him governor of Yemen. "O' Ali, people will appeal to you for justice. If two adversaries come to you for arbitration, do not rule for the one, before you have similarly heard from the other. It is more proper for justice to become evident to you and for you to know who is right." As such, the accused must be informed of what he or she is charged with and be presented with sufficient and valid evidence that supports the accusation. The purpose of the defense is either to deny the accusation by placing doubt on the nature or quality of the evidence or by introducing evidence that proves the person is innocent.

While acknowledging that a person has a right to a defense, this does not necessarily mean that he or she has a right to retain counsel. Islamic law is not explicit in this regard. Moreover, it is interesting to note that scholars have suggested that defendants did not often secure legal counsel. The reason for this was that judges consulted with jurists on complex issues in the course of an investigation and trial. As such, it was often felt that there was no need for an independent and disinterested opinion in the matter at hand, because the jurist had often already provided it to the judge (see Awad, in Bassiouni, 1982).

Criminal Responsibility In Islamic law a person could not be held criminally responsible for his or her actions under the following conditions or circumstances. The first involved the age of the accused. A child under the age of seven was considered not to have reached the age of reason. Children between the age of seven and the beginning of puberty may be partially responsible for their criminal actions. It should be noted that there was a lack of agreement on defining puberty in Islam. Some jurists were of the opinion that one must differentiate between males and females. In addition, there was disagreement over citing a specific age —11 or 12 are often mentioned—or simply making a determination based on the signs of puberty. While children between seven and the onset of puberty could not be held responsible for either a hudud or quesas offenses, they could be disciplined for any tazir crimes. With reference to tazir cases, the Shafii madhhab maintained that any damages imposed by a court should be paid from the child's money, while other madhahib suggested that the family should incur the expense. Once puberty had begun, a person was considered criminally responsible, as long as he or she was of sound mind.

The second condition deals with the mental state of the accused. A person was not held responsible if he or she was insane when they committed the offense. Certain kinds of mental deficiencies, like retardation, may not protect the accused from criminal responsibility unless it was proven that the offender did not know the difference between right and wrong. Voluntary intoxication was another condition. Jurists were of the opinion that hudud or quesas penalties should not be imposed but that tazir sanctions were appropriate.

Investigation In earlier periods of Islamic society, there was often an investigative phase before a trial. What was different at that time was that there was not a clear distinction between the investigative and trial phases. The reason for this was that it was not unusual for a judge to conduct the investigation and then also sit as the trial judge.

On the subject of searching for evidence, the Quran acknowledges that a person should have a right to privacy. "Believers, do not enter other people's houses until you have asked permission to do so and greeted those inside—that is best for you: perhaps you will bear this in mind. If you find no one in, do not enter unless you have been given permission to do so. If you are told, 'Go away', then do so—that is more proper for you. God knows well what you do" (24:27–28). And "Believers, avoid making too many assumptions—some assumptions are sinful—and do not spy on one another or speak ill of people behind their backs:" (49:12). These verses have been interpreted to mean that a person was free from unreasonable searches and seizures. Moreover, the second verse reminds agents of the justice system that they must be sensitive to and cautious of baseless accusations. Generally, the search of a person or their property was achieved by seeking a warrant from the *Mazalim* (Minister of Complaints).

There is a recognition that society benefits from permitting agents of the state to enter a home with the purpose of discovering the truth in a criminal case. As such, a person does not have an absolute right to privacy in their home, as long as the state abides by various criteria and adheres to certain restrictions. Contemporary laws have been approved that provide the individual person with a right to privacy that extends beyond their home. Because the state has a compelling interest in maintaining order and securing the safety of the public, an investigator is permitted to arrest, search, and seize relevant evidence at the home or on the person of the accused and to hold the person in preventive detention. Accused persons are given an opportunity to present a defense to the investigator in the case, which could involve introducing evidence that contradicts that of the accuser or providing witnesses in support of their innocence. This could even involve the use of a technical expert.

The seizure and preventive detention of a suspect is also a concern among Islamic legal scholars. On the one hand, they recognize that preventive detention is a necessary state function. On the other hand, a basic assumption of Islam is that humans should be free. Scholars frequently cite the Quranic verse: "It is He who has made the earth manageable for you—travel its regions; eat His provision—and to Him you will be resurrected" (67:15). As a result, scholars tended to oppose detention unless it was absolutely necessary.

Interrogation A distinction is made within Islamic law between simple questioning and an interrogation. An interrogation involves charging the suspect and presenting evidence that is the basis for the charges. The interrogation enables the suspect either to admit guilt or object to the authenticity of the evidence. If the accused admits guilt, then the interrogation has produced another piece of oral evidence.

During an interrogation, the accused is not required to speak; he or she can remain silent and cannot be forced to admit guilt. Legal scholars are in agreement that neither the Quran, Sunna, nor ijma condone tactics that lead to a forced confession. Of course, torture was an acceptable method of securing a confession throughout the ancient world and on into the European middle ages. According to one scholar, "Islamic law expressly prohibits torture, beating, and other cruel and inhumane treatment. The Prophet forbade torture[,] saying: 'God shall torture on the Day of Recompense those who inflict torture on people in life' " (see Abd-el-Malek al-Saleh, in Bassiouni, 1982). In the modern era, constitutions and due process rules of procedure have prohibited such conduct. Nevertheless, agents of the criminal justice system in many countries continue to use physical coercion, especially psychological techniques, to intimidate a suspect, which often leads to incriminating statements.

According to scholars of Islamic law, a system was established that was designed to reduce the likelihood of abuse during the interrogation stage. In addition to a judge, the Mohtasib was authorized to receive reports of alleged crimes and to investigate them. The work of the Mohtasib was then submitted to the Mazalim (Minister of Complaints), who referred the matter to a judge who would in turn adjudicate the matter. In the event the complaining party did not prosecute the matter, it was the responsibility of the Mohtasib to prosecute the case at trial (see Abd-el-Malek al-Saleh, in Bassiouni, 1982).

In the case of both hudud and quesas crimes, the accused cannot be forced to take an oath during an investigation. With specific reference to hudud offenses, the accused had the right to remain silent and refuse to answer the questions of an investigator. Moreover, exercising the right to remain silent was not admissible as evidence against the accused. Finally, under Islamic law the accused had the right to withdraw a confession before the execution of a sentence. As a result, the confession could not be used as part of the evidence to convict the individual.

Evidence Because the presumption of innocence for the accused is fundamental in Islamic law, an accuser must prove his or her claim that a crime has occurred. The rules that have emerged over time have a basis in the Quranic verse: "As for those who accuse chaste women of fornication, and then fail to provide four witnesses, strike them eighty times, and reject their testimony ever afterwards: they are the lawbreakers, except for those who repent later and make amends—God is most forgiving and merciful" (24:4–5). For a period of time, three madhahib (Hanafi, Shafii, and Hanbali) maintained that evidence was limited to oral testimony, in part because of the aforementioned Quranic verse. In time the acceptance of other types of evidence was accepted. There was one exception; hudud crimes required the testimony of witnesses.

Because of the harsh penalties associated with hudud crimes, the admissibility of evidence had to conform to some specific rules: (1) two eyewitnesses were required for most crimes and four witnesses in cases involving unlawful sexual intercourse; (2) hearsay accounts were unacceptable; (3) the testimony had to be unambiguous; (4) the witnesses had to possess moral integrity; (5) the testimony had to be provided expeditiously from the time of the alleged offense; and (6) the witnesses had to maintain their adherence to their testimony and not deviate from it. With specific reference to the crime of adultery, special conditions for the testimony were established. The four prosecution witnesses had to be male. The testimony of women for the defense was accepted, but it was often required that two females had to testify for every male witness. There was also disagreement among the legal schools over the admissibility of testimony from the husband.

Islamic law established various standards that a person had to meet in order to be a witness. First, it has already been mentioned that the witness had to be an eyewitness and not someone providing hearsay testimony. This rule met the authenticity standard. Second, the witness had to meet a moral integrity standard by being of good character. It should be noted that there was not a consensus on how to determine the probity of a witness. The Maliki and Shafii madhahib maintained that a person's good character was based on their trustworthiness and their avoidance of sin. The character of a person was presumed to be good unless proof was offered to the contrary. Third, the individual must be rational, that is, they must have been in possession of their mental faculties when they observed the event and when they testified. Fourth, the person had to be an adult. The testimony of a minor was inadmissible, unless in a case of homicide where a minor's testimony was used to refute another minor's testimony, and both witnesses had been deemed rational. Fifth, the witness must have the ability to retain and recollect past events. Those who possess a bad memory were deemed not competent to testify. Sixth, the person must be able to speak. Different madhahib had varying opinions on the testimony of people who could not speak or hear. The Malik and Hanbali madhahib accepted the written testimony of a person who could not speak, whereas the Hanafi madhhab rejected the testimony. Seventh, an individual had to have seen the event about which he or she was testifying. As such, most jurists claimed that the testimony of a blind person was inadmissible. Finally, the acceptance of the Islamic faith was a prerequisite to permitting a person to testify in an Islamic law court. This is based on the Quranic verse: "Call two just witnesses from your people and establish witness for the sake of God" (65:2). However, if a Muslim witness did not exist or was not available, a non-Muslim could testify. This deviation from the previous standard was also supported by another verse: "You who believe, when death approaches any of you, let two just men from among you act as witnesses to the making of a bequest, or two men from another people if you are journeying in the land when death approaches" (5:106). With respect to hudud and quesas crimes, most jurists maintained that the witnesses must be male.

Confession is another type of evidence in Islamic law. The admissibility of a confession is based on three standards. First, the confession is being offered freely, that is, the accused is not being tortured or coerced in anyway. Second, the person understands the legal consequences of admitting guilt. Third, the person must describe or explain his or her specific actions that have been deemed criminal. It should be noted that the Hanafi madhhab maintained that a valid confession must occur in court, whereas the Maliki, Shafii, and Hanbali madhahib concluded that a confession was valid outside of court, as long as there were witnesses to the testimony. The judge would determine the admissibility of the confession.

Although eyewitness testimony is the primary form of evidence, secondary forms of proof were considered. Several Quranic verses have been interpreted to support the use of secondary proofs. They included: "Our messengers came to them with clear signs," (5:32); "Say, I stand on clear proof from my Lord," (6:57); "The disbelievers say, 'Why does he not bring us a sign from his Lord?' Have they not been given clear proof confirming what was in the earlier scriptures?" (20:133); and "those who were given the Scripture became divided only after they were sent [such] clear evidence" (98:4). Thus, any kind of evidence was acceptable as long as it enabled the process to reach the truth of the matter at hand. Nevertheless, and not surprising, Islamic law favored criminal evidence that was based on eyewitness testimony.

One scholar of Islamic law concluded that "the Shari'a rules of evidence reflect the idealism of the Muslim jurists. The strict burden of proof imposed upon the plaintiff or prosecutor requires him to establish his claim to a high degree of certainty, on the principle that it is better for several actual offenders to escape liability than for one innocent person to suffer liability." He went on to point out that "the rule of oral testimony places an unrealistic burden on the prosecution," in light of the fact that most crimes are usually not committed in the presence of two adult males that are noted for their integrity (Coulson, 1969).

Rights of the Accused at Trial The Quran emphasizes the importance of justice and equality among people. "So [Prophet] judge between them according to what God has sent down. Do not follow their whims, and take good care that they do not tempt you away from any of what God has sent down to you"(5:49). Also "God commands you [people] to return things entrusted to you to their rightful owners, and, if you judge between people, to do so with justice: God's instructions to you are excellent, for He hears and sees everything"(4:58).

It was the practice of the Prophet Muhammad and the caliphs that succeeded him who established rights for the accused. To illustrate, the admonition of Caliph Omar to a newly appointed judge was:

> The right to adjudication is an absolute duty in accordance with the Sunna. Investigate any case you suspect (to bring about right), for right without execution is futile. Equalize between the parties before you in your expressions and in your judgment. Your judgment should not be on the basis for the noble to hope for your favor, and for the poor to despair from your justice. ... If you render a judgment and after a period of time you find it to be unjust, do not hesitate to revise it, unless it is so old that no one can change it. The revision of judgments is better than preserving injustice (Sanad, 1991).

In the early development of Islamic law, the jurists maintained that trials should not be conducted in private. In addition, the decision of the court should also occur in a public setting. Because Islamic law employed an accusatorial procedural method, the accused was guaranteed certain protections from abuse, especially by the authority of the state. For example, the accused had the right of assistance of counsel in his or her defense to prove either that he or she was not legally guilty or was factually innocent.

The right to assistance of counsel traced its origin to the theory of protected interests, which was mentioned earlier in the section on the principles of Islamic criminal justice. This theory essentially states that people are guaranteed protection from the unwarranted infringement of the state with regard to: religion, life, the mind, posterity, and property. The right to assistance of counsel was specifically designed to protect or assure the accused of his or her right to live with dignity. The right to assistance commenced at the investigative stage of the process and in particular at the interrogation phase. In those cases in which the accuser was a private citizen, both the accuser and the accused had the right to appoint another person to represent their interests before a judge.

It is important to note that there were no attorneys in Islamic law, at least as the term is employed in legal systems that originated in the West. For purposes of legal representation in court, a person hired a *wakil* (an agent). These people were not members of any professional organization, like a bar association, nor were they required to achieve certain conditions, such as passing an examination, in order to serve in this capacity. These wukala (the plural of wakil) were recognized as unique because they did possess a good deal of legal knowledge and were particularly familiar with court procedures.

The ability of a wakil to utilize his powers of persuasion on behalf of his client was indeed important in light of the various procedural rules. To illustrate, a person could not be convicted of hudud or quesas offenses if there was reasonable doubt as to the guilt. This rule prevented a judge from imposing a hadd punishment. In the case of theft, for example, the amputation of the accused's hand would be prohibited if the value of the property was minimal or the items taken were not personal property. Of course, a person found innocent of a hudud offense because of reasonable doubt could be convicted with a tazir punishment. In the event the prosecution failed to provide adequate evidence to make a case or if the evidence presented by the prosecution and defense contradicted one another, the judge would be required to acquit the accused of the crime and not subject the person to a tazir sanction.

Judge A judge (qadi) was a representative of the governor of a region. As such, his authority was not independent but rather a delegated authority. Thus, Sharia courts never attained independent judicial authority, for the judiciary always held office at the pleasure of the political authority. Moreover, because it was a delegated authority, the governor retained the right to administer justice. Obviously, under this arrangement, the concept of separation of power did not apply. The role of the judge was to apply the basic customary law of the Islamic territory. There was no hierarchy of courts to which a trial judge could turn. Thus, the decision was often his personal judgment, based on knowledge of local law and the Quran.

Although judges served at the pleasure of the political authority, there were certain requirements that a person had to attain before seeking such an appointment. First and foremost, an Islamic judge was a religious judge. As such, they had to be a Muslim. Second, they must know the Quran and Sunna, the principal sources of Islam and Islamic law. The judge acquired this knowledge by attending a special school, a *madrassa*, which was an Islamic religious school. Each madrassa was associated with one of the four madhahib, which were discussed previously, that contributed to the development of Islamic legal theory. It has been pointed out that the religious nature of a judge's job also made him qualified to preside over religious functions. This included presiding over Friday prayers, preaching at a mosque, reciting the ritual funeral prayer, opening the Ramadan fast, and being present at the ceremony of conversion of a non-Muslim to Islam (Khadduri and Liebesny, 1955).

During the early period in the development of Islam, a person appointed as a judge did not solely function as a judge. He was often given other delegated responsibilities, such as law enforcement. As mentioned earlier, the right to prosecute belonged to the judge in addition to the pretrial examination of witnesses. In Islamic law, a judge acted only when a request was submitted by an interested party. In the realm of criminal law, this meant that the victim must initiate an action. If the case involved a hudud offense or involved a threat to the public interest, a judge could initiate an action. Only later did a judge focus solely on his judicial duties.

The ultimate responsibility of the judge was at a trial to determine the guilt or innocence of the accused. In the event the accused was found guilty of a tazir offense, the judge determined the appropriate sanction. In the course of reaching a punishment, the judge considered the personality of the criminal, the nature and circumstances of the offense, and the harm caused to the victim. These criteria were important for they were in keeping with a frequent Quranic exhortation that God is most forgiving and merciful. As such, these factors could mitigate the punishment. There could also be grounds to aggravate the sanction, with the most frequent justifications being that the offender committed the same crime in the past or appeared to have embraced a life of crime.

The tradition of permitting a single judge to handle a case in an Islamic court was justified by the fact that the judge often consulted with jurists on technical or difficult legal issues. These jurists were private scholars who were noted for interpreting Islamic law. When they issued an opinion or ruling on a specific interpretation of law, the opinion was known as a *fatwa.* While fatwas were acknowledged as a legal authority, they were not considered law. Thus, although a single judge was imposing a ruling, the ruling was often based on the advice received from a jurist. While a judge was not obligated to consult with jurists, they usually did. Moreover, it was common for jurists to be present during trials.

During the eighth and ninth centuries, a chief judge (*qadi al-qudat*) was appointed to a region that enabled the chief to appoint and dismiss deputy judges on behalf of the political authority. In spite of this development, there were no appellate judges in a court hierarchy as that term is understood in legal systems that emerged in the West. A dissatisfied litigant could ultimately appeal a judgment to the head of state. When the sovereign elected to sit as a court himself or through his designate, it was known as the court of Mazalim (complaints). This was based on the notion that the ruler, whether a caliph or sultan, had a responsibility to correct any wrong and ultimately to guarantee justice to all his people. In the context of criminal cases, the political authority or the delegate exercised a legal prerogative to resolve an apparent wrong that had occurred in an Islamic court. There were no rules or texts that defined the limits of the jurisdiction of mazalim. Whereas judges in the regular Islamic courts were bound by rules based in Islamic law, mazalim judges were free to exercise their discretion beyond such procedural or evidentiary rules in order to achieve the goal of righting a wrong.

In some geographical areas, Sharia courts were restricted to the field of family law, while in other territories they retained an almost comprehensive jurisdiction. It has been pointed out that over time Islamic law had essentially developed two kinds of courts: "the distinction between the Mazalim and Shari'a jurisdictions came very close to the notion of a division between secular and religious courts" (Coulson, 1964). The Sharia court judges were characterized as being representatives of God's law, while Mazalim court judges were portrayed as representatives of the ruler's law.

Police and Sanctions Shurta (police) was a police organization with responsibilities for order maintenance. Because Islamic procedural law did not provide for a prosecutor, the jurisdictional duties of the shurta were extensive. They were authorized to investigate crimes in Sharia that were punishable by a fixed penalty or hudud and carried out the corporal penalties imposed. They carried out the retaliatory sanctions of quesas offenses, such as the death penalty, and they were authorized to identify acts considered devious, although not infractions of law. This kind of power suggests the type of autocratic political authority that was prevalent at that time in territories where Islam was the dominant faith.

Senior police had the authority not only to investigate criminals, but also to serve as a judge and execute a sentence. When the shurta sat as a court, it was supposed to respect Sharia standards of proof, but it was not bound by them. As a result, circumstantial evidence could be introduced, and the testimony of witnesses whose integrity was questionable was admitted. This kind of procedural flexibility led to an enhanced degree of discretion when determining an appropriate sanction. While on some occasions this could be an exercise in compassionate power, there was also the concern that it could illustrate autocratic power.

With regard to sanctions in the context of Islamic law, the primary purpose was deterrence (both specific and general) rather than retribution. The sanctions were ultimately viewed as mechanisms designed to maintain the stability of the umma, the community of believers. The punishments for hudud and quesas crimes are illustrative of a deterrent goal in light of the fact that the sanction is carried out in public. It is important to note, however, that an equally important rationale for imposing some sanctions was the rehabilitation of the criminal.

Imprisonment had been legitimized under Islamic law and employed as a form of punishment for tazir crimes. In this context, there is an acknowledgment that prisoners are entitled to certain protections, for example, against torture or other forms of physical and verbal abuse. In addition, it was thought that imprisonment should be limited to dangerous or recidivist criminals. It is interesting to note that because the state was depriving the prisoner of his or her freedom, it was the state's responsibility to provide the inmate with the necessities of life. This included conjugal visitations of prisoners who were married.

This section has provided the reader with an introduction to Islamic law, Sharia, within the context of criminal justice. Brief mention was made of the historical development of this legal system and the important role played by the madhahib in establishing Islamic jurisprudence. The principal sources of Sharia were identified. The basic assumptions that make this legal system unique from other systems were explained, and the principles associated with Islamic criminal justice were clarified. The various categories of crimes and punishments were described to a considerable degree. Finally, critical issues associated with criminal procedure and the authorities appointed to carry out the procedural rules were described.

Sharia: Three Contemporary Case Studies

The remainder of this chapter will return to the three regions of the Middle East that were identified when discussing the historical reception of Islam: the Arabian Peninsula, Persia, and the Ottoman Empire. By way of an introduction and orientation, it is important to note that the

Ottoman Empire had reached its peak between the sixteenth and eighteenth centuries. In the initial years of the empire, Islamic armies had successfully invaded parts of Christian Europe. These centuries were fairly stable periods for the region of Islam. The various Muslim societies in the Middle East were loosely connected to the notion of the caliphate or successor to the Prophet Muhammad. This period of stability and self-sufficiency, however, was about to change. It is also important to remember that although Islam viewed the ideal Muslim community or umma as under the political administration of one caliph, the reality was that Islam was divided politically into several independent states, both worldwide and in the Middle East.

From the eighteenth through the twentieth century, the Middle East was influenced and at times dominated by Western ideas. Initially, this was limited to European countries, especially under British and French colonial rule. By the twentieth century, they were joined by the Soviet Union and the United States. Part of the influence in the region had to do with trade and strategic military interests. With the advent of the industrial revolution in the eighteenth and nineteenth centuries in Europe and America, modern science and technology were transforming the world with a host of developments, such as steamships, railroads, and the telegraph. No longer could a stable region of the world be free from the significance and power of these technological advances. The discovery of oil and natural gas in the region enhanced the significance of this colonial and Western domination further. The economic and military interests of the West are factors that have created a good deal of tension for a considerable period of time in the Middle East. With the advent of the cinema, radio, television, and most recently the Internet, Western popular culture has had a further significant influence on more recent generations of people living in the Middle East. For older generations, Western culture has often been characterized as decadent, and this has been a factor causing tension in the region. The principal concern for these people was that the Middle East, like Europe, would forsake its religious roots and embrace a more secular society.

The interest in acquiring modern military technology from the West began in the nineteenth century. The importance was not limited to weaponry, however; it included tactics in training and organization. This led to an interest in broader ideas associated with the emerging science of public administration. Of particular interest was the desire to centralize the administrative authority of government further in order to weaken any dissidents. With concerns about government administration, law was singled out for particular benefit. A degree of familiarity with western European legal systems had already been achieved during the colonial period, because European countries arranged to have their citizens, who were residing in the Middle East, subject to the laws of their mother country rather than those of the local jurisdiction. Initially, the Ottoman

Empire adopted legal ideas from the codes of European countries. By the late nineteenth century and with specific reference to criminal justice, they were adopting a Penal Code (1857) and a Code of Criminal Procedure (1879) that was based on the contemporary legal codes of France.

Although there was opposition by Islamic jurists to this reception of European law, there were two long-standing traditions in Islam that justified these adaptations. First, the responsibility for developing procedural rules had always been a delegated authority to the sovereign or ruler. While the process could conform to cultural and societal norms, it ultimately had to be in compliance with Sharia. As mentioned earlier, this delegated authority to a ruler was a feature of siyasa, that is, administrative justice policy. As noted earlier, the term *siyasa sharia* means an administration of justice policy that is in conformity with Sharia. Therefore, a distinction was made between Sharia and siyasa. Sharia is that blend of both a code of law and a code of morals. Siyasa sharia is the method of introducing practical pragmatic policies for the administration of justice that are in conformity with the spirit of Sharia, especially when Sharia does not provide specific guidance.

Second, the Islamic legal tradition had long recognized the right of the sovereign to sit as a court himself or through his designee; it was known as the court of Mazalim (complaints). As mentioned earlier in the chapter, this was based on the notion that the ruler, whether a caliph or a sultan, had a responsibility to correct any wrong and ultimately to guarantee justice to all his people. In the context of criminal cases, the political authority or the delegate exercised a legal prerogative to resolve an apparent wrong that had occurred in an Islamic court. There were no rules or texts that defined the limits of the jurisdiction of mazalim. Whereas judges in the regular Islamic courts were bound by rules based in Islamic law, mazalim judges were free to exercise their discretion beyond such procedural or evidentiary rules in order to achieve the goal of righting a wrong.

In spite of these justifications to borrow from the Western legal tradition, this legal reception was cause for tension. After all, Sharia explains to the umma what is the will of God. According to one legal expert, "Islamic law is the epitome of the Islamic thought, the most typical manifestation of the Islamic way of life, the kernel of Islam, itself"(Schacht, 1964). Moreover, it has been pointed out that the acceptance of Western legal ideas raised questions about "the role and nature of the divine command in law. The attitude of classical and traditional jurisprudence to this question rested upon two fundamental and unassailable propositions; first, that the divine revelation prescribed rules and standards that were valid in all conditions and for all time; second, that divine revelation answered, directly or indirectly, every legal problem. In short the divine command was comprehensive and eternally valid" (Coulson, 1969).

As if these aforementioned tensions were not enough, a final, all-encompassing issue confronting many of the countries in the Middle East centers on a basic societal dilemma: what is at the core of a society? As was mentioned in the introductory chapter to this text, the concept of the nation state emerged in the eighteenth century and has been a significant political unit of analysis throughout the world since that time. The intellectual milieu of the Enlightenment helped foster the qualities associated with this nation state, as the Age of Reason replaced the Age of Faith that had dominated Europe since the Middle Ages. Among the characteristics associated with this nation state are performing political activities over a specific sovereign territory and sharing certain common societal features that may include: language, religion, and a common cultural or historical experience. In addition, the institutional development of a nation state has often placed a good deal of emphasis on secular law, because law has usually played a significant role in establishing various legitimate political processes. Finally, the most successful of the nation states in the modern era have embraced democratic principles. The core ideals associated with a modern secular democracy include: a recognition of the importance of government by rule of law, a goal to achieve equality for all members of the community, an objective to establish a right for all members of the community to participate in the conduct of government, and a policy to control and limit government by representatives of the community. The basis for these ideals is the notion that people have individual rights and freedoms.

The concept of a nation state, however, did not emerge in the Middle East until the twentieth century. As a result, the countries in the region are only now grappling with a host of issues associated with this newfound independence as a nation state. Creating a good deal of tension within each country and among the countries in the region is a central issue confronting each country: the ongoing debate over where their allegiance lies. Is their allegiance to an Islamic society? From the inception of Islam, the most important group associated with it was the umma, the community of believers. Today, because Islam is a worldwide religion, the umma extends beyond the borders of any and all nation states. As God is considered the supreme head of the umma, in countries that have embraced all aspects of Islam, the state is considered subordinate to Islam. This kind of state is often described as a theocratic state. The purpose of such a state is to secure the maintenance and enforcement of God's will or law. This is designed to prepare the believers for life in the hereafter. To assist in that preparation, the state seeks to purge society of all sources that create a decadent secular society.

In this aforementioned debate, the alternative allegiance is toward a secular democratic society. While not precisely mimicking what happened in eighteenth-century Europe, some within the Islamic Middle East want to replace their age of faith with an age of reason. Social scientists have long noted and cautioned that political democracy is impossible without social democracy. The proponents of a secular democratic society see the Muslim world's failure to modernize as the cause of both economic and social poverty among the people and often political tyranny in the governance of the states in the region. One scholar has warned that there is "an unstable mix" of a growing population in the Middle East that includes many uneducated and unemployed young people, especially men, who are increasingly frustrated by their plight (Lewis, 2003).

The choice between an allegiance to an Islamic society or to a secular society offers fundamentally different views of society. To explore how the region is grappling with this significant debate, we turn to the nation states of Saudi Arabia, Iran, and Turkey. The objective is to examine the role that Islamic law plays in the contemporary context of these countries. Specifically, our attention is directed at the law and its application within the context of criminal justice.

KINGDOM OF SAUDI ARABIA

The Kingdom of Saudi Arabia is roughly one-fifth the size of the United States at 784,233 square miles. Much of its territory is desert. It shares land borders with Jordan, Iraq, Kuwait, Qatar, United Arab Emirates, Oman, and Yemen. It has a coastline along the Red Sea and the Persian Gulf. The population is about 28 million, of which 5.6 million are foreigners. Until the 1960s, much of the population was described as being nomadic or semi-nomadic. The development of the economy, especially in the petroleum and petrochemical industries and the mining of natural resources, and urban growth have led more than one-third of the people to settle in four metropolitan areas. Of the native population, 90 percent are Arab and 10 percent are Afro-Asian. Approximately 85 percent are Sunni Muslims, while 15 percent are members of the Shia sect of Islam. Saudi Arabia is also home to two of Islam's holiest sites: Mecca and Medina.

When discussing the Arabian Peninsula, it was pointed out that the region was largely populated by Bedouin patriarchal tribes. Given the desert terrain and sparse vegetation in the region, the most significant social unit was the family. These units often existed in isolation; therefore, people were totally dependent on their family for support and survival. As a result, the importance of the family was a significant Bedouin value that remains part of the Saudi cultural and social tradition. The teachings of Islam simply reinforced the importance of the family further. This attitude about family and tribe led to Arabian society not being terribly receptive to assimilating other peoples or ideas. Today, Saudi society continues to emphasize the family or extended family. Protecting the family and the security of its members is paramount. In addition, the rigid patriarchal familial structure from Bedouin times continues. As such, the notion of individuality is essentially absent. Thus, individual rights and freedoms are alien concepts to many people of the region.

The Arabian Peninsula was the birthplace of Islam and Mecca, the spiritual center. Various military skirmishes with the Persians in the eighth century led to the defeat of the Arabs and the transfer of Islamic political power to Baghdad. As a result of these events, the Arabian Peninsula receded in political and economic significance until oil was discovered and became an important resource in the twentieth century. Throughout these centuries of self-imposed isolation, Mecca retained its status as the spiritual center of Islam.

While the modernization of a society usually follows an evolutionary trajectory, this has not been the case for Saudi Arabia. Efforts at modernization, which were initiated during the last third of the twentieth century, have been abrupt and often have no relationship with the past cultural traditions. It has been suggested: "The people and their leaders believed that they could buy the physical development that they wanted without disturbing the stability of their traditional society. It is an illusion they still fight to preserve" (Mackey, 2002). Today, the most important stabilizing factor of that traditional society is Islam. "Islam for the Saudis is more than a theology, it is an entire way of life. Religion is the central force of their existence. Religion is life and life religion. Such an intense theology immensely complicates the Saudis' accommodation to modernization" (Mackey, 2002).

The Kingdom and Wahhabism

The Kingdom of Saudi Arabia was officially founded in September of 1932. The origins of the kingdom, however, began in the middle of the eighteenth century with an alliance between two men: Muhammad ibn Saud (1710–1765), who was a local ruler in the market town of Dir'iyya, and Muhammad ibn Abd al-Wahhab (1703–1792), who was a religious reformer. Their objective was to establish a Muslim state that would follow the teachings of Islam as explained by the Hanbali madhhab. As mentioned earlier, this legal school claimed that all legal rules could be found in either the Quran or the Sunna of the Prophet. Thus, they strongly favored the traditional approaches or sources of Islamic law and focused on both the legal and moral teachings that could be derived from the Quran. Over the course of 150 years, the Saud family would expand and surrender the territory of their Islamic state through conflicts with other Arabian families and with Egypt and the Ottoman Empire. In 1902, Abdul Aziz al-Saud (1880?-1953) recaptured Riyadh, which the

Saud-Wahhabi alliance had established as their capital back in 1824. He then led a succession of campaigns to recapture more territory throughout the peninsula. In 1932, he proclaimed himself king and named his consolidated territories the Kingdom of Saudi Arabia.

It has been pointed out by a contemporary scholar that:

> Wahhabism is rarely defined. Many of the regimes and movements labeled as Wahhabi in the contemporary era do not necessarily share the same theological and legal orientations. The reality is that Wahhabism has become such a blanket term for any Islamic movement that has an apparent tendency toward misogyny, militantism, extremism, or strict and literal interpretation of the Quran and hadith that the designation of a regime or movement as Wahhabi or Wahhabi-like tells us little about its actual nature. Furthermore, these contemporary interpretations of Wahhabism do not necessarily reflect the writings or teachings of Ibn Abd al-Wahhab (Delong-Bas, 2004).

When Muhammad ibn Saud and Muhammad ibn Abd al-Wahhab formed their alliance in 1744 to establish the Saudi state, it was understood that Saud would serve as emir or independent ruler and Wahhab would assume the duties of imam or leader of the Islamic community. Saud created a political system that merged the religious and secular aspects of life into one. Wahhab was one of several religious reformers in the eighteenth century concerned about the state of the Islamic faith. Part of the decline in piety of the adherents to the faith was associated with increased contact with Europeans. One of Wahhab's goals was to emphasize *tawhid*, that is, the Islamic belief in absolute monotheism. There is only one God, and only God should be worshipped. What had happened over the centuries was the erection of monuments to the companions of the Prophet and to previous caliphs. These monuments attracted people who venerated the memory of the person. For reformers like Wahhab, these displays of reverence should have been reserved for God alone. As a result, his followers destroyed such monuments that venerated either Muslims or non-Muslims.

Wahhab's most important concern was directed at the ulama. As mentioned earlier, the ulama were men who had pursued a religious education of the Quran, Sunna, and Sharia. Because Islam did not have an ordained clergy or a method to certify scholars, they were simply identified by their community for their religious learning. They became the guardians of the beliefs, values, and practices of the umma, the community of believers. Some became noted as famous theological scholars, while others were noted for their legal scholarship and were referred to as jurists. The elite among the ulama were called upon to serve as judges in important courts, as teachers at the famous schools, and as preachers in the major mosques. By Wahhab's time, members of the ulama were not studying the original sources of Islam, the Quran and Sunna in particular, but were relying on legal manuals and secondary literature. The reformers, like Wahhab, called for a return to the study of the original sources of Islam and the gleaning from those sources of the true meaning of Islam and what it meant to be a devout Muslim. As a preacher, Wahhab's message was to return to the original purer form of Islam through a strict obedience to the Quran and a rejection of the newer interpretations of Islam. He maintained that a Muslim should evaluate the context of the messages derived from the Sunna and then make comparisons with the Quran in order to discover the truth. It was during this time that the Saud-Wahhabi state adopted the Hanbali madhhab version of Sharia as the only legitimate law of their state.

In keeping with his approach of relying on the original sources for guidance, Wahhab maintained that the Prophet Muhammad went to war only as a defensive tactic in order to protect the Muslim community. Scholars have pointed out that his writings indicate that *jihad* was a special kind of war that was designed to protect the Muslim community from an aggressor. The ultimate goal was to end the aggression by establishing a truce or a treaty. Moreover, Wahhab has been described as opposing violence because it would reduce the likelihood of converting people to Islam, which was one of the original goals of the Prophet, and he was not a proponent of Muslim martyrdom. On the subject of women, scholars have indicated that Wahhab's writings indicate a concern for the rights of women that were similar to those of the Prophet Muhammad.

Of course, Wahhab's Islamic conservatism was clearly evident in his support for the Hanbali method of Islamic jurisprudence and his rejection of the notion that Islamic law and local custom should be synthesized. It has been pointed out that he was more focused on the intent of a person in a legal case rather than on the act itself. Thus, he was skeptical of legal decisions that were based solely on a literal interpretation of the Quran or Sunna (Delong-Bas, 2004).

Wahhab was recognized as both a theologian and a jurist or legal scholar. While he took strong exception to the ulama of his day and their distortions of the faith, he was also concerned about the lack of knowledge that both religious and political leaders had of Islamic law. His principal means of reform was through education. He was of the opinion that discussion and debate was the approach that should be taken to teach people about their faith, and possibly even to convert people to Islam.

Muhammad ibn Saud's objective of expanding the territory of his state took precedent over Muhammad ibn Abd al-Wahhab's desire to reform Islam. In 1773, Wahhab resigned as imam and withdrew from public life. When he died in 1791, the Saud-Wahhabi alliance had only started to achieve its significance in the region. Today, those who hold the most fundamentalist positions in the Kingdom trace their beliefs to

Wahhab's conservative views. In light of his concern for the rights of women and his opposition to making legal decisions solely on a literal interpretation of the Quran, it is questionable whether he would support the fundamentalists of today that employ his name to describe and advance their social policies.

Government

The government of Saudi Arabia is based on a near absolute monarchial system. The Saudi Arabian king exercises very broad powers in his capacity as head of state and head of the government. From its inception in 1932, the legitimate foundation for the Kingdom of Saudi Arabia was the Sharia. While King Abdul Aziz acknowledged that Sharia was the only law of the kingdom, he astutely expanded his right to legislate through royal decrees. This was justified through siyasa sharia. As mentioned earlier, this is the method of introducing practical pragmatic policies for the administration of justice that are in conformity with the spirit of Sharia, especially when Sharia does not provide specific guidance. With regard to contemporary legal reform, Saudi Arabia is clearly a work in progress. Over the past three decades a number of factors have led to incremental changes in the law and legal system. Those factors include: attempts to grapple with the Kingdom's modern societal changes, pressures from international human rights groups, and events in Iran since 1979 (which will be discussed below in the subsection of this chapter on Iran). To illustrate, a fairly recent and important use of siyasa sharia occurred in 1992 when the Basic Law of Government was adopted by a royal decree from King Fahd. It serves as the constitution of the Kingdom. It is alleged that no government body was consulted on the contents of the Basic Law other than members of the House of Saud (Human Rights Watch, 1992).

Article 1 of the Constitution states: "The Kingdom of Saudi Arabia is a sovereign Arab Islamic state with Islam as its religion; God's Book and the Sunnah of His Prophet, God's prayers and peace be upon him, are its constitution." Even before the Basic Law of Government was adopted, there was a prohibition against the open practice of any other religion in the country. This is generally not the case in other countries where the dominate religion is Islam.

The importance of Islam is ever present in this document. To illustrate, article 7 indicates that "Government in Saudi Arabia derives power from the Holy Qur'an and the Prophet's tradition," while article 8 explains that "Government in the Kingdom of Saudi Arabia is based on the premise of justice, consultation, and equality in accordance with the Islamic Shari'a." This article is an expression of the long-standing uniqueness that the Kingdom of Saudi Arabia exhibits among the various Islamic countries in the world. Whereas many Islamic countries might adhere to various Sharia principles, they have reformed their legal system in light of modern contemporary society. With specific reference to Sharia, that is not the case in Saudi Arabia. One scholar has described this unique character.

> The legal system of Saudi Arabia is an exceptional one in the world of Islam. In most countries where the Shari'a is applied, the state determines which parts of the Shari'a are enforced. Moreover, in order to assert their power to determine what is law, states as a rule have codified—and thereby modernized—those parts of the Shari'a that are applied by the courts. In Saudi Arabia, however, the state does not interfere with the substantive laws of the Shari'a. The Saudi state regards uncodified Shari'a as the law of the land, and enacted law is subordinate to it (Peters, 2005).

Without a modern codified context, judges are trained and refer to commentaries of the Shaira that were written for the most part in the middle ages.

The long-standing policy of the House of Saud to ban any political dissent is given added legal support with article 12 of the Basic Law. It declares: "The consolidation of national unity is a duty, and the state will prevent anything that may lead to disunity, sedition and separation." As such, people do not have the right to assemble unless the government authorizes a demonstration that is in support of one of its policies. Of course, there are people in the country that hold a range of views across the conservative to liberal political spectrum, but there are no formally established political parties in the country. The nature of the political groups that have emerged in the Middle East over recent decades has only reinforced the position of the House of Saud to prohibit organized political groups. Moreover, the notion of the importance of a free press is absent. The government generally determines all the news that it deems fit to print. Finally, the Ministry of Information owns and operates Saudi radio and television.

Constitution The Basic Law of Government or Constitution of Saudi Arabia is divided into nine chapters and includes a total of 83 articles. While some facets of the constitution will be discussed below in other parts of this section on government, it is worth highlighting two chapters that illustrate that Sharia remains intimately part of the constitution and central to an understanding of the Saudi legal system. Chapter 3 of the Basic Law is titled "Features of the Saudi Family." Article 9 declares: "The family is the kernel of Saudi society, and its members shall be brought up on the basis of the Islamic faith, and loyalty and obedience to God, His Messenger, and to guardians; respect for and implementation of the law, and love of and pride in the homeland and its glorious history as the Islamic faith stipulates." Article 10 states: "The state will aspire to strengthen family ties, maintain its Arab and Islamic values and care for all its members, and to provide the right conditions for the growth of their resources and capabilities." Article 11 explains that "Saudi society will be based on the principle of adherence to God's command, on mutual cooperation in good deeds and piety and mutual support and inseparability." These articles illustrate the Saudis ongoing commitment to the most significant social unit of their society, the family, which was also the centerpiece of ancient Bedouin society. Finally, article 13 indicates: "Education will aim at instilling the Islamic faith in the younger generation, providing its members with knowledge and skills and preparing them to become useful members in the building of their society, members who love their homeland and are proud of its history."

Chapter 5 is devoted to rights and duties. The state's duties are placed within the context of Islam and Islamic law. For example, article 23 proclaims: "The state protects Islam; it implements its Shari'a; it orders people to do right and shun evil; it fulfills the duty regarding God's call." Article 26 declares: "The state protects human rights in accordance with the Islamic Shari'a." Individual rights and those associated with criminal justice issues in particular are prominent in this chapter. To illustrate, article 36 indicates: "The state provides security for all its citizens and all residents within the territory and no one shall be arrested, imprisoned, or have their actions restricted except in cases specified by statutes." Article 37 continues along these lines in stating: "The home is sacrosanct and shall not be entered without the permission of the owner or be searched except in cases specified by statutes." Finally, article 38 indicates: "Penalties shall be personal and there shall be no crime or penalty except in accordance with the Shari'a or organizational law. There shall be no punishment except for acts committed subsequently to the coming into force of the organizational law." A more detailed discussion of criminal procedure follows below.

Monarch Many countries in the world that were historically associated with monarchial governance have abandoned this form of government, especially during the course of the twentieth century. Those that have retained the monarchy have often limited the role to symbolic and ceremonial duties. This is clearly not the case in Saudi Arabia. As mentioned previously, article 7 of the Basic Law states: "Government in Saudi Arabia derives power from the Holy Qur'an and the Prophet's tradition." This is in keeping with the Sunni Islam tradition that grants the leader authority in the political realm but does not bestow a theocratic status. Of course, the leader is expected to be a protector and defender of the Islamic faith. Thus, Sunnis believe that an Islamic government is a civil matter without any religious authority. It would be the responsibility of the ulama, the religious scholars, to offer moral and ethical guidance to the community, although they are not actually mandated to govern. Thus, the office of monarch is a sacred trust imposed on and accepted by the individual, which includes protecting Islam. Moreover, article 6 commands: "Citizens are to pay allegiance to the King in accordance with the Holy Qur'an and the tradition of the Prophet, in submission and obedience, in times of ease and difficulty, fortune and adversity."

Chapter 2 of the Basic Law of Government is devoted to monarchy. Article 5 states: "The system of government in the Kingdom of Saudi Arabia is that of a monarchy." The article continues with four statements that outline the act of succession to the monarchy.

> Rule passes to the sons of the founding King, Abd al-Aziz Bin Abd al-Rahman al-Faysal Al Sa'ud, and to their children's children. The most upright among them is to receive allegiance in accordance with the principles of the Holy Qur'an and the Tradition of the Venerable Prophet.
>
> The King chooses the Heir Apparent and relieves him of his duties by Royal order.
>
> The Heir Apparent is to devote his time to his duties as an Heir Apparent and to whatever missions the King entrusts him with.
>
> The Heir Apparent takes over the powers of the King on the latter's death until the act of allegiance has been carried out.

A few comments are in order regarding this method of succession. First, the Saudis have always employed an agnatic order of succession, that is, only males are eligible to become the monarch. This is not surprising in light of the historical and contemporary patriarchal character of the society. It should be noted, however, that countries with monarchies that have long been associated with democratic principles have only recently either adopted or are considering the introduction of cognatic succession, that is, the eldest child (male or female) is the heir. Second, most monarchial methods of succession, whether agnatic or cognatic, claim the right to the eldest child. That is not necessarily the case in Saudi Arabia, where the Basic Law reiterates the tradition of selecting "the most upright among" the heirs of King Abdul Aziz. Because the King had so many children, there is unlikely ever to be a shortage of royal princes eligible for consideration. The king selects his heir, the crown prince, among the royal princes, but this is always done in consultation with senior members of the royal family and religious leaders. Article 8 of the Basic Law speaks of the importance of government by consultation, and this important decision is an illustration of that principle in action. In the past, the selection of the crown prince was a rather secretive and somewhat informal process. In 2006, King Abdullah announced that an Allegiance Commission was formed to handle the selection process and thus bring some sense of transparency to the procedure. Finally, it is noted that the heir apparent would take over upon the king's death. There have been instances in which a crown prince has actually functioned in place of the monarch when the reigning king was incapacitated.

In his capacity as head of state and head of the government, the monarch's duties are extensive, and most are cited throughout the Basic Law of Government. They include: overseeing the administration of the government, chairing the Council of Ministers, appointing ministers to the Council and heads of various departments, appointing members to the Consultative Council, declaring states of emergency as the commander-in-chief of all armed forces, carrying out the policies of the country, overseeing the implementation of Sharia, issuing royal decrees that have the force of law, appointing judges, and implementing judicial rulings. The king delegates some of the breadth and depth of these duties to others.

Although the king's authority is significant, he should not be considered an absolute monarch, for he must adhere to Sharia and Saudi traditions. Thus, the monarch's authority is rooted in two sources: Islam and Bedouin society. It was already mentioned that the Sunni tradition acknowledges that the political leader is responsible for the administration of the Islamic government as a civil matter. He does not have any religious authority, but in his capacity as leader, he is expected to be a protector and defender of the Islamic faith. This is particularly the case in Saudi Arabia, the home of two sacred sites: Mecca and Medina. The king, however, would consult with the ulama, the religious scholars, whose responsibility it is to offer moral and ethical guidance for the community.

As mentioned earlier, Bedouin society was based on a patriarchal tribal social structure. The various tribes initially created unwritten rules that over time established customary laws for a tribe. As such, a single executive or legislative authority did not exist in the Arabian Peninsula. Each sheikh held the leadership position in his tribe. These sheikhs would meet periodically to resolve disputes among the various tribes in the region. When Abdul Aziz declared himself king of the newly formed Kingdom of Saudi Arabia, he became the first sheikh among the sheikhs in the region. To assure their allegiance, King Abdul Aziz continued the Bedouin tradition of consultation with the local leaders. What follows are three examples of the consultative process in Saudi governance. They illustrate the value of forming a consensus on policy matters for the Kingdom.

Council of Ministers In addition to holding the title of king, the monarch is also the prime minister, for he chairs the Council of Ministers.

As article 56 of the Basic Law indicates in part, "The Council of Ministers establishes the prerogatives of the Council regarding internal and external affairs, the organization of and co-ordination between government bodies. It also establishes requirements to be fulfilled by ministers, their prerogatives, the manner of their questioning and all issues concerning them." King Abdul Aziz created the Council 1953 as an advisory body to the king. By 1958, Crown Prince Faisal had enhanced the authority of the Council by giving it both administrative and legislative duties. While the Council can issue decrees, this authority is not separate from that of the king, who must approve all of the Council's decisions.

In addition to the king, the Council is composed of the crown prince, some royal advisors, and the heads of various ministries. The most prominent ministries include: defense and aviation, foreign affairs, finance, interior, justice, education, health, industry, information, labor and social affairs, petroleum and mineral resources, public works and housing, pilgrimage affairs and religious trusts, and the Saudi Arabian National Guard.

Consultative Council Muslims believe that God is the sole source of authority and the lawgiver. As mentioned previously, the Quran states: "Authority belongs to God alone, and he orders you to worship none but Him: this is the true faith, though most people do not realize it" (12:40). While God is the sovereign lawgiver, "God has made a promise to those among you who believe and do good deeds: He will make them successors to the land, as He did those who came before them; He will empower the religion He had chosen for them; He will grant them security to replace their fear" (24:55). This verse has been interpreted as acknowledging that man is God's trustee on earth and thus has the authority to make law, but it must be in conformity with Sharia. Thus, while God is the lawgiver, man has the authority to be a lawmaker.

While the Council of Ministers has both administrative and legislative functions, the Consultative Council can be characterized as a type of legislature within the context of Saudi governance. Article 68 of the Basic Law of Government created this Council in 1992, and article 69 indicates that "The King has the right to convene the Consultative Council and the Council of Ministers for a joint meeting and to invite whoever he wishes to attend that meeting to discuss whatever matters he wishes." Once again, this passage illustrates both the king's broad authority, but also the important role that consultation plays in the governance of the Kingdom.

The Consultative Council is composed of 150 people selected by the king for a four-year term. Half of the members must be newly selected every four years. Membership on the Council consists of men of learning who do not hold governmental or private management positions, unless the king waives this rule. The Council is designed to serve as a sounding board on government policy, and it can propose new or amended legislation. It does not, however, have the independent authority to legislate. Any legislation under consideration must secure the approval of two-thirds of the members of the Consultative Council for it to become law. Ultimately, for legislation to become law, it must be approved by the Consultative Council, the Council of Ministers, and the monarch.

Senior Council of the Ulama In 1971, the Senior Council of the Ulama was created. It is composed of between 30 and 40 of the leading senior religious scholars and is chaired by the Grand Mufti. A *mufti* is a specialist in Islamic law and is authorized to issue fatwas. Although this Council is not part of the legislative process as the aforementioned councils are, it is consulted on various pieces of proposed legislation to seek its guidance on conformity with the moral and ethical teachings of Islam in general and Sharia in particular. One of its principal duties is to provide fatwas that establish general rules regarding questions submitted to it by the government. Traditionally, a fatwa was a legal opinion from any religious scholar or jurist on an issue. While fatwas were acknowledged as a legal authority, they were not considered law. A fatwa is distinct from a judge's ruling in a court of law, although a judge can be guided in his deliberations by a fatwa.

Judiciary

There have been two kinds of courts in Saudi Arabia: Judicial Courts and the Board of Grievances. In October 2007, King Abdullah issued a royal decree designed to modernize the judiciary and impact both types of courts. The Board of Grievances, which is now referred to as Administrative Courts, have a parallel structure to that of the Judicial Courts. The Administrative Courts are responsible for disputes among government departments and cases involving administrative decisions by the government or an independent corporate entity. The other type of courts are referred to as Judicial Courts, and they are of particular interest for our purposes. While some of the reforms are still being introduced, the new judicial system is presented here. It is anticipated that the new system will be completed by 2010. Before the court system is described, however, it may prove beneficial to explain the role of the Supreme Judicial Council, which has a significant responsibility for the administration of justice.

Supreme Judicial Council Prior to the introduction of the 2007 judiciary reforms, the Supreme Judicial Council functioned as the highest court in the court hierarchy. It also had several administrative functions. As a result of the reforms, the Supreme Judicial Council is primarily limited to handling administrative matters. To illustrate, it has supervisory authority over the courts and judges. This includes: appointing judges, issuing regulations on the role of judges, inspecting courts, and addressing court organizational issues. The Ministry of Justice maintains financial control over the judiciary along with some administrative duties.

Members of the Council include: the Chief Judge of the High Court, four chief judges of the Appellate Courts, a deputy Minister of Justice, the Chief of the Bureau of Investigation and Prosecution, and three members who have the qualifications of judges from Appellate Courts. With the exception of the Chief Judge of the High Court, the Chief of the Bureau of Investigation and Prosecution, and the deputy Minister of Justice, all the other appointees are selected directly by the king. The term of the appointment is for four years, which can be renewed.

Judicial Courts There are three tiers in the hierarchy of the Judicial Courts: High Court, Courts of Appeal, and First-Degree Courts (see Figure 7.1).

Figure 7.1

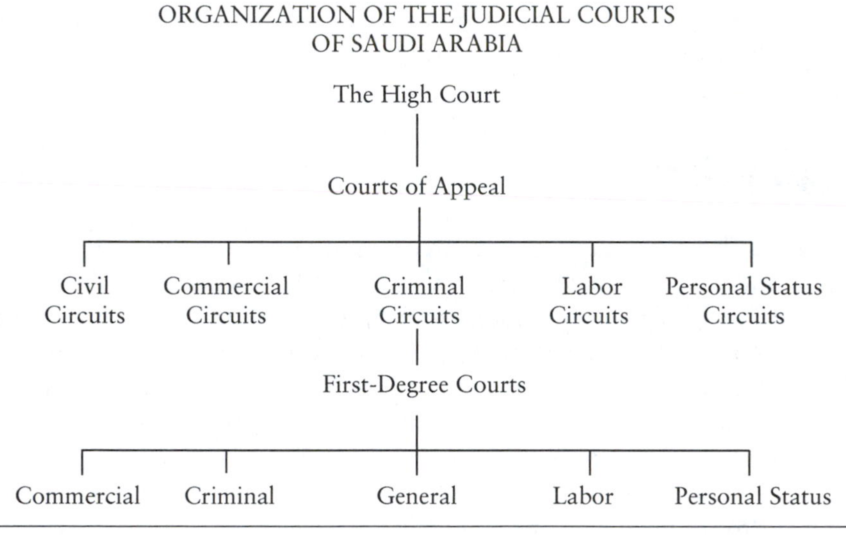

The High Court is located in Riyadh, the capital of Saudi Arabia, and it has two functions. It has certain administrative responsibilities that include overseeing the implementation of Sharia in the courts and regulations decreed by the king. It also reviews the decisions made by and upheld by the Courts of Appeal. The court's other function is to entertain appeals that are essentially based on questions of law or questions of procedure. A panel of three judges would normally hear appeals to the court. There is one exception to this rule. In cases coming from a criminal circuit of a Court of Appeal, the panel will consist of five judges, because the court is mandated to review judgments involving major punishments, such as the death penalty, stoning, amputation, or quesas cases other than death. At least one Court of Appeal is located in each of the 13 provinces of the country. Courts of Appeal are subdivided into specialized circuits: Civil, Commercial, Criminal, Labor, and Personal Status. These circuits entertain appeals from the First-Degree Courts.

First-Degree Courts are located throughout the country. These courts are also subdivided into divisions of specialization: Commercial, Criminal, General, Labor, and Personal Status. With regard to the Criminal Court, it is further subdivided into circuits that specialize in hudud, quesas, tazir, and juvenile offenses. The hudud, quesas, and tazir offenses were explained above in the section, "Crime and Punishment." They indicate the manner in which criminal offenses are categorized in Islamic law. The Criminal Court is composed of a three-judge panel. Any other offense that does not fit under the aforementioned categories would be handled by a single judge.

Judges According to article 1 of the Law of the Judiciary, "Judges are independent and, in the administration of justice, they shall be subject to no authority other than the provisions of Shari'a and laws in force. No one may interfere with the Judiciary." The objective of this statement is to give the appearance that the power of the executive branch of government is reduced regarding the judiciary. The revised Law of the Judiciary has essentially removed the minister of justice from a significant role either in the appointment of judges or in the judicial decision-making process, but the ministry is still responsible for the budget. Ultimately, the executive branch is involved, because of the role that the king plays either directly or indirectly in the appointment of members to the Supreme Judicial Council.

The role of the judge is not that of a disinterested umpire, as common law judges are often described; rather, their task is to seek the truth through an inquisitorial method of probing questions of the parties, witnesses, and evidence, and then concluding by dispensing justice. The judges are guided by one of two types of procedures employed in the adjudication process, depending on the nature of the case. The procedural rules are titled the Law of Procedure before Sharia Courts and the Law of Criminal Procedure.

Article 31 of the Law of the Judiciary explains the qualifications necessary to become a judge. Requirements include: being a Saudi national, of good character and conduct, qualified to hold the position in accordance with the Sharia, meeting the educational requirements, and not having been sentenced for a crime affecting his religion or honor or dismissed from public office for disciplinary reasons, unless the person has been rehabilitated. With regard to the education requirement, the judge must hold a degree from one of the Sharia colleges within the Kingdom. This is designed to assure that the person is capable of practicing ijtihad. As mentioned earlier in this chapter, ijtihad is the process in which jurists determine a rule based on analogy. It is utilized when a rule conflicts with another rule or when a rule is rather vague and somewhat questionable. Originally, jurists turn to ijtihad when neither the Quran nor the Sunna specifically addressed an issue at hand. The ultimate goal of ijtihad is to resolve a conflict or clarify an issue that is in the best interests of the Muslim community.

If a candidate has not been schooled in one of the Sharia colleges but holds an equivalent certificate elsewhere, he must pass a special examination. A candidate must be at least 40 years of age for appointment to an appellate court and at least 22 years of age for appointment to the other courts. Newly appointed assistant judges serve a two-year probationary period. All of their decisions are reviewed by more senior judges before they are announced in court.

One of the criticisms directed at Saudi judges is their overly broad use of discretion when interpreting Shaira. On the one hand, people in the West favor judicial independence and see it as a good thing. In the Saudi context, on the other hand, some features of judicial independence impede the development of a uniform and just legal system. To illustrate, Saudi judges do not rely on precedent; rather, they may depend solely on their own reasoning. Because judges are religiously educated men, they tend to be from a fairly conservative mind-set.

This often extreme conservative interpretation of the law prompted recent efforts at judicial reform. For example, the authority of the Supreme Judicial Council to function as the ultimate court of appeal was removed. The goal is to make the High Court more sensitive to modern legal issues that are associated with a broad range of concerns, from business ventures to human rights. In addition, the very narrow legal schooling that judicial candidates have received at Sharia colleges was another concern. As a result, the Judicial Academy and an Institute of Public Administration were established in 2000 and are designed to offer additional training by enhancing the expertise and skills of members of the judiciary. While these reforms are welcome, it is important to keep in mind that implementing them will be extremely slow given the conservative nature of the society in general and the current judges in particular.

Saudi Arabia is below the international average for the number of judges per 100,000 people. The international standard suggests that the Kingdom should have 5,200 judges, yet the Ministry of Justice identified 662 active judges in 2006 (Human Rights Watch, 2008d). The aforementioned educational reforms are designed to rectify this problem. Nevertheless, the current active judges are overworked, which inevitably leads to errors. Given the nature of the pretrial and trial processes, these errors can contribute to issues associated with human rights violations against those accused of crime.

Bureau of Investigation and Public Prosecution With regard to the Saudi criminal justice process, the Bureau of Investigation and Public Prosecution is the most important component of their system. As the name suggests, the Bureau may investigate crimes, but it does not have exclusive responsibility for that. Other law enforcement agencies might have jurisdictional authority, depending on the nature of the offense and where the crime occurred. The Bureau is also responsible for the prosecution of criminal offenses.

The Bureau is under the administrative leadership of the Ministry of the Interior. The Chairman of the Bureau is responsible for the management of the organization, which has offices throughout the country. Article 14 of the Law of Criminal Procedure states: "The Bureau of Investigation and Prosecution shall conduct its investigation and prosecution in accordance with its Law and the implementing regulation thereof." The Law that article 14 refers to is the Law of the Bureau of Investigation and Public Prosecution. This piece of legislation explains the organization, management, and jurisdiction of the Bureau. It also provides an extensive internal procedure for disciplining members of the Bureau who are accused of either a criminal or noncriminal violation.

While the name of the Bureau explains two of its key responsibilities, article 3 of the Law of the Bureau of Investigation and Public Prosecution offers a more encompassing list of its duties. The article states, in part:

> The Bureau shall have jurisdiction, in accordance with the law and as specified by the implementing regulations, as follows:
>
> (a) Investigating crimes;
>
> (b) Taking action with respect to an investigation through filing a case or taking no action in accordance with relevant regulations;
>
> (c) Prosecuting before judicial bodies in accordance with the implementing regulations;
>
> (d) Appealing judgments;
>
> (e) Supervising the execution of criminal sentences;
>
> (f) Monitoring and inspecting prisons, detention centers and any places where criminal sentences are executed, as well as hearing complaints of prisoners and detainees, insuring the legality of their imprisonment or detention and the legality of their remaining in prison or the detention center after the expiry of the period, taking necessary steps to release those imprisoned or detained without a legitimate cause and applying the law against those responsible for such action. The Minister of Interior shall be informed of any relevant observations, and a report shall be submitted to him regarding the conditions of the prisoners and detainees every six months;
>
> (g) Any other power conferred upon it by the law, regulations issued pursuant to this Law, the resolutions of the Council of Ministers or the High Orders.

Thus, in addition to investigating some cases and prosecuting all offenses, the Bureau appeals court judgments, supervises the execution of sentences, and oversees the management of the prison system and detention centers. Critics have suggested that the Bureau's oversight of prisons and detention centers has been minimal at best. Finally, article 25 of the Law of Criminal Procedure authorizes the Bureau to supervise the overall investigation of an offense that is being handled by criminal investigators from another law enforcement agency. Indeed, this agency wields a significant amount of authority throughout the Saudi justice system. In light of that authority, it has been suggested that the Bureau should not fall under the jurisdiction of the Ministry of the Interior but rather under that of the Ministry of Justice.

Finally, within the Bureau there is a Bureau Administration Committee composed of senior members, including the Chairman and Vice Chairman of the Bureau. While much of the Committee's duties focus on administration, such as studying issues associated with investigation and prosecution and the production of an annual report, it does have one significant substantive responsibility: it is charged with the review of all indictments in which the death penalty, amputation, or stoning are sought. The Saudis are well aware of the objections that many nations and international organizations have with regard to some of the Sharia sanctions. In view of that, in those cases where such a sanction is sought, the Bureau examines the indictment even before the case goes to trial. Because the Saudis have proclaimed their adherence to Sharia in a host of legal documents, they are unlikely to deviate from their support for the sanctions that others find objectionable. From the Saudi point of view there are several steps in their criminal process that are designed to prevent miscarriages of justice. With regard to the aforementioned sanctions, the review of the indictment by the Bureau Administration Committee is the first step, which may be followed by a trial, an appeal, and then ultimately a review by the High Court.

Law

There are three main sources of law in Saudi Arabia: Islamic law, statutory law, and royal orders. The principal sources of Islamic law or Sharia are the Quran and Sunna. These sources, along with ijma and ijtihad, were explained above in the section, "Sources of Sharia." The application of Sharia is guided by the interpretation of the Hanbali madhhab. This is one of the four orthodox madhahib or Islamic legal schools that were discussed earlier in the section on madhahib. It is important to reiterate the importance and uniqueness of Islamic law. Sharia was "the comprehensive and preordained system of God's commands, a system of law having an existence independent of society, not growing out of society but imposed upon society from above" (Coulson, 1969). Moreover, Sharia is considered both a code of law and a code of morals. Thus, a distinction was never made between the two concepts. The Quran, in particular, is the fundamental vehicle that defines what is appropriate in the Islamic community of believers. As mentioned earlier, not only is the law unique, but the Kingdom of Saudi Arabia's application of Sharia is essentially different from other Islamic countries in the world. Whereas many Islamic countries might adhere to various Sharia principles, they have reformed their legal system in light of modern contemporary society. With specific reference to Sharia, that is not the case in Saudi Arabia.

Statutory laws and regulations are the result of deliberations of the Council of Ministers, the Consultative Council, and the monarch. These statutes deal with a host of private and public law issues associated with a modern contemporary society. They include: drug-related offenses, embezzlement, explosives, and official abuses of power. In order to become law, these pieces of legislation had to be in compliance with Sharia. Finally, the king has the authority to issue royal decrees, also, of course, in conformity with Sharia. Royal decrees may or may not be subjected to consultation, either with the Council of Ministers or possibly with that Council as well as the Consultative Council. That decision rests totally with the monarch.

One of the ongoing criticisms directed at the Saudi justice system is the fact that the criminal law has not been codified. A number of Saudis have indicated the merits of codification, but it has not come to fruition. Presently, there are three kinds of crime. The origins of this categorization are explained above in the section, "Crime and Punishment." Crimes of hudud are considered against God, because they threaten the social order and security of the community of believers. Quesas crimes are violations against the rights of an individual. These are associated with retribution and compensation. Finally, tazir offenses are considered less serious, because they essentially do not involve physical injury to a victim. They are also referred to as discretionary crimes, because the judge has the discretion to determine if the action or inaction was a crime and what constitutes an appropriate sentence. Because Saudi judges are not required to follow precedent, they exercise a considerable amount of discretion in this context, which has led to allegations of serious abuse. Obviously, an accused person is placed in a very difficult situation if he or she cannot refer to a formally approved definition of the offense they are accused of committing. Among the examples left to a judge to define are: defrauding people, failure to observe prayer, and lewd behavior (Human Rights Watch, 2008d).

As mentioned earlier, there are two types of procedural law: the Law of Procedure before Sharia Courts and the Law of Criminal Procedure. Some of the contents of the Law of Criminal Procedure were borrowed from Egyptian and French procedural law (Ansary, 2008). Naturally, it is the Law of Criminal Procedure that is of interest for our purpose. Attention is paid to both the pretrial and trial processes.

It is important to point out straightaway that this law was approved in 2001. A number of the provisions of the law have been criticized as deficient in either protecting or securing due process rights. A reoccurring point of contention is that this procedural law suffers from far too many vague statements (Human Rights Watch, 2008d). As is the case with any procedural law, its successful implementation is often totally dependent on a vigilant judiciary. Criticisms have been raised that various aspects of the pretrial and trial processes have not always been implemented or adhered to in the spirit in which they were intended. This may in part be attributed to the document's vagueness, but it may also be an expression of opposition on the part of the judiciary. Only time will tell if these concerns can be resolved, especially with the recent implementation of reforms associated with judges.

Pretrial Procedures Chapter 5 of the Basic Law of Government is devoted to rights and duties. Within this chapter, individual rights and those associated with criminal justice issues in particular are prominently featured. Article 26 declares: "The state protects human rights in accordance with the Islamic Shari'a." To illustrate, article 36 indicates: "The state provides security for all its citizens and all residents within the territory and no one shall be arrested, imprisoned, or have their actions restricted except in cases specified by statutes." Article 37 continues along these lines, stating: "The home is sacrosanct and shall not be entered without the permission of the owner or be searched except in cases specified by statutes."

It is the Law of Criminal Procedure that establishes guidelines for agents of the justice system on how they are to proceed with a criminal investigation. These guidelines are similar to those found in many countries of the world, irrespective of the legal family with which they are associated. Following some general comments about the Saudi investigative process, the rules associated with the right to assistance of counsel, the powers associated with searches and seizures, the powers associated with interrogations, and the powers associated with arrests and detention will be explained.

With regard to the general comments, there are essentially two ways in which a case can be opened and an investigation initiated. The law authorizes the Bureau of Investigation and Prosecution to initiate a criminal investigation. Moreover, article 17 of the Law of Criminal Procedure indicates: "The victim or his representative and his heirs may initiate criminal action with respect to all cases involving a private right of action, and shall follow-up any such case before the competent court." In such cases, the court would inform the prosecutor of the matter, and the prosecutor would then initiate an investigation if it deemed that it would serve the public interest.

According to article 26 of the Law of Criminal Procedure, there are a number of government agencies that are authorized to conduct a criminal investigation within their respective jurisdictions. The agencies include: members of the Bureau of Investigation, directors of police and their assistants, public security officers, secret service officers, passport officers, intelligence officers, civil defense officers, prison directors and officers, border guards, National Guard officers, and military officers. The heads of the Commission for the Promotion of Virtue and the Prevention of Vice are also authorized to conduct investigations with respect to matters falling within their jurisdiction. (The Commission for the Promotion of Virtue and the Prevention of Vice is explained below.) Irrespective of the agency conducting the investigation, article 25 indicates that they are all "subject to the supervision of the Bureau of Investigation and Prosecution." Critics have suggested that the Bureau has not been terribly vigilant in its oversight of other law enforcement agencies, singling out secret service and intelligence officers as examples, which should come as no surprise given the nature of their work. They have also avoided supervising the Commission for the Promotion of Virtue and the Prevention of Vice, which is politically accountable only to the monarch.

With roots both in Islamic procedural law and with modern procedures borrowed from some Romano-Germanic countries, the Saudi procedure acknowledges the standing of the person harmed in the course of the commission of a criminal offense. While the prosecutor is primarily representing the public as a victim in a criminal case, which is referred to as the public right of action, the actual victim also has a claim with respect to a private right of action. In that context, article 69 addresses the pretrial rights of a victim during the course of an investigation. "The accused, the victim, the claimant in respect of the private right of action, and their respective representatives or attorneys may attend all the investigation proceedings. The Investigator may, however, conduct the investigation in the absence of all or some of the above mentioned, whenever that is deemed necessary for determining the truth. Immediately after the necessity has ended, he shall allow them to review the investigation."

With regard to the right to assistance of counsel, article 4 of the general provisions of the procedural law declares: "Any accused person shall have the right to seek the assistance of a lawyer or a representative to defend him during the investigation and trial stages." This right is reiterated at article 64: "During the investigation, the accused shall have the right to seek the assistance of a representative or an attorney." Thus, a person has the right to assistance when suspicion is directed at them. Critics have pointed out that many accused people are never told of their right to representation. Moreover, there is no public defender system. Therefore, when the accused is made aware of the right to assistance, he or she may not, and often does not, have the means to employ an attorney (Human Rights Watch, 2008d).

The powers associated with searches and seizures may involve a person, place, or belongings. Regarding a person, article 42 indicates: "A criminal investigation officer may search the accused where it is lawful to arrest him, which may include his body, clothes, and belongings. If the accused is a female, the search shall be conducted by a female assigned by the criminal investigation officer."

With specific reference to places, article 41 focuses on the importance of a search warrant. It states:

> A criminal investigation officer may not enter or search any inhabited place except in the cases provided for in the laws, pursuant to a search warrant specifying the reasons for the search, issued by the Bureau of Investigation and Prosecution. However, other dwellings may be searched pursuant to a search warrant, specifying the reasons, issued by the Investigator. If the proprietor or the occupant of a dwelling refuses to allow the criminal investigation officer free access, or resists such entry, he may use all lawful means, as may be required in the circumstances, to enter that dwelling.

Article 45 points out that searches are designed to collect information associated with the crime under investigation. It indicates, however, that if a search "incidentally reveals unlawful material the possession of which is unlawful or any evidence associated with any other crime, the criminal investigation officer shall collect such evidence and a note to that effect shall be entered into the record."

Article 51 states: "The search shall be conducted during the daytime, after sunrise and before sunset in accordance with the powers conferred by law. No access to dwellings during the night shall be allowed except during the commission of a crime." Moreover, article 46 indicates that a search of a dwelling should be conducted in the presence of either the owner or his representative. If this is not possible, two witnesses should be secured to oversee the search.

Article 55 indicates: "Mails, cables, telephone conversations and other means of communication shall be inviolable and, as such, shall not be perused or surveiled except pursuant to an order stating the reasons thereof and for a limited period as herein provided for." Article 56 elaborates on this qualification: "The Director of the Bureau of Investigation and prosecution may issue an order authorizing seizure of mail, publications, and parcels and surveillance and recording of telephone conversations, if such procedure is deemed useful in determining the truth related to a crime that has actually been committed. Such order shall state the reasons thereof and shall be for a period not exceeding ten days renewable according to the requirements of the investigation."

With regard to the whole issue of searches and seizures associated with a person, place, or belongings, critics claim that these rights have been violated to a significant degree (Human Rights Watch, 2008d). The lack of compliance with the rules can be attributed in part to the fact that they are still a fairly new feature of the Saudi judicial process. With appropriate training, the next generation of police officers might be more willing to follow these procedural rules. Even this will not totally eliminate abuses, a result to which many democratic countries that embraced due process rights long ago can attest.

In reference to the powers associated with interrogations, article 101 offers only brief guidelines: "When the accused appears for the first time for an investigation, the Investigator shall take down all his personal information and shall inform him of the offense of which he is charged. The Investigator shall record any statements the accused expresses about the accusation. The accused may be confronted with any other accused person or witness. After statements of the accused have been read to him, he shall sign them. If he declines to sign, a note to that effect shall be entered into the record." According to article 126, if the investigator is of the opinion that there is sufficient evidence against the accused, the investigator refers the matter to the court, which would then issue a summons if the accused is not already in custody. It is important to note that the Saudi Law of Criminal Procedure does not provide a person with the right to remain silent. Moreover, a number of claims have been made that the accused is often subjected to various forms of poor treatment and even torture, if the person does not comply with the investigator's interrogation (Human Rights Watch, 2008d).

The Saudi Law of Criminal Procedure addresses issues associated with both arrest and detention. Depending on the circumstances of the case, either a summons or an arrest warrant may be issued. If the person under suspicion ignores the summons, an arrest warrant is issued. Article 104 points out that "an arrest warrant shall instruct the public authority officers to arrest and bring the accused promptly before the Investigator in the event he refuses to appear voluntarily. Furthermore, the detention warrant shall instruct the detention center officer to admit the accused into detention center after explaining the offense with which he is charged and the basis thereof." With specific reference to an arrest, article 109 indicates: "The Investigator shall promptly interrogate the accused, who has been arrested. If this is not possible, he shall be kept in a detention center pending his interrogation. The period of detention shall not exceed twenty-four hours." And article 33 states: "... In all cases, the person under arrest shall not be detained for more than twenty-four hours, except pursuant to a written order from the Investigator."

A good deal of attention in the procedural law is devoted to the issue of detention. For example, article 112 states: "the Minister of the Interior shall, upon a recommendation by the Director of the Bureau of Investigation and Prosecution, specify what may be treated as a major crime requiring detention." This decision is often based on the interrogation of the accused and an evaluation as to whether evidence might be compromised if the person remains free or the possibility that the accused is a flight risk. In such cases, article 113 authorizes the investigator to "issue a warrant for his detention for a period not exceeding five days from the date of arrest." According to article 114, the investigator can seek an extension of the detention order from the provincial branch of the Bureau of Investigation and Prosecution. He may be granted an order that extends "the period of the detention for a period or successive periods provided that they do not exceed in their aggregate forty days from the date of arrest, or otherwise release the accused." If there is a desire to extend the detention further, the article indicates that "the matter shall be referred to the Director of the Bureau of Investigation and Prosecution to issue an order that the arrest be extended for a period or successive periods none of which shall exceed thirty days and their aggregate shall not exceed six months from the date of arrest of the accused. Thereafter, the accused shall be directly transferred to the competent court, or be released."

While the accused is detained, the procedural law notes certain protocols that are to be followed. For example, article 119 states: "In all cases, the Investigator shall order that the accused may not communicate with any other prisoner or detainee, and that he not be visited by anyone for a period not exceeding sixty days if the interest of the investigation so requires, without prejudice to the right of the accused to communicate with his representative or attorney." Article 120 indicates: "An Investigator in charge of the case may, at any time, whether of his own accord or pursuant to a request by the accused, issue an order for the release of such accused, if he considered that there is no sufficient justification for his detention, that his release would not impair the investigation, and that there is no fear of his flight or disappearance, provided that the accused undertakes to appear when summoned."

Once again, a number of claims have been made that agents of the Saudi justice system are not complying with the spirit of the rules associated with detention. In some instances, people are being held without formal charges being brought against them. One justification for this policy is that the person is being reeducated. The person is eventually released upon a successful period of reeducation. "Substituting such a program of involuntary 'reeducation' for an impartial adjudication of criminal charges in a court of law denies defendants the chance to prove their innocence and clear their names. A senior Saudi official told Human Rights Watch that the reeducation approach largely replaces trials." This strategy has been employed for both violent and nonviolent detainees (Human Rights Watch, 2008d).

Trial Procedures As indicated above, trials occur in First-Degree Courts, which are located throughout the country. These courts are also subdivided into divisions of specialization: Commercial, Criminal, General, Labor, and Personal Status. With regard to the Criminal Court, it is further subdivided into circuits that specialize in hudud, quesas, tazir, and juvenile offenses. The hudud, quesas, and tazir offenses were explained above in the section, "Crime and Punishment." They indicate the manner in which criminal offenses are categorized in Islamic law. Recall that the Criminal Court is composed of a three-judge panel. Any offense that does not fit under the aforementioned categories would be handled by a single judge.

In all cases involving a major crime, the accused must appear in person, while accused persons in a minor offense may have their attorney or another person represent their defense. In 2002, the Ministry of the Interior specified 14 offenses as major crimes: murder, rape, kidnapping, drug or intoxicant abuse or dealing, theft through forced entry, using weapons or implements, forming a gang, fighting, firing weapons resulting in serious injury, impersonating a security officer, bribery, embezzlement, and forgery. According to article 140 of the procedural law, the court can order a person to appear in any case. Article 141 indicates that if the accused fails to appear and has not sent a representative, the court can proceed to hear the plaintiff and enter the evidence into the court record: "The judge shall not render a judgment except in the presence of the accused. If the accused fails to appear without an acceptable excuse, the judge may issue a warrant for his detention."

Reference was made earlier to the private right of action in which a person harmed during the course of a crime could seek a private action against the accused. Article 148 indicates that if the private action was rejected following the investigation into the offense, it could be resubmitted to the trial court for their consideration. Moreover, article 149 authorizes the court to appoint a person to pursue the action if the victim "lacks the capacity and has no guardian or trustee." Article 150 provides the same service if the accused is in similar circumstances to that of the victim.

The courtroom work group for a court hearing involving a major crime would consist of the following people: a three-judge panel, in which the senior judge would be recognized as the chair, a prosecutor, and representatives or attorneys for the accused, and any victim seeking a private right of action. Civilians are not used as jurors or as lay judges in Saudi courts.Although the procedural law calls for court hearings to be open to the public, it has been suggested that "few trials appear to be open to the public" (Human Rights Watch, 2008d). Article 155, however, indicates: "The court may exceptionally consider the action or any part thereof in closed hearings, or may prohibit certain classes of people from attending those hearings for security reasons, or maintenance of public morality, if it is deemed necessary for determining the truth." Although the accused is under guard during the proceedings, he or she is not restrained, according to article 158, "unless he gives cause thereof. In that case, the proceedings shall continue and the accused may be admitted to the hearing whenever such cause for his removal ceases to exist. The court shall keep him informed of any action that has been taken during his absence."

When the hearing commences, the court is not "bound by the description included in the memorandum of the charges" (article 159). Moreover, article 160 permits the prosecutor to amend the charges "at any time." The article also indicates that the accused is to be informed of any amendment and given sufficient time to revise his or her defense. These procedural rules again illustrate that the role of the Saudi judge is not that of a disinterested umpire, as common law judges are often described. His task is that of an inquisitor to seek the truth during the hearing and then conclude by dispensing justice.

The standard court hearing would follow these steps:

1. The court would inform the accused of the charges against him and provide him with a copy of the charges.
2. If the accused admits guilt either at the beginning of the hearing or at any time during the hearing, the court would hear his statement and examine him on the details of the matter. If the court was satisfied with the validity of the confession, it would decide the case.
3. If the accused denies guilt in the matter or stands mute, the court would proceed to hear the evidence.
4. The court would first hear from the prosecutor.
5. The accused or his representative would then respond to the charges. The court would examine the accused regarding the charges and the evidence.
6. The court would then hear the claimant of the private right of action.
7. Each of the parties is permitted to comment on the statements of the other parties.
8. All witnesses may be cross-examined by the parties. Moreover, the court may call witnesses to hear or cross-examine them. Witnesses are kept separate from one another and testify separately.
9. The court can assign expert witnesses on technical questions. Their report is provided not only to the court but also to the litigants.
10. The accused has the last opportunity to speak to the court.
11. The court would then render a judgment either by acquitting the accused or convicting the person and imposing a

> sentence. If a private right of action was also being entertained, the court would also rule on that matter.

With regard to determining the outcome of a hearing, article 8 of the Law of Criminal Procedure indicates: "Decisions shall be rendered either unanimously or by majority vote. A dissenting judge shall declare his dissent and explain the reasons thereof, and the majority shall explain their opinion in the response to the dissent, which shall be entered into the record." The procedural law permits the accused, prosecutor, and claimant of the private right of action to appeal the conviction or acquittal. The law also authorizes both the convicted person and the prosecutor the right to appeal the sentence of the court. Following a reading of the judgment in the court, all the parties to the case must receive a copy of the judgment within 10 days from the date of the reading. The parties then have 30 days to file any appeal.

As mentioned earlier, at least one Court of Appeal is located in each of the 13 provinces of the country. Courts of Appeal are subdivided into specialized circuits: Civil, Commercial, Criminal, Labor, and Personal Status. These circuits entertain appeals from the First-Degree Courts. A panel of three judges would normally hear appeals to the court, except in certain criminal cases in which the panel will consist of five judges, because the court is mandated to review judgments involving major punishments, such as the death penalty, stoning, amputation or quesas cases other than death. If a sentence involving the aforementioned major punishments is affirmed by a Court of Appeal, it must still be affirmed by the High Court. If the High Court does not affirm the sentence, then the case is remanded for another hearing before another panel of judges. If the sentence is affirmed for one of these major punishments, it can only be carried out following the issuance of a royal order from either the king or his representative.

Finally, it is interesting to note that article 201 of the procedural law indicates that "A judgment shall be reversed if it contradicts the text of the Qur'an or Sunnah or the consensus of Muslim jurists." Once again, this is another illustration of the Quran as the fundamental source that defines what is appropriate in the Islamic community of believers, and that Islamic law has always been considered both a code of law but also a code of morals.

In 2006, Human Rights Watch conducted a study of the application of the Saudi Law of Criminal Procedure. They interviewed a number of people, including: defendants, lawyers, judges, prosecutors, prison officials, and officials from the Ministry of the Interior. While they offered a good deal of comment and criticism on how the procedural law was either being employed or ignored, they recommended reforms in four general areas. First, the Saudi Law of Criminal Procedure should be more in compliance with international human rights law. Second, there is a need for greater transparency in the procedures associated with the arrest and interrogation of suspects. Third, the rights of defendants should be enhanced, include providing free counsel to indigent defendants. Finally, the Bureau of Investigation and Public Prosecution should not be reporting to the Ministry of the Interior, but rather to the Ministry of Justice. In addition, they contend that the Bureau should not have the power to arrest, detain, and release suspects from prosecution (Human Rights Watch, 2008d).

Critical Issues

While commenting on the Saudi criminal justice system, one Western author who is familiar with the Kingdom pointed out: "Whether it is due to severe punishment or public humiliation, Saudi Arabia unquestionably enjoys a remarkably low rate of crime" (Mackey, 2002). The author also reminded her readers that "the legal system is designed to protect society, not the rights of individuals." As mentioned earlier, a number of nations and several international organizations have objected to some processes employed by agents of the Saudi criminal justice system. This section identifies some examples that illustrate either how the Saudi justice system places a good deal of emphasis on protecting society rather than an individual, or the nature and context of severe punishment or public humiliation.

Status of Women From a Western perspective, a significant amount of humiliation appears to be directed at women. Much condemnation is directed at the Kingdom for the perceived lack of freedom for women. Saudi women must seek permission from their male guardian, who is often either their father or husband, to work, travel, study, or marry. In the case of a widow, her son is often called upon to serve in this capacity as "guardian." For some, male guardianship has led to concerns about family violence and varying levels of potential abuse that are neither easily identified nor likely to be reported given the patriarchal nature of the society.

This secondary status is associated both with Saudi cultural traditions and Islam and is justified by the claim that these traditions are designed to protect the personal honor of women. To understand this justification, one must begin with the understanding that in Saudi society men are considered superior because they are responsible for protecting the family and maintaining it economically. The Quranic verse frequently cited to support this claim is: "Husbands should take good care of their wives, with [bounties] God has given to some more than others and with what they spend out of their own money. Righteous wives are devout and guard what God would have them guard in their husbands' absence" (4:34).

Critics of this logic suggest that this position may have made sense during pre-modern times when "women were more vulnerable to poverty, harm, and exploitation than men," but that it is no longer justified in contemporary society (Human Rights Watch, 2008c).

Some women work, but for a long period of time, professional occupations have been limited primarily to teaching and nursing. There are no female judges, prosecutors, or practicing lawyers in Saudi Arabia. In 2008, the first class of female law students graduated from King Abdul Aziz University, but the Ministry of Justice refuses to grant women the license to practice law (Human Rights Watch, 2008c). It should be noted that many women accept this arrangement of not seeking employment and staying at home for the security of the family. Moreover, one commentator on Saudi society has pointed out: "It is estimated that forty percent of private wealth in Saudi Arabia is held by Saudi women, and even though women are not permitted to hold a business directly, many do so through the front of a male representative, often a family member" (Ahmed, 2008). No doubt, the role that women play in contemporary Saudi society has probably not gone unnoticed by those who recall that the Prophet Muhammad had a similar role after he married Khadija, a 40-year-old widow who was a wealthy merchant and who enabled him to associate with the societal leaders of Mecca.

It is important to point out that the various dress codes, in particular the veil, date back to around 1500 BCE. Thus, these dress codes do not have a basis in Islam, but are rather part of the cultural traditions of the region. The lack of freedom of movement for women is also associated with Saudi cultural traditions, namely, protecting the personal honor of women. Thus, women must often be escorted by a male family member if they leave their home. It was this attitude that led King Saud in 1957 to issue a royal decree that forbade women to drive. Again, this decision was based on Saudi culture and did not have its basis in Islam. Recently, it was announced that the driving ban would be lifted. Some have offered a telling argument that given the male-dominant society, the real honor that is being protected is that of the man. The *ird*, or sexual honor of the females of a family, is often cited in support of this position. Finally, the cases in which a daughter is killed for dishonoring the family is not an issue that was determined by an Islamic court, rather this was a matter associated with *urf* or traditional local law, which predates the emergence of Islam. In fact, a number of commentators have pointed out that when Islam was introduced, it actually granted women some protections by providing them with various legal rights that did not exist in the patriarchal tribal society at that time (Mackey, 2002).

Although the second-class status of women in Saudi society may be traced originally to the cultural traditions of the region that predate Islam, presently senior religious leaders have a significant role to play in perpetuating this attitude through their involvement with determining the social policies of everyday life that impact women. These religious leaders control the educational system, sit as judges, and have a profound influence on the Commission for the Promotion of Virtue and the Prevention of Vice, which will be explained shortly. To illustrate the role that religious leaders play, a few examples should indicate the significant authority associated with the Senior Council of the Ulama that was created in 1971. The Council is composed of between 30 and 40 of the leading senior religious scholars and is chaired by the Grand Mufti. As noted earlier, a mufti is a specialist in Islamic law. It was the Senior Council of the Ulama that caused Saudi Arabia to withdraw from attending a 1994 United Nations conference on population and development that was being held in Cairo, Egypt. Among the topics discussed that the Council claimed were against the laws of God and nature included birth control as well as equality between men and women.

Although this Senior Council is not part of the legislative process, it is consulted on various pieces of proposed legislation to seek its guidance on conformity with the moral and ethical teachings of Islam in general and Sharia in particular. One of its principal duties is to provide fatwas that establish general rules regarding questions submitted to it by the government. Among the fatwas issued by the Council on women, two will suffice to indicate how they impact not only the everyday life of women now but also the prospects of future generations. On the subject of postponing marriage in order to finish secondary or university education, the Council proclaimed:

> For women to progress through university education, which is something we have no need for, is an issue that needs examination. What I see [to be correct] is that a woman finishes elementary school and is able to read and write, and so she is able to benefit by reading the Book of God, its commentaries, and Prophetic hadith, that is sufficient for her. This is so unless she excels in a field that people need, such as medicine or its like, and as long as this study involves nothing prohibited, such as the mixing of the sexes and other things.

On the subject of employment, the Council announced: "God Almighty ... commended women to remain in their homes. Their presence in the public is the main contributing factor to the spread of fitna [strife]. Yes, the Shari'ah permits women to leave their home only when necessary, provided that they wear hijab and avoid all suspicious situations. However, the general rule is that they should remain at home" (Human Rights Watch, 2008c). These examples clearly indicate that the religious leaders of Islam in Saudi Arabia are facilitating the maintenance of a perpetual second-class citizenship for Saudi women. One frequent visitor to the Kingdom, however, has suggested that the "gender apartheid committed in the name of Islam is already dying, rasping its last, soured breaths" (Ahmed, 2008).

Moreover, it is important to note that the encroachment of values associated with Western societies into Saudi Arabia is often considered an attack on the family in general and possibly women in particular. As such, the attitude that women must be protected is advanced further. To illustrate, this Islamic patriarchal society observes modern Western culture forsaking its religious roots and embracing a more secular society. They read of the large number of divorces and the significant number of births to single women throughout the West and conclude that the dignity of women is being compromised. This reinforces their abhorrence of that which is associated with secularism and individualism.

Law Enforcement There are essentially two kinds of police in the Kingdom: the civil or Public Security Police, and the religious police or *matawain*. The Public Security Police are a national law enforcement organization that is accountable to the Ministry of the Interior. It is responsible for the typical law enforcement and order maintenance issues that confront any society. One of the main criticisms directed at the security police is the manner in which they handle foreign guest workers when they skirt Saudi law. The pretrial rules found in the Law of Criminal Procedure may alleviate some of these concerns, once they are further refined in light of the criticisms mentioned above. Within the Public Security Police is a directorate called the *mubahith* or secret police. They are responsible for domestic security and counterintelligence functions of the ministry. There is also a Directorate of Intelligence that collects, analyzes, and coordinates the intelligence work of all agencies; it reports directly to the king.

It is the matawain (matawain is the plural of matawah, an enforcer of religious law) or religious police that are the subject of a good deal of criticism associated with Saudi law enforcement. The matawain is the enforcement arm of the Commission for the Protection of Virtue and the Prevention of Vice that was briefly alluded to earlier. The Commission holds ministerial status, and it is recognized for building mosques, distributing Qurans, and providing religious educational programs. It has also been criticized for being too zealous in its attempts to uphold the morals of Saudi society. Some have suggested that it is too powerful and should be placed under the Ministry of the Interior.

The matawain was created by King Abdul Aziz early in his reign. Although such an enforcement agency seems out of place in contemporary society, there is a certain logic for its existence. Since the establishment of the Islamic faith, the political leader of the umma or community of believers was always expected to be a protector and defender of the faith. The matawain is the group that assists in that endeavor. The focus of their attention is on public morality, and it is the basis for the criticism directed at them.

One of the principal problems associated with the matawain is that the vice they are empowered to prevent has not been defined to any significant degree. As a result, the matawain are associated with the following types of enforcement actions: raiding homes in search of bootlegged alcohol or illegal drugs; reprimanding men and women in cars who are not related; homosexuality; overseeing that shops close for the five daily prayers; identifying those wearing a Christian cross or a star of David; monitoring business establishments to assure that women are not employed in certain occupations, of which there are many; discouraging members of the opposite sex who are not related from congregating in public; detecting gambling; raiding photo-developing labs to evaluate the type of pictures being printed; preventing foreign books and magazines from entering the Kingdom; censoring images in magazines, especially pictures of women and ads for alcohol; preventing barbers from providing Western-style haircuts for men; forbidding women from riding bicycles or jogging; and enforcing a modest dress code. Given the nature of their very broad mandate, matawain have been characterized as a very powerful vigilante force that even politicians are reluctant to confront (Ahmed, 2008; Human Rights Watch, 2008d; Mackey, 2002).

What critics find particularly troubling is the matawain who are out on the streets enforcing this rather vague definition of vice. The matawain consist of two groups of people: the religious police, supplemented with volunteers. Neither group wears a uniform, but they carry a badge. Although both are characterized as religious fundamentalists, the volunteers are identified as people who are recruited from local mosques and who are young, often uneducated, and poor. The matawain carry whips that are often used to encourage virtue and deter vice. They can arrest people, and in some instances, they will take the offender to one of their jails for further harassment. Cases have been reported in which people were not only whipped in public but beaten further while in custody. In some cases, people died from their treatment at the hands of the matawain.

It is unlikely that the government will curb the work of the matawain. They have been a useful tool in maintaining Saudi morality throughout the Kingdom. Moreover, critics acknowledge that they help address two social problems confronting the Kingdom: the high unemployment rates, especially among young people, and the surplus of graduates from various religious studies programs.

Status of Juveniles In addition to the typical petty offenses associated with juveniles throughout much of the world, young people in Saudi Arabia are frequent targets of several of the kinds of vice-related issues that are generally enforced by the matawain. When confronted with the matawain, some incidents are yet another illustration of humiliation for girls and young women. For boys and young men, however, it is not uncommon for them to receive the brunt of the physical abuse. Eating in restaurants with young women or walking in groups in family-only sections of malls have led to punishments such as flogging (see Gilani, in Friday and Ren, 2006).

One of the central criticisms raised regarding juveniles is the matter associated with the age of criminal responsibility and how that is determined. In 2006, the age of criminal responsibility for boys was raised from seven to 12; however, the law did not set a minimum age for girls. Human Rights Watch has argued that this law is not well publicized or enforced (Human Rights Watch, 2008a). Moreover, young people are often treated like adults even though their crime was committed when they were under the age of 18. At issue is when a child can be tried as an adult. In Saudi Arabia, it frequently depends on the child's physical development rather than a consideration of the mental and emotional maturity of the person. Usually, judges decide this question based on the physical signs of puberty. This method has been employed by Islamic judges for centuries and was discussed previously under the subsection on criminal procedure of the section on Sharia.

This situation is exacerbated further by weaknesses in the justice system that directly impact juveniles. For example, the Bureau of Investigation and Public Prosecution does not employ investigators that specialize in juvenile cases. It is also worth repeating that there are no female prosecutors or judges that would likely offer a different perspective on handling young people. Finally, juveniles are most vulnerable in that they frequently are without legal counsel to defend them.

In their 2008 report, *Adults Before Their Time: Children in Saudi Arabia's Criminal Justice System*, Human Rights Watch offered several recommendations for improving the plight of juveniles caught up in the Saudi justice system. Among the recommendations were: detain children only as a last resort and for the shortest period of time; protect children from abuse while in detention; eliminate the use of corporal punishment, solitary confinement, and denial of family visits; provide access to adequate legal assistance; and abolish the sentence of death for those who committed their offense while under the age of 18.

Nature of Punishment It has been pointed out that "Saudi Arabia's criminal justice system, perhaps more than any other, encompasses the true philosophy of 'an eye for an eye and a tooth for a tooth.' In the customs of Arabia, a person convicted of harming his neighbor was punished by the same act suffered by the victim" (Mackey, 2002). In addition to the status of women, also leading to much of the criticism directed at the Saudi criminal justice system are the public beheadings of those sentenced to death, the amputation of a hand or foot for a less serious offense, and the flogging of people for offenses that in some cases are not even considered criminal in most countries. The objections have been led by various international organizations associated with human rights and have been supported by a number of countries.

Thus far, such criticisms have been largely ignored by the authorities within the Kingdom. As mentioned earlier, not only is Sharia unique, but Saudi Arabia's application of it is essentially different from many other Islamic countries in the world. Whereas many Islamic countries might adhere to various Sharia principles, they have reformed their legal system in light of modern contemporary society. With specific reference to Sharia that is not the case in Saudi Arabia.

Most experts on Saudi Arabia maintain that the House of Saud will remain wedded to their highly conservative interpretation of Islam. They do so because the faith of the leaders of the House is rooted in that orthodoxy. From a pragmatic point of view, it is also in their political interests to do so. As described above, the government of Saudi Arabia is based on a near absolute monarchial system. The Saudi Arabian king exercises very broad powers in his capacity as head of state and head of the government. Presently, the greatest concern for the House of Saud is the military and ideological threat that Iran poses in the region. That ideology is associated with the religious and political authority granted to a highly structured clerical organization in Iran following the 1979 revolution. From the House of Saud's perspective, their form of Islam provides them with a degree of security from that Iranian ideology. Where one finds some agreement between the two countries, however, is over the threat that modernization poses to their religious and cultural traditions.

Islamic Republic of Iran

Iran is slightly larger than the state of Alaska, at 636,295 square miles. Its territory consists of both desert and mountains. It shares land borders with Iraq, Turkey, Armenia, Azerbaijan, Turkmenistan, Afganistan, and Pakistan. It has a coastline along the Caspian Sea, the Persian Gulf, and the Gulf of Oman. The population is more than 70 million, of which 51 percent are Persian. Among the important industries are petroleum, petrochemicals, textiles, cement, and building materials. Most Iranians are Muslims with about 89 percent Shia and 9 percent Sunni. Other religions represented in the population are: Zoroastrian, Jewish, Christian, and Bahai.

It was mentioned earlier that Persia's rich intellectual tradition enabled the nurturing and development of the Shia sect of Islam. It would eventually become the state religion of Iran in 1501 when the Safavid dynasty (1501–1736) established it as such. Over time, there emerged the belief among the Shia community that the ulama, the religious scholars, were the only legitimate authority to offer guidance on governance. Although the ulama were not mandated to govern, they were to offer moral and ethical guidance to the Shia community. Within this community the ulama established a clerical hierarchy that assumed the legitimate mantle of authority to offer guidance on governance. This clerical hierarchy is a unique feature of Shia Islam, for Sunni Muslims, who represent the largest number of the adherents to the Islamic faith, do not subscribe to a clerical hierarchy. The role of religious leaders in the Iranian Revolution of 1979 and the subsequent creation of the Islamic Republic of Iran illustrate the most recent chapter in the debate surrounding the amount of power accorded the secular political leaders and the authority granted to the religious leaders of Islam.

To provide context for this struggle over the degree of authority accorded to the secular and religious leaders in contemporary Iran, a brief outline of the country's twentieth-century political events is in order. Historians have pointed out that the Safarid period (1501–1722) had created three institutional sources of authority in Iran. One was the state, which was often weakly centralized because it was vying for power with the second source, the provincial tribal groups. The third source was the independent Shia religious establishment.

The Safavid dynasty was followed by a period of anarchy until the Qajar dynasty (1779–1925) established itself. During its tenure in power, it did not succeed in changing these three centers of authority. At the onset of the twentieth century, the Qajar's were offering the country weak leadership and a bankrupt treasury, in part because of their extravagant royal spending. This led to an alliance among the ulama, merchants, and intellectuals, who were demanding a parliamentary government. They succeeded in forcing Shah Muzaffar ad Din to sign a constitution into law in December of 1906. A good deal of turmoil followed, including civil war, suspending the constitution, and World War I.

Finally, Reza Khan, an army officer, seized power in 1921. Following periods in which he was minister of war and prime minister, the Iranian Majlis (parliament) gave Reza Khan and his heirs the crown, having earlier deposed the Qajar dynasty. Reza Khan became Reza Shah Pahlavi; thus began the Pahlavi period (1925–1979). Reza Shah initiated an effort both to modernize the country along Western lines and to enhance the power of the central government. He modeled his efforts of reform after another army officer who had assumed the position of leadership in another country in the region, Mustafa Kemal Ataturk of Turkey. Reza Shah needed to curb the independent power of the ulama and bring it under the control of his centralized government. He achieved this largely through his efforts at modernizing the country. For example, he created a secular education system and placed religious schools under the oversight of the government. He introduced Western law codes to replace Sharia. As a result, judges were required to hold law degrees from the secular Tehran University faculty of law or a foreign law school, which disqualified members of the ulama from sitting as judges in the secular state courts. While the Islamic law courts were not eliminated, they were noticeably curtailed in the issues they were permitted to address, such as marriage and wills. The position of women was significantly improved in terms of educational opportunities and freedom of movement in public. The Iranian *chador,* or veil, that covered the head and body, but not the face and hands, was outlawed. Finally, Reza Shah changed the name of the country from Persia to Iran.

Reza Khan would serve as shah from 1925 to 1941. He helped extend the institution of Persian kingship that dated back to the fourth century BCE. Part of his success can be attributed to the cultural traditions of the country. It has been pointed out that "Iranian culture has held within itself a deep-rooted authoritarian tradition in which society demands submission to the will of those who hold a position, higher than oneself"(Mackey, 1996). What Iranians often seek from this authority figure is the assurance of internal security and national independence. Clearly, Reza Shah was that authority figure during the 1920s and 1930s. He had removed the independent source of power that the Shia religious establishment had held during the Safavid and Qajar dynasties. The ulama were unable to find among their group a figure that could serve as an alternative religious source of authority to counter the secular vision of Reza Shah.

Reza Shah was succeeded by his son, Muhammad Reza Shah, who ruled from 1941 to 1979. A brief period, 1951 to 1953, marked a time when the weak shah lost control of the country. Muhammad Mossadeq, a popular politician, assumed greater control, which led to the shah fleeing the country. Following a coup that was organized by Britain and the United States, the shah returned to power. While Muhammad Reza Shah continued his father's efforts at modernizing the country, he also enhanced efforts to consolidate more power solely to the House of Pahlavi and to spend lavishly on the royal family. At a time when he was losing the support of his people through his autocratic style of rule, he was also claiming to be God's agent to save his country from both internal and external threats (Hiro, 2005). Hence, the shah perceived himself to be the only authority figure capable of assuring both the internal security and national independence for the country. Both secular and religious opposition grew against the shah; it finally came to a head in 1978, and in early 1979, the Pahlavi dynasty was deposed. For a more detailed examination of the nineteenth- and twentieth-century Iranian political developments, see Keddie, 2006; Lapidus, 2002; and Lewis, 1996.

Shia Islam and Ayatollah Khomeini

Some of the differences between Sunni and Shia Muslims have already been explained above in the section, "Sunni and Shia." To place Shia Islam in the context of twentieth-century Iran, a brief summary of that explanation of Shia Islam is in order. Shia Muslims (from the party of Ali) gradually developed a movement that asserted the hereditary succession of Ali's descendants to the position of leader, because they believed that Muslims should be ruled by a male descendant of Muhammad. Ali was the Prophet Muhammad's cousin who also became his son-in-law when he married the Prophet's daughter, Fatima. With this claim of hereditary succession, the people would have no voice in determining the ruler, because it was considered a prophetic matter. These descendants of Ali were called Imams, and their leadership authority extended to the realms of both religion and politics. As religious leaders, they were considered the interpreters of God's will. Although the Imams do not have the status of a prophet, their speeches and writings are considered important religious texts.

Today, the largest group within Shia Islam is known as Twelver Shias. They believe that Muhammad, the twelfth Imam, who was born in 869, went into hiding in the ninth century. Originally, it was thought that this period of seclusion would not last long. As the period of "Occultation" continued over centuries, there emerged the belief that the Imam Muhammad would return on Judgment Day. While the Imam was in seclusion, there emerged the belief among the Shia community that the ulama, the religious scholars, were the only legitimate authority to offer guidance on governance, for it was the ulama who had undertaken long years of study of the Quran and Sunna. The ulama were not mandated to govern, but they were to offer moral and ethical guidance to the Shia community. The Shia community had its greatest concentration and development in Persia, which is now Iran.

As stated earlier, Persia's rich intellectual tradition helped to nurture the development of the Shia sect of Islam, which would eventually become the state religion of Iran in 1501 when the Safavid dynasty (1501–1736) established it as such. It is important to note that this tradition was associated with the study of philosophy and other subjects, and it represents another difference between Sunni and Shia. Sunni scholars tend to focus only on the Islamic sources, such as the Quran, Sunna, and Shaira. Hence, their intellectual interests tend to emphasize issues associated with Islamic law. Shia scholars are learned not only in the traditional Islamic sources, but their interests also extend to other fields of study. For example, philosophy remains an important area of study, and this no doubt has contributed to their recognition as leaders in theological debates.

It has also been suggested that from the sixteenth to the twentieth century people did not make a pronounced distinction between being a Shia Muslim or a Persian. When these concepts were distinguished, people were more apt to identify with Shia Islam (Keddie, 2006). Within this context there emerged the belief among the Shia community that the ulama were the only legitimate authority to offer guidance to political leaders. This, in turn, led the ulama to establish a clerical hierarchy that assumed the mantle of authority to offer that guidance on governance. The upper echelons of this hierarchy are senior leaders who are called ayatollahs (signs of God), who are noted both for their piety and religious knowledge.

It is important to note that within the clerical hierarchy there is a group who are referred to as *mujtahid*. The mujtahid are jurists who are recognized as qualified to interpret Islamic law through independent reasoning or ijtihad. Ijtihad was discussed above in the section on sources of Sharia. Briefly, it is the process by which jurists determine a rule based on analogy. It is utilized when a rule conflicts with another rule or when a rule is rather vague and somewhat questionable. Jurists turn to ijtihad when neither the Quran nor the Sunna has specifically addressed an issue. Thus, a mujtahid is a cleric who has achieved distinction with the study and interpretation of Shaira. These men hold significant positions throughout the governmental system of the Islamic Republic.

Finally, it should be further noted that the vast majority of Shia clerics have simply studied for a time at an Islamic college, with much of their studies focusing on Islamic jurisprudence. To become an entry -level cleric, the male Muslim need not complete a specific course of study that would lead to a degree, and there is no ceremony of ordination. A person who has achieved a level of competence that is acknowledged by others would be called a *mullah*. Mullahs staff most of the religious posts in Iran; they also serve as judges in the lower courts.

Throughout the twentieth century, the Pahlavi dynasty curtailed the authority of the Shia clerics in general and the clerical hierarchy in particular. Specific examples were mentioned earlier. Throughout the 1960s and 1970s, they were highly critical of Muhammad Reza Shah and his government. When a significant secular opposition emerged in the late 1970s, the ulama joined with them in the Iranian Revolution of 1979 to depose the shah.

Ayatollah Ruhollah Khomeini (1900–1989) had been a leading critic of the shah and his government since the early 1960s. His opposition led to imprisonment for a while and eventually to his exile from 1964 to 1978. It has been suggested that "Khomeini was popular because of his uncompromising attitude to the shah, his anti-imperialist and populist rhetoric, his simple lifestyle and language, and his religious status" (Keddie, 2006). Khomeini had established himself as a serious Shia scholar who had written treatises on ethics, law, and philosophy. He also had a good deal of support from the working class, who deferred their allegiance largely to him. Khomeini would emerge as the cleric who would lead the revolution that would overthrow the shah and his regime.

One of his treatises on Islamic government would become a guide, if not a blueprint, for the form of government that would be created following the removal of the shah. The work, *Velayat-e faqih* or

Guardianship of the Jurist, argued that monarchy was an unsuitable form of government for Islam. Moreover, while God is the lawgiver, as reflected in the Quran and Sunna, man is God's trustee on earth and has the authority to make law, as long as it is in conformity with Sharia. While awaiting the return of the Twelfth Imam, it is left to the Islamic jurists to govern, for it is they who have studied and understand God's law. Thus, Khomeini was arguing that the ulama should not limit their authority only to offering moral and ethical guidance, but rather they should assume a significant degree of actual political power. This thinking became the basis for the establishment of a type of Islamic theocratic state. Finally, it was maintained that the ulama had a responsibility to cleanse Iran, because much of society during the Pahlavi dynasty was corrupted by the many years of secular materialistic ideas from the West.

With the Islamic revolution not only was the type of government changed from a monarchial system to a curious republican theocratic form, but the secular laws introduced by Reza Shah were abandoned and the Sharia prominently reinstated. On the subject of the form of government, Khomeini supported a republic system in which a parliament elected by all citizens would have a role in the legislative process. Not all Shia clerics were supportive of Khomeini's ideas, though. Some maintained that the ulama's historical role of offering guidance to the political authorities should be retained rather than members of the ulama actually assuming positions of governance. Some opposed the proposed form of government on the grounds that it was associated with Western political ideas. Nevertheless, the style of government was eventually formulated, and "the constitution reflects the goals and values of Khomeini's Islamist movement and of Khomeini himself" (Martin, 2003). Finally, one scholar reminds us: "In Iran as elsewhere, the so-called Islamic Revival does not mean that most people are more religious than they used to be: for the majority the degree of religiosity shows no sign of significant change. Rather, it means that Islam is reentering politics and government in a stronger and more militant way than it had in most areas for many decades"(Keddie, 2006).

The Islamic Republic of Iran is unique in that it is the only modern Muslim country that has turned legal and political power over to the clergy. Within that governmental system, Ayatollah Khomeini would hold the ultimate position of authority, as Supreme Leader, until his death in 1989. Other Shia clerics would head many of the other important units of the government. All laws had to conform to Shaira, and all judges had to base their decisions on Shaira. With the secular law of the shah being abandoned, most judges were removed and replaced by Shia jurists. A few secular judges retained their positions after a period of training in Sharia. Today, either all or almost all of the judges are Shia clerics whose knowledge of law is almost exclusively limited to Sharia.

Government

On March 30 and 31, 1979, all Iranians who were at least 16 years of age were encouraged to vote in a referendum on whether the monarchy should be abolished and an Islamic republic created. The provisional government announced that 98 percent of the voters approved the creation of the Islamic Republic of Iran, and its 1979 Constitution was subsequently approved in December of that year. The document was revised slightly in 1989, following the death of Ayatollah Khomeini.

It is in the first chapter of the Constitution that the reader is presented with some general principles regarding governance in this Islamic Republic. First among these is the "long-standing conviction in the rule of truth and justice of the Quran." Article 2 states, in part:

The Islamic Republic is a system based on faith in:

1. The One and only God [There is no God but Allah], His exclusive Sovereignty and Legislation and the necessity of submission to His commands.
2. The Divine Revelation and its basic role in exposition of laws.
3. The concept of Resurrection and its constructive role in the course of evolution of Man toward God.
4. The justice of God in the Creation and Legislation.
5. Perpetual Imamat and leadership and its fundamental role in perpetuation of the Islamic Revolution.
6. Eminent dignity and value of Man, his freedom coupled with his responsibility before God, which provides justice and political, economic, social, and cultural freedom and national unity...

Thus, the criteria for all laws and regulations would be based ultimately on the Islamic sources of the Quran and Sunna.

Another constitutional principle is the importance placed on the development of policy through consultation with various institutions of government, and ultimately, the role that the public plays through elections. Like the Saudi constitution, the Iranian document acknowledges the important role of the family in an Islamic society. Article 10 states: "Since the family is the basic unit of the Islamic society, all laws and regulations and pertinent [plannings] shall strive to facilitate the setting up of a family to protect its sanctity and to stabilize family relations on the basis of Islamic laws and ethics."

Finally, while the official religion of Iran is Shia Islam, article 12 specifically acknowledges that the Sunni branch "shall enjoy full respect." This includes not only how they practice their Islamic faith, but also suggests that deference should be paid to differences in legal interpretations, as a result of the four Sunni legal schools mentioned earlier, when a lawsuit reaches a court. Unlike the Saudis, the Iranians recognize certain rights of three religious minorities: Zoroastrians, Jews, and Christians. Article 13 indicates that they "shall be free to carry out their religious rites and practice their religion in personal status and religious education."

Constitution The Constitution of the Islamic Republic of Iran is divided into 14 chapters and includes a total of 177 articles. Some features of the Constitution will be discussed below in other parts to this section on government. First, it is worth highlighting Chapter 3, which is titled "The Rights of the People." Article 19 states: "The people of Iran, of whatever tribe and clan, shall enjoy equal rights, and color, race, language and the like shall not be a privilege." Article 20 continues: "All members of the nation, both men and women, shall receive equal protection of the law and enjoy all human, political, economic, social, and cultural rights, with due observance of the principle of Islam." The rights of women are singled out, in particular, for attention in article 21.

> The government shall be required to guarantee the rights of women in all respects, by observing the principles of Islam, and shall carry out the following:
>
> 1. To create a suitable environment for the growth of personality of woman and to restore material and moral rights.
> 2. To protect mothers, particularly during the period of pregnancy and custody of children, and to protect children without guardians.
> 3. To create competent courts for preserving the existence and survival of family.
> 4. To create special insurance for widows, elderly women, and women without guardians.
> 5. To grant guardianship of children to worthy mothers for protecting the children's interests, in case there is no legal guardian.

Issues that are often associated with the privacy rights of an individual are also addressed in this chapter. For example, article 23 states: "Investigation of one's beliefs shall be prohibited. No one may be offended or reprimanded simply because of having a certain belief." Article 25 indicates: "It shall be prohibited to inspect or fail to deliver letters, to record and divulge telephone conversations, to disclose telegraphic and telex communications, to censor them or fail to communicate or deliver them, to eavesdrop or to make any other search whatsoever, unless by order of law."

Issues that are often associated with group or societal rights are explained, although there are some generalized qualifiers that are associated with Islam. To illustrate, article 24 notes: "Publications and the press shall have freedom of expression unless they violate the essentials of Islam or public rights. Its details shall be set forth by law." Article 27 states: "It shall be allowed to hold assemblies and marches, without carrying arms, provided that it does not violate essentials of Islam." Finally, the freedom to associate with others is covered in article 26: "It shall be allowed to form parties, societies, political or professional associations and Islamic or other religious societies of the recognized minorities, provided that they do not violate the principles of freedom, independence, national unity, Islamic standards and essentials of the Islamic Republic. No one may be stopped from participating in them or forced to participate in one of them." The formal development of political parties is a relatively new feature. Various reform groups have emerged in recent years. People, however, are more apt around election time to associate with a particular group and its agenda, which then usually disbands following the election.

Finally, Chapter 3 addresses rights that are often associated with protecting the individual from abuse by agents of the criminal justice system. Article 32 points out:

> No one may be arrested unless by order of and in the manner provided for by law. In case of an arrest, the accused person must immediately be served with in writing and made to understand the charges he is accused of and the grounds thereof. The preliminary files must be sent to competent judicial authorities within a maximum period of 24 hours and the trial proceedings must be started within the shortest period of time. The violator of this article shall be punished in accordance with the provisions of law.

Article 34 continues: "It shall be the established right of every one to plead for justice. Every one may refer to competent courts to seek justice. All members of the nation shall have the right to have access to such courts. No one can be stopped from referring to the court to which he has a right to refer according to law." Moreover, article 35 states: "Both parties to a lawsuit have the right to appoint a lawyer in all courts and if they are not able to appoint a lawyer, facilities for appointing a lawyer shall be provided for them."

Article 37 proclaims: "Innocence is always presumed and thus no one shall be regarded as guilty in the eye of law unless his guilt is proven in a competent court." Article 36 indicates: "Penal judgments can only be passed by and enforced through a competent court in accordance with law." Article 38 cautions: "It shall be prohibited to apply any form of torture to obtain a confession or information. It shall not be allowed to force a person to give testimony, make a confession or take an oath; such testimony, confession or oath shall have no validity whatsoever. The violator of this article shall be punished according to law." Finally, article 39 concludes: "Defamation or aspersions in any manner whatsoever of persons arrested, detained, jailed, or exiled by order of law shall be prohibited and punishable by law."

All of these aforementioned rights, whether they are associated with basic human rights, privacy rights, associational rights, or those that focus on procedural protections involving agents of the criminal justice system, are essentially dependent on two factors. First, a country that proclaims these rights in its constitution must have an executive branch of government that is willing to abide by the ideals spelled out in the constitution. Second, it must have a judiciary that is truly independent from other branches of government. As such, there can be no interference with the judiciary, especially when it is exercising its constitutional authority to interpret the spirit and letter of the law. Another important feature of judicial independence is that individual judges are free to exercise their discretion in reaching a judgment that is based on their understanding of the law rather than encumbered by political or ideological considerations. Iran has been criticized by a number of commentators and international human rights groups for failing to adhere to its constitutional provisions.

The Faqih In the office of Faqih or Leader one sees the hand of Ayatollah Khomeini. His treatise, *Velayat-e faqih*, or *Guardianship of the Jurist*, argued that while awaiting the return of the Twelfth Imam, it is left to the Islamic jurists to govern for it is they who have studied and understand God's law. Moreover, while God is the lawgiver, as reflected in the Quran and Sunna, man is God's trustee on earth and has the authority to make law, as long as it is in conformity with Sharia. This thinking became the basis for the establishment of a type of Islamic theocratic state. Article 5 of the Constitution indicates that the Islamic Republic is under the leadership of a Faqih, "who is just, virtuous, has contemporary knowledge, is courageous and an efficient administrator," while article 107 recognized Ayatollah Khomenini as the first person to occupy this office. Thus, the Leader is the head of state.

Article 109 outlines the qualifications and attributes of the Leader. They include: "1. Academic qualifications necessary for issuing decrees on various issues of religious jurisprudence[;] 2. Fairness and piety necessary for leading the Islamic Nation[;] 3. Proper political and social insight, prudence, courage, authority and power of management necessary for leadership." The article further states that "[i]n case there are many individuals who qualify the above conditions, the one who has stronger insight in religious jurisprudence and politics shall be preferred." The Assembly of Experts, which is discussed shortly, is responsible for selecting the Leader when the office becomes vacant.

The functions and authority of the Leader are explained in article 110 and include both general and specific duties. To illustrate, the Leader is tasked: to determine and to supervise the general policies of the Islamic Republic; to decree referendums; to be the Supreme Commander of the Armed Forces; to declare war and to make peace; to resolve disputes among the executive, legislative, and judicial branches of government; to resolve problems that cannot be settled by the Expediency Council; to approve candidates for the presidency, sign the order of appointment once a president has been elected, and dismiss a president impeached by the Majlis or found negligent by the Supreme Court; and to pardon or mitigate sentences of condemned people upon the recommendation of the Head of the Judiciary. In addition to these duties, the Leader has the authority to appoint and dismiss a number of people from specific offices of the central government. These include: the jurists of the Guardian Council, the chief judges of the judicial branch, the head of the Islamic Republic of Iran Broadcasting Corporation, the chief of staff of the armed forces, the chief commander of the Pasdaran or Islamic Revolutionary Guards, and the chief commanders of the armed forces and the police forces.

This office is obviously an extremely powerful position of authority. While only two people have held this office in the relatively recent creation of the Islamic Republic of Iran, the requirements for the office limits the candidates to those Shia clerics who are already members in the upper echelons of the clerical hierarchy. These senior clerics are called ayatollahs (signs of God) and are noted both for their piety and religious knowledge.

President Article 113 of the Constitution states that "the President shall be the highest official State authority who is responsible for the implementation of the Constitution and, as the Chief Executive, for the exercise of the executive powers, with the exception of those matters that directly relate to the Leader." The president of Iran is elected by the people to a four-year term, and can be reelected consecutively to one additional term. As mentioned earlier, the Leader must approve the candidacy of all contestants for the office of president. Candidates must be Shia Muslims of Iranian citizenship and possess distinguished religious and political qualifications. In order to secure the office, a candidate must achieve an absolute majority of the votes. If no candidate achieves the majority, the two candidates that achieved the most votes would participate in a run-off election. Article 99 authorizes the Guardian Council to supervise the presidential election.

The president functions as the head of the government of the Islamic Republic. His duties consist of: responsibility for state planning, the budget, and administering the civil service; appointing members to the Council of Ministers; signing bills approved in the Majlis into law; and signing treaties and other types of international agreements. The Council of Ministers consists of 21 people who head various government departments. The responsibilities of the departments are common to many governments throughout the world and include agriculture, commerce, defense, education, foreign affairs, interior, and justice. There is also a Ministry of Culture and Islamic Guidance.

The Assembly of Experts Articles 107 and 108 explain the singularly important duty of the Assembly of Experts. It is the responsibility of this group to select a Leader when that office becomes vacant either through death, resignation, or removal by the Assembly. The Assembly is composed of 86 clerics, of which some would hold the status of mujtahid, who are elected by the people to an eight-year term. The chairman of the Assembly of Experts holds the rank of ayatollah in the Shia clerical hierarchy.

The Expediency Council This Council was created in 1988 by the Ayatollah Khomeini. Originally, it was called upon to resolve differences between the Majlis and the Council of Guardians over legislative matters. More recently, it has been given the mandate to resolve conflicts throughout the system of governance. The Council is composed of approximately 40 people, and it includes: the president, speaker of the Majlis, the clerical members of the Council of Guardians, the chief justice, and others appointed by the Leader to three-year terms. Again, some of these appointments by the Leader would be from the ranks of those clerics who have attained the status of mujtahid. The chair of the Expediency Council holds the rank of ayatollah in the Shia clerical hierarchy.

Majlis The Majlis or National Assembly is the unicameral legislative branch of the Islamic Republic's government. The Majlis is composed of 290 deputies who are elected by the people to a four-year term. Each deputy represents a specific geographical constituency. Five seats are reserved for the non-Muslim religious minorities: two for Armenian Christians and one each for Assyrian Christians, Jews, and Zoroastrians. Before a person can run for a seat in the Majlis, the person's candidacy must receive the approval of the Council of Guardians.

The leader of the Majlis is the speaker who is selected from among the deputies. The Majlis has a number of permanent committees that focus on specific government departments. Ministers of those departments can be called before the Majlis and questioned about government policies. One responsibility of the Majlis is to approve the president's choice of members to the Council of Ministers. The Majlis can also vote no confidence on a minister's performance or that of the government. While most legislation is presented through bills approved by the Council of Ministers, a deputy may submit a bill if it receives the support of at least 15 other deputies. According to article 72, "The Majlis may not enact laws contrary to the principle and rules of the official Faith of the country or the Constitution."

Council of Guardians The Council of Guardians consists of 12 members. Six of the members are appointed by the Leader, and according to article 91, they are jurists who have a reputation as "just and acquainted with the needs of the time and issues of the day." The other six, also according to article 91, are "jurists specializing in various branches of law, elected by the Majlis from among Muslim jurists proposed to the Majlis by the Head of the Judiciary." Members of the Council hold their position for a six-year term. Half of the membership is changed every three years. No doubt, people who have attained the status of mujtahid would be represented on this Council, and the chairman of the Council holds the rank of ayatollah in the Shia clerical hierarchy.

One of the responsibilities of the Council of Guardians is to assure that laws passed in the Majlis are not contrary to the principles of Islam or of the Constitution. Article 96 specifically mandates: "The majority of faqihs (jurists) of the Guardian Council shall decide whether or not the legislation passed in the Majlis is in conformity with the precepts of Islam. The majority of all members of the Guardian Council shall decide whether or not the same complies with the provisions of the Constitution." If the Council finds inconsistencies in a bill, it is returned to the Majlis for reconsideration. In this context the Council functions like a second house of a parliament. In determining if a bill is in compliance with the Constitution, it is functioning like a constitutional court. Even before such judgments are issued, however, article 97 enables members of the Council to attend the Majlis and "express their views" about bills that are under consideration.

In addition to this legislative function, the Council of Guardians provides oversight for all the major elections. Article 99 indicates that the Council "shall be charged with the responsibility of supervising the elections of the Assembly of Experts, the President, the Majlis, and referendums."

Judiciary

Like the executive and legislative branches of government, the judiciary has a prominent place in the Constitution of the Islamic Republic. Article 156 states:

> The judiciary shall be an independent power that protects individual and social rights, shall be responsible for implementing justice and shall carry out the following functions:

1. To examine and pass judgments in respect of litigations, violations, complaints; to settle lawsuits, resolve hostilities and to take necessary decision and action in respect of that part of matters of personal status to be laid down by law.
2. To restore public rights and to promote justice and lawful freedoms.
3. To supervise the proper implementation of laws.
4. To uncover crimes, to prosecute and punish the criminals and implement hudud and the Islamic codified penal provisions.
5. To take suitable measures for preventing the commission of crime and to reform the offenders.

To reiterate the importance of judicial independence, article 170 indicates that "Judges of courts shall be required to refrain from implementing Government decrees and regulations which are contrary to law or the rules of Islam or beyond the limits of authorities of the Executive." In order to carry out the aforementioned duties of the judiciary, several offices have been created to address specific responsibilities. These, for the most part, are explained in the Constitution.

At the top of the Iranian judicial hierarchy is the head of the judiciary. This person is appointed to the position by the Leader for a five-year term. The person must have attained the status of mujtahid, explained above. Presently, the head holds the rank of ayatollah in the Shia clerical hierarchy. Article 158 authorizes the head to develop an organizational structure to administer justice. The head is also responsible for all things associated with judges. This includes defining their jurisdictional duties and their appointment, transfer, promotion, and dismissal.

The minister of justice is responsible for coordinating relations with the executive and legislative branches of government. The person who holds this position is appointed by the president, but the head of the judiciary proposes individuals who are suitable for appointment to the post. The head of the judiciary can delegate to the minister of justice those administrative responsibilities that fall under his constitutional mandate, for example, dealing with budgetary or personnel issues.

The attorney general is the chief state prosecutor. This person is appointed by the head of the judiciary after consulting with members of the Supreme Court. The attorney general is appointed to a five-year term and has already attained the status of mujtahid. He is responsible for the prosecution of criminal offenses.

Courts There are several courts operating in Iran, with varying degrees of judicial responsibility (see Figure 7.2). At the top of the court hierarchy is the Supreme Court. According to article 161, the Supreme Court supervises "the proper implementation of law by the courts of law, creating uniform and binding judicial precedent and carrying out the responsibilities assigned to it by law." The head of the judiciary determines the rules of the Supreme Court and appoints the president of the court, who would serve a five-year term. The president of the Supreme Court must have attained the status of mujtahid. The Supreme Court essentially has appellate jurisdiction over the Iranian court system.

Figure 7.2

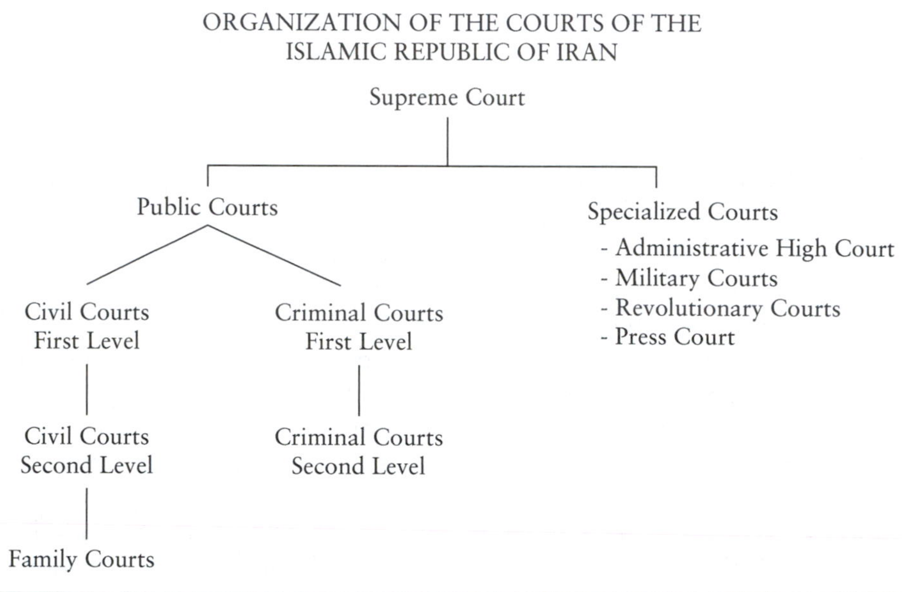

The public courts are essentially divided into two categories: civil and criminal. First- and second-level civil courts deal with a variety of noncriminal issues. The first-level courts deal with issues in which the value of the property in dispute or the level of punitive damages is high, whereas the second-level courts deal with minor civil disputes. Correspondingly, the first-level criminal courts are responsible for the more serious criminal offenses, and the second-level criminal courts handle offenses that may lead to sanctions that are less punitive. There is also a separate civil court that specializes in family law, such as divorce and child custody matters.

According to article 173, the Administrative High Court was established to deal "with complaints, grievances and objections of people against Government employees, institutions or administrative regulations and redressing their rights. Article 172 established special military courts that are designed to investigate "crimes related to the special military or police duties of the members of the Army, Police and Islamic Revolutionary Guard Corps." The article also indicates, however, that ordinary crimes committed by such people "in their capacity as law enforcement officers shall be investigated by the public courts."

As is the case with any successful revolutionary movement, there is an immediate need to establish a system to hold trials against the enemies of the movement. The victors in Iran's revolution continued that tradition by forming revolutionary tribunals that tried opponents quickly and often harshly. Today, the responsibility of the revolutionary courts has been curbed considerably with the creation of the public courts. Nevertheless, they are mandated to handle cases dealing with terrorism or other issues associated with national security.

In recent years, two additional specialized courts were established. The Clerical Court was created in 1987, and it handles cases in which a cleric is charged with a flawed interpretation of Islamic principles. The Clerical Court is unique in that it is not part of the judiciary hierarchy. It is accountable only to the Leader. Finally, a Press Court was formed in 1990 to handle cases involving the media.

Critical Issues

Time and space do not permit a more extensive coverage of the Islamic legal system of Iran, in particular that part associated with the criminal justice system. It is important, however, to mention at least briefly some of the criticisms that have been directed at the justice system of the Islamic Republic of Iran. Some of the criticisms come from those who either live or have lived for extended periods of time in the country since the 1979 revolution or from independent commentators or international human rights organizations.

Constitutional Rights The first criticism is directed at the law, the Constitution of the Islamic Republic of Iran (Tamadonfar, 2001). Three examples should suffice to illustrate the concern. Article 24 states: "Publications and the press shall have freedom of expression unless they violate the essentials of Islam or public rights. Its details shall be set forth by law." This is simply not the case in actuality. There have been a number of instances in which the press has been censored and even required to close down. When the United Nations was preparing its report on human rights in Iran, it found that "some 22 newspapers and journals have been closed, and at least an equal number of publishers and writers have been convicted, jailed or fined, or served with a summons by one of the various tribunals now exercising jurisdiction over the press." The report also stated that the "press court seems to have become simply another control agency dedicated to the suppression of free expression rather than the protection of that right" (Copithorne, 2000). Human Rights Watch has been monitoring the arbitrary detention, torture, and sentences of four Internet journalists, which was initiated in 2004 and has continued into 2009. Furthermore, the government owns the Iranian radio and television broadcasting corporation and thus controls the news that it sees fit to disseminate. With regard to satellite television, the police periodically remove the dishes from houses and apartment buildings (Moaveni, 2009).

Article 27 states: "It shall be allowed to hold assemblies and marches, without carrying arms, provided that it does not violate essentials of Islam." Of course, the crux of the problem here is how the agents of the government interpret violations of the "essentials of Islam." The United Nations report mentioned above was particularly critical of the treatment of students protesting in 1999. Some Iranians have been able to offer eyewitness examples of such violations (Ghahramani, 2009; Moaveni, 2005; Moaveni, 2009; Nafisi, 2003). Human Rights Watch has not only reported on prohibitions against assembly, but also on speech and association (Human Rights Watch, 2008e). The government essentially does not permit demonstrations that question their authority or any aspect of their policies.

A final example of criticism regarding the constitution focuses on the rights associated with protecting the individual from abuse by agents of the criminal justice system. Articles 32 through 38 explain these rights and were cited above. Unfortunately, the United Nations, Human Rights Watch, and independent commentators maintain that people have been subjected to violations of these rights. People have been arbitrarily held without a warrant, deprived of meeting with an attorney, and tortured while being interrogated. The government often justifies such tactics on the grounds that the person is suspected of violating the country's national security. Many of these people are eventually released, but the experience obviously creates a chilling effect regarding how one lives (Ghahramani, 2009).

Status of Women A second criticism is associated with the status of women. Iran and Saudi Arabia are similar in that they are both based on a traditional patriarchal society. They differ in that Iran's House of Pahlavi, for all of its mistakes, introduced a number of rights for women. This involved greater educational opportunities and more equitable treatment in the event of a divorce. Moreover, women were not subjected to a mandatory dress code. However, all or most of that changed with the 1979 revolution. For example, the Family Protection Law was suspended. It had raised the age of marriage for girls to 18 and granted women the right to seek a divorce without their husband's permission. Following the revolution, all matters dealing with the family were delegated to Sharia courts rather than secular courts (as they had been abolished). As a result of these reversals, there has been a concern over the vulnerability of women as victims to violence in general and domestic violence in particular (Copithorne, 2000; Sahebjam, 1994). In addition, when a woman is murdered and her family seeks the death penalty for the perpetrator, her blood price is only half that of a man. It is important to note that this tradition dates back further than the establishment of Islam.

Gender segregation in public places was also reintroduced. With the exception of universities, coeducation was abolished, and in universities, classroom seating segregates men and women. In 1981, the Majlis passed the Islamic Dress Law, which required all women to wear the hijab. They were also required to avoid wearing jewelry, hairstyles, and makeup that was considered un-Islamic. Violators could receive a sentence of up to one year in jail (Hiro, 2005). Women strongly objected to this. While it is still the law, there have been periods when the dress law is not enforced to any significant degree. For example, women can wear a scarf as a veil during times when the political climate is willing to allow people a degree of personal freedom. The political climate can quickly change, however, and women find themselves singled out in particular for public humiliation by the morality police for such transgressions (Moaveni, 2005; Moaveni, 2009; Nafisi, 2003).

Law Enforcement The morality police or basij is the source of a third criticism directed at the Islamic Republic. Iran has two regular law enforcement agencies that are modeled somewhat after the French. The National Police handle the regular law enforcement and order maintenance needs of larger cities, while the Gendarmerie is responsible for the rural areas of the country. Both are accountable to the Ministry of the Interior.

The *basij* (mobilization) is accountable to the Iranian Revolutionary Guard or Pasdaran. The Guard was created by Ayatollah Khomeini to assist in the establishment and protection of the Islamic revolution. The basij are an auxiliary militia force. They are the frontline "soldiers" that have a mandate to protect Islamic society from the threat of cultural and moral decay either from within or influences from Western societies. The basij is composed of both a full-time force as well as volunteers. Members include young boys who are often too young to join a branch of the military and older men who have concluded a military career. The basij is not limited to men, however; there is a large contingent of women who assist in the mission of policing public spaces. Basji are often used to quell demonstrations, which has led to a good deal of criticism regarding the tactics they employ. They have also been employed to secure information about university students. In policing public spaces, they are specifically in search of any behavior that might appear un-Islamic. Road blocks have been set up to check motorists for: alcohol, other drugs, inappropriate CDs or DVDs, passengers of opposite sexes who are not married, and dress code violations. People have been detained, beaten, and in some cases brought to court. The extrajudicial tactics of the basji have been noted by various human rights groups and commented on by independent observers (Copithorne, 2000; Ghahramani, 2009; Hiro, 2005; Human Rights Watch, 2008e; Moaveni, 2005; Moaveni, 2009; Nafisi, 2003).

Nature of Punishment A fourth criticism is directed at the sanctions imposed on people found guilty of crimes in Iran. The types of Sharia sanctions for hudud, quesas, and tazir offenses have already been explained in general and noted in particular in contemporary Saudi Arabia. As was the case with Saudi Arabia, the human rights concern is over the physical harshness of the sanctions. Immediately following the overthrow of the Pahlavi dynasty, revolutionary courts were established and began to dispense justice according to the laws of Islam. In the early 1980s, a series of laws were passed that essentially codified Islamic criminal law. Some of the more modern offenses were incorporated into these laws, but the punishment was changed. For example, driving a car without a license could lead to the offender being flogged. Flogging appears to be the most common of the traditional sanctions employed. Moreover, quesas offenses were associated with retribution, that is, the victim had the right to seek a retaliatory punishment, but it could not be greater than the harm caused to the victim. This characteristic of ancient forms of justice has been retained. To illustrate, in late 2008, an Iranian court ordered a man blinded with acid after he had been convicted of blinding with acid a woman whom he had been stalking. The 1991 Penal Code essentially consolidated these earlier pieces of legislation. The objections to the harshness of a number of sanctions have been led by various international organizations associated with human rights and have been supported by a number of countries (Peters, 2005).

Of particular concern is the use of harsh sanctions imposed on juveniles, especially imposing the death penalty on young people who committed their crime before they reached the age of 18. The Iranian Penal Code exempts children who have not reached puberty from criminal responsibility. The Civil Code of 1991, however, is more specific regarding the age of responsibility by citing boys at 15 and girls at nine. According to Human Rights Watch, the majority of juvenile executions were the result of the child being found guilty of murder (Human Rights Watch, 2008b). Moreover, it is believed that Iran executes more juveniles than any other country. Between 2007 and 2009, it is believed that 26 juveniles under the age of 18 were executed. The common method of carrying out the sentence is by hanging. Moreover, it is estimated that at least 130 juveniles are presently on death row.

In 2008, two policy changes were announced regarding executions. The head of the judiciary ordered a halt to all public executions unless authorized by him. Late in the year, judges were instructed not to impose the death penalty on juveniles.

Democracy or Theocracy A final criticism impacts many of the other concerns and is associated with the political and administrative system of the government. The Islamic Republic has some quasi-democratic features with an elected parliament and presidency. Unfortunately, candidates for either branch of government must first be approved by the Council of Guardians, which is dominated by senior Shia jurists. The Leader, who holds the ultimate and extensive political and spiritual authority, is a senior Shia cleric. He is selected by the Assembly of Experts, whose membership is limited to Shia clerics. The Expediency Council, which is charged with resolving conflicts among the various branches or departments of government, is dominated by Shia clerics. Finally, a number of deputies in the Majlis are also Shia clerics.

While it should be noted that the vast majority of Shia clerics do not hold positions in the government, there is a good deal of criticism over the degree to which Shia clerics control the political system by occupying so many key governmental offices. Among those concerned are Shia clerics themselves, and some are high-ranking clerics in the hierarchy. Nonclerical critics are generally concerned about the theocracy that has been created since 1979. Many Iranians who supported the overthrow of the shah were not seeking to replace him with a theocracy. Within that group there was a good deal of support to establish a democratic system of government. The status quo will continue to inhibit efforts by the political opposition to move the country in that direction.

A number of well-educated people have left the country following the revolution, and that trend continued as the theocracy took hold and stifled various forms of individual freedom. This "brain drain" in a host of professions has had an adverse impact on the country. Since the death of Ayatollah Khomeini in particular, the tension over the desire for more democracy and less clerical hegemony rises and subsides depending on the success of internal political policies, especially those associated with the economy. With regard to the economy, it should be noted that Iran has a large number of young people; two out of three Iranians are under the age of 30. The lack of jobs for people between 25 and 29 years of age is a serious social dilemma, with approximately half of them unemployed. This adds to the social and political tensions confronting the country.

Exacerbating this tension is the often continued visible acquisition of significant wealth by the Shia hierarchy. While some of this wealth is used for worthy causes, it is also noted that a select group of Shia clerics have enhanced their personal wealth considerably since the 1979 revolution. By way of comparison, this is another difference between Iran and Saudi Arabia. The Sunni religious establishment in the Kingdom receives almost all of their finances from the government, which is controlled by the House of Saud (Mackey, 1996). It is important to remember that opposition to clerics in government is not a rejection of Islam.

Finally, a number of commentators have addressed the issue of whether Iran is capable of introducing a truly democratic system of governance. The proponents within the country for establishing a democratic system of government are confronted with two pressing issues. First, democracy tends to advocate support for individual rights. The cultural traditions—namely, the dominant patriarchal society and the tenet within Islam that the most important group is the umma, the community of believers—has long subordinated the individual in Iranian society. While both of these traditions are capable of changing and have done so in other countries, the question for Iran remains how long would this transformation take? Second, conservative elements of society have some reservations about democracy because of its secular nature. For many conservatives, that secular nature is associated as the vehicle that ultimately leads to the moral decay of society.

In spite of these issues, the ongoing decline of support for clerics in positions of government has not abated, and this should enhance the interest to change the status quo. Moreover, it is clear that Islam has not been able to address many of the problems confronting Iran's fairly modern society, a society whose basis for modernity is not rooted in Islam. One scholar has noted: "In the Islamic Republic, Islam is at stake. A vigorous push towards democracy will put an end to the contention over the capacity of religion to foster modernity." He also rightly points out that "[m]odernisation and democratisation are long and continuous processes. The complete transformation of a traditional society requires time and enormous efforts"(Alsaif, 2007). Obviously, the opposition to the Islamic Republic must first grow significantly in numbers and then be in a position to change the system of governance in Iran. If and when that happens, and if the proponents of a truly democratic system assume positions of leadership as agents of change undertaking this long and enormous task, they may be in search of a primer. One might suggest that they look to the far northwest reaches of their own neighborhood—to the Republic of Turkey—as one example for such a transformation.

REPUBLIC OF TURKEY

With our purpose of examining Shaira in contemporary contexts, our coverage of the Republic of Turkey is somewhat brief. Although the overwhelming majority of the population is Muslim, Islamic law no longer influences the justice system of the country. The demise in the significance of Islamic law came about in the 1920s, and Islamic law has remained of little public significance to this day. The Turks are an example of a people that have largely embraced modernity with all of its problems while still remaining devout members to their Islamic faith.

At 300,948 square miles, Turkey is slightly smaller than the combined area of the states of Washington, Idaho, and Montana. Its territory consists of hilly, fertile regions and rugged, mountainous areas. It shares land borders with Bulgaria, Greece, Georgia, Armenia, Iran, Azerbaijan, Iraq, and Syria. It has a coastline along the Black, Mediterranean, and Aegean Seas. The population is more than 70 million, and the principal ethnic groups are Turkish and Kurdish. The Kurds are the largest ethnic minority, representing approximately 12 million. Until recently, they were a nomadic tribal people. They are presently divided among six countries in the region. In each of those countries, with Turkey being but one example, there are tensions over issues associated with Kurdish nationalism. Muslims represent 99 percent of the population of Turkey, with about 80 percent of them Sunni. The Shia population tends to be located in the southeast region of the country. Minority faiths include Christian, Baha'i, and Jewish.

It was mentioned above that the height of the Ottoman Empire was between the sixteenth and eighteenth centuries, and that it was this empire that was "the last great expression of the universality of the world of Islam" (Hourani, 1991). Even before the empire began to decline, two groups had emerged regarding the direction it should take to assure its viability. On the one hand were the restorationists, who essentially looked back to the glorious period of the reign of Sulayman the Magnificient (1520–1566) and wanted to recapture that kind of prominence for the empire. On the other hand, the modernists encouraged the adoption of European ideas, especially those associated with military training, organization, and administration (Lapidus, 2002). By the nineteenth century, the modernists had won that debate. Nevertheless, the Ottoman Empire was in a state of decline. Scholars point out that the decline "was due not so much to internal changes as to their inability to keep pace with the rapid advances of the West in science and technology, in the arts of both war and peace, and in government and commerce" (Lewis, 1996).

Finally, as noted above, the Ottoman Empire from its inception employed three sources of law. First and foremost was Sharia, the Islamic law, derived from the Quran and Sunna. Second were the rules and principles established to address issues that were not explained in the Sharia (and, of course, the very process of creating these rules was guided by the Quran). A third source of law was official rulings or directives to cope with various social circumstances at a particular time and a specific place in the vast empire. A fourth source of law, however, emerged during the nineteenth century. As a result of the importance of commercial enterprises and the borrowing of scientific and technological advances from the West, the empire sought additional assistance with nagging problems in other areas of governance. Initially, the empire adopted legal ideas from the codes of European countries. By the late nineteenth century and with specific reference to criminal justice, they were adopting a Penal Code (1857) and a Code of Criminal Procedure (1879) based on the contemporary legal codes of France.

The large Ottoman bureaucratic state has long been noted for contributing to the longevity of the empire. The Turkish military was also a key component of the Ottoman system of governance. It had a storied tradition before the empire was established and was largely responsible for its creation. At the top of the government was the sultan who had the additional title of caliph. It should be remembered that the title of caliph was given to the successors of the Prophet Muhammad as the temporal rulers of the umma or community of believers. Thus, the sultan was the political and religious head of the Muslim community. The sultan, as caliph, did not have any spiritual responsibilities to the community; rather, his fundamental duty, as the political leader, was to defend and protect the Islamic faith. Because Sunni Islam did not have a clerical bureaucracy, the ulama's official role was limited to that of guardian of the beliefs and practices of Islam. Moreover, the sultan acknowledged the ulama as an important component of his administration.

Ataturk and His Legacy

The dissolution of the Ottoman Empire occurred following the end of World War I in 1918. Although Turkey was a loser in terms of the warfare, it was actually a winner in that it emerged as an independent nation state. It was also fortunate to have a person with leadership skills to step forward during this extraordinary time for the country and lead it toward the establishment of a modern society. That person was Mustafa Kemal (1881–1938), who would later add the surname Ataturk, or "father of the Turks." He was an Ottoman army officer who had been active in the political intrigues among the army, liberals, and Muslim conservatives before and during World War I. It was Ataturk who founded the Republic of Turkey in 1923 and was named president for life. This is the man (briefly mentioned in the section on Iran) to whom Reza Shah turned as a model to emulate when he initiated efforts to modernize Iran along Western lines and to enhance the power of his central government.

Whereas most revolutionary transformations in government, like those in the United States, France, and Russia, are associated with endeavors at the grassroots level, Turkey was somewhat unique in that its revolution is often referred to as a revolution from above. Ataturk's first task was to control the territory that was the new nation state of Turkey. For his fledgling republic he retained the civil service and military from the Ottoman Empire to assist in this process. Those two bureaucracies, along with the Republican People's Party, which he had founded, would serve to carry out his agenda for the country (Sunar, 2004). His principal goal was to emulate the West, and to achieve this his strategy was to transform Turkey both economically and culturally into a modern society. During his tenure as president, Ataturk frequently had to adjust the balance between liberty and order. One established commentator on Turkey has pointed out: "Ataturk's priority was order. It is because the order which he established has largely held, that the Turks can now embrace democracy, as the new secular, universal religion"(Mango, 2004). That order would be of a secular kind; Islam would no longer be needed to secure the social order in this new emerging country. Scholars tend to agree that Ataturk's authoritarian style of governance was undoubtedly necessary initially in order to move his country in the direction of a modern democratic state. Ataturk died in 1938 and was succeeded by his trusty lieutenant, Ismet Inonu, who carried on the pragmatic policies of the founder of the republic.

One of the principal targets of Ataturk's reform efforts was directed at Islam, and this was achieved in several ways. For example, the position of sultan was abolished in 1923, and this was followed in 1924 with the elimination of the office of caliph. The position of caliph had served as an important symbol throughout the Muslim community. A new government office for religious affairs was placed in charge of the ulama. He authorized that people had the right to change their religion. The weekly day of rest was changed from Friday to Sunday. In 1925, he decreed that traditional male headgear should be replaced with European-style hats. Although he did not prohibit the wearing of the veil for women, it has been suggested that the veil was abolished "by a kind of social pressure and osmosis, without the apparatus of legal enforcement" (Lewis, 1996). In addition, a new Latin script was introduced to replace the Arabic alphabet in 1928. He also replaced the Muslim calendar with the Gregorian or Western calendar. Finally, the educational system was secularized.

Of course, the Ottomans had already begun to abandon some aspects of Islamic law in the nineteenth century. The Turks would continue that endeavor and borrowed extensively from European legal codes during the 1920s and 1930s, in particular the Swiss civil law, the Italian criminal law, and French administrative law. Specifically, a new family law was gleaned from the Swiss, replacing Sharia. Legislation abolished polygamy and enhanced efforts at equity in divorce. Muslim women were permitted to marry non-Muslim men. Women had already experienced new economic opportunities because of the shortage of men resulting from World War I. Both employment and educational opportunities were increased for women, with the changes introduced by Ataturk's government. These changes established the foundation for a new type of society: the "crucial difference is that in Turkey women are much more emancipated and better able to realize their potential than in most Islamic countries"(Mango, 2004). All of the aforementioned changes were significant in the cultural transformation of the new secular Turkish society that Ataturk was creating. It is also important to note that he had the full support of the educated classes and professions.

Most scholars agree that the twentieth-century history of Turkey can be divided into two periods. The first occurred from 1921 to 1950 and essentially was dominated by the one-party, authoritarian rule of Ataturk and Inonu. It was during this period that the foundations of a constitutional, democratic, multiparty political system were established and the initial stages of an industrial, modern, economic society were created. Since 1950, Turkey has experienced rapid economic change, which, in and of itself, can create a good deal of tension. Another type of tension is associated with political governance as it relates in particular to the role of the military, a multiparty political system, and ideological conflict (Lapidus, 2002).

While the post-1950 tensions are important in order to understand the country, a detailed examination of them is beyond the scope of our purpose. Nevertheless, two tensions are summarized that are interrelated with the military, politics, and ideology. The first tension is associated with the military. On two occasions, there have been military coups to rescue the country from ineffective governments. The first occurred in 1960 and lasted one year. The generals abolished the Democratic Party, which had been in power and had altered Ataturk's secular policy by supporting greater tolerance of Islam in public life. The generals were also instrumental in writing a new constitution for the country. In 1980, the army would again take control of the country as a result of political and economic instability. They suspended the constitution and dissolved parliament and all political parties. This coup also led to a new constitution that was submitted to the people in a referendum in November of 1982. It was approved by 91 percent of the voters. In addition to these coups, there have been other occasions in which there were threats, subtle and not so subtle, that the military might intervene in the governance of the country.

It is important to note that there are some segments of the population, often referred to as Kemalists (for the founding father of modern Turkey, Mustafa Kemal Ataturk), who have preferred an authoritarian style of government when it is in their economic or political interests. To illustrate, in a poll published in August 2003, 88 percent of the sample stated that the armed forces were the most trustworthy institution in the country. The army has long been viewed as facilitating Turkey's efforts at modernization. One of their specific tasks has been to intervene if politicians are not capable of maintaining the law and order that are vital to achieving modernization. They have been called upon to reintroduce a level of Ataturk's style of authoritarianism in order to assure the continued nurturing of democratization throughout the political process (Mango, 2004). It has been suggested that having the army in the background, ready to intervene when voters make mistakes at the polls and civilian governments become inept at handling issues often of a domestic nature, leads to a "permanently immature" electorate. "It allows them to avoid ultimate responsibility for the consequences of their votes.... As long as the army is around to do the system's dirty work, voters can avoid confronting the urgency of political change. ... It does not, however, serve the cause of democracy" (Kinzer, 2001).

The other tension presently dominating Turkish political life is associated with the Justice and Development Party. To understand the current crisis, it is important to review briefly the tensions created by opposition parties that either have an active Islamic political agenda or are at least willing to accommodate the existence of a religious political party. First, opposition political parties were for the most part suppressed while Ataturk was alive. On only two occasions did parties emerge, but they were short-lived: the Progressive Party 1924 and the Liberal Party of 1929 and 1930. A competitive political party system did not develop until the 1950s. Second, Ataturk's emphasis on the secular state leading the country to modernity and a higher standard of living as seen in the West had led to Islam being removed from having a prominent voice in public life. With the emergence of a multiparty political landscape in the 1950s, those with an Islamic political agenda began to organize themselves. It was the Democratic Party that was instrumental in allowing this to happen. It had won a parliamentary majority in 1950 by defeating the Republican People's Party, the party of Ataturk. One of its agendas was to relax the overly strict secularist policies that Ataturk considered essential to enabling Turkey to transform itself into a modern state. As mentioned above, it was the Democratic Party that was banned as a result of the military coup in 1960.

By 1970, the first Islamic party emerged as the National Order Party, but it was quickly eliminated in 1971 on the grounds that it opposed the secular nature of the state. It was replaced by the National Salvation Party in 1972, and it called for a return to an Islamic way of life. This party lasted until the military coup of 1980, when all political parties were banned. Shortly after the reemergence of a civilian government in 1982, the Welfare Party became the standard bearer for political Islam in Turkey throughout much of the 1980s and 1990s. It was clearly opposed to Western influences. In 1998, it was eliminated with the help of the military, and several of its members were banned from politics for five years. The Virtue Party replaced the Welfare Party and established a position that was not hostile to Western influences. Nevertheless, the Constitutional Court closed its operations in 2001 on the grounds that it advocated an anti-secular position. The ability to ban a religious political party that carries its agenda too far has a basis in Turkish constitutional law. Article 68, which deals with political parties, states in part: "The statutes and programmes, as well as the activities of political parties shall not be in conflict with the independence of the state, its indivisible integrity with its territory and nation, human rights, and principles of equality and rule of law, sovereignty of the nation, the principles of the democratic and secular republic; they shall not aim to protect or establish class or group dictatorship or dictatorship of any kind, nor shall they incite citizens to crime." This has been the legal basis to ban such political activities that are considered in conflict with "the principles of the democratic and secular republic."

Two groups emerged following the demise of the Virtue Party. The more conservative group formed the Felicity Party, while the moderates established the Justice and Development Party. In the 2002 parliamentary elections, the Justice and Development Party won 34 percent of the vote, which was ahead of the Republican People's Party, which received 19 percent of the vote. With 363 seats in the new parliament, the Justice and Development Party formed a government. During this time it was pointed out that "official Islam in Turkey is developing a philosophy of religious humanism as an alternative to the secular humanism of the intellectual elite. ... Turkish Islam is emerging from decades of intellectual stagnation to meet the modern world on its own terms"(Mango, 2004). Moreover, one scholar indicated that "... there are now hurried attempts by even secularist official circles to introduce an Islamic morality and larger doses of nationalism into the socialization process of school children and the young. Islam, therefore, will continue to play an important role in society—not, however, in the form of a mass movement, an Islamic revolution or revolt, but largely as an ethical guide to promote good civic behavior and social peace, and as a private experience for individuals" (Sunar, 2004). As such, the Justice and Development Party attempted to accommodate itself to the secular society that Kemalists were determined to maintain.

For many people, the Justice and Development Party was considered a center-right party rather than a religious party. It had pursued a moderate approach, especially on issues associated with Islam. One of its principal objectives was to initiate reforms in the law and in particular the administration of criminal justice in order to establish grounds for gaining Turkey's admission into the European Union. In the 2007 parliamentary elections, the Justice and Development Party received 46.6 percent of the vote, for 341 seats, while the Kemalist Republican People's Party secured 20.8 percent of the vote, for 112 seats. Following their second victory, the government in early 2008 proposed lifting the ban on women wearing headscarfs at Turkish universities. The ban had been introduced in 1997. This prompted the Chief Public Prosecutor to request that the Constitutional Court ban the Justice and Development Party and 71 of its leading members, which included the President and Prime Minister of the country, from active involvement in politics for five years, because of their active anti-secular activities. In addition to the headscarf controversy, there was a charge that the education minister was attempting to insert Islamic teachings in school textbooks. The leadership of the Justice and Development Party denied that they were attempting to transform the country into an Islamic state.

It is important to interject that "polls show that there is little support in Turkey for an Islamic state. A large majority of Turks, including religious Turks, support the secular state"(Rabasa and Larrabee, 2008). To illustrate, in one respected poll from 2006, only 9 percent of the population supported a state that was based on Sharia. Nevertheless, one commentator of contemporary Turkey has pointed out that: "The relatively low proportion of Islamic fundamentalists revealed by social surveys has not stilled the fears of defenders of secularism or reduced the vigilance of the armed forces, which see themselves, and are seen by society, as the ultimate guarantors of the modern, secular republic"(Mango, 2004).

In the summer of 2008, the Constitutional Court handed down two decisions that would address the concerns that Turkey's secular state was in jeopardy. First, it reimposed the ban on headscarfs, indicating that the government's policy was a violation of the secular principles of the constitution. With regard to banning the Justice and Development Party and its leaders from politics for five years, six of the 11-member Court voted yes, but the rules required a majority of seven members to secure such a decision. Ten of the justices agreed that the party had been involved in anti-secular activity, but they disagreed on the punishment. As a result, the party was fined for its activities. The events of 2008 created both a political and constitutional crisis for the country. At the core of that crisis was the issue of ideology: secularism and Islam.

Government

In the twentieth-century history of Turkey, the country has been guided by four constitutions. The Constitution of 1921 was essentially a transitional document during the Turkish War for Independence. It consisted of 23 articles and introduced the principle of national sovereignty. While it delegated governing authority to the executive and legislature, there was no discussion of a role for the judiciary. The Constitution of 1924 was enacted following the proclamation in 1923 declaring Turkey to be a republic. With this document the authority of the executive, legislature, and judiciary are noted. Ataturk had a fundamental role to play in the preparation of both the 1921 and 1924 constitutions. Following the 1960 coup, the Constitution of 1961 was approved, and it was noted for two things: the establishment of a bicameral legislature and, most important, the acknowledgment of individual human rights. Following the military coup in 1980, the constitution was suspended and parliament dissolved. In 1982, the people voted overwhelmingly in a referendum to approve a new constitution. In form it was modeled in several ways after the 1958 Constitution of the Fifth Republic of France. This does not mean that it functions precisely within the Turkish context like that of the French constitution. For example, the 1982 constitution abandoned the bicameral legislature for a unicameral legislature.

Constitution The 1982 Constitution of the Republic of Turkey consists of seven parts and contains 177 articles. The Preamble to the document begins with the following statement: "In line with the concept of nationalism and the reforms and principles introduced by the founder of the Republic of Turkey, Ataturk, the immortal leader and the unrivalled hero, this Constitution, which affirms the eternal existence of the Turkish nation and motherland and the indivisible unity of the Turkish state." Thus, the father of modern Turkey, Ataturk, remains a revered figure.

Part One of the Constitution establishes the general principles. While article 1 indicates that Turkey is a Republic, article 2 identifies characteristics that are central to the Republic. They state, in part, that Turkey "is a democratic, secular and social state governed by the rule of law; bearing in mind the concepts of public peace, national solidarity and justice; respecting human rights; loyal to the nationalism of Ataturk." Article 4 is of interest because it declares that articles 1 through 3 of the Constitution are irrevocable and indicates that they cannot be amended. What is of particular interest for our purposes is that the article is essentially proclaiming that Turkey is to remain a secular society. Article 6 acknowledges that sovereignty rests in the nation and that it cannot be "delegated to any individual, group, or class."

Part One also indicates that political power and authority will reside in the legislative, executive, and judicial branches of government and that each is subject to the provisions of the Constitution. Although Turkey has two offices associated with the executive branch, it essentially functions as a parliamentary system. Finally, article 10 addresses the issue of equality before the law. It states:

> All individuals are equal without any discrimination before the law, irrespective of language, race, colour, sex, political opinion, philosophical belief, religion and sect, or any such considerations.
>
> Men and women have equal rights and the State is responsible to implement these rights. No privilege shall be granted to any individual, family, group or class.
>
> State organs and administrative authorities shall act in compliance with the principle of equality before the law in all their proceedings.

Of particular interest here, given the previous discussion in the sections on Saudi Arabia and Iran, is the statement that religion and gender are protected by the principle of equality before the law.

Part Two is devoted to a host of fundamental rights and duties that are frequently associated with a modern democracy. It was mentioned earlier about the tension created over the agenda of religious political parties and the constitutional principle of Turkey as a secular state. We return to that theme in the area of fundamental rights and duties. For our purposes, article 24, dealing with freedom of religion and conscience, is of interest. It states, in part: "Everyone has the right to freedom of conscience, religious belief and conviction. Acts of worship, religious services, and ceremonies shall be conducted freely, provided that they do not violate the provisions of Article 14." Article 14 is titled "Prohibition of Abuse of Fundamental Rights and Freedoms." It declares:

> None of the rights and freedoms embodied in the Constitution shall be exercised with the aim of violating the indivisible integrity of the state with its territory and nation, and endangering the existence of the democratic and secular order of the Turkish Republic based upon human rights.
>
> No provision of this Constitution shall be interpreted in a manner that enables the State or individuals to destroy the fundamental rights and freedoms embodied in the Constitution or to stage an activity with the aim of restricting them more extensively than stated in the Constitution.
>
> The sanctions to be applied against those who perpetrate these activities in conflict with these provisions shall be determined by law.

This is another illustration (of which there are several in the Constitution) that adheres to Ataturk's goal of establishing a secular democracy in which Islam would no longer have a prominent independent role in securing or maintaining the social order. Article 24, however, also states: "Education and instruction in religion and ethics shall be conducted under state supervision and control. Instruction in religious culture and moral education shall be compulsory in the curricula of primary and secondary schools."

Whereas secularism in the West has meant a separation of church and state, this is not the case in Turkey. The Kemalist policy toward religion in general, and Islam in particular, was to control or regulate it. This decision was based on the history of Islam in the region and its role not only as a religious faith but also as a source for establishing a system of law and a political philosophy that acknowledges a role for it in the governance of the umma or society of believers. As such, article 136 acknowledges that the "Department of Religious Affairs, which is within the general administration, shall exercise its duties prescribed in its particular law, in accordance with the principles of secularism, removed from all political views and ideas, and aiming at national solidarity and integrity."

Part Three of the Constitution is devoted to the three branches of government. Turkey has a unicameral legislature called the Turkish Grand National Assembly. It consists of 550 deputies who are elected by citizens who have reached the age of 18 through open, free, and competitive elections. The deputy serves a four-year term. The principal duties of the National Assembly consist of proposing, amending, and repealing laws; supervising the Council of Ministers; and approving the budget.

The executive branch is composed of three elements. Until 2007, the president of the Republic was the head of state and elected by colleagues in the National Assembly. The candidate had to achieve a two-thirds majority of the vote, and once elected, he resigned his seat in the Assembly and severed any affiliation with a political party. The term of office was for seven years, and it was not renewable. A constitutional amendment that was approved by the voters in late 2007 now permits the citizens to vote directly for the president to a five-year term that is renewable once. The president has duties that are associated with all three branches of the government. For example, with regard to the legislature, the president calls it into session, promulgates the laws passed, can appeal to the Constitutional Court regarding a law, and calls for new elections of the Turkish Grand National Assembly. Among the executive duties of the president are: appointing a prime minister, appointing ministers to the Council of Ministers on the recommendation of the prime minister, ratifying treaties, mobilizing the Turkish armed forces, appointing the chief of the General Staff, presiding over the National Security Council, proclaiming martial law or a state of emergency, and signing decrees. Although it appears on paper that a good deal of responsibility resides in the office of the president of Turkey, the Constitution illustrates in an important way the parliamentary nature of the system of government. Article 105 deals with presidential accountability and nonaccountability. Essentially, the president is not authorized to sign decrees alone. Rather, a decree must be countersigned by the prime minister and the minister who is responsible for implementing the policy associated with the decree. Finally, with regard to the judiciary, the president has the authority: to appoint members to the Constitutional Court, one-fourth of the members to the Council of State, the chief public prosecutor and deputy chief public prosecutor, members of the Military High Court of Appeals, members of the Supreme Military Administrative Court, and members of the Supreme Council of Judges and Public Prosecutors.

The other two elements of the executive branch are the prime minister and the Council of Minsters. The prime minister is appointed by the president from a member of the Turkish Grand National Assembly. He is the head of the government. The ministers of the Council of Ministers are nominated by the prime minister and appointed by the National Assembly. Ministers are responsible for various departments of the government that include: defense, education, finance, foreign affairs, health, industry and commerce, interior, and justice.

Judiciary

The judiciary is the third branch of government for the Republic of Turkey. Article 9 states: "Judicial power shall be exercised by independent courts on behalf of the Turkish Nation." Article 138 is more specific in its definition of what is meant by independent courts.

> Judges shall be independent in the discharge of their duties; they shall give judgment in accordance with the Constitution, law, and their personal conviction conforming with the law.
>
> No organ, authority, office or individual may give orders or instructions to courts or judges relating to the exercise of judicial power, send them circulars, or make recommendations or suggestions.
>
> No question shall be asked, debates held, or statements made in the Legislative Assembly relating to the exercise of judicial power concerning a case under trial.
>
> Legislative and executive organs and the administration shall comply with court decisions; these organs and the administration shall neither alter them in any respect, nor delay their execution.

It is clear from these provisions that both the executive and legislative branches of government are expected to comply with the decisions of the courts and not interfere with their judicial deliberations.

Before a description of the organization of Turkish courts is presented, it is important to mention three offices associated with the work of the judiciary as well as one court. The Supreme Council of Judges and Public Prosecutors is chaired by the minister of justice and includes a deputy minister of justice and five senior judges appointed by the president of the Republic. They serve a four-year term and may be reappointed. Article 159 of the Constitution explains that the Council is responsible for "the admission of judges and public prosecutors of courts of justice and of administrative courts into the profession." They also determine the appointment, transfer, promotion, discipline, and removal from office of judges and public prosecutors. If a person wishes to become a judge following graduation from a secular law school, he or she would apply to the Ministry of Justice. If selected, the person would serve a two-year apprenticeship before being eligible for appointment by the Council.

It is the minister of justice, a member of the government's Council of Ministers, who proposes the aforementioned personnel issues to the Council. The Ministry of Justice is responsible for preparing any new or amended legislation to the National Assembly. Public prosecution also falls under the authority of the Ministry of Justice. The prosecutorial service exists throughout the country; it is the responsibility of the state to prosecute those cases that it deems appropriate after a preliminary investigation into a matter has been completed. Finally, the chief public prosecutor represents the state in the Constitutional Court and in any of the High Courts of Appeal. The person is appointed by the president of the Republic to a four-year term and may be reappointed to the post.

Constitutional Court A number of countries permit the highest appellate court in the regular court hierarchy to entertain issues associated with the constitutionality of its law. Others have elected to create a separate Constitutional Court that has exclusive judicial control over such matters. Turkey opted to establish such a court in the 1982 Constitution. Article 148 explains the functions and powers of the Court.

> The Constitutional Court shall examine the constitutionality, in respect of both form and substance, of laws, decrees having the force of law, and Rules of Procedure of the Turkish Grand National Assembly. Constitutional amendments shall be examined and verified only with regard to their form. However, no action shall be brought before the Constitutional Court alleging unconstitutionality as to the form and substance of decrees having the force of law issued during a state of emergency, martial law or in time of war.

In its appellate capacity the Constitution Court receives cases in one of two ways. First, article 150 of the Constitution permits the president of the Republic, a parliamentary group of either the government's party or the main opposition party, or one-fifth of the membership of the National Assembly, to raise an issue of unconstitutionality. Second, an individual can seek judicial review with the claim that his or her individual rights have been violated. It should also be noted that the Constitutional Court is authorized to function as a trial court if senior members of the government, the president of the Republic and members of the Council of Ministers, or members of high courts are scheduled for trial for an offense associated with their constitutional functions.

The Constitutional Court is composed of 11 regular members and four alternates. The president of the Republic is authorized to make the appointments to the Court; however, most of the candidates are actually nominated by the other high courts. These include: the Court of Cassation, Council of State, Military Court of Cassation, the High Military Administrative Court, and the Court of Accounts. In addition to these candidates, the president will select one member to the Court from among the nominees put forward by the Board of Higher Education, and he will personally select three members from among the senior civil service and lawyers who have practiced for at least 15 years. Members of the Court retire at the age of 65, which is the retirement age for other members of the judiciary.

Courts Within the civilian justice system there are two kinds of courts: administrative courts and judicial courts. For our purposes, it is the judicial court hierarchy that is associated with criminal justice issues (see Figure 7.3).

At the top of the judicial court hierarchy is the Court of Cassation. It handles all appeals associated with the legality of lower civil and criminal court decisions. This court is divided into chambers that specialize in

Figure 7.3

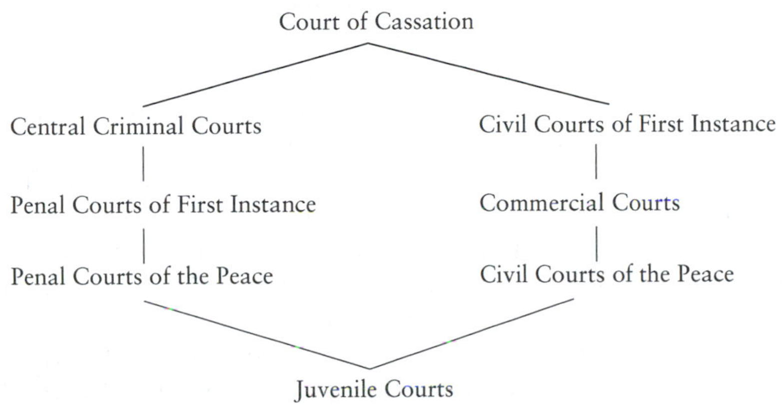

issues associated with the lower courts. Presently, there are 21 civil law and 11 criminal law chambers. Central Criminal Courts handle offenses for which the penalty could be at least 10 years of imprisonment. These cases are handled by a panel of three judges. It should be noted that Turkey does not use a jury of laypersons in any of its courts. Whereas the Penal Courts of the Peace handle minor misdemeanors, the Penal Courts of First Instance are responsible for adjudicating cases not handled by the other two criminal trial courts. Moreover, a single judge would handle cases in the Penal Courts of First Instance and the Penal Courts of the Peace. Finally, Juvenile Courts would handle cases involving people under the age of 18. In Turkey, the age of criminal responsibility is 12. Young people who are found guilty of offenses committed while they were between the ages of 12 and 17 would receive a reduced sentence from that imposed on an adult. For example, if an adult is found guilty of a crime that usually calls for a sentence of life imprisonment, a juvenile found guilty of the same offense would receive a sentence of between seven to nine years.

It should also be noted that while Saudi Arabia and Iran have retained the death penalty, the most severe punishment imposed on people convicted of a crime in Turkey is life imprisonment without parole. The last time the death penalty was carried out in Turkey was in 1984. In 2002, the sanction was abolished for ordinary crimes; in 2004, it was abolished for all crimes.

Critical Issues

For a number of years, agents of the criminal justice system have been the focus of a good deal of criticism associated with Turkey's human rights record. These criticisms have come from international organizations such as Amnesty International, Human Rights Watch, and Transparency International. Concerns have also been expressed by other countries and from the work of journalists and scholars. To illustrate the peculiar nature of the country's problem, it has been suggested: "Of all the countries with bad human-rights records, Turkey is the freest. To put it the other way, Turkey has the worst human-rights record of any free country. This is its deepest and most troubling contradiction" (Kinzer, 2001).

Although this point is troubling, there is, nevertheless, a reasonable explanation for it. First, the authoritarian nature of the government has been an entrenched feature for centuries. It existed throughout the Ottoman period and continued under Ataturk as he began a process that was designed to introduce Western concepts of democratic principles and the rule of law. Second, the Republic of Turkey remains a fairly young country in terms of its adoption of democratic principles. A true parliamentary democracy did not begin to emerge until after the death of Ataturk. Third, the country has suffered from a number of political scandals. One scholar has bluntly noted: "Turkey has a very corrupt political past" (Cerrah, in Haberfeld and Cerrah, 2008). Some of that corruption has infiltrated the criminal justice system. The ebb and flow of corruption, especially political corruption, is one reason why the army has on occasion taken over the governance of the country. While many of the problems associated with human rights are long-standing and will not be resolved overnight, the country has begun in recent years to turn its attention to improving the justice system by addressing problems associated with accountability, transparency, and zero-tolerance for corruption. This was in part prompted by Turkey's interest in joining the European Union.

With regard to police, it should be noted that the country has two kinds of police organizations: the Turkish National Police and the Gendarmerie. Like all units of Turkey's government, the Turkish National Police is a highly centralized organization. For many years their approach to law enforcement and order maintenance was to impose it on the citizenry from above. The Gendarmerie is a highly disciplined military police force that serves rural areas of the country. Because it is a military organization, it has always been somewhat remote from the community of citizens. An illustration of the separateness of the Gendarmerie is that they live in barracks; as such, the opportunities to interact with the citizenry outside the job are reduced considerably.

Some of the criticism directed at the police over human rights concerns involved the style of policing employed by the two agencies. One scholar stated "... policing in Turkey can be described as policing by coercion. Policing by coercion is policing without consent and with the hostility of the community"(Aydin, 1997). It was further pointed out that coercion is a characteristic of any authoritarian regime and over time had become an accepted feature of the state. In recent years, attempts have been made to introduce community policing, that is, inviting the support and participation of the community in reducing crime and maintaining order within their community.

While these efforts at community policing remain a work in progress, two other forms of coercion are in need of solutions. For years, Turkish detectives relied more on informers and rough-handed tactics on an initial suspect to solve crimes rather than a careful attempt to collect evidence to establish a case. The harsh tactics often led to various forms of brutality. Article 94 of the Criminal Law states: "Any public officer who causes severe bodily or mental pain, or loss of conscious or ability to act, or dishonors a person, is sentenced to imprisonment from three years to twelve years." In spite of this provision in the law against torture, prosecutors and judges have looked the other way. This type of abuse continued until human rights groups, both domestic and international, began to complain about the matter. While it remains a problem, it has subsided to some extent. Another example of coercion is associated with problems of police corruption. One survey conducted in 2001 attempted to capture the public's perception of corruption and found the citizenry suspecting the police, in particular, of the practice. According to one commentator, "Official figures confirm the findings: nearly 40,000 policemen were disciplined and nearly 1,000 expelled from the force in the two and a half years to July 2003. These figures show also that action is being taken to improve the service and re-establish public trust" (Mango, 2004).

Coercive tactics with prisoners have not been limited to police, however. The Turkish Human Rights Association has identified the brutal treatment of people detained in both police stations and jails. One recent study of human rights in Turkey concluded: "Due process rights have been frequently violated in Turkey, and abuse in detention or prison, including torture, have been endemic"(Arat, 2007). In addition to the poor treatment, another problem associated with Turkish prisons is the degree of overcrowding. This has been attributed to the lengthy sentences handed out and by the fact that half the prison population often consists of people awaiting a final judgment in their case (Mango, 2004). It is unlikely that some or all of these problems will be addressed soon. This is based on the view that there is a tendency for governments to address problems associated with human rights and policing before they even consider strategies for greater accountability and transparency in the prison system.

The judiciary, that is judges and prosecutors, has also been the subject of a good deal of criticism. They have been part of the problem associated with the other components of the criminal justice system, and many commentators suggest that they are central to the solution of abuses throughout it. To illustrate, Human Rights Watch has accused prosecutors of not conducting effective investigations into allegations of human rights abuses. Moreover, it is claimed that they often do not even initiate a preliminary investigation into a complaint (Human Rights Watch, 2007). To resolve problems like this, one commentator has pointed out that "[j]udges and prosecutors need to become more independent from the state apparatus and, like newspaper editors, begin to think of themselves as servants of the nation rather than of the state" (Kinzer, 2001).

In its investigation on judicial corruption, Transparency International indicated that there is too much political interference by the Turkish Ministry of Justice in filling judicial positions, especially in its control of appointments to the Supreme Council of Judges and Public Prosecutors. Other concerns include the lack of open information about court proceedings and the disciplining of members of the judiciary. It was noted in their report that a number of judges and prosecutors had been found guilty of accepting bribes and trying to influence other courts. This is in part attributed to the inadequate salaries provided to members of the judiciary. Finally, questions were raised about the accuracy of reports submitted by technical experts. Transparency International offered a number of recommendations to address these issues. They included: removing the minister of justice and his deputy from the Supreme Council of Judges and Public Prosecutors; providing the Supreme Council with its own budget and offices separate from the Ministry of Justice; creating more training programs for judges, prosecutors, and lawyers; drafting a code of ethics for judges and prosecutors; and abolishing the private expert pool and establishing a pool of public experts for case analysis (Transparency International, 2007). Finally, it should be noted that in 2006 the High University Board increased the years of study in law school from four to five.

It is also important to note that some of the heavy-handed tactics of the agents of the justice system can be attributed to issues associated with terrorism. For many people in the West, terrorism did not become an issue until September 11, 2001 ("9/11"). From the perspective of the Turks, they have been confronting terrorists for a considerably longer period of time (Mango, 2005). Of course, the old adage that one man's freedom fighter is another man's terrorist comes into play here. Nevertheless, two groups from the Turkish perspective are a threat to the country maintaining the Kemalist goal of a nation state based on democratic and secular principles. Those groups are the Kurdish nationalists and the Islamic revivalists.

The Kurdish people number between 15 and 20 million and are largely Sunni Muslims. They were essentially a nomadic people who lived in the mountainous regions of what is today Turkey, Iran, Iraq, and Syria. After World War I, the aforementioned countries were created into new nation states. Although the Kurds were promised a similar arrangement, it never materialized. Thus, they became a minority group within each of these new countries. Throughout much of the twentieth century, the Kurds have maintained that they should also be given a separate nation state. This would require altering the boundaries of the states of Turkey, Iran, Iraq, and Syria. Because the largest group of Kurds live within the modern boundaries of Turkey, they have often been the most vocal for the establishment of their own nation. Over the years they have employed a number of tactics to voice their plight, and this has included terrorist incidents. The Turkish military and agents of its justice system have responded in kind. Kurdish nationalism remains a concern for Turkey.

Islamic revivalists are those members of the faith that wish to turn the clock back to the Middle Ages, with the reintroduction of Sharia as essentially the only law that governs the region. Ottoman rulers rejected such a position long ago. Part of Ataturk's agenda was to control the role that Islam would play in his secular state. With the success of that strategy, other Islamic activists complain that Islam has been eclipsed and isolated from the lives of Muslims. It has been limited to the basic tenets of prayer, fasting, pilgrimage, and alms-giving (Al-Azam, in Ozdalga and Perssin, 1997). In the view of the revivalists, Islam can offer much more for the betterment of the umma, community of believers. This kind of tension is why the headscarf issue mentioned earlier in this chapter created such a stir, and explains in part why the Constitutional Court eventually had to resolve the matter. Today, some Kemalists fear that radical Islamic groups outside the country might enhance the efforts of the revivalists through various methods of social conflict, which could include violence. Admittedly, this is not as pressing a concern as the issues associated with the Kurds. Nevertheless, as long as various radical groups that claim allegiance to Islam attempt to wreak havoc in various Muslim countries throughout the world, the agenda of Islamic revivalists will remain a concern for Turkey.

Among the countries in the region that have overwhelming Muslim majorities, Turkey is unique. Its government is democratic, and its policies are modern. It can serve as a model for those who wish to embrace a Western style of governance, while accommodating the faithful of Islam and the role Islam can play in society. The process of achieving such a goal will take some time to implement, as is the case with Turkey. Like all democratic countries, Turkey is and will remain a work in progress.

Summary

This chapter has offered an introduction to Islamic law, specifically as it relates to criminal justice. Some countries view the purpose and function of law in a different context from that which emerged in the West, and Islamic law is an example of that difference. Because Islam is primarily a religion, which espouses a specific moral code, it was important to sketch out some of the basic characteristics of the religion. As such, the principal sources of the faith, the Quran, and Sunna were explained. Moreover, the Pillars of Islam, the basic tenets of the faith, were described. The difference between Sunni and Shia Muslims was also summarized. Finally, the development of Islam was outlined in the regions called the Arabian Peninsula, Persia, and the Ottoman Empire.

A large section of the chapter was devoted to explaining Sharia or Islamic law. The section began with the historical development of Sharia, noting that religion and law were interrelated in the region, which was a common feature among societies at that time. An outline was provided of the different madhahib or legal schools that emerged, especially those associated with Sunni Islam. Islamic law is characterized as a series of standards that are religious and moral in nature and that are designed to establish and to explain appropriate conduct of the believers of Islam. The sources for those standards were examined next, and they included the Quran, Sunna, ijma, and ijtihad.

The three principles that highlight how justice is pursued within the realm of Islamic criminal justice were also identified. These included: criminal responsibility and the degrees of accountability, legality related to crime and punishment, and the nonretroactivity of the criminal law. Sharia recognizes two categories of crime and punishment. Determined crimes and the corresponding sanctions refer to those offenses and punishments that have been specified either by God in the Quran or by the Prophet Muhammad in the Sunna. Determined crimes are further subdivided between hudud and quesas offenses. The other category of crime and punishment is discretionary, and these are referred to as tazir offenses. Because Sharia did not provide a detailed method of criminal procedure, this process was left to the delegated authority of the sovereign or ruler. The nature of the process that emerged is also explained, and the treatment touches on such issues as the presumption of innocence, criminal responsibility, the investigation and nature of evidence, the trial process, and what today is referred to as the courtroom workgroup.

The third and final section of the chapter returns to the regions where Islam developed but as contemporary case studies. Thus, attention focuses on the Kingdom of Saudi Arabia, the Islamic Republic of Iran, and the Republic of Turkey. These countries were selected in part because each views Islam and the role of Sharia in a different historical and contemporary context. The Kingdom of Saudi Arabia has long been noted for its embrace of a very conservative interpretation of Sunni Islam. The Islamic Republic of Iran is an example of a country that recently established a curious republican theocratic form of government that is based on principles of Shia Islam. What is also unique about Iran is that for much of the twentieth century it had established a secular legal system that reduced significantly the role of Islamic law. Finally, the Republic of Turkey is an example of a country in which the overwhelming majority of the population is Muslim, but Islamic law no longer influences the justice system of the country. The Turks are an example of a people that has largely sought to establish a secular and democratic system of governance while remaining devout members to their Islamic faith.

By way of backdrop to the examination of these three countries, it was pointed out that a good deal of tension exists throughout the region. Part of that tension has been caused by the economic and military interests of the West that have existed since the eighteenth century. Throughout the twentieth century, generations of people living in the Middle East were exposed to Western popular culture. For some of the older generations, that Western culture has often been characterized as decadent, and this belief has been another factor causing tension in the region. The principal concern has been that the Middle East, like Europe, would forsake its religious roots and embrace a more secular society.

Another factor that has created tension in some circles within the Middle East is the extent to which the countries in the region have borrowed ideas and whole codes from the Western legal tradition of Europe. Although there was opposition by Islamic jurists to this reception of European law, some rulers introduced Western ideas in order to address practical pragmatic policies for the administration of justice in areas for which the Sharia did not provide specific guidance. In spite of this justification to borrow from the Western legal tradition, the legal reception was cause for tension, for the Sharia had long been viewed as the only law necessary to guide Muslims because it represented the will of God.

A final factor creating tension in the region is an all-encompassing issue that is associated with the concept of the secular nation state. The nation state did not emerge in the Middle East until the twentieth century. As a result, the countries in the region are only now grappling with a host of issues associated with this newfound independence as a nation state. A central issue confronting each of them is the ongoing debate over where their allegiance lies. Is their allegiance to an Islamic society? From the inception of Islam, the most important group associated with it was the umma, the community of believers. Today, because Islam is a worldwide religion, the umma extends beyond the borders of any and all nation states. In countries that have embraced all aspects of Islam, the state is often considered subordinate to Islam. This kind of state is often described as a theocratic state. The purpose of such a state is to secure the maintenance and enforcement of God's will or law. This is designed to prepare the believers for life in the hereafter. To assist in that preparation, the state seeks to purge society of all sources that create a decadent secular society.

In this aforementioned debate over allegiance, an alternative lies with a secular democratic society. While not precisely mimicking what happened in eighteenth-century Europe, some within the Islamic Middle East want to replace their age of faith with an age of reason. Social scientists have long noted and cautioned that political democracy is impossible without social democracy. The proponents of a secular democratic society see the Muslim world's failure to modernize as the cause for both economic and social poverty among the people and often political tyranny in the governance of the states in the region.

Whether allegiance is to an Islamic society or to a secular society depends on different views of society. By describing the political and legal system of Saudi Arabia, Iran, and Turkey, an attempt was made to show how three countries in the region are grappling with this significant debate and the other tensions associated with it, especially within the context of criminal justice.

Bibliography

General

Abraham, Henry J. (1980). *The Judicial Process*, 4th ed. New York: Oxford University Press.

Becker, Harold K. (1973). *Police Systems of Europe*. Springfield, IL: Charles C Thomas.

Bell, John (2006). *Judiciaries within Europe: A Comparative Review*. Cambridge, UK: Cambridge University Press.

Brewer, John D., et al. (1996). *The Police, Public Order and the State*, 2nd ed. London: Macmillan.

Brodeur, Jean-Paul, Peter Gill, and Dennis Tollborg (2003). *Democracy, Law and Security: Internal Security Services in Contemporary Europe*. Aldershot, UK: Ashgate.

Cavadino, Michael, and James Dignan (2006). *Penal Systems A Comparative Approach*. Thousand Oaks, CA: Sage.

Chang, Dae H. (ed.) (1976). *Criminology: A Cross-Cultural Perspective*. 2 vols. Durham, NC: Carolina Academic Press.

Christie, Nils (2000). *Crime Control as Industry*, 3rd ed. London: Routledge.

Clifford, W. (1978). "Culture and Crime—In Global Perspective." *International Journal of Criminology and Penology* 6:61–80.

Cole, George F., Stanislaw J. Frankowski, and Marc G. Gertz (eds.) (1981). *Major Criminal Justice Systems*. Beverly Hills: Sage.

Conrad, John P. (1965). *Crime and Its Correction: An International Survey of Attitudes and Practices*. Berkeley: University of California Press.

David, René, and John E.C. Brierley (1985). *Major Legal Systems in the World Today*, 3rd ed. London: Stevens & Sons.

David, René, and John E.C. Brierley (1968). *Major Legal Systems in the World Today*. London: Stevens & Sons.

Delmas-Marty, Mireille, and J.R. Spencer (2002). *European Criminal Procedures*. Cambridge, UK: Cambridge University Press.

Derrett, J. Duncan M. (ed.) (1968). *An Introduction to Legal Systems*. London: Sweet & Maxwell.

Dodge, Calvert R. (1979). *A World Without Prisons*. Lexington, MA: Lexington Books.

Ehrmann, Henry W. (1976). *Comparative Legal Cultures*. Englewood Cliffs, NJ: Prentice Hall.

Fairchild, Erika (1993). *Comparative Criminal Justice Systems*. Belmont, CA: Wadsworth.

Fogel, David (1988). *On Doing Less Harm Western European Alternatives to Incarceration*. Chicago: Office of International Criminal Justice.

Friday, Paul, and Xin Ren (eds.) (2006). *Delinquency and Juvenile Justice Systems in the Non-Western World*. Monsey, NY: Criminal Justice Press.

Glos, George E. (1979). *Comparative Law*. Littleton, CO: Fred B. Rothman.

Haberfeld, M.R., and Ibrahim Cerrah (eds.) (2008). *Comparative Policing: The Struggle for Democratization*. Los Angeles: Sage.

Hall, Jerome (1963). *Comparative Law and Social Theory*. Baton Rouge: Louisiana State University Press.

Ingraham, Barton L. (1987). *The Structure of Criminal Procedure*. New York: Greenwood Press.

Jacob, Herbert, Erhard Blankenburg, Herbert M. Kritzer, Doris Marie Provine, and Joseph Sanders (1996). *Courts, Law, and Politics in Comparative Perspective*. New Haven: Yale University Press.

Kangaspunta, Kristiina (ed.) (1995). *Profiles of Criminal Justice Systems in Europe and North America*. Helsinki: HEUNI.

Macridis, Roy C. (ed.) (1978). *Modern Political Systems: Europe*, 4th ed. Englewood Cliffs, NJ: Prentice Hall.

Matthews, Roger, and Peter Francis (eds.) (1996). *Prisons 2000: An International Perspective on the Current State and Future of Imprisonment*. New York: St. Martin's Press.

Muncie, John and Barry Goldson (eds.) (2006). *Comparative Youth Justice*. London: Sage.

Reichel, Philip L. (2002). *Comparative Criminal Justice Systems: A Topical Approach*, 3rd ed. Englewood Cliffs, NJ: Prentice Hall.

Ruggiero, Vincenzo, Mick Ryan, and Joe Sim (eds.) (1995). *Western European Penal Systems A Critical Anatomy*. London: Sage.

Schlesinger, Rudolph B. (1974). "Comparative Criminal Procedure: A Plea for Utilizing Foreign Experience." *Buffalo Law Review* 26:361–385.

Schultz, Ulrike, and Gisela Shaw (eds.) (2003). *Women in the World's Legal Professions*. Oxford, UK: Hart.

Skolnick, Jerome H., and David H. Bayley (1988). *Community Policing: Issues and Practices Around the World*. Washington, DC: National Institute of Justice.

Tonry, Michael (ed.) (2007). *Crime, Punishment, and Politics in Comparative Perspective*. Chicago: University of Chicago Press.

Transparency International (2008). *Global Corruption Report 2008*. Cambridge, UK: Cambridge University Press.

Transparency International (2007). *Global Corruption Report 2007*. Cambridge, UK: Cambridge University Press.

Vagg, Jon (1994). *Prison Systems A Comparative Study of Accountability in England, France, Germany, and The Netherlands*. Oxford, UK: Clarendon Press.

Wicks, Robert J., and H.H.A. Cooper (1979). *International Corrections*. Lexington, MA: Lexington Books.

Wigmore, John Henry (1928). *A Panorama of the World's Legal Systems*. Washington, DC: Washington Law Book.

Winterdyk, John (ed.) (1997). *Juvenile Justice Systems International Perspectives*. Toronto: Canadian Scholars' Press.

Wise, Edward M., and Gerhard O.W. Mueller (1975). *Studies in Comparative Criminal Law*. Springfield, IL: Charles C Thomas.

Zvekic, Ugljesa (ed.) (1994). *Alternatives to Imprisonment in Comparative Perspective*. Chicago: Nelson-Hall.

England

Abel, Richard L. (1988). "England and Wales A Comparison of the Professional Projects of Barristers and Solicitors." In Richard L. Abel and Philip S. C. Lewis (eds.), *Lawyers in Society The Common Law World*, Vol. 1. Berkeley: University of California Press.

Alderson, J.C., and Philip John Stead (eds.) (1973). *The Police We Deserve*. London: Wolfe.

Astor, Hilary (1986). "The Unrepresented Defendant Revisited: A Consideration of the Role of the Clerk in Magistrates' Courts." *Journal of Law and Society* 13:225–239.

Baker, J.H. (1971). *An Introduction to English Legal History*. London: Butterworths.

Baldwin, John, and Michael McConville (1978). "Plea Bargaining Legal Carve-Up and Legal Cover-Up." *British Journal of Law and Society* 5:228–235.

Baldwin, John, and Michael McConville (1978). "Sentencing Problems Raised by Guilty Pleas: An Analysis of Negotiated Pleas in the Birmingham Crown Court." *Modern Law Review* 41:544–558.

Banton, Michael (1964). *The Policeman in the Community*. New York: Basic Books.

Barclay, Gordon C. (ed.) (1995). *Information on the Criminal Justice System in England and Wales*. London: Home Office Research and Statistics Department.

Belson, William (1975). *The Public and the Police*. London: Harper & Row.

Bennion, Francis (1986). "The Crown Prosecution Service." *Criminal Law Review* 3–15.

Berlins, Marcel, and Clare Dyer (1986). *The Law Machine*, 2nd ed. Harmondsworth, UK: Penguin.

Borrie, Gordon (1976). "The Membership of Boards of Visitors of Penal Establishments." *Criminal Law Review* 281–298.

Brazier, Rodney (2008). *Constitutional Reform Reshaping the British Political System*. 3rd ed. Oxford, UK: Oxford University Press.

Bridges, Lee (1994). "Normalizing Injustice: The Royal Commission on Criminal Justice." *Journal of Law and Society* 21:20–38.

Bridges, Lee, and Mike McConville (1994). "Keeping Faith with Their Own Convictions: The Royal Commission on Criminal Justice." *Modern Law Review* 57:75–90.

Brogden, Michael (1982). *The Police: Autonomy and Consent*. London: Academic Press.

Brown, David (1987). *The Police Complaints Procedure: A Survey of Complainants' Views. Home Office Research Study 93*. London: Her Majesty's Stationery Office.

Bryans, Shane, and Rachel Jones (eds.) (2001). *Prisons and the Prisoner: An Introduction to the Work of Her Majesty's Prison Service*. London: Her Majesty's Stationery Office.

Burney, Elizabeth (1979). *J.P. Magistrate, Court and Community*. London: Hutchinson.

Cameron, Neil (1980). "Bail Act 1976: Two Inconsistencies and an Imaginary Offence." *New Law Journal* 130:382–83.

Cavadino, Michael, and James Dignan (2007). *The Penal System: An Introduction*, 4th ed. London: Sage.

Cavadino, Michael, and James Dignan (2004). *The Penal System: An Introduction*, 3rd ed. London: Sage.

Cornish, W.R. (1968) *The Jury*. Harmondsworth, UK: Penguin Books.

Critchley, T.A. (1967). *A History of Police in England and Wales 900–1966*. London: Constable and Company.

Crow, Iain, Paul Richardson, Carol Riddington, and Frances Simon (1989). *Unemployment, Crime, and Offenders*. London: Routledge.

Curtis, Sarah (1989). *Juvenile Offending: Prevention through Intermediate Treatment*. London: B.T. Batsford.

Davis, Gwynn, Jacky Boucherat, and David Watson (1989). "Pre-Court Decision-Making in Juvenile Justice." *British Journal of Criminology* 29:219–235.

Dennis, Ian (1995). "The Criminal Justice and Public Order Act 1994: The Evidence Provisions." *Criminal Law Review* 4–18.

Devlin, Patrick (1979). *The Judge*. Oxford, UK: Oxford University Press.

Douglas, Gillian (1984). "Dealing with Prisoners' Grievances." *British Journal of Criminology* 24:150–167.

Evans, Peter (1980). *Prison Crisis*. London: George Allen & Unwin.

Evans, Peter (1974). *The Police Revolution*. London: George Allen & Unwin.

Feldman, David (1990). "Regulating Treatment of Suspects in Police Stations: Judicial Interpretation of Detention Provisions in the Police and Criminal Evidence Act 1984." *Criminal Law Review* 452–471.

Freeman, John C. (1986). "Alternatives to the Prosecution of Juveniles and the Rights of Children." Resource Materials No. 29, pp. 77–89. Tokyo: UNAFEI.

Friesen, E.C., and I.R. Scott (1977). *English Criminal Justice*. Birmingham, UK: Institute of Judicial Administration.

Goldson, Barry (ed.) (2000). *The New Youth Justice*. Lyme Regis, UK: Russell House.

Griffith, J.A.G. (1991). *The Politics of the Judiciary*, 4th ed. Hammersmith, UK: Fontana Press.

Hall-Williams, J.E. (1975). *Changing Prisons*. London: Peter Owne.

Hall-Williams, J.E. (1970). *The English Penal System in Transition*. London: Butterworths.

Hall-Williams, J.E. (1987). "New Kinds of Non-Custodial Measures The British Experience." Resource Materials No. 32, pp. 121–134.. Tokyo: UNAFEI.

Harding, Alan (1966). *A Social History of English Law*. Baltimore: Penguin Books.

Harris, Brian, and Roger Rickard (1974). *Legal Aid and Advice*. Chichester, UK: Barry Rose.

Hayes, Mary (1981). "Where Now the Right To Bail?" *Criminal Law Review* 20–24.

Hazell, Robert (ed.) (1978). *The Bar on Trial*. London: Quartet Books.

Holdaway, Simon (ed.) (2001). *The British Police*. Beverly Hills: Sage.

Home Office (2001). *Criminal Justice: The Way Ahead*. CM 5074, London: The Stationery Office.

Home Office (1997). *No More Excuses—A New Approach to Tackling Youth Crime in England and Wales*. CM 3809. London: Her Majesty's Stationery Office, 1997.

Home Office (1989). *Criminal Statistics, England and Wales, 1988*. London: Her Majesty's Stationery Office.

Hough, Mike, and Julian V. Roberts (2004). *Youth Crime and Youth Justice: Public Opinion in England and Wales*. Bristol, UK: The Policy Press.

Jason-Lloyd, Leonard (2005). *An Introduction to Policing and Police Powers*, 2nd ed. London: Cavendish.

Jason-Lloyd, Leonard (2003). *Quasi-Policing*. London: Cavendish.

King, Roy D., and Rodney Morgan (1979). *Crisis in the Prisons: The Way Out*. Bath, UK: University of Bath and University of Southampton.

Lamford, T.G. (1978). "The Police College, Bramshill: Toward a Coherent and Comprehensive Command Training Structure." *Police Studies* 1:5–12.

Leigh, L.H. (1975). *Police Powers in England and Wales*. London: Butterworths.

Leng, Roger, and Colin Manchester (1991). *A Guide to the Criminal Justice Act 1991*. London: Fourmat.

Lewis, Roy (1976). *A Force for the Future*. London: Temple Smith.

Livingstone, Stephen, and Tim Owen (1993). *Prison Law: Text and Materials*. Oxford, UK: Clarendon Press.

Lustgarten, Laurence (1986). *The Governance of Police*. London: Sweet & Maxwell.

Lyon, Bryce (1960). *A Constitutional and Legal History of Medieval England*. New York: Harper & Row.

Maguire, Mike, Jon Vagg, and Rod Morgan (eds.) (1985). *Accountability and Prisons: Opening Up a Closed World*. London: Tavistock.

Mair, George. (ed.) (2004). *What Matters in Probation*. Portland, OR: Willan.

Malleson, Kate (2007). *The Legal System*, 3rd ed. Oxford: Oxford University Press.

Mansfield, Graham, and Jill Peay (1987). *The Director of Public Prosecutions*. London: Tavistock.

Mark, (Sir) Robert (1977). *Policing a Perplexed Society*. London: George Allen & Unwin.

Marre, Lady (1988). *A Time for Change: Report of the Committee on the Future of the Legal Profession*. London: The General Council of the Bar and The Law Society.

Matthews, Roger, and Jock Young (eds.) (2003). *The New Politics of Crime and Punishment*. Portland, OR: Willan.

Maxim, Paul S. (1986). "Cohort Size and Juvenile Delinquency in England and Wales." *Journal of Criminal Justice* 14:491–499.

McConville, Sean (1987). "Some Observations on English Prison Management." In *International Corrections: An Overview*, pp. 37–43. College Park, MD: American Correctional Association.

Morgan, Rod, and Tim Newburn (1997). *The Future of Policing*. Oxford, UK: Clarendon Press.

Morgan, Rod, and David J. Smith (1989). *Coming to Terms with Policing*. London: Routledge.

Morrison, Fred L. (1973). *Courts and the Political Process in England*. Beverly Hills: Sage.

Oliver, Dawn (2003). *Constitutional Reform in the UK*. Oxford, UK: Oxford University Press.

Oliver, Ian (1987). *Police, Government and Accountability*. London: Macmillan.

Parsloe, Phyllida (1978). *Juvenile Justice in Britain and the United States: The Balance of Needs and Rights*. London: Routledge & Kegan Paul.

Pattenden, Rosemary (1995). "Inferences from Silence." *Criminal Law Review* 602–611.

Pearson, Rose, and Albie Sachs (1980). "Barristers and Gentlemen: A Critical Look at Sexism in the Legal Profession." *Modern Law Review* 43:400–414.

Pitts, John (1988). *The Politics of Juvenile Crime*. London: Sage.

Pratt, John (1986). "A Comparative Analysis of Two Different Systems of Juvenile Justice: Some Implications for England and Wales." *The Howard Journal* 25:33–51.

Prins, Herschel (1975). "Psychiatric Services and The Magistrates' and Juvenile Courts." *The British Journal of Criminology* 15:315–332.

Punnett, R.M. (1988). *British Government & Politics*, 5th ed. Chicago: The Dorsey Press.

Raine, John W., and Michael J. Willson (1995). "Just Bail at the Police Station?" *Journal of Law and Society* 22:571–585.

Reiner, Robert (1985). *The Politics of the Police*. Sussex, UK: Wheatsheaf Books.

Richardson, Genevra (1984). "Time to Take Prisoners' Rights Seriously." *Journal of Law & Society* 11:1–32.

Rose, Richard (1989). *Politics in England*, 5th ed. Glenview, IL: Scott, Foresman.

Rowe, Michael. Ed. (2007). *Policing Beyond Macpherson Issues in Policing, Race and Society*. Portland, OR: Willan.

Samuels, Alec (1986). "Non-Crown Prosecutions: Prosecutions by Non-Police Agencies and By Private Individuals." *Criminal Law Review* 33–44.

Sanders, Andrew (1986). "An Independent Crown Prosecution Service?" *Criminal Law Review* 16–27.

Sanders, Andrew, and Lee Bridges (1990). "Access to Legal Advice and Police Malpractice." *Criminal Law Review* 494–509.

Scarman, Lord (1981). *The Brixton Disorders, 10–12 April 1981*. London: Her Majesty's Stationery Office.

Smith, David J., and Jeremy Gray (1985). *Police and People in London. Policy Studies Institute Report*. Aldershot, UK: Gower.

Smith, Graham W. (1985). "The Community Corrections Option." Resource Materials No. 28, pp. 131–148. Tokyo: UNAFEI.

Southgate, Peter (ed.) (1988). *New Directions in Police Training. Home Office Research and Planning Unit*. London: Her Majesty's Stationery Office.

Spencer, J.R. (ed.) (1989). *Jackson's Machinery of Justice*. Cambridge, UK: Cambridge University Press.

Stern, Vivien (1987). *Bricks of Shame: Britain's Prisons*. Harmondsworth, UK: Penguin Books.

Stevens, Robert (2005). *The English Judges: Their Role in the Changing Constitution*. Oxford, UK: Hart, 2005.

Stewart, Gill, and David Smith (1987). "Help for Children in Custody." *British Journal of Criminology* 27:302–310.

Terrill, Richard J. (1992). "Organizational Change For England's Police: An American Perspective." *Policing & Society* 2:173–191.

Terrill, Richard J. (1989a). "Complaints Against Police in England." *The American Journal of Comparative Law* 31:599–626.

Terrill, Richard J. (1989b). "Margaret Thatcher's Law and Order Agenda." *The American Journal of Comparative Law* 37:429–456.

Terrill, Richard J. (1984). "Police Theorists and the Enlightenment." *The Anglo-American Law Review* 13:39–56.

Terrill, Richard J. (1980a). "Police Theorists and the 'New Enlightenment.'" *The Anglo-American Law Review* 9:48–64.

Terrill, Richard J. (1980b). "Politics, Government, and the Eighteenth-Century Committees of Inquiry into the Police of Metropolitan London." *Police Journal* 53:110–123.

Terrill, Richard J. (1980c). "Politics, Reform, and the Early-Nineteenth-Century Reports of the Committees on the Police of the Metropolis." *Police Journal* 53:240–256.

Thomas, D.A (1979). *Principles of Sentencing*, 2nd ed. London: Heinemann.

Thorpe, D.H., D. Smith, C.J. Green, and J.H. Paley (1980). *Out of Care: The Community Support of Juvenile Offenders*. London: George Allen & Unwin.

Timmons, John (1986). "The Crown Prosecution Service in Practice." *Criminal Law Review* 28–32.

Uglow, Steve (1984). "Independent Prosecutions." *Journal of Law and Society* 12:233–245.

Uglow, Steve, with Venous Telford (1997). *The Police Act 1997*. Bristol, UK: Jordan.

Wadham, John, and Helen Mountfield (2000). *Blackstone's Guide to the Human Rights Act 1998*, 2nd ed. London: Blackstone Press.

Walker, Nigel (1972). *Sentencing in a Rational Society*. Harmondsworth, UK: Penguin Books.

Walker, Nigel (1970). *Crime and Punishment in Britain*. Edinburgh, UK: Edinburgh University Press.

Ward, Richard (1997). *Criminal Sentencing the New Law*. Bristol, UK: Jordan.

Watson, David (1988). "Close Encounters of the Utilitarian Kind: Mediated Reparation for Young Offenders." *Children & Society* 2:43–52.

Weatheritt, Mollie (ed.) (1989). *Police Research: Some Future Prospects*. Aldershot, UK: Avebury.

Wolchover, David, and Anthony Heaton-Armstrong (1990). "Nearly There on the Questioning Code?—2." *New Law Journal* (November 16):1615–1617.

Wolchover, David, and Anthony Heaton-Armstrong (1990). "A Flawed Code—1." *New Law Journal* (March 9):320–322.

Wolff, Michael (1967). *Prison*. London: Eyre & Spottiswoode.

Younger, Sir Kenneth (1977). "Sentencing." *The Howard Journal* 16:17–21.

Zander, Michael (1994). "A Reply to Bridges and McConville on the Report of the Royal Commission." *Modern Law Review* 57:264–269.

Zander, Michael (1989). *A Matter of Justice*. Oxford, UK: Oxford University Press.

France

Ancel, Marc, and Jacques Verin (1973). "The Politics of Criminal Law Reform in France." *The American Journal of Comparative Law* 21:263–268.

Anonymous (1978a). "Juvenile Protection Unit of the Paris Police Headquarters," tr. Technassociates Inc. National Criminal Justice Reference Service. International Summaries, Vol. 1, pp. 99–109. Washington, DC: U.S. Government Printing Office.

Anonymous (1978b). "The Police Officer and the Juvenile Problem," tr. Technassociates Inc., National Criminal Justice Reference Service. International Summaries, Vol. 1, pp. 1111–1124. Washington, DC: U.S. Government Printing Office.

Asso, Bernard (1978). "National and Municipal Police—France, Parts 1 and 2," tr. Deborah Sauve, National Criminal Justice Reference Service, pp. 197–208. International Summaries, Vol. 1. Washington, DC: U.S. Government Printing Office.

Balmford, Peter (1979). "Some Changes Affecting the Legal Profession in Three European Countries." *Law Institute Journal* 501–504.

Blakesley, Christopher (1978). "Conditional Liberation (Parole) in France." *Louisiana Law Review* 39:1–41.

Boigeol, Anne (1988). "The French Bar: The Difficulties of Unifying a Divided Profession." In Richard L. Abel and Philip S.C. Lewis (eds.), *Lawyers in Society The Civil Law World*, Vol. 2. Berkeley: University of California Press.

Carbonneau, Thomas E. (1980). "The French Legal Studies Curriculum: Its History and Relevance as a Model for Reform." *McGill Law Journal* 25:455–477.

Carr-Hill, Roy A. (1987). "'O Bring Me Your Poor': Immigrants in the French System of Criminal Justice." *The Howard Journal* 26 :287–302.

Chemithe, Philippe, and Paul Strasburg (1978). "France's 'Sentence Judge.'" *Corrections Magazine* 4:39–45, 65.

Cooper, Jeremy (1980). "Legal Services in France." *New Law Journal* 130 (February 14):157–158.

David, René (1972). *French Law: Its Structure, Sources, and Methodology*, tr. Michael Kindred. Baton Rouge: Louisiana State University Press.

Davis, Michael H. (1986). "The Law/Politics Distinction, the French Conseil Constitutionnel, and the U.S. Supreme Court." *The American Journal of Comparative Law* 34:45–92.

de Maillard, Jacques, and Sebastian Roche (2004). "Crime and Justice in France." *European Journal of Criminology* 1:111–151.

Dunbar, N.C.H. (1969). "The French Magistracy." *University of Tasmania Law Review* 3:159–173.

Dunbar, N.C.H. (1968). "The French Criminal Jury." *University of Tasmania Law Review* 3:68–81.

Ehrmann, Henry W. (1976). *Politics in France*, 3rd ed. Boston: Little, Brown.

Elliott, Catherine, and Catherine Vernon (2000). *French Legal System*. Harlow: Pearson Education.

Esmein, Adhemar (1968). *A History of Continental Criminal Procedure*, tr. John Simpson, Rothman Reprints, Inc. New York: Augustus M. Kelley.

Ezratty-Bader, Myriam (1989). "Some Illustrations of the Implementation of Standard Minimum Rules for Non-Custodial Measures and Sentences in French Law." In *The Elaboration of Standard Minimum Rules for Non-Institutional Treatment*. Proceedings of the Sixth International Colloquium of the International Penal and Penitentiary Foundation in Poitiers, France, October 1987. Bonn, Germany: International Penal and Penitentiary Foundation.

Fogel, David (1987). "The Investigation and Disciplining of Police Misconduct: A Comparative View—London, Paris, Chicago." *Police Studies* 10:1–15.

Gleizal, J.J. (1981). "Police, Law, and Security in France: Questions of Method and Political Strategy." *International Journal of the Sociology of Law* 9:361–382.

Goldstein, Abraham S., and Martin Marcus (1977–78). "The Myth of Judicial Supervision in Three 'Inquisitorial' Systems: France, Italy, and Germany." *Yale Law Journal* 87:240–283.

Goutal, Jean (1976). "Characteristics of Judicial Style in France, Britain, and the U.S.A." *The American Journal of Comparative Law* 24:43–72.

Hackler, Jim, and Antoine Garapon (1986). "Stealing Conflicts in Juvenile Justice: Contrasting France and Canada." Centre for Criminological Research. Discussion Paper 8. Edmonton: University of Alberta.

Hackler, Jim, Antoine Garapon, Chuck Frigon, and Kenneth Knight (1986). "Closed Custody for Juveniles: Comparisons between Canada and France." Centre for Criminological Research. Discussion Paper 7. Edmonton: University of Alberta.

Hawkins, H.J. (1971). "The C.R.S." *Police Journal* 44:129–132.

Hawkins, H.J. (1970). "The Police Career in France." *Police Journal* 43:214–221.

Herzog, Peter, and Brigitte E. Herzog (1973). "The Reform of the Legal Professions and of Legal Aid in France." *International and Comparative Law Quarterly* 22:462–491.

Hodgson, Jacqueline (2005). *French Criminal Justice: A Comparative Account of the Investigation and Prosecution of Crime in France*. Oxford, UK: Hart.

Hodgson, Jacqueline (2004). "The Detention and Interrogation of Suspects in Police Custody in France." *European Journal of Criminology* 1:163–199.

Honore, A.M. (1973–74). "The Background to Justinian's Codification." *Tulane Law Review* 48:859–893.

Hoquet-McKee, Sophie (1981). "The French Supreme Court: The Cour de Cassation." *City of London Law Review*:1–6.

Horton, Christine (1995). *Policing Policy in France*. London: Policy Studies Institute.

Howarth, David, and Georgios Varouxakis (2003). *Contemporary France: An Introduction to French Politics and Society*. London: Arnold.

Ingleton, R. (1970). "French Police Training." *Police Journal* 43:313–320.

Journes, Claude (1993). "The Structure of the French Police System: Is the French Police a National Force?" *International Journal of the Sociology of the Law* 21:281–287.

Kania, Richard R.E. (1989). "The French Municipal Police Experiment." *Police Studies* 12:125–131.

Kensey, Annie, and Pierre Tournier (1997). *French Prison Population: Some Features*, tr. Rosalind Greenstein. Paris: Ministry of Justice.

King, Michael (1987). "The French Approach to Youth Crime." *Police* 20:29, 42.

Laffargue, Bernard, and Thierry Godefroy (1989). "Economic Cycles and Punishment: Unemployment and Imprisonment." *Contemporary Crises* 13:371–404.

Laurence, Jonathan, and Justice Vaisse. *Integrating Islam: Political and Religious Challenges in Contemporary France*. Washington, DC: Brookings Institution Press.

"Le Plan de Modernisation" (1985). *Revue de la Police Nationale*. Novembre 1985.

Leigh, L.H. (1977). "Liberty and Efficiency in the Criminal Process—The Significance of Models." *International and Comparative Law Quarterly* 26:516–524.

Levy, René (1993). "Police and the Judiciary in France Since the Nineteenth Century." *British Journal of Criminology* 33:167–186.

Levy, René, and Frederic Ocqueteau (1987). "Police Performance and Fear of Crime: the Experience of the Left in France Between 1981 and 1986." *International Journal of the Sociology of Law* 15:259–280.

Levy, René, and Philippe Robert (1984). "Police, Etat, Insecurite." *Criminologie* 17:43–58.

Macridis, Roy C., and Bernard E. Brown (1960). *The DeGaulle Republic*. Homewood, IL: The Dorsey Press.

Maillet, Jean (1969–70). "The Historical Significance of French Codifications." *Tulane Law Review* 44:681–692.

McArthur, Brigid (1984). "French Judicial Decisions." *Victoria University of Wellington Law Review* 14:463–475.

Ministry of Justice (2001). *Key Justice Figures in 2000*. Paris: Ministry of Justice.

Nicholas, Barry (1978). "Fundamental Rights and Judicial Review in France." *Public Law* 82–101.

Noonan, Lowell G. (1970). *France: The Politics of Continuity in Change*. New York: Holt, Rinehart, and Winston.

Olivier, Michel (1979). "The Future of the Legal Profession in France." *Australian Law Journal* 53:502–508.

Piffaut, Gina (1989). "Concrete Achievements Toward the Implementation of the Fundamental Principles of Justice for Victims." In *Changing Victim Policy: The United Nations Victim Declaration and Recent Developments in Europe*. Helsinki: Helsinki Institute for Crime Prevention and Control, No. 16, pp. 113–134.

Plantard, Jean Pierre (1970). "Judicial Conflicts of Interest in France." *The American Journal of Comparative Law* 18:710–715.

Poullain, Bernard, and Laurence Cirba (1976). "France: Notes on the Juvenile Justice System." *Juvenile Justice: An International Survey*. No. 12, pp 141–173. Rome: UNSDRI.

Pradel, Jean (1989). "Which Offenders Are to be Given Non-Institutional Treatment, Particularly According to French Law?" In *The Elaboration of Standard Minimum Rules for Non-Institutional Treatment*. Proceedings of the Sixth International Colloquium of the International Penal and Penitentiary Foundation in Poitiers, France, October 1987. Bonn, Germany: International Penal and Penitentiary Foundation.

Pradel, Jean (1987). "Community Service: The French Experience." In *Community Service as an Alternative to the Prison Sentence*. Proceedings of the Meeting of Coimbra, Portugal, September 1986. Bonn, Germany: International Penal and Penitentiary Foundation.

Pugh, George W. (1975–76). "Ruminations Re Reform of American Criminal Justice (Especially Our Guilty Plea System): Reflections Derived From a Study of the French System." *Louisiana Law Review* 36:947–971.

Pugh, George W., and Jean H. Pugh (1982). "Measures for Malaise: Recent French 'Law and Order' Legislation." *Louisiana Law Review* 42:1301–1321.

Remington, Michael J. (1976–77). "The Tribunaux Administratifs: Protectors of the French Citizen." *Tulane Law Review* 51:33–94.

Richert, John P. (1977). "Recent Changes in the Administration of Parole in France." *Federal Probation* 41:19–22.

"The Role of Supervising Judges in the Granting of Parole in France: A Critical Evaluation" (1978). *International Journal of Comparative and Applied Criminal Justice* 2:35–47.

Rudden, Bernard (1973–74). "Courts and Codes in England, France, and Soviet Russia." *Tulane Law Review* 48:1010–1028.

Safran, William (1985). *The French Polity*, 2nd ed. New York: Longman.

Schmidt, Vivien A. (1990). "Unblocking Society by Decree: The Impact of Governmental Decentralization in France." *Comparative Politics* 22:459–481.

Simon, M. (1975). "Pre-trial Detention in France." *Kingston Law Review* 31–41.

Sowle, Claude R. (ed.) (1962). *Police Power and Individual Freedom*. Chicago: Aldine.

Stead, Philip John (1983). *The Police of France*. New York: Macmillan.

Stead, Philip John (1965). "The Police of France." *Medico-Legal Journal* 33:3–11.

Stead, Philip John (1957). *The Police of Paris*. London: Staples Press.

Tallon, Denis (1979). "The Constitution and the Courts in France." *The American Journal of Comparative Law* 27:567–587.

Tomic-Malic, Mirjana (1973). "Probation in France: Its Operation and Results." *International Journal of Criminology and Penology* 1:279–288.

Tomlinson, Edward A. (1983). "Nonadversarial Justice: The French Experience." *Maryland Law Review* 42:131–195.

Towe, Thomas E. (1963–64). "Criminal Pretrial Procedure in France." *Tulane Law Review* 38:469–496.

Trouille, Helen (1994). "A Look at French Criminal Procedure." *Criminal Law Review* 735–744.

Volcansek, Mary L., and Jacqueline Lucienne Lafon (1988). *Judicial Selection: The Cross-Evolution of French and American Practices*. New York: Greenwood Press.

von Bar, Carl Ludwig (1968). *A History of Continental Criminal Law*, tr. Thomas S. Bell, Rothman Reprints, Inc. New York: Augustus M. Kelley.

Vouin, Robert (1970). "The Role of the Prosecutor in French Criminal Trials." *The American Journal of Comparative Law* 18:483–497.

Wells, Michael (1994). "French and American Judicial Opinions." *Yale Journal of International Law* 19:81–133.

West, Andrew (1991). "Reforming the French Legal Profession; Towards Increased Competitiveness in the Single Market." *Legal Studies* 11:189–203.

Wilcox, A.F. (1982). "Criminal Investigation in the Hands of Lawyers." *Medico-Legal Journal* 50:89–101.

SWEDEN

Akermo, Karl E. (1986). "Organizational Changes and Remodeling of the Swedish Police." *Canadian Police College Journal* 10:245–266.

Amilon, Clas (1987). "The Swedish Model of Community Corrections." *International Corrections: An Overview*, pp. 11–16. College Park, MD: American Correctional Association.

Andenaes, Johs (1968). "The Legal Framework." *Scandinavian Studies in Criminology* 2:9–17.

Andersson, Tommy, et al. (1997). "Early Aggressiveness and Hyperactivity as Indicators of Adult Alcohol Problems and Criminality: A Prospective Longitudinal Study of Male Subjects." *Studies on Crime and Crime Prevention* 6:7–20.

Anonymous (1986). "Summary Report on Non-Prosecution in Sweden." Non-Prosecution in Europe: Proceedings of the European Seminar. Helsinki: Institute for Crime Prevention and Control, No. 9, pp. 291–298.

Aspelin, Erland, et al. (1975). *Some Developments in Nordic Criminal Policy and Criminology*. Stockholm: Scandinavian Research Council for Criminology.

Becker, Harold L., and Einar O. Hjellemo (1976). *Justice in Modern Sweden*. Springfield, IL: Charles C Thomas.

Berg, Gunnar, and Throsten Cars (1978). "Protection of Human Rights in Criminal Proceedings." *Revue Internationale de Droit Penal* 49:340–355.

Bishop, Norman (ed.) (1980). *Crime and Crime Control in Scandinavia 1976–80*. Stockholm: Scandinavian Research Council for Criminology.

Bishop, Norman, Ann Sundin-Osborne, and Tomas Pettersson (1988). "The Drug-Free Program at the Hinseberg Prison for Women." *International Summaries*. Washington, DC: National Institute of Justice.

Board, Joseph B., Jr. (1970). *The Government and Politics of Sweden*. Boston: Houghton Mifflin.

Boëthius, Maria-Pia (1999). "The End of Prostitution in Sweden?" *Current Sweden*, No. 426 (October).

Bogdan. Michael (ed.) (2000). *Swedish Law in the New Millennium*. Stockholm: Norstedts Juridik.

Brush, Michael (1968). "The Swedish Penal Code of 1965." *Duke Law Journal* 67–93.

Christie, Nils (1968). "Change in Penal Values." *Scandinavian Studies in Criminology* 2:161–172.

Doleschal, Eugene (1977). "Rate and Length of Imprisonment: How Does the United States Compare with The Netherlands, Denmark, and Sweden?" *Crime & Delinquency* 23:51–55.

Dolmen, Lars (ed.) (1990). *Crime Trends in Sweden 1988*. Stockholm: National Council for Crime Prevention, Report 1990, p. 4.

Douglas, Gillian (1984). "Dealing with Prisoners' Grievances." *British Journal of Criminology* 24:150–167.

Edqvist, Bjorn, and Suzanne Wennberg (1983). "Recent Legislation and Research on Victims in Sweden." *Victimology* 8:310–327.

Eriksson, Maria, Marianne Hester, Suvi Keskinen, and Keith Pringle (2005). *Tackling Men's Violence in Families: Nordic Issues and Dilemmas*. Bristol: The Policy Press.

Falkner, Sten (1989). "Recent Legislation in Sweden Improving the Situation of Victims of Crime." In *Changing Victim Policy: The United Nations Victim Declaration and Recent Development in Europe*, No. 16, pp. 83–92. Helsinki: Helsinki Institute for Crime Prevention and Control.

Feld, Barry C. (1994). "Juvenile Justice Swedish Style: A Rose by Another Name?" *Justice Quarterly* 11:625–650.

Forslin, Jan (1980). "Work Adjustment of Swedish Policemen." *Scandinavian Studies in Criminology* 7:157–176.

Friday, Paul C. (1976). "Sanctioning in Sweden: An Overview." *Federal Probation* 48–55.

Fry, Lincoln J. (1985). "Drug Abuse and Crime in a Swedish Birth Cohort." *British Journal of Criminology* 25:46–59.

Ginsburg, Ruth (1963). "The Jury and the Namnd: Some Observations on Judicial Control of Lay Triers in Civil Proceedings in the United States and Sweden." *Cornell Law Quarterly* 48:253–273.

Ginsburg, Ruth, and Anders Bruzelins (1962). "Professional Legal Assistance in Sweden." *International and Comparative Law Quarterly* 11:997–1026.

Government Commission on the Police (1979). *The Police: A Summary*. Stockholm: Ministry of Justice.

Hellner, Jan (1968). "Unification of Law in Scandinavia." *The American Journal of Comparative Law* 16:88–106.

Hodgins, Sheilagh, and Carl-Gunnar Janson (2002). *Criminality and Violence among the Mentally Disordered: The Stockholm Project Metropolitan*. Cambridge, UK: Cambridge University Press.

Jagerskiold, Stig (1967). "Roman Influence on Swedish Case Law in the 17th Century." *Scandinavian Studies in Law* 11:175–209.

Jareborg, Nils (1994). "The Swedish Sentencing Law." *European Journal on Criminal Policy and Research* 2:67–83.

Joutsen, Matti (1985). "From Theory to Research to Policy: Scandinavian Developments in Juvenile Crime Prevention and Control." In *Selected Issues in Criminal Justice*, No. 4, pp. 78–90. Helsinki: Helsinki Institute for Crime Prevention and Control.

Klinteberg, Britt Af (1997). "Hyperactive Behaviour and Aggressiveness as Early Risk Indicators for Violence: Variable and Person Approaches." *Studies on Crime and Crime Prevention* 6:21–34.

Knutsson, Johannes (1984). *Operation Identification—A Way to Prevent Burglaries?* Report No. 14. Stockholm: The National Swedish Council for Crime Prevention.

Knutsson, Johannes (1977). *Labeling Theory: A Critical Examination*. Report No. 3. Stockholm: The National Swedish Council for Crime Prevention.

Knutsson, Johannes, and Eckart Kuhlhorn (1996). "Changes in Social Values and Criminal Policy." *Studies on Crime and Crime Prevention* 5:203–220.

Knutsson, Johannes, Eckart Kuhlhorn, and Albert J. Reiss (1979). *Police and the Social Order*. Report No. 6. Stockholm: The National Swedish Council for Crime Prevention.

Kuhlhorn, Eckart (nd.). *Crime Trends and Measures against Crime in Sweden*. Sixth United Nations Congress on the Prevention of Crime and the Treatment of Offenders.

Kuhlhorn, Eckart (1979). *Non-Institutional Treatment and Rehabilitation*. Report No. 7. Stockholm: The National Swedish Council for Crime Prevention.

Kuhlhorn, Eckart (1978). *Deprivation of Freedom and the Police*. Report No. 4. Stockholm: The National Swedish Council for Crime Prevention.

Kuhlhorn, Eckart (1975). *Non-Institutional Treatment: A Preliminary Evaluation of the Sundsvall Experiment*. Report No. 1. Stockholm: The National Swedish Council for Crime Prevention.

Lithner, Klas (1967). "The Prosecutor's Role." *Annales Internationales de Criminologie* 6:437–457.

Marnell, Gunnar (1981). "Treatment of Long-Term Prisoners: The Swedish Approach." In David A. Ward and Kenneth F. Scheen (eds.), *Confinement in Maximum Custody*, pp. 131–146. Lexington, MA: Lexington Books.

Marnell, Gunnar (1974–75). "Penal Reform: A Swedish Viewpoint." *The Howard Journal of Penology and Crime Prevention* 14 (1974–75):8–21.

Marnell, Gunnar (1972). "Comparative Correctional Systems: United States and Sweden." *Criminal Law Bulletin* 748–760.

Martens, Peter L. (1997). "Parental Monitoring and Deviant Behaviour Among Juveniles." *Studies on Crime and Crime Prevention* 6:224–244.

Martinsson, Bo (1987). "Imprisonment, Rehabilitation and Parole in Sweden." In Edward E. Rhine and Ronald W. Jackson, eds., *Observations on Parole: A Collection of Readings from Western Europe, Canada, and the United States*, pp. 43–48. Boulder, CO: National Institute of Corrections.

Ministry of Justice (2000). *Principles for the Treatment of Women Sentenced to Imprisonment*. Stockholm: Swedish Government Offices.

Ministry of Justice (1997a). *Current Swedish Legislation on Narcotic Drugs and Psychotropic Substances*. Stockholm: National Council for Crime Prevention.

Ministry of Justice (1997b). *Our Collective Responsibility: A National Programme for Crime Prevention*. Stockholm: National Council for Crime Prevention.

Ministry of Justice (1986). *The General Goals of Police Activities: A Summary*. Stockholm: Swedish Governments Printing.

Molander, Eva (1995). "Sweden—A Drug-free Society?" *Current Sweden*, No. 409.

Morris, Norval (1966). "Lessons From the Adult Correctional System of Sweden." *Federal Probation* 30:3–13.

The National Prison and Probation Administration (1994). *Basic Facts about Corrections in Sweden*. Forlaget, Sweden: Norrkoping.

The National Prison and Probation Administration (1990). *Measures of De-Institutionalization, 1980*. Report 1990:1. Stockholm: National Council for Crime Prevention. Crime and Criminal Policy in Sweden.

The National Prison and Probation Administration (1978). *A New Penal System: Ideas and Proposals*. Report No. 5. Stockholm: The National Prison and Probation Administration.

The National Prison and Probation Administration (1975). *General Deterrence: A Conference on Current Research and Standpoints*. Report No. 2. Stockholm: The National Prison and Probation Administration.

Nelson, Alvar (nd.). *Crime and Responses to Crime*. Sixth United Nations Congress on the Prevention of Crime and the Treatment of Offenders.

Nelson, Alvar (1973). "The Politics of Criminal Law Reform in Sweden." *The American Journal of Comparative Law* 21:269–286.

Nelson, Alvar (1972). *Responses to Crime: An Introduction to Swedish Criminal Law and Administration*, tr. Jerome L. Getz. New York: New York University School of Law.

Nilsson, Anders (2003). "Living Conditions, Social Exclusion and Recidivism Among Prison Inmates." *Journal of Scandinavian Studies in Criminology and Crime Prevention* 4:57–83.

Nylen, Lars, and Gun Heimer (2000). "Sweden's Response to Domestic Violence." *Current Sweden*, No. 428.

Orfield, Lester B. (1953). *The Growth of Scandinavian Law*. Philadelphia: University of Pennsylvania Press.

Petersson, Olof (1994). *Swedish Government and Politics*, tr. Frank Gabriel Perry. Stockholm: Fritzes.

Petersson, Olof, Klaus von Beyme, Lauri Karvonen, Birgitta Nedelmann, and Eivind Smith (1999). *Democracy the Swedish Way*. Stockholm: SNS Förlag.

Pettersson, Tomas, Ann Sundin-Osborne, and Norman Bishop (1987). "Results of the Drug Abser Treatment Program at the Osteraker Prison." *International Summaries*. Washington, DC: National Institute of Justice.

Roskin, Michael (1977). *Other Governments of Europe: Sweden, Spain, Italy, Yugoslavia, and East Germany*. Englewood Cliffs, NJ: Prentice Hall.

Ross, Alf (1970). "The Campaign Against Punishment." *Scandinavian Studies in Law* 14:109–148.

Salomon, Richard A. (1976). "Lessons From the Swedish Criminal Justice System: A Reappraisal." *Federal Probation* 40:40–48.

Sandalow, Terrance (1971). "Local Government in Sweden." *The American Journal of Comparative Law* 19:766–785.

Sarnecki, Jerzy (nd.). *Juvenile Delinquency in Sweden*. Sixth United Nations Congress on the Prevention of Crime and the Treatment of Offenders.

Sarnecki, Jerzy (1989). *Juvenile Delinquency in Sweden: An Overview*. Stockholm: The National Council for Crime Prevention.

Sarnecki, Jerzy (1986). *Delinquency Networks*. Report 1986:1. Stockholm: The National Council for Crime Prevention.

Sarnecki, Jerzy, and Stefan Sollenhag (1985). *Predicting Social Maladjustment*. Report No. 17. Stockholm: The National Council for Crime Prevention.

Serrill, Michael S. (1977). "Inmates Work For Free Market Wages at Tillberga Prison." *Corrections Magazine* 3:22–34.

Shapiro, Perry, and Harold L. Votey Jr. (1986). *Econometric Analysis of Crime in Sweden*. Report No. 1986:3. Stockholm: The National Council for Crime Prevention.

Snortum, John R. (1984). "Controlling the Alcohol-Impaired Driver in Scandinavia and the United States: Simple Deterrence and Beyond." *Journal of Criminal Justice* 12:131–148.

Snortum, John R. (1983). "Police Practice and Crime Prevention: Swedish Perspectives and U.S. Problems." *Police Journal* 56:224–240.

Snortum, John R. (1979). "Crime Prevention Programs in Sweden." *Social Change in Sweden*, No. 12.

Snortum, John R, and Kare Bodal (1985). "Conditions of Confinement within Security Prisons: Scandinavia and California." *Crime & Delinquency* 31:573–600.

Sperling, Sven (1980). "Violent Criminality and Social Control During Stockholm's Urbanization." *Scandinavian Studies in Criminology* 7:125–146.

Sundberg, Jacob W.F. (1969). "Civil Law, Common Law, and the Scandinavians." *Scandinavian Studies in Law* 13:179–205.

Svensson, Bo (1995). *Criminal Justice Systems in Europe: Sweden*. Stockholm: National Council for Crime Prevention.

Svensson, Bo (1986). "Measuring Drug Incidence—The Swedish Experience." *Information Bulletin of the National Swedish Council for Crime Prevention*, No. 2.

Sveri, Knut (1986). "The Juvenile Justice System of Sweden." Resource Material Series No. 29, pp. 134–146. Tokyo: UNAFEI.

Sveri, Knut (1981). "Recent Changes in Correctional Policies and Practices in Sweden." Resource Material Series No. 19, pp. 97–109. Tokyo: UNAFEI.

Tham, Henrik (2005). "Swedish Drug Policy and the Vision of the Good Society," *Journal of Scandinavian Studies in Criminology and Crime Prevention* 6:57–73.

The Swedish Committee on Juvenile Delinquency (1993). *Reaction to Juvenile Crime Summary*. Stockholm: Forlaget.

Thornstedt, Hans (1986). "The Day-Fine System in Sweden." *Information Bulletin of the National Swedish Council for Crime Prevention*. No. 3.

Thornstedt, Hans (1975). "The Day-Fine System in Sweden." *Criminal Law Review* 9:307–312.

Toyra, Annika, and Jennie Wigerhoit (2008). *The Swedish Crime Survey 2007*. Stockholm: Swedish National Council for Crime Prevention.

Von Hofer, Hanns (2003). "Prison Populations as Political Constructs: The Case of Finland, Holland and Sweden." *Journal of Scandinavian Studies in Criminology and Crime Prevention* 4:21–38.

Von Hofer, Hanns (2000). "Criminal Violence and Youth in Sweden: A Long-term Perspective." *Journal of Scandinavian Studies in Criminology and Crime Prevention* 1:56–72.

Wikstrom, Per-Olof (ed.) (1990). *Crime and Measures Against Crime in the City*. Report 1990, 5. Stockholm: National Council for Crime Prevention.

Zagaris, Bruce (1977). "Penal Reform in Sweden." *Southwestern University Law Review* 9:111–156.

JAPAN

Allen-Bond, Marc (1984). "Policing Japan." *Law and Order* 32:46–52.

Ames, Walter L. (1981). *Police and Community in Japan*. Berkeley: University of California Press.

Angata, Shizuo (1971). "Anatomy of Volunteer Probation Officer System." Resource Materials No. 2, pp. 192–202. Tokyo: UNAFEI.

Anonymous (1978). "Japanese Police Systems," tr. Virginia Allison, National Criminal Justice Reference Service. International Summaries, Vol. 1, pp. 189–195. Washington, DC: U.S. Government Printing Office.

Araki, Nobuyoshi (1985). "The Flow of Criminal Cases in the Japanese Criminal Justice System." *Crime & Delinquency* 31:601–629.

Archambeault, William G., and Charles R. Fenwick (1988). "A Comparative Analysis of Culture, Safety, and Organizational Management Factors in Japanese and U.S. Prisons." *The Prison Journal* 68:3–23.

Asakura, Kyoichi, et al. (1978) "A Study on Rehabilitation Activities in Prison Facilities—Japan," tr. Michael McCaskey, National Criminal Justice Reference Service. International Summaries, Vol. 2, pp. 59–64. Washington, DC: U.S. Government Printing Office.

Bayley, David H. (1976). *Forces of Order: Police Behavior in Japan and the United States*. Berkeley: University of California.

Bayley, David H. (1976). "Learning About Crime—The Japanese Experience." *Public Interest* 44:55–68.

Becker, Carl B. (1988) "Report from Japan: Causes and Controls of Crime in Japan." *Journal of Criminal Justice* 16:425–435.

Berat, Lynn (1992). "The Role of Conciliation in the Japanese Legal System." *American University Journal of International Law and Policy* 8:125–154.

Bolz, Herbert F. (1980). "Judicial Review in Japan: The Strategy of Restraint." *Hastings International and Comparative Law Review* 4:87–142.

Clifford, William (1976). *Crime Control in Japan*. Lexington, MA: Lexington Books.

Dando, Shigemitsu (1970). "System of Discretionary Prosecution in Japan." *The American Journal of Comparative Law* 18:518–531.

Dando, Shigemitsu (1965). *Japanese Criminal Procedure*, tr. B.J. George Jr. South Hackensack, NJ: Fred B. Rothman.

Dean, Meryll (1997). *Japanese Legal System: Text and Materials*. London: Cavendish.

Dean, Meryll (1994). "Capital Punishment in Japan." *New Law Journal* (June 17):836–837.

Dore, R.P. (ed.) (1967). *Aspects of Social Change in Modern Japan*. Princeton, NJ: Princeton University Press.

Fenwick, Charles R. (1985). "Culture, Philosophy and Crime: The Japanese Experience." *International Journal of Comparative and Applied Criminal Justice* 9:67–81.

Fenwick, Charles R. (1983a). "The Juvenile Delinquency Problem in Japan: Application of a Role Relationship Model." *International Journal of Comparative and Applied Criminal Justice* 7:119–128.

Fenwick, Charles R. (1983b) "Law Enforcement, Public Participation and Crime Control in Japan: Implications for American Policing." *American Journal of Police* 3:83–109.

Foote, Daniel H. (1992). "From Japan's Death Row to Freedom." *Pacific Rim Law & Policy Journal* 1:11–103.

Fukuda, Masa-Aki (1988). "A Critical Analysis of Juvenile Justice Systems in Japan." Unpublished paper.

Futaba, Igarashi (nd.). "Forced to Confess." In Gavan McCormack and Yoshio Sugimoto, *Democracy in Contemporary Japan*. Sydney: Hale and Iremonger.

George, B.J., Jr. (1990). "Rights of the Criminally Accused." *Law and Contemporary Problems* 53:71–107.

Goodman, Carl F. (2003). *The Rule of Law in Japan: A Comparative Analysis*. The Hague: Kluwer Law International.

Haley, John O. (1998). *The Spirit of Japanese Law*. Athens: University of Georgia Press.

Hall, John Whitney, and Richard K. Beardsley (1965). *Twelve Doors to Japan*. New York: McGraw-Hill.

Hamai, Koichi, Tamaki Yokochi, and Kazuya Okada (2000). *Victims of Crime in Criminal Justice in Japan*. Tokyo: Ministry of Justice.

Hamilton, V. Lee, and Joseph Sanders (1992). *Everyday Justice Responsibility and the Individual in Japan and the United States*. New Haven: Yale University Press.

Henderson, Don Fenno (ed.). (1968). *The Constitution of Japan: Its First Twenty Years*. Seattle: University of Washington Press.

Hill, Peter B.E. (2003). *The Japanese Mafia Yakuza, Law and the State*. Oxford, UK: Oxford University Press.

Horii, Yasunobu (1973). "Problems Involved in the Implementation of the Parole System in Japan." Resource Materials No. 6, pp. 183–186. Tokyo: UNAFEI.

Huang, Frank F.Y., and Michael S. Vaughn (1992). "A Descriptive Analysis of Japanese Organized Crime: The Boryokudan From 1945 to 1988." *International Criminal Justice Review* 2:19–57.

Human Rights Watch/Asia (1995). *Prison Conditions in Japan*. New York: Human Rights Watch.

Ito, Shigeki (1986). "Characteristics and Roles of Japanese Public Prosecutors." Resource Materials No. 30, pp. 67–75. Tokyo: UNAFEI.

Itoh, Hiroshi (1990). "Judicial Review and Judicial Activism in Japan." *Law and Contemporary Problems* 53:169–179.

Itoh, Hiroshi (1970). "How Judges Think in Japan." *The American Journal of Comparative Law* 18:775–804.

Johnson, Elmer H. (1996). *Japanese Corrections: Managing Convicted Offenders in an Orderly Society*. Carbondale, IL: Southern Illinois University Press.

Johnson, Elmer H. (1991). "Managing Prisoners in Japan: "Attica" is Not Probable." *Social Justice* 18:155–170.

Johnson, Elmer H., and Hisashi Hasegawa (1987). "Prison Administration in Contemporary Japan: Six Issues." *Journal of Criminal Justice* 15:65–74.

The Joint Committee of the Three Tokyo Bar Associations for the Study of the Daiyo-kangoku (Substitute Prison) System (1989). "Torture and Unlawful or Unjust Treatment of Detainees in Daiyo-Kangoku (Substitute Prisons) in Japan."

The Judicial Reform Council (1999). *The Points at Issue in the Judicial Reform*, December 21, 1999.

The Justice System Reform Council (2001). *Recommendations of the Justice System Reform Council For a Justice System to Support Japan in the 21st Century*, June 12, 2001.

Kasai, Akio (1973). "Some Causes of the Decrease of Crime in Japan." Resource Materials No. 6, pp. 134–137. Tokyo: UNAFEI.

Kato, Takao (1980). "Ten Pillars for Improvement of Police Investigation." Report for 1979 and Resource Material Series No. 18, pp. 115–119. Tokyo: UNAFEI.

Katzenstein, Peter J. (1996). *Cultural Norms & National Security Police and Military in Postwar Japan*. Ithaca, NY: Cornell University Press.

Kersten, Joachim (1993). "Street Youths, Bosozoku, and Yakuza: Subculture Formation and Societal Reactions in Japan." *Crime & Delinquency* 39:277–295.

Kim, Yongjin (1987). "Work—The Key to the Success of Japanese Law Enforcement." *Police Studies* 10:109–117.

Kikuta, Koichi (1993). "The Death Penalty in Japan: Why Hasn't It Been Abolished?" *International Journal of Comparative and Applied Criminal Justice* 17:57–75.

Koide, Jun-ichi (1971). "Commitment System for Juvenile Guidance." Resource Materials No. 2, pp. 157–162. Tokyo: UNAFEI.

Kurata, Seiji, and Koichi Hamai (1998). *Criminal Justice System at Work: Outline of Crime Trends, Criminal Procedure, and Juvenile Justice System in Japan*. Tokyo: Japan Criminal Policy Society.

Leishman, Frank (1993). "From Pyramid to Pencil: Rank and Rewards in Japan's Police." *Police Studies* 16:33–36.

Lempert, Richard (1992). "A Jury for Japan?" *American Journal of Comparative Law* 40:37–71.

Leonard, Sherill A. (1992). "Attorney Ethics and the Size of the Japanese Bar." *Japan Quarterly* 39:86–100.

Levine, Andrew (1987). "Professionalization of the Japanese Attorney and the Role of Foreign Lawyers in Japan." *International Law and Politics* 19:1061–1086.

Lorenzo, Richard M. (1974). "The Judicial System of Japan." *Case Western Reserve Journal of International Law* 6:294–303.

McMahon, Margaret Mary (1974). "Legal Education in Japan." *American Bar Association Journal* 60:1376–1380.

Matsuda, Jiro (1958). "The Japanese Legal Training and Research Institute." *The American Journal of Comparative Law* 7:366–379.

Matsumoto, Yoshie, et al. (1978). "Resistance in Prisoners to Group Psychotherapy," tr. Keiko Nichimoto, National Criminal Justice Reference Service. International Summaries, Vol. 2, pp. 65–74. Washington, DC: U.S. Government Printing Office.

Minear, Richard H. (1970). *Japanese Tradition and Western Law*. Cambridge, MA: Harvard University Press.

Miyazawa, Setsuo (1992). *Policing in Japan: A Study on Making Crime*. Albany: SUNY Press.

Ochiai, Kiyotaka (1984). "Offenders' Rehabilitation in Japan." *New Zealand Law Journal* 407–409.

Ono, Morikazu (1980). "Prevention of Crime in the Field of Probation and After-care Services." Report for 1979 and Resource Material Series No. 18, pp. 120–123. Tokyo: UNAFEI.

Parker, L. Craig, Jr. (1984). *The Japanese Police System Today*. Tokyo: Kodansha International/USA.

Rabinowitz, Richard W. (1956). "The Historical Development of the Japanese Bar." *Harvard Law Review* 70:61–81.

Reischauer, Edwin O. (1977). *The Japanese*. Cambridge, MA: Harvard University Press.

Reischauer, Edwin O., and Marius B. Jansen (2005). *The Japanese Today: Change and Continuity*. Tokyo: Tuttle.

Research Department (2000). Executive Summary of Research Department Report 1999. Tokyo: Ministry of Justice.

Rosch, Joel (1987). "Institutionalizing Mediation: The Evolution of the Civil Liberties Bureau in Japan." *Law & Society Review* 21:243–266.

Saito, Toyoji (1993). "Juvenile Delinquency in Japan in the 1980s." *EuroCriminology* 5–6:91–122.

Satsumae, Takeshi (1978). "Suspension of Prosecution: A Japanese Longstanding Practice Designed to Screen Out Offenders from Penal Process." Report for 1977 and Resource Material Series No. 15, pp. 100–111. Tokyo: UNAFEI.

See, Harold (1982). "The Judiciary and Dispute Resolution in Japan: A Survey." *Florida State University Law Review* 10:339–368.

Shikita, M., and S. Tsuchiya (1976). "The Juvenile Justice System in Japan." Juvenile Justice: An Introduction Survey. No. 12, pp. 55–81. Rome: UNSDRI.

Shikita, Minoru (1981). "Law Under the Rising Sun." *Judges Journal* 20:42–47.

Sinnosuke, Inami (1992). "Going After the Yakuza," *Japan Quarterly* 39:353–358.

Someda, Kei (2005). "Community-Based Treatment of Offenders in Japan." Lecture.

Suzuki, Chuichi (1970). "Problems of Disqualification of Judges in Japan." *The American Journal of Comparative Law* 18:727–743.

Suzuki, Yoshio (1979). "Dispositional Decision-Making in the Criminal Justice Process: Objectives, Discretion and Guidance." Report for 1978 and Resource Material Series No. 16, pp. 64–96. Tokyo: UNAFEI.

Suzuki, Yoshio (1978). "Some Thoughts on Decriminalization and Depenalization." Resource Material Series No. 14, pp. 24–31. Tokyo: UNAFEI.

Suzuki, Yoshio (1978). "Speedy Administration of Criminal Justice: The Right of the Accused and the Interest of Society." Report for 1977 and Resource Material Series No. 15, pp. 91–99. Tokyo: UNAFEI.

Suzuki, Yoshio (1977). "Criminal Law Reform in Japan." Report for 1976 and Resource Material Series. No. 13, pp. 84–96. Tokyo: UNAFEI.

Tanaka, Hideo (ed.) (1976). *The Japanese Legal System*. Tokyo: University of Tokyo Press.

Tanizawa, Tadahiro (1979). "Sentencing Standards in Japan." Report for 1978 and Recourse Material Series No. 16, pp. 197–221. Tokyo: UNAFEI.

Thompson, Mark (1985). "The Paradox of Japanese Law Schools." *Student Lawyer* 13:16–21.

Thornton, Robert Y. (1971). "The Kidotai." *Police Chief* 38:65–73.

Tokuoka, Hideo, and Albert K. Cohen (1987). "Japanese Society and Delinquency." *International Journal of Comparative and Applied Criminal Justice* 11:13–22.

Tsubouchi, Toshihiko (1973). "Diversion in the Criminal Justice System of Japan." Resource Materials No. 6, pp. 151–156. Tokyo: UNAFEI.

Ueno, Haruo (1979). "The Japanese Police: Education and Training." *Police Studies* 2:11–17.

von Mehren, Arthur T. (1963). *Law in Japan*. Cambridge, MA: Harvard University Press.

Wren, Harold G. (1968). "The Legal System of Pre-Western Japan." *Hastings Law Journal* 217–244.

Yajima, Masami (1988). "Predelinquent Student Subcultures in Japan: A Comparative Analysis of Junior High School Students and Adults." *International Journal of Comparative and Applied Criminal Justice* 12:159–175.

Yanagimoto, Masaharu (1973). "The Juvenile Delinquent in Japan." *The British Journal of Criminology* 13:170–177.

Yanagimoto, Masaharu (1970). "Some Features of the Japanese Prison System." *The British Journal of Criminology* 10:209–224.

Yoder, Robert Stuart (2004). *Youth Deviance in Japan*. Melbourne: Trans Pacific Press.

Yokoyama, Minoru (2005). "Analysis of Political Corruption in Japan." *Kokugakuin Journal* 42:1–49.

Yokoyama, Minoru (2004a). "Policing the Right Wing Violence in Recent Fifteen Years in Japan." Unpublished paper.

Yokoyama, Minoru (2004b). "Structural Corruption and Individual Corruption in Japanese Police." In Menachem Amir and Stanley Einstein (eds.), *Police Corruption: Challenges for Developed Countries—Comparative Issues and Commissions of Inquiry*. Huntsville, TX: Office of International Criminal Justice.

Yokoyama, Minoru (2001). "Analysis of Japanese Police from the Viewpoint of Democracy." In Menachem Amir and Stanley Einstein (eds.), *Policing, Security and Democracy: Theory and Practice*, pp. 187–209. Huntsville, TX: Office of International Criminal Justice.

Yokoyama, Minoru (1994). "Treatment of Prisoners under Rehabilitation Model in Japan." *Kokugakuin Journal of Law and Politics* 32:1–24.

Yokoyama, Minoru (1992). "Guarantee of Human Rights in Juvenile Justice System in Japan." *Kokugakuin Journal of Law and Politics* 30:1–30.

Yokoyama, Minoru (1989). "Net-Widening of the Juvenile Justice System in Japan." *Criminal Justice Review* 14:43–53.

Yokoyama, Minoru (1986). "The Juvenile Justice System in Japan." In M. Brusten, et al. (eds.), *Youth Crime, Social Control and Prevention*, pp. 102–113. Pfaffenweiler, Germany: Centaurus-Verlagsgesellschaft.

Yokoyama, Minoru (1981). "Delinquency Control Programs in the Community in Japan." *International Journal of Comparative and Applied Criminal Justice* 5:169–178.

RUSSIA

American Bar Association Central and East European Law Initiative (1996). *Analysis of the Draft Criminal Procedure Code for the Russian Federation*. Washington, DC: American Bar Association.

Amnesty International (1975). *Prisoners of Conscience in the USSR: Their Treatment and Condition*. London: Amnesty International.

Anashkin, G.Z. "Tasks and Trends in the Development of Socialist Justice." *Soviet Law and Government* 5 (1966–67):29–40.

Anonymous (1988). "A Dangerous Proclivity Drugs and Addicts—Three Aspects of the Problem." *Soviet Law and Government* 26:19–35.

Anonymous (1986). "Rules of Internal Order of Corrective Labor Institutions (1977)." *Review of Socialist Law* 12:29–83.

Arshavaskii, A. Iu., and A. Ia. Vilks (1991). "Antisocial Manifestations in the Youth Environment: An Attempt at Regional Prognosis." *Soviet Review* 32:71–81.

Barron, John (1985). *KGB Today: The Hidden Hand*. New York: Berkley Books.

Barron, John (1974). *KGB: The Secret Work of Soviet Secret Agents*. New York: Bantam Books.

Barry, Donald D., and Carol Barner-Barry (1978). *Contemporary Soviet Politics: An Introduction*. Englewood Cliffs, NJ: Prentice Hall.

Barry, Donald D., and Harold J. Berman (1968). "The Soviet Legal Profession." *Harvard Law Review* 82:1–41.

Bassiouni, M. Cherif, and V.M. Savitski (eds.) (1979). *The Criminal Justice System of the USSR*. Springfield, IL: Charles C Thomas.

Beermann, R. (1975). "The Role of Law and Legality in the Soviet Union." *Review of Socialist Law* 1:97–111.

Berman, Harold J. (1992). "Christianity and Democracy in the Soviet Union." *Emory International Law Review* 6:23–34.

Berman, Harold J. (1966). *Soviet Criminal Law and Procedure: The RSFSR Codes*. Cambridge, MA: Harvard University Press.

Berman, Harold J., and John B. Quigley Jr. (1969). *Basic Laws on the Structure of the Soviet State*. Cambridge, MA: Harvard University Press.

Brokhin, Yuri (1975). *Hustling on Gorky Street*. New York: The Dial Press.

Burrage, Michael (1993). "Russian Advocates: Before, During, and After Perestroika." *Law and Social Inquiry* 18:573–592.

Burrage, Michael (1990). "Advokatura: In Search of Professionalism and Pluralism in Moscow and Leningrad." *Law and Social Inquiry* 15:433–478.

Butler, William E. (2003). *Russian Law*, 2nd ed. Oxford, UK: Oxford University Press.

Butler, William E. (ed. and tr.) (1998). *Criminal Code of the Russian Federation*, 2nd ed. London: Simmonds & Hill.

Butler, William E. (1988). *Soviet Law*, 2nd ed. London: Butterworths.

Butler, William E. (ed.) (1987). *Justice and Comparative Law*. Dordrecht, The Netherlands: Martinus Nijhoff.

Butler, William E. (1977). *Russian Law: Historical and Political Perspectives*. Leyden, The Netherlands: A.W. Sijthoff.

Celmina, Helene (1985). *Women in Soviet Prisons*. New York: Paragon House.

Chalidez, Valery (1977). *Criminal Russia*. New York: Random House.

Chen, Lauren (2004). "Power Plays: Reallocating Power Under the New Russian Federation Code of Criminal Procedure." *North Carolina Journal of International Law & Commercial Regulation* 30:429–472.

Connor, Walter D. (1972). *Deviance in Soviet Society*. New York: Columbia University Press.

Conquest, Robert (1968). *Justice and the Legal System in the U.S.S.R.* New York: Frederick A. Praeger.

Conquest, Robert (1968). *The Soviet Police System*. New York: Frederick A. Praeger.

Corson, William R., and Robert T. Crowley (1986). *The New KGB: Engine of Soviet Power*. New York: William Morrow.

Dobek, Mariusz Mark, and Roy D. Laird (1990). "Perestroika and a 'Law-Governed' Soviet State: Criminal Law." *Review of Socialist Law* 16:135–161.

Fedorchuk, V.V. (1985–86). "Strengthening the Scientific Foundations of the Activity of the Organs of Internal Affairs." *Soviet Law and Government* 24:18–31.

Feldbrugge, F.J.M. (1990). "The Constitution of the USSR." *Review of Socialist Law* 16:163–224.

Feldbrugge, F.J.M. (1986). "The Soviet Penitentiary System and the Rules of Internal Order of Corrective Labor Institutions in Historical Perspective." *Review of Socialist Law* 12:5–29.

Feldbrugge, F.J.M. (ed.) (1979). *The Constitution of the USSR and the Union Republics*. Alphen aan den Rijn, The Netherlands: Sijthoff & Noordhoff.

Feldbrugge, F.J.M (1975). "Soviet Penitentiary Law." *Review of Socialist Law* 1:123–147.

Filimonov, V. (1975). "Criteria for Correction of Convicted Persons." *Soviet Law and Government* 12:79–84.

Filippov, Victor V. (2003). "New Russian Code of Criminal Procedure: The Next Step on the Path of Russia's Democratization." *Demokratizatsiya* 11:3 (Summer).

Finckenauer, James O. (1995). *Russian Youth: Law, Deviance, and the Pursuit of Freedom*. New Brunswick, NJ: Transaction.

Finckenauer, James O., and Linda Kelly (1992). "Juvenile Delinquency and Youth Subcultures in the Former Soviet Union." *International Journal of Comparative and Applied Criminal Justice* 16:247–261.

Gabrichidze, B.N (1986–87). "Interrelations Between Local Soviets and Law Enforcement Agencies." *Soviet Law and Government* 25:82–94.

Gamaiunov, Igor (1991). "Without Hypnosis Supervising the KGB—Myth or Reality?" *Soviet Review* 32:3–14.

Ginsburgs, George (1985). "The Soviet Judicial Elite: Is It?" *Review of Socialist Law* 11:293–311.

Gooding, John (1990). "Gorbachev and Democracy." *Soviet Studies* 42:195–231.

Gustafson, D. Mauritz (1987). "Soviet Human Rights Under Gorbachev: Old Wine in a New Bottle?" *Denver Journal of International Law & Policy* 16:177–189.

Handelman, Stephen (1995). *Comrade Criminal Russia's New Mafiya*. New Haven, CT: Yale University Press.

Hazard, John N. (1983). *Managing Change in the U.S.S.R.* Cambridge, UK: Cambridge University Press.

Hazard, John N. (1979). *Law and Social Change in the USSR*. Westport, CT: Hyperion Press.

Hazard, John N., William E. Butler, and Peter B. Maggs (1984). *The Soviet Legal System: The Law in the 1980s*. New York: Oceana.

Hazard, John N., William E. Butler, and Peter B. Maggs (1977). *The Soviet Legal System*, 3rd ed. Dobbs Ferry, NY: Oceana.

Henderson, Jane (1990). "Law of the USSR: On the Status of Judges in the USSR." *Review of Socialist Law* 16:305–338.

Hingley, Ronald (1970). *The Russian Secret Police*. London: Hutchinson & Co.

Huskey, Eugene (1990). "Between Citizen and State: The Soviet Bar (Advokatura) Under Gorbachev." *Columbia Journal of Transnational Law* 28:95–116.

Huskey, Eugene (1986). "The Politics of the Soviet Criminal Process: Expanding the Right of Counsel in Pre-Trial Proceedings." *American Journal of Comparative Law* 34:93–112.

Iakovlev, Aleksandr (1990). "Constitutional Socialist Democracy: Dream or Reality?" *Columbia Journal of Transnational Law* 28 :117–132.

Isham, Heyward (ed.) (1995). *Remaking Russia: Voices from Within*. Armonk, NY: M.E. Sharpe.

Jack, Andrew (2004). *Inside Putin's Russia*. Oxford, UK: Oxford University Press.

Jordan, Pamela A. (2005). *Defending Rights in Russia: Lawyers, the State, and Legal Reform in the Post-Soviet Era*. Vancouver: UBC Press.

Juviler, Peter (1990). "Guaranteeing Human Rights in the Soviet Context." *Columbia Journal of Transnational Law* 28:135–155.

Juviler, Peter (1976). *Revolutionary Law and Order: Politics and Social Change in the USSR*. New York: The Free Press.

Juviler, Peter, and Brian E. Forschner (1978). "Juvenile Delinquency in the Soviet Union." *The Prison Journal* 58:18–28.

Kahn, Jeffrey (2002). "Note: Russian Compliance With Articles Five and Six of the European Convention of Human Rights as a Barometer of Legal Reform and Human Rights in Russia." *University of Michigan Journal of Law Reform* 35:641–694.

Kaiser, Robert G. (1976). *Russia: The People and the Power*. New York: Pocket Books.

Kaminskaya, Dina (1982). *Final Judgment*. New York: Simon and Schuster.

Karklins, Rasma (1990). "The Organisation of Power in Soviet Labour Camps." *Soviet Studies* 41:276–297.

Karpets, Igor Ivanovich (1977). "Principal Directions and Types of Activity of the Militia in the Soviet Union." *International Review of Criminal Policy* 33:34–38.

Katz, Alyssa (1987). "Soviet Jews Under Soviet Law: A Practical Guide." *Loyola of Los Angeles International & Comparative Law Journal* 9:711–750.

King, Roy D. (1994). "Russian Prisons After Perestroika: End of the Gulag?" *British Journal of Criminology* 34:62–82.

Kiralfy, Albert R. (1976). "The Child in Soviet Law: The Juvenile Delinquent." *Review of Socialist Law* 2:67–77.

Korenev, A.P. (1983–84). "The Rights of the Soviet Police and Socialist Legality." *Soviet Law and Government* 22:81–94.

Korobeinikov, B.V. (1985). "Sociopolitical and Legal Principles of Crime Prevention in the U.S.S.R." *Crime and Social Justice* 23:29–50.

Kudriavtsev, V.N. (1978). "The Constitution of the State of the Entire People." *Soviet Law and Government* 17:3–17.

Lapenna, Ivo (1975). "The Contemporary Crisis of Legality in the Soviet Union: Substantive Criminal Law." *Review of Socialist Law* 1:73–95.

Lapenna, Ivo (1961). "The New Russian Criminal Code and Code of Criminal Procedure." *International and Comparative Law Quarterly* 10 :421–453.

Larin, A.M., et al. (1985–86). "Enhancing the Role of the Defense Lawyer in Providing Legal Assistance to Citizens." *Soviet Law and Government* 24:3–17.

Levitsky, Serge L., intro. (1988). "The Legislation of Perestroika." *Soviet Statutes & Decisions* 25:1–96.

Levytsky, Boris (1972). *The Uses of Terror: The Soviet Secret Police 1917–1970*, tr. H.A. Piehler. New York: Coward, McCann & Geoghegan.

Loone, Eero (1990). "Marxism and Perestroika." *Soviet Studies* 42:779–794.

Matthews, Mervyn (1974). *Soviet Government: A Selection of Official Documents on Internal Policies*. London: Jonathan Cape.

McClellan, Dorothy S. (1987). "Soviet Youth: A View from the Inside." *Crime and Social Justice* 29:1–25.

Mikhlin, Alexander S. (1999). *The Death Penalty in Russia*, tr. W.E. Butler. London: Simmonds & Hill.

Ministry of Internal Affairs (1997). Latest Data on the Performance of Internal Affairs Agencies and Internal Troops in 1996. Russia: Ministry of Internal Affairs.

Minkovsky, G.M. (1976). "USSR: Effectiveness of Treatment: Measures and Problems of the Typology of Juvenile Delinquents." *Juvenile Justice: An Introduction*, Survey. No. 12, pp. 221–241. Rome: United Nations Social Defence Research Institute.

Morn, Frank, and Vladimir Sergevnin (1994). "Police Training in Modern Russia." *International Journal of Comparative and Applied Criminal Justice* 18:119–128.

Moskal'Kova, Tat'iana N. (1992). "Rehabilitation of the Innocent in the Russian Federation." *Review of Central and East European Law* 18:475–484.

Myagkov, Aleksei (1976). *Inside the KGB*. New Rochelle, NY: Arlington House.

Ochs, Brian A. (1983) "Procedural Rights of Juvenile Offenders Before Soviet Courts and Commissions for Juvenile Affairs." *Review of Socialist Law* 9:61–83.

Oleinik, Anton N. (2003). *Organized Crime, Prison and Post-Soviet Societies*. Aldershot, UK: Ashgate.

Orland, Leonard (2002). "A Russian Legal Revolution: The 2002 Criminal Procedure Code." *Connecticut Journal of International Law* 18:133–207.

Osakwe, Christopher (1983). "The Public Interest and the Role of the Procurator in Soviet Civil Litigation: A Critical Analysis." *Texas International Law Journal* 18:37–106.

Osakwe, Christopher (1975–76). "Due Process of Law Under Contemporary Soviet Criminal Procedure." *Tulane Law Review* 50:266–317.

Partanen, Juha (1987). "Serious Drinking, Serious Alcohol Policy: The Case of the Soviet Union." *Contemporary Drug Problems* 14:507–538.

Pastrevich, Ivan (1971). "Co-operation between Government and Volunteer Community Groups in the Prevention and Control of Crime in the Byelorussian Soviet Socialist Republic." *International Review of Criminal Policy* 29:40–47.

Patterson, David W., and Anne Doak (1980). "Constitutional Changes and the Russian Philosophy of Justice." *International Journal of Comparative and Applied Criminal Justice* 4:29–35.

Piacentini, Laura (2004). "Barter in Russian Prisons." *European Journal of Criminology* 1:17–45.

Pipko, Simona, and Albert J. Pucciarelli (1985). "The Soviet Internal Passport System." *The International Lawyer* 19:915–919.

Pridemore, William A. (ed.) (2005). *Ruling Russia Law, Crime, and Justice in a Changing Society*. Boulder, CO: Rowman & Littlefield.

Quigley, John (1990). "Law Reform and the Soviet Courts." *Columbia Journal of Transnational Law* 28:59–75.

Quigley, John (1988a). "The New Soviet Law on Appeals: 'Glasnost' in the Soviet Courts." *International and Comparative Law Quarterly* 37:172–177.

Quigley, John (1988b). "Soviet Courts Undergoing Major Reforms." *The International Lawyer* 22:459–473.

Savitsky, V.M. (1991). "Fear Confessions of a Well-Known Legal Expert Who Has Criticized the Draft Law on the KGB." *Soviet Review* 32:15–23.

Savitsky, Valery (1993). "Will There Be A New Judicial Power in the New Russia?" *Review of Central and East European Law* 19:639–660.

Sakwa, Richard (2008). *Putin: Russia's Choice*. 2nd ed. London: Routledge.

Sakwa, Richard (1996). *Russian Politics and Society*, 2nd ed. London: Routledge.

Schroeder, Friedrich-Christian (1990). "The Reform of Legal Consultation in the Soviet Union." *Review of Socialist Law* 16:127–133.

Serio, Joseph (ed.) (1992). *USSR Crime Statistics and Summaries: 1989 and 1990*. Chicago: The University of Illinois at Chicago.

Shelley, Louise I. (1990a). "Policing Soviet Society: The Evolution of State Control." *Law & Social Inquiry* 15 :479–520.

Shelley, Louise I. (1990b) "The Soviet Militsiia: Agents of Political and Social Control." *Policing & Society* 1:39–56.

Shelley, Louise I. (1987a). "The Political Function of Soviet Courts: A Model for One Party States?" *Review of Socialist Law* 13:263–283.

Shelley, Louise I. (1987b). "Inter-personal Violence in the U.S.S.R." *Violence, Aggression and Terrorism* 1:41–67.

Shelley, Louise I. (1987c). "The Structure and Function of Soviet Courts." In F.J.M. Feldbrugge (ed.), *The Distinctiveness of Soviet Law*, pp. 199–216. Dordrecht, The Netherlands: Martinus Nijhoff.

Shelley, Louise I. (1984). *Lawyers in Soviet Work Life*. New Brunswick, NJ: Rutgers University Press.

Shevtsova, Lilia (2003). *Putin's Russia*, tr. Antonina W. Bouis. Washington, DC: Carnegie Endowment for International Peace.

Skuratov, Yuri (1994). "Crime Institute Profile: Research Institute on The Problems of Strengthening Legality and Legal Order." *European Journal on Criminal Policy and Research* 2:114–118.

Slovenko, Ralph (1983). "Psychiatric Postdicting and the Second Opinion on Grigorenko." *Journal of Psychiatry & Law* 11:387–412.

Smith, Gordon B. (1996). *Reforming the Russian Legal System*. Cambridge, UK: Cambridge University Press.

Smith, Gordon B. (1992). *Perestroika and the Procuracy: The Changing Role of the Procurator's Office in the USSR*. Washington, DC: Bureau of Justice Statistics, 1992.

Smith, Gordon B. (1978). *The Soviet Procuracy and the Supervision of Administration*. Alphen aan den Rijn, The Netherlands: Sijthoff & Noordhoff.

Smith, Hedrick (1976). *The Russians*. New York: Ballantine Books.

Solomon, Peter H. (2003). "New Justices of the Peace in the Russian Federation: A Cornerstone of Judicial Reform?" *Demokratizatsiya* 11:3 (Summer).

Solomon, Peter H. (1981–82). "Criminalization and Decriminalization in Soviet Criminal Policy, 1917–1941." *Law & Society Review* 16:9–43.

Solomon, Peter H. (1978). *Soviet Criminologists and Criminal Policy*. London: Macmillan.

Solovyov, Vladimir, and Elena Klepikova (1987). *Behind the High Kremlin Walls*. New York: Berkley Books.

Solzhenitsyn, Aleksandr I. (1973–78). *The Gulag: Archipelago 1918–1956, Vols. 1–3*, tr. Thomas P. Whitney and Harry Willetts. New York: Harper & Row.

Solzhenitsyn, Aleksandr I. (1963). *One Day in the Life of Ivan Denisovich*, tr. Ronald Hingley and Marx Hayward. New York: Bantam Books.

Stetsovsky, Yuri (1982). *The Right of the Accused to Defence in the USSR*. Moscow: Progress.

Subtelny, Orest (1984). "Law and Repression in the Soviet Union." *Harvard Journal of Law and Public Policy* 7:109–176.

Taylor, Telford (1976). *Courts of Terror*. New York: Vintage Books.

Terebilov, V. (1983). "Immediate Tasks Before the Organs of Justice and the Courts in Light of the Decisions of the November 1982 Plenum of the CPSU Central Committee." *Soviet Law and Government* 22:27–38.

Terebilov, V. (1973). *The Soviet Court*. Moscow: Progress.

Van Den Berg, Ger P. (1992). "Human Rights in the Legislation and the Draft Constitution of the Russian Federation." *Review of Central and East European Law* 18:197–251.

Van Den Berg, Ger P. (1987). "Judicial Statistics in a Period of Glasnost." *Review of Socialist Law* 13:299–311.

Vengerov, Anatoli, and Anatoli Danilevich (1985). *Law, Morality and Man: The Soviet Legal System in Action*. Moscow: Progress.

White, Stephen (1990). "'Democratisation' in the USSR." *Soviet Studies* 42:3–25.

Williams, Phil (ed.) (1997). *Russian Organized Crime: The New Threat?* London: Frank Cass.

Wolin, Simon, and Robert M. Slusser (eds.) (1957). *The Soviet Secret Police*. New York: Praeger.

Zeldes, Ilya (1981). *The Problems of Crime in the USSR*. Springfield, IL: Charles C Thomas.

CHINA

Bakken, Borge (1995). "Editor's Introduction." *Chinese Sociology and Anthropology* 27:3–18.

Bakken, Borge (ed.) (2005). *Crime, Punishment, and Policing in China*. Lanham, MD: Rowman & Littlefield.

Benewick, Robert, and Paul Wingrove (eds.) (1995). *China in the 1990s*. Vancouver: UBC Press.

Binglei, Chen (1993). "Rank System and Regularized Management of Chinese Police." *China Policing Studies* 32–36.

Bodde, Derk, and Clarence Morris (1967). *Law in Imperial China*. Philadelphia: University of Pennsylvania Press.

Boya, Liao (1993). "The People's Courts of the People's Republic of China a Brief Introduction." *EuroCriminology* 5–6:123–135.

Brown, Ronald C. (1997). *Understanding Chinese Courts and Legal Process: Law with Chinese Characteristics*. The Hague: Kluwer Law International.

Chang, Jung (1991). *Wild Swans*. London: Flamingo.

Chang, Ting (2004). *China Always Says "No" to Narcotics*. Beijing: Foreign Language Press.

Chenguang, Wang, and Zhang Xianchu (1997). *Introduction to Chinese Law*. Hong Kong: Sweet & Maxwell Asia.

Clark, Donald C. (1991). "Dispute Resolution in China." *Journal of Chinese Law* 5:245–296.

Cohen, Jerome Alan (1968). *The Criminal Process in the People's Republic of China 1949–1963: An Introduction.* Cambridge, MA: Harvard University Press.

Cowen, Jonathan M. (1993). "One Nation's 'Gulag' is Another Nation's 'Factory Within a Fence': Prison-Labor in the People's Republic of China and the United States of America." *UCLA Pacific Basin Law Journal* 12:190–236.

Dai, Yi Sheng (1994). *On the Policies of Public Security.* Chongqing, China: Chongqing Publisher.

Dai, Yi Sheng, and Pi Yijun (2004). *Traditional Crime Control Meets Modernization: An Introduction of Juvenile Justice System in China.* Unpublished paper.

Damin, Kang (1993). "Chinese Police and Criminal Justice." *China Policing Studies* 12–21.

Daosheng, Shao (1992). *Preliminary Study of China's Juvenile Delinquency.* Beijing: Foreign Languages Press.

Davies, Robert H. (2001). *Prisoner 13498: A True Story of Love, Drugs and Jail in Modern China.* London: Mainstream.

Davis, Michael C. (ed.) (1995). *Human Rights and Chinese Values.* Oxford, UK: Oxford University Press.

Ding, Yijiang (2001). *Chinese Democracy after Tiananmen.* Vancouver: UBC Press.

Dutton, Michael (2005). *Policing Chinese Politics: A History.* Durham, NC: Duke University Press.

Fairbank, John K. (1992). *China: A New History.* Cambridge, MA: Harvard University Press.

Fang, Wang (1993). "Drug Menace Must Be Eliminated." *China Policing Studies* 22–31.

Finder, Susan (1993). "The Supreme People's Court of the People's Republic of China." *Journal of Chinese Law* 7:145–224.

Friday, Paul C. (1998). "Crime and Crime Prevention in China." *Journal of Contemporary Criminal Justice* 14:296–314.

Gelatt, Timothy A. (1991). "Lawyers in China: The Past Decade and Beyond." *New York University Journal of International Law and Politics* 23:751–799.

Guo, Xiang (1999). "Delinquency and Its Prevention in China." *International Journal of Offender Therapy and Comparative Criminology* 43:61–70.

Guoqing, Dang (1995). "Analysis of Inmates of Reeducation-Through-Labor Institutions Ganging Up Against Reform (June 1984) (Excerpts)." *Chinese Sociology and Anthropology* 27:88–94.

Hangwei, Du (1995). "The Basic Situation and Characteristics of Chinese Juvenile Crime at the End of the 1980s and the Start of the 1990s." *Chinese Sociology and Anthropology* 27:27–36.

Hook, Brian (ed.) (1996). *The Individual and the State in China.* Oxford, UK: Clarendon Press.

Hua, Liu (1995). "Hooliganism." *Chinese Sociology and Anthropology* 27:57–63.

Huaide, Shu (1993). "Comprehensive Management of Public Order." *China Policing Studies* 8–11.

Joseph, William A. (ed.). (1994). *China Briefing, 1994*. Boulder, CO: Westview Press.

Joseph, William A. (ed.) (1993). *China Briefing, 1992*. Boulder, CO: Westview Press.

Junren, Li (1993). "Recidivism: Its Prevention and Control in China." *China Policing Studies* 37–44.

Kaltman, Blaine (2007). *Under the Heel of the Dragon Islam, Racism, Crime, and the Uighur in China*. Athens, OH: Ohio University Press.

Klofas, John M. (1991). "Considering Prison in Context: The Case of the People's Republic of China." *International Journal of Comparative and Applied Criminal Justice* 15:175–186.

Leng, Shaao-chuan (1967). *Justice in Communist China*. Dobbs Ferry, NY: Oceana.

Leng, Shaao-chuan, and Hungdah Chiu (1985). *Criminal Justice in Post-Mao China*. Albany: SUNY Press.

Li, Victor H. (1978). *Law Without Lawyers: A Comparative View of Law in China and the United States*. Boulder, CO: Westview Press.

Li, Xiancui (1998). "Crime and Policing in China." Canberra: Australian Institute of Criminology.

Liang, Bin (2008). *The Changing Chinese Legal System, 1978–Present*. New York: Routledge.

Lin, Gang, and Xiaobo Hu (eds.) (2003). *China After Jiang*. Washington, DC: Woodrow Wilson Center Press.

Liu, Jianhong, Lening Zhang, and Steven Messner (eds.) (1994). *Crime and Social Control in a Changing China*. Westport, CT: Greenwood Press.

Lo, Carlos Wing-hung (1995). *China's Legal Awakening: Legal Theory and Criminal Justice in Deng's Era*. Hong Kong: Hong Kong University Press.

Lu, Xiaobo (2000). *Cadres and Corruption: The Organizational Involution of the Chinese Communist Party*. Stanford, CA: Stanford University Press.

Lubman, Stanley B. (ed.) (1996). *China's Legal Reforms*. Oxford, UK: Oxford University Press.

Ma, Yue (1997). "The Police Law 1995: Organization, Functions, Powers and Accountability of the Chinese Police." *Policing: An International Journal of Police Strategy and Management* 20:113–135.

Madsen, Richard (2000). "Understanding Falun Gong." *Current History* (September): 243–247.

McKnight, Brian E. (1981). *The Quality of Mercy: Amnesties and Traditional Chinese Justice*. Honolulu: The University Press of Hawaii.

Ministry of Public Security (2004). *Chinese Public Security Statistical Data*. Beijing: Ministry of Public Security.

Ministry of Public Security (2003). *Policing in China, 2004*. Beijing: Ministry of Public Security.

Ministry of Public Security (1997). '96 *Policing in China*. Beijing: Ministry of Public Security.

Office of the Fifth Bureau, Ministry of Public Security (1995). "The Basic Situation and Characteristics of Recent Juvenile Crime in China." *Chinese Sociology and Anthropology* 27:19–26.

O'Biren, Kevin J. (ed.) (2008). *Popular Protest in China*. Cambridge, MA: Harvard University Press.

Qinzhang, Han (1993). "Chinese Cities Adopt Police Patrol System." *China Policing Studies* 54–56.

Peerenboom, Randall (2008). *China Modernizes: Threat to the West or Model for the Rest?* Oxford, UK: Oxford University Press.

Peerenboom, Randall (2002). *China's Long March Toward Rule of Law*. Cambridge, UK: Cambridge University Press.

Perry, Elizabeth J., and Mark Selden (eds.) (2000). *Chinese Society Change, Conflict and Resistance*. London: Routledge.

Scobell, Andrew (1990). "The Death Penalty in Post-Mao China." *The China Quarterly* 123:503–520.

Seymour, James D., and Richard Anderson (1999). *New Ghosts, Old Ghosts, Prison, and Labor Reform Camps in China*. Armonk, NY: M.E. Sharpe.

Shapiro, Sidney (1990). *The Law and the Lore of China's Criminal Justice*. Beijing: New World Press.

Soled, Debra E. (ed.). (1995). *China: A Nation in Transition*. Washington, DC: Congressional Quarterly.

Spence, Jonathan D. (1981). *The Gate of Heavenly Peace: The Chinese and Their Revolution, 1895–1980*. Harmondsworth, UK: Penguin Books.

Sun, Yan (2004). *Corruption and Market in Contemporary China*. Ithaca, NY: Cornell University Press.

Troyer, Ronald J., John P. Clark, and Dean G. Rojek (eds.). (1989). *Social Control in the People's Republic of China*. New York: Praeger.

Wang, Shizhou (1995). "The Judicial Explanation in Chinese Criminal Law." *American Journal of Comparative Law* 43:569–579.

White, Lynn T. (1999). *Unstately Power, Vol. 2: Local Causes of China's Intellectual, Legal and Governmental Reforms*. Armonk, NY: M.E. Sharpe.

White Paper on Narcotics Control (2001). State Council of the People's Republic of China.

Wu, Hongda Harry (1992). *Laogai: The Chinese Gulag*. Boulder, CO: Westview Press.

Xichuan, Du, and Zhang Lingyuan (1990). *China's Legal System: A General Survey*. Beijing: New World Press.

Xiguang, Yang, and Susan McFadden (1997). *Captive Spirits: Prisoners of the Cultural Revolution*. Hong Kong: Oxford University Press.

Xincai, Peng (1995). "Trendiness and Juvenile Crime." *Chinese Sociology and Anthropology* 27:79–87.

Yang, Cheng (1994). "Public Security Offences and Their Impact on Crime Rates in China." *British Journal of Criminology* 34:54–68.

Yu, Olivia, and Lening Zhang (1999). "The Under-Recording of Crime by Police in China: A Case Study." *Policing: An International Journal of Police and Strategies Management* 22:252–263.

Yuzhen, Xu (1993). "Police Science and Technology Forge Ahead in China." *China Policing Studies* 73–76.

Zhang, Lening, Dengke Zhou, Steven F. Messner, Allen E. Liska, Marvin D. Krohn, Jianhong Liu, and Zhou Lu (1996). "Crime Prevention in a Communitarian Society: Bang-Jiao and Tiao-Jie in the People's Republic of China." *Justice Quarterly* 13:199–222.

Zhang, Zheng (1995). "The Current Situation and Characteristics of Chinese Juvenile Crime." *Chinese Sociology and Anthropology* 27:37–42.

Zhengchang, Zhang (1993). "Traffic Accidents and Countermeasures in China." *China Policing Studies* 77–81.

Zhibin, Mao, and Cheng Liangwen (1993). "Guaranteeing Human Rights is a Cardinal Principle for Chinese Public Security Departments." *China Policing Studies* 45–53.

Zhihua, Hu (1993). "Create a Fine Investment Environment." *China Policing Studies* 82–85.

Zhou, Joseph (1991). "The Chinese Correctional System and Its Development." *International Journal of Comparative and Applied Criminal Justice* 15:15–32.

Zikang, Wang (1993). "Police Education in China." *China Policing Studies* 63–67.

Zongren, Liu (1995). *Hard Time: Thirty Months in a Chinese Labor Camp*. San Francisco: China Books & Periodicals.

ISLAM

Ahmed, Qanta A. (2008). *In the Land of Invisible Women: A Female Doctor's Journey in the Saudi Kingdom*. Naperville, IL: Sourcebooks.

Alsaif, Tawfiq (2007). *Islamic Democracy and its Limits: The Iranian Experience Since 1979*. London: SAQI.

Ansari, Ali M. (2006). *Iran, Islam and Democracy: The Politics of Managing Change*, 2nd ed. London: Chatham House.

Ansary, Abdullah F. (2008). "A Brief Overview of the Saudi Arabian Legal System." *GlobaLex* Internet: http://www.nyulawglobal.org/globalex/saudi_arabia.htm. New York University School of Law.

Ansay, Tugrul, and Don Wallace Jr. (eds.) (1987). *Introduction to Turkish Law*, 3rd ed. Deventer, The Netherlands: Kluwer Law and Taxation.

Arat, Zehra F. Kabasakal (ed.) (2007). *Human Rights in Turkey*. Philadelphia: University of Pennsylvania Press.

Aslan, Reza (2006). *No God but God: The Origins, Evolution, and Future of Islam.* New York: Random House.

Aydin, Ahmet H. (1997). *Police Organisation and Legitimacy Case Studies of England, Wales and Turkey.* Aldershot: Avebury.

Baer, Gabriel (1977). "The Transition from Traditional to Western Criminal Law in Turkey and Egypt." *Studia Islamica* 45:139–158.

Bassiouni, M. Cherif (ed.) (1982). *The Islamic Criminal Justice System.* London: Oceana.

Beeley, Brian W. (ed). (2002). *Turkish Transformation: New Century, New Challenges.* Huntingdon, UK: The Eothen Press.

Bozdogan, Sibel, and Resat Kasaba (eds.) (1997). *Rethinking Modernity and National Identity in Turkey.* Seattle: University of Washington Press.

Copithorne, Maurice (2000). *Situation of Human Rights in the Islamic Republic of Iran.* United Nations Report.

Coulson, N.J. (1964). *A History of Islamic Law.* Edinburgh: Edinburgh University Press.

Coulson, Noel J. (1969). *Conflicts and Tensions in Islamic Jurisprudence.* Kuala Lumpur: The Other Press.

Curtis, Glenn E., and Eric Hoogland (eds.) (2008). *Iran: A Country Study*, 5th ed. Washington, DC: U.S. Government Printing Office.

DeLong-Bas, Natana J. (2007). *Wahhabi Islam From Revival and Reform to Global Jihad.* London: I.B. Tauris.

Encyclopaedia Britannica (2006). "Iran: The Essential Guide to a Country on the Brink." Hoboken, NJ: John Wiley & Sons.

Esposito, John (2002). *What Everyone Needs to Know About Islam.* Oxford, UK: Oxford University Press.

Ghahramani, Zarah (2009), with Robert Hilman. *My Life as a Traitor.* London: Bloomsbury.

Goldziher, Ignaz (1981), tr. Andras Hamori and Ruth Hamori. *Introduction to Islamic Theology and Law.* Princeton, NJ: Princeton University Press.

Green, Penny (2002). "Turkish Jails, Hunger Strikes and the European Drive for Prison Reform." *Punishment & Society.* 4:97–101.

Green, Penny, and Tony Ward (2000). "State Crime, Human Rights, and the Limits of Criminology." *Social Justice* 27:101–115.

Habibzadeh, Jafar (2005). "The Legality Principle of Crimes and Punishments in the Iranian Legal System." *Global Jurist Topics* 5:1–14.

Hiro, Dilip (2005). *The Iranian Labyrinth: Journeys Through Theocratic Iran and Its Furies.* New York: Nation Books.

Hourani, Albert (1991). *A History of the Arab Peoples.* London: Faber and Faber.

Human Rights Watch (2008a). *Adults Before Their Time: Children in Saudi Arabia's Criminal Justice System.* New York: Human Rights Watch.

Human Rights Watch (2008b). *The Last Holdouts.* New York: Human Rights Watch.

Human Rights Watch (2008c). *Perpetual Minors: Human Rights Abuses Stemming from Male Guardianship and Sex Segregation in Saudi Arabia*. New York: Human Rights Watch.

Human Rights Watch (2008d). *Precarious Justice Arbitrary Detention and Unfair Trials in the Deficient Criminal Justice System of Saudi Arabia*. New York: Human Rights Watch.

Human Rights Watch (2008e). "*You Can Detain Anyone for Anything*"*: Iran's Broadening Clampdown on Independent Activism*. New York: Human Rights Watch.

Human Rights Watch (2007). *Retrograde Human Rights Trends and Stagnation of the Human Rights Reform Process*. New York: Human Rights Watch.

Human Rights Watch (1992). *Empty Reforms: Saudi Arabia's New Basic Laws*. New York: Human Rights Watch.

Jacoby, Tim (2005). *Social Power and the Turkish State*. London: Routledge.

Kamali, Mohammad Hashim (1989). *Principles of Islamic Jurisprudence*. Cambridge, UK: Islamic Texts Society.

Kamali, Mohammad Hashim (2008). *Shari'ah Law An Introduction*. Oxford, UK: Oneworld.

Keddie, Nikki R. (2006). *Modern Iran Roots and Results of Revolution*. Updated ed. New Haven, CT: Yale University Press.

Khadduri, Majid (1961). *Islamic Jurisprudence: Shafi'i's Risala*. Baltimore: The Johns Hopkins Press.

Khadduri, Majid, and Herbert J. Liebesny (eds.) (1955). *Law in the Middle East*. Washington, DC: The Middle East Institute.

Kinzer, Stephen (2001). *Crescent & Star: Turkey Between Two Worlds*. New York: Farrar, Straus and Giroux.

Lake, Michael (ed.) (2005). *The EU & Turkey A Glittering Prize or a Millstone?* London: Federal Trust for Education and Research.

Lapidus, Ira M. (2002). *A History of Islamic Societies*, 2nd ed. Cambridge, UK: Cambridge University Press.

Lewis, Bernard (2003). *The Crisis of Islam Holy War and Unholy Terror*. New York: Random House.

Lewis, Bernard (1996). *The Middle East: 2000 Years of History From the Rise of Christianity to the Present Day*. London: Phoenix.

Mackey, Sandra (1996). *The Iranians: Persia, Islam and the Soul of a Nation*. New York: Plume.

Mackey, Sandra (2002). *The Saudis Inside the Desert Kingdom*. New York: W.W. Norton & Company.

Mango, Andrew (2005). *Turkey and the War on Terror: For Forty Years We Fought Alone*. London: Routledge.

Mango, Andrew (2004). *The Turks Today*. New York: The Overlook Press.

Mansfield, Peter (1992). *The Arabs*, 3rd ed. London: Penguin Books.

Mansfield, Peter (1991). *A History of the Middle East*. London: Penguin Books.

Martin, Vanessa (2003). *Creating An Islamic State: Khomeini and the Making of a New Iran*. London: I.B. Tauris.

Ministry of Interior (1980). *The Effect of Islamic Legislation on Crime Prevention in Saudi Arabia*. Rome: United Nations Crime Prevention Research Center.

Moaveni, Azadeh (2009). *Honeymoon in Tehran: Two Years of Love and Danger in Iran*. New York: Random House.

Moaveni, Azadeh (2005). *Lipstick Jihad: A Memoir of Growing Up Iranian in America and American in Iran*. New York: PublicAffairs.

Nafisi, Azar (2003). *Reading Lolita in Tehran: A Memoir in Books*. New York: Random House.

Nafisi, Azar (2008). *Things I've Been Silent About: Memories*. New York: Random House.

Ozdalga, Elisabeth, and Sune Persson (eds.). (1997). *Civil Society Democracy and The Muslim World*. Istanbul: Swedish Research Institute in Istanbul.

Patai, Raphael (2002). *The Arab Mind*. Rev. ed. New York: Hatherleigh Press.

Peters, Rudolph (2005). *Crime and Punishment in Islamic Law: Theory and Practice from the Sixteenth to the Twenty-first Century*. Cambridge, UK: Cambridge University Press.

Pfaff, Richard H. (1963). "Disengagement from Traditionalism in Turkey and Iran," *The Western Political Quarterly* 16:79–98.

The Qur'an. (2004). M.A.S. Abdel Haleem (tr.). Oxford, UK: Oxford University Press.

Rabasa, Angel, and F. Stephen Larrabee (2008). *The Rise of Political Islam in Turkey*. Santa Monica, CA: RAND.

Rahmdel, Mansour (2006). "The Role of the Courts in the Reform of Iranian Criminal Law Policy." *Criminal Law Forum* 17:59–70.

Sahebjam, Freidoune (1994), tr. Richard Seaver. *The Stoning of Soraya M*. New York: Arcade.

Sanad, Nagaty (1991). *The Theory of Crime and Criminal Responsibility in Islamic Law: Shari'a*. Chicago: University of Illinois at Chicago.

Schacht, Joseph (1964). *An Introduction to Islamic Law*. Oxford, UK: Clarendon Press.

Schwartz, Stephen (2002). *The Two Faces of Islam: The House of Sa'ud from Tradition to Terror*. New York: Doubleday.

Sunar, Ilkay (2004). *State, Society and Democracy in Turkey*. Istanbul: Bahcesehir University Publication.

Tamadonfar, Mehran (2001). "Islam, Law, and Political Control in Contemporary Iran," *Journal for the Scientific Study of Religion* 40:205–219.

Subject Index

Name Index